D0271863

The Origin
of Wealth

The Origin of Wealth

EVOLUTION, COMPLEXITY, AND
THE RADICAL REMAKING
OF ECONOMICS

Eric D. Beinhocker

RANDOM HOUSE

BUSINESS BOOKS

Published by Random House Business Books in 2006

1 3 5 7 9 10 8 6 4 2

Copyright © McKinsey & Company, Inc., 2006

Eric D. Beinhocker has asserted his right under the Copyright, Designs and Patents Act, 1988
to be identified as the author of this work

First published in the United States in 2006 by Harvard Business School Press

Random House Business Books
The Random House Group Limited
20 Vauxhall Bridge Road, London SW1V 2SA

Random House Australia (Pty) Limited
20 Alfred Street, Milsons Point, Sydney,
New South Wales 2061, Australia

Random House New Zealand Limited
18 Poland Road, Glenfield, Auckland 10, New Zealand

Random House (Pty) Limited
Isle of Houghton, Corner of Boundary Road & Carse O'Gowrie,
Houghton 2198, South Africa

Random House Publishers India Private Limited
301 World Trade Tower, Hotel Intercontinental Grand Complex,
Barakhamba Lane, New Delhi 110 001, India

The Random House Group Limited Reg. No. 954009
www.randomhouse.co.uk

A CIP catalogue record for this book is available from the British Library

Papers used by Random House are natural, recyclable products made from wood grown in sustainable forests.
The manufacturing processes conform to the environmental regulations of the country of origin

ISBN 0 7126 76589
ISBN-13 978 0 7126 7658 8 (from Jan 2007)

The author grateful acknowledges permission to reprint the following figures: 4-1, 4-2, 4-3, 4-4: Joshua M. Epstein and Robert Axtell, *Growing Artificial Societies*. Copyright © 1996 the Brookings Institution Press. Reprinted with permission. 5-6, 8-2: John Sterman, *Business Dynamics*. Copyright © 2000 the McGraw-Hill Companies, Inc. Reprinted with permission. 6-1: W. Brian Arthur, "Inductive Reasoning and Bounded Rationality (the El Farol Problem)," *American Economic Review (Papers and Proceedings)* 84, pp. 406–411. Copyright © 1994 American Economic Association. Reprinted with permission. 8-1: David Hackett Fischer, *The Great Wave: Price Revolutions and the Rhythm of History*. Copyright © 1996 David Hackett Fischer. Used by permission of Oxford University Press, Inc. 8-3, 8-4: Benoit B. Mandelbrot, *Fractals and Scaling in Finance*. Copyright © 1997 Benoit B. Mandelbrot. Reprinted with permission of Springer-Verlag New York, Inc. 8-5: Mark Buchanan, *Ubiquity: The Science of History*. Copyright © 2000 Mark Buchanan. Reprinted with permission of Weidenfeld & Nicholson, a division of the Orion Publishing Group. 9-1, 9-2: Karl Sims, "Evolving Virtual Creatures," *Computer Graphics, 2004 Annual Conference on Computer Graphics and Interactive Techniques*, ACM SIGGRAPH'94, pp. 15-22. Copyright © ACM, Inc. Reprinted with permission. 9-3: From *Darwin's Dangerous Idea: Evolution and the Meanings of Life* by Daniel C. Dennett (Penguin Press, 1995). Copyright © Daniel C. Dennett. Reprinted with permission. 9-7, 9-8, 9-9: Eric D. Beinhocker, "Robust Adaptive Strategies," *Sloan Management Review* 40 (3), pp. 95-106. Copyright © 1997 Massachusetts Institute of Technology. Reprinted with permission. 10-4: Reprinted from *Physica D*, 75, Kristian Lindgren and Mats D. Nordhal, "Evolutionary Dynamics of Spatial Games," pp. 292-309, copyright © 1994, reprinted with permission from Elsevier. 17-1: Copyright © 2001 CFA Institute. Reproduced and republished from J. Doyne Farmer, "Toward Agent-Based Models for Investment," *Developments in Quantitative Investment Models*, CFA Institute Conference Proceedings, pp. 61-70, with permission from CFA Institute. All rights reserved. 17-2, 17-3, 17-4: J. Doyne Farmer, "Market Force, Ecology and Evolution," *Industrial Corporate Change* 11 (5), pp. 895-953. Copyright © 2002 Oxford University Press. Reprinted with permission. 18-1: From *Culture Matters*, by Lawrence E. Harrison and Samuel P. Huntington. Copyright © 2000 by Lawrence E. Harrison and Samuel P. Huntington. Reprinted by permission of Basic Books a member of Perseus Books, LLC.

Printed and bound in Great Britain by
Mackays of Chatham plc, Chatham, Kent

FOR TILLY

A door like this has cracked open five or six times since we got up on our hind legs. It's the best possible time to be alive, when almost everything you thought you knew is wrong.

—Tom Stoppard, *Arcadia*

CONTENTS

Preface and Acknowledgments   xi

Part I   A Paradigm Shift

ONE   The Question   3
        How Is Wealth Created?

TWO   Traditional Economics   21
        A World in Equilibrium

THREE   A Critique   45
        Chaos and Cuban Cars

Part II   Complexity Economics

FOUR   The Big Picture   79
        Sugar and Spice

FIVE   Dynamics   99
        The Delights of Disequilibrium

SIX   Agents   115
        Mind Games

SEVEN   Networks   141
        Oh What a Tangled Web We Weave

EIGHT   Emergence   161
         The Puzzle of Patterns

NINE   Evolution   187
         It's a Jungle Out There

Part III **How Evolution Creates Wealth**

TEN   Design Spaces   221
         From Games to Economies

ELEVEN   Physical Technology   241
         From Stone Tools to Spacecraft

TWELVE   Social Technology   261
         From Hunter-Gatherers to Multinationals

THIRTEEN Economic Evolution   279
         From Big Men to Markets

FOURTEEN A New Definition of Wealth   299
         Fit Order

Part IV **What It Means for Business and Society**

FIFTEEN Strategy   323
         Racing the Red Queen

SIXTEEN Organization   349
         A Society of Minds

SEVENTEEN Finance   381
         Ecosystems of Expectations

EIGHTEEN Politics and Policy   415
         The End of Left Versus Right

         Epilogue   451

         Notes   455
         Bibliography   491
         Index   509
         About the Author   527

As I write this, the field of economics is going through its most profound change in over a hundred years. I believe that this change represents a major shift in the intellectual currents of the world that will have a substantial impact on our lives and the lives of generations to come. I also believe that just as biology became a true science in the twentieth century, so too will economics come into its own as a science in the twenty-first century. The great historian and philosopher of science, Thomas Kuhn, observed that scientific inquiry does not advance through steady, even progress. Rather, as one scholar of Kuhn's work described it, science moves forward through "a series of peaceful interludes punctuated by intellectually violent revolutions . . . in each of which one conceptual world view is replaced by another . . ."[1] Kuhn called these periods of upheaval "paradigm shifts," and while the phrase has lost some of its power owing to overuse, this book will argue that what we are witnessing in economics today is in fact the early stages of just such a paradigm shift.

Why does a paradigm shift in economics matter? Why should anyone care other than economists? Most people view economics as a dry, academic, and highly technical field—the "dismal science" as Thomas Carlyle famously put it.[2] Economic ideas matter because they are deeply infused in the intellectual fabric of society. They influence our individual choices ranging from what kind of mortgage we take out, to the investments we make for retirement, to whom we vote for. Economic ideas also provide a critical framework for how business and government leaders make decisions that affect us all. Just as abstract scientific theories are made real in our lives through the airplanes we fly in, the medicines we take, and the computers we use, economic ideas are made real in our lives through the organizations that employ us, the goods and services we consume, and the policies of our governments. As John Maynard Keynes wrote in the conclusion of his *General Theory of Employment, Interest and Money*, "The ideas of economists and political philosophers, both when they are right and when they are wrong, are more powerful than is commonly understood. Indeed, the world is ruled by little else."[3] Throughout history, bad economic ideas have led to misery for millions, while good economic ideas have been fundamental to prosperity.

Despite the importance of economic thinking, few people outside the hushed halls of academia are aware of the fundamental changes under way in the field today. This book is the story of what I will call the Complexity Economics revolution: what it is, what it tells us about the deepest mysteries in economics, and what it means for business and for society at large.

Some scientific revolutions are born whole, the product of a single genius, such as Einstein's development of relativity theory. Others are the product of many people working over multiple decades, for example, the quantum physics revolution from 1900 to 1930. The Complexity Economics revolution is similar to the latter. It is a revolution that is the result of many years of work by scores of people around the world. While many of the ideas in Complexity Economics have deep historical roots, the revolution did not begin brewing until the late 1970s when advances in the physical sciences caused a small number of economists and social scientists to begin to wonder if there might be a fundamentally new way to look at the economy. The advent of cheap and plentiful computing power in the 1980s and 1990s then enabled researchers to explore these ideas in new and often unforeseen ways, kicking the Complexity Economics revolution into full gear.

But it is a revolution still very much in-progress, and as such, it is controversial. Some economists will enthusiastically agree with the ideas in this book, some will vehemently disagree, and many more will agree with some points and disagree with others (as the old joke goes, if you want four opinions, just ask two economists). Nevertheless, I believe that the intellectual tide has turned firmly in the direction of Complexity Economics, and that its concepts will provide the foundation of economic theory and practice for many decades to come. The role of this book is to tell the story of the Complexity Economics revolution and make it accessible to a general audience. In doing so, I will also offer my own views on what the ideas mean, and how they can be applied to the practical worlds of business, finance, and government.

Whom This Book Is For

I've written this book with three audiences in mind. The first is the business leaders, investors, and policy makers who are interested in how new ideas from economics and science might impact their work. For this audience I should note that this is not intended to be a "What do I do Monday morning?" book. Complexity Economics contains a set of very powerful concepts that are highly relevant to some of the most difficult problems executives and policy makers face. However, readers will not find detailed case examples of how leading companies are using Complexity Economics, nor any easy ten-step programs, in this book. Many management books promise readers ideas that are cutting edge and yet have also been proven to work by successful application in scores of companies over many years—of course, you can't have it both ways. My claim is that the ideas of Complexity Economics are indeed cutting-edge, and thus by definition have not yet been widely applied. A few companies have experimented with them, and others, through instinct and serendipity, have stumbled into practices that are consistent with Complexity Economics thinking. Although there have been a few attempts to turn these experiences into management tools, I believe it is still too early to say specifically how these ideas will be applied.[4] Rather than cases and tools, my focus will be on helping readers rewire their thinking about how economic systems work. Rather than a "Monday-morning book," I would think of this as a "Sunday-morning book"—its goal is not to tell you what to do, but to change how you think.

The second audience is anyone with a general interest in economics, social issues, public policy, and science. It is not often that one gets to witness a scientific revolution in the making, particularly one that will have such a large impact on the world. For this audience, I hope that this book can provide a front-row seat for what I believe will be one of the most exciting changes in the intellectual landscape during this century. The book does not assume a prior background in economics or science, and the discussions are not overly technical. However, I will introduce a number of terms that may not be familiar to all readers, and have italicized those terms where they are defined in the text. In fact, one of the important contributions of Complexity Economics is a new language for discussing and understanding economic, business, and social issues.

The third audience is scholars and students. For this group my hope is that this book will be a useful nontechnical review of where we are and where we might go. I also hope it helps clarify (although surely will not resolve) some of the ongoing debates in economics, as well as instigate new ones. For scholars and other readers with a deeper interest in the material, the chapter endnotes should be viewed as an integral part of the discussion. They provide detailed references, as well as more technical discussions and excursions into debates not presented in the main text. For readers interested in pursuing their questions in the original source material, a full bibliography is given at the back.

Acknowledgments

Just as Complexity Economics is the emerging product of many researchers' efforts, this book is the result of the generous support and intellectual contributions of many people to whom I am deeply grateful.

I should begin with Richard Emmet at the Buckingham Browne & Nichols School, whose high school economics class provided the spark for my lifetime interest in the field. Barry Richmond, my professor at Dartmouth, fanned the flames and opened my eyes to the wider world of dynamic systems. Barry remained a friend long after I left Dartmouth, and has been missed since his untimely passing in 2002. At MIT, Rebecca Henderson was an inspirational thesis adviser who taught me to appreciate both the power and intellectual beauty of economic ideas. My other adviser, John Sterman, taught me to also question those very same ideas, and he first introduced me to the concepts of complexity theory. John has been a friend and mentor for many years, and generously read and commented on the entire manuscript.

McKinsey & Company is a truly unique institution and has been remarkable in its support for this work. The Firm provided me with the intellectual freedom to pursue my interests (even when it wasn't always clear where those interests were leading) and a group of highly supportive colleagues to challenge and test my thinking. Current and former colleagues who have played a substantial role in shaping the thinking in this book include Bill Barnett, Lowell Bryan, Hugh Courtney, Kevin Coyne, Jonathan Day, Andrew Doman, John Hagel, Ron Hulme, Bill Huyett, Sarah Kaplan, Tim Koller, Wilhelm Rall, Charles Roxburgh, Somu Subramaniam, Patrick Viguerie, and Adil Zainulbhai. I have also benefited from the support of Stuart Flack, Lang Davison, Saul Rosenberg, Trish Clifford, and Sallie Honeychurch, as well as McKinsey's superb research staff.

There are two individuals from McKinsey who deserve particular mention. First, Dick Foster, who has been a friend and mentor since my earliest days at the Firm. Dick has been an inspiration through his own work, and if any of the ideas in this book have merit, it is likely they were the result of one of our many conversations. Second is Ian Davis, McKinsey's managing director, who has provided unflagging encouragement, support, and more than occasional air-cover during a project that took far longer than I or anyone else expected.

I am also grateful to a number of scholars whose work is discussed in, and informs, this book. Over the years they have given me their valuable time to answer questions about their work and exchange ideas. They include Robert Axtell, Yaneer Bar-Yam, Larry Blume, Eric Bonabeau, Sam Bowles, Joshua Epstein, Duncan Foley, John Geanakoplos, Murray Gell-Mann, John Holland,

Stuart Kauffman, Kristian Lindgren, Benoit Mandelbrot, Phil Mirowski, Melanie Mitchell, Richard Nelson, Tim Ruefli, Didier Sornette, Gene Stanley, Duncan Watts, and Peyton Young.

The most valuable gift one can receive is thoughtful criticism, and several people read major portions of the manuscript and provided insightful feedback, including Vince Darley, David Lane, Scott Page, Eric Smith, Mike Ross, and James Tugendhat. A special thanks to Michael Mauboussin and Laurence Holt, who, along with John Sterman, read and provided detailed comments on the entire manuscript, as well as to two anonymous referees provided by Harvard Business School Press. Not only were the comments of this group unfailingly perceptive, but given the length of the original version, theirs was a true test of endurance.

As readers will see, the Santa Fe Institute (SFI) has, and continues to play, a central role in the story of Complexity Economics. I am very grateful to the Institute for hosting me for a sabbatical several years ago, for inviting me to innumerable conferences and symposia, as well as allowing me to just hang out and talk to people. SFI is a truly special place and I would like to thank its current president Geoffrey West, and its past presidents Ellen Goldberg and Bob Eisenstein for their support, as well as Suzanne Dulle and Susan Ballati.

Two other individuals affiliated with SFI have played key roles in this book. I have received tremendous intellectual inspiration from Brian Arthur and Doyne Farmer, who have never failed to be generous with their time, have deeply influenced (and often corrected) my thinking, and commented on substantial portions of the manuscript.

Naturally, not all of these people may agree with everything in this book, and they bear no responsibility for its errors or other flaws.

Various sections of the book have been presented at conferences over the years, including the 2002 University of Michigan Complexity Workshop, the 2002 Strategy World Congress at Oxford, the 2004 London School of Economics Complexity Symposium, the 2005 System Dynamics Conference, and a number of McKinsey and Santa Fe Institute events. I am grateful to the participants of these conferences for their feedback.

My agent Amanda Urban has been instrumental in making this project possible. No writer could ask for a more skilled and supportive agent, and her colleagues Margaret Halton and Kate Jones have been terrific as well.

I have also been extremely fortunate to have Hollis Heimbouch of the Harvard Business School Press as my editor. She believed in this project from the very beginning, and steadfastly supported it through its long gestation. Her consistently wise counsel and patience have always been appreciated, as have the efforts of the Press staff including Todd Berman, Mark Bloomfield, Erin Brown, Constance Devanthery-Lewis, Mike Fender, David Goehring,

Zeenat Potia, Brian Surette, Christine Turnier-Vallecillo, Jennifer Waring, and Leslie Zheutlin. The manuscript benefited significantly from the thorough and thoughtful copyediting of Patricia Boyd, as well as earlier editing assistance from William Patrick.

Clare Smith of Random House UK played a crucial role in encouraging me to undertake this book in the first place, and I'm grateful to her for her efforts as well as to Susan Sandon, Nigel Wilcockson, and Rina Gill who have taken leadership of the project at Random House following Clare's moving on to new challenges.

I have also benefited from the tireless support of three assistants over the course of writing this book, Claire Tully, Sarah Prescod, and Belinda Marks, who helped in innumerable areas.

Finally, none of it would have been possible without my family. To my parents Gilbert and Barbara, and my sister Elizabeth, and brother Rob, I will always be grateful for their love and encouragement. My daughter Anna was born while I was writing this book, and provided endless joy and wonderful distractions crawling, and eventually toddling, around my study, as well as eating occasional bits of manuscript.

Greatest thanks of all go to my wife Tilly. Not only was she my most trusted source of advice during the project, but she supported me in every possible way, from being a "single mum" during weekends before editing deadlines, to words of encouragement during late-night writing sessions. This was doubly hard for her while juggling a new baby and her own high-pressure career. This book is dedicated to her with my deepest love, respect, and gratitude.

—Eric Beinhocker
London
February 2, 2006

PART I

A Paradigm Shift

*It may be that universal history is
the history of a handful of metaphors.*

—Jorge Luis Borges, *Labyrinths*

CHAPTER ONE

The Question

HOW IS WEALTH CREATED?

I SAT PERCHED on a small ledge, with my back pressed against a dung wall, in the smoky center room of a thatched hut belonging to an elderly Maasai tribesman. The hut was in a remote village in southwestern Kenya. The Maasai elder, with his wise, weather-beaten face and sharp eyes, had been asking me polite questions about my family and where I came from. Now he wanted to get the measure of me. He fixed his gaze on mine across the cooking fire and asked, "How many cattle do you own?" I paused for a moment and then quietly replied, "None." A local Maasai teacher, who had befriended me and was acting as my guide, translated my reply. There was a murmur around the small room as various members of the village, curious about the stranger, digested this piece of information. After a few moments' consideration, the elder replied, "I am very sorry for you." But the pity evident in his voice and on his face was also tinged with puzzlement as to how someone so poor could afford to travel such long distances and own a camera. As the discussion turned back to questions about my family, I remarked that I have an uncle who once owned a large herd of cattle on his farm in Maryland. There was then a quick nodding of understanding as the mystery was solved— the visitor was clearly the ne'er-do-well nephew of a rich uncle, traveling and living off his relative's bovine wealth.

The Mysteries of Wealth

What is wealth? For a Maasai tribesman, wealth is measured in cattle. For most of the readers of this book, it is measured in dollars, pounds, euros, yen, or some other currency. Over two hundred years ago, the great economist

Adam Smith noted the rich variety of ways that people have measured their wealth throughout history: "In the [earlier] ages of society, cattle are said to have been the common instrument of commerce; though they must have been a most inconvenient one . . . Salt is said to be the common instrument of commerce and exchanges in Abyssinia; a species of shells in some parts of the coast of India; dried cod at Newfoundland; tobacco in Virginia; sugar in some of our West India colonies; hides or dressed leather in some other countries; and there is at this day a village in Scotland where it is not uncommon, I am told, for a workman to carry nails instead of money to the baker's shop or the alehouse."[1]

Is wealth an intrinsic, tangible thing? Is there something inherent in cows, cod, and nails that gives them value? For a Maasai tribesman, the wealth embedded in his cattle is there for all to see. It provides him and his family with milk, meat, bone, hide, and horn. Yet, as Smith showed in his *Wealth of Nations,* wealth is not a fixed concept; the value of something depends on what someone else is willing to pay for it at a particular point in time. Even for a Maasai, the value of a cow today may not be the value of a cow tomorrow. For those who measure their wealth in the paper of currencies, wealth is an even more ephemeral concept. Most people in developed countries never see or touch the bulk of their wealth—their hard-earned savings exist only as electronic blips on a bank's faraway computer. Yet those ghostly blips can be converted into the tangible goods of cows, cod, nails, or whatever else one desires (or can afford) with the swipe of a credit card or the click of a mouse.

But where does wealth come from in the first place? How does the sweat of our brows and the knowledge of our brains lead to its creation? Why has the world grown richer over time? How have we gone from trading cattle to trading microchips? This line of inquiry ultimately leads us to perhaps the most important mystery of wealth: how can we create more of it? We can ask this question out of narrow self-interest, but we can also ask the larger question of how the wealth of society can be increased. How can managers grow their companies to provide more jobs and opportunities for people? How can governments grow their economies and address issues of poverty and inequality? How can societies around the world create the resources needed for better education, health care, and other priorities? And, how can the global economy grow in a way that is environmentally sustainable? Wealth may not buy happiness, but poverty does buy misery for millions around the world.[2]

The questions this book will explore—What is wealth? How is it created? How can it be increased?—are among the most important questions for society and among the oldest questions in economics. Yet, they are questions economics has historically struggled to answer. The thesis of this book is that new answers to these fundamental questions are beginning to emerge from work carried out over the past few decades. These new answers come not just from the work of economists, but also from biologists, physicists, evolutionary theorists, computer scientists, anthropologists, psychologists, and cognitive scientists. We will see that modern science, in particular evolutionary theory and the theory of complex adaptive systems, provides us with a radically new perspective on these long-standing economic questions.

In this chapter, I will outline the major themes of the book and give a brief preview of the ideas we will explore. But before we develop a new perspective on the answers, we need to shift our perspective on the questions. The economy is something most people take for granted in their daily lives and don't often think about. When we do think about the economy, it is often in the context of what Princeton economist Paul Krugman has called "up and down economics," as in "the stock market is up" and "unemployment is down."[3] But we need to step back from the wiggling graphs of the economy's short-term ups and downs for a moment and consider the economy as a whole, as a system.

Humanity's Most Complex Creation

Take a look around your house. Take a look at what you are wearing. Take a look out your window. No matter where you are, from the biggest industrialized city to the smallest rural village, you are surrounded by economic activity and its results. Twenty-four hours a day, seven days a week, the planet is abuzz with humans designing, organizing, manufacturing, servicing, transporting, communicating, buying, and selling.[4]

The complexity of all this activity is mind-boggling. Imagine a small rural town, the kind of quiet, simple place you might go to escape the hurly-burly of modern life. Now imagine that the townspeople have made you their benevolent dictator, but in exchange for your awesome powers, you are responsible for making sure the town is fed, clothed, and sheltered each day. No one will do anything without your say-so, and therefore each morning, you have to create a to-do list for organizing all the town's economic activities.[5] You have to write down all the jobs that must get done, all the things that need to get coordinated, and the timing and sequence of everything. No detail is too small, whether it is making sure that Mrs. Wetherspoon's flower shop gets her delivery of roses or that Mr. Nutley's insurance claim for his lumbago is processed. Even for a small town, it would be an impossibly long and complex list. Now think about what a similar to-do list might look like for managing the global economy as a whole. Think of the trillions of intricately coordinated decisions that must be made every minute of every day around the world to keep the global economy humming. Yet, there is no one in charge of the global to-do list. There is no benevolent dictator making sure that fish gets from a fisherman in Mozambique to a restaurant in Korea to provide the lunch for a computer worker who makes parts for a PC that a fashion designer in Milan uses to design a suit for an interest-rate futures trader in Chicago. Yet, extraordinarily, these sorts of things happen every day in a bottom-up, self-organized way.

The most startling empirical fact in economics is that there is an economy at all. The second most startling empirical fact is that day in and day out, for the most part, it works. It provides most (but sadly not all) of the world's 6.4 billion people with employment, food, shelter, clothing, and products ranging from Hello Kitty handbags to medical lasers. If one thinks of other highly complex human-made systems, such as the International Space Station, the government of China, or the Internet, it is clear that the global economy is orders of magnitude more complex than any other physical or social structure ever built by humankind.[6]

The economy is a marvel of complexity. Yet no one designed it and no one runs it. There are, of course, CEOs, government officials, international organizations, investors, and others who attempt to manage their particular patch of it, but when one steps back and looks at the entirety of the $36.5 trillion global economy, it is clear that no one is really in charge.[7]

Yet how did the economy get here? Science tells us that our history began in a state of nature, literally "without a shirt on our backs." Our immediate ancestors were hominid protohumans who had large brains and nimble hands and who roamed the African savanna not far from where I sat with the Maasai tribespeople. How did humankind travel from a state of nature to the stunning self-organized complexity of the modern global economy?

2.5 Million Years of Economic History in Brief

Intuitively, many people imagine that humankind's upward climb in economic sophistication was a slow, steady journey, a linear progression from stone tools to DVD players. The actual story, pieced together by archaeologists, anthropologists, historians, and economists, is not at all like that. It is far more dramatic.[8]

The story begins when the first hominids appeared on earth around 7 million years ago and their descendents, *Australopithecus africanus,* began to walk upright around 4 million years ago.[9] By about 2.5 million years ago, *Homo habilis* began to use its relatively large brain to begin making crude stone tools. We can think of these stone tools as the first products, and we can imagine that at some point two of our hominid ancestors, probably from the same band of close relatives, sat in the dust of the savanna and traded tools. We will use this very approximate point of 2.5 million years ago as the marker for the beginning of the human "economy." It then took roughly another million years for *Homo erectus* to discover fire and begin to produce a wider range of tools made out of stone, wood, and bone. Biologically modern humans, *Homo sapiens,* appeared around 130,000 years ago and developed increasingly sophisticated and diverse tools. At some point—there is much debate on when—*Homo sapiens* evolved the critical skill of language. The economic activity of these first modern humans was primarily limited to foraging in roving bands of close relatives and to basic tool manufacturing.

It is not until around 35,000 years ago that we begin to see the first evidence of a more settled lifestyle, with burial sites, cave drawings, and decorative objects. During this period, archaeologists also begin to see evidence of trading *between* groups of early humans; the evidence included burial-site tools made from nonlocal materials, seashell jewelry found with noncoastal tribes, and patterns of movement suggesting trading routes.[10] One of the great benefits of trade is that it enables specialization, and during this period, the record shows a dramatic increase in the variety of tools and artifacts. As Paul Seabright of the University of Toulouse notes, cooperative trading between nonrelatives is a uniquely human activity.[11] No other species has developed the combination of trading among strangers and a division of labor that characterizes the human economy. In fact, Richard Horan of Michigan State University and his colleagues argue that it was this unique ability of *Homo sapiens* to trade that gave them the critical advantage in their competition with rival hominid species such as *Homo neanderthalensis* (the Neanderthals), enabling our ancestors to survive while the other hominids became extinct.[12]

With permanent settlements, a variety of tools, and the creation of trading networks, our ancestors achieved a level of cultural and economic sophistication that anthropologists refer to as a *hunter-gatherer lifestyle.* From the archaeological record, we have some knowledge of how our hunter-gatherer ancestors lived and what their economy looked like, but we also have another rich source of information on this way of life. There are still a few very isolated places on earth where hunter-gatherer tribes continue to live with very little contact with the modern world, virtually unchanged from tens of thousands of years ago. Anthropologists think of these tribes as living time capsules of an earlier era.

A Tale of Two Tribes

Consider two tribes. First, we have the Yanomamö, a stone-tool-making hunter-gatherer tribe living along the Orinoco River on the remote border of Brazil and Venezuela.[13] Second, we have the New Yorkers, a cell-phone-talking, café-latte-drinking tribe living along the Hudson River on the border of New York and New Jersey. Both tribes share the same thirty thousand or so genes that all humans do and thus, in terms of biology and innate intelligence, are essentially identical. Yet, the lifestyle of the New Yorkers is vastly different from the well-preserved hunter-gatherer lifestyle of the Yanomamö, who have yet to invent the wheel, have no writing, and have a numbering system that does not go beyond *one, two,* and *many.*

If we take a closer look at the economies of the two tribes, we see that Yanomamö employment is focused on collecting food in the forest, hunting small game, gardening a limited number of fruits and vegetables, and maintaining shelters. The Yanomamö also make items such as baskets, hammocks, stone tools, and weapons. They live in villages of forty to fifty people and trade goods and services among each other, as well as among the 250 or so other villages in the area. The average income of a Yanomamö tribesperson is approximately $90 per person per year (this, naturally, is an estimate as they do not use money or keep statistics), while the average income of a New Yorker in 2001 was around $36,000, or 400 times that of a Yanomamö.[14] Without any judgments on who is happier, morally superior, or more in tune with their environment, there is clearly a wide gap in material wealth between the two tribes. The Yanomamö have shorter life expectancies than the New Yorkers, and during their lives, the Yanomamö must endure uncertainties, diseases, violence, threats from their environment, and other hardships that even the poorest New Yorkers do not face—one is eight times more likely to die in a given year living in a Yanomamö village than living in a New York borough.[15]

But it is not just the absolute level of income that makes New Yorkers so wealthy; it is also the incredible variety of things their wealth can buy. Imagine you had the income of a New Yorker, but you could only spend it on things in the Yanomamö economy.[16] If you spent $36,000 fixing up your mud hut, buying the best clay pots in the village, and eating the finest Yanomamö cuisine, you would be extraordinarily wealthy by Yanomamö standards, but you would still feel far poorer than a typical New Yorker with his or her Nike sneakers, televisions, and vacations in Florida. The number of economic choices the average New Yorker has is staggering.[17] The Wal-Mart near JFK Airport has over 100,000 different items in stock, there are over 200 television channels offered on cable TV, Barnes & Noble lists over 8 million titles, the local supermarket has 275 varieties of breakfast cereal, the typical department store offers 150 types of lipstick, and there are over 50,000 restaurants in New York City alone.

Retailers have a measure, known as *stock keeping units*, or *SKUs*, that is used to count the number of types of products sold by their stores. For example, five types of blue jeans would be five SKUs. If one inventoried all the types of products and services in the Yanomamö economy, that is, the different models of stone axes, the number of types of food, and so on, one would find that the total number of SKUs in the Yanomamö economy can probably be measured in the several hundreds, and at the most in the thousands.[18] The number of SKUs in the New Yorker's economy is not precisely known, but using a variety of data sources, I very roughly estimate that it is on the order of 10^{10} (in other words, tens of billions).[19] To put this enormous number in perspective, estimates of the total number of species on earth range from 10^6 to 10^8. Thus, the most dramatic difference between the New Yorker and Yanomamö economies is not their "wealth" measured in dollars, a mere 400-fold difference, but rather the hundred-million-fold, or eight orders of magnitude difference in the complexity and diversity of the New Yorkers' economy versus the Yanomamö economy.

The lifestyle of the Yanomamö is fairly typical of our ancestors circa 15,000 years ago.[20] This sounds like a long time ago, but in terms of the total economic history of our species, *the world of the Yanomamö is the very, very recent past*. If we use the appearance of the first tools as our starting point, it took about 2,485,000 years, or 99.4 percent, of our economic history to go from the first tools to the hunter-gatherer level of economic and social sophistication typified by the Yanomamö (figure 1-1). It then took only 0.6 percent of human history to leap from the $90 per capita 10^2 SKU economy of the Yanomamö, to the $36,000 per capita 10^{10} SKU economy of the New Yorkers.

Zooming in for a more granular look into the past 15,000 years reveals something even more surprising. The economic journey between the hunter-gatherer world and the modern world was also very slow over most of the 15,000-year period, and then progress exploded in the last 250 years. According to data compiled by Berkeley economist J. Bradford DeLong, it took 12,000 years to inch from the $90 per-person hunter-gatherer economy to the roughly $150 per-person economy of the Ancient Greeks in 1000 BC.[21] It wasn't until 1750 AD, when world gross domestic product (GDP) per person reached around $180, that the figure had finally managed to double from our hunter-gatherer days 15,000 years ago. Then in the mid-eighteenth century, something extraordinary happened—world GDP per person increased 37-fold in an incredibly short 250 years to its current level of $6,600, with the richest societies, such as the New Yorkers, climbing well above that.[22] Global wealth rocketed onto a nearly vertical curve that we are still climbing today.

FIGURE 1-1

The Explosive Growth in Human Wealth

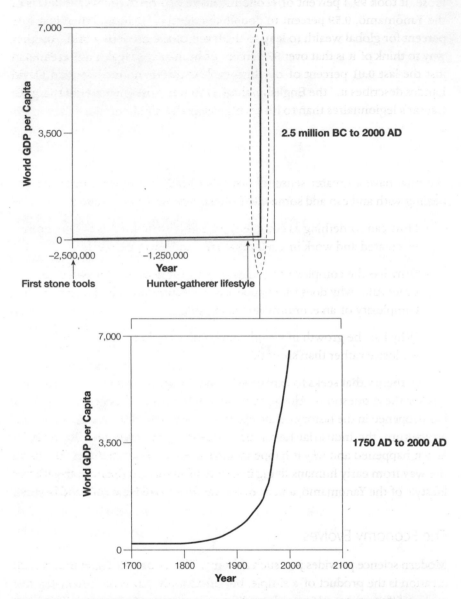

2.5 million BC to 2000 AD

First stone tools

Hunter-gatherer lifestyle

1750 AD to 2000 AD

Source: Estimates for 1 million BC to 2000 AD from J. Bradford DeLong, University of California, Berkeley. Estimates for 2.5 million BC to 1 million BC are an extrapolation. GDP per capita is measured in 1990 international dollars.

To summarize 2.5 million years of economic history in brief: for a very, very, very long time not much happened; then all of a sudden, all hell broke loose. It took 99.4 percent of economic history to reach the wealth levels of the Yanomamö, 0.59 percent to double that level by 1750, and then just 0.01 percent for global wealth to leap to the levels of the modern world. Another way to think of it is that over 97 percent of humanity's wealth was created in just the last 0.01 percent of our history.[23] As the economic historian David Landes describes it, "the Englishman of 1750 was closer in material things to Caesar's legionnaires than to his own great-grand-children."[24]

We now have a greater sense of just what kind of a phenomenon we are dealing with and can add some additional questions to our inquiry:

- How can something as complex and highly structured as the economy be created and work in a self-organized and bottom-up way?

- Why has the complexity and diversity of the economy grown over time? And, why does there appear to be a correlation between the complexity of an economy and its wealth?

- Why has the growth in wealth and complexity been sudden and explosive rather than smooth?

Any theory that seeks to explain what wealth is and how it is created must answer these questions. Although we know the historical narrative of *what* has happened in the history of the economy, for example, the advent of settled agriculture, the Industrial Revolution, and so on, we still need a theory of *how* it happened and *why* it happened. We need a theory that can take us all the way from early humans living in a state of nature, to the hunter-gatherer lifestyle of the Yanomamö, and from the Yanomamö to New York and beyond.

The Economy Evolves

Modern science provides just such a theory. This book will argue that wealth creation is the product of a simple, but profoundly powerful, three-step formula—differentiate, select, and amplify—the formula of evolution. The same process that has driven the growing order and complexity of the biosphere has driven the growing order and complexity of the "econosphere."[25] And the same process that led to an explosion of species diversity in the Cambrian period led to an explosion in SKU diversity during the Industrial Revolution.

We are accustomed to thinking of evolution in a biological context, but modern evolutionary theory views evolution as something much more general. Evolution is an *algorithm;* it is an all-purpose formula for innovation, a formula that, through its special brand of trial and error, creates new designs and solves difficult problems. Evolution can perform its tricks not just in the "substrate" of DNA, but in any system that has the right information-processing and information-storage characteristics.[26] In short, evolution's simple recipe of "differentiate, select, and amplify" is a type of computer program— a program for creating novelty, knowledge, and growth. Because evolution is a form of information processing, it can do its order-creating work in realms ranging from computer software to the mind, to human culture, and to the economy.

Economics and evolutionary theory have a long history together (something we will return to). One of the criticisms of that history is that there has been too much loose analogizing about how the economy might be *like* an evolutionary system. For example, one might say that the computer industry is like an ecological niche, with different "species" of players such as chip designers, hard-drive manufacturers, software providers, and so on, engaged in a "survival of the fittest" struggle within that niche. Paul Krugman calls such metaphorical comparisons of economic and biological systems "biobabble."[27] Most of the researchers discussed in this book would agree with Krugman that such "biobabble" is neither good science nor very illuminating. Modern efforts to understand the economy as an evolutionary system avoid such metaphors and instead focus on understanding how the universal algorithm of evolution is literally and specifically implemented in the information-processing substrate of human economic activity. While both biological and economic systems share the core algorithm of evolution and thus have some similarities, their realizations of evolution are in fact very different and must be understood in their individual contexts.

From a scientific standpoint, the distinction between a metaphorical versus a literal understanding of the global economy as an evolutionary system is critical. Saying that economic systems are *like* biological systems does not tell us much that is scientifically useful. But saying that both economic and biological systems are subclasses of a more general and universal class of evolutionary systems tells us a lot. This is because researchers believe that there are general laws of evolutionary systems.[28] Scientists consider certain features of nature universal. For example, gravity works the same way on the earth as it does in the farthest reaches of the universe, and it works the same way on atoms, apples, and galaxies. Modern evolutionary theorists believe that, like gravity, evolution is a universal phenomenon, meaning that no matter whether the algorithm is running in the substrate of biological DNA, a computer program, the economy, or in the substrate of an alien biology on a distant planet, evolution will follow certain general laws in its behavior.

If the economy is truly an evolutionary system, and there are general laws of evolutionary systems, then it follows that there are general laws of economics—a controversial notion for many. Saying that there are laws of economics does not imply that we will ever be able to make perfect predictions about the economy, but it does imply that we might someday have a far deeper understanding of economic phenomena than we do today. It also means that economics in the future may be able to make prescriptive recommendations about business and public policy with a level of scientific authority that it has not had before.

Some might see the prospect of a more scientific economics as tremendously exciting and offering many potential benefits for the world. Others might see this as yet another misguided attempt to apply science to the problems of human society. Such critics would remind us of the often-repugnant views that came out of the Social Darwinist movement during the late nineteenth and early twentieth centuries, when philosophers such as Herbert Spencer attempted to crudely and metaphorically apply Darwin's theories to the social and economic realm.[29] The Social Darwinists viewed the principle of "survival of the fittest" (a phrase often misattributed to Darwin, but actually from Spencer) as justifying class inequalities, racism, colonialism, and other social injustices. The new views of economic evolution that we will discuss have nothing in common with the old views of Social Darwinism. In fact, they point in the opposite direction, noting that cooperation is as vital an ingredient in economic development as "survival of the fittest" individualism. Likewise, critics might point to the numerous disasters in social engineering caused by the "scientific" theories of Marxism. The cautions on social engineering are duly noted, and the new theories we will discuss help reveal why economic phenomena are so unpredictable and why most efforts at large-scale social engineering have historically failed.

The Creation of Fit Design

Just what kind of an algorithm is evolution? What does it do? The evolutionary philosopher Daniel Dennett calls evolution a general-purpose algorithm for creating "design without a designer."[30] Take for example, *Lumbricus terrestris*, the common earthworm, an ingenious design for the purpose of surviving and reproducing in the soil environment of forests, meadows, and household gardens of North America and Europe. It is in essence a tube that propels itself through the earth, ingesting soil in one end and passing it out the other, absorbing lots of nutritious microorganisms in between and gaining sufficient calories for it to find more food and reproduce. This particular biological design comes fully equipped with touch and vibration sensors to help it avoid predators, and backup systems in most of its body segments so that if it is cut in two, it can regenerate itself. It can also reproduce in sufficient numbers to increase the odds that a good many of its offspring will survive to reproduce themselves. The brilliant design for *Lumbricus terrestris* was created by the algorithm of evolution without a rational designer (in this book I will take an unapologetically scientific stance toward evolution and not address religious debates around creationism or so-called "intelligent design").[31]

Evolution creates designs, or more appropriately, discovers designs, through a process of trial and error. A variety of candidate designs are created and tried out in the environment; designs that are successful are retained, replicated, and built upon, while those that are unsuccessful are discarded. Through repetition, the process creates designs that are fit for their particular purpose and environment. If the conditions are right, competition between designs for finite resources drives the emergence of greater structure and complexity over time, as evolution builds on the successes of the past to create novel designs for the future.[32] Then as the world changes, so too do the designs that evolution creates, often in brilliant and sometimes surprising ways. Evolution is a method for searching enormous, almost infinitely large spaces of possible designs for the almost infinitesimally small fraction of designs that are "fit" according to their particular purpose and environment. As Dennett puts it, evolution is a search algorithm that "finds needles of good design in haystacks of possibility."[33]

Perhaps one needs "design without a designer" to explain biological evolution, but why do we need "design without a designer" to explain the process of wealth creation in the economy when we have lots of human designers around? Aren't we the gods of our own economic creation? We are accustomed to thinking of human rationality and creativity as the primary driving forces behind wealth creation. Wealth, after all, is created by smart, innovative people coming up with new ideas for products and services and lots of hard work to make and sell them. I will argue that human rationality and creativity do play an important role in wealth creation, but not the role we usually think of. Rationality and creativity feed and shape the workings of the evolutionary algorithm in the economy, but do not replace it.

Consider the shirt, the blouse, or any other kind of top you are wearing— where did its design come from?[34] Well, you might reply, it's obvious; a clothes designer designed it. But there is more to the story than just that. What really happened was more or less the following. A number of clothes designers took preexisting ideas of what a shirt should look like and used their rationality and creativity to create all sorts of variations of "shirts" and sketched them out. Those clothes designers then looked at their various sketches and selected a subset of the designs that they thought consumers would like, and made a limited number of samples. The designers then showed those samples to the management of a clothing company, which selected a subset of the designs that it thought consumers would like, and arranged for their manufacture. The clothing company then showed its wares to various retailers, which likewise selected a subset of the designs that they thought consumers would like. With orders in hand, the clothing company then scaled up its manufacturing and supplied the retailer with the shirts. You then walked into a store, browsed through a wide variety of shirts, and selected the one you liked and bought it. Differentiation of designs, selection according to some criterion of fitness, and amplification or scaling up of the successful designs to the next stage of the process—all of this happened both within the clothing company itself and within the overall fashion marketplace. Your shirt was not designed; it was evolved.

But why does the fashion industry go through this iterative, and in many ways, wasteful, process? The reason that your shirt was evolved rather than designed is that no one could predict exactly what kind of shirt you would want out of the almost infinite space of possible shirt designs. The old Soviet Union tried this kind of rational prediction in its infamous five-year plans, and the results included both economic disasters and major fashion errors. As we will see, despite all the strengths and virtues of human rationality, prediction in a system as complex as the economy over anything but the very short term is next to impossible. We use our brains as best we can in economic decision making, but then we experiment and tinker our way into an unpredictable future, keeping and building on what works and discarding what does not. Our intentionality, rationality, and creativity do matter as a driving force in the economy, but they matter *as part of a larger evolutionary process*.

Economic evolution is not a single process, but rather the result of three interlinked processes. The first is the evolution of technology, a critical factor in economic growth throughout history. Most notably, the sharp bend in economic growth around 1750 coincides with the great technological leap of the Industrial Revolution. But the evolution of technology is only part of the story. The evolutionary economist Richard Nelson of Columbia University has pointed out that there are in fact two types of technology that play a major role in economic growth.[35] The first is *Physical Technology;* this is what we are accustomed to thinking of as technology, things such as bronze-making techniques, steam engines, and microchips. *Social Technologies,* on the other hand, are ways of organizing people to do things. Examples include settled agriculture, the rule of law, money, joint stock companies, and venture capital. Nelson notes that while Physical Technologies have clearly had an immense impact on society, the contributions of Social Technologies have been equally important and in fact, the two coevolve with each other.[36] During the Industrial Revolution, for example, Richard Arkwright's invention of the spinning frame (a Physical Technology) in the eighteenth century made it economical to organize cloth-making in large factories (a Social Technology), which in turn helped spur numerous innovations in the application of water power, steam, and electricity to manufacturing (back to Physical Technologies).[37] The stories of the agricultural, industrial, and information revolutions are all largely stories of the reciprocal dance between Physical and Social Technologies.

Yet the coevolution of Physical and Social Technologies is only two-thirds of the picture. Technologies alone are nothing more than ideas and designs. The Physical Technology for a cloth-spinning frame is not itself a cloth-spinning frame—someone actually has to make one. Likewise, the Social Technology for a factory is not a factory—someone actually has to organize it. In order for technologies to have an impact on the world, someone, or some group of people, needs to turn the Physical and Social Technologies from concepts into reality. In the economic realm, that role is played by business. Businesses fuse Physical and Social Technologies together and express them into the environment in the form of products and services.

Businesses are themselves a form of design. The design of a business encompasses its strategy, organizational structure, management processes, culture, and a host of other factors. Business designs evolve over time through a process of differentiation, selection, and amplification, with the market as the ultimate arbiter of fitness. One of the major themes of this book is that it is the three-way coevolution of Physical Technologies, Social Technologies, and business designs that accounts for the patterns of change and growth we see in the economy.

Complexity Economics

The notion that the economy is an evolutionary system is a radical idea, especially because it directly contradicts much of the standard theory in economics developed over the past one hundred years. It is far from a new idea, however. Evolutionary theory and economics have a long and intertwined history.[38] In fact it was an economist who helped spark one of Charles Darwin's most important insights. In 1798, the English economist Thomas Robert Malthus published a book titled *An Essay on the Principle of Population, as It Affects Future Improvements of Society,* in which he portrayed the economy as a competitive struggle for survival and a constant race between population growth and humankind's ability to improve its productivity. It was a race that, Malthus predicted, humankind would lose. Darwin read Malthus's work and described his reaction in his autobiography:

> In October 1838, that is fifteen months after I had begun my systematic enquiry, I happened to read for my amusement "Malthus on Population", and being well prepared to appreciate the struggle for existence which everywhere goes on from long-continued observation of the habits of animals and plants, it once struck me that under these circumstances favorable variations would tend to be preserved and unfavorable ones to be destroyed. The result of this would be the formation of new species.
> Here then I had at last got a theory by which to work.[39]

Darwin's great insight into the critical role of natural selection in evolution was thus inspired by economics.[40] It was not long after Darwin published his *Origin of Species* that the intellectual currents began to flow back the other way from evolutionary theorists to economists. In 1898, the economist Thorstein Veblen wrote an article that still reads remarkably well today arguing that the economy is an evolutionary system.[41] Not long afterward, Alfred Marshall, one of the founders of modern economic theory, wrote in the introduction to his famous *Principles of Economics,* "The Mecca of the economist lies in economic biology."[42] Over the following decades, a number of great economists, including Joseph Schumpeter and Friedrich Hayek, delved into the relationship between economics and evolutionary theory.[43] In 1982, Richard Nelson and Sidney Winter published a landmark book titled *An Evolutionary Theory of Economic Change.* It was the first major attempt to marry evolutionary theory, economics, and the then recently developed tool of computer simulation.[44]

Despite these efforts by some of the finest minds in economics, evolutionary thinking has had relatively little impact on mainstream economic theory. Beginning at about the same time as Darwin's *Origin of the Species,* economics took a turn down a very different road. Since the late nineteenth century, the organizing paradigm of economics has been the idea that the economy is an *equilibrium system,* essentially a system at rest. As we will see, the primary inspiration for economists from the late nineteenth through the mid-twentieth centuries was not biology, but physics, in particular the physics of motion and energy. Traditional economic theory views the economy as being like a rubber ball rolling around the bottom of a large bowl. Eventually the ball will settle down into the bottom of the bowl, to its resting, or equilibrium, point. The ball will stay there until some external force shakes, bends, or otherwise shocks the bowl, sending the ball to a new equilibrium point. The mainstream paradigm of economics over the past hundred years has portrayed the economy as a system that moves from equilibrium point to equilibrium point over time, propelled along by shocks from technology, politics, changes in consumer tastes, and other external factors.

While economists were pursuing their vision of the economy as an equilibrium system, during the latter half of the twentieth century, physicists, chemists, and biologists became increasingly interested in systems that were far from equilibrium, that were dynamic and complex, and that never settled into a state of rest. Beginning in the 1970s, scientists began to refer to these types of systems as *complex systems*. This is a term we will look at in detail later, but in brief, a complex system is a system of many dynamically interacting parts or particles. In such systems the micro-level interactions of the parts or particles lead to the emergence of macro-level patterns of behavior. For example, a single water molecule sitting in isolation is rather boring. But if one puts a few billion water molecules together and adds some energy in the right way, one gets the complex macro pattern of a whirlpool.[45] The pattern of the whirlpool is the result of the dynamic interactions between the individual water molecules. One cannot have a whirlpool with a single water molecule; rather, the whirlpool is a collective or "emergent" property of the system itself.

During the 1970s, as scientists came to know more about the behaviors of complex systems, they became increasingly interested in systems in which the particles were not simple things with fixed behaviors like water molecules, but were things with some intelligence and the capability of adapting to their environment. Water molecules cannot adapt their behavior, but ants, for example, can. An ant may not be terribly smart by human standards, but it can nonetheless process information from other ants and from its environment and modify its behavior accordingly. Like a water molecule, a single ant on its own is not terribly exciting. However, if you put a few thousand ants together, they interact with each other, communicate using chemical signals, and can coordinate their activities to do things such as build elaborate anthills and organize sophisticated defenses against attackers. Scientists refer to parts or particles that have the ability to process information and adapt their behavior as *agents* and call the systems that agents interact in *complex adaptive systems*.[46] Other examples of complex adaptive systems include the cells in your body's immune system, interacting organisms in an ecosystem, and users on the Internet. With the advent of inexpensive, high-powered computers in the 1980s, scientists began to make rapid progress in understanding complex adaptive systems in the natural world and to see such systems as forming a universal class, with many common behaviors. In fact, many biologists have come to view evolutionary systems as just one particular type, or subclass, of complex adaptive systems.

Social scientists following this work increasingly began to wonder whether economies too might be a type of complex adaptive system. The most obvious characteristic of economies is that they are collections of people interacting with each other in complex ways, processing information, and adapting their behaviors. In the 1980s and early 1990s, researchers began to experiment with models of economic phenomena that were radically different from traditional models.[47] Rather than portraying the economy as a static equilibrium system, these models presented the economy as a buzzing hive of dynamic activity, with no equilibrium in sight. Just as the pattern of a whirlpool arises from interacting water molecules, these models showed complex patterns of boom and bust and waves of innovation emerging from the interactions of simulated agents, just as they do in the real economy. Interest and research in understanding the economy as a complex adaptive system has grown rapidly during the past decade, and over the course of this book, we will undertake a review of that work.

I will refer to this body of work as *Complexity Economics* (credit—or blame—for coining this term goes to the economist Brian Arthur, formerly of Stanford University and the Santa Fe Institute).[48] One should not assume from this label that there is currently a single, synthetic theory of Complexity Economics. Rather, my use of the term is intended to cover the broad range of theories, hypotheses, tools, techniques, and speculations that we will survey in this book. At this stage in its development, Complexity Economics is a work in progress, or what philosophers of science refer to as a "program" rather than a unified theory.[49]

The Road Map Ahead

If the economy is indeed a complex adaptive system, then this has four important implications. First, it means that for the past century, economists have fundamentally misclassified the economy and that the mainstream economic theory reflected in textbooks, management thinking, and government policies today is either wrong or, at best, only approximately right. This is an argument we will explore over the remainder of part 1.

Second, viewing the economy as a complex adaptive system provides us with a new set of tools, techniques, and theories for explaining economic phenomena. We will discuss these new approaches in part 2.

Third, it means that wealth must be a product of evolutionary processes. Just as biological evolution summoned complex organisms and ecosystems out of the primordial soup, economic evolution has taken humankind from a state of nature to the modern global economy, filling the world with order, complexity, and diversity along the way. In part 3, we will develop and discuss an evolutionary explanation for the creation of economic wealth.

Fourth and finally, history shows that each time there has been a major shift in the paradigm of economic theory, the tremors have been felt far beyond the academic world. Adam Smith's ideas had an important influence on the growth of free trade in the nineteenth century; Karl Marx's vision inspired revolutions and the rise of socialism in the early to mid-twentieth century; and the intellectual dominance of Anglo-American Neoclassical economics coincided with the ascendancy of global capitalism in the latter decades of the twentieth century. It will probably be several decades before the full socio-politico implications of Complexity Economics become clear. Nonetheless, the outlines of Complexity Economics are sufficiently formed that in part 4 we can begin to explore its implications for business and society.

We will arrive at the end with a message of optimism: if we can better understand the processes of wealth creation, then we can use that knowledge to develop new approaches to create economic growth and opportunity for people. Complexity Economics will not be a cure-all for the challenges of management or the ills of society. But just as a more scientific understanding of natural phenomena has been a major contributor to bettering the human condition, a more scientific understanding of economic phenomena has the potential to help improve the lives of people around the world.

CHAPTER TWO

Traditional Economics

A WORLD IN EQUILIBRIUM

IT WAS 1984 and John Reed had a problem.[1] At the age of forty-five, he had just been elected chairman and CEO of one of the world's largest companies, Citicorp. But Reed was inheriting a company that had recently been through a major trauma. Throughout the 1970s, Citicorp, along with other major American banks, had lent aggressively to the governments of developing countries, in particular to those in Latin America. Reed's predecessor, Walter Wriston, had proclaimed that such lending was "safe banking" because sovereign governments did not default on their debts. Wriston was proved badly wrong when in August 1982 the Mexican government was unable to roll over its massive debt. This set off a chain of events that resulted in a global financial crisis. The next several years saw widespread defaults, currency devaluations, and economic collapse in several countries. When the dust settled, millions of poor people found themselves even poorer, and the banks found that $300 billion had evaporated from their balance sheets. Citicorp alone had lost $1 billion in one year and was still sitting on $13 billion in bad debts.

Reed wanted to understand why the crisis had happened, how it had happened, and, most importantly, how it could be prevented from happening again. How had the best brains at Citibank and all the other major banks so badly misjudged the risks involved? Why had no one been able to foresee the problems these loans would create? How had a set of local events in Mexico spiraled into a global crisis? And why had governments around the world been so ineffectual in their responses?

Reed consulted various experts, including leading economists from academia, Wall Street, and government. Reed himself was well versed in economics from his student days at the Massachusetts Institute of Technology (MIT). If

21

it was anyone's job to be able to answer these types of questions, surely it must be the economists. Yet, the economists had little new or useful to say about the crisis. In fact, Reed believed that their recommendations during the crisis had been dead wrong. According to the science writer Mitchell Waldrop, "When it came to world financial markets, Reed had decided that professional economists were off with the fairies . . . Reed thought that a whole new approach to economics might be necessary."[2]

The Need for a New Approach

Reed is not alone in questioning the state of economics. Over the past decade there has been a surge in criticism of economic theory.[3] For example, in 1996, John Cassidy wrote a controversial and widely read article for *The New Yorker* titled "The Decline of Economics."[4] Cassidy charged that economics had disappeared into an ivory-tower world of highly idealized theory, untested by data, and packed with unrealistic assumptions. He claimed that economics had become a "giant academic game" in which economists wrote papers for each other, showing off their mathematical brilliance, but demonstrating little interest in the relevance of their theories to the real world. He argued that most businesses had given up on economics, and he noted that companies such as IBM and GE had shut down their economics departments.

But it is not only businesspeople and journalists who are critical of the current state of economics; economists themselves are their own toughest critics.[5] In the *New Yorker* piece, Cassidy quoted Joseph Stiglitz, a former chairman of the U.S. President's Council of Economic Advisors, chief economist at the World Bank, and a Nobel Prize winner, saying, "Anybody looking at these models would say they can't provide a good description of the modern world."[6] In the same piece, Gregory Mankiw of Harvard, and also a former chairman of the Council of Economic Advisors, suggested that, given the low useful output of economists, less money should go into their research, and he compared them to over-subsidized dairy farmers. Even Alan Greenspan, the former chairman of the U.S. Federal Reserve and one of the most highly respected figures in economic policymaking, once remarked to his Federal Reserve colleagues, "We really do not know how [the economy] works . . . The old models just are not working," and in earlier comments noted, "A surprising problem is that a number of economists are not able to distinguish between the economic models we construct and the real world."[7]

Although dissatisfaction with the state of economic theory has been growing, few critics would argue that the field has been completely useless or un-influential. On the contrary, most business leaders, policy makers, and even self-critical economists will admit that economics has produced some enormously powerful and influential ideas, ranging from the efficiency of markets to the benefits of free trade and the importance of individual choice. One measure of the success of economic theory can be found in the wealthy economies of the G7 countries (Britain, Canada, France, Germany, Italy, Japan, and the United States), where these ideas have been implemented to a greater extent than in most of the rest of the world. What most people in the G7 take for granted today—the use of interest rates to manage inflation; monetary and fiscal policies to dampen the business cycle; active encouragement of competition; a social safety net to take the rough edges off the market system; and product safety, environmental, and labor regulations to protect people from market failures—were all not quite so common one hundred, fifty, or even twenty years ago. All are ideas developed by academic economists during a century of very hard work.

Rather, the issue is a growing sense in the academic, business, and policy communities that economics is not fulfilling its true potential as a science.[8] Many of the "big ideas" of the field are now well over a century old, and too many of the field's formal theories and mathematical models are either hamstrung by unrealistic assumptions or directly contradicted by real-world data. The point is not to denigrate the contributions of the past, but rather to say "economics can do better" and it is time to move on.

In this chapter and the next, we will look at why a fundamentally new approach is needed. We will begin by defining the conventional wisdom in the field, or what I will refer to as *Traditional Economics*. We will then take a whirlwind tour of the history and key concepts of Traditional Economic theory and, in chapter 3, look at a synthesis of what the critics have to say. Inevitably we will only skim the surface of over two hundred years of economic ideas and leave out much important work. But the purpose of these two chapters is not to provide a textbook account of Traditional Economics or a comprehensive survey of the criticisms (far more complete accounts are referenced in the notes and listed in the bibliography).[9] Rather, the goal is to highlight a set of ideas that have been central to the development of modern economics, examine their strengths and weaknesses, and lay some groundwork for our discussions of Complexity Economics in part 2. As we will see, in order to fully appreciate where economics is going in the future, it is important to first understand its past.

Defining Traditional Economics

I will use the term *Traditional Economics* to refer to the set of ideas that have dominated economic theory for the past century. At this point, it is appropriate to define what I mean by the term. In general, Traditional Economics is the economics one finds in university textbooks, discussed in the news media, and referred to in the halls of business and government—it is the mainstream view of academic economics.[10] In order to add some more precision to the term, I will follow the lead of two prominent critics of Traditional theory, Richard Nelson of Columbia University and Sidney Winter of the University of Pennsylvania, and use the literature of economics itself as the basis for my definition:[11]

> Traditional Economics *is the set of concepts and theories articulated in undergraduate and intermediate graduate-level textbooks. It also includes the concepts and theories that peer-reviewed surveys claim, or assume, that the field generally agrees on.*[12]

Textbooks represent a consensus view of the profession and include the basic ideas that anyone being introduced to the field needs to know.[13] But textbooks inevitably omit more-advanced material. I have thus added survey books and articles to my definition as they summarize the state of the field at a given point in time. The limitation of both textbooks and surveys, of course, is that they typically focus on the conventional rather than the cutting edge.[14] But this restriction is intentional; I mean for Traditional Economics to refer to the *historical* core of economics, the stuff for which the Nobel Prizes have already been awarded.[15] The ideas that I will lump under the "Traditional" label will generally refer to what economists call Neoclassical economics, a term that will be defined later in the chapter.[16]

Inevitably, what is and is not included under the Traditional label will be somewhat subjective, and there will be a gray zone of ideas that are half in and half out. Nonetheless, the label will prove useful to our later discussions as we draw a distinction between the historical paradigm and the new ideas from Complexity Economics that are challenging it. With these caveats in mind, now that we have labeled the Traditional Economics box, let's look inside it.

Pin Making and the Invisible Hand

We will begin with perhaps the most famous economist of all, Adam Smith. Smith was not the first economist (that honor arguably goes to the ancient Greek philosopher Xenophon; the word *economics* is derived from the title of his work, *Oikonomikos*), but Smith's influence is such that he provides an appropriate jumping-off point for our discussion.[17] Smith was born in Kircaldy, a small town near Edinburgh in Scotland, and lived from 1723 to 1790, during what historians refer to as the *Classical* period of economic theory (circa 1680–1830).[18] Smith was educated at Oxford, but spent most of his career at the University of Glasgow. His first significant work was not in economics but in moral philosophy. *The Theory of Moral Sentiments* was published in 1759 and made him a key figure in the Scottish Enlightenment at a relatively young age. While at Glasgow he came to the attention of a wealthy young Scottish duke who took him on as his well-paid private tutor. Smith traveled with the duke to France, where the young tutor was exposed to the economic ideas being debated on the Continent at the time, in particular by the Physiocrats, a group of intellectuals who held the radical idea that governments should limit their interference in the economy and let markets do most of the work. Financially secure with his income from the duke, he returned to Kircaldy, where he lived with his mother in relative isolation for six years working on the manuscript for his *Wealth of Nations.* The book was published in 1776 and was instantly recognized as a great work.

There are two fundamental questions that economists have grappled with throughout the history of their field: how wealth is created and how wealth is allocated.[19] Smith addressed both in *The Wealth of Nations.*[20] His answer to the first question was simple but powerful: economic value is created when people take raw materials from their environment and then, through their labor, turn those materials into something that people want. For example, a potter might take clay from the ground and use it to create a bowl. Smith's great insight was that the secret to wealth creation was improving the *productivity* of labor. The more bowls a potter can make in an hour, the richer he or she will be. The secret to greater productivity in turn was the division of labor and the specialization that it enables.[21] Smith famously cited the example of a pin factory, where he observed ten men at work, each of whom specialized in one or two steps of the pin-making process.[22] Smith noted that this specialization and cooperation enabled the group to make 48,000 pins per day, or 4,800 pins per man. Without this division of labor, he estimated, the factory would have only been able to make twenty pins per man per day, or in the case of the less-skilled men, none.

A growing population will increase the total wealth of a society as the amount of available labor grows. But growing wealth on a per-person basis (thus raising individual standards of living) requires increasing productivity, and increasing productivity requires specialization. This logic led Smith to the second great question of economics: What determines how wealth and resources are allocated in a society? If creating wealth requires specialization, then specialization requires trade—after all, the pin makers couldn't eat their pins, they had to trade them for other goods they needed. But if pin makers, farmers, fishermen, carpenters, and other producers are all trading their wares in an economy, what determines the way in which goods are allocated? How many pins equals a bushel of wheat? How many fish for a carpenter's chair? Who will be richer, the pin maker or the fisherman? The natural corollary for Smith, the moral philosopher, was not just the question of how resources *are* allocated, but how they *should be* allocated; what is a fair or just allocation of resources both for the individual and for society as a whole?

Smith's view was that the most just mechanism for allocating resources from the point of view of the individual was one that enabled people to pursue their own self-interest and make their own choices. After all, people are usually the best judges of their own happiness. At the same time, the best allocation of resources for society as a whole was the one that put resources to their most efficient uses, thus maximizing the total wealth of society. Wasting resources was morally unjust (especially to a frugal Scotsman) because it reduced the overall wealth available to society. Smith's maxim was taken from his mentor at Glasgow, Francis Hutcheson, who argued for "the greatest happiness of the greatest number."[23] Smith's view on how this objective should be achieved was (and to some people still is) a radical one: that competitive markets are the most morally just mechanism for allocating a society's resources. He argued that if people were left to trade freely, self-interest would drive them to provide the goods and services people need: "It is not from the benevolence of the butcher, brewer, or the baker that we expect our dinner, but from the regard to their own interest."[24] Furthermore, the combination of the profit motive and competition would drive them to provide those goods and services as efficiently as possible: "Every individual is continually exerting himself to find out the most advantageous employment for whatever capital he can command."[25]

Smith argued that this pursuit of self-interest would in turn benefit society as a whole: "[The merchant] intends only his own gain, and he is in this, as in many other cases, led by an invisible hand to promote an end which was no part of his intention . . . By pursuing his own interest he frequently promotes that of the society more effectually than when he really intends to promote it."[26]

The "invisible hand" that led society to the happy result of efficient resource allocation was the mechanism of competitive markets. Smith described how price provides the key mechanism through which producers and consumers meet in the marketplace.[27] If there is too little supply for the available demand, then prices rise, producers increase production, and consumers decrease consumption. If there is too much supply for the available demand, then prices fall, producers decrease production, and consumers increase consumption. At some point the market reaches a price at which the two opposing forces come into balance: supply meets demand and the market clears. Smith argued that left to their own devices, the combination of self-interest and competitive markets would naturally bring the economy to this point of balance. Smith's point can be re-phrased in modern terms by quoting the character Gordon Gekko from the 1980s movie *Wall Street*, "greed is good"—a rather surprising conclusion coming from Smith the moral philosopher.

A Healthy Balance

The notion that the economy has a balancing point to which it naturally progresses is a theme that stretches back well before Smith to the field's earliest days and remains a core concept of Traditional Economics today. Competition for finite resources inevitably means that there are opposing forces or tensions in the economy. For the seventeenth-century Irish financier Richard Cantillon, the central tension in the economy was between population and the food-growing capacity of land. Cantillon believed that the brutal mechanisms of overpopulation and starvation would cause wages and prices in the economy to self-adjust to a point where the two would eventually come into balance.[28] For the eighteenth-century French intellectual François Quesnay (the leader of the Physiocrats, with whom Smith spent much time in France), the central tension was between agriculture, manufacturing, and the land-owning aristocracy. With his famous *Tableau Economique* (in essence a flow diagram of the economy), Quesnay claimed to be able to calculate the prices and levels of production that would bring the economy into balance.[29] For Quesnay, who had been a physician prior to venturing into economics, a balanced economy was a healthy economy, just as in eighteenth-century medicine a body was healthy if its "humours" were in balance. For Smith, the central tension in the economy was between consumers and producers, and the balance to be achieved was that between supply and demand (we should note, though, that Smith's view of supply and demand was not the complete theory presented in textbooks today, which would be created later by John Stuart Mill and Alfred Marshall).

While Smith described the role of markets in achieving the balance between supply and demand, he did not describe in detail the decision-making process by which self-interested producers determined *how much* product to supply, or how self-interested consumers determined *how much* to demand. The core ideas on this would come from two of Smith's Classical contemporaries: Jacques Turgot and Jeremy Bentham.

Jacques Turgot was a minister in the government of Louis XV and a famous proponent of *laissez-faire*, or the philosophy that governments should minimize their interference in the workings of markets.[30] Despite Turgot's views, the French government at the time was very much involved in running the economy *(plus ça change, plus c'est la même chose)*, and one of Turgot's jobs as a minister was to deal with food shortages.[31] In 1767 he observed that if a farmer simply throws seed on a plot of land, he will only get a very small crop. If he tills the soil just once before seeding, he will get a much larger crop. If he tills the land twice, he might not merely double but triple his output. As the farmer works the soil harder and harder, he will get progressively larger crops. But at some point the soil will become exhausted and each incremental unit of effort invested by the farmer will yield a smaller and smaller return. On the basis of these observations, Turgot articulated what has come to be known as the *law of diminishing returns*. In most production processes, whether it is farming, manufacturing, or a service business, as one inputs more and more of a particular factor (e.g., labor, raw materials, or machinery), at some point one gets progressively less output bang for the input buck. The law of diminishing returns is a critical force in helping the economy achieve balance. Given a price in the market, a producer will keep adding more inputs and expanding output until the payoff is no longer worth it, that is, until the incremental cost of producing the next unit of output is greater than the incremental revenue one would receive for it. Thus a farmer will work his land just the right amount demanded by the market, no more, no less. If the price of his crop goes up, he will work the land harder (or put more land under the till), while if the price goes down, he will grow less. If returns on production did not diminish at some point, then the farmer would keep expanding output infinitely—an absurd result.[32] Turgot's law provided a crucial concept linking producer costs into the supply side of supply and demand.[33]

At approximately the same time, an English philosopher, Jeremy Bentham, was making a similarly important contribution to the demand side. Bentham, born in London in 1748, was a child prodigy who learned Latin at age four and went to Oxford at age twelve.[34] Like Adam Smith, Bentham viewed himself as a moral and political philosopher. Smith had identified human self-interest as the motivating force that drove the economy, but did not have much to say on just how that self-interest translated into specific economic decisions. Bentham argued that the pursuit of self-interest was a rational activity based on a calculus of pleasure and pain. Bentham identified a quantity that he termed *utility* to measure individual pleasure and pain.[35] He argued that economic choices were the result of an individual's calculations as to what actions would maximize his or her utility.[36] If you like apples and dislike bananas, when faced with a choice between an apple and a banana, you will calculate that consuming the apple will provide you with greater utility and therefore choose it. For another person the utility of the banana might be higher. Bentham's ideas developed a strong following in late-eighteenth-century intellectual and political circles and came to be known as Utilitarianism. The credo of the Utilitarians was that society should be organized in such a way as to maximize its collective utility, or happiness.

Some fifty years later the German economist Hermann Heinrich Gossen built on Bentham's ideas and gave us the *law of diminishing marginal utility*.[37] This was in essence the flip side of Turgot's law. Just as Turgot showed that there were diminishing benefits to increased production, Gossen showed that there were also diminishing benefits to increased consumption. For example, if one is very hungry and buys a doughnut, its consumption might provide quite a lot of satisfaction, or utility. If one was still hungry and bought a second doughnut, it too might be satisfying, but according to the law of diminishing marginal utility, it would be incrementally less so than the first. By the time one gets to the fifth or sixth doughnut, one's incremental satisfaction is likely to be pretty small (or perhaps even negative as one gets a stomachache). At some point, one will say, "I'm full and the next doughnut is just not worth the money." Just as a farmer will increase production if the price rises and will reduce production if the price falls, the point at which a consumer says "it is not worth it" and stops consuming will be lower or higher, depending on price. Thus, demand falls as price rises, and vice versa. Also, just as diminishing marginal returns keep farmers from growing an infinite quantity of crops, diminishing marginal utility keeps consumers from consuming an infinite quantity of doughnuts.

The combination of diminishing marginal returns on production and diminishing marginal utility on consumption means that markets have a natural balancing mechanism—price. Price is the key piece of information that producers and consumers share. A price increase will simultaneously lower the consumption point of consumers and raise the production point of producers, while a price decrease will accomplish the reverse.

Thus the Classical period of economics ended with a compelling framework in place for describing how markets balance the needs of consumers with the economics of production, and naturally progress to a point that satisfies both. But an important question remained unanswered: For a given commodity, a given set of utilities, and a given production process, what exactly would the price be? Could we calculate it? Could we predict it?

Dreams of a New Science

The work of the Classical economists was followed by the Marginalist era (circa 1830–1930). The central figure of this period was Léon Walras, who was born in 1834 in Evreux, France. The young Walras had a very shaky start to his career, and there was little foreshadowing of his later greatness. As a student, he was twice rejected from the prestigious École Polytechnique due to poor mathematical skills. He instead went to the École des Mines but failed as an engineer, then tried his hand as a novelist but was unsuccessful at that as well. One evening in 1858, a depressed Walras took a walk with his father, a teacher and writer, discussing what he should do with his life.[38] The elder Walras, a great admirer of science, said that there were two great challenges remaining in the nineteenth century: the creation of a complete theory of history, and the creation of a scientific theory of economics. He believed that differential calculus could be applied to economics to create a "science of economic forces, analogous to the science of astronomical forces."[39] The younger Walras was inspired by his father's vision of a scientific economics and decided to make achieving that vision his life's work. Walras then spent several years struggling as a newspaper writer and a bank employee, while in his spare time writing articles and pamphlets on economics. In 1870, after much debate by the other professors, he was finally appointed to the faculty of the Lausanne Academy and, in 1872, completed his masterwork, *Elements of a Pure Economics*.[40]

Prior to Walras's *Elements*, economics was not a mathematical field. Many earlier economists, such as Smith and Bentham, regarded themselves as philosophers rather than scientists, and the mathematics of the Classical period is generally limited to a few numerical examples and a bit of algebra, but nothing more sophisticated.[41] Walras and his fellow Marginalists radically changed that. They lived in an era of great scientific progress. Following Newton's monumental discoveries in the seventeenth century, a series of scientists and mathematicians, including Leibniz, Lagrange, Euler, and Hamilton, developed a new mathematical language using differential equations to describe a staggeringly broad range of natural phenomena. Problems that had baffled humankind since the ancient Greeks, from the motions of planets to the vibrations of violin strings, were suddenly mastered. The success of these theories gave scientists a boundless optimism that they could describe any aspect of nature in their equations.[42] Walras and his compatriots were convinced that if the equations of differential calculus could capture the motions of planets and atoms in the universe, these same mathematical techniques could also capture the motion of human minds in the economy.

In particular, Walras saw a parallel between the idea of balancing points in economic systems and balancing points in nature.[43] Many systems in nature have balancing points, or in the language of physics, *equilibrium points*. As described in the previous chapter, imagine you have a large glass bowl with a smooth, round bottom and a small, hard rubber ball in your hand. You place the ball on the lip of the bowl and let it go. The ball rolls around for a while, swinging back and forth, but eventually it comes to rest at the bottom of the bowl. The ball is now in equilibrium. Equilibrium is achieved when all the forces acting on the system cancel each other out and the system is in balance. In this case, the force of gravity pushing down on the ball is met exactly by the force of the bowl underneath pushing up. The ball will stay precisely in this position, at the bottom of the bowl, forever, unless some new force disturbs it. Notice that in this example, there is only one equilibrium point—the lowest point in the bowl. No matter how many times we drop it into the bowl, the ball will always come to rest at this same point.

Physical systems have a wide variety of types of equilibrium. For example, imagine balancing a pencil exactly on its tip. If you got it just right and were able to make the pencil stand up, it would be in equilibrium. However, unlike the ball in the bowl, this state would be a very *unstable equilibrium,* as the slightest breeze would tip the pencil over. There are also *dynamic equilibrium* states. When a planet is in orbit around a star, the gravitational force of the star pulling the planet inward is exactly counterbalanced by the centrifugal force of the planet's motion pushing it outward. This balance will be maintained and the planet will travel in a stable orbit until some outside force disturbs it. Finally, we could also imagine a bowl with a bumpy bottom that would have *multiple equilibrium* points for the ball to land in.

One of Walras's objectives in bringing mathematics to economics was to make economic systems predictable. Unfortunately, unstable equilibriums are inherently hard to predict, as small changes can send the system in one direction or another. Likewise, during Walras's time, determining whether a dynamic system was in a stable equilibrium was considered such a difficult problem that King Oscar II of Sweden offered a prize of 2,500 crowns to anyone who could solve it.[44] Finally, if a system has multiple equilibriums, then predicting which equilibrium the system will settle in is at a minimum difficult and in many cases an impossible problem. Walras wanted predictability, and that meant he needed a single, stable equilibrium point. Specifically, Walras saw the balance of supply and demand in a market as metaphorically like the balance of forces in a physical equilibrium system. He conjectured that for each commodity traded in a market, there was only one price, one equilibrium point, at which traders would be satisfied and the market would clear. Prices in a market would predictably settle to a single equilibrium level, just as a ball would predictably settle into the smooth bottom of a bowl.

To turn his conjecture into equations, Walras raided the physics textbooks of his time. One such textbook, *Elements of Statics,* published in 1803 by the French mathematician Louis Poinsot, was particularly influential on Walras (even to the extent that Walras echoed its title in his own *Elements*).[45] As Walras's biographer William Jaffé has pointed out, it was specifically from chapter two of that book, titled "On conditions of equilibrium expressed by means of equations," that Walras imported the concept of equilibrium from physics into economics and laid the mathematical foundations for the Traditional Economics found in textbooks and journals today.[46] This historical detail is noteworthy, because, as we will see in the next chapter, some critics argue that this borrowing of equilibrium from physics was a crucial scientific misstep that has had lasting consequences for the field.

In building his equilibrium model, Walras put to one side the production half of the economy and focused on trading between consumers. In his model, he assumed that various goods already exist in the economy and the problem is to determine how prices are set and how the goods would be allocated among the individuals involved. To see how Walras's model works, imagine a big room full of people. Each person is endowed with a random sampling of all the goods available in the economy. For example, I might be given five bananas, a washing machine, two pairs of shoes, five car tires, and so on, while you might be given a pair of blue jeans, two umbrellas, a telephone, three avocados, and other goods. Each person, however, has an individual set of utilities for the various goods. For example, you might like bananas and I might like avocados, but we both might value the telephone. Given that the initial endowment of goods was random, it is highly unlikely that all the participants will be happy with what they have been given, and so they will want to trade. Walras regarded this desire to trade as a sign that the system was out of equilibrium. It meant that there was a different allocation of goods that would make the group happier. The problem, then, is to find the allocation of goods that leaves everyone in the room as satisfied as possible, and to find the prices for trading that would enable the people to move from their initial state to the more satisfied state. This new state would be in equilibrium because once everyone was as satisfied as possible, given the goods available and prices, no one would want to trade anymore.[47]

To make the trading more organized (and mathematically simpler), Walras imagined that the group had an auctioneer. He assumed that one of the goods in the economy could be used as a form of money (e.g., gold pieces, glass beads, shells) and then the auctioneer would price things in terms of that commodity (e.g., an avocado might be worth ten glass beads). The auctioneer would call out prices for each of the goods and take down bids. If there was more demand than supply for the good, he would raise the price; if there was more supply than demand, he would lower the price. He would do this for all the goods in the economy until he reached a point at which supply and demand was balanced across all of them. With all the prices set, then and only then would everyone trade, thus ensuring that all the participants maximized the value they received from their trades. The trading would then move the group from their initial random, out-of-equilibrium state, into the happier, equilibrium state. Walras called this state the *general equilibrium* point. Walras referred to his auction process as *tâtonnement,* French for "groping," as the auctioneer groped for the general equilibrium point by trying out different prices for different goods.

While Walras's ideas were novel, what was truly revolutionary was his use of sophisticated mathematics borrowed from physics. If one accepted Walras's assumptions that people had different utilities, and that they were rational and self-interested in maximizing those utilities, then one could predict with mathematical precision how they would trade and the relative prices that would be set in the economy. There were a few minor details, like the existence of his godlike auctioneer and questions as to how one could observe and measure individuals' utilities, but these issues could be addressed in the future, a small price to pay for the ability to make mathematically precise, scientific predictions about things like prices in the economy for the first time.[48] Walras's willingness to make trade-offs in realism for the sake of mathematical predictability would set a pattern followed by economists over the next century.

As Predictable as Gravity

Walras was not the only economist during his era raiding physics textbooks in search of inspiration. William Stanley Jevons was born in 1835 in Liverpool, the ninth of eleven children in a prosperous industrial family.[49] Like Walras he was a late bloomer, leaving university without a degree and spending his twenties as an assayer at the Sydney mint during the Australian gold rush. Nevertheless, he had a restless mind, became fascinated by railroads (the Internet of their day), and in his spare time attempted to build mathematical models of railroad economics. This experience convinced him that economics needed to become a mathematical science. He decided to return to England to finish his degree by studying economics. Like Walras, he was a man on a mission determined "to define the foundations of our knowledge of man" and "re-establish the Science [of economics] on a sensible basis."[50]

In 1867, two prominent British scientists, Sir William Thomson (later Lord Kelvin) and Peter Guthrie Tait, published a new textbook titled *A Treatise on Natural Philosophy,* which consolidated recent discoveries in energy physics.[51] One of the eager readers of that book was Jevons. In Thomson and Tait's book, Jevons found new theories developed by Michael Faraday and James Clerk Maxwell for describing gravity, magnetism, and electricity as "fields of force." For example, a mass such as the sun has a gravitational field that pulls objects toward it; the bigger the mass the stronger the gravitational field of force. Jevons saw man's self-interest as a force very much like gravity:[52] "Utility only exists when there is on the one side the person wanting and on the other the thing wanted . . . Just as the gravitating force of a material body depends not alone on the mass of that body, but upon the masses and relative positions and distances of the surrounding material bodies, so utility is an attraction between a wanting being and what is wanted."[53]

Jevons took Bentham's notion of utility, along with Gossen's theory of diminishing returns to consumption and, in his 1871 *Theory of Political Economy*, used equations derived from field theory to turn their ideas from a philosophical concept into a mathematical model.[54] In short, Jevons wanted to make human behavior as predictable as gravity. In order to predict how an object will move in a gravitational field, one must know two things: the direction gravity is acting in, and the shape of any constraints on the motion of the object. To go back to our earlier example, if we roll a ball into a bowl, gravity pulls the ball downward and the sides of the bowl constrain the motion of the ball. We can predict where the ball will eventually land (its equilibrium point) if we know which direction is "down" and the shape of the bowl constraining the motion of the ball. Likewise, we can predict the equilibrium point of a pendulum if we know which direction gravity is pulling it, and the length of the string that constrains its motion. In Jevons's conception, self-interest provides the force, like gravity, that pulls us to maximize our happiness or utility. But we also live in a world of finite resources, and this provides the constraints on our actions. The trick then is to find the combination of goods and services that maximizes our happiness within the constraints of finite resources, and as in Walras's model, we use trade to get to this state.

Let's imagine an economy with two goods, say, wine and cheese. I might generally prefer wine over cheese, but at some point the law of diminishing marginal utility says that I will have had enough wine and would rather have some cheese than another glass of wine. You, on the other hand, might generally prefer cheese to wine, but also at some point would be happy to have some wine rather than more cheese. Now let's imagine there is a finite amount of wine and cheese in this economy and we are both randomly given some of each. Just as in Walras's model, it is unlikely that we will have been given the exact amount that matches our utilities, so we will trade until we each hold an amount of wine and cheese that provides the most satisfaction possible given the total amounts available to us.

Jevons's lasting contribution was to portray the problem of economic choice as an exercise in constrained optimization. That is, given the amounts available, a consumer will calculate what quantities of various goods will make him or her the most happy. In Jevons's view, differences in individual utilities create a kind of potential energy for trade. He wrote in his *Principles of Economics*, "The notion of value is to our science what that of energy is to mechanics."[55] Just as a ball in a bowl seeks its minimum energy state within the constraints of the sides of the bowl, human beings will seek their maximum happiness state within the constraints of their finite resources and will trade their way to get there.

The Panglossian Economy

Adam Smith postulated that human self-interest drives markets to a form of balance, a stable state where prices are agreed on, trades are made, and the market clears. Walras demonstrated that this balanced state could be regarded as an equilibrium point that could be mathematically calculated. Jevons showed that if people attempt to maximize their happiness in a world of individually differing utilities and finite resources, they would inevitably trade their way to the market equilibrium point. Adam Smith had gone farther in his claims, however—not only would self-interest drive markets into balance, but it would result in the best possible outcome for society as a whole.

Vilfredo Pareto was an Italian contemporary of Walras and Jevons. Having been trained as an engineer and written his doctoral dissertation on "the elastic equilibrium of solid bodies," Pareto was as well or even better versed in the physics of his day than Walras and Jevons.[56] He was an eccentric personality who spent his later years as a recluse in a Swiss mountain chalet with twenty angora cats. However, he achieved immortality in the world of economics by having his name attached to one of the field's most important concepts.

Ever since Smith's *Wealth of Nations* was published, economists had wanted to determine whether competitive markets truly maximized social welfare and, if so, under what circumstances. Although Jevons had significantly advanced the theoretical treatment of utility, there was still the problem that utility was unmeasurable—one couldn't simply look inside peoples' heads, measure their utilities, and add them up. How then could one tell if social welfare had in fact gone up, or if it had been maximized.

Pareto got around this problem through an ingenious logical argument. He reasoned that there are four kinds of trades that people can make. First, there are win-win trades, in which both parties gain; in this case it is clear that welfare has gone up. Second, there are trades, in which one party gains, but no one loses, and again welfare has unambiguously gone up. Third, there are trades, in which no one gains, but someone loses, and in this case welfare has unambiguously gone down. Fourth and finally, there are trades, in which some parties win and some lose, but without the ability to directly measure utility, it is impossible to determine what the net impact is. Pareto argued that since it takes two consenting people to trade and people aren't stupid, they would only engage in trades that were either win-win or at least win-no-lose, both of which raise the total welfare of the participants. These trades later came to be called *Pareto superior* trades, and Pareto contended that in free markets, people would keep trading until they had exhausted all the Pareto superior trades. At that point trading would stop since any further trades would make someone worse off, and the market would reach an equilibrium point that later economists called *Pareto optimal*. The Pareto optimal is thus the point at which no further trades can be made without making someone worse off. The Pareto optimal is not necessarily the point at which value is maximized for the entire group, as there might be some trades that would harm some people for the benefit of others, but would nonetheless raise the sum total utility of the group. Without a way to precisely measure utilities and a dictator to force trades that reduce the welfare of some for the benefit of others, the Pareto optimal is the best that one can do in a free society.[57]

Thus, according to the theories of Walras, Jevons, Pareto, and the other Marginalists, in a market economy the participants freely trade their way to a state where they are as satisfied as possible, given the resources available. Through this trading the economy glides to an equilibrium, a natural resting point, where supply equals demand, where resources are put to their most efficient use, and where the welfare of society is Pareto optimal. As Voltaire's Dr. Pangloss put it, "In this best of possible worlds . . . all is for the best."[58] What was perhaps most remarkable about the Marginalists' achievement was that economics now had a mathematical theory that showed how, left to its own devices, a free-market economy would reach this Panglossian state with the inevitability of a ball rolling to the bottom of a bowl. Walras declared that his "pure theory of economics is a science which resembles the physico-mathematical sciences in every respect." Jevons believed that he had created a "calculus of moral effects." And Pareto proclaimed, "The theory of economic science thus acquires the rigor of rational mechanics."[59] In their view, the Marginalists had succeeded in their dream of turning economics into a true mathematical science.

The Neoclassical Synthesis

In the twentieth century, a pantheon of great economists consolidated and built on the foundations laid by the Marginalists. At the turn of the century, the English economist Alfred Marshall bridged Jevons's model of a single market in isolation (partial equilibrium) with Walras's model of many inter-linked markets in an economy (general equilibrium). Marshall was also responsible for first drawing the crossed supply and demand curve graphs that have vexed introductory economics students ever since. In the 1930s, John Hicks (who was appropriately the Jevons Professor at the University of Manchester) synthesized the work of Walras, Marshall, and Pareto into a coherent theory in his opus *Value and Capital*. As Europe descended into war in the middle of the twentieth century, the locus of innovation shifted across the ocean, where a generation of Americans as well as refugees from Hitler's Europe created the modern core of economic theory that has come to be called the *Neoclassical synthesis*. Two of the most prominent figures of that era are Paul Samuelson and Kenneth Arrow.

Samuelson was a true prodigy.[60] His ambitiously titled *Foundations of Economic Analysis,* completed in 1941 when he was twenty-six, was written as a thesis while he was still a graduate student at Harvard. In it he essentially took Hicks's synthesized theory, added his own innovations, and turned it into a dazzling mathematical theory that become the standard model for the workings of markets.[61] One of Samuelson's key breakthroughs was solving a problem that had bedeviled economists since the days of Bentham. Utility had become a core part of economic theory, yet it was still a mysterious, unob-servable, unmeasurable quantity. Pareto and Hicks had already debunked the idea that a "util" was a fixed unit of measure (like a kilogram or a watt) and argued that utility only had meaning in a relative fashion, as in "to me that apple has twice as many utils as it does relative to an orange." But that still begged the question of how one measured even relative utility. Samuelson's reply was that one didn't have to look inside people's heads and measure util-ity directly; rather, people would reveal their preferences through the choices they made. All one had to do was assume that people are logical and consis-tent in their behaviors. If, for example, you gave someone a choice between an apple and an orange and he or she chose the apple, you would predict that if next given a choice between an apple, an orange, and a banana, the person would *not* choose the orange (logically, he or she should still prefer the apple to the orange and thus either choose it or the banana). While such observa-tions do not allow one to say that "an apple has twice as many utils as an orange," one could definitely say that in this case the person in question "prefers apples to oranges." Samuelson argued that this simple statement was good enough to build a theory of demand upon, and he thus replaced utility theory with a set of basic, logical rules for the ordering of people's *prefer-ences*. These rules became the foundation for the theory of consumer behav-ior in Traditional Economics and the backbone of the notion that people are rational in their economic choices.[62]

Samuelson's slightly younger contemporary, Kenneth Arrow, also displayed superb mathematical skills from an early age. Arrow has made a number of fundamental contributions to the field, but one of his most famous is a theorem he proved with the French economist Gérard Debreu in 1954. Arrow and Debreu connected Walras's notion of a general equilibrium with Pareto's concept of optimality in a very general way, thus creating the Neoclassical theory of general equilibrium. Their theorem showed that all the markets in the economy together would automatically coordinate on a set of prices that was Pareto optimal for the economy as a whole, and that this would occur even when there was uncertainty in the market (Walras required in his model that everything be certain).[63] This automatic coordination occurs because markets are linked with each other by the ability of some goods to act as *substitutes* for others (e.g., if the price of coffee goes up, one can switch to tea) and by the tendency of other goods to be consumed together as *complements* (e.g., a rise in the price of gasoline can reduce the demand for large, gas-guzzling cars). Arrow and Debreu showed that prices act like a nervous system, transmitting signals about supply and demand throughout the economy, and that self-interested people react to those price signals and inevitably drive the system to its socially optimal equilibrium point—the invisible hand is powerful indeed.

Perhaps the most stunning achievement of the Arrow-Debreu general equilibrium theory was that this powerful result was built up from just a small set of axioms. Some of the assumptions were fairly uncontroversial, such as you can't have negative labor or negative consumption. However, some of the assumptions were more problematic. For example, the theorem assumed that everyone is endowed with at least some amount of every commodity, that futures markets exist for every product and service, that everyone is extremely rational in calculating decisions, and knows the probabilities of all possible future states of the world. As with Walras's original model, these assumptions were viewed as necessary simplifications, details to be addressed at another time. The important thing was that one could start with a simple set of axioms and rigorously, mathematically, build up to a very general result: rational self-interest operating in competitive markets would drive the economy to its optimal point. When the theorem was published in 1954, it was hailed by economists as a major breakthrough. At the height of the Cold War, it was eventually interpreted in the political realm (albeit incorrectly) as final mathematical proof of the superiority of market capitalism over socialism.[64] To be sure, Arrow and Debreu's model was a highly simplified picture of an economy, and it was missing real-world features such as monopolistic industries, labor unions, government regulations, taxes, and so on, but its political message was clear. The closer we reach the ideal state of perfect market competition, without distortions and interference, the closer we would be to the optimal equilibrium point.

By the 1960s, there emerged a largely complete theory that began with axiomatic assumptions about individual consumers and producers and built up to sweeping conclusions about markets and economies. Economists refer to such bottom-up theories of individuals and markets as *microeconomics*. Much work had also been going on during this period in *macroeconomics* as well, where economists look at the economy from the top down, and ask questions such as why unemployment exists, what causes business cycles, and how interest rates and inflation are linked. These are subjects we will return to later, but the critical point for the moment is that in the 1960s and 1970s, the Chicago economists (so called because many were on the faculty of the University of Chicago) such as Milton Friedman and Robert Lucas began to apply the techniques of Neoclassical microeconomics to macroeconomics, and concepts such as rational utility-maximizing consumers and optimal equilibriums became a core part of Traditional macroeconomic theory as well.

From Allocation to Growth

Earlier in the chapter, I noted that economics has historically been concerned with two great questions: how wealth is created and how wealth is allocated. Between the Classical era of Adam Smith and the mid-twentieth-century era of Samuelson and Arrow, the first question was largely overshadowed by the second. The models of Walras, Jevons, and Pareto began with the assumptions that an economy already exists, producers have resources, and consumers own various commodities. The models thus view the problem as how to allocate the existing finite wealth of the economy in a way that provides the maximum benefit for everyone. An important reason for this focus on allocation of finite resources was that the mathematical equations of equilibrium imported from physics were ideal for answering the allocation question, but it was more difficult to apply them to growth. Equilibrium systems by definition are in a state of rest, while growth implies change and dynamism.

An important figure who recognized the contradiction between equilibrium and growth was Joseph Schumpeter (1883–1950), often referred to as an Austrian economist, even though he was born in what today is the Czech Republic.[65] Schumpeter was a colorful character renowned for wearing riding boots to Harvard faculty meetings and formal evening dress for dinners at home. He was famed for proclaiming that he had three goals in life: to be the greatest lover in Vienna, the greatest horseman in Europe, and the greatest economist in the world. Alas, he would say, he had failed in his second goal. Schumpeter was sympathetic to the equilibrium notions of his Neoclassical contemporaries on the question of wealth allocation, but he did not believe that it was the right framework for answering the growth question. The Neoclassical view of production was very static. Firms were assumed to have fixed technologies and product sets, and all they did was calculate the quantity of production that would maximize their profits. As Schumpeter observed, however, economic growth is not just a matter of increasing the quantity of what is already produced; there must be a role for innovation: "Add successively as many mail coaches as you please, you will never get a railway thereby."[66] In the terms described in chapter 1, Schumpeter wanted to explain SKU growth as well as quantity growth.

The Neoclassicals tended to view innovation as an external, or *exogenous*, factor: a random variable that affected the economy—like the weather—but was outside the bounds of economic study. Schumpeter, however, believed that innovation had to be viewed as internal, or *endogenous*, to the economy and central to its understanding. He insisted that for growth to occur, there must be "a source of energy within the economic system which would of itself disrupt any equilibrium that might be attained."[67] For Schumpeter, that source of energy was the figure of the entrepreneur, whom he wrote about in almost heroic terms. According to Schumpeter, technological progress occurred in a random stream of discoveries. The commercialization of new technologies, however, faced numerous barriers, ranging from the need for financing to the intransigence of old habits and mind-sets. Thus, like water behind a dam, the random rain of discoveries built up over time. In Schumpeter's theory, entrepreneurs played the role of dam breakers, unleashing a flood of innovation into the marketplace. In this way, growth comes to the economy not in a steady stream, but as Schumpeter famously put it, in "gales of creative destruction." The origin of wealth, according to Schumpeter, lies in the heroic efforts of individual entrepreneurs. Schumpterian wealth creation occurs when people like Richard Arkwright, Henry Ford, Thomas Alva Edison, and Steve Jobs battle the odds to turn the technologies of their time into successful commercial enterprises.

Schumpeter's theory was in essence a human and historical theory, and this was both its strength and its weakness. While the descriptive richness of Schumpeter's ideas still resonates today, he was never able to translate his theories into the rigorous language of mathematics. This meant that his ideas could never be reconciled with the mathematical Neoclassical framework—a shortcoming that ultimately limited their impact.[68] The lack of a mathematical approach also made growth theory something of an intellectual backwater for the next forty years, until the arrival of Robert Solow.[69]

Solow was born in Brooklyn, was trained at Harvard, and spent his career at MIT.[70] Solow did not suffer from Schumpeter's lack of mathematical acumen and sought to reconcile growth with the ball-in-the-bowl predictability of Neoclassical theory. In his 1987 Nobel Prize lecture, Solow described his motivation for developing his theory.[71] Earlier mathematical work on growth had been fairly simplistic and assumed that the productivity of capital, that is, the return one got from investing in such things as tools, machines, and equipment, was constant. This assumption was clearly unrealistic. Changes in technology through history have dramatically increased the productivity of capital—the productivity of a tractor is far higher than that of an ox-driven plough. Solow wanted to find a way to incorporate this important effect. But unlike Schumpeter, who saw innovation as a disruptive disequilibrium force, Solow wanted to account for innovation in a way that would be consistent with Neoclassical theory and maintain equilibrium in the economy.

Growth and equilibrium do not sound like very compatible concepts. The ball-in-the-bowl is not a system that grows. In a landmark paper in 1956, however, Solow reconciled the two by viewing the economy as being in a kind of dynamic equilibrium, or what he called *balanced growth*.[72] Imagine a circus act where a brave performer rides a bicycle across a high wire. In order to maintain balance and keep from falling off the wire, the performer holds a long pole extended horizontally. Even though the performer is in motion while pedaling forward across the wire, at each point in time, the rider is balanced in a kind of equilibrium. Similarly, Solow saw the economy as being balanced in equilibrium, even as it grew. He treated two key variables in the model as exogenous: the rate of population growth and the rate of technological change. These two variables drove the growth rate (you can think of these as the energy the high-wire bicycle rider is putting into pedaling). Solow then showed that other factors in the economy, such as the rate of savings and the total amount of capital in the economy, would automatically be balanced in response to changes in population growth and technology, just as our circus performer would shift the pole to stay balanced. In Solow's model, the role of the balancing bicycle rider is played by the markets for labor and capital, which work to keep everything in Pareto optimal equilibrium, even as the economy grows.

Solow's model was consistent with Adam Smith's insight that while population growth might increase the *total* wealth of a nation, only improvements in productivity could make a nation richer on a *per capita* basis—it is not how much capital a country has that makes it rich; it is how productive that capital is, and according to Solow the key to productivity is technology. Solow's model implied that the United States and other Western countries did not become rich because of a lucky endowment of natural resources or because of capital falling like manna from heaven. Rather, they became rich through a virtuous cycle in which technology improvements led to capital's becoming more productive, which in turn led to more savings, which in turn led to more capital investment. Without technology growth, capital would only grow in proportion to population, and wealth per capita would simply level off. Back in 1956, long before the term became fashionable, Robert Solow had discovered the knowledge economy.[73]

Solow's work set off renewed interest in the topic of growth. A stream of work that provided variations on his basic model soon followed. In the mid-1980s, however, a group of researchers, led by Stanford economist Paul Romer, became increasingly dissatisfied that the real driver of growth in Solow's model, technology, was exogenous, just as Schumpeter had been frustrated fifty years earlier, when economics considered innovation exogenous.[74] Like Schumpeter, Romer thought that the "energy" for growth should be considered endogenous to the economy, and in 1990, Romer published a paper that kicked off the development of what has come to be known as *endogenous growth theory*.[75]

Romer located the source of energy for growth not in the heroism of the entrepreneur, but in the nature of technology itself. He noted that technology has a cumulative, accelerating quality to it. The more stuff we know, the greater the base of existing human knowledge, and the greater the payoff from the next discovery. Knowledge is what economists refer to as an *increasing returns* phenomenon. As discussed earlier, in the eighteenth century Jacques Turgot showed that most production processes exhibit the opposite quality of decreasing returns. For most types of production processes, whether it is farming, manufacturing, or services, as one inputs more and more resources, the marginal returns get smaller and smaller. Romer argued that in the case of the production of technology (i.e., think of research and development as a process for producing technology), this logic is reversed; the more we invest in knowledge cumulatively over time, the higher the payoffs. An hour of R&D invested in microchips and biotech today has a higher payoff than an hour of R&D invested in steam locomotives and telegraphs in 1900. Romer created a positive feedback loop in his model, a virtuous circle, in which the more society invests in technology over time, the richer the society gets, and the greater the payoffs to further investments in technology. The result is unbounded, exponential growth. If we think of the image of a bicycle rider on a high wire again, the increasing returns to investment in technology pushes the pedals of growth at an ever-faster rate.

The Legacy of Traditional Economics

By the end of the twentieth century, Traditional Economics was thoroughly dominated by the Neoclassical paradigm with its foundational notions of rational, optimizing consumers and producers making choices in a world of finite resources, and (with the exception of investments in technology) those choices being bounded by decreasing returns. This combination of self-interest and constraints then drive the economy to the Pareto optimal point of equilibrium. The methodology of economic analysis was also dominated by the use of mathematical proofs that began with a set of assumptions and then built logically up to a set of conclusions. The Neoclassical growth theory pioneered by Solow claimed to answer the great question of wealth creation, while the Neoclassical general equilibrium theory of Arrow and Debreu ostensibly answered the great question of wealth allocation. These canonical models, of course, had many variations, including models that featured uncertainty, imperfect competition, and incomplete information. But these were indeed variations on a theme rather than new symphonies themselves.

The twentieth-century economists had thus realized their ambition to create a set of rigorous, well-defined mathematical models for describing the workings of the economy. Although the dream of completely integrating the micro and macro perspectives under the Neoclassical paradigm had not been fully realized, one could nonetheless travel from the atomistic world of individual decision makers to the sweep of national economies within a logically consistent framework and set of assumptions.[76]

The Traditional paradigm has, without a doubt, had a major impact on the worlds of public policy, business, and finance. Policy makers ranging from central bankers to presidential advisers and finance ministers all rely on the concepts and models of Traditional Economics. Likewise, concepts from Traditional Economic theory are commonly used to inform decisions in the business world—decisions ranging from competitive strategy to whether to undertake a merger or an acquisition.[77] Also, it would not be an exaggeration to say that trillions of dollars are traded each day in world financial markets using calculations made from the theories of Traditional Economics. The ideas of Traditional Economics have made tremendous contributions to our understanding of the economy and of society more generally.

Nonetheless, despite the unquestionably significant impact of Traditional Economics, the unease expressed at the beginning of the chapter remains valid. The economist Werner Hildenbrand once compared general equilibrium theory to a gothic cathedral, of which Walras and his contemporaries were the architects, and the great economists of the twentieth century were the master builders.[78] Unfortunately, as we will see in the next chapter, the cathedral was built on very shaky ground.

CHAPTER THREE

A Critique

CHAOS AND CUBAN CARS

DESPITE HIS OCCASIONAL frustrations with economists, John Reed maintained active connections with the academic community and served on the board of the prestigious Russell Sage Foundation, an organization that supports social science research. During a coffee break at a board meeting in New York, a fellow trustee, Bob Adams, the secretary of the Smithsonian Institution, told Reed about a radical new research organization that was being set up in the desert of New Mexico.[1] The group was led by a former White House science adviser and Los Alamos National Laboratory research head, George Cowan. His co-conspirators were an A-list of scientific super-stars, including Nobel Prize winner and discoverer of the quark, Murray Gell-Mann, fellow Nobel laureate Phil Anderson of Princeton University, and several Senior Fellows of the Los Alamos Lab.

The group had set itself the modest ambition of fundamentally changing the way in which scientific research is conducted. Historically, science had taken a top-down, reductionist approach, breaking the universe into ever-smaller pieces, moving from the level of galaxies to subatomic particles in search of ultimate laws. The Santa Fe scientists believed that while this approach had been extraordinarily successful, many of the hardest problems in nature are "complex systems" that have collective or emergent character-istics that are better understood though a bottoms-up, holistic approach.[2] For example, the group felt that a question such as "What is life?" would never be cracked by only looking top-down at the chemistry of organisms.[3] An organ-ism is a complex system whose emergent whole is greater than the sum of its chemical parts. Answering the "What is life?" question would require a view of organisms as systems, and a bottoms-up understanding of how billions of

45

molecules interact to create the complex dance called life. The group felt that for a broad class of phenomena, including the brain, biological ecosystems, the Internet, and human society itself, the sum was in some way greater than the constituent parts, and such an approach was needed. The group also believed that such hard scientific problems require perspectives from multiple disciplines. Progress on a question such as "What is life?" would need the contributions of biologists, physicists, chemists, computer scientists, and others, working together. Yet most universities and research labs were organized in departmental silos that discouraged such collaboration. In 1984 the group created the Santa Fe Institute (SFI) as a nonprofit research organization to pursue the cross-disciplinary study of complex systems, and a short while later set up shop in a disused convent, with Cowan ensconced in the mother superior's office, and views of the Sangre de Cristo Mountains to inspire them.[4]

Reed was intrigued by Adams's description of SFI. Understanding a system as complex as the global economy was surely a hard scientific problem, and perhaps SFI's bottoms-up, interdisciplinary approach could provide economics with a needed kick in the intellectual pants. Adams introduced Reed to SFI's founders, and in 1987, Reed and Citicorp agreed to fund a cross-disciplinary workshop on economics.

The Clash of the Titans

The meeting was set up like a rugby match.[5] Squaring off on one side were ten leading economists captained by Nobel Prize winner Kenneth Arrow, co-originator of the Arrow-Debreu general equilibrium theory described in the last chapter. On the other side were arrayed ten physicists, biologists, and computer scientists, captained by Phil Anderson. The economists' side had luminaries such as Larry Summers, who would later become U.S. secretary of the treasury and then president of Harvard University; Brian Arthur of Stanford University, whose theories would provide key arguments in the Microsoft antitrust trial; and José Scheinkman, who would go on to become chairman of the legendary University of Chicago economics department. The physical scientists' team was no less impressive, with scholars such as David Ruelle, one of the pioneers of chaos theory; John Holland, a researcher in artificial intelligence; Stuart Kauffman, a University of Pennsylvania biologist who had won a MacArthur Foundation "genius" award; and Doyne Farmer, a young hotshot physicist from the Los Alamos National Laboratory who was infamous for his exploits using nonlinear physics to win at roulette in Las Vegas.

Each side presented the current state of its field and then spent ten days debating economic behavior, technological innovation, business cycles, and the workings of capital markets. The economists were excited by the physical scientists' ideas and techniques, but thought the scientists were naive and even a bit arrogant about economic problems. On the other side, the physical scientists were impressed by the mathematical virtuosity of the economists and genuinely surprised by the difficulty of economic problems.

But what really shocked the physical scientists was how to their eyes, economics was a throwback to another era. One of the participants at the meeting later commented that looking at economics reminded him of his recent trip to Cuba. As he described it, in Cuba, you enter a place that has been almost completely shut off from the Western world for over forty years by the U.S. trade embargo. The streets are full of Packard and DeSoto automobiles from the 1950s and relatively few cars of more recent vintage. He noted that one had to admire the ingenuity of the Cubans for keeping these cars running for so long on salvaged parts and the odd piece of Soviet tractor. For the physicists, much of what they saw in economics had a similar "vintage" feeling to it. It looked to them as if economics had been locked in its own intellectual embargo, out of touch with several decades of scientific progress, but meanwhile ingeniously bending, stretching, and updating its theories to keep them running. What the physicists were seeing was the legacy of Walras and Jevons. The mathematical Packards and DeSotos were the equations and techniques that the Marginalists had plundered from physics textbooks a hundred years ago.

Not only did the mathematics of economics seem like a blast from the past, but the physicists were also surprised by the way the economists used simplifying assumptions in their models. Ever since the days of Galileo, scientists have used simplifications such as perfect spheres and ideal gases to make their models easier to analyze. But scientists are generally careful to ensure that while their assumptions might simplify reality, their simplifications don't actually contradict it. And scientists also carefully test whether their assumptions matter to the answers given by their theories. In the view of the scientists at the workshop, the economists had taken the use of assumptions to an extreme. One assumption that got the scientists particularly exercised was what economists refer to as perfect rationality. Traditional Economics simplifies human behavior by assuming that people know everything possible about the future and crunch all that information through incredibly complex calculations to make such basic decisions as whether to buy a pint of milk. Even without being fully aware of the long history of debate on this subject, the physical scientists vociferously objected to the use of a model so clearly at odds with day-to-day reality. The science writer Mitch Waldrop quotes one of the economists, Brian Arthur, who describes the exchange:

The physicists were shocked at the assumptions the economists were making—that the test was not a match against reality, but whether the assumptions were the common currency of the field. I can just see Phil Anderson, laid back with a smile on his face, saying, "You guys really *believe* that?"

The economists backed into a corner would reply, "Yeah, but this allows us to solve these problems. If you don't make these assumptions, then you can't do *anything*."

And the physicists would come right back, "Yeah, but where does that get you—you're solving the wrong problem if that's not reality."[6]

In this chapter, I will argue that despite the field's many successes, the concerns of the scientists at the Santa Fe meeting were valid. When Walras imported the concept of equilibrium from physics into economics, he gained mathematical precision and scientific predictability. But he paid a high price for that gain—realism. The mathematics of equilibrium required Walras and later economists to make a set of highly restrictive assumptions that have increasingly detached theoretical economics from the real world. Traditional Economics has what computer programmers call a "garbage in, garbage out" problem. If you feed a computer bad inputs, it will with absolute precision and flawless logic grind out bad outputs. Likewise, most Traditional Economic models begin with unrealistic assumptions and then, with mathematical inevitability, work their way to equally unrealistic conclusions. As we will see, this is why there is little empirical support for many core ideas of Traditional Economics, and in some cases empirical evidence directly contradicts the theory's predictions. We will look at the assumptions that so vexed the Santa Fe scientists, and then move on to an examination of the empirical record of Traditional Economics. We will close with a return to the history of economics and see how a historical accident sent Traditional Economics down a century-long wrong turn.

Unrealistic Assumptions

The Santa Fe meeting was not the first time economists and physical scientists had clashed over the use of assumptions. In 1901, Léon Walras sent Henri Poincaré, the legendary French mathematician, a copy of his *Elements of a Pure Economics,* asking him for his opinion. Poincaré replied, "*A priori,* I am not hostile to the application of mathematics to the economic sciences, as long as one does not go beyond certain limits." In a follow-up letter, the mathematician made clear what those limits were by noting that Walras's theory contained a number of "arbitrary functions" (referring to Walras's use of assumptions). Poincaré commented that the conclusions drawn from Walras's equations were mathematically correct, but "if the arbitrary functions reappear in these consequences," the conclusions of the theory will be "devoid of all interest."[7] Just like the Santa Fe scientists a century later, Poincaré was particularly concerned about Walras's assumption of the unlimited foresight of economic actors. As Poincaré put it, "you regard men as infinitely selfish and infinitely farsighted. The first hypothesis may perhaps be admitted in a first approximation, the second may call for some reservations."[8]

During this period, there was quite a lot of correspondence between economists and the leading scientists of the day, including the French physicists Joseph Bertrand and Hermann Laurent, the American pioneer of thermodynamics J. Willard Gibbs, and the great Italian mathematician Vito Volterra. All echoed Poincaré's complaint that, while it was laudable for economics to become more mathematical and rigorous, throwing out reality for the convenience of making the equations solvable was not the way to go about it.[9] For the most part, however, the economists ignored these criticisms, and the program of building the Neoclassical theory of economics continued apace. The controversy over assumptions didn't go away, but for many decades bubbled along in the field at a low level.

Then in 1953, the University of Chicago's Milton Friedman brought the debate back up to a full boil when he published an essay titled "The Methodology of Positive Economics."[10] The essay argued that unrealistic assumptions in economic theory simply do not matter so long as the theories make correct predictions. If the economy behaves "as if" people were perfectly rational, then it really doesn't matter whether people are perfectly rational or not. Assumptions need no further justification as long as the results are correct. In other words, if it wasn't "garbage out" it didn't matter what was going "in." The essay was widely read and immediately controversial.[11] At a meeting of the American Economic Association several years later, Herbert Simon of Carnegie Mellon University delivered the counterargument.[12] He noted that the purpose of scientific theories is not to make predictions, but to explain things—predictions are then tests of whether the explanations are correct. But one has to test the whole logical chain of explanation, not just the conclusion reached at the end.

I will use a simple example to illustrate Simon's point. One could propose a theory that would explain that the sky is blue by assuming the existence of giants who paint it blue every night while we are sleeping.[13] Taken to an extreme, Friedman's logic would say that the assumption of giants is irrelevant as long as the theory makes the correct prediction, that the sky is blue, which it does. Simon would argue, however, that one can't just test the correctness of the conclusion. Rather, to accept such a theory, one would also have to observe the giants in action. As the economic philosopher Daniel Hausman has put it, one must "look under the hood" of a theory to see that the causal chain of explanation is valid as well.[14]

What, then, is the proper role of assumptions in theory? Why can Galileo and Newton get away with perfect vacuums and idealized spheres while Walras cannot get away with perfectly rational people and godlike auctioneers? Philosophers of science generally agree that there are two golden rules for the use of assumptions.[15] First, the assumptions must be appropriate for the purpose of the model, and second, they must not affect the answers the model provides for that purpose. The source of these two rules comes down to what philosophers of science call *fine* versus *coarse graining*.

A good way to illustrate this is to imagine scientific theories as being like maps.[16] Maps are approximate pictures of an underlying reality; a map of Oskaloosa, Iowa, is only an approximate representation of the real Oskaloosa. The only perfect map of Oskaloosa is Oskaloosa itself, which is too big to fit in the glove compartment of your car and thus not very useful. Just as map makers idealize and leave out certain features of the terrain, scientists simplify and idealize their theories. What is included or left out will depend on the purpose of the map or theory. If you are driving across the country, you might need just a coarse-grained map that shows the major highways. If, on the other hand, you were going to visit your great-aunt on Ford Avenue in Oskaloosa, you would need a fine-grained map that shows the street grid of Oskaloosa, but not all the highways in the country. Likewise, a cosmologist might be looking at the universe at the level of galaxies while a chemist might be looking at it at the level of atoms; each researcher needs different types and amounts of idealization. The key is that both the coarse- and fine-grained maps (and theories) *must agree with each other and the observations of underlying reality*. If a highway map places a river in a particular location, the river must be in the same location on the local map, and must agree with observations of where the river actually is. Likewise, even though the models of the cosmologist and the chemist may focus on different things, the models should not contradict each other, and both should be consistent with empirical and experimental evidence. In map making, one cannot just move roads and rivers around for the purpose of making the maps easier to draw. To many critics, the assumptions of Traditional Economics do not look like a legitimate case of coarse graining. Instead, it appears that beginning with Walras and Jevons, economists began arbitrarily making up assumptions about perfect rationality, godlike auctioneers, and so on, with the sole purpose of making the equilibrium math work. We will now take a closer look at some of the most troubling assumptions in Traditional theory.

Incredibly Smart People in Unbelievably Simple Worlds

Of all the assumptions in Traditional Economics, perhaps the strongest and most obviously unrealistic is its model of human behavior, a topic we will discuss in detail in chapter 6. The standard model, often referred to as *perfect rationality*, is built on two fundamental assumptions. The first is that people pursue their self-interest in economic matters. Economists recognize that in the real world, people occasionally do engage in acts of genuine altruism (though this is notoriously tricky to define), but argue that as a simplification, it is reasonable to assume that people will generally do whatever is in their economic self-interest. The second part of the assumption is that people pursue their self-interest in fantastically complex and calculating ways. Economists regularly assume that we take into account factors such as inflation rates, estimates of future government spending, and the trade deficit in our daily decision making. Economists also assume that we process all this information using equations and calculations that they themselves find difficult to solve.

Furthermore, in order to make human behavior predictable, economists traditionally assume that these superhuman robots live in theoretical worlds that are much simpler than the real world people actually inhabit. For example, to take into account projected interest rates for the rest of your life when deciding whether to put your money into a savings account or buy a six-pack of beer, you need information about what those rates are likely to be. Traditional models typically assume that all the information needed to make decisions is completely and instantly available for free. The reality, of course, is that we often have to make decisions with incomplete or ambiguous information, or if we wanted more information, it would cost us time and money to get it. Other typical assumptions about the world we live in include:

- There are no transaction costs (e.g., no fees, taxes, legal restrictions, or other costs or barriers to buying and selling)

- All products are pure commodities sold only on price (e.g., no brands or differences in product quality)

- Companies are always working as efficiently as possible

- Consumers can purchase insurance for any possible eventuality

- Economic decision makers only interact with each other through price, usually through an auction mechanism (when was the last time your supermarket held an auction?)

This combination of assumptions has caused Axel Leijonhufvud, a macroeconomist at the University of California, Los Angeles, to comment that

Traditional Economics models "incredibly smart people in unbelievably simple situations," while the real world is more accurately described by "believably simple people [coping] with incredibly complex situations."[17] There is a mountain of evidence to support Leijonhufvud's claim (which, again, we will review in chapter 6). Behavioral economists such as Herbert Simon, Daniel Kahneman, and Amos Tversky have shown that while people are intelligent in their decision making, they are intelligent in ways very different from the picture presented by Traditional Economics.[18] Real people are actually quite poor at complex logical calculations, but are very good at quickly recognizing patterns, interpreting ambiguous information, and learning. Real people are also fallible and subject to biases in their decision making. Finally, they engage in what Herbert Simon called *satisficing,* whereby one looks for a result that is "good enough" rather than the absolute best. For example, Traditional Economics would assume that the moment you need gas for your car, you drive to every gas station in your area in search for the one with the lowest price. Simon, on the other hand, would argue that you simply have a rough idea of what gas costs and pull into the nearest station that appears to have a reasonable price.[19] It makes sense that in a world where information is costly, incomplete, and rapidly changing, our brains would be wired to make fast decisions that are "good enough" rather than perfectly optimal.

In recent years, mainstream economists have begun to accept the unreality of these Traditional assumptions. In 2001 the Nobel Prize was awarded to George Akerlof, Michael Spence, and Joseph Stiglitz, whose models recognize that not everyone has access to perfect information. Then in 2002 the Nobel went to Daniel Kahneman and Vernon Smith for their work on more realistic theories of behavior. There has also been much work on "non-Walrasian markets" (i.e., markets without auctioneers) by researchers such as Frank Hahn and Takashi Negishi. Despite these advances, models that incorporate all these effects simultaneously and thus portray realistic people in a realistic environment have remained elusive.[20] Equilibrium is a strict master, and while economists are able to relax one or two assumptions at a time, the limitations of equilibrium mathematics mean that truly realistic models require a more radical break from the Traditional framework.

Time Waits for No One

One of the other prices that Traditional Economics has paid for its reliance on equilibrium is a strange view of time. Most Traditional Economic models don't actually consider time; instead they simply assume that the economy clicks along instantly from one equilibrium to another and that the transient conditions between equilibrium states do not matter. If a model does have time, it is typically a "short run" and a "long run," or an imaginary index time (e.g., rounds in game-theory models, or generations in many macroeconomic models). Few models actually have time in the normal sense of minutes, hours, days, and weeks.[21] Yet, time is undoubtedly important in real-world economic phenomena. It takes time to design things, make things, transport things, sell things, get information, and make decisions. How much time these things take matters in understanding the dynamics of the economy.

This can be illustrated using a well-worn joke about an old economist and a young economist walking down the street. The young economist looks down and sees a $20 bill on the street and says, "Hey, look a twenty-dollar bill!" Without even looking, his older and wiser colleague replies, "Nonsense. If there had been a twenty-dollar bill lying on the street, someone would have already picked it up by now."

In the Traditional Economics view, when a $20 bill hits the street, the world is suddenly out of equilibrium. As rational, self-interested people have an incentive to pick up $20 bills, someone will come along, pick up the bill, and move the world back to equilibrium. What matters is that we know what the equilibrium state is—one with no $20 bills lying on the streets—how long it takes to find and scoop up the bill and the specific path the world follows as it moves between equilibrium states are of no real concern.

In the real world, of course, there is a time delay between a $20 bill's landing on the sidewalk and someone's seeing it and picking it up. It then stands to reason that at any point in time, there are at least some undiscovered $20 bills lying on sidewalks somewhere. It is important to be explicit about the timescales in this process, because the amount of money lying on the streets will be a function of the rate at which bills are dropped and the average time to discovery. By varying the timescales, one can paint scenarios in which the streets are littered with money (rapid rate of loss, long delay until discovery) or in which $20 bills are very rare (slow rate of loss, short delay until discovery) or any scenario in between. One can even construct scenarios in which the world oscillates wildly between piles of money lying around and none.[22] The point is that unless we know the relative timescales involved, we can't say much about how the system will behave.

This lack of explicit timescales was one of Alfred Marshall's favorite complaints about economics a hundred years ago. During the intervening century, there have been some important attempts to introduce dynamics into Traditional theory, including work by Richard Day of the University of Southern California and macroeconomic models that feature time lags.[23] But, as with the assumptions on behavior, it is all but impossible to create models that combine equilibrium with complex dynamics and real-world timescales.[24]

Making the Interesting Exogenous

If Traditional models don't typically include explicit notions of time, then it is reasonable to ask just how they handle change in the economy. Returning to our image of Traditional theory as like a ball in a bowl, every time we try to roll the ball somewhere else in the bowl, the ball returns to the same equilibrium point it started from. But we know that economies are highly dynamic phenomena; things change all the time as production goes up and down, prices fluctuate, tastes and technologies change, and so on. How do we get this kind of dynamism into the inherently static picture of equilibrium? How do we get the ball-in-the-bowl to move over time?

What if we picked up our ball-in-the-bowl and gave it a good shake, bent one of the bowl's sides, and disturbed its equilibrium? The shock would initially send the ball out of its equilibrium point rolling around the bowl. As we bent the bowl's sides (imagine the bowl is made of rubber) and changed the shape of the constraints, eventually the ball would settle down into a new equilibrium point based on the reshaped bowl (figure 3-1).

In effect, this is what economists do to their models when they introduce *exogenous shocks*. All models have boundaries. If one tries to incorporate too much into a model, it will become so large and complex that it loses its usefulness. For example, population growth clearly affects economic systems, but it might not make sense to have a model of birth and death built into an economic model. Instead, for simplicity, one might just take a table of projected

FIGURE 3-1

Equilibrium, Shock, New Equilibrium

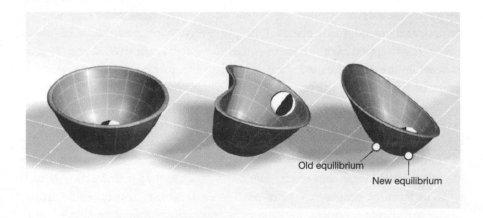

Old equilibrium

New equilibrium

population figures as an external input. As mentioned earlier, variables outside the bounds of a model are known as *exogenous variables,* while variables inside the bounds of a model are *endogenous variables.* Typical examples of exogenous variables include changes in consumer tastes, technological innovations, government actions, and the weather. For example, a change in technology, such as the invention of the Internet, can be seen as an exogenous shock to the economic system. This change affects both producer costs (e.g., Dell can sell computers more cheaply by taking orders online) and consumer preferences (e.g., consumers like the convenience of buying books online from Amazon.com). Such changes affect the constraints in the system (i.e., the shape of the bowl) and thus the location of the equilibrium point. As the economy is buffeted by shocks from exogenous variables, the equilibrium point moves over time. Thus the dynamism of the economy comes from a process of equilibrium, then shock, then new equilibrium, then shock, then new equilibrium, and the economy moves from one *temporary equilibrium* to another.

The problem with this approach is that it gives economists an escape hatch and allows them to put the most difficult and often most interesting questions outside the bounds of economics. For example, if technological change is treated as a random, outside force (like the weather), then one doesn't need a fundamental theory of the interaction between technological change and changes in the economy.[25] Likewise, one can attribute the waves of the business cycle to mysterious outside forces such as changes in consumer confidence, or crashes in the stock market to news. There is a parallel to this approach in biology. For years, evolutionary theorists pondered the puzzle of mass-extinction events. Our natural instinct is to look for a proximate and proportionate cause; that is, a big event must have had a big cause. For example, in the 1980s the geologist Walter Alvarez and his father, Nobel Prize laureate physicist Luis Alvarez, proposed a theory that the dinosaurs were wiped out by a massive asteroid colliding with the earth at the end of the Cretaceous period, and indeed, some evidence supports this hypothesis. Yet when other researchers stepped back and examined the long-term fossil record, they found that while the asteroid theory might explain the particular mass extinction event of the Late Cretaceous, it did not account for the ten other major extinction spasms (some much bigger) evident in the fossil record. More recent work has shown that extinction spasms are probably caused by the internal dynamics of evolution itself, without a major external event.[26] As we will see in chapter 8, in complex adaptive systems, small, innocuous events can occasionally set off avalanches of change.

In economics, exogenous "asteroids" do sometimes hit the economy, such as the worldwide economic impact of the September 11 terrorist attacks. But what about the stock market crash of October 19, 1987, when the market plummeted 20 percent? The *New York Times* headline that day was "Worry over dollar decline and trade deficit"; surely such a headline could have been written on many other days when major crashes did not happen.[27] Or what about the recession of 1982, when unemployment jumped from 7.5 percent to 11 percent in twelve months? Throughout the year, a panel of twenty leading economists consistently made forecasts that unemployment would decline. If some major exogenous event that could cause a recession had been going on at that time, wouldn't the forecasters have predicted that unemployment would grow?[28] In each case, it seems that endogenous factors are driving the truly interesting economic behavior—that some incompletely understood internal dynamic is causing stock market crashes and recessions.[29]

Again, one must draw model boundaries somewhere, but for a science to progress, it must extend its scope of explanation over time. In Traditional Economics, the straitjacket of equilibrium has forced the models to put some of the field's most interesting and fundamental questions outside the exogenous wall.

Keeping a Lid on Things

Many people have had the embarrassing situation of stepping up to a microphone to speak and being greeted by a loud squealing sound—the result of positive feedback. Positive feedback happens when a microphone is held too close to a loudspeaker and the sound bounces between the mike and loudspeaker in an amplifying cycle until the result is an earsplitting screech. Positive feedback is an accelerating, amplifying, self-reinforcing cycle. Negative feedback is the opposite: a decelerating, dampening, self-regulating cycle. A classic example of negative feedback is a thermostat. If your house gets cold, the thermostat switches on the heat. As the heat rises past a set point, the thermostat switches off, until the house cools back down below the set point. The thermostat dampens the fluctuations of heat in the house, keeping the temperature close to the set point.

Traditional Economics assumes that economic processes are dominated by dampening, negative feedback. This is the decreasing, or diminishing, returns to production and consumption that we discussed earlier. As we noted, Traditional Economics assumes that the twentieth worker on the production line is incrementally less productive than the tenth, and the fifth doughnut incrementally less desirable than the first. Like the sides of a bowl, negative feedback keeps things contained, keeps things heading toward equilibrium, and prevents the world from being awash in infinite quantities of cars and doughnuts.

The real world clearly does exhibit decreasing returns. But as former Stanford and SFI economist Brian Arthur has argued, the real world also exhibits positive feedback, or *increasing returns*.[30] As more teenagers wear a trendy pair of sneakers, the shoes become more desirable. As more information becomes available on the Web, the more useful the Web becomes. And sometimes, the more people who buy a stock, the more other people pile in to catch its rise. All these increasing-returns phenomena eventually peter out. The hot trend today is tomorrow's fashion blunder, the Web runs into information overload, and stock-market bubbles inevitably pop. But again, timing is everything. Traditional Economic theory tends to assume a long run, in which all increasing returns have exhausted themselves and the economy can safely go to equilibrium. But what if the long run never arrives? What if before one fashion peters out another starts to rise? What if someone invents Google to help us navigate the Web? What if some investors still believe they can beat the market, even after seeing a bubble pop? In a system such as the economy, there are always new sources of positive feedback to liven things up. There is no long run in the real world, or as John Maynard Keynes famously put it: "This long run is a misleading guide to current affairs. In the long run we are all dead. Economists set themselves too easy, too useless a task if in tempestuous seasons they can only tell us that when the storm is long past the ocean is flat again."[31]

In his novel *Crotchet Castle*, the nineteenth-century English satirist Thomas Love Peacock describes a debate between two gentlemen on whether the world has progressed or gone backward since the days of the ancient Greeks. One of the gentlemen cites as evidence of progress the invention of economics, "the science of sciences," as he puts it. His opponent replies that economics is "a hyperbarbarous technology, that no Athenian ear could have borne. Premises assumed without evidence, or in spite of it; and conclusions drawn from them so logically, that they must necessarily be erroneous."[32]

In order to fit the complex, dynamic world economy into the simple, static equilibrium box, economists have been forced to make "premises without evidence," and these premises raise serious questions about the results of the models built with them. Without these assumptions, the neat ball-in-the-bowl model degenerates; the smooth bottom of the bowl sprouts bumps, the ball never settles down, the equations cannot be solved, and the predictability of equilibrium is lost. A Traditional economist might justifiably reply that a great deal of effort has been expended over the years building models that add a dose of reality by relaxing some of these assumptions.

Economists have built models with less-than-perfect rationality, with imperfect information, with market frictions, with dynamics, and with endogenous treatments of formerly exogenous variables. But one can ask where in Traditional Economics are the models that relax *all of these assumptions at once* and therefore actually look something like a real economic system? To do this, one has to give up on the idea that the economy is an equilibrium system, something that until recently Traditional Economics has not been ready to do.

Reality Test

But let's say we give Milton Friedman the benefit of the doubt and imagine that we don't need to "look under the hood" at the assumptions in Traditional Economics. How does Traditional theory fare against Friedman's empirical test?

Many noneconomists are skeptical of the scientific credentials of economics because of its notoriously bad record at predicting things such as economic growth, interest rates, and inflation. We should keep in mind, however, that the hallmark of a science is not its ability to forecast the future, but its ability to *explain* things—to increase our understanding of the workings of the universe.[33] As mentioned before, the role of prediction in science is to help us distinguish between competing explanations. A well-formulated theory will have logical implications that can be tested. For example, meteorologists and climatologists can tell us quite a lot about the chemistry of the atmosphere, and their theories can be tested by drilling ice cores in the Arctic and sending weather balloons into the upper atmosphere. However, this does not mean that anyone can tell you with certainty whether it will rain on your barbecue next Sunday. This is because the earth's atmosphere, like the economy, is a complex, highly dynamic system that is far from equilibrium. In fact, meteorology and climate science can explain *why* weather forecasting is so inherently inaccurate. Science is full of examples of fields where researchers can explain phenomena and test the validity of their explanations, without necessarily being able to make accurate forecasts. For example, biologists can explain but not forecast the folding of proteins, and physicists can explain but not forecast the exact motion of a turbulent fluid.

Science is a continuous learning process in which the logical implications of competing explanations are tested and a body of evidence is accumulated over time. As Sir Karl Popper showed in the 1930s, there is no "final proof" that a theory is correct, but one *can* say whether a theory is disproved by data, whether one theory fits the data better than another, and whether a theory has yet to be contradicted by data.[34] For example, one cannot say that Einstein's theory of relativity has been proven, but one can say that its predictions have been well tested, it has yet to be contradicted, and it fits the data better than any alternative explanation proposed thus far. Science thus goes through a process of proposing various explanations, rigorously articulating them in ways that can be tested, eliminating theories that fail the tests, and building on the ones that succeed.[35]

Given this standard, we can then ask, how well are the predictions of Traditional Economics supported by data? The answer is "not well." As the highly respected microeconomist Alan Kirman, director of studies at L'Écoles des Hautes Études en Sciences Sociales in France, observes:

> Much of the elegant theoretical structure that has been constructed over the last one hundred years in economics will be seen over the next decade to have provided a wrong focus and a misleading and ephemeral idea of what constitutes an equilibrium. If we consider two standard criteria for a scientific theory—prediction and explanation—economic theory has proved to say the least, inadequate. On the first count, almost no one contests the poor predictive performance of economic theory. The justifications given are many, but the conclusion is not even the subject of debate. On the second count, there are many economists who would argue that our understanding of how economies work has improved and is improving and would therefore contest the assertion that economic theory, in this respect, has proved inadequate. The evidence is not reassuring, however. The almost pathological aversion to facing economic theory with empirical data at anything other than the most aggregate level is indicative of the extent to which "explanation" is regarded as being a self-contained rather than a testable concept.[36]

As Kirman points out, not only is there a problem with data that contradicts Traditional theories, but many theories have simply never been properly tested. One branch of economics, called *econometrics*, deals with data analysis.[37] Rather than testing theoretical models, however, much econometric work is devoted to finding statistical relationships between variables (often for public policy or other applied purposes). Unfortunately, statistical correlations don't provide a causal explanation of the phenomena. Furthermore, as many economists would point out, there is often a lack of readily available data to test theories with, and even data that is available is frequently noisy or otherwise problematic (though economists would find little sympathy from physicists or biologists, who have to build particle colliders and space telescopes and map the human genome to get data for their theories).

In two areas, however, Traditional theory has undergone rigorous testing. The first is finance theory, for which the availability of minute-by-minute data from financial markets and huge amounts of computing power have enabled an unprecedented level of testing of Traditional theory. Unfortunately for Traditional Economics, this encounter with data has produced a steady stream of work refuting many of the theory's most basic predictions, a topic we will return to in chapter 17.[38] The second area of rigorous testing is experimental economics. There is a popular perception that economics is different from other sciences in that one cannot readily carry out controlled experiments to test hypotheses. The Federal Reserve, for example, can't radically raise interest rates just to see at what point they would trigger a recession. While it may be challenging to conduct experiments on the economy as a whole, it is, however, possible to conduct experiments on economies in miniature. Researchers take groups of people and have them bargain with each other, bid in auctions, play economic games, invest in simulated stock markets, go shopping in fake stores, and participate in all sorts of contrived situations to capture specific aspects of economic behavior. This has produced a rich body of work, some of which we will review in chapter 6. Again, the encounter with data has generally not been kind to many of the core ideas of Traditional Economics.[39]

Naturally, much of the work testing Traditional Economics has been highly technical (and those interested can refer to the notes). Nevertheless, over the next few sections, we will look at a few intuitive examples for which the key predictions of Traditional theory do not meet the standards of a scientific reality test.

The "Law" of Supply and Demand

As discussed in the previous chapter, one of the oldest principles of Traditional Economics is the law of supply and demand. A basic prediction of this "law" is that the counterbalancing forces of supply and demand will drive a market to an equilibrium price and quantity level where the market clears. As a first approximation, this theory works pretty well. For example, if a car company introduces a new model that suddenly becomes popular, the company will typically raise the price while demand exceeds supply, expand production, and then lower the price once demand has cooled off and supply has caught up. All just as the theory would predict.

If, however, we zoom into a more fine-grained level, we see that real-world markets are almost never in equilibrium, supply rarely equals demand, and markets rarely come into balance. In fact, virtually all markets are built around the assumption of disequilibrium rather than equilibrium. Most markets have stocks of inventory, order backlogs, slack production capacity, and middlemen to help smooth out the disequilibria. Your local car dealer has a parking lot full of vehicles that are slower selling and an order backlog of "hot" vehicles that customers are waiting for. Your local supermarket is rarely in equilibrium, as its inventory stock floats up and down soaking up the imbalances between the supply of food being delivered through the back door and the demand being carried out through the front door. Service businesses such as lawyers and accountants rarely utilize their professionals at 100 percent, thus keeping some swing capacity available for fluctuations in demand. Even financial markets, which are viewed as the closest markets to the theoretical ideal, have mechanisms for dealing with inevitable supply-demand imbalances. The New York Stock Exchange has "specialists," and the NASDAQ exchange has "market makers," both of whom stand between supply and demand to smooth things out.

The law of supply and demand isn't a law after all (at least not in any scientific sense); rather, it is more appropriately "the rough approximation of supply and demand." Some Traditional economists might argue that the existence of inventories and slack production capacity doesn't matter, that they are just noise in the supply-demand balance. This is actually wrong. As we will discuss later in the book, the dynamics of inventories and production capacity can help explain phenomena such as price fluctuations and business cycles—phenomena that Traditional Economics usually looks to exogenous forces to explain.[40] And as we will see in chapter 18, the existence of inventories in stock markets may even help explain stock market volatility.[41]

The Law of One Price

The second most famous "law" in Traditional microeconomics is the law of one price, which states, "In the absence of transportation costs and trade barriers, identical goods must sell at the same price in all markets."[42] For example, the price of gold in New York should be the same as that in London, and any difference should be accounted for by the cost of shipping it from one market to the other (plus import duties, taxes, and any other transaction costs). Otherwise, one could arbitrage the difference and make a risk-free profit by buying gold in the low-price market and selling it in the high-price market. The buying and selling of arbitrageurs would then bring the price of the two markets back to equilibrium. Like supply and demand, the law of one price does often work as a first approximation. Highly liquid commodities such as gold rarely do show significant "arbitrageable" deviations in prices across markets.

Nonetheless, it is an approximation that often breaks down, both at the macro level of economies as a whole, as well as at the more micro level of individual products and services. For example, an important test of the theory has been the integration of the majority of European economies into the European Union and in particular the introduction of the euro currency. The theory predicts that this large-scale dropping of trade barriers, increased mobility of people, reduction in currency transaction costs, and greater price transparency should have led to a greater convergence of prices across the European Union. But in fact the opposite has happened. According to Eurostat, the EU's statistical agency, price differences have widened since the euro was introduced in 1999. The standard deviation of prices within the euro zone rose from 12.3 percent in 1998 to 13.8 percent in 2003, the exact opposite of the theory's prediction. Francisco Caballero-Sanz, head of economic analysis at the EU internal market directorate, attributed the lack of convergence to consumers being "not as 'rational' as economic theory would like them to be."[43]

Zooming in to a more fine-grained level, we often see a wide divergence in the prices of individual goods and services. For example, James Montier, the head of global equity strategy at the investment bank Dresdner Kleinwort Wasserstein, conducted a somewhat whimsical study of the London ketchup market and found that the price of the same bottle of ketchup could vary widely at area supermarkets.[44] He found deviations of up to 43 percent from the theoretically predicted price. There are thus opportunities for risk-free profits in the London ketchup market. In the theoretical world of Traditional microeconomics, such an opportunity would be arbitraged away instantly. But in the real world, arbitrage opportunities take time to be discovered, come and go, may or may not be worth exploiting, and may have various barriers to being exploited.

Again, some Traditional economists might ask, does it matter if the law of one price is an idealization? To most scientists, however, a 13.8 percent standard deviation across the euro zone, or a 43 percent error in ketchup prices, sound like pretty big idealizations. The point is *not* that the basic idea behind the law of one price is wrong; of course people have incentives to arbitrage price differences "in the absence of barriers." But in the real world, barriers of some kind almost always exist, whether it is the fact that no one has the time to search all the stores in an area for the lowest-priced ketchup, or whether there are still various transaction costs and transport, legal and other issues affecting trade in the European Union. In fact, the scientifically interesting question around price convergence is the dynamic interplay over time between the incentives to arbitrage and the changing nature of the various barriers. Yet, the mathematical requirements of the equilibrium framework force economists to strip away this complexity, leaving a "law" whose predictions are of questionable value. More useful would be a theory that could handle the complexity of prices in the real world.[45]

Equilibrium in a Few Quintillion Years

Perhaps the most fundamental prediction of Traditional Economics is that the economy as a whole must at some point reach equilibrium (this is a prediction made by both the general equilibrium theory of microeconomics, as well as by standard macroeconomics).[46] As noted earlier, Traditional Economics does not imagine equilibrium as a permanent state, but describes the economy as going through a sequence of shock, temporary equilibrium, shock, temporary equilibrium over time. Again, we can imagine whacking our ball-in-the-bowl, watching the ball settle back down, whacking it again, and so on. But for the system to reach equilibrium, the time in between shocks to the bowl must be long enough for the ball to settle. If that isn't the case, and we keep hitting the bowl with rapid shocks, then the ball will simply rattle around forever, randomly buffeted and never reaching equilibrium.

An important question, then, is, How long does it take for the economy to reach equilibrium? What is its "settling" time? In the 1970s, the Yale economist Herbert Scarf determined that the time to equilibrium scales exponentially with the number of products and services in the economy to the power of four.[47] The intuition behind this relationship is straightforward: the more products and services, the longer it takes for all the markets to interact with each other, and the longer it takes for all the prices and quantities to adjust. If we take the rough estimate from the first chapter that a modern economy has something on the order of 10^{10} SKUs in it, and if we optimistically assume that *every* decision in the economy is made at the speed of the word's fastest supercomputer (currently IBM's Blue Gene, at 70.72 trillion floating-point calculations per second), then using Scarf's result, it would take a mere 4.5 quintillion years (4.5×10^{18}) for the economy to reach general equilibrium after each exogenous shock. Given that shocks from factors such as technology change, political uncertainty, weather, and changes in consumer tastes buffet the economy every second, and the universe is only about 12 billion years old (1.2×10^{10}), this clearly presents a problem.[48]

Nonrandom Walks

As mentioned earlier, perhaps the area of Traditional Economics with the best opportunity to empirically test its theories is finance. But again, while the predictions of Traditional finance are not bad as a first approximation, they break down under closer examination.

One of the best known predictions of Traditional finance is that stock prices should follow a "random walk." We will look at this in more detail later in the book, but briefly, a random walk implies that there should be no patterns in the movement of prices, and that looking at past prices should not provide any clues about future prices. At first glance, stock prices do look very much like a random walk, particularly when they are relatively quiet and behaving "normally." For decades, researchers believed that the prices were, in fact, random. More recent analyses with better data and more powerful tools, however, have shown conclusively that prices do not follow a random walk. For example, Andrew Lo of the Massachusetts Institute of Technology (MIT) and Craig MacKinlay of the Wharton School at the University of Pennsylvania put the random-walk hypothesis through a series of tests on a 1,216-week sample of stock prices from 1962 to 1985; they tested individual stocks, portfolios of stocks, and stock indices, and in all cases rejected the random-walk hypothesis.[49] Numerous other studies using different samples and different techniques have also rejected the random-walk hypothesis.[50]

Interestingly, the departure of stocks from a random walk is statistically clearest when markets are making major moves, in other words, when they are the farthest from equilibrium.[51] There is also clear dynamic structure and information in stock price data, and while it is debatable whether anyone can systematically make money from that information, the fact that the prediction of random walks is wrong certainly does little to enhance Traditional finance's scientific credibility.[52]

The predictions of Traditional Economic theory are usually not completely crazy. Supply does roughly, approximately, equal demand. Prices do sometimes (but not always) converge. Markets may never actually reach equilibrium, but can act as if they are in a form of equilibrium. And, financial markets do superficially appear as if they follow a random walk when they are quiet and well behaved, that is, until they are no longer quiet and well behaved. If these statements don't sound very scientific, it is because they are not. As Friedman's nemesis, Herbert Simon, put it: "To be sure, economics has evolved a highly sophisticated body of mathematical laws, but for the most part these laws bear a rather distant relation to empirical phenomena, and usually imply only qualitative relations among observables."[53]

Traditional Economics is built on a shaky foundation of assumptions that has led to equally shaky conclusions. The next logical question is to ask why the field has ended up in this position. The explanation for the troubles with Traditional Economics goes back to over a hundred years ago, to the crucial step Walras took when he imported the concept of equilibrium into economics from physics. Without realizing it, Walras fundamentally misclassified the economy.

Misused Metaphors

Human beings are skillful pattern recognizers and use metaphors to help them understand and reason about the world. Saying that something resembles or has qualities of something else enables us to quickly, and in just a few words, grasp the essence of a complex phenomenon. Shakespeare could have given us a long passage about how Juliet was central to Romeo's life, brought him happiness, and so on. Instead, with the simple phrase "Juliet is the sun!" Shakespeare conveyed those meanings in a far richer and more powerful way.

Science uses metaphor as well, both to inspire creativity and to help communicate complex ideas. For example, the metaphor of tiny, vibrating loops of string has helped inspire the physicists who are developing string theory (an attempt to unify the fundamental forces of the universe and explain the origins of subatomic particles) to think in radically different ways from their predecessors.[54] Likewise, the phrase *loops of string* helps metaphorically communicate the key idea of string theory to a lay audience more easily than does "eleven-dimensional Calabi-Yau space." But while metaphor is useful in inspiring and communicating science, science itself is based on more than metaphor. Scientific theories do not merely make claims that one thing resembles another. As discussed in chapter 1, scientists make claims that something literally *is* a member of a universal class of phenomena. Similarity is not sameness. When a cosmologist says our sun is a star, the scientist doesn't just mean it is similar in some way to a star. Rather, our sun is a member of a universal class of phenomena, which are called stars, that share certain empirically observable characteristics.[55]

There is no doubt that when Walras read Poinsot's physics textbook, he was metaphorically inspired by the similarity between notions of balancing forces in physical systems and notions of balancing forces in economic systems.[56] This similarity motivated him to apply the mathematical tools of equilibrium analysis to economic systems. A hundred years later, at the meeting of scientists and economists in Santa Fe, the key question on the table was, is the concept of equilibrium in economics based merely on superficial similarities between physical and economic systems, or are economic systems *literally* equilibrium systems, which thus share the universal properties of such systems?[57] In other words, is the equilibrium framework in Traditional Economics a metaphor or science?

To Walras and his Marginalist compatriots, such a question would not have occurred to them. First, at that point in time, the philosophy of science and an understanding of the legitimate and illegitimate roles of metaphor were not as well understood as they are today. Second, the question begs another question. If economic systems are not equilibrium systems, then what are they? This second question would have baffled Walras as well. To the physicists of Walras's time, there were simply equilibrium systems, which could be mathematically analyzed, and "other" systems, some of which could be analyzed, but most of which could not. There weren't many alternative ways one could categorize a phenomenon such as the economy. Given Walras's goal of bringing mathematical rigor and predictability to economics, it is not surprising he went down the well-trodden path of equilibrium analysis.

Half-Baked Physics

Unfortunately, Walras was on his mission to turn economics into a science when science itself was at a peculiar point in its development and missing a critical concept. All science is a work in progress, and the physics that the Marginalists knew was not yet the classical thermodynamics that one would see in a textbook today; in fact, one could say it was only half-baked. The physics that the Marginalists borrowed included the First Law of Thermodynamics, but was missing the Second Law.

The *First Law of Thermodynamics,* which states that energy is neither created nor destroyed and is otherwise known as the *Conservation of Energy Principle,* had been developed in the early to mid-nineteenth century and was clearly spelled out in the texts that Walras, Jevons, and the others read. To see how the First Law works, imagine that a ball is held high on the side of our now familiar bowl. It has *potential energy* that can be released when the ball is dropped. If you put your hand at the bottom of the bowl, you would feel the ball whack into it as gravity pulls it down and its energy is released into your hand. That release of energy is referred to as *work* (because it potentially could be used to do something useful, like drive a machine). When the ball is let go and begins to roll around, it also encounters friction from the side of the bowl, and that friction generates heat. The potential energy of the ball is thus turned into work and heat. The great English physicist James Prescott Joule showed that nature is very parsimonious with energy and that energy is neither created nor destroyed, but merely converted from one form into another. If one added up the amount of potential energy stored in the ball at the top of the bowl and the amount of work plus heat released as it rolled down, the two amounts would be equal. Likewise, if one measured the amount of energy stored in a lump of coal and then burned the coal to do some work (e.g., propel a steam locomotive), the energy stored in the coal would equal the energy used to do the work plus the waste heat going up the locomotive smokestack.[58]

One of the properties of the First Law is that if the total energy in a system is fixed, that is, "conserved," then the system is *guaranteed* to eventually reach equilibrium. Once the potential energy of the ball is done turning into work and heat, and the ball is resting at its minimum energy state at the bottom of the bowl, it is in equilibrium. Likewise, once the burning coal has been turned into work and waste heat, it will stop burning and reach an equilibrium state. Only by *adding energy from the outside,* for example, by shaking the bowl or adding another lump of coal, can we keep the system out of equilibrium.

As Philip Mirowski of Notre Dame has pointed out, one of the consequences of Walras's borrowing equilibrium is the mathematical need for fixed or conserved quantities in Traditional models. This is why Traditional Economics typically portrays value as a fixed quantity that is converted from one form to another (i.e., resources are turned into goods, which are exchanged for money, which is exchanged back for goods, which are consumed, creating utility).[59] New wealth isn't actually created; rather, the world begins with a finite set of resources that are allocated among producers who in turn create a finite set of commodities that are allocated among consumers. One can allocate that wealth in ways that are more or less efficient, just as one can burn a lump of coal in ways that are more or less efficient, but in general equilibrium models the economy can't create new wealth any more than a lump of coal can reproduce.[60] This emphasis on a fixed pie of wealth caused the English economist Lionel Robbins in 1935 to famously call economics "the science of scarcity."[61] This is still reflected in modern economics textbooks, for example, Paul Samuelson and William Nordhaus's widely used book defines economics as "the study of how societies use scarce resources to produce valuable commodities and distribute them among different people."[62] The legacy of the First Law that metaphorically inspired Walras and Jevons lives on in Traditional Economics today.

However, the First Law is only half of the thermodynamic story. The Second Law, which was missing from the physics Walras and Jevons knew, states that *entropy,* a measure of disorder or randomness in a system, is always increasing. The Second Law says that the universe as a whole is inevitably drifting from a state of order to a state of disorder—the ultimate end point of the universe is a random, featureless miasma of perfectly even temperature. Over time, all order, structure, and pattern in the universe breaks down, decays, and dissipates. Cars rust, buildings crumble, mountains erode, apples rot, and cream poured into coffee dissipates until it is evenly mixed. Entropy is what gives time its arrow. The great physicist Murray Gell-Mann, one of the founders of SFI, illustrates this by noting that if you have young children (or in his case, grandchildren), you are likely to have jars of both peanut butter and jelly in the cupboard. Over time, the peanut butter eventually gets in the jelly and jelly gets in the peanut butter as the children make sandwiches. Gell-Mann notes that if he showed you a time-lapse movie of the peanut butter jar getting progressively more and more flecks of jelly in it, and then showed a movie where the flecks disappear as the peanut butter spontaneously cleaned itself up, you would immediately know which was the forward and which was the backward version.[63] Without entropy and the inevitable drift from order to disorder, there would be no way to tell what was the past, present, or future. Since its discovery, entropy has become a central concept in the way physicists view the universe.[64]

Unfortunately for Walras, Jevons, and the other builders of Traditional Economics, this supreme law of nature was missing from their framework. The Second Law was one of those scientific concepts that had a long gestation and was built through the work of a number of people, including Sadi Carnot, Rudolph Clausius, and Sir William Thomson (a.k.a. Lord Kelvin), over the period 1824 to 1865. Its significance, however, was not fully appreciated until the end of the nineteenth century, and many of its important implications were not worked out until well into the twentieth century (and indeed are still being worked out today). Entropy would have been considered still too new and too poorly understood to be put into introductory texts that inspired Walras and Jevons at the time.[65]

Open Sesame

With an understanding of both the First and Second Laws of Thermodynamics, we can move on to another concept that would have been unavailable to Walras and Jevons at the time: that of closed and open systems (these terms have another meaning in economics relating to whether an economy engages in international trade, but we will use them in the physicists' sense). First, a thermodynamic *system* is any defined set of space, matter, energy, or information that we care to draw a box around and study. The universe itself is a system, and within that largest of all systems, one can define any number of smaller systems. For example, our planet is a system, as is your body, your house, or a bathtub full of water. A *closed* system is a system having no interaction or communication with any other system—no energy, matter, or information flowing into or out of it. The universe itself is a closed system. There is no "outside" the universe, no other system beyond its boundaries that it can interact with.[66] Energy might be converted into matter, and vice versa, and energy might be converted into different forms within the system, but the total amount is constant, according to the First Law. In addition, the total entropy in a closed system is always increasing to its maximum level, as order decays into disorder and the system eventually comes to rest.

The second type of system is an *open* system, with energy and matter flowing into and out of it. Such a system can use the energy and matter flowing through it to temporarily fight entropy and create order, structure, and patterns for a time. Our planet, for example, is an open system; it sits in the middle of a river of energy streaming out from the sun. This flow of energy enables the creation of large, complex molecules, which in turn have enabled life, thus creating a biosphere that is teaming with order and complexity. Entropy has not gone away; things on the earth do break down and decay, and all organisms eventually die. But the energy from the sun is constantly powering the creation of new order. In open systems, there is a never-ending battle between energy-powered order creation and entropy-driven order destruction. Nature's accounting rules are very strict, and there is a price to be paid when order is created in an open system. For order to be created in one part of the universe, order must be destroyed somewhere else, because the net effect must always be increasing entropy (decreasing order). Thus, as the sun powers order creation on earth, all of that life and activity creates heat, which is radiated back into space. The heat has a randomizing effect wherever it ends up, thereby increasing entropy. The earth thus imports energy and exports entropy.

For an example closer to home, let's imagine you've been very busy at work and the Second Law has driven your house from a state of order to one of disorder. You decide to invest some energy to fight entropy and clean it up. You input energy into your house through the calories you burn scrubbing and picking things up, and you use electricity to power your vacuum cleaner, dishwasher, and washing machine. In addition, matter flows into your house in a highly ordered state in the form of food, clothing, cleaning products, and so forth. The universe gets its entropy payback, however, when you and all the devices you use radiate heat back into the environment. Moreover, the electricity you use also causes waste heat and smokestack emissions at the generating plant, and matter flows back out of your house into the world in a disordered state in the form of trash. Thus the system of your house imports energy and matter, which is then used to create the order within its confines, and then sends back into the universe heat and disordered matter, thereby exporting its entropy.

Closed systems always have a predictable end state. Although they might do unpredictable things along the way, they always, eventually, head toward maximum entropy equilibrium. Open systems are much more complicated. Sometimes they can be in a stable, equilibrium-like state, or they can exhibit very complex and unpredictable behavior patterns that are far from equilibrium—patterns such as exponential growth, radical collapse, or oscillations. As long as an open system has free energy, it may be impossible to predict its ultimate end state or whether it will ever reach an end state.

In chapter 1, I defined a complex adaptive system as a system of interacting agents that adapt to each other and their environment. Complex adaptive systems are a subcategory of open systems. It takes energy to process information, sustain order, and create complex patterns. For example, an ant colony takes in energy and matter through the food and material it brings into the nest; it uses that energy and material to fight entropy as the colony builds its nest and organizes its activities. The presence of free energy is what enables a complex adaptive system such as an ant colony to stay away from equilibrium, create order, and be dynamic over time. If you remove that energy, then entropy takes over and the system decays and eventually reaches a state of stasis or equilibrium. As one of the participants at the SFI meeting, University of Michigan theorist John Holland, once put it, "in fact, if the system ever does reach equilibrium, it isn't just stable. It's dead."[67]

The Misclassification of the Economy

Walras and Jevons were not familiar with the Second Law and thus were not aware of the distinction between open and closed systems, or the existence of complex adaptive systems. In fact, a detailed understanding of open systems emerged only gradually during the twentieth century, accelerating with the work of the Russian-born chemist Ilya Prigogine in the 1960s and 1970s. The Traditional model, then, was created with the implicit assumption that the economy is a thermodynamically closed equilibrium system, even though, at the time, Walras, Jevons, and their fellow Marginalists did not know that they were building this assumption into their theories. For the next one hundred years, as economics and physics each went their separate ways, this assumption lay buried in the mathematical heart of Traditional Economics.[68]

Unfortunately for economic theory, this unawareness of the Second Law meant that the Marginalists and their successors fundamentally (though unwittingly) misclassified the economy. The economy is not a closed equilibrium system; it is an open disequilibrium system and, more specifically, a complex adaptive system. The proof for this lies just outside your window, right under your nose. It is so obvious, in fact, that it has escaped the attention of most economists until relatively recently.[69] If the economy were a closed equilibrium system, its defining characteristic would be a trend toward *less* order, complexity, and structure over time, as entropy sends any closed equilibrium system inevitably toward a featureless stasis. Closed equilibrium systems do not spontaneously self-organize; they do not generate patterns, structures, and complexity; and above all, they do not create novelty over time.[70] All the movement, buzz, organization, and activity of the economy outside your window *cannot be the product of a closed equilibrium system.* As we saw in the first chapter, the defining characteristic of the economy has been an immense rise in economic complexity throughout its journey from the

10^1 SKU economy of *Homo habilis* to the 10^{10} SKU economy of the modern world. The growth of economic activity from the Stone Age until now has been one long story of fighting entropy on a grand scale—something that could only happen in an open disequilibrium system.

A Traditional economist might well ask what all this physics of open and closed systems has to do with economics. Open and closed systems are physical concepts, while the economy is a social phenomenon. Am I engaging in the kind of inappropriate metaphorical reasoning I have accused Walras of using? The answer is no. We have to remember that social systems are not just abstract mathematical models that exist in the minds of economists or in the equations of textbooks. They are real physical systems made of matter, energy, and information; they are made up of people and all of that stuff outside your window, and they are just as subject to the laws of physics as any other phenomenon. Real, physical economies have enormous amounts of real, physical energy pouring into them every day—that is what makes them tick.[71] Our hunter-gather ancestors powered their economies with the food they ate and the firewood they collected. Modern economies power themselves with Big Macs and microwavable ready-meals, as well as with oil, natural gas, coal, hydropower, nuclear power, and any other energy source we can get our hands on. Energy comes into economies to power the fight against entropy and create order. Likewise, economies obey the Second Law and export disorder back into the universe around them as they throw off waste, pollution, greenhouse gases, and heat.

Economies are not just metaphorically *like* open systems; they literally and physically *are* a member of the universal class of open systems. If one were to cut off the supply of energy to an economy—shut off the food, oil, gas, and coal—then entropy would be unopposed, and the economy would drift toward a true equilibrium. Sadly, we see something like this when a country has been wracked by war, such as in the Democratic Republic of Congo, or is isolated by its political leaders, such as in North Korea. Such economies inevitably decline as entropy begins to win and they head toward a literal equilibrium of misery and starvation, whereas a growing, vibrant economy is by definition far from equilibrium.

Even a market that is "pure information" such as the NASDAQ stock market, which exists only on the computer screens of traders, still has a basis in the physical world. There was a surprising reminder of this a number of years ago, when a squirrel burrowed its way into an electricity transformer near the NASDAQ's main computer center in Connecticut. The creature got zapped, knocked out the power, and briefly shut down the market.[72] As we will discuss in chapter 14, all wealth creating economic activities require some form of energy and involve manipulations of matter and/or information (although the reverse is not true, not all energy using, matter and information manipulating activities are wealth creating). Economic activity is firmly rooted in the real, physical world, and thus economic theory cannot escape the laws of thermodynamics.

A Traditional economist might concede that economies are real physical systems and even open systems, but argue that the physics of open and closed systems does not matter because economists model economies at a higher level of abstraction than their physical basis (in other words, economic models are more coarse-grained than physical science models). Just as a biologist might model a cell without reference to subatomic physics, an economist might model an economy without explicit reference to physical thermodynamics. Economics has its own concepts, such as preferences, prices, and production functions, that exist as abstractions in the social realm, just as biologists have their own high-level abstractions (e.g., the gene) that are relevant to the biological realm. A Traditional economist might argue that by borrowing some math tricks from physics textbooks, all Walras and Jevons were guilty of was trying to make the abstractions of economics more rigorous. Equilibrium analysis is just a math technique, nothing more. Both physics and economics also use algebra—why is equilibrium such a problem?[73]

There are actually two points embedded in this pro-equilibrium argument. The first is the "different levels of abstraction" point; the second is the "it's just math" point. Certainly, science requires different levels of abstraction for different phenomena. As we noted before, scientific theories can be big picture and coarse grained like a highway map, or fine grained like a local street map. Both are equally valid; they just need to agree with each other and conform with reality. Thus, it is fine for economics to have its own high-level, coarse-grained concepts that are not addressed in physics and that may omit explicit references to physical laws. However, economic theories cannot be *inconsistent* with basic physical laws. A claim that the economy is a closed equilibrium system would be in obvious violation of basic physical laws. Thus, for the "levels of abstraction" response to be valid, we must believe that, even though the economy is in reality an open disequilibrium system, it is for some reason better to model it as a closed equilibrium system. In fact, the reverse is true. As we will see in part 2, the problems of unrealistic assumptions and lack of empirical validation stem from the mis-modeling of the open disequilibrium economy using closed equilibrium techniques.[74]

The second part of the pro-equilibrium argument—"it's just math"—misunderstands both what equilibrium is about and what math is about. Math is a form of language, it is a symbolic system that we use to describe and explain our world.[75] It is a special language because of the high degree of agreement on what its various symbols mean and the rules for manipulating those symbols. There have been various attempts to create a "pure" mathematics, which is just an abstract language whose symbols are purely logical constructs with no connection to the real world.[76] While these exercises have been valuable in pushing the boundaries of the field, the current consensus among mathematicians and philosophers is that one cannot separate mathematics from its meaning in the physical world.[77] Of course, mathematicians can create mathematical fantasy worlds that do not exist in physical reality, including forty-three-dimensional objects that one cannot see or touch. But we do this with natural language as well—we write novels or make movies about things that do not exist in the real world. Yet our *interpretation* of these fantasy objects, whether the latest Hollywood blockbuster, or a forty-three-dimensional hypersphere, is unavoidably tied to our experience with the real world.[78] There is no such thing as "just math."

If "economic equilibrium" does have a meaning in the real world, the next question is, What does it mean? There is no rule that says researchers in two fields must use their terminology in the same way. We can thus ask whether the term *equilibrium* means the same thing in economics as it does in physics? Perhaps the economists mean something completely different by *equilibrium* and the problem I've pointed out is just a case of confused terminology. If *equilibrium* were being used to mean different things in different fields, then we should be able to translate from one definition to the other. Yet, I know of no definition of *equilibrium* in economics that defines it in any way that is distinct from what physicists mean by it. On the contrary, the two fields use the word in precisely the same way. The *Oxford Dictionary of Physics* defines *equilibrium* as "[a] state of a system in which forces, influences, reactions, etc. balance each other out so that there is no net change."[79] Meanwhile the *Collins Dictionary of Economics* defines *equilibrium* as "a state of balance with no tendency to change."[80] In addition, the mathematical techniques used by economists and physicists for equilibrium analysis are identical.

This leads to some uncomfortable questions for economics. Does Traditional Economics claim that economies and markets *literally* are equilibrium systems? Is this a case of legitimate theory extension, in which we have a universal class, called equilibrium systems, that includes things like weights hanging off springs *and* the market for pork bellies? Yet, how can the economy be a closed equilibrium system when it has energy and matter pouring in one end and entropy leaking out the other? Wouldn't this claim violate the laws of physics? Or, are economies and markets merely *like* equilibrium systems? Is it all just a misused metaphor arising from the peculiar history of economics?[81]

The answer, I believe, is yes; the Neoclassical model that lies at the heart of Traditional theory was built on a misused metaphor. Without realizing it and with the best intentions, the late-nineteenth-century economists borrowed from physics a set of ideas that fundamentally misclassified the economy as a closed equilibrium system. This approach set the framework for the Traditional Economics we see today. Unfortunately, this misclassification has acted as a straitjacket, forcing economists to make highly unrealistic assumptions and limiting the field's empirical success.

Beyond Walras's Cathedral

When the Santa Fe meeting ended after ten days, there was a sense of both exhilaration and exhaustion.[82] Despite the intensity of debate and occasional clashing of egos, the meeting ended with a profound sense of mutual respect. The economists had seen some of their own doubts about Traditional economic theory reinforced and had their eyes opened to new ways of thinking about long-standing economic problems. The physical scientists, for their part, had gotten a glimpse into a phenomenon as fascinating, complex, and challenging as anything in nature. Many of the connections and collaborations forged at the meeting continued, and SFI launched an interdisciplinary program in economics, initially cochaired by Brian Arthur and John Holland and funded by Citicorp. Like a snowball starting down a hill, the idea of viewing the economy as a complex adaptive system gathered pace. SFI remained a central driving force, hosting a variety of workshops and conferences over the years on topics ranging from finance to economic inequality, including a sequel to the original conference a decade later.[83] Perhaps even more importantly, the network of researchers working on these issues spread dramatically. Today, virtually every major economics department has at least one or two people working on some aspect of what I will define in the next chapter as Complexity Economics. And the interdisciplinary collaborations have grown as well; it is not uncommon now to see economics papers in journals such as *Physical Review Letters, Nature,* and even the *Journal of Theoretical Biology.*

The critique presented in this chapter is not intended as a broadside at economics or economists generally. Rather it has been a critique of the specific theories that comprise Traditional Economics. Economics is a broad church, and within the field there has been a wide variety of work outside the Traditional Economics orthodoxy and much recent work pushing the Traditional boundaries. As we will see in part 2, many economists themselves have left the Traditional fold and are taking the lead in developing the new theories of Complexity Economics, oftentimes alongside colleagues from other disciplines. Nor am I criticizing economics' aspirations as a science, or the use of mathematics by the field. There are many critics who pine for the simpler pre-Walrasian days, when economics was a branch of political and moral philosophy and one did not need sophisticated mathematical skills to be an economist. While economics undoubtedly has a number of unique characteristics as a science, it would have little hope of creating scientifically credible explanations without the precision and rigor of mathematics.[84] The issue I have raised is whether economics is using the right math.

This critique also does not in any way take away from the accomplishments of the field over the past century. As discussed earlier, scientific theories are always approximations of the underlying reality they attempt to describe. In part 2, I will argue that Complexity Economics is a better approximation of economic reality than Traditional Economics, just as Einstein's relativity is a better approximation of physical reality than Newton's laws. Nonetheless, I believe that Traditional Economics has been at least approximately or directionally right on many important issues, and its ideas have helped improve the lives of billions of people. In addition, the theories of Traditional Economics have a true intellectual beauty to them and have been developed by some of the finest minds to grace the sciences. Science progresses by the ideas of one generation building on, and occasionally replacing, the ideas of another. Nothing would better honor the legacy of the builders of Walras's cathedral than to see the field progress beyond the paradigm that they constructed.

PART II

Complexity Economics

The real voyage of discovery consists,
not in seeking new landscapes,
but in having new eyes.

—Marcel Proust

CHAPTER FOUR

The Big Picture

SUGAR AND SPICE

MARIA LUZ OCHONDRA lives on one of the world's largest garbage dumps, a place incongruously called the Promised Land, just outside Manila in the Philippines.[1] No one knows exactly how many people live on and around the Promised Land, but at least a couple thousand desperately poor adults and children spend their days picking through the garbage looking for anything useful. Father Joel Bernardo, a Catholic priest who works with the residents, notes that they are the "leftovers" of the world, the poorest of the poor. Another resident, Paz Calopez, describes conditions in the Promised Land this way: "There's always smoke, there's always fire, even when it rains. The garbage is glowing, even at night, and you hear popping sounds. We think it's batteries exploding. It smells worse than a bathroom, especially when the bulldozers come through." Tragically, during July 2000, weeks of monsoon rains soaked and loosened the mountain of garbage, causing it to suddenly collapse, killing more than two hundred people and two of Mrs. Ochondra's sons.

It is hard to believe that in this most hellish of places on earth, populated by some of the most desperate people imaginable, there is a sophisticated and, one could even say, vibrant economy. In 1994, the Philippine government closed a large dump in another location, greatly increasing the amount of garbage going to the Promised Land. Almost as soon as the Promised Land began to fill up, its economy sprang to life. At the base of the Promised Land economy are the scavenger families who live on the dump and spend their days picking through the garbage, looking for scrap metal, plastic bottles, rubber tires, and other useful materials. Sometimes they find discarded appliances, pieces of furniture, clothing, children's toys, even edible food. The scavengers keep some of the material for their own use, but sell most of it to middlemen, who are the next link in the chain. The middlemen tend to specialize by type of material and have relationships with recyclers and manufacturers that purchase the metal, plastic, and rubber that the middlemen consolidate from the scavengers. Some middlemen even have recycling contracts with large companies and hotel chains. These contracts allow the middlemen to hire scavengers on a piecework basis to pick through their clients' garbage first, culling the choice material before the trucks tip it into the general dump. The middlemen enjoy more efficient access to better materials, and their client companies are charged reduced tipping fees.

At the next level of the economic chain are the various businesses that have sprung up to service the scavengers, middlemen, and their families. Various shanty shops sell products ranging from soap to shoes, bicycle parts, ice cream, and school supplies. Although the scavengers have a very difficult, unhealthy, and dangerous existence, the dump nonetheless provides a relatively steady income that keeps the majority of its residents from starving—an all-too-real risk in a country with 74 million people who earn less than one dollar per day. As Father Bernardo observed, "It's raw capitalism working here. And it really generates money. Millions of pesos revolve through here every day."

Where do economies come from? How is a complex economic ecosystem such as the Promised Land economy conjured out of a pile of garbage? How do the behaviors, relationships, institutions, and ideas that underpin an economy form, and how do they evolve over time? Questions of origins play prominent roles in most sciences. It would be difficult to imagine modern cosmology without the Big Bang, or biology without evolution. Likewise it would be hard to believe that economics could ever truly succeed as a science if it were not able to answer the question "Where do economies come from?" Yet the question of the origin of economies has not played a central role in Traditional Economics.[2] As discussed, Traditional Economics has tended to focus on how the economic pie is allocated rather than how the pie got here in the first place. Even Traditional growth theory implicitly begins with "assume an economy." The process of economy formation presents us with a first-class scientific puzzle and one of the sharpest distinctions between Traditional Economics and what I will describe as Complexity Economics.

Welcome to the Sugarscape

Joshua Epstein and Robert Axtell are researchers at the Brookings Institution, one of the leading public-policy think tanks in Washington, D.C. In

1995, they decided to conduct an experiment to see if they could grow an economy from scratch. Like biologists trying to cultivate life in vitro in a petri dish, Epstein and Axtell wanted to see if they could spark economic life *in silico,* in the simulated world of a computer.[3]

Traditional microeconomic models typically start out with assumptions that there are consumers, producers, technologies, and markets. Macroeconomic models likewise start out with assumptions that there are things like money, labor markets, capital markets, governments, and central banks. Epstein and Axtell wanted none of that. They wanted to go back to the very beginning, to a state of nature, and have a model that included nothing more than people with a few basic abilities, and an environment with some natural resources. They wanted to find out the minimum conditions required to set off a chain reaction of economic activity. What would it take to get the system to start climbing the ladder of increasing economic order?[4]

To picture Epstein and Axtell's model, imagine a group of people shipwrecked on a desert island, except that both the island and the castaways are simulations inside a computer. The computer island is a perfect square with a fifty-by-fifty grid overlaid on top of it, like a giant chessboard. The virtual island has only one resource—sugar—and each square in the grid has different amounts of sugar piled on it. The heights of the sugar piles range from four sugar units high (the maximum) to zero (no sugar). The sugar piles are arranged such that there are two sugar mountains, one mountain at the northeast corner and one at the southwest corner, each with sugar piled three and four units high (figure 4-1). Between the two mountains is a "badlands" area with little or no sugar. Epstein and Axtell called their imaginary sugar island Sugarscape.

The Sugarscape landscape is, of course, a vast simplification of an actual island, but it highlights three essential features of real-world islands: (1) There is a notion of physical space. That is, you can move north, south, east, and west on it. (2) There is a source of energy, namely, the sugar. And (3) the terrain is differentiated; it has mountains, valleys, fertile areas, and desert areas.

Likewise, the virtual castaways on Sugarscape are vast simplifications but share some key characteristics with real people. Each virtual person, or "agent," is an independent computer program that takes in information from the Sugarscape environment, crunches that information through its code, and then makes decisions and takes actions. In the most basic version of the simulation, each agent on Sugarscape can only do three things: look for sugar, move, and eat sugar. That's it. In order to find food, each agent has vision that enables it to look around for sugar, and then has the ability to move toward this source of energy. Each agent also has a metabolism for digesting sugar.

FIGURE 4-1

The Sugarscape

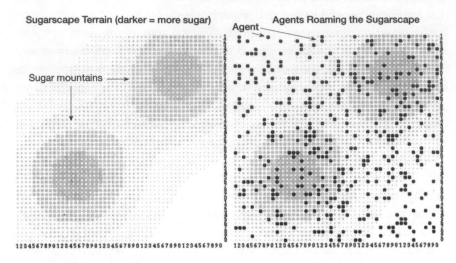

Source: Epstein and Axtell (1996).

Epstein and Axtell wanted to see if simple agents in a simple landscape could create something like an economy. Thus, each agent had a basic set of rules that it followed during each turn of the game:[5]

- The agent looks ahead as far as its vision will allow in each of four directions on the grid: north, south, east, and west (the agents cannot see diagonally).

- The agent determines which unoccupied square within its field of vision has the most sugar.

- The agent moves to that square and eats the sugar.

- The agent is credited by the amount of sugar eaten and debited by the amount of sugar burned by its metabolism. If the agent eats more sugar than it burns, it will accumulate sugar in its sugar savings account (you can think of this savings as body fat) and carry this savings through to the next turn. If it eats less, it will use up its savings (depleting fat).

- If the amount of sugar stored in an agent's savings account drops below zero, then the agent is said to have starved to death and is removed from the game. Otherwise, the agent lives until it reaches a predetermined maximum age.

In order to carry out these tasks, each agent has a "genetic endowment" for its vision and metabolism. In other words, associated with each agent is a bit of computer code, a computer DNA, that describes how many squares ahead that agent can see and how much sugar it burns each round. An agent with very good vision can see sugar six squares ahead, while an agent with very poor vision can only see one square ahead. Likewise, an agent with a slow (good) metabolism needs only one unit of sugar per turn of the game to survive, versus an agent with a fast (bad) metabolism, which requires four. Vision and metabolism endowments are randomly distributed in the population; thus, the population of agents is *heterogeneous* (meaning that not all agents are alike). Some agents have poor vision, but great metabolisms; others have great vision and poor metabolisms, while some are well endowed with both, and the genetically unlucky are poor on both. Each agent also has a randomly assigned maximum lifetime, after which a computer Grim Reaper comes and removes it from the game. Finally, as sugar is eaten, it grows back on the landscape like a crop, at the rate of one unit per time period. So if a sugar pile of height four is eaten, it will take four periods to grow back to its original level.

The game begins with 250 agents randomly dropped on the Sugarscape. Some agents happen to land on the rich sugar mountains and thus are born into sugar wealth, while others have bad luck and are born in the poor areas of the badlands. At first, when the game begins, things are a bit chaotic as the agents rush around looking for sugar, and many of the agents who start off in the badlands die of starvation. Pretty quickly, however, order begins to emerge. As one might expect, the agents discover the two sugar-rich mountains and begin to coalesce around them (figure 4-2, note that numbers 1, 2, 3, and 4 are sequential points in time). Thus geographic destiny comes into play almost right away. The structure of the island with its two fertile areas of the sugar mountains leads to a splitting of the agents into two groups.[6] If we focus on a specific area of the Sugarscape, we notice something else. The agents are remarkably efficient grazers. There is very little sugar left lying around for long; the agents, even with their highly simplistic rules, very efficiently suck the maximum value out of the landscape. Almost as soon as a pile of sugar grows back to its capacity, it is hit by a grazing agent. Thus, we almost immediately see a basic form of self-organization. Agents quickly organize themselves into two concentrated "tribes," one on each mountain, efficiently harvesting its sugar crop.

The Rich Get Richer

Epstein and Axtell collected and tracked various statistics on the Sugarscape population over the course of the simulation. One of the variables they

FIGURE 4-2

Order Emerging on the Sugarscape, from Time 1 to Time 4

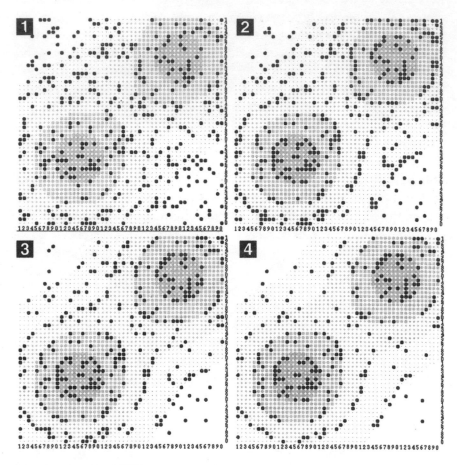

Source: Epstein and Axtell (1996).

tracked was agent wealth—how much sugar the agents had in their savings accounts at a given moment. At each period, the researchers took the richest agent (e.g., those with wealth 100) and divided the distance measured in savings between the richest agent and the poorest agent into ten bins, for example, 0–10, 11–20, 21–30, and so on. They then counted how many agents fell into each bin (two agents had wealth 0–10, six had 11–20, etc.). From this histogram, Epstein and Axtell noticed something very interesting about how the distribution of wealth evolved over time (figure 4-3). At the beginning of the simulation, Sugarscape is a fairly egalitarian society and the distribution of wealth is a smooth, bell-shaped curve with only a few very rich agents, a few

FIGURE 4-3

How the Distribution of Wealth Evolves in Sugarscape

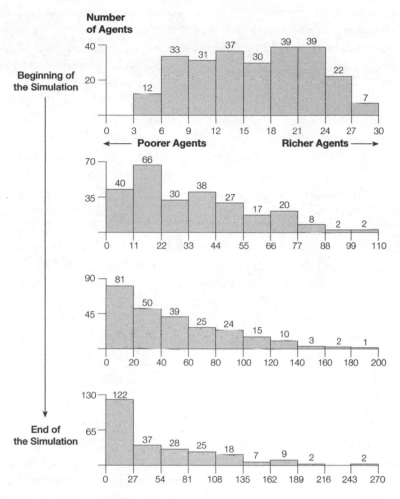

Source: Epstein and Axtell (1996).

very poor, and a broad middle class. In addition, the distance between the richest and the poorest agents is relatively small. As time passes, however, this distribution changes dramatically. Average wealth rose as the agents convened on the two sugar mountains but the distribution of wealth became very skewed, with a few emerging superrich agents, a long tail of upper-class yuppie agents, a shrinking middle class, and then a big, growing underclass of poor agents (note in the diagram that the scale of the axes changes over time, the richest agents at the beginning have only 30 units of sugar, but by the end the richest have 270).

In chapter 2, we briefly discussed the work of the nineteenth-century economist Vilfredo Pareto. In addition to developing the concept of Pareto optimality, the Italian economist was also very interested in the distribution of wealth in society. In 1895, he collected income data from a number of countries and fit the data with a distribution curve that became known as the *Pareto distribution*. Rather than being a bell-shaped normal distribution, the Pareto curve has a lot of people at the bottom end of the wealth distribution, a wide range in the middle class, and then a few superrich. The Pareto distribution is where the so-called 80-20 rule comes from, as roughly 80 percent of the wealth is owned by 20 percent of the people. Over the past century, economists have confirmed that income and wealth tend to roughly follow a Pareto distribution and that this result is remarkably consistent across different countries and over different periods of time. The wealth distribution that the simple Sugarscape model produced was just this kind of a real-world Pareto distribution.[7]

One can then ask, why does this happen? Why even in Sugarscape do the rich get richer and the poor get poorer? In the controlled world of Sugarscape, it is very easy to test various hypotheses. First, we can ask, is it nature—does it have something to do with the genetic endowments of the players? That is, are all the agents with great eyesight and slow metabolisms getting all the wealth? The answer is no. Genetic endowments are given out in a uniform random distribution. If wealth correlated with genetic endowments in Sugarscape, then the distribution of wealth should be very even, with roughly equal numbers of rich, middle class, and poor. We can then ask, is it nurture—is it caused by the circumstances the agents are born into? That is, are all the agents born on top of sugar mountains getting all the wealth and those with the bad luck of being born in the badlands staying poor? The answer to this is no as well. An agent's place of birth, like its genetic endowment, is perfectly random, so if that were the cause of an agent's ultimate economic class, the distribution would also be evenly distributed. How, then, from these random initial conditions do we get a skewed wealth distribution?

The answer is, in essence, "everything." The skewed distribution is an *emergent property* of the system. It is a macro behavior that emerges out of the collective micro behavior of the population of agents. The combination of the shape of the physical landscape, the genetic endowments of the agents, where they were born, the rules that they follow, the dynamics of their interactions with each other and with their environment, and, above all, luck all conspire to give the emergent result of a skewed wealth distribution.

To see how this works imagine Agent 1 and Agent 2, both born in the middle of the range of genetic endowments, and both born in middle-class sugar neighborhoods. At birth, their chances of success or failure are equal. But Agent 1, on his first move in life, looks in each direction and sees other agents already occupying the landscape to the east, west, and south. So he heads north, eating sugar along the way. By chance, north takes him into the heartland of one of the sugar mountains and to an area that, also by chance, is only sparsely occupied. He then spends the next several turns feasting on the maximum levels of sugar, racking up large savings, until other agents discover the area and start to move in. This initial golden period, however, has boosted Agent 1's wealth far above the average, and as one of the first onto the sugar mountain, he is able to stay there and live out the rest of his life in comfort. Meanwhile, Agent 2 isn't so lucky. On his first move, he heads south, toward the badlands. By the time he realizes his error, other agents have filled in the rich northern area, preventing him from heading back to the fertile region for several turns. During those turns, his savings dwindles and he falls further and further behind the average. Once he finds his way back toward more fertile ground, it is already very full, so there are fewer periods when he finds unoccupied grazing land. Agent 2 survives, but falls further and further behind the equally endowed Agent 1 as the game progresses. Thus, even when the agents had the same initial endowments, small, chance events early on were magnified by the dynamics of the game, leading to very different outcomes for the two agents. This result is something economists call *horizontal inequality* and is strictly prohibited in Traditional Economic theory. In the equilibrium world of Traditional Economics, people with the same abilities, preferences, and endowments should end up with the same level of wealth, and if there is any difference, it should be randomly distributed noise. But in the disequilibrium world of Sugarscape, horizontal inequality is a fact of life. It is important to note that the difference in outcome between Agents 1 and 2 is not just due to the randomness in the system (and thus not what a Traditional Economist would call noise). Randomness plays a role in sending the agents down different paths, but the dynamics of the game cause those paths to diverge widely, leading to a result that is more skewed than random chance alone can account for.

To see how these dynamics work, imagine if Agent 1 also had slightly superior genetics or had been born in a slightly better position to begin with—then he would have pulled ahead even faster and farther. Likewise, if Agent 2's initial endowments had been slightly poorer, his spiral into poverty could have been much worse, potentially causing him to starve. Thus, individual capabilities, circumstances at birth, and, even more importantly, the little twists and turns of fate at the individual level all combine to create a particular path for an agent through simulated life. The key is that small differences at one point (i.e., a lucky or a bad break somewhere) can lead to major differences down the road. This acceleration of small differences tends to send some individuals to riches and others to rags. Imagine the bell-shaped curve from the beginning of the simulation. Now, take the tails at the two ends and pull them outward. The right side of the tail stretches out to include a few super-rich, while the bump in the middle shrinks. As we stretch the left (poor) end of the distribution, you cannot be poorer than having zero sugar (at which point you die), so that part of the tail gets chopped off. This stretched, chopped distribution gives us the result we see at the bottom of figure 4-3.

All this means that even in Sugarscape, there is no simple cause-and-effect relationship driving poverty and inequality. Instead, it is a complex mix of factors. It is not easy to come up with solutions for the poverty problem even in the highly simplified world of Sugarscape. Epstein and Axtell note that Sugarscape is too simple to draw specific conclusions about real-world poverty and inequality. But, the model does make clear that one-dimensional views, whether on the left (e.g., poverty is caused by the rich's exploiting the poor) or on the right (e.g., if you are poor, you must be dumb, lazy, or both) are likely to be wrong, and any effective solutions must address the problem systemically. Complexity economists have gone beyond the simple world of Sugarscape to better understand the causes of inequality in the real world. We will look at their work in chapter 18.

Birds Do It, Bees Do It . . . and So Do Agents

Epstein and Axtell added into Sugarscape one more factor that they knew, as in real life, would turn the place upside down—sex. Economists have noted the effects of sex on economics at least since the days when Thomas Robert Malthus wrote his famous tract on population in the early nineteenth century. Luckily, a computer model such as Sugarscape enables us to observe the effects of population growth and evolution in real time, and experiment with various conditions and assumptions.

Epstein and Axtell decided to give each agent a tag indicating its age and whether it was male or female.[8] Once an agent reaches "child-bearing age," and if that agent has a minimum amount of sugar savings, he or she is considered fertile. Each period, fertile agents scan their immediate neighborhood of one square to the north, south, east, and west. If they find another fertile agent of the opposite sex, they reproduce. The DNA of the resulting baby agent is then chosen randomly, half from the mother, and half from the father. Thus the child's vision and metabolism characteristics will be some mix of the two parents. In addition, the baby agent inherits wealth from both parents, receiving an amount equal to half the father's wealth plus half the mother's wealth. The baby agent is born in an empty square next to its mother and father, so if the parents live in a rich or poor sugar neighborhood, the child agent will start its life there as well. This highly simplified setup has two important effects: the least fit members of the population will be less likely to have offspring, and the progeny of the most fit members of the population start life with some significant biological and environmental advantages.

When Epstein and Axtell hit the "run" button on this newly eroticized Sugarscape, the agents buzzed around as usual, harvesting sugar. Fertile agents quickly found each other, romance blossomed, and as summer follows spring, the pitter-patter of little agent feet was soon heard on the Sugarscape matrix. Then three things began to happen:

First, the least fit members of the population died off, while the most fit members had more and more offspring. Over time, both average vision and average metabolic efficiency began to climb. As the average of these attributes rose, so too did wealth.

Second, the new birth-death dynamics introduced population swings. Before the advent of sex, the population was constant and roughly balanced with the carrying capacity of the landscape. However, with sex came cycles of feast and famine. Fit agents built up savings and had multiple offspring, but eventually, the increase in population started to exceed the carrying capacity of the landscape. Agents started overgrazing the sugar stocks, triggering a famine, which then brought the population crashing back down. Eventually, the landscape regenerated and the cycle began all over again.

And, third, the gap between rich and poor widened even further. In the previous section, we saw how even a simple model without sex could generate a skewed wealth distribution. The introduction of genetic inheritance as well as wealth inheritance across generations further accelerated the trend toward the rich getting richer and the poor getting poorer.

The Invisible Hand Comes to Sugarscape

Thus far, the agents of Sugarscape have been pure hunter-gatherers, collecting and consuming what they can find on the landscape. But Epstein and Axtell added a further dose of realism to their artificial world.[9] They introduced a second commodity, called spice. Each square on the board now had a value for how much sugar it held and a value for how much spice it held. As with sugar, spice was concentrated in two mountains. In addition to the sugar mountains as before in the northeast and southwest, there were now spice mountains in the southeast and northwest. Epstein and Axtell also tweaked their agents' metabolisms so that they all required some of each commodity to survive. However, some agents needed lots of sugar and only a little spice, while others needed more spice than sugar—again, this was determined by their DNA. In Traditional Economic terminology, these differences in needs can be thought of as the agent's *preferences*.[10] As before, agents could save both sugar and spice that they didn't consume.

As a final step, Epstein and Axtell made it possible for the agents to trade. There was no assumption of a market or an auctioneer as in typical Traditional Economic models. Instead, there was just straightforward bartering between individuals. As agents move around the Sugarscape, they encounter other agents. At each turn in the game, each agent looks one square to the north, south, east, and west and asks any players in its neighborhood if they want to trade. If one agent has a lot of spice and needs sugar and another agent faces the reverse situation, both agents could improve their circumstances by trading. Once the agents agree to trade, they go into a little bargaining session, whereby they each make offers to the other until they agree on a price. There is no money in Sugarscape, so *price* means the relative value of sugar to spice, or vice versa.

Epstein and Axtell seeded Sugarscape with randomly endowed agents who could now trade, and hit the switch. The agents started to buzz around, and immediately a brisk business in sugar and spice took off. In many ways, the pattern of trading looked a lot like what is predicted by Traditional Economics. Epstein and Axtell compared model runs where agents were allowed to trade with runs where everyone was on their own to find their sugar and spice, and saw that trading made the Sugarscape society much richer. The increase in wealth from trading is one of the most basic predictions of economics, going back to the days of Adam Smith. Epstein and Axtell illustrate this wealth effect with an extreme case: imagine there is a pair of neighboring agents, one of whom has sugar but is close to death from spice deprivation and another who has spice but is close to death from sugar deprivation. If we forbid trade, both die; if we allow it, both live. Trade has an effect equivalent to increasing the carrying capacity of the landscape, thus making everyone better off.

Epstein and Axtell also traced the development of trading networks. They tracked who was trading with whom and found that, not surprisingly, there was some clustering in the trading networks by geographic region. Agents tended to trade most frequently with other agents in their region, and since the gains from trade are self-reinforcing, trading begat trading. Clusters of concentrated trading networks became established, almost like local market towns. In addition, the introduction of the second commodity made the movements of the agents more complicated. They could no longer simply cluster on top of their two sugar mountains with their tribe. They also needed to get out and search for spice, as well as for trading partners. The combination of geography and population dynamics created heavily trafficked trading routes, the computer equivalent of the ancient Silk Road, as agents shuttled back and forth between the sugar and spice mountains.

Epstein and Axtell could look inside each agent during each period of play and determine how much sugar or spice the agent was willing to buy or sell at a series of possible prices. These figures were then added up across all the agents to create supply-and-demand curves for each of the two Sugarscape commodities. What resulted was an almost textbook downward-sloping demand curve, along with an upward-sloping supply curve, even though Epstein and Axtell did not explicitly build anything about supply and demand into their model (figure 4-4). Rather, the curves emerged as a purely bottom-up phenomenon from the simple interactions of the population of agents.

FIGURE 4-4

No Equilibrium on the Sugarscape

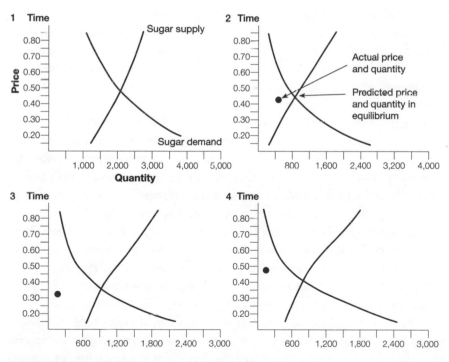

Source: Epstein and Axtell (1996).

Equilibrium Lost

In chapter 3, we discussed how many of the core predictions of Traditional Economics work well as a first approximation, but break down under closer examination. This was also true in Sugarscape. While the Sugarscape economy spontaneously produced nice X-shaped supply and demand curves, the actual prices and quantities traded (indicated by the dot in figure 4-4) never settled on the theoretically predicted equilibrium point (at the intersection of the supply and demand X in the figure). Prices fluctuated in the vicinity of the equilibrium point, and under some conditions, there was even modest convergence toward it over time. However, the variations in price away from equilibrium remained significant throughout even very long model runs. A Traditional economist might respond that this was just "noise around the equilibrium," but we should note that there is no noise in this model. The initial conditions were randomly set, but once the model got going, all the behavior was perfectly deterministic as the computer just crunched along. Rather, the correct interpretation is that prices in Sugarscape move dynamically around an "attractor" (a term we will discuss in chapter 5) but never actually settle down into an equilibrium. Thus, in Sugarscape, as in the real world, the law of supply and demand is only a rough approximation.

Epstein and Axtell also found that there was far more trading than there would be if the system was reaching equilibrium. A corollary to the Traditional prediction of equilibrium prices is that there should be only a minimal amount of trading—just enough to bring supply and demand into balance. One of the most important mysteries in Traditional Economics is why trading volume in both goods markets and financial markets is much higher than the theory predicts.[11] This same mystery is replicated in Sugarscape with more price volatility and trading volume than predicted under Traditional theory. In Traditional models, the entire population is simply assumed to make the minimum number of trades necessary to reach equilibrium. In Sugarscape, there is no mechanism for coordinating the whole population, and as agents are separated by physical distance (and it takes time to move), agents simply trade with other agents in their local neighborhood, never finding the global equilibrium. Thus new opportunities for trade arise as the agents move around and bump into each other, and this results in lots of trading volume.

As discussed earlier, another central prediction of Traditional Economics is the law of one price: in a given market, a commodity should only trade at the equilibrium price. In Sugarscape, however, at any point in time there is a wide variance in prices—on some parts of Sugarscape, you are likely to get ripped off, while in other neighborhoods, there are bargains to be had, just as in the London ketchup market. This is because, unlike an equilibrium model, in which everything is assumed to happen all at once, Sugarscape unfolds over time—and it takes time to find trading partners. If there are bargains in one part of the world, it takes time for agents to discover them and travel there; just as was the case with the economists finding the $20 bill on the street. As soon as arbitraging agents close down one bargain, another pops up somewhere else, but the dynamics are such that the agents can never keep up with the constant changes in the economy, and thus never drive price completely to equilibrium.

Another basic tenet of Traditional Economics is Pareto optimality—markets always lead to a perfect allocation of resources; no reallocation of resources can make someone better off without making someone else worse off. The Sugarscape market, however, operates at less than Pareto optimality. There are always trades that could have happened, that would have made people better off, but didn't. Again, this is because the agents' trades are separated in time and space, so Agent A in the southwest corner simply does not know that Agent B in the northeast corner would be a great trading partner. What's more, even if they found out, it would take some time for them to travel to get together (and by then, prices might have changed). A Traditional economist would immediately note that this is exactly the problem that markets cure—they bring buyers and sellers together in time and space and thus make the parties' trades more efficient. We could easily improve Sugarscape's economic efficiency by bringing all the agents together to one spot at noon each day, and having a sugar and spice auction as in Walras's model. Traditional Economics simply *assumes* that the real world is made up of such "Walrasian auctions" going on all the time. But this is not what actually happens in the real world. Outside of financial markets and eBay, real-world auctions are actually quite rare. The reason? While auctions are very good at finding the "right price," they are very slow at processing transactions (e.g., it can take hours or days to buy something on eBay). Most transactions in the real world are more like Sugarscape—they are bilateral, in other words, between two parties, such as you and your corner grocery store, or IBM and Ford. Although bilateral transactions create more spread in prices, they are more time efficient (or more specifically, computationally efficient); think how annoying it would be if you had to sit through an auction at your local supermarket every time you just wanted to pick up some milk.[12] Bilateral trading in the real world spreads trading out in space and time, just as it does in Sugarscape, and thus makes it highly unlikely that any kind of global equilibrium is ever reached. The only reason that Traditional Economics assumes that trading happens in auction markets is that the assumption allows the math to produce an equilibrium result.

While trade in Sugarscape does "lift all boats," making the society richer as a whole, it also has the effect of further widening the gap between rich and poor. In the basic version of the model, we had a small but still significant gap between rich and poor simply from the dynamics of the game. This gap was further widened when we introduced sex and families, which allowed abilities and wealth to be inherited. Finally, the introduction of trade widened the gap further (though again, making everyone significantly richer), to the point that, according to Epstein and Axtell, the skewed distribution of wealth started to approach that of modern real-world economies.[13]

The Evolution of Hierarchy

So far, the economy of Sugarscape has just been a collection of individuals—there is no hierarchy of bosses and workers, or suppliers, middlemen, and retailers. This is because the interactions between agents have been short-lived (they meet, they trade, they leave), and because they have been symmetrical. Yet hierarchy is one of the signature features of real-world economies. Epstein and Axtell made one more simple change to the behavior of the agents. This modification led to the creation of stable structures in trading relationships and the development of a hierarchy: the researchers enabled borrowing and lending.

In Sugarscape, there is only one reason to become a borrower—to have children. All agents in Sugarscape have a basic desire to procreate, but some are too poor to support offspring, while others have surplus sugar and spice lying around and nothing to spend it on. Thus Epstein and Axtell introduced a rule that said that an agent can be a lender if it is too old to have children, or if it has more savings than it needs for its own reproductive needs. In turn, an agent can be a borrower if it has insufficient savings to have children, but has a sustainable income of sugar and spice. For simplicity, Epstein and Axtell fixed the interest rate and duration of the loans and made basic provisions for borrower default. Then any agent who was creditworthy and needed resources to have children was free to borrow from neighbors who had the resources to lend.

What surprised Epstein and Axtell was not that significant borrowing and lending activity occurred, but that a complex, hierarchical capital market emerged. Epstein and Axtell traced the relationships between borrowers and lenders and found that some agents became simultaneously both borrowers and lenders—in effect, middlemen. Sugarscape had evolved banks! As the simulation proceeded, things got even more complicated. Certain really rich agents took on a wholesale role, lending to middlemen, who then made loans to the ultimate borrowers. In some simulations, the hierarchical chain grew to five levels deep. The simulation not only evolved banks, but also evolved the Sugarscape equivalent of institutional investors, investment banks, merchant banks, and retail banks.

As with the other emergent patterns in Sugarscape, the evolution of these credit networks was not in any way imposed from the top down on the model. Rather, these large-scale macro patterns grew from the bottom up, from the dynamic interplay of the local micro assumptions.

An Economy *in Silico*

When scientists compare two theories, they do so according to the *correspondence principle*. According to the correspondence principle, a new theory should reproduce the successes of the old theory, explain the failures of the old theory, and offer new insights that the old theory does not. Neither Epstein nor Axtell would claim that Sugarscape on its own represents a full-blown economic theory; nor would they claim that the model fully answers the "origin of wealth" question. Sugarscape, however, does follow the correspondence principle and point us in interesting new directions. The model reproduced many of the most basic and commonsense elements of Traditional Economics. The law of supply and demand worked in an approximate way (just as it does in the real world), and there were significant gains from trade. It would be hard to believe a model that did not have those results. Yet, Epstein and Axtell reproduced these classic economic results with a model that is remarkably free of the unrealistic assumptions typically found in Traditional models. Its agents were not assumed to have superhuman powers of rationality; the model did not assume preexisting social or economic structures. Nor did it assume that everything happens instantaneously.

But perhaps even more interesting, Sugarscape also reproduced some of the major anomalies found in Traditional Economics, including violations of the law of one price, the existence of horizontal inequality, and higher levels of price volatility and trading volume than would be predicted by Traditional Economics. This was because the approach Epstein and Axtell took was fundamentally different from the Traditional methodology. They did not a priori assume that Sugarscape was an equilibrium system. Instead, Epstein and Axtell gave Sugarscape a basic structure of agents and a landscape, but once it was set up, they let it evolve on its own to see where it would go. Sugarscape *could* have gone to equilibrium, but it did not. Instead, Sugarscape spontaneously evolved complex order, structure, and diversity, including what could (with a bit of imagination) be interpreted as tribes, market towns, trading routes, and capital markets, none of which was preprogrammed. Rather, it all emerged from the bottom up, from the simple starting rules that Epstein and Axtell gave the system.

Further Defining Complexity Economics

Sugarscape provides just one illustration of what I believe to be a genuinely new approach to economics. Although models like Sugarscape are a relatively recent development (largely because they depend on the availability of fast computers), they are built on a long and rich intellectual history. That history includes figures such as John von Neumann, the inventor of game theory and cellular automata; members of the "Austrian school" such as Friedrich Hayek; behavioral economists such as Herbert Simon and Daniel Kahneman; institutional economists such as Douglass North; evolutionary economists such as Richard Nelson and Sidney Winter; political scientists such as Robert Axelrod and Thomas Schelling; and computer scientists such as John Holland and Christopher Langton.[14]

Over the chapters in part 2, we will discuss the work of these researchers and many others and see how, taken together, their work comprises a new paradigm for the field. In describing various aspects of this work, economists use a number of terms, including computational economics, agent-based modeling, social dynamics, evolutionary economics, behavioral game theory, the Santa Fe school, and interactions economics.[15] All these terms mean slightly different things, and thus, by adopting any one of them, I would risk taking too narrow a view of what is happening in the field. I have thus chosen the umbrella term *Complexity Economics*. As mentioned before, at this point in its development, Complexity Economics is still more of a research program than a single, synthesized theory, and thus there are many gray areas regarding what falls under this umbrella term. But there are five "big ideas," described in table 4-1, that help define Complexity Economics and distinguish it from work that has gone before it.

An important aspect of the Complexity Economics approach is that these five areas cannot be analyzed using mathematical theorems alone. Brian Arthur has referred to Traditional Economics' reliance on mathematical proofs as being stuck with "quill pen and parchment technology." Rather, Complexity Economics uses a broad toolkit of approaches. Theorems, equilibrium analysis, game theory, and other Traditional approaches remain a part of that toolkit, but Complexity researchers also take full advantage of Moore's law to apply liberal doses of computing power to their work. In addition, Complexity researchers have imported new mathematical and statistical tools from physics, biology, and other fields to help them better understand the economy as an open, dynamic system. Finally, Complexity economists have been utilizing experimental economics and advances in economic data analysis to begin to build a body of empirical evidence for their theories.

Over the next five chapters, we will look at each of these "big ideas" in more depth. Then, in part 3, we will see how they come together to provide the foundations for a new way of looking at the origin of wealth.

TABLE 4-1

Five "Big Ideas" That Distinguish Complexity Economics from Traditional Economics

	Complexity Economics	Traditional Economics
Dynamics	Open, dynamic, nonlinear systems, far from equilibrium	Closed, static, linear systems in equilibrium
Agents	Modeled individually; use inductive rules of thumb to make decisions; have incomplete information; are subject to errors and biases; learn and adapt over time	Modeled collectively; use complex deductive calculations to make decisions; have complete information; make no errors and have no biases; have no need for learning or adaptation (are already perfect)
Networks	Explicitly model interactions between individual agents; networks of relationships change over time	Assume agents only interact indirectly through market mechanisms (e.g., auctions)
Emergence	No distinction between micro- and macroeconomics; macro patterns are emergent result of micro-level behaviors and interactions	Micro- and macroeconomics remain separate disciplines
Evolution	The evolutionary process of differentiation, selection, and amplification provides the system with novelty and is responsible for its growth in order and complexity	No mechanism for endogenously creating novelty, or growth in order and complexity

CHAPTER FIVE

Dynamics

THE DELIGHTS OF DISEQUILIBRIUM

AT THE BEGINNING of the twentieth century, just as economics was separating from its encounter with physics and retreating into its intellectual Cuba, the physical sciences took a radical change in direction. Over the next one hundred years, physicists would tear up the very theories that Walras and company had borrowed, and replace them with relativity, quantum mechanics, the thermodynamics of nonequilibrium systems, chaos theory, and complexity theory. Scientists came to recognize that the universe is neither deterministic like a clock, nor random like a casino; in fact, systems that are either perfectly deterministic or truly random are quite rare. Most phenomena in the universe are somewhere in the middle; they mix determinism and randomness in complex and unpredictable ways. In the twentieth century, science came to accept the messy and the indeterminate.

In chapter 3, I argued that the economy had been misclassified by Traditional Economics as an equilibrium system, but in fact is a complex adaptive system. In chapter 4, using the example of Sugarscape, we began to explore what complex adaptive systems are and how they behave. In this chapter, we will continue to refine our picture of what the economy is and what our new characterization implies. Since the 1980s, terms such as *chaos, dynamic,* and *nonlinear* have all entered the popular consciousness, as a result of best sellers such as James Gleick's *Chaos* and even fictional books and Hollywood movies. We will look at what those terms mean in an economic context and discuss how phenomena such as booms and busts in industries ranging from aircraft manufacturing to real estate might be connected to them.

Dynamics and Feedback

A useful starting point is to observe that the economy is a *dynamic system*. All this means is that the economy changes over time. This is obvious: prices bounce up and down, wages change, and companies enter and exit markets. This dynamism is something that Traditional Economics has recognized, but as discussed, has generally viewed as generated from exogenous sources such as technology changes, political events, and changes in consumer taste. The interesting question for us is how such dynamic behavior might be generated endogenously, as a result of the structure of the economy itself.

When scientists talk about a system's being dynamic, what they mean is that the state of the system at the current moment is a function of the state of the system at the previous moment, and some change in between the two moments.[1] A simple example of a dynamic system is a bank account.[2] The state of the account, or balance, changes over time. Your balance tomorrow is dependent on your balance today, plus any changes during the intervening day, such as deposits, withdrawals, or interest payments. We can create a simple formula to describe the account balance (B) at any point in time with t for today, $t + 1$ for tomorrow: $B_{t+1} = B_t +$ (deposits − withdrawals + interest). Thus, a savings account clicks along over time, the output of the equation during one period becomes the input for calculating the next period in an iterative loop. Changes in dynamic processes can either be discrete, like a bank account, in which the changes occur at specific points in time (e.g., interest is paid on a particular day), or they can be continuous and smooth, like the orbiting of planets.

A convenient way to describe a dynamic system is in terms of *stocks* and *flows*.[3] A stock is an accumulation of something, such as the balance in a bank account or water in a bathtub. The rate at which a stock changes over time is known as a flow, for example, the rate of money flowing into or out of a bank account, or water flowing into and out of a bathtub. The economy is full of different stocks that change over time, for example, the total supply of money or the number of people employed. Each of these stocks has corresponding flows, or rates of change over time; for example, the central bank might increase or decrease the money supply, or companies might hire or fire employees. Note that flows are always per some unit of time. Stocks and flows don't always have to be tangible things such as money and people; they can also be less tangible, but nonetheless important, factors. For example, consumer confidence can be thought of as a stock that rises and falls over time.[4]

When one starts thinking of the economy as a collection of stocks and their related flows, it quickly becomes apparent that the various stocks and flows are connected to each other in complex ways. For example, if the stock of employment fell to a low level, a policy maker might decide to cut interest rates in order to encourage borrowing, which would expand the stock of money available for investment, which then would be used by businesses to invest in new productive capacity, creating more demand for employees, thus raising the stock of employment, which finally would feed back to affect future interest rate policy. Such chains of relationships between stocks and flows in a dynamic system are known as *feedback loops*.

Feedback occurs when the output of one part of a system is the input for another, so, for example, A affects B, which affects C, which comes back to affect A again. *Positive feedback* occurs when the connections are reinforcing—if I push A, it pushes B even harder, which pushes C even harder, which pushes A harder than my original push, and so on. As mentioned earlier, a classic example of positive feedback is when a microphone is held too close to an amplifier and creates a screeching sound. Despite the word *positive* in the phrase, downward spirals are also a form of positive feedback. For example, a drop in consumer confidence can lead to decreased spending, which leads to decreased production, which leads to unemployment, which leads to even lower consumer confidence and thus a further drop in spending, spiraling right down into a recession. This was the dynamic loop that John Maynard Keynes famously identified in his *General Theory of Employment* in 1936.[5] It is an example of positive feedback, even though it is not very positive for the people in it. The key thing to remember is that positive feedback reinforces, accelerates, or amplifies whatever is happening, whether it is a virtuous cycle or downward spiral. Systems with positive feedback can thus exhibit exponential growth, exponential collapse, or oscillations with increasing amplitude.

The opposite is *negative feedback*. Negative feedback is a dampening cycle—instead of reinforcing, it pushes in the opposite direction. While positive feedback accelerates change, negative feedback dampens change, controls things, and brings things back in line. As mentioned previously, a classic example is a thermostat. Systems with negative feedback tend to get pushed back to some set point, an equilibrium, or oscillate with decreasing amplitude and peter out over time.[6]

Dynamic systems also have a third ingredient—*time delays*. You have probably had the experience of taking a shower in an unfamiliar place such as a hotel room, turning on the hot water, noticing it isn't hot enough, turning it up some more, and then it turns scalding, so you turn it down, it is still too hot, so you turn it down some more, then it is freezing, and so on. The problem is that there is a small time delay between your actions on the water knobs and the feedback from the shower temperature. The delay causes you to overshoot and oscillate around the desired temperature. Eventually, you figure it out and the oscillations get smaller and smaller until you hit the desired temperature.

The longer the time delay, however, the harder it is to control the shower and the more oscillations you get.

It is not difficult to see how dynamic systems can quickly become quite complex if one has multiple stocks and flows interacting via both positive and negative feedback loops. The positive feedbacks drive the system, accelerating it, but at the same time the negative feedbacks are fighting back to dampen and control it. When time delays are thrown in, the driving and damping can get out of balance, and out of synch, causing the system to oscillate in highly elaborate ways.

The Science of "Nonpachydermology"

Our second observation about the economy is that it is a *nonlinear system*. This term is often a source of confusion (even among economists). Since *nonlinear* literally means "not a straight line," people sometimes assume this means that any function that produces a curve is nonlinear. In static systems, this is true. The equation $y = mx + b$ is linear; if we graph it, we get a straight line. On the other hand, the equation $y = x^2$ is nonlinear; if we graph it, we get an exponential curve. A good rule of thumb is if the right-hand side of the equation is all pluses, minuses, multiplication, and division, then it is linear; but if the equation has powers, sines, cosines, or other fancy stuff, it is nonlinear.

We have to be a bit more careful, however, when we talk about dynamic systems, because dynamic systems that are linear can exhibit curved behavior when plotted over time. We noted earlier that a bank account is a dynamic system. We can create a simple linear equation for calculating how the account grows with interest payments over time. Let's say the interest rate is 10 percent (and we will assume no deposits or withdrawals). Then the equation for the balance (B) would be $B_{t+1} = B_t(1 + 0.10)$. Thus, if our balance is currently 100, it will be 110 next period. Again, this relationship is linear because the right-hand side is only pluses and multiplication. However, if we plot the balance (B) over time (t), we get a nice exponential curve (figure 5-1a). Even though the behavior over time is a curve, the equation is still said to be linear because the *rate of change is linear,* in this case, a constant 10 percent. One can see this most easily by plotting the graph of the next period ($t + 1$) against the current period (t) (figure 5-1b). This is called a *cobweb diagram.* The way to interpret cobweb diagrams is to note that the x-axis shows the balance in the current period, and the y-axis shows what the balance will be in the next period. This gives us a way to see whether the rate of change is accelerating, decelerating, or constant. In the case of figure 5-1b we see a nice, straight line which indicates that the rate of change is constant and the system is thus linear. Linear dynamic systems can exhibit a number of behav-

FIGURE 5-1

An Exponentially Growing Bank Balance

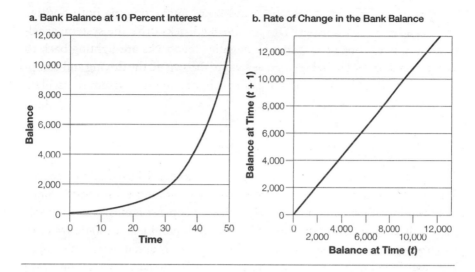

a. Bank Balance at 10 Percent Interest

b. Rate of Change in the Bank Balance

iors over time, including stasis, straight-line growth or decline, and exponential growth or decay—in each case, the rate of change is linear.

Things get more interesting when we look at *nonlinear dynamic systems*. Going back to our bank account, we can imagine a somewhat strange account in which the balance is calculated as follows: $B_{t+1} = rB_t - rB_t^2$, where r is a constant. Note the square sign on the right indicating the relationship is nonlinear—we can also rewrite the equation in the easier-to-read form $B_{t+1} = rB_t (1 - B_t)$, a form known as the quadratic map equation. For example, if your current balance was 100 and r was 0.10, then your balance next period would be –990. Even though this nonlinear equation does not make for a very good savings account, it does have some interesting properties. We can use the term r like a gas pedal and accelerate or decelerate the rate of change and, as a result, kick the equation into some very different modes of behavior.

For example, if we set the initial balance at 0.1 and r at 1.5, the balance will rise to 0.3333 and then stay there forever in a steady state (figure 5-2a). If we look at the cobweb diagram (figure 5-2b), we see that the rate of change rises in a gentle curve until the balance hits 0.3333, and then it stops. This is our old friend equilibrium, or in the parlance of dynamic systems, a *fixed-point attractor,* so called because the system is pulled or attracted to a single fixed point in the cobweb diagram (in this case, 0.3333). If we set r to 3.3, we get a very different result. The system goes into regular oscillations, like a pendulum

FIGURE 5-2

A Fixed-Point Attractor Account

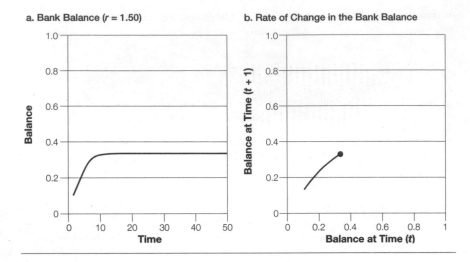

a. Bank Balance (r = 1.50)

b. Rate of Change in the Bank Balance

swinging back and forth (called a *periodic limit cycle*) (figure 5-3). If we nudge *r* just a tiny bit up to 3.52, the simple oscillation turns into a more complex pattern of oscillations within oscillations, like the pattern of a heartbeat (a *quasi-periodic limit cycle*) (figure 5-4). Some nonlinear systems can exhibit extremely complex patterns that go on for a very long time, but then eventually do repeat themselves. Finally, if we bump *r* to 4, we get *chaos* (figure 5-5a). A chaotic system has three important characteristics. First, although it might look random, it is actually deterministic. For example, our chaotic bank account formula has no random factors. Second, unlike a periodic system, you can run the formula forever and it will never exactly repeat itself (although sometimes it can be difficult to tell a truly chaotic system from one that just has very long, complex oscillations). And third, the system is bounded. Even though the system's trajectory is all over the place, there are some places it won't go. In the bank balance case, the values stay between 0 and 1, and in the cobweb diagram, we can see the system traces out a rough triangular pattern with a hole in the middle (figure 5-5b). If you find it is a bit tricky to mentally relate the diagrams of the balance over time on the left to the cobweb diagrams showing the rates of change on the right, you are not alone. Nonlinear dynamic systems are not always intuitive, and as we will see later, this can create problems when people try to make decisions in them.

The fact that we can get such widely varying behaviors simply from tweaking one variable demonstrates an important characteristic of nonlinear

FIGURE 5-3

A Periodic Limit Cycle Account

a. Bank Balance (r = 3.30)

b. Rate of Change in the Bank Balance

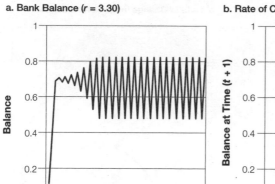

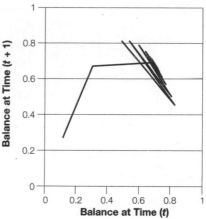

FIGURE 5-4

A Quasi-periodic Limit Cycle Account

a. Bank Balance (r = 3.52)

b. Rate of Change in the Bank Balance

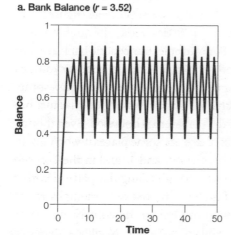

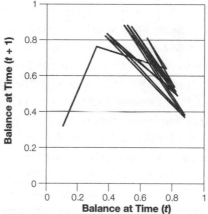

FIGURE 5-5

A Chaos Account

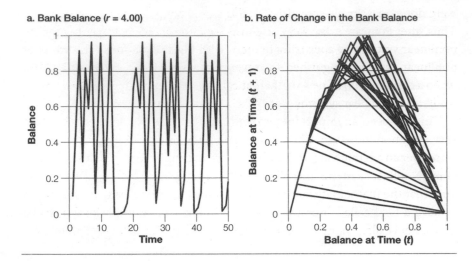

a. Bank Balance (r = 4.00)

b. Rate of Change in the Bank Balance

dynamic systems: *sensitivity to initial conditions.* Imagine that a golfer hits a putt on a very tricky green with lots of dips and bumps and ridges on it. If the golfer hits two putts, but they are ever-so-slightly different in terms of the starting position of the ball, or the angle and force of the swing, the two balls will diverge, follow very different paths, and end up far apart on the green. Nonlinearities cause small differences in initial conditions to be magnified over time, and thus unless you know the beginning state of the system with almost infinite precision, you cannot know the end state.

A related characteristic is that nonlinear dynamic systems are *path depen-dent,* or in other words, history matters. The bank balance at $t + 1$ depends on the balance at t, and likewise, where a golfer lies on her fourth shot on a hole is a function of where she was on her third shot, which is a function of the second shot, and so on. Any changes in this chain of events can yield a very different outcome; for example, a very different second shot would ulti-mately have implications for the fourth shot.

These two characteristics, sensitivity to initial conditions and path depen-dence, make nonlinear dynamic systems notoriously difficult to work with and in many cases impossible to predict. In fact, around the time Walras was plundering physics textbooks, the French mathematician Henri Poincaré dis-covered chaos and proved that many kinds of nonlinear dynamic systems could not be solved with the mathematical tools available at that point in time.[7] Because the equations could not be solved analytically, there were no shortcuts to seeing what a nonlinear dynamic system would do. The only way to see how the system would play out was to let it play out. While letting the system play out is easy on a computer (e.g., the bank account examples were done on a simple spreadsheet), it is incredibly tedious to do it by hand. Thus, after Poincaré's discovery, scientists had little choice but to either ignore nonlinear systems or approximate them with linear equations. The study of nonlinear systems languished for seventy years until the 1960s and 1970s, when a combination of new mathematical tools and computers reopened their study, and nonlinear systems are now a bread-and-butter topic for physicists.[8]

This has been an important development, because nonlinear systems are very common in nature. They show up in phenomena ranging from turbulence over an aircraft wing, to weather, lasers, and the firing of synapses in your brain. Nonlinear systems are so common, and truly linear systems so relatively rare, that the mathematician Ian Stewart thinks it is just as silly for physicists to have a field called "nonlinear systems," as it would be for zoologists to have a field called "nonpachydermology"—the study of all nonelephants.[9]

The Economy Is Complex but Not Chaotic

We have already noted that the economy is a dynamic system. We can now further characterize it as a nonlinear system. Economists have recognized the existence of nonlinear relationships in economics since Turgot articulated the law of diminishing returns in the eighteenth century. We can also see nonlinearities intuitively in our daily economic life, ranging from the accelerating pace of technological change to our tendency to pay less attention to an advertisement the fifth time we have seen it than the first. Statistical work has also shown evidence of nonlinearities in macroeconomic data ranging from industrial output to unemployment figures.[10] While economics has long recognized the existence of nonlinearities, it has had a more difficult time incorporating those nonlinearities in a dynamic way. Because nonlinear dynamic systems were not well understood until relatively recently, Traditional economists historically made do by either using nonlinear relationships in static models or using linear relationships in dynamic models, where in each case the equations could be solved. In contrast, the Complexity Economics approach recognizes that the economy is both nonlinear and dynamic and as a result uses mathematical tools and computer simulations that have been more recently developed.

A natural question to ask is whether the economy is chaotic. This question generated a lot of interest in the 1980s, particularly around whether the stock market was chaotic (and, of course, whether knowing this would enable anyone to make loads of money).[11] There has been much subsequent work on this question, and the current consensus is "probably not." It is hard to be conclusive about this question, because chaos is difficult to distinguish from other complex but nonchaotic behavior and certain types of random behavior. Testing for chaos also requires enormous amounts of data, and not even financial markets are data-rich enough for conclusive results.[12]

Most researchers would say that calling the economy chaotic would be too simple and narrow a categorization. Truly chaotic systems tend to have relatively few variables and few degrees of freedom. It is more appropriate to call the economy complex. As we have noted, the economy has a massive number of stocks and flows dynamically connected in an elaborate web of positive and negative feedback relationships; those feedback relationships have delays and operate at different timescales, and the system is riddled with nonlinearities. Such a system is likely to have a staggering number of degrees of freedom and be capable of the full collection of behaviors in the zoo of nonpachyderms. Thus it is probably fair to say that at some times, and in some dimensions, the economy may exhibit chaotic behavior, but the economy also exhibits growth, decay, periodic limit cycles, quasi-periodic limit cycles, and a whole panoply of other behaviors.

The full dynamic complexity of the economy becomes even clearer when we think of it as what scientists call an n-body problem. The motivation for Poincaré's original study of chaos was a prize of 2,500 crowns offered in 1887 by King Oscar II of Sweden to anyone who could tell him whether the solar system was stable, or whether the planets would someday crash into the sun, or fly off into space.[13] This is a particularly hard problem because not only is the solar system dynamic as the planets whiz around the sun, and not only is the force of gravity nonlinear, but all the interactions have to be worked out between ten planets plus the sun. Poincaré realized that he couldn't even solve the problem for three bodies, let alone the eight planets known in his day and the sun. King Oscar's problem wouldn't be solved until the twentieth century (you don't have to worry: the sun will blow up well before the earth's orbit becomes unstable), but n-body problems remain very difficult to work with. The economy, then, is an n-body problem on a massive scale. Each individual person in the economy has his or her own set of stocks (savings, debt, skills, etc.) and flows (income, expenses, learning, etc.) just as each individual agent in the highly simplified Sugarscape economy had its own stock of sugar and flow of sugar consumption and digestion. And just as the dynamics of Sugarscape were a product of all the interactions between the agents in that imaginary economy, the dynamics of the real economy are a product of the nonlinear interactions of billions of people. It is a system whose complexity makes Poincaré's sorting out of the solar system look easy—it is not just a three-body problem, it is a 6.4-billion-body problem.

One can thus begin to appreciate why economic forecasters have such a tough job and an even lower reputation than weather forecasters. The combination of sensitivity to initial conditions, path dependence, and immense dynamic complexity makes the economy, like the weather, unforecastable over all but the very short term. Weather forecasters have significantly improved their track record over recent years through much better data from satellites and radar and through more sophisticated analysis from computer models. It is likely that economic forecasting will improve too over time with better data and models. However, just as highly accurate long-range forecasting of the weather will always be impossible, so too will highly accurate long-range forecasting of the economy.

The impossibility of long-range forecasting in the economy, however, is not a barrier to the field's growth as a science. As noted earlier, science is about explaining, not forecasting, and understanding the dynamic nature of the economy will significantly help in developing testable explanations of economic phenomena.

The Invisible Hand Sometimes Shakes

John Sterman, a professor at MIT's Sloan School of Management, is a researcher who has spent much of his career using nonlinear dynamic techniques to develop new explanations of economic and business phenomena.[14] A question that has been of particular interest to him has been why so many commodities go through complex boom and bust cycles. The types of industries that are cyclical run the gamut, as Sterman puts it, "from aircraft to zinc" (figure 5-6).[15] What these diverse industries have in common is that their cyclical swings in prices and industry capacity are much more volatile than the swings in underlying demand or in the economy overall. We thus have big effects without any obvious big causes.

The cycles also have the interesting property of being not quite regular and not quite random. Looking at them, we see that the data clearly aren't just random fluctuations; they have a definite periodicity. But the cycles aren't exactly regular, either; they aren't perfectly periodic. One could certainly say the cycles are complex. Many people, from commodity traders to industry executives, have tried to forecast these cycles, with little success. Sterman decided to build a model to investigate what was driving this not-quite-regular, not-quite random behavior.

The most important negative feedback loop in Traditional Economics is the role played by price in supply and demand. If demand goes up, price will rise, causing supply to increase, which then causes price to fall until supply and demand are back in balance—just like a thermostat. As we discussed,

FIGURE 5-6

Examples of Cyclical Industries

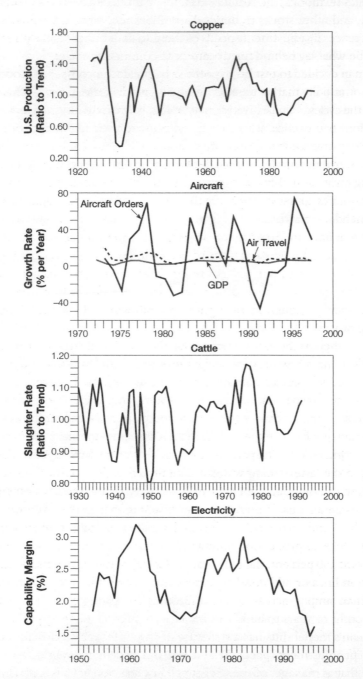

Source: Sterman (2000). Copper and cattle data from the Commodity Research Bureau, *Commodity Yearbook*. Aircraft data from Pugh-Roberts Associates, Cambridge, MA. Electricity data from the Edison Electric Institute, *Statistical Abstract of the US*.

however, Traditional Economics usually assumes this all happens at once, ignoring the role of time delays.[16] Thus, while supply and demand balance in economics textbooks, the real world is full of inventories, excess production capacity, and other stocks to buffer disequilibrium. Sterman postulated that the differences in adjustment speeds of these various buffer stocks might ultimately be what lay behind the dynamics of commodity cycles.

Sterman decided to test his hypothesis by building a computer model of a simple commodity market to see if he could reproduce the statistical characteristics of the cycles.[17] Unlike Traditional models, his model (a "system dynamics" simulation) had explicit stocks for inventory and production capacity, positive and negative feedback loops, time delays, and nonlinear relationships. To see how Sterman's model worked, let's imagine you work at a generic manufacturing business making widgets (the mythical product of many introductory economics courses). There are three critical buffer stocks against supply and demand mismatches.

First, you have an inventory of widgets. The inventory acts as a buffer between the uncertain demand from your customers and the production from your factory. If customer orders are less than production, your inventory rises; if they are more than production, inventory falls. Inventories adjust almost instantly (though there might be a small delay between receiving and shipping orders).

Second, there is the stock of immediately available productive capacity. If you start running low on your widget inventory, you can ask the factory to boost production. Under normal circumstances most factories run at something less than 100 percent of capacity (80 percent is typical)—this gives them some short-term flex capacity. If you put in a call to boost production, the factory manager can run the widget production line a bit faster, add an extra shift of workers, open a spare line, or convert a line from a slower-selling product to the faster-selling widgets. The time delay in boosting short-term production can range anywhere from hours to months—the key point is that it is not instantaneous. It is a slower adjustment loop than the inventory loop.

The third and final stock is the total amount of long-term production capacity. Once all production lines are running at maximum speed and utilization is at 100 percent, the only way to expand output is to build additional production lines or add another factory. Adding new long-term capacity is slower than simply increasing the utilization of existing capacity. It usually takes months or years to build a new factory, hire more people, and so on.

Sterman's model thus has a structure of three feedback loops all running at different adjustment speeds. To see how this structure plays out over time, imagine that as manager of the widget product line, you get a weekly product report. As you sit down to read this week's report, you notice that widget demand has increased and inventories have dropped a bit. Inventories rise and fall all the time, just due to random fluctuations in demand, so the first question you have to consider is whether to ask the factory for an increase in production. A natural reaction would be to wait a little while to see if the rise will persist or is a temporary blip before you order an expensive increase in production that could create too much inventory. The next question, then, is, should you raise price? Well, again you want to see whether the increase in demand is a real uptick. Raising prices takes time and effort (new prices have to be programmed in computers, customer contracts changed, and so on), and price rises always run the risk of alienating customers. Thus you decide to wait some more.

In your next inventory report, you see the rise in demand has continued and you now believe there is a definite trend. Inventories have dipped dangerously low, and you have had to put some customers on back order. Now you jump into action and put in a request to increase production. Corporate headquarters grinds through its bureaucracy, the factory takes some time to make the adjustments, and it is not until several weeks later that production actually increases. In the meantime, demand has continued to rise, but now there are stock-outs and order backlogs as customers have exhausted your inventory. Given the robust demand and looming product shortages (you also note your competitors are going through the same thing), you decide that now is also the time to raise prices.

The price increase doesn't immediately affect demand. Your customers' inventories of your product are depleted because of the shortages, they can't find substitutes or alternative sources immediately, and so they are willing, at least in the short term, to pay the higher prices. With surging demand and higher prices, your profit-and-loss statement looks terrific and the CEO thinks you're a hero. Your only problem is making enough of the product. The factory is running at nearly 100 percent, and you are losing orders and market share to competitors that have more capacity. You then put in a capital investment proposal to the executive committee to build another factory. On the basis of the stellar performance of your business, they approve. You break ground on the new site, and construction begins.

About six months before the new factory is scheduled for completion, you notice a worrying trend. Demand is beginning to flatten out. The price rises and shortages of several months ago have begun to have an effect. Your customers have found substitutes for your product and ways to use less of it. In addition, while you were running your factory hotter to meet demand, so were your competitors, and now there is plenty of inventory out there. You start hearing from your sales force that you are getting pressure to lower prices again as the combination of softening demand and increased availability from competitors hits home. You accede to your sales force's cries and authorize some discounting.

Now it is the day of the opening ceremony for the new factory. Just after the CEO cuts the ribbon, you get a report that turns your blood cold. Demand has continued to soften, but even worse, prices are in free fall. Everyone in the industry is sitting on piles of inventory and discounting heavily to keep it moving. Despite the falling prices and your increasingly ugly profit-and-loss statement, you go ahead and fire up the capacity in the new factory. It has been built, after all—largely a sunk cost—and it can't be used for much else. Even with prices low, you can at least cover the cost of your labor and materials.

A few months later, you are at an industry trade show, sitting at a bar with other executives bemoaning the decline in your industry. It turns out that during the boom years, they were doing just what you were doing, and they all have shiny new factories coming online, too. You suspected that your competitors were building new capacity, but because of industry secrecy, you didn't know exactly how much and assumed that rising demand would cover it. You also assumed people wouldn't go crazy and over-build.

During the next year, the industry becomes awash in capacity, and prices collapse. The whole cycle starts to happen in reverse. After time, with mounting losses, the industry begins to shut down lines, reduce shifts, and otherwise scale back capacity. As the bloodletting gets worse, the companies go to the next step of shutting down whole factories and laying off large numbers of people. It takes many years for all the excess capacity to get squeezed out of the system. But it is no longer your concern, because you were fired in one of the rounds of downsizing.

Several years later, a fresh-faced young manager is put in your old job. She was just a college student during the last cycle and doesn't remember any of it. One day, she is at her desk and receives the latest widget product report. She is excited to see a nice uptick in demand . . .

This dynamic story is the essence of Sterman's model. When he ran it, he found that it generated commodity cycles that were statistically similar in important ways to real-world cycles.[18] The model shows that the combination of the different timescales in the feedback loops and human fallibility make such cycles almost inevitable. Sterman and his colleague Mark Paich also conducted experiments in which real people were asked to play the part of the manager and attempt to minimize the cycles.[19] The researchers found, however, that people have a very difficult time mentally processing systems with complex feedbacks and delays of varying lengths (just as the sluggishly responding shower tap always gets us). One of the implications of Sterman's model and experiments is that the only way to mitigate the cycles is to change the structure of the system itself. For example, one could reduce the time delays in the system (e.g., time to add new capacity), make capacity less chunky (e.g., building "mini-mills" rather than big factories), get more forward visibility on customer orders, or increase transparency on how much capacity is actually in the industry and how much is under construction.

One of the most interesting aspects of Sterman's work is that it highlights just how difficult it is for our mental models to grasp and develop an intuition for nonlinear dynamic systems.[20] The problem is not that people are stupid; rather, it is just that our brains are not wired to think this way. Managers and policy makers do the best they can, but their actions often have unforeseen consequences or can even make things worse. In the next chapter, we will look more generally at the foibles of human cognition. In later chapters we will return to investigating how the combination of human behavior and dynamic structure in the economy may help explain complex phenomena, ranging from economy-wide cycles of growth and recession to volatility in the stock market.

CHAPTER SIX

Agents

MIND GAMES

AT THE CORE of any economic theory, there must be a theory of human behavior. Economies are ultimately made up of people. A theory of economic behavior must answer questions such as, How do we make economic decisions? What kinds of information do we use? And, are there some types of decisions that we are better or worse at making?

Many people have a natural resistance to the idea that human behavior can be understood in a scientific way. After all, how can we possibly understand something as complex and unpredictable as the human mind, with its emotions, creativity, imagination, and ability to learn? How can we put loving, hating, poetry-writing human beings into a mathematical formula? In Isaac Asimov's classic science fiction trilogy *Foundation*, scientists in the far future invent a new field called psychohistory, with which they are able to reduce the behavior of individual humans down to mathematical equations, enabling them to make precise predictions about the future course of history. Psychohistory sounds like an economist's ultimate fantasy. However, we do not need a "psychohistory"-like predictive theory of human behavior to understand the workings of the economy. Our standards are much lower. All we need is for there to be some basic regularities in human behavior, and then by understanding those micro-level regularities, we can better understand the macro-level behavior of the economy. As we will see in this chapter, human behavior is full of regularities.

As discussed earlier, all scientific theories are approximations and simplifications of the real world; thus, our goal in creating an economic model of human behavior is not to create a perfect copy. Rather, our model of human economic behavior should be like a good map; it should capture the essential features of the terrain, but strip out extraneous details. But the model should also not add anything that does not exist in the real world (e.g., the model should not give us mental telepathy or other capabilities that real people do not have) nor contradict things we know to be true. Sugarscape showed us an example of this kind of simplification. The behavior of the agents in Sugarscape was vastly, vastly simpler than the behavior of real people. The agents in Sugarscape could only eat, move, reproduce, and trade, and even the way they did those things was almost trivially simple. Nonetheless, physical movement, reproduction, and trading are all real human activities that are potentially relevant for understanding economic phenomena. There was nothing in Sugarscape that real people do not or cannot do.

Economists like to refer to their standard model of human behavior as *Homo economicus* ("economic man"). In this chapter, we will see that the Complexity Economics approach to *Homo economicus* is a radical departure from the Traditional approach. As we have discussed briefly, the Traditional model of human behavior was one of the more controversial assumptions in Traditional theory. We will now take a closer look, and I will argue that the *Homo economicus* of Traditional Economics is a "bad map" that both ignores important details about how real human beings behave and at the same time adds critical features that real humans do not have.

Spock Goes Shopping

Spock, the Vulcan in the *Star Trek* series, portrayed a perfectly rational being. Spock could remember the number π to fifty decimal places and perform incredibly complex calculations, all while under enemy phaser fire and without the slightest trace of emotion. Spock is a good example of how Traditional Economics portrays human behavior. Imagine you walk into your local grocery store and see some tomatoes. The following paragraphs outline what Traditional Economics says you go through in deciding whether to buy them.[1]

You have well-defined preferences for tomatoes compared with everything else you could possibly buy in the world, including bread, milk, and a vacation in Spain. Furthermore, you have well-defined preferences for everything you could possibly buy at any point in the future, and since the future is uncertain, you have assigned probabilities to those potential purchases. For example, I believe that there is a 23 percent chance that in two years, the shelf in my kitchen will come loose and I will need to pay $1.20 to buy some bolts to fix it. The discounted present value of that $1.20 is about $1.00, multiplied by a 23 percent probability, equals an expected value of twenty-three cents for possible future repairs, which I must trade off with my potential purchase of tomatoes today, along with all of my other potential purchases in my lifetime. In the Traditional Economics model, all these well-defined preferences are also ordered very logically. So if I prefer tomatoes to carrots, and prefer carrots to green beans, I will always take the tomatoes over the green beans. Likewise, if I prefer tomatoes to carrots, I won't suddenly go for the carrots simply because I saw some green beans.

Traditional Economics also assumes that you know exactly what your budget is for spending on tomatoes. To calculate this budget, you must have fully formed expectations of your future earnings over your entire lifetime and have optimized your current budget on the basis of that knowledge. In other words, you might hold back on those tomatoes because you know that the money spent on them could be better spent in your retirement. Of course, this assumes that your future earnings will be invested in a perfectly hedged portfolio of financial assets and that you take into account actuarial calculations on the probability that you will live until retirement at age sixty-five, as well as your expectations of future interest rates, inflation, and the yen-to-dollar exchange rate. While standing there, staring at those nice, red tomatoes, you then feed all this information into your mind and perform a cunning and incredibly complex optimization calculation that trades off all these factors, and you come up with the perfectly optimal answer—to buy or not to buy! This Spocklike method is known as the *perfect-rationality* model, one of the bedrock assumptions of Traditional Economics.[2]

In contrast, at the core of the emerging Complexity Economics view of behavior lies another method known as *inductive rationality,* and it goes like this: "Hmmm . . . tomatoes. They look nice and fresh. I kinda feel like salad tonight. Price looks okay." And into the shopping basket they go . . .

Cognitive Dissonance

Like much else in Traditional Economics, perfect rationality goes back to our friends Walras and Jevons. They did not come up with this model by actually studying human behavior. No one has ever seen people making all these calculations or behaving this way. Instead, economics adopted perfect rationality as an *assumption* in order to fit economics into the nineteenth-century equilibrium framework.

As we have discussed, in the ball-and-the-bowl framework of equilibrium economics, perfect rationality plays a role akin to the force of gravity. If we know the constraints on people's actions, and if we assume that everyone is behaving perfectly rationally, then they will all react to those constraints in the same way. Their decisions will thus be predictable and drive the system to equilibrium. It is important to note that the key behavioral assumptions of Traditional Economics were not developed because anyone thought they were a good description of real human behavior; *they were adopted to make the math work in the equilibrium framework*. Walras and later economists tried to justify ex post facto the lack of realism in the assumptions by arguing that even if the assumption of perfect rationality was not a good description of how people *do* behave (in economics lingo, a "positive model"), it could be interpreted as a description of how they *should* behave (a "normative" model). We can model a perfectly rational economy and then see how far the real world is from this ideal.

There are two problems with justifying perfect rationality on the basis that it is how people should behave. First, it does not necessarily follow that if everyone else is behaving in some other way, one should be the lone "perfectly rational" person in the crowd. As in the case of our discussion of dynamics, timing is everything. For example, if one had been shorting dot-com stocks in 1998, one would have had a lonely two years of losing lots of money before being vindicated in 2000. And second, as we will see shortly, perfect rationality is not a good normative model, because even if people wanted to act this way, they actually cannot.

As discussed in chapter 3, the perfect-rationality assumptions were challenged and criticized right from their introduction, but economists continued to use the assumptions anyway because perfect rationality enabled the models to be mathematical and no one had a better alternative. Then in the 1950s, Herbert Simon and his colleagues at Carnegie Mellon, James March and Richard Cyert, provided a more direct challenge. They did something quite radical; they actually watched and studied real people making decisions, in particular real managers in real companies. These experiences, as well as the work they drew on by psychologists, convinced them that real-world behavior looked nothing like the picture presented in economics textbooks. Simon put forward a competing theory of decision making—a theory he called *bounded rationality*.[3] Basically, it said that humans are economically self-interested and smart—but not that smart. Simon's theory took into account our lack of perfect information and the large but still finite processing power of our brains. As we mentioned before, Simon claims that instead of following perfect rationality, we *satisfice*—basically, we take the information we have, and we do the best we can.

For his efforts, Simon won a Nobel Prize in 1978, and most economists today mention him in reverential tones. Nonetheless, his work has had only a limited impact on the core of Traditional Economic theory.[4] Most standard economic textbooks don't even mention Simon or bounded rationality.[5] An important reason for this neglect is that, despite various attempts over the years, researchers have never succeeded in turning Simon's ideas into a mathematical model.[6]

Following Simon's pioneering work, two generations of economists and psychologists began to build a mountain of empirical and experimental evidence against the Traditional model of *Homo economicus.* In the 1970s, Daniel Kahneman of Princeton and Amos Tversky of Stanford published a series of seminal papers showing how real, human decision making directly contradicted some of the most basic assumptions of the Traditional model.[7] In the 1980s and 1990s, a number of researchers, including Paul Slovic, Colin Camerer, Alvin Roth, Reinhard Selten, Richard Thaler, George Lowenstein, Mathew Rabin, Drazen Prelec, Herbert Gintis, Ernst Fehr, John Kagel, and Vernon Smith, created what is known today as *behavioral economics.*[8] This research has confirmed again and again that real people simply do not form preferences, judge risk, or make decisions in the way the Traditional theory describes. By the new millennium, behavioral economics had entered the mainstream, and in 2002, Daniel Kahneman and Vernon Smith won the Nobel Prize (and as Nobel Prizes are not given posthumously, many noted that Kahneman's longtime collaborator, the late Amos Tversky, was the missing "third man").[9]

The rise of behavioral economics has left the field in a strange state of cognitive dissonance: many economists admit the validity of criticisms against perfect rationality, but they plug away using the Traditional assumptions because they lack an alternative that they can use in a formally stated model. But as behavioral economists, psychologists, and computer scientists have increased their collaborations, an alternative model has begun to emerge. Over the next few sections, we will look at some of the evidence compiled by the behavioral economists and then examine what a new *Homo economicus* might look like.

You Selfish Pig!

Imagine that you are traveling on an airplane, sitting on the aisle next to an eccentric-looking woman in the middle seat.[10] Next to her in the window seat is a business traveler whom you don't know. Halfway into the flight, the eccentric-looking woman says to both of you that she is very wealthy and gets very bored on long flights. She says she will give you and the businessman $5,000 together if you can agree on how to split up the money. However, the process for this is as follows: the businessman will decide how to make the split and offer you a portion of the money. If you accept his offer, then you both get to keep your portions. If you reject his offer, you both get nothing. The businessman thinks for a minute, then turns to you, and says,

"My offer is that I get $4,990 and you get $10." What do you do? Do you accept his offer or reject it?

If you are like most people, you will reject it. Why? Because it is unfair—the businessman is a selfish pig! Yet in economic terms, a rejection of his offer is completely irrational. You should accept anything he offers you, even if it is just one dollar. After all, even if the selfish businessman gets $4,999, isn't it better for you to get a dollar than nothing?

Versions of this "ultimatum game" have been played with real people, thousands of times, in places as different as Japan, Israel, Slovenia, Chile, Zimbabwe, Indonesia, and the United States. The game has also been played with college students, businesspeople, Torguud tribespeople in Mongolia, and Sangu herders in Tanzania. The results are remarkably consistent; real behavior looks nothing like the economic textbooks and most people reject offers that are perceived as unfair, even if it means walking away from a sure financial gain (exactly what is considered unfair differs by culture, though it is generally anything less than 30 percent).[11] Does this mean that people are simply emotional and irrational?

Some economists would argue that turning down the ten dollars is still perfectly rational. We can look at the situation as what economists call a "repeated game." By declining the offer and punishing the businessman, you might be implicitly assuming that there will be future interactions, and now that the businessman knows that you aren't a sucker, he will be more likely to give you a bigger share in future transactions. Thus, you are rationally trading off ten dollars now for the potential of a bigger payoff later. However, this interpretation does not hold up under scrutiny. In a set of carefully designed experiments, Ernst Fehr and Simon Gächter of the University of Zurich showed that even when it is clear to the participants that there will be no future interactions between the parties, and thus no chance to trade losses now for gains later, the same behavior emerges.[12]

Not only does our sense of fairness and reciprocity prompt a desire to punish people who treat us unfairly, we also naturally reward people who help us and give us things. For example, researchers studying behavior in restaurants observed that tips to the waiters were 18 percent higher when the waiters left a piece of candy with the bill (two pieces of candy got an even higher tip).[13]

The Traditional model implicitly assumes that people only care about the outcome of economic decisions, and not the process that people go through in making them. Things like bargaining, fairness, and coercion don't enter the picture. In addition, the model assumes that people only care about what they personally gain and lose and don't look at the results for other people. Experiments with the ultimatum game are direct evidence against those assumptions. In a survey of recent behavioral research, Herbert Gintis, of the University of Massachusetts and the Santa Fe Institute, and a group of colleagues note that Adam Smith portrayed humankind as a selfish, materialistic creature in his *Wealth of Nations*.[14] Gintis and company comment that many people forget that Smith also wrote another book, *The Theory of Moral Sentiments*, in which Smith presented a more nuanced view of human nature, portraying it as capable of both selfishness and generosity. Evidence from the ultimatum game and other experiments shows that the second Smith was right. Humans have strongly ingrained rules about fairness and reciprocity that override calculated "rationality." Gintis and his colleagues observe that humans are "conditional cooperators" who will behave generously as long as others are doing so, and "altruistic punishers" who will strike back at those perceived to behave unfairly, even at the expense of their own immediate interests.

That we are conditional cooperators and altruistic punishers should not be surprising. Our hominid ancestors spent about 2 million years of their existence living in small bands for which cooperative behavior and survival were highly correlated. Today, people still inhabit networks of social interactions in which reciprocity—I'll scratch your back if you scratch mine—is important. We are all better off if we help each other out, but this creates the potential for abuse by those who take benefits without giving back. A small amount of free riding can be tolerated, but if it becomes widespread, then the system of mutual back scratching collapses, which makes everyone worse off. Thus it makes sense that we have deep rooted behaviors that reward cooperation and punish free riders.[15] While some economists might view these behaviors as irrational, we will see in later chapters that these behaviors in fact provide the cornerstone for the social cooperation that is essential for wealth creation.

To Err Is Human

Another important way that real people deviate from the Traditional model is that they make mistakes. The Traditional model assumes that its Spock-like agents are perfect and never make mistakes, or if they do, their mistakes are randomly distributed noise around the correct answer. In other words, in the Traditional model people share no common errors or biases.

The behavioral economics view, on the other hand, is that "to err is human." One behavioral researcher, Jon Elster of Columbia University, even claims that "those who are most likely to make unbiased cognitive assessments are the clinically depressed."[16] Some of the common errors and biases that researchers have uncovered in normal, nondepressed people include these:[17]

- FRAMING BIASES. Exactly how an issue is framed can affect how we think about it. Compare, for example, the two questions "Should Britain adopt the euro?" and "Should Britain abolish the pound?" Under perfect rationality, this framing should not matter.

- REPRESENTATIVENESS. People have a bad habit of drawing big conclusions from very small and biased samples. For example, we might talk to three friends in the office, each of whom has coincidentally had a bad day, and conclude that the company is falling apart.

- AVAILABILITY BIASES. People tend to make decisions based on data that is easily available as opposed to finding the data that is really needed to make a good decision. This is, in effect, "looking for your lost keys under the lamppost" because that is where the light is best.

- DIFFICULTIES JUDGING RISK. Most people have a tough time reasoning with probabilities and assessing risks. In October 2000, a train crashed in Hatfield, England, tragically killing four people and injuring thirty-four. In response, the British government proposed to invest an additional $3 billion in rail safety. However, as The Economist newspaper pointed out, the real probability of dying in a train crash is quite low compared with other forms of transportation, and this expenditure would mean spending 150 times as much per expected life saved traveling by railway versus what is spent on road safety.[18]

- SUPERSTITIOUS REASONING. We tend to only look for the most proximate causes of things and often confuse random chance with cause and effect. Examples range from sports stars wearing their "lucky socks" to governments trying to reduce unemployment by simply making it more difficult to fire people.

- MENTAL ACCOUNTING. Traditional Economics treats all money the same. However, people tend to put money into different mental compartments. For example, many people make a monthly contribution to a retirement plan even if they have outstanding credit-card balances. This is not economically rational, because the return on investment in the retirement account (even after tax savings) will likely be less than the credit-card interest. Nevertheless, people often view their retirement contribution as sacred and wall it off from current spending. This mental compartmentalizing of different types of expenditures is deeply rooted—an anthropologist has even found this kind of behavior among Luo tribespeople in Africa.[19]

That Does Not Compute

Traditional economists sometimes reply to this catalog of human frailties by saying that sure, most people are subject to deviations from rationality, but all it takes is a small number, or even just one superrational player in a market, to take advantage of everyone else's mistakes and drive the market to the perfect rationality equilibrium. Even if most investors are fools, a few Spock-like traders will arbitrage everyone else's foolishness, make a lot of money, and drive prices to the level predicted by perfect rationality.[20] Aside from the practicalities of how this arbitrage process would work (can anyone have enough information or capital to do it, can it work in less-than-"perfect" markets such as the London ketchup market, and what about time delays, search costs, etc.?), there is another big problem: it is not possible for anyone, even Mr. Spock, to be smart enough to actually do this.

In 1985, a mathematician named Alain Lewis used some sophisticated techniques from the theory of computation to prove that no one, not even the smartest arbitrageur, could actually make the calculations described by perfect rationality.[21] Lewis proved that perfect rationality might be possible in economic theory, but is not possible in any practical sense because it is simply not computable. The theory of computation has a notion called a Turing Machine (named after the mathematician Alan Turing), which is a kind of imaginary all-purpose computer.[22] If something can be computed on a Turing Machine, it is at least theoretically (if not always practically) possible to build a physical computer that can compute it as well. However, if something cannot be computed on a Turing Machine, then no computer, no matter how powerful, even if it were the size of the universe itself, will ever be able to solve the problem. What Lewis proved was that perfect rationality as Traditional Economists define it is not computable by a Turing Machine.

Although cognitive scientists and philosophers debate whether, technically, our brains are Turing Machines, Lewis's proof shows that the computational demands of perfect rationality are enormous (this is also related to our earlier discussion about it taking a few quintillion years for the economy to reach equilibrium).[23] It is an amount, and type, of calculating power that our brains are very unlikely to have.

Arthur's Bar Problem

In addition to being noncomputable, many types of economic problems turn out simply to have no perfectly rational solution at all—not in theory and not in practice.[24] Brian Arthur, one of the participants in the original Santa Fe Institute meeting and a former director of the SFI economics program, pointed this out with the following example.[25] A popular Santa Fe bar, El Farol, offers live Irish music on Thursday nights. It is not a large bar, however, so you have a comfortable and pleasant evening if no more than sixty people show up. But if more than sixty people fill the bar, it becomes overcrowded and uncomfortable. You decide that you will go to the bar on Thursday night if you expect there to be sixty people or fewer, and you stay at home if you expect more than sixty people to show up. You have no way of communicating with other people who might go to the bar, and you can't call El Farol to ask how big the crowd is. Let's also assume that everyone else will make the decision to go to the bar or not in the same way. Do you show up? Do you stay at home? How do you decide?

It turns out there is no perfectly rational solution to this problem. There is an infinite circularity to it—what you do depends on what you expect me to do, which in turn depends on what I expect you to do, and so on. Instead of an analytic answer, the only way to make a decision in the El Farol problem is for the participants to look at their past visits to the bar, try to see if there is some pattern, and then make a judgment call such as "I went the last two Thursdays and it wasn't too crowded, so I'll go again."

Arthur has run computer simulations of agents following such rules of thumb and found that the bar never settles into an equilibrium. Some nights, it is quite full, some nights it is half empty, but the fluctuations average out to an attendance of sixty (figure 6-1). A Traditional economist might look at this and say, "Aha, see it does reach the perfectly rational attendance level of sixty

FIGURE 6-1

Attendance at the El Farol Bar

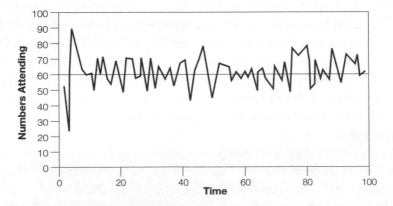

Source: Data from Arthur (1994).

where the bar is at its maximum comfortable capacity—so we can say it has found an equilibrium, albeit with some noise around it." But this is not correct. The average attendance of sixty is not an equilibrium, and the fluctuations cannot be dismissed as just noise. There is nothing random in the system other than the starting conditions, so it is completely deterministic and noise free. Rather, the proper interpretation is that the problem has no equilibrium, no fixed-point attractor.[26] The dynamics of the participants all using various rules of thumb create a dynamic attractor around sixty, and the high volatility of the attendance level is generated endogenously by the interactions of the agents and will never die down—attendance levels will always swing wildly and there will never be a convergence to an equilibrium.

Arthur notes that there are many economic decisions that, like the bar problem, are dynamic, self-referential, and ill defined. Company A thinking about cutting price will worry not just about its own situation, but what companies B and C will do; they in turn will partly base their strategies on their perception of what company A will do. Adopting a new technology standard, positioning a new product in the market, or assessing the value of a stock all have self-referential expectations built into them. The only way people can muddle through such decisions is by looking for patterns and rules of thumb from their past experience. Such a world of evolving, interacting, muddling agents will never reach equilibrium. Arthur's bar problem raises the intriguing possibility that much of the volatility we see in the real-world economy may be generated by the dynamics of people's decision rules, rather than by exogenous, random shocks.[27]

Inductive Rationality

So where does this leave us? The label *perfect rationality* is an unfortunate and emotionally loaded turn of phrase because it implies any alternative is imperfect and irrational, and none of us wants to be imperfect and irrational—least of all economists. Is our only choice simply to throw our hands up in the air, mutter about the capricious ways of humans, and give up on trying to understand *Homo economicus?* Fortunately, there is an alternative way of looking at human behavior—a way that can provide us with the foundation for a new view of *Homo economicus:* the theories of modern cognitive science.

Cognitive science is the label given to the field that studies the "software" of the human mind (as opposed to the "hardware" of the brain). This field draws on many areas, including neuroscience, psychology, artificial intelligence, linguistics, evolutionary theory, anthropology, and philosophy.[28] It is one of the most rapidly advancing areas of science at the beginning of the twenty-first century.

Modern cognitive science views the human mind from two perspectives. First, the mind is thought of as (to use a phrase from MIT's Steven Pinker) an "information-processing organ," in other words, a "thing that computes."[29] Cognitive scientists, however, don't like to use the word *computer*, because it has the negative connotations of the dumb white plastic thing sitting on your desk and whose only known emotion is a gleeful sense of cruelty when it crashes just before you have a big deadline. And while our minds do compute, they do it in ways very different from any human-made computer. The term *information-processing organ* connotes that the brain housing your mind is a part of your biological equipment, but it has a specialized function: the processing of information. The term also connotes that, while our brains may be extraordinarily complex, there is nothing magic or ultimately unknowable about them. Rather, the brain is a material object that can be understood by science, although it may take us a very long time to do so. The second perspective brought to the subject by modern cognitive science is evolution. The information-processing organ of *Homo sapiens* has been shaped by the forces of natural selection and is a product of our species' history and environment. Our minds were not designed by engineers starting from a clean sheet of paper, but were designed by tens of millions of years of evolution as primates, and then two million years of evolution as hominids, living primarily in the environment of the African savanna.

The picture that is emerging from cognitive science research is that the human mind is capable of incredible feats of information processing and learning—just in ways that are very different from the picture portrayed by perfect rationality. For example, humans may not be brilliant at calculating long equations, but they are amazing storytellers and story listeners. Roger Schank, the director of the Institute for Learning Sciences at Northwestern University and the former director of the Yale Artificial Intelligence Laboratory, has conducted research showing the centrality of stories to our mental processes for understanding, remembering, and communicating.[30] As Plato said, "Those who tell the stories rule society." The next time you are at a dinner with friends, sit back for a minute and observe the goings-on. What is everyone doing? Most of the evening will probably be taken up exchanging stories, funny ones, sad ones, stories about friends, stories read in the newspaper, and so on. Why do we do that? Why is storytelling and story listening so important to the way we think?

Stories are vital to us because the primary way we process information is through *induction*. Induction is essentially reasoning by pattern recognition. It is drawing conclusions from a preponderance of evidence. For example, although no one saw the butler do it, the butler's fingerprints were on the knife, the butler was caught leaving the scene, and the butler had a motive;

therefore, the butler did it. One cannot logically prove the butler did it; it is logically possible that someone else did. After all, no one saw the butler do it. But the pattern of evidence leads us to conclude inductively that the butler did it.

We like stories because they feed our inductive thinking machine, they give us material to find patterns in—stories are a way in which we learn. For example, by reading Shakespeare, we can learn all sorts of useful lessons about love and family relationships (be suspicious if your father suddenly dies and your mother marries your uncle, etc.). The best-selling business books are often stories of successful individuals or companies; everyone wants to read stories about how Jack Welch or Bill Gates "did it," hoping to glean patterns of success.

Humans particularly excel at two aspects of inductive pattern recognition. The first is relating new experiences to old patterns through metaphor and analogy making.[31] The next time you are in a meeting, see how frequently people reason by analogy, saying things like "this is just like the industry shake-out of 1987" or "this customer reminds me of Company X." When the Internet first hit the business scene in the early 1990s, people struggled to define it as like or unlike television, radio, magazines, software, and the telephone.

Second, we are not just good pattern recognizers, but also very good pattern-completers. Our minds are experts at filling in the gaps of missing information. The ability to complete patterns and draw conclusions from highly incomplete information enables us to make quick decisions in fast moving and ambiguous environments.

Pattern recognition and storytelling are so integral to our cognition that we will even find patterns and construct narratives out of perfectly random data. Sports commentators and fans enjoy coming up with detailed stories for why so-and-so is suddenly on a hot streak and scoring lots of goals or hitting lots of home runs. In a famous analysis, Thomas Gilovich, Robert Vallone, and Amos Tversky looked at this phenomenon and showed that the vast majority of these so-called hot hands in sports are completely explained by random chance—if you have enough players in the game, someone is bound to hit a hot streak sometime. In essence, people just make up stories to explain what they think is a pattern.[32]

Why Deep Blue Can't Tie Its Shoes

The opposite of induction is *deduction*. Deduction is a process of reasoning in which the conclusions must logically follow from a set of premises, for example, "Socrates is a man, and all men are mortal. Therefore, Socrates is mortal." Humans use deduction as well as induction, but we are not as good at deduction. Interestingly, while humans are relatively good at induction and relatively poor at deduction, computers are the opposite. Any of us is capable of instantly recognizing a face (an inductive task), yet most of us would have a tough time quickly doing the deductive calculation: $(239.46 \times 0.48 + 6.03) \div 120.9708$. At the same time, a simple pocket calculator can quickly and perfectly do the latter (the answer is 1), while it is a very hard programming challenge to get even a powerful computer to accurately recognize a face.

Nonetheless, we supplement our strong inductive capabilities with an occasional foray into deduction. We usually do this when we are stumped, when our storehouse of patterns isn't coming up with the answer, or if we are not confident of the answer our inductive instinct is giving us. Then, we will hunker down and painfully (and not always accurately) apply logic to find our way through a problem. To help us in this process, we have invented crutches such as pencils and paper, algebra, abaci, calculators, computers, and even the scientific method itself. Once we do the crunching, however, the experience goes into our storehouse of patterns so we don't have to repeat the complete exercise. We then constantly evaluate the success or failure of our pattern-based judgments and thus learn through experience.

A good illustration of how our inductive and deductive sides work together is the game of chess. Top chess players use induction to look globally at the patterns on the board, while they use deduction to analyze specific local positions. According to Andy Clark, director of the cognitive science program at Indiana University, grand master chess players can distinguish at a glance roughly fifty thousand different board positions.[33] This incredible storehouse of inductive patterns enables them to respond almost automatically to many situations, for example, "this is a bit like Bobby Fischer's attack at the World Championships in 1971." But chess has an enormous number of possible states of play, and so there will always be situations that don't fit a pattern. This is where the grand masters then grit their teeth and try to deductively grind their way through the possible decision tree of moves and countermoves for a specific position. Most top chess players can go three levels deep in the deductive tree.

The human method of mixing inductive pattern recognition with a little bit of deductive logic is in stark contrast to the brute-force deductive approach of IBM's chess-playing Deep Blue computer. Deep Blue can evaluate up to 200 million potential moves per second and map out up to six levels of moves and countermoves. The example of Deep Blue, however, shows why we tend to favor induction over deduction. Deduction only works on very well-defined problems such as chess moves; for deduction to work, the problem cannot have any information missing or ambiguity. Deduction is thus a powerful method of reasoning, but inherently brittle. While induction is more error prone, it is also more flexible and better suited for the incomplete and ambiguous information that the world throws at us. It thus makes evolutionary sense that we would be built this way. Deep Blue may be able to play chess at the level of Gary Kasparov, but Gary Kasparov's inductive machinery allows him not only to play chess, but also to tie his shoes in the morning and order food at a restaurant—tasks that would leave Deep Blue immediately lost.[34]

The modern cognitive science view of human behavior is thus almost the exact inverse of the Traditional Economic view of perfect rationality.[35] Perfect rationality assumes we are 100 percent deductive and, like Deep Blue, always work on unambiguous, well-defined problems. It also assumes that we don't learn; after all, there is no need to learn if we are already perfect.

The cognitive science view also helps provide an explanation for the anomalous results that experimental economists have come up with. The framing problems, availability biases, anchoring, and other effects fit with the picture of humans as fast pattern-recognizers and pattern-completers. Sometimes in our inductive haste, we make mistakes and miss logical connections. Evolution has made us fast, flexible, and usually right, as compared with being slow, brittle, but perfectly logical.

But this leaves us in a quandary. A key benefit of perfect rationality is that it is very specific; you can write it down in a set of equations and build models around it. For economics to be a science, it needs that sort of precision. How can we do that with ideas as squishy as pattern recognition, induction, learning, and analogy making?

The Mind of an Agent

At the moment, there is no standard, widely agreed-upon model of inductive reasoning, but various researchers have shown that it is at least possible to build precisely stated, mathematical models of induction. Models featuring pattern recognition and learning have become a staple of computer science research, and many of these models are used in practical applications that range from recognizing the faces of terrorists at airports, to recognizing fraudulent charge patterns on credit cards.

John Holland, a computer scientist at the University of Michigan, Keith Holyoak, a psychologist at UCLA, Richard Nisbett, a psychologist at Michigan, and Paul Thagard of Princeton's Cognitive Science Laboratory have devised a general model of induction that is an example of what a new *Homo economicus* might look like.[36] The basic structure of Holland and company's model is as follows:

- AGENT. There is an agent interacting with other agents and its environment.

- GOALS. The agent has some goal or goals it is trying to achieve, and thus the agent can perceive gaps between its current state and its desired state, for example, "I'm hungry" or "I'm in danger." The agent's job is to make decisions that bring it closer to its goals.

- RULES OF THUMB. The agent has rules of thumb that map the current state of the world to actions. These are called *condition-action* rules, or better known as IF THEN rules. For example, IF <hot stove> THEN <do not touch>. An agent's collection of rules of thumb at any point in time is referred to as the agent's *mental model*.

- FEEDBACK AND LEARNING. The agent's mental model keeps track of which rules have helped it achieve its goals and which rules have moved the agent farther from its goals. Historically successful rules are used more often than unsuccessful rules. Feedback from the environment thus causes the agent to learn over time.

Portrayed in this way, induction is essentially a problem-solving tool that an agent uses to further its goals. The collection of rules, shaped by feedback from the agent's environment, creates an internal model of the agent's external world. The agent then uses this internal model to make predictions about what will be the best responses to the various situations that it encounters in pursuit of its goals.

This kind of inductive problem solving, learning, and reasoning by analogy sounds like pretty sophisticated stuff. Yet, as Holland points out, the setup just described is pervasive in the biological world, albeit in varying levels of complexity. Even the lowly bacterium uses inductive problem solving; as it encounters varying concentrations of food, it moves in the direction of higher concentrations, thus making the implicit prediction that more of the molecules it likes lie in that direction. The bacterium's DNA provides a model of the bacterial world that says, if the concentration of food is going up, then it is likely to keep going up (if food molecules were distributed completely randomly, this would not be true). The bacterium has a goal (food), recognizes a pattern (chemical gradient), makes a prediction (food that way), and acts on it (wiggle flagellum). The bacterium then gets very direct feedback from its environment—if the rule works it lives and reproduces, if not it dies.

Frog Learning

Imagine a frog—Kermit—sitting happily on his lily pad in a pond.[37] His goals in life are pretty simple: to avoid danger and to eat flies. In Kermit's mental model, he has various *detectors* that check for conditions in his environment via his senses, for example, <moving>, <striped>, <large>, <near>, <buzzing>. Kermit also has a collection of *effectors* that prescribe various actions he can take, for example, <flee>, <pursue>, <extend tongue>, <do nothing>. The job of Kermit's mental model, then, is to put together detectors and effectors in IF THEN rules in ways that best achieve Kermit's goals. So, for example, Kermit might have a rule that says IF <small> <flying> <in center of vision> THEN <extend tongue>.

But how does Kermit get the rules in the first place, and how does Kermit learn over time? There is a basic set of rules hardwired into Kermit by his DNA, so that even as a tadpole, he has a start on being able to eat and avoid danger. However, once out in the wide world, Kermit's rule set quickly begins to expand. Let's say Kermit is born with the rule IF <small> <flying> <in center of vision> THEN <extend tongue>. However, after a few unpleasant encounters with bees and wasps, he might modify this rule to IF <small> <flying> *<blue>* <in center of vision> THEN <extend tongue> to more accurately capture flies. Likewise, his bad bee and wasp experience might add a new rule that says IF <small> <flying> <striped> THEN <do nothing>.

As Kermit's rule set is modified and expanded by feedback from his environment, he inevitably runs into conflicts. Imagine that one day, Kermit sees a small flying blue thing, and at the same time, a shadow passes overhead. His detectors then fire two rules: IF <small> <flying> <blue> <in center of vision> THEN <extend tongue>, and IF <shadow> <overhead> THEN <flee>. These two rules are now competing for Kermit's attention. We will assume that, to resolve this conflict, Kermit's mental model has a process of *credit assignment,* whereby rules are given scores based on how well they have performed in achieving Kermit's goals in the past. Successful rules get high scores, while unsuccessful or harmful rules get low scores. Let's say the IF <shadow> <overhead> THEN <flee> rule is important for helping Kermit avoid becoming lunch for a predatory bird. Let's imagine that in the scoring system of Kermit's mental model that this rule is assigned a score of one hundred. At the same time, the fly-catching rule is important, but not as important, so it is assigned a score of eighty. Thus, both rules fire, but Kermit's mental model will select the higher-score rule, and he will flee. Kermit's mental model will then take note of how well the <flee> rule worked in light of his goals and update its score.

This process then leads very naturally to learning. Let's say Kermit has a rule that says IF <hear buzzing> <left> THEN <turn head left> <extend tongue>. By random chance, however, one day Kermit turns his head right instead of left and just happens to get a fly. Now he also has the rule IF <hear buzzing> <left> THEN <turn head *right*> <extend tongue>. Both rules are in direct conflict and both rules have led to fly lunches in the past, so they are tied with a score of ten. We can think of these two rules now as competing hypotheses about what leads to lunch in frog-world. As long as the scores are even, Kermit will try them both. We can clearly see, however, that over time, the <turn left> rule will produce better results than the <turn right> rule, and the <turn left> score will climb.

There are two problems, however. First, we don't want the system to be so rigid that, as soon as one rule moves from a score of ten to eleven, Kermit never tries the other rule again. After all, if Kermit tried the <turn right> rule next and by random chance got a fly, which would push the rule's score to eleven, he would then never try the <turn left> rule again and probably starve to death. So a higher score should increase the *probability* of a rule's being fired, but not guarantee it. We still want some experimenting with rules that are relatively close in score, and we may even want to try an out-of-favor rule occasionally to see if the world has changed. Second, we have a problem in that action and reward are sometimes separated in time. How would such a system learn to behave strategically where it does things that have a cost in the near term, but a payoff in the long term?

Holland and company's answer will warm the hearts of economists—we have a market. Their hypothesis is that the rules in your mental model compete with each other by bidding for your attention using their credit scores.[38] The higher the credit score, the greater the probability, but not certainty, that a rule will win. For example, a five-point difference in the bidding rules might mean a fifty-fifty chance of either rule's being selected, while a ten-point difference might mean sixty-forty odds in favor of the higher bid, and so on. In addition, bids are not usually made by single rules acting on their own, but by complex chains of rules. For example, Kermit might have a strategy of seeking out a place with lots of flies, approaching it (temporarily scaring off the flies), sitting still for a while until the flies return, and then zapping them with his tongue. The complex chain of rules involved in making this happen means there is some separation between the rule that got the reward (IF <fly> THEN <stick out tongue>) and the rule that set it all up in the first place (IF <smelly stuff that attracts flies> THEN <approach>).

In our rule market, we can think of the rules in this chain as suppliers and customers to each other. For example, the <stick out tongue> rule buys from the <sit still> rule, which buys from the <approach smelly stuff> rule. Thus, when the <stick out tongue> rule gets the reward, it must pay its supplier rules, which pay their suppliers, and so forth. Thus, rules that make a profit—i.e., they contribute to the chain's ability to get a reward—grow in strength over time and get used more frequently. As rules get farther and farther back in the chain, however, the trickle-down of payments diminishes, owing to all the middlemen. This resulting lower payment puts a natural limit on the distance between cause and effect. Such a structure is consistent with experimental evidence showing that we are able to act strategically to some extent, but have a difficult time reasoning through long, complex chains of cause and effect.

Frog Poetry?

We can begin to see how a relatively simple system of competing rules, scores, and feedback from the environment can result in a flexible pattern-recognition system that learns over time. We will now make one more assumption about the system to greatly enhance its performance. We will assume that over time, the rules in the system self-organize into hierarchies. Because there is regularity in Kermit's world, there will be regularities in the firing patterns of the rules in Kermit's mental model. For example, rules dealing with <small> <flying> <blue> things will tend to fire together. When rules often fire together, they become associated, and we can think of them as organized in a category. So the various rules that fire when Kermit encounters <small> <blue> things can be put under the category <fly>; likewise things that fire <large> <flying> <flapping> rules might go under the category <bird>. Kermit's mental models will have a host of experiences and responses associated with flics and birds.

This hierarchical structure gives the inductive system two important advantages. First, the structure allows the system to respond to novelty. Any mental model will by necessity always be simpler than the world it lives in. So Kermit will always encounter situations he hasn't experienced before and will need some response (even if the response is <do nothing>). Thus, we will assume that Kermit's rules are arranged in a *default hierarchy*. When Kermit encounters a pattern, his mental model will scan to see if he has a specific response to that pattern, but if not, he will fall back on a default response.[39] For example, Kermit might have the default response IF <object moving> <no other information> THEN <flee>. This is a very general, conservative rule designed to keep Kermit out of trouble. Under this general default rule, however, Kermit might encounter several situations for which he has more information as well as a more situation-specific response, for example, IF <object moving> <small> <near> THEN <approach> <slowly>. Thus, Kermit will tend to be cautious when faced with novelty and fall back on tried-and-true rules, but over time, he will develop a tailored repertoire of responses to the new situations.

The second advantage of a rule hierarchy is that it makes possible reasoning by analogy.[40] Frogs may not be able to come up with metaphors in the literary sense (so no frog poetry), but frogs or any other agent using an inductive system can reason by analogy enough to say that one thing is like another. Collections of rules arranged in a hierarchy lend themselves quite naturally to this type of reasoning. Let's say most of Kermit's experience with birds has been with seagulls and he has a category called <birds>, which is fired by detection of <large> <flying> <flapping> things. One day Kermit sees something that is <large> <flying> but is not flapping. Thus, the encounter fires some but not all of the <bird> detectors. To Kermit, this new object is "birdlike," but does not exactly fit his experience with birds. Kermit's mental model scans his other categories for matches and sees that it is more birdlike than flylike or doglike, and so on. Thus Kermit uses his default hierarchy and goes for the most general <bird> response, which is <flee>. This reasoning by analogy gives Kermit a big advantage in an ambiguous world that is constantly throwing novelty at him. By seeing that something is birdlike, he has a much better probability of generating the correct response than if the new unidentified object just went into an <I don't know what it is> category. For example, what if Kermit's nonflapping thing was a soaring hawk looking for a frog snack? It also could have been an airplane or something else harmless, but seeing it as birdlike is still a reasonable, conservative response. The point is, even if his response isn't perfect, his odds of doing something appropriate are improved. Over time, if hawks or airplanes were important to Kermit's world, then his definition of birdlike would evolve and he would develop more tailored responses to those objects in his default hierarchy.

Stock Bots

While we can see how one might build a model of a frog catching flies, how does Holland and company's inductive model apply to human economic decision making? Shortly after the 1987 Santa Fe Institute economics meeting, Holland began a collaboration with Brian Arthur. Although Arthur was an academic, he had spent some time early in his career working in the business world, including a stint at McKinsey & Company while he was a graduate student. He had seen firsthand that the decision-making processes of the real world hardly resemble the cool, dry, perfect rationality of economic models, and thus he had a long-standing interest in trying to find a better way to reflect this. The two men decided to team up and apply Holland's ideas to modeling the behavior of the stock market. The model they built along with Blake LeBaron, Richard Palmer, and Paul Tayler, the Santa Fe Institute Artificial Stock Market, has since become a classic in the Complexity Economics literature.[41]

Following the general model of induction just outlined, the agents in the SFI model are viewed as information-processing entities, they are essentially little computer programs. They collect information from their environment, process that information, generate decisions, and then receive feedback on those decisions from the environment.

Like the agents in Sugarscape, the agents in the stock market model are subject to the forces of evolution. Just as the most economically successful Sugarscape agents survived and reproduced, in the SFI stock market, the most successful stock-trading agents are rewarded and the least successful go bankrupt and exit. Arthur, Holland, and company, however, added a second layer of evolution to their model. In the stock market model, evolution is also at work *inside the heads of the agents* to enable them to learn.

To see how this works, let's imagine you win a modest amount in the lottery and want to invest it. You call up a broker and ask for some general advice on investment strategy. In response, your broker gives you some rules of thumb, such as "Buy and hold is the best strategy for the long term," "Always ensure your portfolio is diversified," and "Beware of stocks whose price-to-earnings ratios are way above the rest of their sector." Nevertheless, you decide to shop around for advice. You call up a few more brokers, plus you ask your crazy uncle and a few friends what they think you should do. Pretty soon you have a collection of investment advice, and inevitably, some of it conflicts. Your job is then to sort through all the potential strategies floating around in your head and figure out what to do.

In this scenario there are two levels of competition going on in the market. First, there is the general competition among investment strategies in the market itself: who will do better, the growth investors or the value investors, the bulls or the bears? And second, there is the competition among the conflicting potential investment strategies fighting for airtime in your head: who should I listen to, my broker or crazy Uncle Herbie? Arthur and Holland conjectured that both follow an evolutionary learning process.

To explore this idea, Arthur, Holland, and their colleagues set up a simulated trading environment on a computer with a single stock that paid a random dividend. They then created one hundred trading agents that would buy and sell the stock. The stock's price would then be determined by the buying and selling of the agents in the market. Each agent had a simple goal, to make as much money as possible, and in order to achieve that goal, each agent had to decide when to buy and when to sell. The agents had access to three pieces of information to make their decisions: the historical price pattern of the stock, its historical dividend payout, and a risk-free interest rate. Next, Arthur, Holland, and company had to decide how the agents would process that information to make their decisions.

Just as in the frog example, the researchers used condition-action rules to map patterns in the market to an agent's expectation for the value of the stock. For example, one rule might be IF <price rose 5 percent last period> THEN <forecast next-period price as current-period price plus 5 percent>. An agent following such a rule would then decide whether to buy or sell the stock by simply comparing its forecast price with the current price; if the forecast price was higher, the agent would buy, and if it was lower, the agent would sell. Rules constructed this way could also be made much more complicated. For example, IF <price has risen in the last three periods> AND <price is not larger than sixteen times the dividend divided by the risk-free rate> THEN <forecast next-period price plus dividend as 106 percent of current-period price plus dividend>. The rules of thumb used by the agents could be based on fundamentals (e.g., buy stocks in a certain range of price-to-earnings ratio), on trends in the market (e.g., buy stocks that are going up in price), or on any mixture of the two. In the model there was no effective limit to how complex a rule could get.

Consistent with our imaginary lottery winner sorting through conflicting stock advice, instead of giving each agent in the model just one rule of thumb, Arthur and Holland gave each agent one hundred rules of thumb. One can think of the one hundred rules in each agent's software head as competing hypotheses on what leads to success in the stock market. In other words, each of the rules is a potential investment strategy, and the agent's job is to sort through its own set of potential strategies and figure out which ones will help the agent make money.

We can then ask how an agent sorts through its one hundred competing investment strategies? The answer is fairly straightforward; just like Kermit the frog, the agent uses what has worked in the past. Arthur and Holland set up an evolutionary process working inside the heads of the agents. Each condition-action rule was coded as a string of 1s and 0s, and one can think of these strings as computer DNA representing various investment strategies. Thus 011000100101 might represent IF <dividend dropped 10 percent averaged over the past five periods> THEN <forecast price to drop 2 percent next period>, while 100011010101 might represent IF <dividend is less than three times the risk-free rate> THEN <forecast price to rise 5 percent next period>. Thus, each agent had in its software head a population of investment strategy DNA. Each piece of strategy DNA was then given a fitness score. If that strategy led to the agent's making money, its fitness score was increased; if it led to losing money, its score was decreased.

During each turn of the game, each agent went through the following process. The agent was given information on the historical stock price, dividend, and risk-free rate. The agent then compared this information with its population of potential strategies and its storehouse of patterns and looked for a match. If more than one rule matched, the agent would look at the fitness scores and choose the rule with the higher score. Thus, rules that worked in the past tended to get used more often. After a rule is used, the agent then looks and sees how it did—did the agent make money or lose money? If the agent made money, the result further strengthens the rule; if the agent lost money, the rule is weakened.

Thus far, we have a system that can learn within a fixed population of rules. Let's say we start each agent with a population of one hundred randomly constructed rules. Using the above system, through trial and error, the agent eventually will learn which of those rules helps it make money and which don't. But we know that in real stock markets, people are constantly innovating new investment strategies—how do we get the agents to innovate and create new rules?

Arthur, Holland, and company built the following process into their model. Every now and then, at random intervals, each agent's set of one hundred rules undergoes an evolutionary process: the bottom-performing twenty rules are eliminated and new rules are generated to fill their place. Some of the remaining eighty more successful rules are given mutations to individual elements of their computer DNA. For example, a random 1 might be flipped to a 0, or vice versa. Some of the remaining strategies are also recombined in what is, essentially, computer sex. One DNA string is snipped in two at a random point and combined with another string, also snipped in two, to create something new. The effect of this process of mutation and recombination is to create new strategies in the agent's pool of one hundred rules. Many of these new rules will be nonsense, or even harmful, but some will be successful innovations—perhaps even more successful than many of the other strategies active in the market.

With their inductive stock market ready to go, Arthur, Holland, and their colleagues hit the switch and ran a series of experiments. Before running the full model with a hundred rules per agent, they conducted a run where every agent had the same, single rule—perfect rationality—and a learning rate of zero.[42] In this run, the results looked very much like what is predicted by Traditional Economics. The model quickly settled down to a price that was close to the theoretical equilibrium price, which corresponded to the fundamental value of the stock. There was relatively little trading volume or volatility, and no one earned particularly higher returns than anyone else earned. This run showed that if *everyone* was behaving according to the Traditional model of rationality (or a close approximation), things would look more or less as predicted by Traditional theory.

They then performed a second run, in which they turned on the one hundred competing rules in each agent's head, initialized those rules with a random scattering of strategies, and raised the learning rate above zero. This had a dramatic impact on the behavior of the model. Trading volume went way up, volatility climbed, and the stock price had far more complex dynamics, including bubbles and crashes, over time. The market also developed a pattern of periods of relative quiescence interspersed with intense stormy periods. In addition, there were large differences in the relative performance of agents; some super-performing Warren Buffett agents emerged, while others plunged into bankruptcy. As we will see in more detail in chapter 17, real financial markets look much more like this picture than the equilibrium predicted by Traditional Economics.

What caused this change to a more dynamic and realistic-looking market is as follows. If everyone starts with the same perfect rationality rules and sticks to them with little learning, then the market trundles along in a herd, with price roughly at equilibrium. As soon as heterogeneity and learning are introduced, things get much richer and more complex. Let's say that for some reason, the price of the stock takes a blip upward. Some members of the agent population have active rules that look for growth in the stock's price and then buy. As the price rises, more and more of these players will pile in, which in turn causes the price to run up higher and higher. Some other players, however, focus on fundamental value and at some point begin to sell because they think the stock is overvalued. If enough of them come in at once, they could tip the stock back down, in turn triggering the entry of players who have rules to sell declining stocks, sending the share price plunging as the growth players run for the exit. New rules might even evolve that look specifically for this up-and-down pattern and then try to exploit it. All this price movement is driven by the dynamic interactions of various rules in the population and has little or nothing to do with changes in the underlying economic value of the stock. Nor are the complex patterns due merely to random noise. Instead, there is a complex battle of beliefs going on within the heads of agents and among the agents, which leads to volatility and complex patterns in the market. In chapter 17, we will further explore how competition between different types of agents and their strategies may account for important aspects of market behavior.

In the complex adaptive system of the economy, understanding the micro-level behaviors of individuals is essential to understanding how the system as a whole behaves. For over a hundred years, economics has made do with a model of human behavior that most economists now recognize as overly simplistic and fundamentally at odds with an enormous body of evidence, simply for the sake of mathematical tractability. Today, however, collaborations with psychologists, computer scientists, and cognitive scientists are producing a new model of *Homo economicus*. This model portrays humans as *inductively rational* pattern-recognizers who are able to make decisions in ambiguous and fast-changing environments and to learn over time. Real people are also neither purely self-regarding, nor purely altruistic. Rather, their behavior is attuned to eliciting cooperation in social networks, rewarding cooperation and punishing free riders. But alas, none of us is perfect, and we also have our foibles and biases.

There is, however, one final defense of the perfect-rationality model. Some might argue that there is only one way to be perfectly rational, and at least economics has had a standard, agreed-upon method for modeling behavior, however flawed and simplistic. One cannot say that about inductive rationality. Cognitive science is still in its infancy, with no single agreed-upon approach. I would argue, though, that we are better off using a model that is at least consistent with the facts than one we know is wrong. Moreover, there will probably never be a single *Homo economicus* for all purposes. The simplified behavioral assumptions needed for a stock market model may be different from those required for a macroeconomic model. But again, if one thinks of theories like maps, the various approaches to *Homo economicus* should at least be consistent with each other and with what we know about real human behavior. In the meantime, cognitive science will continue to progress at its rapid pace, modeling technology will continue to improve, and while economics will never become "psychohistory," we will have a far better understanding of how behavior drives the economy than we do today.

CHAPTER SEVEN

Networks

OH WHAT A TANGLED WEB WE WEAVE

NETWORKS ARE AN ESSENTIAL INGREDIENT in any complex adaptive system. Without interactions between agents, there can be no complexity. For example, the biological world comprises a massive hierarchy of networks: molecules interact in cells, cells interact in organisms, and organisms interact in ecosystems. The human body is a highly complex collection of networks within networks interacting with other networks, including the brain, nervous system, circulatory system, and immune system. If you took away the network structure of the human body, we would each be nothing more than a small box of chemicals and half a bathtub's worth of water.

The economic world likewise depends on networks. The earth is girdled by roads, sewers, water systems, electrical grids, railroad tracks, gas lines, radio waves, television signals, and fiber-optic cables. These provide the highways and byways of the matter, energy, and information flowing through the open system of the economy. The economy also contains massively complex virtual networks: people interact in companies, companies interact in markets, and markets interact in the global economy. Just as in biology, the networks of the economic world are arranged in hierarchies of networks within networks.

Yet, despite the importance of networks to economic activity, they have not been a central concern of economists until quite recently. Sociologists have studied networks for many years, but generally in the context of sociopolitical relationships rather than economics.[1] Traditional Economics has tended to gloss over networks because they don't fit neatly into the equilibrium paradigm. Traditional models typically assume that agents only interact through auctions (or some other price-setting mechanism) or in one-on-one negotiations. This assumption came about because auctions and two-person games can be portrayed as equilibrium systems, while larger groups of people involved in complex interactions are much more difficult to model mathematically and in many cases require computer simulation.

In contrast, networks have been a topic of interest in the physical sciences for many years. Much of the pioneering work on the subject was done by the Hungarian mathematicians Paul Erdös and Alfréd Rényi in the 1950s and 1960s.[2] In recent years, new mathematical tools and computers have greatly accelerated research on networks in both the physical and the social sciences. This research has shown that networks have a number of very general properties that apply whether one is talking about a network of particle interactions, a web of neurons in the brain, or people in an organization.[3] In this chapter, we will see what some of these newly discovered "laws of networks" imply for economic systems.

Before exploring the properties of networks, however, we should define a few terms. Take a piece of paper, draw some dots on it, and draw some connections between the dots—you have created a picture of a network. Mathematicians call these dots *nodes,* and the lines connecting them *edges*. The overall picture of the network itself is called a *graph*. If, when you connected the dots, you drew the lines randomly, then the network you drew is called a *random graph* (figure 7-1). If the connections you drew were in a regular pattern—for example, each dot is connected to its four nearest neighbors, making a checkerboard pattern—then it is called a *lattice graph*. Both random and lattice graphs show up in the economy, and some of the most interesting networks are combinations of the two.

FIGURE 7-1

Random and Lattice Graphs

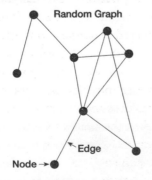

Random Graph

Node → Edge

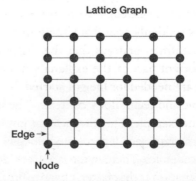

Lattice Graph

Edge →

Node

How Networks Catch Fire

Economists have long recognized that certain products, such as e-mail, faxes, and telephones, share a property whereby the greater the number of people who use them, the more useful they become. This is called, appropriately enough, a *network effect*. Traditional Economics, however, has not historically had much to say about why these types of products tend to suddenly catch fire and take off in popularity.

Stuart Kauffman, a mathematical biologist, believes that the random-graph theory developed by Erdös and Rényi holds the answer.[4] Picture a thousand buttons scattered on a hardwood floor. Imagine you also have in your hand pieces of thread; you then randomly pick up two buttons, connect them with the thread, and put them back down. As you first start out, the odds are that each button you pick up will be unconnected, so you will be creating a lot of two-button connections. As you work away, however, at some point you will pick up a button that is already connected to another button and you will thus be adding a third. Eventually, as there are fewer and fewer unconnected buttons, you will get more and more little clusters of three buttons, and then some four- and five-button clusters will begin to form, like little islands scattered in a sea of buttons.

Then, as you keep stringing together buttons, isolated clusters of connected buttons will suddenly begin to link up into giant superclusters—two fives will join to make a ten, a ten and a four will make fourteen, and so on. Physicists call such a sudden change in the character of a system a *phase transition*. For example, if you take steam and lower the temperature one degree at a time, when you reach 100°C, the steam will suddenly transform into liquid water and then, at 0°C, into ice. In random networks, the phase transition from small clusters to giant clusters happens at a specific point, when the ratio of segments of thread (edges) to buttons (nodes) exceeds the value of 1 (i.e., on average, one thread segment for every button).[5] One can think of the ratio of one edge to one node as the "tipping point" where a random network suddenly goes from being sparsely connected to densely connected.[6]

Kauffman believes that this "tipping point" in network formation is an important part of the explanation for how the chemical reaction networks that are needed for life got started. But we also see this effect at work in economic and technology contexts. The Internet is probably the most dramatic recent example. The Internet was invented back in the 1960s as a Defense Department project. It percolated along in obscurity for twenty years, used mostly by academics. Then, in the late 1990s, its usage suddenly exploded. A plausible explanation is that faster, cheaper modems and better user interfaces pushed the edge-to-node ratio in people's social networks above the magic ratio of 1, thus creating an explosion in usage.

Random-graph theory gives us a way of modeling such phenomenon and seeing that network effects are not smooth and gradual, but highly nonlinear. By analyzing such networks, we may be able to better understand why some fashions become hot, how political movements can suddenly take off, and even what makes the stock market sometimes so volatile.[7]

It's a Small World

In 1967, the psychologist Stanley Milgram decided to conduct an experiment.[8] He sent letters to a group of people in Kansas and Nebraska with instructions that the letters were to be forwarded to one of two recipients in Boston. But he only identified the name, profession, demographics, and approximate location of the recipient. He instructed the Kansan and Nebraskan participants to forward their letters to someone they knew on a first-name basis, someone who in turn could forward it to someone he or she knew on a first-name basis (like a chain letter), until it reached the intended recipient. Thus, if you were one of the participants, you might not have known anyone in Boston, but you might have sent it to a cousin in Ohio who went to college on the East Coast, and that cousin then forwarded it to a college friend living in Boston, who then sent it to a doctor because the intended recipient was a doctor, and so on. What Milgram found, much to his surprise, was that first, most of the letters got through, and second, the median number of links in the chain was six. This result became the basis for the phrase "six degrees of separation," the notion that everyone on earth is within six connections of each other.

Duncan Watts of Columbia University and Steve Strogatz of Cornell University provided a more recent and somewhat whimsical test of the "six degrees" principle using the "Kevin Bacon game."[9] According to Watts, the game was invented by a group of William and Mary College fraternity brothers who were movie buffs and decided that Kevin Bacon was the center of the movie universe. In the game, one thinks of a random actor and then determines how many links he or she is to a Bacon film. Kevin Costner, for example, has a Bacon number of one because he starred with Bacon in *JFK*. Bruce Willis, on the other hand, has never starred with Bacon, but has a Bacon number of two because he was in *Armageddon* with J. Patrick McCormack, who in turn was in *Hollow Man* with Bacon. Using data from Brett Tjaden of the University of Virginia, Watts and company found that the highest Bacon number for any American actor is four. They then did an exhaustive search on the Internet Movie Database and found that 90 percent of the roughly

570,000 actors in the world had some connection to Bacon, the highest Bacon number in the world was ten, and 85 percent had a number of three or less.[10] Similar studies have been done on other social networks, including scientists and corporate board members, and have yielded similar results.[11] It is a small world after all.

How on a planet of 6.4 billion people can we all be just six or so handshakes from each other? A mathematician might note that if everyone in the world had on average 100 friends, then the number of friends' friends would be 10,000 (100 × 100), and friends' friends' friends 1 million, and so on, until at five degrees, we reach 10 billion.[12] But there are two problems with this. First, 100 is probably too high for the average number of friends for every person on earth. But, second and more importantly, groups of friends tend to have considerable overlap. That is, my 100 friends are not completely different from my friends' friends. So, the *small-world effect,* as it is called, must be due to something else.

Watts and another colleague, Mark Newman of the University of Michigan (both are also affiliated with the Santa Fe Institute), have come up with an interesting answer: the small-world effect is due to the structure of the network itself. What Watts and Newman found is that social networks have evolved to become highly efficient mixtures of the regular and the random.[13] Imagine a map of the United States on which we have placed a dot to mark all the cities with populations greater than 100,000. Now let's draw a line between each city and its four nearest neighbors. Boston, for example, might be connected to Worcester, Cambridge, Providence, and Manchester. What we have just created is a lattice network. Such a lattice network would not look quite as neat as the idealized one in figure 7-1, but its "four nearest neighbors" connection rule would mean that the network has regularity and structure to it. We can look at the cities connected to Boston and think of them as a region, for example, southeastern New England. The downside of this regularity, though, is that moving through the network requires a great many hops. For example, if we wanted to connect Boston to San Diego, we would have to use Boston's link to Providence, and then Providence's link to Hartford, and then Hartford's link to New York City, and so on, creeping one city at a time across the country. Because lattice graphs have high degrees of separation, it might take as many as twenty or thirty hops to hook one coast up to the other.

Now imagine instead of our nearest-neighbor rule, we said that each city was randomly connected to four other cities. One hop from Boston might include Albany, New York; Topeka, Kansas; Sarasota, Florida; and Spokane, Washington. Some random lines will inevitably be quite short, say, between Washington, D.C., and Philadelphia. Some will be more medium length, say, between Denver and Cleveland. But others will be quite long, say, from San Diego to Charlotte. Because the connections are random, there will be equal numbers of short, medium, and long connections. This means that it will take far fewer hops to link any two cities together, because for any two cities, one will be able to piece together a trip of short, medium, and long connections as appropriate to span the distance. When moving from a lattice to a random graph, the number of degrees of separation collapses to a handful.

The Value of Random Friends

Social networks are like lattice graphs because they have order and structure in them. Your collection of friends most likely includes people you grew up with, people you went to school with, colleagues from work, people in your profession, and your current neighbors. This means that, because we tend to draw friends from social pools, your friends have a greater-than-average likelihood of knowing each other. All social networks have very identifiable clusters, or cliques. For example, dentists in St. Louis tend to know each other, as do airplane enthusiasts in Stuttgart. The existence of these clusters shows that the network is not random but has order and structure.

Although our social networks are structured, we also all have a few random friends as well, people who are not in our normal social circle or just outside it, but who we have somehow met and become friendly with. It might be someone you got to know while on vacation, or in the waiting room of a doctor's office. These people who don't fit in our normal cluster are bridges out of our social networks and connect us to other social networks. It turns out that if you take a nicely structured lattice graph and then throw in a few random connections scattered around it, you get the best of both worlds. You get identifiable clusters, but with short degrees of separation, for instance, "most of my friends might be dentists in St. Louis, but I know this guy at my gym who used to work in Hollywood . . ." and pretty soon you are talking to Madonna. Thus, our random friends are like the express flight from Charlotte to San Diego.

Newman and Watts have been able to quantify this effect. Let's say we have a population of 1,000 people with 10 friends each and no "random" friends. That is, everyone's friends are drawn only from a strictly defined social circle. Then the average degree of separation is 50; in other words, on average it will take fifty hops to get from one randomly selected person to another. But if we now say that 25 percent of everyone's friends are random, that is, drawn from outside their normal social circle, then the average degree of separation drops dramatically to 3.6.[14] Interestingly, the idea of random friends runs somewhat counterintuitive to our idea of what constitutes a good networker. We tend to think of someone as being well connected if he or she knows a particular world very well. But Watts and Newman's research shows that the best-connected people are really the ones who have the most diverse group of contacts. We all know people who seem to be able to talk to just about anyone and pick up friends from all walks of life and circumstances— these are the people who are truly well connected.

The structure of social networks is not only important for us as individuals, but also makes a big difference in the functioning of large organizations. If an organization keeps people in strict career ladders and has silo-like business units and divisions, then the social network will be overly structured, with insufficient randomness. This, in turn, means long chains of hops for information to be transmitted around, resulting in poor communications and slow decision making. In contrast, some organizations quite deliberately move people across functions and businesses in their careers, thus creating within the company social networks that have a greater diversity of connections. Too much churning of people can turn a social network into a random mush, but a moderate amount can dramatically improve its functioning. General Electric, for example, is famous for moving people across organizational boundaries and for using training programs to give people from different geographies an opportunity to forge lasting social connections.

"The Network Is The Computer"

For a number of years Sun Microsystems has advertised itself with the slogan "The Network Is The Computer."[15] This is an unusually insightful strap-line because it speaks to fundamental truths about both networks and computers. Computers are in fact networks, and networks are in reality computers. If you crack open a computer and look inside, you will see a bunch of chips wired together in a network. If you crack open one of those chips and look inside, you will see a few tens of millions of transistors wired together in a network. The only thing those transistors do is flip between two states: 0 and 1. A computer doesn't get its power from the individual transistors; it gets its power from the way they are put together in a network. Likewise, individual computers can be strung together in networks to create computers that are still more powerful; in fact, most modern supercomputers are really networks of individual computers.

Networks of nodes that can be in a state of 0 or 1 are called *Boolean networks,* after the mathematician George Boole, who invented them.[16] In Boolean networks, the 0 or 1 state of the nodes is determined by a set of rules. Stuart Kauffman illustrates this with the image of a string of Christmas tree lights that blink on or off.[17] Imagine just three lights strung together in a loop; call them A, B, and C. Each light bulb can be either on or off, which we can represent with a 1 or 0, respectively. Each bulb receives inputs from the two bulbs on either side of it telling it whether they are on or off. We can then imagine that each light bulb has a rule that it follows to determine what it does next period, based on the inputs from the other two bulbs. For example, bulb A might have a rule that says if both bulbs B and C are 1, then it will be 1, too, but under any other circumstances, it will be 0 (this is known as the *Boolean AND rule* and is one of the basic building blocks of computation). We can imagine all sorts of other rules we might give the bulbs, for example, if A and B are 0, then C will be 0, too, and in any other circumstance, C will be 1 (this is the *Boolean OR rule*). The rules we give the bulbs then determine the pattern that the lights blink over time. The network clicks through each state, each bulb looking at its two inputs and its rules, then determining whether it will turn on or off during the next period. The rules thus map the state of the network from one period to the next.

Boolean networks range from transistors on computer chips to chemical reaction networks (researchers have even been able to build "chemical computers"). Even though our brains don't work using the same 0 and 1 logic of computers, individual neurons can be mathematically portrayed that way and thus most researchers believe that the brain, a mass of neurons, is a form of Boolean network (albeit a staggeringly complex one). If we think of the economy as a massive network of brains, then in effect the economy is a Boolean network, too (an even more staggeringly complex one). Admittedly, this is a bit of a conceptual jump, but we can speculate about what this might mean for the economy if it is true.[18]

After more than thirty years of research on Boolean networks, their properties are fairly well understood. While Boolean networks can do amazing things such as form the World Wide Web, build your body, and create your mind, they are in fact simple creatures at heart. Basically, three variables guide the behavior of such networks. The first is the number of nodes in the network. The second is a measure of how much everything is connected to everything else. And the third is a measure of "bias" in the rules guiding the behavior of the nodes. Let's look at each of these in turn and their implications for economic and other types of organizations.

Big Is Beautiful: Informational Scale

The first important fact about Boolean networks is that the number of states a network can be in scales exponentially with the number of nodes. A network with 2 nodes can be in four, or 2^2, states: 00, 10, 01, and 11. Likewise, a network with 3 nodes can be in eight, or 2^3, states. This simple fact has an astounding consequence. If we have a network with *just 100 nodes,* and we click through each possible state of the network at the speed of the world's fastest supercomputer, it would take 568 million years to completely explore all the possible states.[19] Just add 5 more nodes to make 105, and we are beyond the lifetime of the universe. If we can't even fully explore these small networks, then there is no hope of ever exploring all the possible states of an Intel Pentium processor, or a human brain.[20] Only the most infinitesimally small fraction of the possible states will ever be visited. The positive side of this is that as a network grows in size, the amount of information it can capture, or the things it can do, also grows exponentially. Not only has Moore's law been growing raw processing power exponentially, but *what* that power can do has been growing exponentially.

Biology provides a good example of the power of network growth. Genomes can be thought of as massively complex chemical networks that switch genes on and off. Before starting the Human Genome Project, scientists estimated that the human genome had about 100,000 genes. When the mapping was complete, they were surprised to find that humans only have about 30,000 genes.[21] By comparison, the humble roundworm has about 19,000, or two-thirds the number of human genes. Humans are clearly more than 33 percent more complex than roundworms; how can a gloriously complex *Homo sapien* have only 33 percent more genes than a simple nematode? The answer may lie in the fact that our genes regulate the growth of our bodies in a Boolean network, and thus with a scant 10,000 more genes, the human genetic network can produce results that are vastly more complex than what the roundworm network can do.

The exponential growth in possible states creates a very powerful kind of economy of scale in any network of information-processing entities. Traditional economists have usually thought of economies of scale as a function relating cost and volume, for example, as the quantity of widgets produced rises, the cost per widget declines. The laws of Boolean networks, however, cause us to think of another kind of economy of scale. As the size of a Boolean network grows, the *potential for novelty* increases exponentially. A Boolean network with 10 nodes can be in 2^{10} possible states, while a Boolean network with 100 nodes can be in 2^{100} states. The space of possible states for a 100-node network is not merely ten times greater than that for a 10-node network; it is thirty orders of magnitude (10^{30}) greater. The jump from the 10 people who work at my local coffee shop to the 180,000 people who work at Boeing is only four orders of magnitude in terms of the number of employees, but the jump in complexity from making café lattes to making jumbo jets is many, many more orders of magnitude greater, just as a human is many more orders of magnitude complex than a roundworm. An organization the size of Boeing also has inherently more headroom for innovation in the future—the larger number of states in the Boeing organizational network means that there are more *potential* ways for Boeing to make a living than for my corner coffee shop.

If Traditional economies of scale were all there were to the economic growth story, then we would simply be making stone tools more cheaply today than we did 2 million years ago. But if we think of human organizations as a kind of Boolean network (admittedly, with far more states than *on* or *off*), then we can see that as organizations grow in size, the space of possible innovations unfolds exponentially. Human economic organizations have in fact been growing in size over time. In particular, jumps in organization size have corresponded with changes in technology. The development of settled agriculture enabled the creation of villages that were significantly larger than the hunter-gatherer bands, the previous unit of organization. Likewise, the Industrial Revolution resulted in the creation of large-scale factories and industrial cities, while the information revolution of the late twentieth century has enabled the creation of enormous global companies. In a virtuous circle, technology change enables larger units of economic cooperation, which in turn can leverage greater informational scale, which in turn creates more potential for future innovations. We will explore this theme further in part 3.

The mathematics of Boolean networks leaves us with a quandary, however. If large organizations have more headroom for innovation than do small organizations, then why does the mythos of business hold that small organizations out-innovate large ones? Why do the Silicon Valley Davids seem to regularly beat the big, corporate Goliaths?

Big Is Bad: Complexity Catastrophes

Network theory shows us another, darker side to size. There are important diseconomies of scale driven by the second control variable of Boolean networks: the degree of connectedness. You can imagine a network that is very sparsely connected, say, each node is only connected to one node on either side of it, as in our earlier string of Christmas tree lights. Or you can imagine a network that is very densely connected—say you had a thousand nodes and every node was wired to every other node. The number of connections per node has an important effect on the behavior of a network. Kauffman and his colleagues at the Santa Fe Institute have studied this relationship in depth.[22] One of their key findings derives from the simple observation that if a network has on average more than one connection per node, then as the number of nodes grows, the number of connections will scale exponentially with the number of nodes. This means that the number of interdependencies in the network grows faster than the network itself. This, then, is where the problems start to arise. As the number of interdependencies grows, changes in one part of the network are more likely to have ripple effects on other parts of the network. As the potential for these knock-on effects grows, the probability that a positive change in one part of the network will have a negative effect somewhere else also increases.

To illustrate, let's imagine you are the cofounder of a small start-up company with only two departments: product development and marketing. You run product development and have an idea for a new product. So you have a meeting to discuss your plan, the marketing department agrees to it, and you are ready to go—simple enough. Your new product is a success. Your company begins to grow, and you decide you need to create a finance department and a customer service department. However, like all start-ups, yours is a bit disorganized. None of the new groups talk to each other, but because you are one of the founders, they all talk to you. You now have another new product idea, so you have a meeting with marketing, a meeting with finance, and a meeting with customer service to ensure they all support the new offering. More complex than before, but not too bad. The total number of meetings only grew by the number of departments, which is to say, from one with your first product to three with the second.

But you are getting tired of being the communications hub, and so you tell each of the department heads that he or she should be regularly talking directly with the other heads, sharing information, and coordinating. Soon the e-mails are flying and the conference rooms are full of meetings—your initiative to improve communications is a success. You now have an idea for your third-generation product, but something bizarre has happened. You have your usual meeting with marketing, but now before you get the department's OK, the marketing managers say they have to check the impact on their budget, which was approved by finance. The finance folks say they can't approve your project until they get an estimate from customer service on the cost of the additional support needed. And customer service has to check with marketing to make sure its plans are consistent with the company's brand and pricing strategy. All of a sudden, you have gone from three meetings to ten (if all the permutations occur) even though the size of the company is the same. The sole reason for this is the increase in the density of communications connections. Imagine what would happen if the company continues to grow and keeps this same wiring, namely, the rule that everyone must talk to everyone else. If you added just one more department, say, a legal department, the number of meeting permutations would jump to twenty-five. With nothing but the best intentions—all you wanted to do was grow and have better communications—your company has created a bureaucratic quagmire.

You find something else curious about this meeting explosion. The decisions made in each meeting have become interlinked with each other such that small changes in one part of the organization lead to cascades of change throughout the network. Your plan causes marketing to need more budget, which finance takes from customer support, which then says you need to change the product to make it easier to support, which you incorporate into your plans, which then circles back to cause more changes in marketing, and so on. Likewise, delays in one part of the network can lead to widespread traffic jams. For example, legal holds up your product plans for review, which means marketing can't finalize its budget, which means finance can't tell customer service its budget, which means customer service doesn't know how many people they can hire, and so on.

This kind of interdependency in a network creates what Kauffman calls a *complexity catastrophe*. The effect occurs because as the network grows, and the number of interdependencies grows, the probability that a positive change in one part of the network will lead to a cascade resulting in a negative change somewhere else grows exponentially with the number of nodes. This in turn means that *densely connected networks become less adaptable as they grow*.

Complexity catastrophes help explain why bureaucracy seems to grow with the tenacity of weeds. Many companies go through bureaucracy-clearing exercises only to find it has sprung back a few years later. No one ever sits down to deliberately design a bureaucratic muddle. Instead, bureaucracy springs up as people just try to optimize their local patch of the network: finance is just trying to ensure that the numbers add up, legal wants to keep us out of jail, and marketing is trying to promote the brand. The problem isn't dumb people or evil intentions. Rather, network growth creates interdependencies, interdependencies create conflicting constraints, and conflicting constraints create slow decision making and, ultimately, bureaucratic gridlock.

Degrees of Possibility Versus Degrees of Freedom

We thus have two opposing forces at work in organizations: the informational economies of scale from node growth, and the diseconomies of scale from the buildup of conflicting constraints. Taken together, these opposing forces help us understand why big is both beautiful and bad: as an organization grows, its *degrees of possibility* increase exponentially while its *degrees of freedom* collapse exponentially.

Put simply, large organizations inherently have more attractive opportunities before them than small organizations do (the large can theoretically do everything the small can do, plus more). But reaching those future opportunities involves trade-offs, and the more densely connected the organizational network, the more painful those trade-offs will be. The politics of organizations are such that local pain in particular groups or departments is often sufficient to prevent the organization from moving to a new state, even if that state is more globally fit.

For example, for decades IBM used its size and global scale to dominate the computer industry, and thru the 1980s, it had the lion's share of the world's personal-computer business.[23] Yet, in 1984, a nineteen-year-old named Michael Dell, using $1,000 of capital saved from a teenage stamp-trading business, started a company that thirteen years later would eclipse IBM as the world's leading seller of PCs, and eventually cause IBM to exit the PC business and sell its operations to a Chinese company.

How could one of the world's greatest corporations, a company with billions of dollars in assets, with hundreds of thousands of talented employees around the world, and with Nobel Prize–winning technical research, lose out to a teenager with pocket money from his stamp collection? We can speculate that as Dell began eating into IBM's PC market share in the early 1990s, some smart person in IBM must have said, "Customers seem to like buying computers through the mail and Dell is growing fast—why don't we sell computers through the mail?" Selling computers through the mail was certainly not beyond the capabilities of IBM; it could buy boxes and bubble wrap and put things in the mail as well as anyone else. So why did the company wait until several years after Dell had passed it in market share to begin selling computers directly to its customers? The reason is that IBM fell prey to a complexity catastrophe.

At the time Dell got started, IBM sold significant quantities of PCs to consumers through retail channels and to corporate customers through their in-house sales force. If IBM had begun selling through the mail, it would have caused a revolt among both its retailers and its sales force, probably leading to an instant drop in sales. There were also undoubtedly questions about whether the cheap and cheerful direct-mail image was appropriate for IBM's blue-chip brand. In fact, such a change would have set off a chain reaction in IBM's entire business system, right from manufacturing to customer service. Although IBM executives probably realized at some point that Dell was a threat, and they surely would have liked to recapture Dell's share of the market, the interdependencies of IBM's business system meant that there were many opportunities for people to say no. The more interactions required to get something done, the higher the probability of a conflict or a constraint. The reality in most organizations is that if enough people say no, it won't happen. In the early days of the IBM–Dell battle, IBM had far more degrees of possibility than Dell. For example, IBM could have penetrated the corporate market with the direct-order model far faster than Dell did, but the older company had fewer degrees of freedom to take advantage of those opportunities.[24]

This tension between interdependencies and adaptability is a deep feature of networks and profoundly affects many types of systems. Software designers see it when a program becomes so complex that any enhancement or bug fix introduces five new bugs. Architects see it when a client asks them to move a wall just one foot, and it has knock-on effects that send the project's cost sky-high. Some biologists, such as Stuart Kauffman, believe that this tension creates upper limits on the complexity of organisms.[25] In economic organizations, there is a clear trade-off between the benefits of scale and the coordination costs and constraints created by complexity. The next question then is, what can be done about it?

Two Cheers for Hierarchy!

Network theory shows that organizations can take two actions. One is to reduce the density of connections, and the other is to increase the predictability of decision making. We will briefly look at each.

Thus far, we have been discussing networks in which the pattern of connections is the same for every node, say, three connections each. But what if we arranged the network in a hierarchy? Let's imagine that three worker nodes report into a manager node, three manager nodes report into an executive node, and so on. What happens then? The network has a different look to it and is a mixture of dense and sparse patches (figure 7-2). Kauffman argues that an effective way to increase adaptability and avoid conflicting constraints is to break things up.[26] Organizing the network into hierarchies reduces the density of connections and thus reduces the interdependencies in the network. Hierarchies are critical in enabling networks to reach larger sizes before diseconomies of scale set in. This is why so many networks in the natural and computer worlds are structured as networks within networks.

In an organizational context, the conventional wisdom is that hierarchy is a feature of bureaucracy that reduces adaptability. Managers are told that they should de-layer and flatten their organizations. But counterintuitively, hierarchy can serve to increase adaptability by reducing interdependencies and enabling an organization to reach a larger size before gridlock sets in.[27] A simple example will illustrate. The hierarchical structure in figure 7-2 has forty nodes (we'll think of them as people). Let's imagine that the organization has to make a decision and we need to "get everyone on board." If we imagine an extreme case with no hierarchy at all, then everyone would have to meet with everyone else—that would mean sixteen hundred meetings. But in the hierarchical structure in the figure, we can assume that each team of peers meets with their boss, agrees, and then kicks its decision up to the next level, who then meet, kick the decision up to the next level, and so on.

FIGURE 7-2

Dense Versus Hierarchical Networks

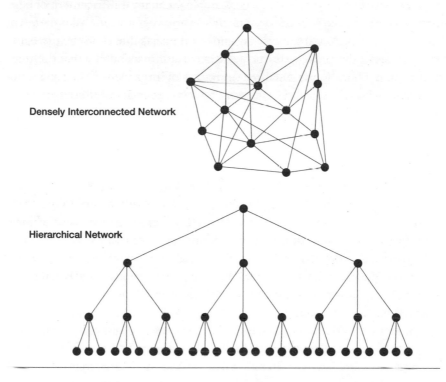

Densely Interconnected Network

Hierarchical Network

Thus, we have nine meetings at the bottom level, three at the middle layer, and then a last meeting with the CEO—thirteen meetings in total versus sixteen hundred. Who would have thought that hierarchy actually saves meetings? Hierarchy does, of course, have its problems; for example, information can degrade as it travels up the chain, the top may become out of touch with the front line, and a poor performer in a senior role can do a lot of damage. But just assuming that hierarchy is inherently bad is simplistic and misses its crucial role as an interdependency breaker.

A related move is to give the units within a hierarchical structure more autonomy. This was one of Alfred P. Sloan's great insights when he invented the concept of autonomous divisions, enabling General Motors to grow to become, at the time, the largest company in the world. Sloan essentially created five car companies within a car company, each with its own brand and a high degree of independence. The move by many companies in the 1980s and 1990s to more autonomous business units with their own profit-and-loss accountability was to a large degree a response to the complexity that came with organizational growth.

Finally, it may make sense to give units the ultimate measure of autonomy by spinning them off or breaking up the corporation. When private equity firms buy out the divisions of large companies, there is often a step-change improvement in the performance of the business. Much of this is certainly due to the incentives and stock ownership given management. But at least some of the effect is likely due to the removal of constraints and increased degrees of freedom. Likewise, we often see the reverse when a high-performing small company is bought by a large company, which then proceeds to smother it in constraints.

Boring Is Better

When Kauffman and his colleagues did their original work, they found that nonhierarchical networks exhibit spontaneous order with one or two average connections per node, but went into chaos (thus creating cascades of change and the potential for a complexity catastrophe) at four connections per node or more.[28] Subsequently, two physicists at the École Normale Supérieure in Paris, Bernard Derrida and Gerard Weisbuch, discovered a parameter that could change the point at which this phase transition takes place.[29] They called the parameter *bias*.

Recall that inside each of our Boolean Christmas tree lights, there is a rule that transforms inputs received from neighboring lights into an output. For example, if A and B are off, then C will be off, too. Let's now imagine that we do not know what the rules inside any of the bulbs are—each bulb is a black box. Nonetheless, we can study the behavior of individual bulbs by feeding them inputs and then observing their outputs. Let's say we pick a bulb and start feeding it 1s and 0s at random. Our input stream will thus be approximately 50 percent 1s and 50 percent 0s. If the output stream was also fifty-fifty 1s and 0s, then we could say that the output was *unbiased*, but if the output was say 90 percent 1s, then we could say it was *biased* toward 1, or likewise, if 90 percent 0s, then biased toward 0. We know that the output the bulb produces is calculated by applying a deterministic rule to the input, so a low bias (fifty-fifty output) does not imply that the bulb is behaving randomly; it merely implies that the mystery decision rule is equally likely to produce a 1 or a 0. From the viewpoint of an outsider who does not know what the rule is, the behavior of a low-bias node is difficult to predict, while a high-bias node is easier to predict.

Derrida and Weisbuch found that the higher the bias, the more densely connected a network can be before the transition to chaos occurs. If the average bias is fifty-fifty, then the transition to chaos happens in the range between two and four average connections per node, as it did in Kauffman's study. If the average bias is closer to 75 percent, then the transition happens above four connections per node. At higher bias levels, the network can go up to six connections per node before it trips into chaos. The key point is, *the more regularity there is in the behavior of the nodes, the more density in connections the network can tolerate.*

In an organizational context, we can think of bias as being a measure of predictability. If there is predictability in the decision making of an organization (the equivalent of the light bulbs' rules), then the organization can function effectively with a more densely connected network. If, however, decision making is less predictable, then less-dense connections, more hierarchy, and smaller spans of control are needed. Thus, for example, in an army, where regular, predictable behavior of troops is highly valued, it might be possible to get away with larger unit sizes than, say, in a creative advertising agency. It also means that factors that make behavior less predictable, such as office politics and emotions, can limit the size an organization can grow to before being overwhelmed by complexity. One can see a recipe for creating a dysfunctional organization: just mix unpredictable behavior, a flat hierarchy, and lots of dense interconnections—the chances of getting anything done would be roughly zero.

The Edge of Order

The work by Kauffman and the others leads to a counterintuitive insight. IBM's problem with Dell was not that the blue chip company was insensitive to change, but rather that it was *too sensitive* to change. The dense interconnections and tangles of interaction in IBM's business system meant that small changes ("let's sell computers by mail") could cascade into big problems ("here are the thousand reasons why we cannot sell computers by mail").

This illustrates one of the dangers of interpreting complexity theory at a merely metaphorical level. Many popular management books and articles have been written about the "edge of chaos." This is the boundary between order and chaos, where it is claimed that nature is at its most adaptable. The popular interpretation of this idea is that companies fail to adapt because they are stuck too far in the ordered regime and thus need to let a bit more chaos into their organizations to spur further innovation. While this sounds appealing, the correct interpretation of the science is actually more subtle and leads to different implications.

To understand this, let's go back to Kauffman's network of blinking light bulbs. In Kauffman's studies, if each light bulb had on average just two connections to another lightbulb, then the network's behavior was quite orderly— small changes would not lead to any big changes in the pattern of blinking lights. When he connected each bulb to four other bulbs, however, the behavior was quite different. A small change in one part of the network (say we slightly modify one of the switching rules governing a bulb's behavior) led to cascades of change and made it impossible to predict the patterns of lights. In an organizational context, it is these cascades of change that then run into conflicting constraints.[30] Moving from two to four connections per bulb, there was a sudden phase transition between the network's being rigid and insensitive to change and its becoming chaotic and overly sensitive to change. For reasons we will look at more closely later in the book, evolutionary systems work best when their sensitivity to change is in a medium, in-between range. If an evolutionary system is too insensitive to change, then the system will not be able to keep up with the pace of change in its environment. However, if a system is overly sensitive to change, then small changes can have large consequences. This oversensitivity is a problem because if a system has been successful in the past, then few major changes are likely to improve it. Rather, the odds are that the vast majority of possible major changes will harm it.

Kauffman found that when each bulb in the Boolean network had on average between two and four connections, the system went into a highly adaptable, in-between state. In this state, the system was generally orderly, with large islands of structure, but vibrant percolating disorder around the edges of the structures. Small mutations in the switching rules of the system generally led to small changes in outcomes, but occasionally, a small change would set off larger cascades of change, which sometimes degraded the performance of the system, but sometimes led to improvements. Although this particular network was highly adaptive, Kauffman was troubled by the observation that two to four connections per node was still pretty sparsely connected, by the standards of most networks in nature or in human organizations.

If we combine Kauffman's original result with the later results on hierarchy and bias, however, the phase transition shifts to the range of six to nine nodes. Interestingly, the numbers that come out of the analysis of Boolean networks are quite close to what we typically see for the size of effective working groups in human organizations.[31] For example, company boards and executive committees often have five to eight members under a Chairman or CEO. The United States Supreme Court has eight associate justices and a chief justice, while the European Union's executive has five vice presidents and a president. Some anthropologists have speculated that these typical group structures and sizes come from our long evolutionary heritage as hunter-gatherers, and that such group sizes made for effective hunting bands. Evolution tends to be quite efficient over time at finding balances between trade-offs.

So it is likely that these typical working group sizes evolved because they represented a balance between the benefits of scale (a hunting band can get more food per calories expended than a lone individual can), and the diseconomies of complexity. Our ancestors would not have survived for long if hunting groups of thirty people spent hours debating whether they should hunt bison or antelope that day.

CHAPTER EIGHT

Emergence

THE PUZZLE OF PATTERNS

AROUND THE YEAR 1315, the English economy went into a state of free fall.[1] After two bad harvests in a row due to poor weather, the price of a bushel of wheat rocketed eightfold, from five shillings to forty shillings. The rising price of wheat meant that millers could not afford grain for milling, and bakers could not afford flour for baking. Farmers could not afford to feed their livestock, which then sickened and died. The loss of livestock meant fields went unplowed, causing further shortages. As the food supply collapsed, the peasantry became desperate and began feeding off cats, rats, insects, trees, anything they could find. As the peasants starved, the collapse spread to the merchant sector, with carpenters and seamstresses going under as well. The aristocracy was not immune, and even the court of King Edward II found it difficult to procure food. The slide in the English economy soon began to spread to the continent, and depression set in from Paris to Utrecht.

Depressions, recessions, and inflation are not exclusively modern phenomena; they are patterns that have recurred since the beginning of recorded history.[2] There are other patterns in economics that are equally old, including the long-run growth in wealth per person discussed in chapter 1, and the distribution of wealth discussed in chapter 4. For these patterns to be so old, they must be the result of causes that are deep in the workings of economies, causes that are independent of the technologies, government policies, or business practices of a particular age.

When one looks at graphs of economic time-series data, whether it is output, unemployment, or inflation, one notices that the data is very noisy—the lines wiggle all over the place. But despite the noisy wiggles, there are patterns in the data. For example, figure 8-1 shows an index created by David

161

FIGURE 8-1

The Price of Consumables in England, 1201–1993

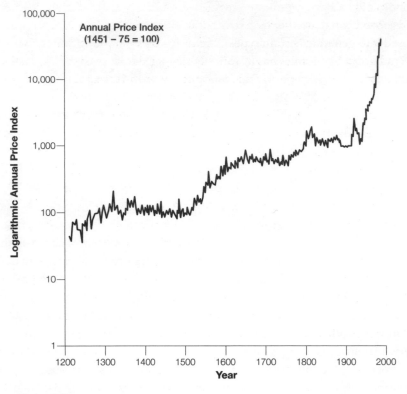

Source: Fischer (1996).

Hackett Fisher of Brandeis University that provides a picture of price inflation in England over almost eight hundred years, from 1201 to 1993. One can
clearly see multiple patterns in the data. First, one notices a long-term growth
trend (the graph is logarithmic, so the growth is actually an exponential curve);
then layered on top of that growth are three humps or waves each lasting a
few hundred years and then lots of shorter up and down cycles each lasting
just a few years. The data in the graph is neither perfectly regular, nor perfectly random.

Other time series have a similar not-quite-regular, not-quite-random character to them. For example, the ups and downs of the U.S. business cycle
exhibit a clear oscillatory pattern, but the frequency of the oscillations ranges
from as little as eighteen months to as long as nine years, and the amplitude
ranges from mild slowdowns to deep depressions.[3] Economists have had

very little success in trying to use the irregular historical patterns in economic data to predict the behavior of the economy in the future. We thus have two questions that economics needs to explain. First, why do patterns in economic data have a not-quite-regular, not-quite-random quality to them? And second, what are the deep structural features of the economy that have caused it to generate certain types of patterns over very long periods?

Traditional Economics has historically struggled to answer these questions. As discussed earlier, economics is split into two halves: microeconomics and macroeconomics. Microeconomics is the bottom-up view of the economy and starts with individual decision makers and then builds up to markets and economies. Macroeconomics is the top-down view that starts with questions such as why there is unemployment and then drills down to find an answer. Thus far, we have mostly been concerned with microeconomic issues, but in this chapter, we will step up to the macro level. Most economists agree that ideally, there should not be a separate microeconomics and macroeconomics. One should be able to start with micro behaviors and work up, or with macro patterns and work down, and be able to use either approach seamlessly within one theory. Although the two halves of the field share many ideas, techniques, and the overall Traditional equilibrium framework, they unfortunately have yet to achieve that aspiration. Like the two teams that built the transcontinental railroad across the United States in the nineteenth century, microeconomists and macroeconomists have been working toward each other from different sides of the field. Unfortunately, after a century of laying tracks, they have failed to meet in the middle. We will briefly look at what each side of the micro-macro split has to say about the puzzle of patterns, and then look at the issues from a Complexity Economics perspective.

Are Business Cycles Like Wiggling Jelly?

A phenomenon such as the oscillations of the business cycle presents a basic challenge to Traditional micro theory. As discussed, the Neoclassical equilibrium model does not dance, wiggle, or otherwise oscillate of its own accord. The model has to be livened up with exogenous shocks. In this way, the equilibrium model acts as a *propagation mechanism*.[4] We input a shock into the model, which propagates the shock and then produces an output pattern. To picture this, imagine you have a big mound of grape jelly on a plate. You start randomly tapping the jelly mound with a spoon and observe what happens. The taps are propagated through the jelly and come out the other side, causing the jelly to wiggle and jiggle. We can think of the taps as exogenous inputs and the wiggling at the other side as the pattern of output. In the Traditional Economics literature, models that work this way are known as *real business cycle* models. These models were pioneered by Fynn Kydland and Edward Prescott in the 1980s.[5]

There is a problem, however, with the Traditional wiggling-jelly model. Traditional theory usually portrays the exogenous inputs as random (or at least not having a pattern that can be forecast). But if the input to the jelly is truly random, then the output will be random as well. The signal might be transformed in some way by the propagation mechanism, but the output will still be random. Imagine you make graphs of both your input spoon taps and the output wiggles of the jelly. The output wiggles won't exactly match the input taps, because the jelly adds time delays to the taps (i.e., it takes a while for the tap to propagate through the jelly) and it may add oscillations (i.e., one tap may yield three or four wiggles). However, while the output wiggling might look different from the input tapping, it is still random. The jelly alone cannot take a random, disordered input stream and add complex order to it.[6] The jelly is an equilibrium system; if you stop tapping, it will eventually settle down and stop moving. The only way for the jelly to produce truly ordered wiggles is if the input tapping is ordered as well. For example, if you tapped the Morse code for "SOS" into the jelly (three quick taps, three long taps, three quick taps), the output wiggles would no longer be random, but would have the structure of the SOS signal in them.

Thus, the real business cycle approach of microeconomics has a problem. One can input random data, in which case the output doesn't look like much like the real world. Or, one can input data that has structure to it, and the model then adds some effects making the output have the not-quite-regular, not-quite-random character of real data. But in this latter case, one is not really explaining the causes of the cycles, just shifting the explanation to exogenous factors.[7]

We're All (New) Keynesians Now

If we go to the other side, where the macroeconomists have been working away, we see a different approach. They have to start with the data and then try to come up with an explanation. Throughout the history of macroeconomic theory, the only way that macroeconomists could credibly explain the not-quite-regular, not-quite-random character of the economy has been to back away from the orthodoxy of Traditional microeconomics. Thus, they have had to lay their train tracks in a somewhat different direction.

The departure from the rational-equilibrium fold took perhaps its most important turn when John Maynard Keynes wrote his *General Theory of Employment, Interest and Money* in 1936. During the 1930s, Keynes witnessed one of the most tragic disequilibrium events of modern times, the Great

Depression.[8] Since Neoclassical microeconomic theory held that an economy in equilibrium was one with full employment, clearly a story had to be developed that could explain how the economy could so significantly depart from this condition, and what might be done to hasten its return. The story that Keynes developed, his General Theory, was a dynamic story.[9]

Let's say that for some reason people in the economy get nervous—for example, there might be a source of political uncertainty, a natural disaster, or a war. Consumers and businesspeople then start to become more conservative, spend less, and hold on to more cash. As there is a fixed amount of cash in the economy at any one point in time, these behaviors take money out of circulation. This means less income for the farmers, manufacturers, shopkeepers, and other producers, who then get nervous and start spending and investing less themselves, which takes away money from someone else, and so on. Eventually the drop in spending and investment causes people to lose their jobs, which leads to further nervousness and even less spending. This then creates an accelerating downward spiral of falling spending and investment, rising unemployment, and increasing anxiety among consumers and businesspeople.

Equilibrium economics says that such a contraction in the money supply eventually should self-correct—prices and wages should drop to reflect less money in circulation, and eventually everything should get back to normal full-employment equilibrium. In the Great Depression, prices and wages did indeed drop, but this deflation caused people to spend even less (in a deflationary environment your money is worth more in the future, so it is best to hang on to it), further exacerbating the downward spiral. Keynes argued that these dynamics could cause economies to get stuck out of equilibrium for very long periods. So to knock the economy back to full employment, Keynes advocated that the government play a role by injecting money into the system. This injection of money causes spending to stop dropping, unemployment to stop rising, and confidence to return, reversing the vicious downward cycle into a virtuous upward cycle.

Keynes's ideas were widely accepted by Western governments in the postwar years, but remained controversial in economic circles in the decades that followed. The debate came to a head in the 1960s and 1970s, when Milton Friedman argued that the kind of government spending Keynes advocated would not lead to long-term growth, but only to higher inflation. Friedman's arguments took on particular poignancy during the high-inflation, low-growth years of the 1970s. Then Friedman's University of Chicago colleague Robert Lucas made the argument that even if one acknowledged the dynamics of Keynes's story, if people were perfectly rational, they would understand what was going on, figure out that the economy was in a downward spiral, adjust their behavior accordingly, and thus return the economy to full-employment equilibrium. In addition, perfectly rational consumers and producers would see through any government attempt to intervene, anticipate the government's actions, and act in ways that would negate the effects of the policies. Government intervention would not only fail to prevent recessions, but was likely to just make things worse. Lucas's theory was mathematically brilliant, and he was awarded a Nobel Prize in 1995, but its extra-strong version of rationality stretched the credulity of even many Traditional economists.

Following Lucas's work, George Akerlof, a professor at the University of California at Berkeley and cowinner of the 2001 Nobel Prize, built on Herbert Simon's ideas to suggest that it actually might not be rational for people to try to estimate the future government budget deficit as they purchase tomatoes in the supermarket. Collecting and processing such information would simply be too costly and time-consuming to be worth it. Although Akerlof did not build the kind of inductively rational model we saw earlier, he did show that even if consumers and producers were a little bit less than perfectly rational (regardless of precisely how they made their decisions), then that would be enough to set off the Keynesian dynamics, sending the economy spiraling into a recession.[10] Akerlof also acknowledged that time delays play an important role in the dynamics of the economy, particularly the "stickiness" of prices and wages and their inability to adjust instantaneously. His model showed that the government could play a constructive role in counteracting this spiral by increasing liquidity in the market. Akerlof's work was synthesized with the work of figures such as Edmund Phelps, Olivier Blanchard, and Gregory Mankiw, to become what is now called New Keynesian economics.[11] While New Keynesian economics remains somewhat controversial among economic theoreticians, in the practical worlds of government and Wall Street, people generally accept that government management of factors such as interest rates and budget deficits do have an impact on economic performance.

At the beginning of the twenty-first century, Traditional Economics thus offers us two competing hypotheses to explain the oscillating patterns we see in the economy.[12] On one side we have the microeconomics-based real business cycle theory, which holds on to the rational-equilibrium view and sees the economy as merely propagating external shocks. Under this theory, the key causes of economic oscillations are exogenous political events, changes in technology, and other factors. But such models cannot tell us why the cycles have been so persistent throughout history, despite enormous changes in the exogenous factors posited as causes. On the other side of the tracks, we have the macroeconomics-based New Keynesianism. This body of work has backed away from Traditional orthodoxy and incorporated less-than-perfect rationality, dynamics, and time delays in order to find endogenous explanations. In many ways, New Keynesianism is a step in the Complexity Economics direction, but the New Keynesians have not been prepared to abandon equilibrium, and as a result, the empirical success of the theory has thus far been limited.[13]

"More Is Different"

We have previously discussed how the micro-level interactions of agents in a complex adaptive system create macro-level structures and patterns. We saw, for example, how the interactions of even the very simple agents in Sugarscape could give rise to patterns such as economic growth and income inequality. The ultimate accomplishment of Complexity Economics would be to develop a theory that takes us from theories of agents, networks, and evolution, all the way up to the macro patterns we see in real-world economies. Such a comprehensive theory does not yet exist, but we can begin to see glimmers of what it might look like.

Such a theory would view macroeconomic patterns as *emergent* phenomena, that is, characteristics of the system as a whole that arise endogenously out of interactions of agents and their environment.[14] We have touched on emergence briefly in previous chapters, but the concept probably still has a somewhat mystical feel to it. How can something be more than the sum of its parts? Or as the physicist Phil Anderson put it so well, "Why is more different?"[15]

Emergence may seem mysterious, but it is actually something that we experience every day. For example, a single water molecule of two hydrogen atoms and an oxygen atom does not feel wet (assuming you could feel a single molecule). But a few billion water molecules in a cup feel wet. That is because wetness is a collective property of the slippery interactions between water molecules in a particular temperature range. If we lower the temperature of the water, the molecules interact in a different way, forming the crystal structure of ice, losing its emergent characteristic of wetness and taking on the characteristic of hard. Similarly, what we call a symphony is a pattern of sound that emerges out of the playing of individual instruments, and what we call a kidney is a pattern of cells working together to provide a higher-level function that none of the cells could do on its own.[16]

Complexity Economics likewise views economic patterns such as business cycles, growth, and inflation as emergent phenomena arising endogenously out of the interactions in the system. Complex adaptive systems tend to have signature emergent patterns that are common across many types of systems. These patterns help us better understand the workings of those systems. We will look at three such signature patterns: oscillations, punctuated equilibrium, and power laws.

Oscillations: Boom and Bust in Beer World

A pendulum swinging back and forth, the vibrations of a guitar string, and your heartbeat are all examples of oscillatory systems. As we have discussed, economies also oscillate with the ups and downs of the economy-wide business cycle, the industry-level commodity cycles discussed in chapter 5, and perhaps longer-term waves of change as well.[17] Why do these oscillations exist, and why have they been so persistent throughout history?

Oscillations are a common feature in complex adaptive systems. For example, populations in biological ecosystems go through patterns of oscillation. In the early twentieth century, a Ukrainian chemist, Alfred Lotka, and an Italian mathematician, Vito Volterra, built a famous model to describe the oscillations created by the interactions between predators and prey.[18] If we imagine a population of foxes and rabbits, the Lotka-Volterra model shows how as the population of rabbits grows, the foxes eat more rabbits, causing the fox population to rise and the rabbit population to fall. This decline in rabbits in turn leads to less food per fox, and eventually the fox population falls, allowing the rabbit population to rise again, thus creating oscillations of fox and rabbit populations. This dynamic system never settles but oscillates ad infinitum. In Lotka and Volterra's model, there are no exogenous shocks driving the oscillations. The ups and downs emerge from the structure of the system itself rather than from any outside source.

So how might the structure of an economic system generate endogenous oscillations? In fact, it is not very difficult to get economic systems to endogenously oscillate; all one needs is a few undergraduate students and some imaginary cases of beer. In the 1950s, Jay Forrester of MIT invented a game called the Beer Distribution Game, which demonstrates how a combination of human behavior and dynamic structure can interact to produce oscillations in a simple economic system.[19]

Four volunteers are asked to play a game simulating the manufacture and distribution of a commodity. It could be any commodity, but to make it more fun for his students, Forrester chose beer. One person plays the role of the brewer, another is the beer distributor, another the wholesaler, and another the retailer. This supply chain of manufacturer, distributor, wholesaler, and retailer is, of course, common to many industries. In the game there is no person playing the beer consumer, rather consumer demand is provided by a stack of cards lying facedown next to the retailer.

The game is played as follows. Each participant has an inventory of cases of beer (represented by chips on the game board). At the beginning of each turn, the retailer turns over one card from the deck to get the order from the consumers (e.g., four cases) and then submits an order to the wholesaler. The wholesaler looks at his or her orders from the retailer and submits an order to the distributor, who in turn submits an order to the brewer. Once everyone gets his or her orders, the player then fills them by shipping cases of beer. The brewer ships to the distributor, who ships to the wholesaler, who ships to the retailer, who sells it to the consumers. Thus, orders flow up the supply chain from consumer to brewer, and beer flows back down in reverse. Once orders have been submitted and beer shipped, the next round starts.

Players incur costs of $0.50 per case for holding inventory (e.g., the cost of storing and securing the beer), and costs of $1.00 per case for running out of beer (e.g., angry customers and lost sales). Therefore, the players want to hold just enough inventory to meet their orders without running out. Given the asymmetry in costs, though, players will tend to err on the side of having a bit of extra inventory. The winner of the game is the one who incurs the lowest cost. This sounds easy, but there are a few twists. As in real life, there is a time delay between ordering the beer and when it is actually received; you can imagine that it takes some time to produce the beer and ship it on trucks. Likewise, there is a small delay between when orders are submitted and when they are processed; you can imagine this as representing the time it takes for someone to receive the order, enter it in the computer system, do a credit check, and so on. Finally, no communications are allowed between the players other than through the orders. Thus, the brewer doesn't know what the customer demand is down at the retailer's end; all he or she sees are the orders coming from the distributor.

These time delays make things a bit tricky. Let's say you are the distributor, and you get a big order from the wholesaler, which causes your inventory to take a sudden drop. You then put in a big order with the manufacturer to replace your stock, but it will take several turns to receive the beer, and what happens if there is another big order in the meantime? Should you make your order even larger in anticipation of continued high demand next turn? But what if it is just a temporary blip? Then you might be flooded with beer two turns later. Humans don't do well when there is a time delay between their actions and the response to those actions—just remember chapter 5's example of your oscillating between scorching and freezing while you try to get the water temperature right in an unfamiliar shower.

The game starts out in equilibrium, with each player getting an order for four cases of beer and shipping exactly that many. The delivery pipeline also starts full, so each player receives exactly four cases of beer during the first turn, thus keeping inventory levels across the supply chain constant. From then on, the players are on their own and must make decisions on how much to order. Unbeknownst to the participants, the first several cards in the consumer deck remain at four. Some players may order a bit more or a bit less than four, depending on how risk averse they are. Otherwise, not much happens. Then, suddenly, on one turn, the consumer-order card jumps from four to eight. The players do not know it, but the customer-order level will stay at eight for the rest of the game; it is a onetime step-up in orders. This step-up in orders, however, sends a perturbation down the supply chain. According to Traditional Economics, this exogenous shock in demand should simply cause the players to move to a new equilibrium after a few turns of adjustment, with everyone ordering eight, and everyone's inventories staying constant once the new equilibrium is reached.

In experiments with real people, however, the players inevitably overreact to the jump in demand by over-ordering as their inventory falls. As this wave of over-ordering travels up the supply chain, it is amplified. Perhaps the retailer, surprised by the jump from four to eight, needs to restock inventory and orders twelve. Then the wholesaler, seeing her orders jump to twelve, orders sixteen, and so on. In addition to overreacting, the participants don't properly account for the delay between ordering and receiving beer. So the retailer might have ordered twelve cases last period, but they haven't arrived yet and the inventory is running out, so he orders twelve more. The inevitable consequence of this is that large amounts of beer eventually start flowing back down the supply chain and everyone gets swamped with inventory. The overreaction cycle swings the other way, and players drastically cut their orders, some even to zero. Thus oscillating waves of over-ordering and under-ordering wash up and down the supply chain, and our imaginary beer industry incurs very costly cycles of boom and bust (figure 8-2).

MIT professor John Sterman and others have conducted the Beer Game experiment hundreds of times with people from all around the world, including MBA students, businesspeople, and people selected at random.[20] They have even tried it with professional inventory managers and highly rational economists. Yet the result is always the same—wild oscillations.[21] Traditional Economic theory says that if the players were perfectly rational

FIGURE 8-2

Typical Results from the Beer Game

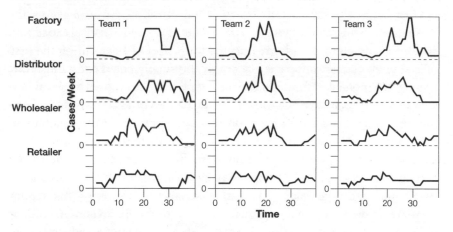

Source: Sterman (2000).

(in the game they have all the needed information to be perfectly rational), the wild oscillations should not occur; the game should just step neatly from one equilibrium to another. If one calculates the costs generated in the experiments versus those in the theoretically rational case, the costs generated by the real humans are on average *ten times* the perfectly rational costs.

Just what kind of behavior leads to such wild oscillations in a relatively simple environment? Sterman has been able to statistically derive the decision rule used by the participants.[22] This rule is based on a behavior known in the psychology literature as *anchor and adjust.* Rather than deductively calculate their future beer needs by looking at all the inventory on the board (which they can see) and incorporating the effects of the time delays and so on, the participants simply look at the past pattern of orders and inventory levels, and inductively anchor on a pattern that seems normal. Their IF THEN rules consequently try to steer them to maintain that normal pattern. Thus, a participant might anchor on four cases as the normal pattern of orders and then struggle to adjust when things are not normal, for example, "My inventory is dropping, order more!" In an environment with time delays, the anchor-and-adjust rule causes individuals to both overshoot and undershoot, which in turn leads to the emergent pattern of cyclical behavior.

The Beer Game is not a mere wiggling-jelly propagation mechanism. The game receives a single exogenous shock—the increase in orders from four to eight. But unlike a jelly given a single tap, once the oscillations start in the Beer Game, the system never returns to equilibrium.[23] This is because the ultimate source of the oscillations in the Beer Game is *not* the exogenous shock itself (it just gets things started), but the behavior of the participants and the feedback structure of the system. The system is not propagating exogenous dynamics; it is endogenously creating them.

The point of this example is not simply to put another arrow in the chest of perfect rationality (although it does a nice job), but rather to show how the vagaries of individual behavior at the micro level can lead to big, emergent consequences at the macro level—in this case, how the anchor-and-adjust rule leads to oscillations. One can reasonably ask whether the gyrations of the macroeconomy are the result of something like a vastly more complex version of the Beer Game. The economy is, after all, chock full of supply chains, inventories, and time delays. The actual causes of macroeconomic oscillations are no doubt multifarious, but the lesson of the Beer Game is that the causes of the cycles may ultimately lie in the way in which the inductive rules people use in their decision making interact with the dynamic structure of the economic system.

If the economy is something like a giant Beer Game, then one implication is that the standard solutions of interest-rate cuts and increased government spending do not address the root causes of the cycle; they merely address the symptoms. We may never be able to eliminate business cycles entirely (and in fact we might not want to, as periodic contractions flush out inefficient uses of resources and spur innovation), but if governments wanted to attenuate cyclical effects in a more fundamental way, then they would need to look at the structure of the economic system itself.

There is evidence, in fact, that the dynamic structure of the economy is changing, even without explicit government intervention. There are two ways to dampen the cycles in the Beer Game: one is to reduce the time delays, and the other is to give the participants more information (e.g., giving the brewer direct visibility into what is happening at the retail level).[24] The information technology revolution that began in the 1960s has directly affected both factors. Data shows that the volatility of the U.S. business cycle has been dampening since 1959, with a particularly sharp reduction beginning in the 1980s that coincided with the widespread adoption of fast, cheap computers.[25] Computers have enabled companies to speed order processing, adopt just-in-time inventory practices, and electronically link producers with their supply chains. There is some debate about how much of the reduced volatility is attributable to these changes in technology and business practices, versus other factors.[26] But it is clear that the macroeconomic Beer Game has been changing.[27]

Punctuated Equilibrium: Are There "Keystone" Technologies?

Over the century that followed the publication of Darwin's *Origin of Species,* biologists assumed that evolution proceeded in a stately and relatively linear fashion, leading to a smooth pattern of speciation and extinction. Then, in a landmark paper in 1972, the paleontologists Niles Eldredge and Stephen Jay Gould overturned this conventional wisdom and argued that the fossil record shows that biological evolution has not followed a smooth path.[28] Rather, it has gone through long periods of relative stasis interspersed with periods of explosive innovation and periods of massive extinction. For example, during the Cambrian period about 550 million years ago, a burst of evolutionary innovation saw the takeover of the earth by multicellular life and the creation of most of the major phyla on earth today. Then, about 245 million years ago, during the late Permian period, there was what Gould called "the grand-daddy of all extinctions"; when 96 percent of all marine species on earth disappeared.[29] Gould coined the term *punctuated equilibrium* to describe this pattern of alternating calm and storm (the term is not quite technically correct as biological evolution is never in a mathematical sense truly in equilibrium; Gould himself notes that what he intended to convey with the term was periods of quiescence or stasis interspersed with periods of change, but the phrase punctuated equilibrium has stuck, so we will use it).[30]

Patterns of punctuated equilibrium show up not just in biological evolution, but in other complex systems ranging from the slides of avalanches to the crashes of stock markets.[31] Complexity researchers have been studying these patterns and their origins since the 1980s. One of the conclusions of this research is that an important contributor to this behavior is the network structure of the interactions in the system. As discussed in chapter 7, work by Duncan Watts and Mark Newman of the Santa Fe Institute has shown that many types of networks self-organize into a structure that has a mixture of very dense connections and very sparse connections.[32] Sanjay Jain, a researcher at the Indian Institute of Science, and his colleague Sandeep Krishna of the Nehru Centre believe that it is just such a network structure that underlies the emergence of punctuated equilibrium in biological ecosystems.[33]

Jain and Krishna created a simulation of an evolving ecosystem of computer creatures. The researchers found that if they randomly removed "species" from their simulated ecosystem, typically not much happened. Yet, once in a while, removing a random species would set off a cascade of events leading to a mass extinction. Certain species are very densely connected to other species in the web of food relationships and niche competition. Biologists call these *keystone species.* For example, one might imagine a species of amoeba that was a source of food for various insects and filter-feeding worms, which in turn were food for a variety of birds and mammals, which in turn also had an impact on various plant species, and so on. A sudden drop in the amoeba population at the bottom of this food chain could radiate widely throughout the ecosystem.

In their ecosystem simulations, Jain and Krishna noted three distinct phases to the punctuated equilibrium pattern. First, in a *random phase*, the network percolates along without much structure, and random changes occur without much effect—this is a period of "equilibrium" in the punctuated equilibrium pattern. Then, an innovation sends the network suddenly into a *growth phase*. The innovations that trigger these phases tend to catalyze other innovations in a positive feedback loop whereby innovation leads to further innovation. As new species arise and take their place in the ecosystem, they create an ordering of the food and niche network. The growth phase eventually flattens out and then is followed by an *organized phase*. In this phase, the changes are consolidated, the network is highly structured, and keystone species appear at critical points in the interaction web—like hub cities in an airline route map. The network continues to bubble along for a while in the organized phase (another period of "equilibrium"), but then an innovation or a random change hits a keystone species. Changes influencing the keystone species radiate into the structure, and the network crashes in a wave of extinction. The process then begins again with a new random phase, leading to a growth phase.

Many observers, not the least of whom include Karl Marx and Joseph Schumpeter, have noted that technological innovation proceeds in similar patterns of calm and storm.[34] Most technological innovations have a limited impact. In 1957, for example, General Electric invented the quartz halogen lamp. The technology eventually became cheap enough in the 1980s that halogen lighting became a popular consumer item. Halogen lights were an important improvement over standard incandescent bulbs, but nonetheless, one cannot say they have had a dramatic impact on society.

Contrast this with another invention that was also initially an incremental improvement over a predecessor technology. In December 1901, Guglielmo Marconi sent three Morse code clicks via radio waves from Cornwall, England, across the Atlantic to Newfoundland. Marconi's invention was meant to be nothing more than a cheaper, more convenient alternative to wired telegraphy, and not many people at the time were impressed with his invention. The Anglo-American Cable Company, quoted in the *Financial Times*, was dismissive of the new technology: "the possibilities of wireless telegraphy commercially are so remote that we look forward to the future without alarm."[35] The rest, as they say, is history. The radio had an enormous impact on its own, but also in turn led to the invention of television, microwave communications, radar, the mobile phone, and, now, wireless Internet access. Marconi's invention created an avalanche of change that has dramatically reshaped popular culture, entertainment, politics, and even military strategy.

Over the years, there has been a great deal of study of technology development as an evolutionary process.[36] This is a topic we will return to in chapter 11. But two key observations from this work are relevant to the discussion of punctuated equilibrium. The first is that no technology is developed in isolation. All technologies depend on a web of relationships with other technologies; the invention of the mobile phone, for example, drew not only on radio technology, but on many other areas, such as computer technology and coding technology.[37] These interrelationships are not just technological, but economic. The economic web that has grown around the automobile, for example, includes industries ranging from steelmaking to oil, hotels, and fast food.[38]

The second observation is that, as Kim Clark of Harvard Business School has noted, technologies are inherently modular: a car, for example, is made up of an engine, a transmission, a body, and so on.[39] Modules are then assembled into "architectures," in this case, the design of the car itself. Innovations in modules can enable new architectures (e.g., the microchip enabling the PC), but it is innovations in architectures (e.g., the PC revolution itself) that tend to have the big catalyzing ripple effects on innovation. We thus have two of the key features that led to the punctuated equilibrium pattern in Jain and Krishna's model—sparse-dense networks of interaction, and catalyzing effects from individual nodes. We will explore this in more detail in chapter 11, but one can see how technology webs might be subject to cascades of change leading to the emergent pattern of punctuated equilibrium, and that certain technologies could play the role of keystones in those webs.

Power Laws: Earthquakes and Stock Markets

Earlier in the book, I briefly noted that one prediction of Traditional Economics is that stock prices should follow a *random walk*. To envision a random walk, place a pen on a piece of paper, start pulling the pen from left to right, but as you do so, move the pen in random increments either up or down—if you imagine a drunk person staggering across your pad, you get the idea. Now look at figure 8-3, taken from work by the Yale mathematician Benoit Mandelbrot. One of the graphs is the price of IBM stock from 1959 to 1996 (plotted on a logarithmic scale), and the other is a sample of random-walk data (this random walk has a growth trend in it). The graphs look qualitatively very similar, and if they weren't labeled, it would be very hard to guess which graph was IBM and which was the random walk. It is not

FIGURE 8-3

IBM's Stock Price Versus a Random Walk

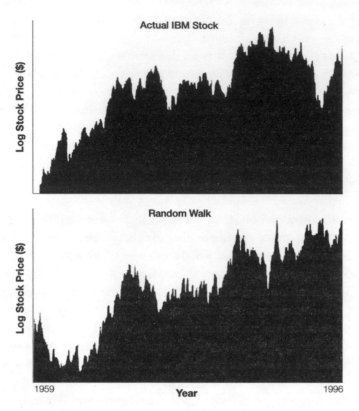

Source: Mandelbrot (1997).

difficult to see why the random walk has been a core part of finance theory for over one hundred years.

But instead of looking at the absolute price level, let's look at how much the stock price moved up or down on each particular day, as shown in figure 8-4. We now see that the two graphs look strikingly different. The graph on the top is quite spiky, with periods of big price swings and periods of smaller price movements clustered in time. Meanwhile, the graph on the bottom is fuzzier, with big and little moves randomly mixed together over time. Looked at this way, the spiky IBM data obviously does not look much like the fuzzy random-walk data (and as mentioned in chapter 3, several researchers have shown statistically that stocks do not follow a random walk). The clumpy pattern for IBM shows that the volatility of price movements is correlated in time. This is the stormy–quiet–stormy pattern of punctuated equilibrium

FIGURE 8-4

Changes in Stock Price, IBM Versus a Random Walk

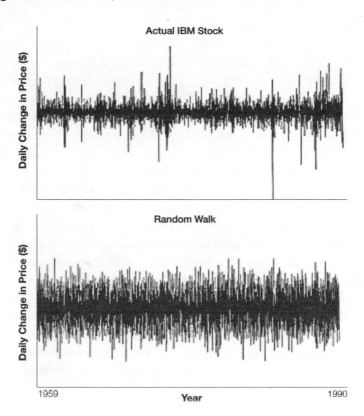

Source: Mandelbrot (1997).

we discussed in the last section. But you will notice something else. In the random-walk data, there are some large price movements, but none that really stand out way above the others. But in the real data, a few points sky-rocket above, or plunge far below, the rest of the sample. What could lead to such dramatic movements in prices?

Traditional Economics tells us that stock prices move when a piece of news hits the market. One of the predictions of Traditional theory is that big price movements should correspond with big, unexpected news. David Cutler, James Poterba, and Larry Summers tested this prediction in a study in 1989.[40] They looked at the biggest U.S. stock market movements from 1941 to 1987 and then went through the newspapers of the time to determine the news that corresponded with those events. They found that, typically, there was really not much news to speak of on the days around the biggest crashes. As we noted earlier, the *New York Times* explanation for the 20 percent drop in the S&P 500 on October 19, 1987, was "Worry over dollar decline and trade deficit." On September 3, 1946, the date of another big crash, the lead story was "No basic reason for the assault on prices." Cutler and his colleagues also took the reverse view. They looked at the biggest news events of the period and measured the market movements on those days. For example, when the Japanese bombed Pearl Harbor, the market only dropped 4.4 percent. When the Cuban Missile Crisis was peacefully resolved, the market rose a mere 2.2 percent. We thus have a mystery: why is there so much news-less volatility in the market? The answer to this mystery lies in an interesting observation: while stock price movements don't look much like a random walk, they do look like another phenomenon: earthquakes.

In the 1950s, two geophysicists from the California Institute of Technology, Beno Gutenberg and Charles Richter, went into Cal Tech's library and dug up materials describing earthquakes.[41] The scientists went as far back in history as they could. They were interested in seeing how many earthquakes occurred at various levels of strength. For example, are powerful quakes common or rare? Is an earthquake with a magnitude of 2 twice as likely as a quake with a magnitude of 4? They divided their data into bins, one bin for magnitudes 2.0–2.5, one for 2.5–3.0, and so on. They then drew a distribution curve of their data, similar to the graph of income data in Sugarscape.

The best-known distribution is the bell curve, known as the *normal,* or *Gaussian distribution* (named after its nineteenth-century discoverer, Karl Friedrich Gauss). If we collected data on the height of women in a population, created bins for ranges of height (e.g., 50–52 inches, 52–54 inches, etc.), and counted the number of occurrences in each bin, we would see a smooth, bell-shaped curve. The hump in the middle of the curve shows that a typical woman is between 60 and 70 inches tall, while the tails indicate that there are very few extremely short women and very few extremely tall women.

For earthquakes, one might expect the graph to look similar to the Gaussian distribution of heights. We might expect that there is a typical size of earthquake, with most quakes falling in that range, and very few superlarge or supersmall quakes. But when Gutenberg and Richter graphed their data, they found something quite different. To make their results easier to see, they graphed the data with logarithmic scales on both axes. The result on the log-log graph was almost a dead straight line (figure 8-5). This straight line on a log-log scale meant that, with earthquakes, there is no "typical" size in the middle of the distribution as there is in body heights. Rather, earthquakes occur across all size scales, but the bigger the quake, the rarer it is—specifically, with each doubling in earthquake energy, the probability of a quake of that size occurring drops by a factor of four. It is thus a slippery slope down

FIGURE 8-5

An Example of a Power Law Distribution: Earthquake Magnitudes

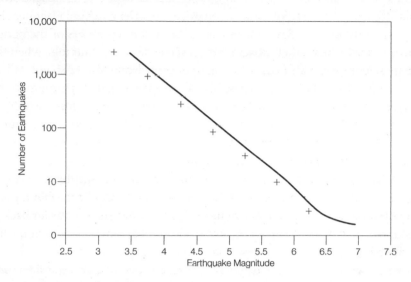

Source: Data from the Southern California Earthquake Center. Graph from Buchanan (2000).

the distribution from the smallest to largest quakes. Physicists call this kind of relationship a *power law*, because the distribution is described by an equation with an exponent, or power.[42]

Power laws have been discovered in a wide variety of phenomena, including the sizes of biological extinction events, the intensity of solar flares, the ranking of cities by size, traffic jams, cotton prices, the number of fatalities in warfare, and even the distribution of sex partners in social networks.[43] Power laws, along with oscillations and punctuated equilibrium, are another signature characteristic of complex adaptive systems.

Earthquakes, however, were not the first power law to be discovered. In fact, the first discovery of a power law was in economics by our friend Vilfredo Pareto in 1895, although it wasn't recognized as a power law at the time.[44] As discussed in chapter 4, Pareto's study of income found a lot of poor, a middle class that stretched over a wide range, and a very few superrich. He found that for every increase of income by 1 percent, there was a corresponding decline in the number of households by 1.5 percent—graphed on log-log paper, this produces a straight line—a power law. Pareto did not have the mathematical tools to fully appreciate the significance of his finding.[45] Power laws reemerged briefly in economics in the 1960s, when Benoit Mandelbrot became interested in the fluctuations of cotton prices on the Chicago Mercantile

Exchange. When Mandelbrot graphed the data, he quickly noticed that the price fluctuations, like the graph of IBM's stock, had far more large movements than Traditional Theory would predict. In addition, he noticed that the fluctuations seemed to have no natural timescale. If he took one section of the graph, say, one hour, and stretched it out to the length of a day, one could not tell which graph was the hourly data and which was the daily data. He then looked at data from other commodities, including gold and wheat, and saw the same pattern—power laws.[46] When Mandelbrot first made his discovery, his work was largely ignored by economists, partly because he was a mathematician from outside the field, and partly because the data simply does not fit in with Traditional theory.

The startling nature of Pareto's and Mandelbrot's findings lay largely unappreciated until the 1980s and 1990s, when ideas about the economy's being a complex adaptive system sparked a renewed interest in power laws. Physicists had much experience analyzing power laws from natural systems, and a number of "econophysicists" began to look at stock market data. One of them, Gene Stanley of Boston University, has calculated that if stocks followed a random walk as Traditional Economics posits, then the probability of the 1987 Black Monday crash's occurring was 10^{-148} percent. Just to put this incredibly small number in perspective, the smallest known measure in the universe, the Planck length, is 10^{-33} centimeters. Thus, it is stupendously unlikely that the market could have just randomly walked its way into a crash of that magnitude. Gaussian, random walks almost never have fluctuations greater than five standard deviations, yet in real economic data, such as stock market crashes, five-standard-deviation events, and even larger-deviation ones, do in fact occur.[47]

To try to figure out what was going on, Stanley and his team took every stock market transaction, sampled every five minutes, from 1994 to 1995, for one thousand of the largest U.S. companies—all 40 million data points—and began crunching the data through their computers. They found that the fluctuations in stock prices follow clear power laws in the tails of the distribution. Just to be sure, they also looked at the 30 million daily records for six thousand U.S. stocks over the thirty-five year period from 1962 to 1996. Again, the records formed power laws. A Traditional economist might reply that perhaps the data is non-Gaussian for the short, five-minute ticks that Stanley was looking at, but things should become Gaussian over longer periods. Stanley varied his time periods over three orders of magnitude, from 5 minutes to 6,240 minutes (sixteen days—beyond that, it is difficult to have enough data for strong conclusions). The data did look somewhat more Gaussian than the shorter periods did, but it still very clearly followed a power law.[48]

One of the consequences of this result is that financial markets are far more volatile than Traditional Economics leads us to believe. If the markets follow a power law, then the probability of a Black Monday event is more like 10^{-5} (which means there is a good chance one will happen in any hundred-year period) rather than 10^{-148}, an enormous difference. This clearly has major implications for how investors think about and manage risk. Stunningly clear power laws have shown up in other economic data sets as well. Using 1997 U.S. census data, Robert Axtell (of Sugarscape fame) has conducted an analysis of all 5.5 million firms with one employee or more and showed that the size of companies as measured by employees also scales according to a power law.[49] Stanley and his group have found that company sales growth, as well as the GDP growth of nations, likewise scales according to a power law.[50] We will look at the implications of these findings in later chapters.

Why Are Stock Markets So Volatile?

Why are stock markets so much more volatile than Traditional theory predicts? And why does that volatility follow the pattern of a power law? Doyne Farmer, a physicist who was at the original Santa Fe Institute economics meeting, and his team of collaborators believe they have found the answer to these questions.[51] The key is that there are two types of trades one can make on most stock exchanges. The first is a *market order,* in which a trader says buy (or sell) stock X right now for the best available price. The second is a *limit order,* in which a trader says buy stock X if the price falls to $100 (or conversely, sell stock X if the price rises to $100). In this example, $100 is the limit at which the trader is prepared to trade. For every stock in the market, there is a *limit order book* that keeps track of the limit orders. In the old days, the book used to be a ledger with buy orders on one side and sell orders on the other; today the book is electronic.

In effect, the limit order book is an inventory or storage device for unfilled orders. If a trader places a buy limit order for stock X at $100 and the current price is $110, then the order will be stored in the book until it is either filled by the stock's dropping to $100 or canceled. At any point in time, one can look at the limit order book and see what the best-buy and best-sell offers are. For example, the best buy offer might be $100 and the best sell offer $102; the gap between the best buy and sell offers is known as the *bid-ask spread.*

Now let's see what happens when a new *market* order hits the limit order book. The specific details of how orders are filled vary somewhat by stock exchange, and some exchanges such as New York involve people, while others such as London are all-electronic, but there are two rules that most exchanges share: *price priority* and *time priority*. Remember, a market order says *fill me at the best price you can get right now*. So price priority means that we start with the best price in the book, fill the order as much as we can, then move to the next best price, and so on. Time priority means that if there are two limit orders in the book at the same price, the earlier order gets filled first.

To illustrate, imagine the following scenario. You call your broker with a market order to buy 1,000 shares of stock X and he or she transmits your order to the exchange. The current best sell offer in the book is a limit order for $102 and there are 200 shares available at that price. The system fills 200 shares of your order at that price, leaving 800 shares still to be filled. The system then looks further up the limit order book for the next best price which is a limit sell order for 300 shares at $105. You buy those shares, leaving 500 unfilled in your order. Marching further up the book, the next best price is a limit sell order for 200 shares and another limit sell order for 600 shares, both at $107. Let's imagine the 200 share order has been in the book longer, so using time priority, the system allocates those shares, plus 300 from the second block to you for a total of 500. Your order is now complete and has been transacted at an average price of $105.40. Given the current state of the book, that was the best price for buying 1,000 shares. Following the completion of your 1,000 share transaction there are still 300 shares remaining available at $107, so that is now the new best asking price. The impact of your 1,000 share market order was to drive the asking price from $102 to $107. As Farmer puts it, we can imagine limit orders sprinkling into the book over time like falling snow, and accumulating in the book at different price levels. Then once in a while a market order (or a limit order inside the bid-ask spread) hits the book and zaps out a bunch of limit orders, moving the price of the stock up or down.

Farmer and his team wanted to understand how this process of order fulfillment and the structure of the limit order book affect prices. They analyzed a data set from the London Stock Exchange that shows trade-by-trade data with complete visibility into the order book, for sixteen of the largest and most highly traded stocks. Overall, the researchers analyzed more than 40 million "events" (order placements and cancellations). Farmer and his team found that the cause of large price fluctuations was the structure of the order book itself—large fluctuations occurred when there were large gaps between the price levels in the book. They cited a moment of trading in the stock of AstraZeneca, a global pharmaceutical company, as an example. At the particular point in time they studied, AstraZeneca's limit order book had a small limit sell order at £31.84 and then a big gap, after which the next limit sell order was £32.30. A single, very small market buy order then came in, and the asking price jumped from £31.84 to £32.30 in one trade, an increase

FIGURE 8-6

Big Price Movements from Small Orders in AstraZeneca's Limit Order Book

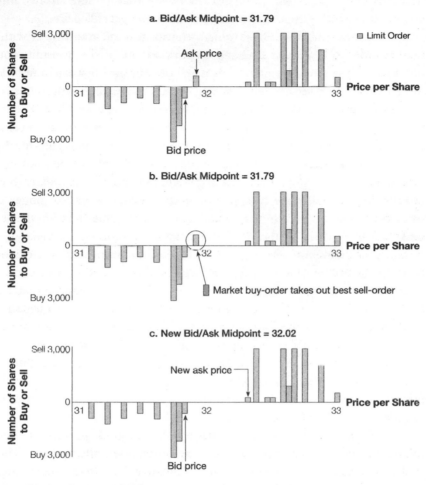

Source: Data from Farmer et al. (2004).

of 46 pence, or 1.4 percent (figure 8-6). This one tiny trade, worth only £16,000 ($28,000) moved the share price by 23 pence (calculated as the mid-point of the bid-ask spread, so half the 46 pence movement in the asking price) and added £374 million ($658 million) to AstraZeneca's total market value. Yet there was no exceptional news in the newspapers that day, and AstraZeneca had done nothing to change its value as a company—this large change in market value was merely an artifact of the pattern of orders that had been stored in the book over time. On further analysis, Farmer and team found that such events were fairly common, and that limit order books in general tend to be quite chunky and sparsely populated. Even the biggest, most liquid stocks typically have only thirty or so price levels populated with limit orders, and lots of unpopulated prices and therefore gaps. You would expect that most limit orders would be clustered around the best bid and ask, and that turned out to be somewhat true, but the team also found orders spread around all over the book. For example, someone might just stick in a sell order way above the current price and leave it there hoping the price eventually moves up, thereby creating a patchy pattern of orders and gaps in the book.

Professional traders have always known that even in big stocks, there is less liquidity than one might think, and that order books are quite patchy. That is why they have to dribble out large trades over time—a big trade hitting the market all at once would move the price too much. But until Farmer and company's work, it wasn't appreciated just how much this patchiness of order books contributed to stock volatility. The team built a mathematical model of the order book and showed that with just random trading (again, no real news), the structure of the order book on its own was a significant source of volatility. They also showed that, as one might expect, smaller, more thinly traded stocks were more volatile than large, more liquid stocks.

In a subsequent study, Farmer and his colleague Mike Szabolcs went the next step and took a closer look at the pattern of order placement in the limit order book.[52] The variable they focused on was the distance of a new limit order from the current best bid-ask spread. For example, if the current bid-ask spread was $100 to $102, what would the probability be of a sell limit order arriving at a price of $101, $102, $103, and so on, or a buy limit order at $101, $100, $99 and so on. They found that the orders followed a very regular pattern, known as a *student distribution* (instead of a bell curve imagine a witch's pointy hat) anchored around the center of the bid-ask spread. Farmer and Szabolcs noted that the regularity of the order pattern implied that there was also some regularity in the behavior of the traders placing the orders—a result at odds with the Traditional theory that all trading is driven by unpredictable news events. When Farmer and Szabolcs combined their result with the earlier study of the limit order book, they were able to reproduce the power law volatility exhibited by the stocks they studied to a very close degree.

This result *does not mean* that real news does not matter to stocks. If AstraZeneca announces results that surprise investors, its stock will respond. In many ways the limit order book serves as a form of memory, or a storehouse of past news, as the pattern of orders in it may have been influenced by news at the time the orders were placed. But the result does mean that there can also be a lot of stock price movement that has nothing to do with current news, but instead is an artifact of the interactions between new order flow and the particular pattern of orders that happens to be stored in the book at a moment in time. Some Traditional economists might be tempted to just dismiss this movement as short-term noise that can be safely ignored. But Farmer's reply was twofold. First, the impact of the limit order book isn't just over the short term; he and the team showed that the same distribution of volatility shows up across much longer timescales, too. Second, it isn't random noise. The power-law pattern of price movements emerges from the structure of the system itself, just as the oscillations in the Beer Game emerge from the structure of that system. Farmer's results were just for individual stocks, but in chapter 17, we will look at how "news-less volatility" can combine with the behavioral rules of real, human stock traders to create earthquakes in the market as a whole.

In many ways, the lessons of the Beer Game and the Farmer team's model are the same. Complex emergent phenomena such as business cycles and stock price movements are likely to have three root causes. The first is the behavior of the participants in the system. As we have seen, real human beings have real behavioral regularities, whether it is the anchor and adjust rule of the Beer Game participants, or the yet to be understood regularity that leads to student distributions in stock ordering. Second, the institutional structure of the system makes a big difference. In the case of the Beer Game, the structure of the supply chain between the manufacturer and retailer created dynamics, that when combined with participant behavior, led to oscillations. In the case of the stock market, the structure of the limit order system, when combined with trader behavior, led to power law volatility. Third and last, are exogenous inputs into the system. In the case of the Beer Game it was the onetime jump in customer orders, and in the case of the stock market it is news. These exogenous shocks undoubtedly initiate and help drive the dynamics of the system. While exogenous factors play a role, the equilibrium straitjacket of Traditional Economics has unfortunately led to an overemphasis on this factor at the expense of the other two.

Complexity Economics does not have all the answers to the puzzle of economic patterns, but it provides us with new tools to begin to understand how these various factors combine to result in the behaviors we observe. The real-world economy is a far more interesting place than the equilibrium world imagined by Traditional Economics. Oscillations that do not settle down, punctuated equilibrium, and power laws—these are all signature behaviors of a complex adaptive economy at work.

CHAPTER NINE

Evolution

IT'S A JUNGLE OUT THERE

HOW MANY TIMES have you heard the expression "It's a jungle out there"? Or "It's survival of the fittest"? Businesspeople, journalists, and academics all gravitate quite naturally to using images of ecosystems and evolution when they speak about the economy. One of the strongest claims of Complexity Economics is that this language is no mere metaphor—organizations, markets, and economies are not just like evolutionary systems; they truly, literally are evolutionary systems. In this chapter, we will see that evolution is not just about biology. Rather, evolution is a general-purpose and highly powerful recipe for finding innovative solutions to complex problems. It is a learning algorithm that adapts to changing environments and accumulates knowledge over time. It is the formula responsible for all the order, complexity, and diversity of the natural world. And as we will see in part 3, it is the same formula that lies behind all the order, complexity, diversity, and, ultimately, wealth in the economic world.

Design Without a Designer

Daniel Dennett, an evolutionary theorist and the director of the Center for Cognitive Studies at Tufts University (whose work I will draw on heavily in this chapter), calls evolution a method for "creating design without a designer."[1] When we think of something as having *design*, we think of it as having a purpose—it is fit for a task. A hammer is designed to drive nails, and a bacterium is designed to survive and reproduce in a particular environment. We also think of things that are designed as having a degree of complexity, order, and structure to them. We wouldn't think of the random grains of sand on a beach as designed, but we would think of the complex structure of a jet engine, the spiraling chambers of a nautilus shell, or the intricate arrangement of notes in a piece of music as all exhibiting design. It is this combination of fitness for purpose and complexity that distinguishes designed things from non-designed things. A striated rock outcropping might be beautiful to the human eye, it might have complex patterns, and it might even look like a piece of art. But it does not have a function, it is not fit for any particular purpose, it is instead the accidental creation of random geological forces. Things that are designed have low entropy. They are far from being random creations.

There are two realms (and only two realms) in which we see design: in biology and in the artifacts created by biological creatures. In biology, there are kangaroo legs for jumping, bat sonar receivers for finding things in the dark, and flower stamens cleverly disguised as bee sex organs to encourage pollination. In the human world, there are screwdrivers for turning screws, spatulas for turning pancakes, and jumbo jets for transporting people. But humans are not the only creatures to create artifacts that exhibit design; there are also the elaborate nests built by termites, and complex dams built by beavers.

William Paley, an Anglican priest and philosopher, famously pointed out in his 1802 *Natural Theology* that something as complex and designed as a watch presupposes a watchmaker. Therefore, he argued, the complexity and design of the natural world requires the existence of a divine watchmaker. Highly designed things don't just spring up in the world on their own. After all, designs exhibit purpose, intelligence, and problem solving (this of course is the same argument currently being made two centuries later by proponents of the so-called "theory of intelligent design").[2]

Yet this is exactly what evolution does—it creates design on its own. Richard Dawkins, the Oxford evolutionary theorist whose work also informs much of this chapter, has called evolution "the blind watchmaker."[3] It is a mindless, mechanical, and simple formula, but at the same time, it is astonishingly effective at creating clever designs.

Artificial Life

In 1994, Karl Sims, a former member of the MIT Media Lab and now at GenArts, Inc., wanted to study evolution in action. But he wanted to do it in a way that was faster and gave him more control than he would get experimenting with bacteria and fruit flies in a lab. So he created a simulated evolutionary world on a supercomputer populated by animated computer creatures. (Those without a supercomputer and Karl Sims's programming genius can experience simulated evolution through a variety of commercial computer

FIGURE 9-1

Karl Sims's Block Creatures

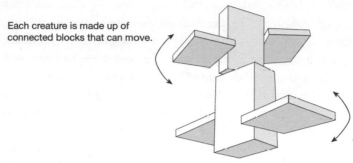

Each creature is made up of
connected blocks that can move.

Source: Sims (1994).

games such as Maxis's SimLife and Microsoft's Impossible Creatures.)[4] Each
creature's body was made up of a series of interlinked rectangular blocks. A
creature could have any number of body blocks, which could be any dimension (e.g., cubes, short fat rectangles, long thin rectangles). The blocks were
linked to each other in such a way that they were hinged and could flex (figure 9-1). A block creature could control the movement of its hinged-block
body parts by virtue of a simple computer brain that coordinated movement.
Sims gave each block creature a goal, and the creature then used sensors on
its body to assess where it stood in relation to its goal. It then tried to take
actions to achieve its goal by moving its hinged-block body parts in some
way. In his first experiment, the goal of the creatures was to swim as fast as
they could through simulated water.

Sims then gave his block world a biological twist by endowing each block
creature with a form of computer DNA that described (1) the layout of the
creature's body, (2) how its hinged-block body parts could move, and (3) the
initial state of its simulated brain. Sims then ran a set of experiments. He
started each experiment with a population of three hundred block creatures
with completely random computer DNA, and thus completely random
block bodies. He then set the creatures loose in a simulated swimming pool
inside his computer. Being randomly designed, most of the creatures flailed,
tumbled, or sank. However, by random chance, a few had just a glimmer of
potential—some motion that propelled them forward, or some ability to
steer themselves. Sims then applied a simple evolutionary formula to his first
generation of random creatures: those who were the most successful swimmers were kept, and the least successful swimmers were removed. Then the

most successful swimming creatures had "computer sex," swapping parts of their computer DNA with each other to create new creatures that inherited features from both parents. In addition, some of the new creatures had random mutations that altered their DNA.

Thus, the population of block creatures exhibited *variation;* at any point in time, there were creatures with varying swimming abilities. There was also a process *selecting* the fittest creatures and then *replicating* successful creatures and thus propagating their designs. This simple formula of variation, selection, and replication was repeated over and over for a hundred or so generations. Typically, after a mere twenty to thirty generations, ungainly, random, flailing, tumbling block creatures began to evolve into creatures that could actually swim (figure 9-2). Some creatures developed large core bodies, with a flapping tail at the back; some tails flapped up and down like a dolphin, while others flapped side to side like a shark. Several creatures sprouted stabilizing fins in various fishlike designs. Others developed long, thin bodies with many segments, which they swished like a snake. Still others developed many small arms, which they gyrated like a millipede, and yet another evolved into a very elegant seahorse shape.

The evolutionary algorithm found no single best way to swim, no optimum, but to use a phrase from Daniel Dennett, the evolutionary formula discovered a variety of "Good Tricks for survival."[5] The basic physics of water allows for a large, but not infinite, number of ways of locomotion. Maneuvering in the water also requires some ability to stabilize oneself with something such as fins, or a hydrodynamic body shape. The physics of water thus provides constraints on what successful swimming designs look like. This is why all real aquatic life consists of variations on certain themes, as do human-made aquatic machines such as submarines, and why Sims's block creatures quickly "discovered" these successful designs through the evolutionary process.

The success of Sims's computer evolution at finding Good Tricks in a world of complex constraints was not just limited to the problem of swimming. Sims also conducted a similar set of experiments in which the creatures were given the goal of walking on a flat surface with simulated gravity. Again, after twenty or thirty rounds of the evolutionary formula, random flailing block creatures evolved into scurrying crablike creatures, slithering snakelike creatures, as well as creatures that crawled, hopped, rolled, and even walked on legs. In a further set of experiments, block creatures competing with each other to grab a simulated food block evolved arms, claws, and mouths.

Sims did not include beforehand any of the solutions that emerged from the evolutionary process. Although he created the conditions for evolution to work in his program (e.g., the computer DNA and the selection process),

FIGURE 9-2

Sims's Block Creatures After Virtual Evolution

Examples of creatures
evolved for swimming

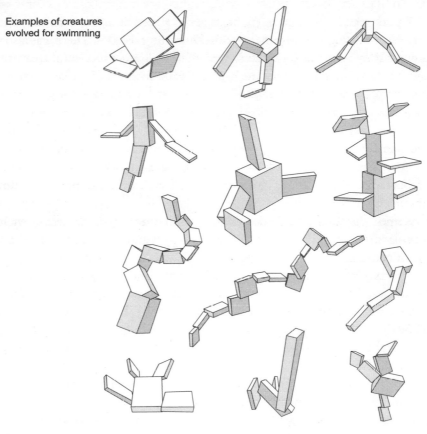

Source: Sims (1994).

he did not "design" anything about the creatures—there was nothing in the program about fins, tails, legs, or claws. All these designs were discovered and emerged bottom-up from the grinding of the evolutionary process over many generations.[6] It is the same process that, over millions of years, has given biological creatures such incredibly innovative designs as eyeballs, armor plating, poisonous sprays, wings, and opposable thumbs.

Yet, how exactly does evolution produce such a variety of innovative Good Tricks for survival?

An Algorithm for Innovation

I have referred several times to evolution as an *algorithm,* but what exactly does that mean? You can think of an algorithm as a recipe that takes some set of inputs (e.g., flour, eggs, sugar, butter), mechanically works them through some process (e.g., stir together well, bake at 350°F or 175°C for fifteen minutes), and, if the instructions are followed, reliably produces some set of outputs (e.g., cookies). Dennett uses the example of a tennis tournament that has quarterfinals, semifinals, and finals as another example of an algorithm—somebody or some organization inputs players, and the process grinds along according to a set of rules and then reliably outputs a result, the winner. The tournament process is a fairly generic algorithm and is not restricted to tennis. It can be used for golf, soccer, computer games, tiddlywinks, or any number of *substrates.* The substrate can be thought of as the material or information on which the algorithm acts.

Some algorithms are *substrate-neutral,* that is, they can be stripped down to a basic core that works on a wide variety of substrates as long as some basic setup conditions are in place. For example, you can imagine an algorithm that sorts things from biggest to smallest. Such an algorithm might be useful for sorting buckets of apples or the lengths of last names in a list. What defines the algorithm is not the particular substrate, but rather the logic the algorithm uses to process information. A sorting algorithm doesn't physically sort apples or names; rather, the algorithm *does its work on information* about the weight of apples or the spelling of names. Algorithms are formulas for processing information. They are in effect computer programs.[7]

Evolution is an algorithm that is substrate-neutral. It takes information about designs for things and mindlessly grinds that information through a process. Evolution is also *recursive:* its output from one cycle is the input for the next round. This circularity means that it will keep cranking along infinitely until something stops it. Dennett's example of a tennis tournament is also recursive in that the output of the previous round (e.g., the quarterfinals) is the input for the next round (e.g., the semifinals), and the process keeps going until a winner has been identified. Biological evolution, however, has no predefined stopping point and will keep cranking along recursively until the sun blows up or the planet otherwise becomes uninhabitable.

The Library of LEGO[8]

One year at a Christmas party, the biologist and evolutionary theorist Stuart Kauffman won a LEGO set in a contest.[9] It was a particularly apt gift for Kauffman because one of his research topics is looking at how evolution constructs incredibly complex designs from very simple building blocks. As any child knows, the great appeal of LEGO is that its simple and colorful plastic blocks can be snapped together in myriad ways to produce interesting and complex structures.

Even the simplest blocks can be attached in a large number of permutations; for example, two of the little rectangular blocks that are one dimple wide by two dimples long (we will call it a 1-by-2 block) can be put together in fourteen distinct permutations of attachment positions (assuming the two blocks are non-identical, e.g., different colors), and two 2-by-2 blocks can be attached in thirty-three ways. As the number of blocks, their size, and the number of attachment options grow, the number of possible permutations explodes. The total number of possible structures that can be constructed from even a modest-sized LEGO set is mind-bogglingly enormous.

Nonetheless, the number is finite. Evolutionary theorists call such a set of possible permutations a *design space.* There are five hundred pieces of varying shapes and colors in the appropriately named LEGO "Creator" set, and we can thus say that there are (roughly) 10^{120} unique possible LEGO block designs that can be created from that set. To borrow some more phraseology from Daniel Dennett, we'll call this the "Library of All Possible LEGO Designs."[10] We can imagine this library, which is vastly larger than the universe itself (the universe has only around 10^{80} atoms), as having shelves and shelves stacked with paper note cards, each with instructions for creating a unique LEGO design on it. If we wandered the Library of LEGO, randomly picking up note cards, we would see that the vast, vast majority of the designs are really boring. There would be thirty-three designs that had simply one blue 2-by-2 block attached in different ways to a red 2-by-2 block, another thirty-three designs with a blue 2-by-2 block attached to a yellow 2-by-2 block, millions of other ways of connecting just two blocks, trillions of ways of just connecting three blocks, and so on.

But buried somewhere deep in the heart of the library is a fabulous 384-block design for a LEGO spaceship that would make the heart of any seven-year-old race. Likewise, there is a fascinating 220-block LEGO horse, as well as a 405-block LEGO castle. There is also a design for a 406-block castle that is identical to the previous design except for the added block. In fact, there are 1-block variants of all the designs. But despite the trillions of variants on castle designs, such "interesting" designs are exceedingly rare in the Library of LEGO. There are far, far more boring, random, gibberish designs. There are also lots of designs that simply won't work—designs that, while theoretically possible, would tip over and break, or collapse under their own weight when faced with real-world gravity. To paraphrase Dennett, you would have a better chance of finding a specific drop of water in the world's oceans than finding a specific interesting design amid all the junk in the Library of LEGO.

Let's imagine, however, that we have been given the thankless task of searching the Library of LEGO for interesting designs. How would we go about it? How would we find the castles, spaceships, and horses in the vastly-bigger-than-the-universe sea of boring, random designs? If we wandered the library at random, peeking on its shelves, it might be millions of years before we found a single design that was even vaguely interesting. We need an algorithm that can reliably and quickly find good designs in enormous design spaces. It turns out that evolution is just such an algorithm. In fact, it is the grand champion.

The Setup for Evolution

All algorithms need a bit of setup to do their work. Algorithms process information, so we first need some way to turn potential LEGO designs into "information." We could codify a LEGO design in many ways: we could write out a description using English-language sentences, for example, "Attach a red 2-by-6 block on top of a blue 2-by-2 block." We could draw a diagram of the design in the way architects create blueprints. Or we could create a special code for describing LEGO designs, for example, RED26TOPBLUE22AT56TO12, or we could represent the design on a computer as a string of 1s and 0s, such as 101011100100101, and so on. It doesn't matter exactly how this coding is done; it just matters that it can be done in a way that reliably codes and decodes accurate descriptions of the designs. Such a coding of designs is called a *schema*.[11] Once we have established our schema, we can then represent any possible design in the design space with the schema.

Next, we need some device for storing the information represented by the schema. In the case of the Library of LEGO, let's imagine that designs for LEGO structures are stored by writing the schemata down on paper note cards. For example, one card might have RED26TOPBLUE22AT56TO12, and another card might have YELLOW26TOPBLUE22AT56TO12.

Next, we need a mechanism for converting theoretical designs represented by the schema into actual plastic LEGO constructions in the real world. What we need is a *schema reader*. In the biological world, a schema reader is a mechanism that turns DNA into living creatures. For example, in birds it is a fertilized egg that is capable of converting a DNA design for a chick into an actual living chick. For humans and other mammals, the schema-reader is a fertilized egg implanted in a female womb. As Dennett points out, this was the fatal flaw to the plot of the novel and movie *Jurassic Park* in which scientists recreate dinosaurs from dinosaur DNA—in order to do this the scientists would have needed a dinosaur schema reader, in other words a female dinosaur and her eggs.

An important feature of biological systems is that the schemata code for the designs of their own schema readers. In humans, by the time a female fetus is just twenty weeks old, she will have already developed ovaries and the millions of eggs that they contain. Thus, even before a woman gives birth, not only will she have her own daughter in her womb, but inside her daughter are the eggs for creating her future grandchildren.

LEGO toys, however, have not yet advanced to the state where they are self-replicating. Thus, let's imagine that the LEGO schema reader is a seven-year-old child who knows the schema code. We will dump a big box of LEGO pieces in front of the child and hand this young builder a card with the code for a design on it. The child will then dutifully scoop up the necessary plastic parts and assemble them into the design described by the code on the slip of paper. We'll call this child the "Reader."

We then need a word to describe what the Reader is building; we need a term to distinguish between theoretical, potential designs in the design space and real live designs that actually have been built. We will use a term from the evolutionary philosopher David Hull: an *interactor*.[12] Interactors are designs that have been rendered from the space of possible designs and made "real" (although "real" can also mean existing on a computer) in an environment. *Interactor* is an appropriate term because in an evolutionary system, once a design is rendered and made "real," it in some way interacts with its environment and is then subject to the selection pressures of that environment.

The last required piece of our evolutionary setup is a *fitness function*. So far I've been pretty vague about what we are looking for in the Library of LEGO. I've only said that we're looking for "interesting designs." But interesting to whom or what? In Karl Sims's model, the fitness function was defined by swimming speed. As mentioned, designs exhibit purpose and since the purpose of a LEGO toy is to entertain children, we will imagine that we have a second seven-year-old child who will serve as our arbitrator of LEGO design fitness. The Reader will assemble LEGO toys as specified by various schemata and hand them to the fitness-determining child (whom we'll call the Judge). The Judge will then look at the various toys handed to her and rate them on a scale from 0 ("yuck, boring") to 100 ("really cool").

The Evolutionary Process: Child's Play

With all the information-processing machinery in place for evolution to do its work, we need to initialize the system. Let's imagine the pieces of the LEGO set are spilled out on the floor in front of the Reader. We pull one hundred cards with LEGO designs encoded on them at random from the Library of LEGO and hand them to the Reader. He then dutifully constructs each of the toys specified on the cards and puts them in front of the Judge. The Judge then rates each of the toys on the boring-to-cool scale. Since the toys are completely random constructions, most are rated at or near zero, but some are just a bit more interesting than others and get slightly higher ratings. We will call the process whereby the Judge applies the fitness function and rates the toys *selection*.

The Reader then takes the top two rated toys and makes *variants* on their designs. He does this by taking their schema cards, cutting them randomly in half, and swapping the halves. Thus, the new variants have design features from each of the two toys that got high ratings. In evolutionary lingo, this swapping of parts of schema is called *crossover*. An important requirement of the evolutionary algorithm is that the more fit a design is, the more variants on average will be made of it. This helps ensure that characteristics that make designs fit are *amplified* in the population. However, we also have a constraint on the size of the population of LEGO toys because there are a finite number of LEGO pieces that the Reader can use to construct the toys. To amplify the characteristics of fit toys in the population and de-amplify the characteristics of less fit toys, we will implement the following rule: the top twenty fittest designs will have four variants made per pair using crossover, the next twenty will have three variants per pair, the next twenty will have two per pair, the next twenty get one per pair, and the least fit twenty will have none. We will break any ties in fitness by flipping a coin. Thus, from the original one hundred designs, we will make a total of one hundred variants (40 + 30 + 20 + 10 + 0). Once the variants are made, we will then destroy the original one hundred and return their parts to the box. We will also have a rule that if a highly rated design needs more parts than are available in the box, we will break up the lowest-rated design to provide the necessary parts—even in LEGO world, there is competition for finite resources.

Finally, we will assume that the Reader child is not perfect. Occasionally, errors will creep into the process. For example, he might make a mistake transcribing a schema from one card to another and accidentally change, delete, or add a symbol that wasn't there before. Most of these errors will go unnoticed, perhaps just changing the color of a part here or there, or slightly changing the orientation of a particular brick. But once in a great while, such a random error might have a significant effect on the subsequent toy's fitness. Such random errors are *mutations*.

Now, let's imagine that the pair of children go through this cycle a few dozen times—what would we see happen? Just as in Karl Sims's computer simulation, initially we would see a population of random, low-fitness toys.

The children might churn through a large number of uninteresting designs for quite a while. But eventually a design or two would catch the Judge's eye and those designs would begin spawning variants. We would soon start seeing more fit and more interesting (at least to the Judge's eye) designs. Fitness across the population of toys would begin to rise. We would also see common features arise in the toys, Good Tricks for meeting the Judge's taste. If, for example, the Judge liked toys that are images of people and animals, we would begin to see toys with limbs and faces. If the Judge liked yellow, we would see lots of shades of yellow running through the toys. At some point, we would begin to see complex structures emerge, LEGO people, LEGO horses, LEGO dogs, whatever caught the fancy of the fitness-determining Judge. On a relative scale, this discovery of fit designs would happen very quickly when compared to a random search of the Library of LEGO.

The appearance of common features and Good Tricks in the population of interactors leads us to another important point. Complex designs are inherently modular.[13] Our bodies have a bewildering array of systems, subsystems, and other components, from the cardiovascular system, to the heart, to an individual red blood cell, which in turn has its own systems and subsystems. Complex human-made designs have the same characteristic, such as a car's braking system, the brakes themselves, and an individual brake pad. A complex design can be viewed as a hierarchical collection of modules and submodules. In an evolutionary system, each of these systems, subsystems, and component parts has corresponding pieces of code for it in the schema. Thus, the schema for an evolutionary construction is full of such *building blocks* combined into higher-level building blocks that are combined into still higher-level building blocks. In biology, the building blocks of our DNA schemata are individual genes that code for things ranging from eye color to the chemical cycle that converts toxic ammonia into less dangerous urea. In our LEGO example, we would see chunks of schemata that code for things such as LEGO limbs and the color yellow. If a building block contributes to the fitness of interactors, then over time we would see the building block become more prevalent in the population. For example, every human has the highly useful gene for breaking down ammonia, and if our Judge really liked yellow, we would start seeing the yellow building block pop up in lots of schemata.

In fact, as Dawkins has pointed out, selection does not actually act on the interactors themselves; it acts on the building blocks.[14] We can think of each LEGO toy as a collection of features coded for by building blocks. The Judge prefers certain features (although we don't know what they are), and by dangling different combinations in front of the Judge, the evolutionary process tests which features capture the Judge's eye, and then builds more things with those features. Over time, those features (and the building blocks that code for them) become more common in the population. Thus, in effect the evolutionary process isn't selecting individual toys, it is saying, "The Judge likes yellow things with limbs."

Now imagine we remove the Judge and replace her with another judge (Judge 2). Suddenly what is fit and what is unfit in the LEGO environment would change. We would quickly see a collapse in fitness, as many of the toys that met the tastes of the previous Judge are now deemed "yuck" by Judge 2. But at some point after this collapse, the evolutionary algorithm would again get a foothold and begin to put forward just slightly better designs. Once this happened, it would start spawning more and more variants of the better designs and eventually the fitness of the LEGO toy population would begin to climb again. If, let's say, Judge 2 liked airplanes, cars, and the color green, we would soon start seeing designs emerge with wings, wheels, and lots of green.[15]

Evolution is thus a process of sifting from an enormous space of possibilities. It tries a bunch of designs, sees what works, and does more of what works and less of what doesn't, repeated over and over again. There is no foresight, no planning, no rationality, and no conscious design. There is just the mindless, mechanical grinding of the algorithm.

Replicators Just Want to Replicate

"But hold on!" you might cry. "Is that really design without a designer?" It might be true that the algorithm itself grinds along without any help, but what about all of that setup? What about Karl Sims doing all that programming? What about the way we parachuted in a human Reader and a human Judge into our LEGO thought experiment?

The best way to appreciate the logic of *endogenous evolution,* or evolution unassisted by an outside designer or programmer, is to look at the one known instance of it (so far): the development of life on earth.[16] The earth is approximately 4.6 billion years old. For about the first billion years of its existence, there was no life of any kind. Over this period, though, the rich chemical brew of the early earth sloshed around in its cooling oceans, was churned in its forming landmasses, and was spewed up into the atmosphere by volcanoes. Astronomically large numbers of molecules interacted and reacted with each other as they were heated, cooled, sloshed around, and electrically charged. With all of this interacting and reacting, ever-increasingly complex molecules were created.

Eventually, at some point around 3 to 3.5 billion years ago, a remarkable accident occurred—molecules were created that could make copies of themselves. The first self-copying molecules were undoubtedly quite simple, not much more than a template, really. One self-copying molecule probably attracted some "opposite" molecules from the surrounding sea of chemicals, which in turn would attract their "opposites," thus making a copy of the original (like making a photographic negative and then the print). Even a simple self-copying molecule is a highly unlikely thing to be created by random chance. But one-in-a-trillion-trillion chances become pretty likely with a few trillion trillion molecules having a few quintillion quintillion interactions over a billion or so years. Some scientists also believe that the odds might have been significantly improved by the laws of thermodynamics. The early earth had tremendous amounts of free energy from volcanic and other geothermal activity, and the reaction networks and complex organic molecules that are basic to metabolism and self-replication may have been a natural and likely way for all of that energy to percolate through the chemistry of the earth's oceans.[17]

Scientists don't yet know the exact composition of the first self-copying molecule (or perhaps, molecules), and this is a major area of research. We do know, however, that at least one molecule must have looked something like a precursor to RNA (all life on earth has common genes on ribosomal RNA— DNA is a more recent evolutionary invention). But once the first self-copying molecules arose from the random chemical sloshing-around of the early earth, a peculiar logic took over. As Richard Dawkins points out in the *Selfish Gene,* no copying process is perfect. Eventually, an error slips in, a bit is changed here or there, and the self-copying molecule makes something that is almost, but not quite, identical to itself. Imagine that the error was not large enough to harm the self-copying process. After some time, the chemical soup would be filled up with a variety of slightly different self-copying molecules. Would the numbers of the various self-copying molecules in the soup be the same? As Dawkins argues, inevitably not. Some molecules would be more chemically stable than others and thus "live" longer (even though they were still not technically alive) or be faster at copying themselves. Thus longer-"lived" and better, faster copiers would be more prevalent in the population. In addition, there would be a finite supply of raw materials for replication in the immediate neighborhood of the self-replicating molecules to feed their replication. If random changes made one molecule better at chemically attracting raw materials than another, then such a molecule would be able to make more copies of itself. Competition for finite resources was a theme of evolution from its very beginnings.

Eventually, some molecules might stumble on chemical structures that destabilize and break up the structures of their fellow self-replicators, and then enable the attacking molecule to incorporate the newly freed molecules of its victim for its own use. Such an accidental innovation would instantly provide an enormous advantage because it is much easier to take preassembled raw materials from a fellow self-replicator than to find and assemble them yourself. Molecules that were vulnerable to disruption and having their chemicals stolen would quickly decline in the population, while good disruptors would replicate quickly. But then, some copying molecules might by chance have had some chemicals, for example, lipids, in their outer layers that provide a buffer between their self-replicating machinery and the outside world. With a defense against the disruptors, the protected molecules would successfully replicate more frequently and become more prevalent in the population. Once we get to the stage at which we have replicating disruptors with barriers against the outside world, we have something recognizable to our modern eyes—a virus. A virus may or may not be viewed as alive, but it is certainly on the way.

The logic underlying these molecular wars is very simple: good replicators get replicated.[18] It sounds like a tautology, but its simple, circular logic is one of the most subtle and powerful drivers of evolution. If random chance creates differences in the ability to replicate, any difference that promotes replication will become more common in the population over time. Evolution ultimately selects for building blocks that support replication. This is the essence of Dawkins's famous *selfish-gene* theory.[19] By *selfish,* Dawkins did not mean, as is sometimes misunderstood, that our genes make us (or other creatures) inherently selfish in our quest to survive—in fact, cooperation is a critical survival technique for many species, including our own. What he was referring to was the logic of replication, that genes (or more generally, building blocks) that are good at supporting their own replication (i.e., "selfish") will be replicated. Any other strategy will not survive in a world of competition.

We see the logic of "good replicators get replicated" play out in the viruses that sometimes plague our computers. A "successful" computer virus (from the hacker's or virus's point of view) is one that makes lots of copies of itself. Most viruses copy themselves by using the recipient's e-mail address book. Thus for a virus to be copied, it must trick the recipient into opening the e-mail in which it arrived. Thus, viruses come in e-mails with subject lines ranging from "I love you" to "Nude pictures of . . ." A particularly tricky one I received recently was from "Admin" and had the subject line "Your e-mail account to be closed." All these are Good Tricks evolved by the hacker community to help their creations replicate. Since good replicators get replicated, if we did a survey of the virus population on the world's computers, we would expect to see these Good Tricks disproportionately represented in the population.

Eventually, about 3.8 billion years ago, the self-replicating molecule wars progressed to a point at which the good replicators had a self-replication process that looked like modern RNA, and a basic membrane between them and the outside world, but not much else—no mitochondria, chloroplasts, nucleus, or other organelles found in cells of higher organisms. Rather, these first life-forms were not much more than self-replicating molecules in a sack, like simple blue-green algae, floating in scummy mats on the world's seas. Once the self-replicating molecules got to this point, however, evolution was off to the races, creating an immense variety of single-cell organisms that developed more-complex internal organizations and could do things such as move, process sunlight, and eat each other. Eventually, about 1.8 billion years ago, evolution discovered designs for multicellular life-forms, leading to an explosion of diversity that created plants, animals, and, eventually, us.

While there are still many important scientific details to be worked out in this story, its logic does not require any exogenous factors. As soon as there was a schema, a schema reader, and a fitness function, the logic of the evolutionary algorithm could be established. In the story of life, the schema and schema reader were one in the same, as self-copying molecules are both code and reader. Even the technology for replication evolved over time, eventually developing innovations such as DNA, nuclear membranes to protect the DNA, sexual reproduction, and then, of course, the myriad strategies for attracting the opposite sex.

In the LEGO experiment, the fitness function was supplied exogenously by the Judge. In biology, the fitness function is endogenous. Some fitness-determining constraints are fixed, such as the laws of physics and chemistry. But other important aspects of fitness *coevolve* with the system. A critical part of an organism's environment is other organisms. The evolutionary moves and countermoves of each organism affect the fitness of other organisms. A predator might evolve faster running speed (good running genes increase the odds of replication), but then its prey might develop camouflage, the predator's eyesight might consequently improve, and so on in a coevolutionary arms race ad infinitum. But with each move, the fitness function changes. Even the earth's climate, another component of fitness, has changed as life has evolved. For example, the development of plant life increased the amount of oxygen in the atmosphere, paving the way for oxygen-breathing life. And of course, human evolution is now further changing the climate and the fitness functions of all life on the planet.

The setup for evolution thus boils down to information processing. In order for evolution to get a foothold, the algorithm needs an information-processing medium: something to store, modify, and copy schemata. Evolution could not get started in the biological world until a combination of thermodynamics and random chance created the first self-copying molecules to store, modify, and replicate molecular designs. In part 3, we will see that the information-processing medium that gave evolution a foothold in the economy was spoken language and, later, writing. Once the information-processing medium is established, the processes of differentiation, selection, and replication can begin. Good replicators replicate, and what is fit is defined by the environment, which includes competition with other replicators. Evolution then starts its march through design space, seeking out designs that are better and better replicators.

We have thus seen *how* evolution works. The next big question is *why* it works so well.

Explorations on the Fitness Landscape

Imagine the design space of all possible creatures that can be coded for by DNA. The DNA alphabet contains four letters (C, G, A, and T, representing the four nucleotide bases cytosine, guanine, adenine, and thymine), each arranged in base pairs, which in turn are arranged in the familiar double helix of DNA. The human genome has about 6 billion DNA base pairs. Just to give us some headroom for the evolution of creatures with longer DNA strands than humans, let's imagine a design space that would hold all possible permutations of the DNA alphabet across 10 billion base pairs. Further imagine that we write each permutation down in a thick book and lay all the books on a table (which is, of course, vastly larger than the size of the universe). Somewhere on the table is a three-thousand-page book with your own personal entire DNA sequence in it, as well as about 10^{900} different books with various *E. coli* sequences, $10^{12,000}$ books for typical plant species, and so on.[20] Daniel Dennett calls this design space of all possible DNA creatures the Library of Mendel, after the nineteenth-century monk who first discovered the gene.[21] Just as with the Library of LEGO, most of what is here is junk—genetic nonsense that, if it were ever built, would produce at best a stillborn mutant. While there are unimaginably large numbers of designs for things that could live successfully in their environment, relative to the even more unimaginable size of the design space, they are exceedingly rare.

As with the Library of LEGO, the Library of Mendel is finite, but it is only finite at a point in time.[22] In fact, the history of life on earth has seen an expansion in the length of DNA strings over time, from simple bacteria to more complex mammals, and thus an expansion in the size of the DNA design space. One can think of design space as like the surface of a balloon—it is finite at a point in time, but it can grow, just as the surface of a balloon expands as it is inflated. While the finiteness of a design space such as the Library of Mendel has some important mathematical implications, for all practical purposes, it might as well be infinite—all of the possible designs for humans or any other creature could never be fully explored in many lifetimes of many universes.

Borrowing another image from Dennett, let's imagine that each DNA book in the Library of Mendel has a metal rod towering above it.[23] We will make the height of each rod represent the fitness of the particular DNA sequence underneath it—the higher the rod, the fitter the design. Of course, by *fit*, we mean fit for a particular environment at a particular point in time. We will make a further assumption that the DNA books in our Library of Mendel are arranged in order such that they are just one "bit" apart; for example, the sequence AGCCT is next to CGCCT, which is next to GGCCT, and so on. Thus right next to the book with your DNA in it are all the 36 billion variants of you that differ by just one genetic letter.[24] We can thus move about the landscape "one letter at a time," going from book to book and seeing the corresponding change in fitness indicated by the height of the rod for each DNA sequence.

Surveying our construction, we now have a vast mountainous landscape of rods of different heights (figure 9-3). This way of portraying a design space so that we can see which designs are better than other designs is what biologists call a *fitness landscape*, a concept first developed by the evolutionary theorist Sewall Wright in 1931.[25] The fitness landscape shows us visually (and to researchers mathematically) where the good designs in a design space are located. We can think of good designs as high fitness peaks, and our problem of finding good designs in the near infinity of design space can then be reconceived as finding high peaks in the fitness landscape.

What would this immense, mountainous landscape of fitness rods look like? Stuart Kauffman points out that one could imagine two extremes. First, one might imagine that every rod has a different height from every other rod, thus the landscape would look like a completely random, spiky, jumble (figure 9-4). At the other extreme, we could imagine a perfectly orderly landscape where there is a smooth progression from low fitness to high fitness leading up to a single Mount Fuji–like peak towering above the landscape (figure 9-5). The reality, Kauffman claims, is somewhere in between (figure 9-6).[26] A DNA book that is only one letter different from your DNA book will in all likelihood have the same fitness as you (unless it is a particularly lucky or unlucky mutation). A DNA book that is two letters different will also probably have identical fitness. As we head further away from your DNA book to books that are tens, hundreds, or thousands of letters different, the odds start climbing that these changes will affect fitness. The further out we get, the more different the corresponding fitness of the book is likely to be. The changes will not be perfectly smooth with distance, however, because some small changes might have very large effects, while some larger changes might only have a small effect. Thus, the fitness between any two neighboring points is only roughly correlated. As we move longer distances between books, things get bumpy. Kauffman observes that the effect of this *rough correlation* in the landscape is to create a geography that is more like the Swiss Alps than either a random jumble or a Mount Fuji.

FIGURE 9-3

Building a Fitness Landscape

Imagine a rod above each possible DNA permutation.

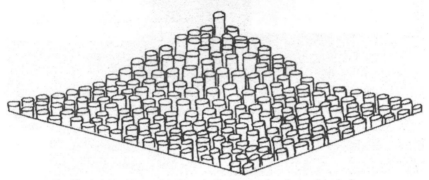

The height of the rod represents the fitness of each possible design.

Source: Dennett (1995).

Other researchers, including Jim Crutchfield of the Santa Fe Institute, have studied the mathematical shape of fitness landscapes and noticed additional features.[27] First, unlike a normal mountain landscape, the fitness landscape is pocketed with flat spots. As mentioned, the vast majority of small changes in an organism's DNA code do nothing either positive or negative, for fitness. Thus, there will be a large, flat spot in the landscape around the 36 billion or so one-letter variants of your DNA, and the trillions and trillions of few-letter variants, and so on. However, within these flat plateaus are deep holes or crevasses; the landscape is pockmarked like Swiss cheese. A step into one of these holes results in a dramatic drop in fitness. This is because even though the vast majority of small mutations do little, some are quite dangerous. For instance, if the instruction for making a key protein in brain function is

FIGURE 9-4

A Random Fitness Landscape

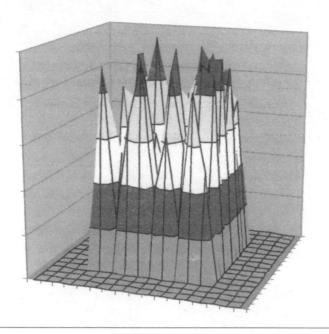

FIGURE 9-5

A Mount Fuji–like Fitness Landscape

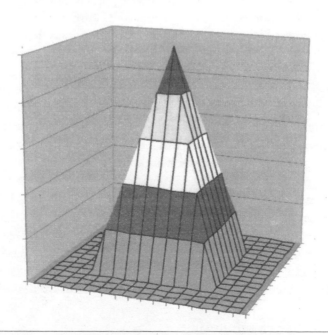

FIGURE 9-6

A Rough-Correlated Fitness Landscape

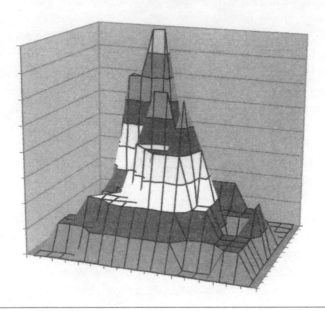

deleted from your DNA, then you're in big trouble. But the flip side is that while there are some highly negative small mutations, there are some highly positive ones as well. These small mutations can have a dramatic improvement in fitness or, sometimes even more importantly, can open the way for still further fitness-enhancing mutations. Crutchfield calls these spots in the landscape *portals,* they are fast routes up the mountain, like land bridges from one plateau on the mountain to another. In the previous chapter, we looked at a model that explained punctuated equilibrium through the network structure of species relationships in an ecosystem. According to Crutchfield, the flat spots, Swiss cheese holes, and portal routes characteristics of the landscape also contribute to punctuated equilibrium by creating a nonlinearity in the impact of genetic changes. Most changes have little or no effect, but some changes have a big impact on fitness (for good or ill) and thus may have a disproportionate effect on the web of species relationships.

Any design space for which *most* small changes in schemata lead to small or no changes in fitness, but *some* small changes have large effects, will have the rough-correlated shape of the biological fitness landscape. This is an important point, because it is this rough-correlated characteristic that makes evolution the ideal algorithm for searching fitness landscapes.

The Grand Champion Search Algorithm

Let's imagine we have been given the task of searching the Library of Mendel's mountainous fitness landscape for high peaks. Our task, though, is not to find the highest peak. First, there might not necessarily be a single, unambiguously highest peak; there could be multiple peaks of the same height spread far from each other in the landscape. But more importantly, even if there were one fitness rod that was just ever-so-slightly higher than any other rod, the chances of ever finding it would be infinitesimally small. Also, as we will discuss in a moment, the height of peaks constantly changes in the landscape, so by the time we found the one highest rod, undoubtedly it would have shrunk, or another would have grown higher. Thus, rather than search for some global optimum, we will simply look for the highest peaks we can find at any given time.

Before we start our hiking trip, we are going to introduce three additional challenges to our search. First, we have to imagine that it is a pitch-black, moonless night. You can sense if your wanderings are taking you higher or lower, but that is about it. This represents evolution's inability to "look ahead" in any sense; all evolution can do is try something to see if it works.

Second, this landscape has a dangerous feature to it. Kauffman uses the image of a poisonous fog that clings to the low-fitness valleys and crevices of the landscape. If you go too low in your wanderings, you will descend into the fog, choke, and die. The fog represents natural selection—at some point if your fitness is too low, you will be selected out.

Third, the landscape is not static, but is changing all the time. As the environment changes, the fitness function changes, and therefore what is a high-fitness peak today might not be a high peak tomorrow. As the environment shifts, the landscape bucks and heaves as low-fitness valleys are thrust up into new mountains while formerly high peaks collapse into lowlands below the poison fog. At any point in time, some regions of the landscape may be stable, others may be shifting gradually like the movement of tectonic plates, while still others might be highly active, the equivalent of fault lines full of dramatic upheavals, earthquakes, and eruptions.

Some of the changes to the landscape, such as an asteroid's hitting the earth and altering the climate, represent random changes to the environment. But much of the bucking and heaving is the result of the evolution of species themselves. Previously we noted that all species exist in complex webs of relationships with other species: predators, prey, symbiotic, parasitic relationships, and so forth. As species coevolve, engage in arms races between offense and defense and between cooperating and competing, an evolutionary change in one species can set off a chain reaction in the fitness of other species.

In order to search the landscape, we might first pick a random starting point and then use the following simple rule: take a step in a random direction; if the step led you up, stay there and take another random step. If not, return to where you were before and try again. You can imagine that if your starting point were down in a valley and you were following this rule, you would initially wander the valley floor in random directions. But eventually you would find a path up and pretty quickly scale the nearest peak. This rule is called an *adaptive walk* (figure 9-7).[28] While the adaptive walk is efficient at climbing individual peaks, it has an important limitation; once you reach the top of a peak, you stop and are stuck on a local maximum. There might be a much higher peak just a short way over the valley, but you will never find it, because you would have to go down first to get to it. The adaptive walk could even get stuck on a molehill right in the middle of a field of Everests.

Another strategy would, again, start with a random point. This time however, instead of walking, imagine you have a very powerful pogo stick. When you push a button on the pogo stick, it launches you in a random direction over a random distance. Thus, you keep hitting the button hoping to land on a high spot. This strategy is called a *random jump* (figure 9-8). The random jump has the advantage over the adaptive walk of not getting stuck on local maxima—you might hop clear over the intervening valley from a low peak to a higher peak. However, it also has the disadvantage that you might also find yourself down in a death valley. Thus, the random jump is a riskier strategy than the adaptive walk because at least the adaptive walk keeps you out of the lowest lowlands and avoids the poisonous fog. The random jump also faces very long odds of actually finding a high peak. Think of the geometry

FIGURE 9-7

An Adaptive Walk

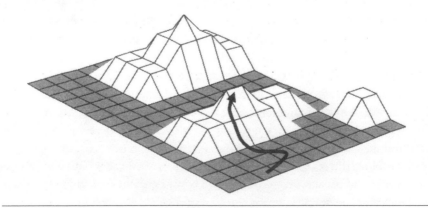

FIGURE 9-8

Random Jumps

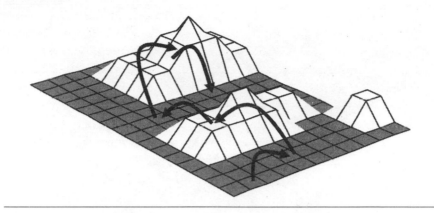

of a mountain—roughly cone shaped. If you take the cone and slice it in half horizontally, the surface area of the bottom half of the cone will always be greater than the surface area of the top half. Thus, more surface area of the landscape will be covered with areas that are lower fitness than high fitness, and on average, your random pogo jumps will put you in low-fitness spots, with the occasional lucky break. For anyone who is searching a fitness landscape and has found a point of even moderately high fitness, there will always be many more ways to make yourself worse off than better off—remember, the number of good designs in a design space is, to use Dennett's phrase, "vanishingly small."

So far, we seem to face a Hobson's choice. We must pick either a strategy that is low risk, but is unlikely to ever get us to any very high peaks, or a risky one that has a chance of landing us on a high peak, but has an even greater chance of landing us below the poison fog.

Next, let's try an algorithm that mixes the two choices, an algorithm that does an adaptive walk to keep us climbing higher and higher in the landscape, but also gives us a few random jumps to keep us from getting stuck on local peaks (figure 9-9).[29] We'll also weight our random jumps toward smaller jumps (the longer the jump, the lower its probability of occurring). This will still help keep us from getting stuck on local peaks, but reduce the odds of ending up in a really low valley. Let's add one more twist. Instead of just one hiker searching, let's imagine we have a whole army of hikers to help us explore the landscape. How would this search method do?

If we took (to use a phrase from Kauffman) a "god's-eye" view over the fitness landscape, each hiker would look like a little black dot on the immense

FIGURE 9-9

Combining an Adaptive Walk with Random Jumps

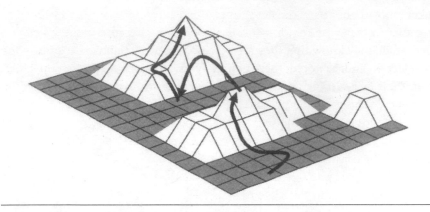

terrain and our army would look like a buzzing cloud as each hiker looked for higher peaks.[30] We would see the buzzing cloud slowly oozing its way up the side of a mountain as everyone engaged in adaptive walks. Eventually the cloud would hit a local plateau and randomly diffuse around it as the hikers spread out looking for more ways up. As they continued their adaptive walk, some hikers would disappear down a Swiss cheese hole, but most would spread out around the local plateau. Every now and then, however, we would see the group spit out a few random jumpers, who land farther afield from the main body of the group. Like advance scouts, these jumpers would seek out new routes up in the landscape. Some of the jumpers would leap right off the edge of the plateau and into the poison fog below. But some of them might stumble upon a new route up; they might find one of Crutchfield's portal land bridges that takes them across a low-fitness valley and into a new high-fitness plateau.

We thus get the best of both worlds. The bulk of our hiking resources are applied to the relatively low-risk adaptive walk, marching away through the landscape. But we have a dispersal of our bets, with some hikers fanning out farther from the center, and a few scouts taking real fliers and searching quite far from the main group. Such a strategy will inevitably lose some hikers, but will also have a greater likelihood of finding high-fitness regions of the landscape without getting stuck on local plateaus.

This kind of spreading of bets across a population is exactly what evolution does—each interactor (or in biology, organism) can be considered a hiker. The process of replication powers the adaptive walk. If high-fitness hikers tend to recombine their schemata with other high-fitness hikers and have more offspring then low-fitness hikers, then the cloud of hikers tends to grow at higher altitudes and shrink at lower ones. But the process of differentiation (in biology, through crossover and mutation) ensures that we have hikers spread out across the landscape. Most will be bunched relatively close together in the same region—this is a good thing because if the hikers are alive at all, they know that they are at least somewhere above the poison fog of selection and, as noted, there are always more ways down than up. However, there will also be at least a few outliers providing a chance of finding some new ways to higher ground.

If the outlying scouts do find a new way up, say, by crossing a portal land bridge to a new high-fitness region, their higher fitness will mean that they will reproduce faster, creating a new population cloud in the new high-fitness region. From our god's-eye view, we would see a buzzing population cloud on a plateau—in other words, a new species.[31]

This dispersal of bets created by differentiation is critical not only for discovering new ways up in fitness, but also for increasing the odds that some hikers will survive if the landscape changes. The bulk of our hiker population might be buzzing around enjoying life on a nice high-fitness plateau when suddenly the landscape changes and their plateau collapses beneath the fog. The only ones left would be the scouts who were further afield and who then must rebuild the population. Likewise, some of the scouts who were at low-fitness spots on the landscape before suddenly might find themselves at a new, higher altitude as the landscape shifts. This is the important role that genetic diversity plays in a population; without spreading your bets across the landscape, you risk losing it all when the environment suddenly changes.

By creating a spread of jump lengths, evolution manages what John Holland calls the tension between *exploration* and *exploitation*.[32] If evolution finds a high-fitness plateau, most of the population remains clustered around that area, replicating and growing, thus exploiting its good fortune and utilizing the successful adaptations it has discovered. But there will always be some hikers farther afield stumbling in the dark, searching for new ways up hills and guarding against "overadaptation."

Interestingly, Holland has shown that evolution automatically strikes the right balance between exploration and exploitation. When things are good, when evolution has found a high plateau, evolution will devote proportionally more population resources to exploiting. But when things are bad, when the population is down in the valley, proportionally more resources will be devoted to exploring. Every time evolution occupies a new part of the fitness landscape, it is placing bets to sample the unknown. But like any bettor, as evolution gets more information, it wants to double up on the bets that look most promising. Holland has worked out the optimal formula for balancing exploitation and exploration and has shown that evolution comes very close to achieving the optimal balance.[33] Evolution is a gambler, but one that plays the odds very well.

Good Tricks, Forced Moves, and Path Dependence

I have already mentioned Dennett's notion of *Good Tricks*.[34] Good Tricks are moves on the fitness landscape that are not required on pain of extinction, but rather are so attractive that there is a strong probability they will be repeatedly and independently discovered by evolutionary searches of the landscape. For example, imagine in our landscape a great, high mountain region called "creatures with eyes," for which all the DNA books have instructions for making sensors that detect light. The ability to detect and interpret light signals through eyes makes such a significant contribution to fitness, virtually regardless of the environment (unless the world went dark), that in terms of the fitness landscape, the region of DNA books with "creatures with eyes" is a very large, stable region of high fitness. The size, height, and stability of the region make it highly likely that any evolutionary search process will eventually find it. Large, high-mountain regions will also probably have multiple evolutionary paths leading up to them. Thus, the Good Trick might arise independently in multiple species and each with somewhat different designs, such as mammal eye designs and insect eye designs.

Dennett also refers to another factor—*Forced Moves*.[35] In the game of chess, players sometimes find themselves in a position in which they have no choice on what to do next. They are boxed into a position in which any other move is suicidal. Likewise, in a fitness landscape, the movements of evolutionary search are constrained by what is fit in a given environment. That is, one can run along a ridge that is above the poisonous fog of low fitness, but if one deviates from the ridgeline, one is dead. Some Forced Moves are created by the constraints imposed by the laws of physics and chemistry. For example, the laws of thermodynamics dictate that all biological creatures must have some kind of boundary between themselves and the rest of the world to provide a barrier between their low-entropy interior and the high-entropy outside world. Thus, all living things have some kind of skin, membrane, exoskeleton, protein shell, or other container. Other Forced Moves may or may not be permanent, being defined by the current state of the environment or by coevolution between species.

A third and final consequence of fitness landscape topography is path dependence, a concept we discussed briefly earlier in the book. In evolutionary systems, history matters; where you can go in the future depends on where you have been in the past. Differentiation can spread populations out in a neighborhood of the landscape, but you can't just go instantly from one part of the landscape to another at will (remember our random jumps are both random in where they take you and weighted toward smaller jumps). Imagine a peak occupied by the design for a certain type of fish. However, the fish's environment is changing; its niche is disappearing and its peak is sinking into the poison fog. From our god's-eye vantage point, we can see that nearby is a peak for another type of fish design that doesn't exist yet—it is high above the poison and appears stable. Between the two designs in the landscape, however, there is no path, no land bridge that stays above the poison fog. The designs are too far apart to be bridged by random jumps. Because there are no sustainable, intermediate niches along the way between the first fish design and the second, the fish is a prisoner of its history. Its particular path led to the cul-de-sac on its particular peak, and its options for the future are limited by its past.

Mathematicians and evolutionary theorists have explored a variety of alternative search algorithms on different landscape shapes. Some are better for searching perfectly random landscapes, and some are better for searching highly ordered and regular landscapes. But for landscapes that are in between, are rough-correlated, and have complex features such as plateaus, holes, and portals, evolution is hard to beat. And when the landscape is constantly changing, when the search problem is a dynamic one, when one must balance the tension between exploring and exploiting—evolution truly is the grand champion.[36]

Stripping Evolution Back to Its Basics

To recap the substrate-neutral version of evolution we have been building, here are the *necessary conditions* for evolution to do its work:

- There is a *design space* of possible designs.

- It is possible to reliably code those designs into a *schema*.

- There is some form of *schema reader* that can reliably decode schemata and render them into *interactors*. In endogenous evolution, schemata code for the building of their own readers.

- Interactors are made up of modules and systems of modules that are coded for by *building blocks* in the schemata.

- The interactors are rendered into an *environment*. The environment places *constraints* on the interactors (e.g., the laws of physics, climate, or the LEGO Judge), any of which can change over time. A particularly important constraining factor is *competition* among interactors for finite resources.

- Collectively, the constraints in an environment create a *fitness function* whereby some interactors are fitter than others.

The process of evolution can then be thought of as an algorithm that searches the design space for designs that are fit, given the fitness constraints of the environment. The algorithm conducts its search of the design space as follows:

- There is a process of *variation* of schemata over time. Schemata can be varied by any number of *operators*, for example, crossover and mutation.

- Schemata are rendered into interactors creating a *population*.

- Acting on the interactors is a process of *selection*, whereby some designs are deemed by the fitness function to be fitter than others. Less fit interactors have a higher probability of being removed from the population.

- There is a process of *replication*. Fit interactors have on average a greater probability of replicating, and more variants are made of them than of less-fit designs.

- Thus over time, *building blocks* that contribute to interactor fitness are replicated more frequently and become more common in the population.

- Finally, the algorithmic process of variation, selection, and replication is conducted *recursively* on the population, with output from one round acting as the input for the next round.

When the algorithm is running in an appropriately setup information-processing substrate with the right parameters, we can then expect to see the following results:[37]

- The creation of *order from randomness*. From simple random beginnings, the algorithm creates complex designs that are "ordered" from the point of view of the fitness function. All evolutionary processes operate in open systems, so in effect the algorithm harnesses energy to decrease local entropy and turn randomness into order.

- The discovery of *fit designs*. The algorithm provides a fast and efficient way of searching the enormity of design space for fit designs. In endogenous evolution, designs are fit if they survive and replicate under the constraints of their environment ("good replicators get replicated").

- Continuous *adaptation*. The algorithm "learns" what the fitness function wants and seeks out designs that meet those criteria. If the fitness function changes, evolution produces designs that reflect the new selection pressures.

- The accumulation of *knowledge*. The evolutionary process accumulates knowledge over time. If we were to freeze the LEGO evolutionary process and analyze the schema cards for all the toys at a particular point in time, we could say that the information in those cards reflected learning or knowledge about the fitness environment in which the toys had historically evolved. Likewise, DNA contains immense amounts of information about which biological designs have worked in the past. If you were an alien from another planet and had never seen the earth, but somehow obtained a piece of DNA from an earthly organism, you could learn much about the earth's environment just from that piece of code (assuming you had a DNA reader). Schemata are like the hard drives of the evolutionary process; they fill up with information over time.

- The emergence of *novelty*. During the evolutionary process, the algorithm continuously creates new variants of designs. In a theoretical sense, all possible designs already exist in the design space, but by discovering and rendering them, evolution introduces "new" designs into the real world. In our LEGO example, the evolutionary algorithm would undoubtedly churn out some designs that the children themselves had not thought of beforehand, and experiments using computer-simulated evolution to design things from jet-engine fan blades to computer chips have also resulted in novel designs.[38]

- *Growth* in resources devoted to successful designs. Populations of successful designs grow, and populations of unsuccessful designs shrink as successful designs win in the competition for resources. The larger populations mean that successful schemata "control" more resources in terms of matter, energy, and information than do unsuccessful schemata. Growth, however, may not follow a smooth pattern, but may follow a pattern of punctuated equilibrium due to a combination of network effects from coevolution and the shape of the fitness landscape itself.

Evolution is highly effective at finding fit designs in massive design spaces with *rough-correlated fitness landscapes* because:

- Evolution employs *parallel search*. In effect, each member of the population is an individual experiment in design, so there are many hikers out looking for high peaks.

- Evolution creates a *spectrum of jumps* on the landscape. It doesn't pursue just short, incremental jumps that could get stuck on local optima; nor does it pursue too many crazy long jumps that have a greater chance of failing than succeeding.

- Finally, evolution is a process of *continuous innovation*. The recursive nature of the algorithm never stops. This is essential, given the constantly changing nature of the landscape. There may be periods of more or less active search as evolution balances exploration and exploitation, but the search is never complete. The system has no equilibrium—in evolutionary systems, stasis is a recipe for extinction.

In effect, evolution says, "I will try lots of things and see what works and do more of what works and less of what doesn't." But in this process of sifting, remarkable things happen. The algorithm learns what the fitness function "wants," knowledge of that learning accumulates in the population of schemata, and the evolutionary process generates novelty as it searches for fitter and fitter designs.

Evolution is like a play. The cast of characters and the plot are fixed, but the particular actors, the setting, and many of the details are not. The evolutionary process can be set in biology, computer simulations, games with LEGO toys, or, as we will see, human culture, technology, and the economy. The universal evolutionary process produces the general results just described as long as the conditions are in place, no matter what the substrate.

From Evolutionary Theory to Economic Reality

As mentioned earlier in the book, evolution and economics have a mutually intertwined history stretching back to Darwin's time some 160 years ago. Although many of the great minds of economics, from Alfred Marshall to Friedrich Hayek, wrestled with incorporating evolution into economics, they were ultimately limited by two things. First, they struggled with trying to map an understanding of biological evolution onto economic evolution, raising questions such as, What is the economic equivalent of a gene? Is a group of companies a population? What constitutes a parent and an offspring in economic systems?[39] Often, these early efforts were just as guilty of metaphorical reasoning as Walras, Jevons, and the other Marginalists. Instead of biology, our starting point in part 3 will be the generic, algorithmic picture of evolution that we just discussed. The claim of the modern algorithmic view of evolution is that evolutionary systems are a universal class with universal laws. We can then ask whether the economy is a part of that class and subject to those laws. If the answer is yes, then the economic and biological worlds are both members of that universal class. They may be very different in their implementations of the algorithm, and thus asking what a parent and an offspring are in economics may make no sense. Nonetheless, the two worlds are still subject to the same general laws of evolutionary systems, thus explaining the strong (pardon the metaphor) family resemblance.

Perhaps the first pioneers down this road were Richard Nelson and Sidney Winter, with their seminal *Evolutionary Theory of Economic Change*. But from their vantage point in the late 1970s and early 1980s, the substrate-neutral, algorithmic theory of evolution was only just beginning to form. John Holland's landmark *Adaptation in Natural and Artificial Systems* was published in 1975, Richard Dawkins's *Selfish Gene* in 1976, John Maynard Smith's *Evolution and the Theory of Games* in 1982, and Stuart Kauffman's *Origins of Order* not until 1993. The ideas in these works and others provided germ seeds that have fed flourishing research programs since the mid-1980s, with important work continuing today.[40]

But Nelson and Winter and their economic predecessors also lacked another important ingredient—the massive amounts of cheap computing power available today. As we have seen, evolution is the relentless grinding of a simple algorithm thousands, millions, or billions of times across large populations. Such a process is almost impossible to model in the analytical style traditionally used by most economists, and only became possible in the 1990s as computers became more powerful.

We now have the roles and plot of our evolutionary play and are ready to begin casting the parts with economic actors and building the settings of organizations, markets, and national economies. The story of this play is the story of wealth creation, and the time has now come, in the words of Shakespeare's Falstaff, to "play out the play."[41]

PART III

How Evolution Creates Wealth

There is grandeur in this view of life, . . . [that]
from so simple a beginning endless forms most beautiful
and most wonderful have been, and are being evolved.

—Charles Darwin, *The Origin of Species*

CHAPTER TEN

Design Spaces

FROM GAMES TO ECONOMIES

TWO PEOPLE ARE ARRESTED for a crime, but the police lack sufficient evidence to convict either one. An interrogator puts the two suspects in separate cells so they can't communicate with each other. The interrogator tells each suspect that if he testifies against his partner, he will be given a reward for his help and released, provided his compatriot does not testify against him. If he testifies but his compatriot also testifies, then he will go to jail, but be given a reduced sentence for being helpful. But if he keeps quiet, he then faces two possibilities: If his partner also keeps quiet, then they will both go free due to a lack of evidence. However, if he keeps quiet and his partner testifies, then he will go to jail for a very long time.

This is the setup for the Prisoner's Dilemma—an economic problem that is so ubiquitous that Robert Axelrod of the University of Michigan, one of the pioneers of Complexity Economics, once called it "the *E. coli* of the social sciences."[1] Just as biologists often start with bacteria, fruit flies, and other simple organisms before moving on to the complexity of humans, we will start with a simple model and build up in increments our intuition for how the economy works. In this chapter, we will use the Prisoner's Dilemma as our *E. coli* model, and see how the evolutionary algorithm can be used to evolve designs for strategies in simple games. Over the course of part 3, we will graduate from games to the evolution of the economy as a whole.

The Prisoner's Dilemma

The choices in the Prisoner's Dilemma can be portrayed as a payoff matrix giving the results of different combinations of decisions (figure 10-1). The

FIGURE 10-1

Payoffs in the Prisoner's Dilemma

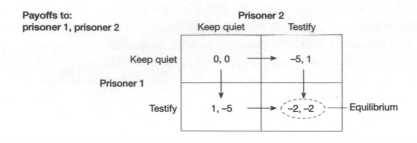

payoffs show that both prisoners have a strong incentive to testify. If you do not know what your partner will do and have no way of coordinating with him, you are always better off testifying. Specifically, if your partner keeps quiet, you're better off testifying (you get a 1 versus a 0), while if your partner testifies, you're still better off testifying (you get a –2 versus a –5). Since both players face the same incentives, the game slides into an equilibrium solution of both prisoners singing like birds and both going to jail. From the prisoners' point of view, this, of course, is not the optimal outcome, because if they could somehow coordinate their actions, they could both go free.

The Prisoner's Dilemma presents a classic trade-off between following one's narrow self-interest (testify, limit your own downside, and hope the other guy keeps his mouth closed) and trying to cooperate with someone else for a greater gain (if we both keep quiet, we can go free). This trade-off arises in situations as varied as nuclear arms control, business strategy, and marital relations. The Prisoner's Dilemma is an example of a *game theory* problem. As its name implies, game theory is used to study situations in which one can define a set of players (e.g., the two prisoners), a goal (getting rewards or avoiding jail time), a decision (to testify or not), and a set of rules that map the decisions to a set of payoffs for the players.[2]

The Prisoner's Dilemma is particularly interesting because it is an example of a *non-zero-sum game*. In a non-zero-sum game, cooperation between two or more people leads to some greater gain for the group. In the Prisoner's Dilemma, the total payoff to both players is maximized by their cooperating with each other; that is, if both stay silent, their combined payoff is 0, versus –4 for the alternatives. The maxim "you scratch my back and I'll scratch yours" is a non-zero-sum game, because cooperation enables us to capture a gain we could not attain on our own. In contrast, in a *zero-sum game,* for each winner there must be a loser—one person's gain is another person's loss. For example, in a bet between two people on the outcome of a football game, one will win and one will lose; there is no possibility of both being winners. As we will see, the existence of non-zero-sum games and the resultant tension between self-interest and cooperation play a central role in Complexity Economics.

The Prisoner's Dilemma presents us with a conundrum. The economy depends on cooperative activity—people need to work together to produce things, to trade with each other, and so on—yet, when people look at their narrow, short-term self-interest, they have an incentive to slack off at work, to cheat in trading, and generally not to cooperate. Even when people don't actually cheat, being the first to extend the hand of cooperation for the greater good might have risks when one doesn't know what others will do. In his book *Microeconomics,* the Santa Fe Institute economist Samuel Bowles illustrates this problem with a discussion he once had with local farmers in Palanpur, a small village in rural India:

> Palanpur farmers sow their winter crops several weeks after the date at which yields would be maximized. The farmers do not doubt that earlier plantings would give them larger harvests, but no one, the farmer explained, is willing to be the first to plant, as the seeds on any lone plot would be quickly eaten by birds. I asked if a large group of farmers, perhaps relatives, had ever agreed to sow earlier, all planting on the same day to minimize the losses. "If we knew how to do that," he said looking up from his hoe at me, "we would not be poor."[3]

Such dilemmas are called *coordination* problems. When people do not cooperate, game theorists refer to them as *defecting*. How is coordination achieved in the economy? How do we avoid the defection trap?

What if our prisoners made their decision, saw their results, and then had a chance to decide again—would it change the outcome? You would think that after ending up in jail a few times, the two prisoners eventually would learn that they could do better by cooperating with each other and keeping silent. Likewise, if the Palanpur farmers tried to coordinate their planting and some farmers cheated, the cheaters could be punished or sanctioned in the next growing season.

Unfortunately, there is a problem with this logic. If the game is repeated but has a fixed number of rounds, then we collapse back into a state in which the players defect again. In the Prisoner's Dilemma, if both players know that, for example, round five is the last round, then logic forces them to play as if it were just a single-round game. There is no round after round five, so that round, both players should automatically defect. However, we now face the same dilemma in round four. We know there will be no reward for cooperation in round five, so why not defect in round four as well? And so on, all the way back to round one.

But in the real world, we usually don't know in advance exactly how many rounds a game will be played. What if the game is played for a finite, but unknown number of rounds? A Palanpur farmer knows that he will only have a finite number of planting seasons in his lifetime, but he does not know how many seasons that will be. In this case, the game loses its equilibrium and conventional economic analysis does not tell us what the best strategy is. We have to look at a different way of thinking about the game.[4]

The Tournament of Champions

In the late 1970s, Robert Axelrod tried to answer the question of how to play a repeated Prisoner's Dilemma game with an unknown number of rounds using a very unconventional approach. He decided to conduct an experiment that has since become quite famous.[5] Instead of attacking the problem with mathematical analysis, he held a contest. He asked fourteen social-science researchers from around the world to submit a candidate for the best strategy. He then played the various entries against each other in a round-robin tournament. Some of the strategies were very elaborate and employed complex mathematical formulas. But the strategy that won the tournament was extremely simple. It was submitted by Anatol Rapoport, a professor of psychology and mathematics at the University of Toronto. Rapoport's strategy was memorably called Tit for Tat, and its first move was to cooperate, and from then on, it simply looked at the last move its opponent made and repeated the opponent's move. If its opponent cooperated, Tit for Tat cooperated; if its opponent defected, it defected. Axelrod was surprised at the success of this simple strategy and ran a second, larger tournament to test it further. This time there were sixty-two entries from leading scholars in economics, mathematics, physics, computer science, and evolutionary biology. Tit for Tat won again.

Axelrod was intrigued. How could such a simple strategy consistently outplay designs that were far more elaborate? Was Tit for Tat really the best, or was there some better strategy out there waiting to be discovered? Also, while Tit for Tat was generally successful, it did less well against certain strategies than others. In a sense, it was quite brittle. Imagine two Tit for Tat strategies playing against each other. Things are going swimmingly well with both players cooperating, when suddenly one player makes a random error and defects—the two Tit for Tat players then become stuck in a vicious cycle defecting against each other forever. This disastrous result from a simple error had particularly worrisome implications for one of Axelrod's areas of interest—nuclear arms control.

Axelrod wanted to explore other strategies but did not want to deal with the hassles of holding another, even larger, tournament. Then, Axelrod's University of Michigan colleague John Holland introduced him to the technique that Holland had invented in the mid-1970s for simulating evolution on a computer. (This is the same technique used by Holland in the stock market model with Brian Arthur and discussed in chapter 6.) Axelrod decided to try out Holland's simulated evolutionary algorithm and see if, instead of having humans propose strategies for the Prisoner's Dilemma, he could simply evolve strategies on the computer and then let nature take its course in a battle for survival of the fittest.

Strategies in Silico

Axelrod published his results in 1987, starting a chain of very fruitful research combining evolutionary simulation and game theory.[6] A recent contribution to this research is a model built by Kristian Lindgren, a physicist at the Chalmers University of Technology and Göteborg University in Sweden.[7] Lindgren's model is particularly interesting because rather than having pairs of agents play the Prisoner's Dilemma against each other in a tournament, Lindgren's model has multiple agents playing the game simultaneously on a computerized landscape, much as the agents interacted with each other in Sugarscape.

Lindgren's simulation of the evolving Prisoner's Dilemma provides us with a relatively simple *E. coli* model that captures several critical aspects of how evolution works in the complex adaptive system of the real-world economy. There are four key points to note: First, the inherent trade-off between cooperating and competing creates a central tension that keeps the system in a constant disequilibrium boil. This tension leads to a shifting pattern of cooperative structures that self-organize, grow, and break up over time, just as they do in the real economy. Second, consistent with our discussion in chapter 6, the agents playing the Prisoner's Dilemma in Lindgren's model have no way to globally optimize their behavior. All they can do is look at their own situation and their own history and do the best they can. Third, as discussed earlier, the dynamic interactions of agents can often lead to complex emergent patterns of behavior, many of which are inherently unpredictable, and Lindgren's model is no exception. Fourth, and perhaps most interestingly, this is a model that innovates. Like Karl Sims's evolutionary search for creatures that can swim, Lindgren uses evolution to find successful strategies for playing the Prisoner's Dilemma. In effect, we can think of Lindgren's model as using evolution to search the astronomically large design space of all possible Prisoner's Dilemma strategies.

The overall structure of Lindgren's model actually combines two games: the Prisoner's Dilemma and the Game of Life. The Game of Life was developed by the mathematician John Horton Conway and is played on a two-dimensional grid like a large checkerboard (figure 10-2). Each square on the grid is a *cell,* and each cell can either be ON or OFF at any point in the game. If a cell is ON, it is colored black; if it is OFF, it is white. Each cell has eight neighboring cells—four adjacent cells and four diagonals. Whether a cell is ON or OFF depends on the states of its neighbors, with each cell following a simple rule: Count how many neighboring cells are ON. If the number is exactly two, then the center cell will stay in its current state (whether ON or OFF) in the next round. If the number is exactly three, then the center cell will be ON in the next round, regardless of its current state. Under all other conditions, the cell will be OFF in the next round.

The Game of Life gets its name because as a result of setting up this grid of cells with these simple rules, one gets patterns of cells blinking on and off in a way that seems at times to almost be alive. Sometimes the grid appears to be a random mess of blinking lights; sometimes the cells self-organize into complex patterns, looking like bacteria growing across a *petri* dish. (One might notice a similarity between the Game of Life and Kauffman's Boolean networks, discussed in chapter 7. Both are types of *cellular automata,* a highly general class of computational systems developed by John von Neumann in the 1960s.)[8]

FIGURE 10-2

The Game of Life

For each cell, count its
eight nearest neighbors.

If exactly two neighbors are ON,
then the cell stays in its present state.

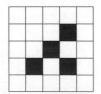

If exactly three neighbors are ON,
then the cell becomes ON,
no matter its present state.

In all other circumstances,
the cell becomes OFF.

Lindgren created a Game of Life grid in his model, but instead of having the cells on the lattice blink ON and OFF according to the normal rules of the Game of Life, he had them blink ON and OFF based on how the cells play the Prisoner's Dilemma game with each other. We will refer to the cells on the grid as agents, and each agent plays its four nearest neighbors (north, south, east, and west) in the Prisoner's Dilemma game (figure 10-3). Each agent might have a different strategy for playing. For example, one might be playing Tit for Tat, another might be playing Anti–Tit for Tat (always do the opposite of your opponent), one might always be cooperating, and so on. Lindgren colored each cell on the grid according to the strategy being played by the agent that occupies the cell (e.g., Tit for Tat might be blue). He then took the scores from each agent's four individual games with its neighbors and averaged them. The agent with the highest average score at the end of a round was declared the winner. The winner would then take over the square at the center of its neighborhood—like a virus, it would inject its winning strategy into that cell, in effect reproducing itself.[9] If, for example, an Anti–Tit for Tat agent won the round in its neighborhood, the center player would be taken over by Anti–Tit for Tat and use that strategy in the next round.

Now, how does each agent on the grid decide what strategy to play? We could just randomly seed different strategies across the grid and see what happens. Doing this produces a fairly dull result, as eventually, the lattice settles down into either some kind of equilibrium or a cycle of simple, repeated patterns. This also wouldn't help much with Axelrod's problem of looking for strategies that are better than Tit for Tat, because the probability of finding something good by testing randomly created strategies is quite low.

Instead, Lindgren decided to let evolution search the design space of all possible Prisoner's Dilemma strategies, looking for high-scoring strategies. Each agent on the board was given a schema, a computer DNA string of 1s and 0s that encoded its strategy. Lindgren assumed that the agents made

FIGURE 10-3

Combining the Game of Life and the Prisoner's Dilemma

Each cell plays its four nearest neighbors in the Prisoner's Dilemma.

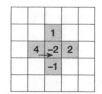

The cell with the highest score takes over the center cell.

their strategic decisions inductively, that is, they looked back at the history of moves and countermoves in the game and used that historical pattern to form an expectation of what a successful move in the next round would be. Thus, the input to each agent's computer DNA was the history of moves and countermoves, and the output was a decision on whether to cooperate or defect.

Lindgren initialized the game with agents that could only remember one move back. There are only four possible strategies for an agent that can only remember one move back:

- ALWAYS DEFECT. Always defect, no matter what your opponent did in the last round.

- ALWAYS COOPERATE. Always cooperate, no matter what your opponent did.

- TIT FOR TAT. Always do exactly what your opponent did.

- ANTI–TIT FOR TAT. Always do exactly the opposite of what your opponent did.

At the beginning of the game, Lindgren randomly endowed each agent with one of these four possible strategies. He then put the agents through a process of evolutionary variation by periodically zapping their DNA with random mutations. Lindgren's model employed three types of mutations. First, in *point mutations,* a bit of the agent's computer DNA was simply flipped, so 01 might become 00. Second was *gene duplication,* in which a piece of the DNA was replicated and tacked on at the end (e.g., 01 might become 011). One effect of gene duplication was that the agent's memory would grow to include more moves in its history. Thus, instead of just looking one move back, the agent might be able to look two or three moves back. With more memory, an agent could have more complex strategies, such as "If my opponent defected, then I defected, and then my opponent defected again, I will cooperate." Third and last, there were *split mutations* where one end or the other of the DNA was simply hacked off; for example, 011011000110001 might become just 011011. This has the effect of shrinking memory size and thus reducing the complexity of strategies.

In addition to mutations, Lindgren also gave another little random stir to the pot by having the agents occasionally make mistakes; an agent's strategy might indicate cooperation, but it would "accidentally" defect instead.

A Rain Forest of Bits

To begin the game, Lindgren created a playing board that was 128 by 128 squares. The board thus had a population of 16,384 squares, with one agent per square, each randomly initialized with one of the four basic strategies. Lindgren then hit the switch and started the players playing, and the evolutionary process began grinding away. Strategies started mutating, and the fittest strategies got the highest scores and started replicating into their neighboring squares.

An ecology was born. At first, the landscape of randomly scattered simple agents began to percolate and bubble as the four initial strategies interacted with each other—Tit for Tat and Always Cooperate agents got into love fests of cooperation, racking up high scores together. Meanwhile, Always Defects ruthlessly exploited poor helpless Anti–Tit for Tats, and Always Cooperates continued to cooperate, even as the Always Defects kept defecting. Pretty soon, however, large seas of noncooperating Always Defects began to ooze out over the board. But in these seas of distrust, islands of cooperation emerged. These islands were often arranged with a cluster of Always Cooperates in the middle, furiously cooperating and raising their scores, surrounded by a ring of Tit for Tats, which were keeping the evil Always Defects at bay. Yet, these colonies of cooperation were not stable. Sometimes, invading defectors would break into a cooperative island, dragging everyone down. At other times, an island of cooperation would grow rapidly like a bacterial colony, pushing out its bounds into the hostile sea of defection. From the chaos of the initial board, patterns of squares, zigzags, swirls, and other shapes emerged as the strategies organized themselves geographically in their titanic battle between cooperation and defection.

Soon, something else began to happen in the pulsing soup of strategies—innovations began to appear. Mutations that added genes caused agent memory sizes to grow, thus enabling the agents to look further back in history and devise strategies that were more complex. Many of the mutants were nonsensical strategies that died off quickly. But, in general, more memory is a big advantage, and new strategies that were successful began to emerge and reproduce. For example, Lindgren called one new strategy Simpleton. It cooperated if the two players chose the same move in the previous round (whether it was cooperate and cooperate, or defect and defect), but defected if the two players chose different moves. Another, which I will refer to as Vengeful, started out cooperating, but then, if its opponent defected, it would defect once (like Tit for Tat), but then defect a second time just to give the other agent a piece of its mind before returning to cooperating. Some of the strategies were quite clever. As mentioned before, one problem with Tit for Tat is that if two Tit for Tats are playing each other and one makes a mistake and accidentally defects, the two agents get stuck defecting with each other forever. One strategy, called Fair, starts out cooperating, but if its opponent defects, Fair gets "angry" and punishes its opponent by defecting until the opponent starts cooperating again. However, if Fair makes a mistake itself, it will then "apologize" by cooperating until it is forgiven by its opponent and then the two start cooperating again. Thus, Fair strategies tend to perform well in noisy, error-prone environments.

The King of the Forest

So who was the winner? What was the best strategy in the end? What Lindgren found was that this is a nonsensical question. In an evolutionary system such as Lindgren's model, there is no single winner, no optimal, no best strategy. Rather, anyone who is alive at a particular point in time, is in effect a winner, because everyone else is dead. To be alive at all, an agent must have a strategy with something going for it, some way of making a living, defending against competitors, and dealing with the vagaries of its environment. "Everyone is a winner" may sound like a cop-out, but survival is no mean feat. As Stuart Kauffman likes to point out, the vast majority of species that have ever lived on this planet are now extinct. Only the most infinitely minuscule portion of the fitness landscape is expressed into reality at any one point in time.

To get a sense for why "who won?" is a nonsensical question, take a walk through a typical patch of forest, a highly complex ecosystem of plants, insects, birds, and animals. All are agents using different strategies to make a living, some cooperating with each other, and some competing. So who is the king of the forest? Who has the best strategy for surviving and reproducing? Is it we humans, *Homo sapiens*? We seem to think we are running the show, but we've only been around for the blink of an evolutionary eye, and our long-term prospects remain uncertain. How about the little field mouse? This creature has been around longer than humans and certainly outnumbers us. How about a cockroach scurrying along the ground? Cockroaches have been around a lot longer than even mice and seem able to survive just about anything, from exterminators to nuclear blasts. What about the weeds that seem equally impervious to our efforts to eliminate them? Or the *E. coli* bacteria happily hitching rides in the stomachs of all the mammals running around the woods, including you? An even further complication is that if you did an *In Search of Excellence*–style study of your local patch of forest and somehow ranked the top one hundred most successful strategies for surviving and reproducing, and then looked at your list a hundred years from now (a mere moment in biological time), it would look completely different. Highly successful strategies today might be real losers in a hundred years, and the most successful strategies in a century might be ones that were only modestly successful today, or don't even exist yet.

Likewise, we cannot say any single strategy in the Prisoner's Dilemma ecology was a winner. Lindgren's model showed that once in a while, a particular strategy would rise up, dominate the game for a while, have its day in the sun, and then inevitably be brought down by some innovative competitor. Sometimes, several strategies shared the limelight, battling for "market share" control of the game board, and then an outsider would come in and bring them all down. During other periods, two strategies working as a symbiotic pair would rise up together—but then if one got into trouble, both collapsed. There were also the cockroaches of the game, simple strategies like Tit for Tat, which never dominated, but seemed somehow to survive and make a living, no matter what else was going on.

The game also proceeded in patterns of punctuated equilibrium. Over time, an established order of strategies would emerge and the game would go into a relatively stable period in which certain strategies dominated. During these periods, everyone cooks along, the agents' strategies are relatively stable, and no one has a particular incentive to change, thus establishing what the evolutionary theorist John Maynard Smith has called *evolutionary stable strategies*.[10] But sooner or later, a small innovation would appear and gather momentum, and suddenly the whole board would turn into a seething froth of change as the old order was wiped out and a new order was built to replace it. Sometimes the model had boom years that were favorable to cooperative strategies and during which everyone racked up great profits. Then, for no clear reason, the economic clouds would gather and a dark age of defection and losses would set in (figure 10-4).

Unpredictable but Understandable

All of this turbulence occurs because the success or failure of any strategy is highly dependent on the other strategies in the environment at a particular moment. One can think of the board as a giant ecological web, very much like the Jain and Krishna keystone model from chapter 8. As in the keystone model, small changes in one part of the system can ripple through and create big changes somewhere else. For example, imagine an island of Always Cooperate strategies surrounded by a protective layer of Tit for Tats who are keeping the Always Defects out and preventing them from exploiting the Always Cooperates. Then a few small mutations send the Tit for Tats into a downward spiral and create an entry for the Always Defects to invade. The Always Cooperate island quickly collapses and disappears.

This sensitivity to small changes means that one cannot predict the model's outcome using equations. It is as "un-forecastable" as the real economy. One

FIGURE 10-4

The Population of Strategies over Time

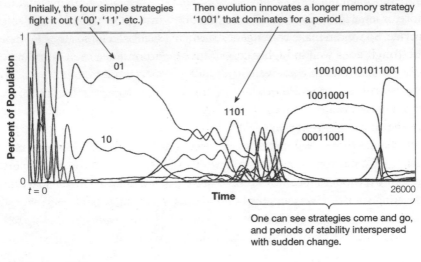

Initially, the four simple strategies fight it out ('00', '11', etc.)

Then evolution innovates a longer memory strategy '1001' that dominates for a period.

One can see strategies come and go, and periods of stability interspersed with sudden change.

Source: Lindgren (1997).

might think that this inability to forecast is due to the random factors in the model—the random mutations and the random errors in the agents' actions. Being a computer program, however, the model is actually perfectly deterministic. If one generates a table of random numbers to use for the mutation rates and errors and then reuses that same table in a second run, one will get results that are identical to the first run. One can know the exact starting positions of all the agents, their rules for behavior, and even what all the "random" numbers in the game will be in advance. However, even with all this information, there is no way to forecast the model's precise behavior in advance—it is simply too complex.

The only way to see what happens is to run the model and evolve it—there is no shortcut. While we cannot forecast such a model's behavior, we can, in a scientific sense, understand it. For example, we can see that there are certain tuning parameters for the model. These include the mutation rate, the error rate, and the relative payoffs in the game, all of which affect the game's macro behavior. For some values of these parameters, we might get highly cooperative, high-scoring outcomes. Other values might send the model into a depressed, low-cooperation state that is very difficult to get out of. We can also see that some values might lead to more innovation in new strategies than other values might produce. So, even though we can't make specific forecasts, we can make statements such as "A mutation rate of 0.001 or less leads to low innovation and low cooperation," or "From 0.001 to 0.01, the environment switches to being highly dynamic and innovative with high cooperation and profits." Likewise, some parameter values might provide a more or less favorable environment for some strategies than other variables provide. So we can make contingent statements such as "The strategy Friendly But Tough does well in highly cooperative environments, even with lots of noise, while Iron Fist does well in very low-cooperation environments." We can also run the model thousands of times with the same parameters, but with different random shocks to see how robust the outcomes are. We may then be able to say things like "For parameter settings of X, there is a 60 percent chance that a high-profit environment will emerge and a 40 percent chance of a collapse into low profits." Thus, while we may not be able to forecast the model's specific outcomes, by exploring the parameter space and collecting statistics, we can learn a good deal about the model's behavior. In many ways, a deep understanding of how the system works may ultimately be more valuable than being able to make forecasts.

In the previous chapter, we saw how Karl Sims used evolution to find good solutions to the problem of swimming. In Lindgren's model, we saw how evolution could be used to search for effective strategies in an economic problem. We discovered that there is no one best strategy; rather, the evolutionary process creates an ecosystem of strategies—an ecosystem that changes over time in Schumpeterian gales of creative destruction. We can now ask, if evolution can search the design space of simple economic games, could it also search the design spaces of more complex games? Could it search the design space of the biggest game of all—the $36.5 trillion global economy?

The Library of Babel

If a design space for the global economy sounds like an absurd idea, let's briefly consider another absurd idea—the Design Space for All Possible Literature. In his book *Darwin's Dangerous Idea*, Daniel Dennett asks us to imagine an astronomically large library that contains all the possible 500-page books that could possibly be written in the English language.[11] He calls this imaginary library the *Library of Babel*, after a Jorge Luis Borges story. A standard book page holds about two thousand character spaces, so a 500-page book gives us one million character spaces per book. As there are about one hundred English-language characters, including small letters, capitals, numbers, and punctuation marks, this means there are approximately $100^{1,000,000}$ possible books in the Library of Babel. As with the Library of Mendel and the Library of LEGO, the Library of Babel is vastly larger than the universe itself and thus can only be a theoretical construction.

Let's think about what we might find in the Library of Babel. There is a volume that consists of just blank pages and a volume with a single letter *a* and then all blank pages after that. There is also a volume with just five hundred pages of question marks. The overwhelming majority of books in the library are just random gibberish. As Dennett notes, there is a "vanishingly small chance" of finding a volume with even a single grammatical sentence in it. However, this library also holds a perfect copy of *Moby Dick*, as well as the complete works of William Shakespeare. It also contains a book that is identical to *Moby Dick* in every way except that the whale is called *Boby Dick*. There is also a *Coby Dick* and a *Doby Dick*. One bizarre feature is that somewhere in the library is a perfectly accurate 500-page biography of your life, including all the things that have not happened to you yet, and an account of your own death.

If a book is shorter than five hundred pages, say, Albert Camus' *The Myth of Sisyphus*, at 192 pages, there will be a 500-page volume whose first 192 pages are an exact copy of *The Myth of Sisyphus*, and its remaining 308 pages are blank. Likewise, books longer than 500 pages are represented in the library by multivolume sets; for example, James Joyce's *Ulysses*, at 933 pages, can be split into a 500-page first volume and a second volume with the remaining 433 pages followed by 67 blank pages. One can even claim that all books in all languages are somewhere on the shelves, as the library contains English translations of every possible book in every other language. Likewise, the best-selling book of the year 2042 sits in the library, even though it is yet to be written.

Some readers might accept that there are a finite number of LEGO designs that can be created out of a particular LEGO set, but might balk at the claim that there are a finite number of books that can ever be written—even if it is a beyond-astronomically-large number that will never be fully explored in the lifetimes of many universes. It is a mathematical fact, however, that such design spaces are indeed finite. Nonetheless, our intuition that such a design space grows over time as new works are created is not wrong, either. The notion of design spaces contains a paradox: on the one hand, they are finite, but on the other, they are unbounded and can grow, as mentioned earlier, like the surface of a balloon. The only thing that makes the number of books in the Library of Babel finite is Dennett's limitation of each book to 500 pages (and the trick of box sets), but this is an arbitrary limit. In theory, there is no fixed limit on the length of a book.[12] Nonetheless, there is always a book that is the longest in existence at a particular point in time, and thereby defines the upper bound of book length at that moment. Currently, according to the *Guinness Book of World Records,* the longest book ever written is Marcel Proust's thirteen-volume, 9,609,000-character *Remembrance of Things Past.* However, before Proust's book, the upper bound was something shorter, and in all likelihood, someone will someday write a book over 10 million characters. *But no one will ever write or read an infinitely long book.* This is because the laws of physics do not allow schema readers to read infinitely long codes.[13] Any design that is physically rendered in the real world therefore *must* have a finite schema, and a finite schema means a finite design space.

Design spaces are finite, but can expand or contract over time as the outer envelope of the longest renderable schema grows or shrinks. As mentioned in the previous chapter, the design space of DNA-based creatures on earth has grown as DNA has lengthened over time and as species' ability to render through "technology" (eggs, wombs, etc.) has kept up with that growth. Likewise, we could imagine that the size of literary design space changes over time. Books were undoubtedly shorter when printing technology consisted of chipping hieroglyphs onto stone tablets, and perhaps in the future, Proust will look pithy when books can be downloaded at high speed directly into our brains.

The Library of Babel illustrates another important point about design spaces—we can construct a design space for anything whose design can be represented by a string of symbols, such as the letters in the alphabet, or numbers, pictures, or the chemical codes of DNA. In other words, anything that can be digitized, and therefore stored on your computer, is eligible for a design space. We can thus imagine finite, but unbounded, Libraries of All Music, Art, Cooking Recipes, and Building Designs.

Now let's imagine we have stumbled upon the lost laptop of a businessperson, who perhaps accidentally left it at an airport X-ray machine. What might we find on that computer? We might find a few MP3 music files, photos of his or her family, and documents such as sales presentations, budgets, and e-mails describing various projects—and we might even find something called a business plan.

The Library of Smith

How might you describe the design of a business? Well, you might write down a description of the purpose of the business, its strategy for competing, its products and services, how it is organized, its marketing and sales plan, its production plan, the technology and skills required, its economic model, and so on. In short, you would write down a *Business Plan.*[14]

Rarely do even large, sophisticated companies have a single, all-encompassing Business Plan. Rather, the contents of such a plan might be scattered around the organization in various individual business unit plans, strategy presentations, organization charts, budgets, annual reports, regulatory filings, notes, and information carried in people's heads. At the same time, many small businesses don't have formal Business Plans at all; again, the information is in people's heads. The key point is that even if such a single document doesn't exist, it could, in principle, be created if anyone wanted to go to the trouble of doing it.

Following Dennett's Library of Babel, let's imagine a larger-than-astronomical library that contained every possible Business Plan that could ever be written in a 500-page volume or in boxed sets combining multiple volumes. Thus, instead of shelves of literature, we would have shelves and shelves of Business Plans stretching across the vast reaches of the universe. In fact, this Library of All Possible Business Plans would be a special subsection of the Library of Babel. I will call this sublibrary of Business Plans the *Library of Smith*, after Adam Smith.

If we searched the shelves of the Library of Smith, we would find the Business Plan for setting up a one-man shoe-shine stand in Times Square, a Business Plan that perfectly describes IBM's strategy today, the Business Plan for General Electric in 1952, the Business Plan for a wheat farmer in Lebanon in 8500 BC, and the Business Plan for a Yanomamö hunting party. The Library of Smith also contains the Business Plan for a company that manufactures and markets supernano neural-blastule tubes, even though supernano neural-blastule tubes won't be invented until 2023. The Library of Smith contains descriptions of all the ways that humankind has ever created or will create for organizing human beings to make a living. Of course, like all design spaces, the vast, vast majority of volumes in the library contain Business Plans that are utter nonsense, and only the tiniest fraction of the plans will ever be turned into reality.

But how detailed do these imaginary plans have to be? And how can we distinguish a Business Plan from a copy of *Moby Dick*?

We will use the same test that we would use on any other schema. The key test as to whether a volume in the Library of Smith is a valid Business Plan is whether a *Business Plan Reader* could use that plan to organize and create the economic activity described in the plan. What is a Business Plan Reader? It is a management team.

Let's imagine it is the year 2006, and we pull from one of the shelves in the Library of Smith a document titled "Cisco Systems Business Plan for 2007," which we hand to the existing Cisco management team. If the team could take the information in that plan, act on it, and realize the design described therein, then it would be a valid Business Plan. We could imagine feeding the Cisco management team various 500-page texts. If the text was gibberish, nothing would happen. If the text was *Moby Dick*, the team would have a nice read, but Cisco's business would not change. However, if we gave management a document that it could render into a new design for Cisco, then that qualifies as a Cisco Business Plan and a candidate design for Cisco. There would, of course, be an astronomical number of potentially valid Business Plans. One plan might advocate aggressive international expansion, another might push new product development, another might recommend scaling back investments, and others might be combinations of these strategies. Some plans would be profitable; most would not. There would also be plans that range from tiny, incremental changes to Cisco's existing business to absurdly radical changes, such as a plan that recommends it exit the computer communications business and go into fast food.

One objection might be that no imaginary Cisco Business Plan, even written over thousands of pages, would be sufficient in every detail for building Cisco. The objection, however, holds for any process of rendering a schema into a design. Schemata are inevitably a form of shorthand, a compression of the design they attempt to describe. Thus, not every tiny detail needed to run Cisco would be described in a valid plan. The Business Plan would rely on the Reader's already having implicit knowledge, context, and skills, just as our LEGO schemata could assume that the child Reader had certain skills in picking up and snapping together plastic bricks, or DNA assumes the existence of an egg and a womb with the requisite abilities. Thus, to be valid, a plan would have enough information so that the Cisco management team of 2006 would know what to do with it, but no more.

Like biological systems, the schemata of Business Plans and their readers coevolve. For example, the Cisco Business Plan for 2005 (again, whether it was written or just in people's heads) influenced what kind of management team would be in place in 2006, what kind of skills its members would have, what kind of knowledge they would possess, and what kinds of experiences they would have under their belts. This in turn would define the types of plans the team could read and act on for 2007, and the 2007 plan would consequently influence the future evolution of the management team, and so on in a coevolutionary circle.[15] If we gave the Cisco management team a Business Plan for a Yanomamö hunting party, it might be a perfectly valid plan for a group of rain forest tribespeople, but the Cisco team could act on it. Likewise, giving the Cisco Business Plan to a group of Yanomamö would not result in their suddenly building an Internet router company.

A Model of Economic Evolution

The economy evolves as evolution searches for fit designs in the Library of Smith, whether it is designs for Yanomamö hunting parties, IBM, or supernano neural-blastule tube companies in 2023. Just as the churning of the evolutionary algorithm through the Library of All Prisoner's Dilemma Strategies created patterns of innovation, growth, and creative destruction, so too does the churning of evolution through the Library of Smith lead to these patterns in the real economy.

If we return to our generic model of evolution from chapter 9, we can next ask how the process of variation, selection, and replication works in the substrate of Business Plans. Over the next four chapters, we will examine the process of evolutionary search for fit designs in the economy. We will see that variation occurs as people continually experiment with, tinker with, and invent new business strategies and organizational designs. Selection works at multiple levels in the economy, causing some Business Plans to succeed and others to fail. Likewise, replication occurs in economic systems as successful designs are rewarded with more resources and are widely copied.

Economic evolution is not the result of evolution in a single design space, but rather, as I will propose, the result of coevolution across three design spaces. In chapter 1, I briefly introduced two terms from Richard Nelson of Columbia University: Physical and Social Technologies.[16] *Physical Technologies* are what we usually think of when we think of the word *technology*. Physical Technologies are designs and processes for transforming matter, energy, and information in ways that are useful for human purposes, for example, turning sand into glass or into silicon chips. *Social Technologies* are equally important, but often less at the forefront of our minds. They are the designs, processes, and rules that humans use to organize themselves. Villages, armies, matrix organizations, paper money, the rule of law, and just-in-time inventory management are all examples of social technologies.

Business Plans play the critical role of melding Physical and Social Technologies together under a *strategy*, and then operationally expressing the resulting designs in the economic world. We need to think of Business Plans, Physical Technologies, and Social Technologies as three distinct design spaces because each has its own unique fitness functions at work. Business Plans tend to be selected for economic reasons, but Physical and Social Technologies may evolve for other purposes. Many important Physical Technologies have been invented to fill military, health care, or other societal needs, or developed simply because of the curious tinkering of scientists and inventors. Likewise, many Social Technologies, such as the rule of law or universal education, have critical economic functions, but may have been originally developed for other purposes. As we will see, a common feature of evolutionary systems is that an innovation evolved for one purpose may become co-opted for another, a process called *exaptation*.[17]

The model I will outline views economic evolution as the joint product of evolution in Physical Technology space, Social Technology space, and Business Plan space. We can think of these as three distinct, but interlinked and coevolving design spaces. In each space, evolution is at work, churning through possible designs, finding and amplifying ones that work, discarding those that don't, and thereby creating the order that we see in our technological, social, and economic worlds.

CHAPTER ELEVEN

Physical Technology

FROM STONE TOOLS TO SPACECRAFT

STANLEY KUBRICK'S film masterpiece, *2001: A Space Odyssey,* opens with a scene entitled "The Dawn of Man." The sun rises over the timeless beauty of the east African savanna, and we see a group of apelike creatures begin to stir with the morning. The creatures are early hominids—not quite ape, not quite human. The hominids make their way to a water hole, a scarce resource in the parched landscape, where they confront another troop of protohumans. The first troop is slightly larger, more aggressive, and better organized in its attack. It is a close fight, but the first group manages to chase off the others and get access to the water. Size, aggression, and social organization confer an advantage. This result is not an evolutionary surprise; the same story could be told about many other species.

In the second scene, some hundreds of thousands of years later, a slightly larger, more upright hominid is shown scavenging through the bones of a wild pig. His nimble hands, evolved for grasping tree branches, wrap around the pig's thigh bone, and he slowly begins to swing it around, smashing the other bones in the process. As he smashes up the pig's bones with growing enthusiasm, a critical connection is made in his bigger-than-an-ape, but smaller-than-a-human brain. The connection is that he can use the thigh bone as a club and smash the skulls of live pigs, just as he is doing with the skull of a dead one—a highly useful insight (in the movie, this critical moment is accompanied by the strains of Strauss's *Also sprach Zarathustra*). Now, this development is a bit more unusual in evolutionary terms, but not completely unique. Other species, in particular primates, use found objects as tools. For example, Capuchin monkeys use stones to smash open nuts, and chimpanzees use sticks to fish insects out of tree holes.

241

In the third and final scene, things get really interesting. A few hundred thousand years later, a group of hominids is shown sitting around, fashioning bones and sticks into recognizable clubs. Once our ancestors started actually making tools as opposed to simply finding them—or as anthropologists put it, creating *artifacts* as opposed to just picking up *naturefacts*—humankind took an important evolutionary step away from every other species on the planet.

The scene also shows an adult hominid teaching a child how to make a club, thus transmitting the knowledge of toolmaking to future generations through culture rather than genes. Neither the teaching of young nor the cultural transmission of knowledge is unique to humans; mother lions teach their cubs to hunt, and according to evolutionary theorist Richard Dawkins, once British tit birds learned to pry open milk bottles with their beaks the skill spread throughout the population by imitation.[1] But the *combination* of fashioning tools and transmitting that knowledge to peers and the young *is* something uniquely human—it was at this point that evolution literally leaped out of our bodies and into our social culture. That was the moment Physical Technology was born.

We next see Kubrick's hominids putting their newfound skills to good use, enthusiastically clubbing wild pigs to death and enjoying the resultant calorie and protein feast. But then the action returns to another confrontation at the water hole with a less developed hominid tribe. This time it is no contest; the club-wielding artifact creators pummel their competitors. In celebration, the alpha male of the victorious troop flings his club, which spins into the air and then poetically turns into a spinning spaceship circling the earth (to the tune of a Strauss waltz). Kubrick's point was made. Once the initial breakthrough in toolmaking and culturally transmitted knowledge occurred, it was just an evolutionary hop, skip, and jump to the modern world of spaceships and all our other technology.

The Dawn of Economic Man

In the non-Hollywood version of the story, this breakthrough in toolmaking probably occurred around 2.5 million years ago. The first evidence of hominid toolmaking is the crude, flaked-stone hand axes created by *Homo habilis* and found in the Olduvai Gorge of Tanzania. By the time we get to *Homo erectus,* around 1.0 million years ago, the tools are quite sophisticated, with fine strike marks and flaking on both sides, and a variety of designs. In addition, it was *Homo erectus* who discovered another highly useful tool—fire. Thus, between 2.6 and 1.0 million years ago, our ancestors began using their large brains to bend matter and energy to do their will and began sharing that knowledge with their children and peers.

Of course, no one knows exactly where, when, or how human economic activity first sprang into existence. But at some time during this period, two hominids, let's call them Harry and Larry, must have sat down next to each other and one of them, let's say Harry, grunted and used body language, to ask his colleague, "So, do you want a piece of meat for that ax?"[2] Perhaps Harry had had a lucky day hunting and had some extra meat lying around, and perhaps he wasn't very good at making axes or just didn't like doing it. And perhaps Larry, who found ax making easy and fun, was hungry after an unlucky day hunting. Larry grunted, "Yeah, sure," they traded, and the economy was born (cue Strauss . . .).[3]

Economies rely on the existence of two factors: Physical Technologies to enable people to create products and services that are worth trading, and Social Technologies that smooth the way for cooperation in creating and trading those products and services among nonrelatives. Evidence points to the presence of both these factors in the societies of *Homo habilis* and *Homo erectus*. Thus, we can say that at that point, the economy came into being (although long-distance trading did not begin until much later).[4]

Early hominid toolmaking was undoubtedly a process of limited but nonetheless logical deductive insight (e.g., "perhaps if I use a harder rock for striking, the softer one will flake more easily"), which led to experimentation (e.g., trying various stones of different hardness). Successful experiments then produced inductive rules of thumb for making tools (e.g., "this type of rock is good for flaking hand axes"). These inductive technology recipes could then be transmitted to children and peers, thus avoiding everyone's having to "reinvent the ax." With these socially transmitted technology recipes, humans began a bootstrapping process of Physical Technology evolution, as each generation of tools built on the successes and failures of those that had gone before, leading to tools of greater and greater functionality and complexity over time. We see evidence for this in the archaeological record, in which recognizable generations of tools appear over time at an accelerating rate.

Physical Technology Space

We can see the same evolutionary patterns in generations of more modern technologies, such as automobiles progressing from the Model T to a modern car jammed with microprocessors, or mobile phones progressing from suitcase size to "so small I forgot I had it in my pocket" size.[5] One can also see relationships between technologies that look very much like speciation—the airplane is related to hot-air balloons, dirigibles, and hang gliders in a sort of phylum of artifacts for flying. We can also observe technologies going "extinct." For example, in the middle of Washington, D.C., one can find the remnants of an old nineteenth-century canal system that in its heyday was packed with barges full of coal, food, and other goods. Today, the canal is used as a jogging trail, but one can still see a few old barges tied along the side, lovingly preserved, like stuffed mastodons in a museum of extinct technology species.

But is technology evolution merely a misused metaphor of the kind I have pledged to avoid? We can avoid the metaphor trap by showing that technology evolution can be mapped onto the general model of evolution outlined in chapter 9. A good starting point is developing a more precise definition of Physical Technology:[6]

> Physical Technologies *(PTs) are methods and designs for transforming matter, energy, and information from one state into another in pursuit of a goal or goals.*

For example, hominid Larry takes a couple of rocks (matter) and burns some calories smashing them up (energy) to create a hand ax (a design) in order to have a tool for chopping animal bones (a goal). Or a programmer uses calories from vending-machine food to power his or her brain, and electricity running into a computer (energy) to transform software bits (information) from one state to another to create a video game (a design) that people can use for entertainment (a goal). Some PTs result in the production of an artifact (e.g., a hand ax or computer program), but others result in the provision of a service. For example, one could imagine a set of PTs for making a bank loan or providing a Shiatsu massage. Services, like artifacts, involve transformations of matter, energy, and information for a purpose; for example, a Shiatsu massage involves transforming energy (the massager's calories) into specific motions (a design) for the purpose of relaxing the recipient's muscles.

A PT is not the thing itself (the hand ax, the software, or the massage), but rather, it is both the design for the thing, and the instructions and techniques for making it. One way of envisioning a PT is to think about what an instruction manual for the artifact or service would look like. For example, a manual for making stone hand axes might include diagrams of the completed ax, a description of the types of stones needed, and a guide to the method for banging them together to create the intended design. Just as with the Library of Smith, we can then define a schema for PTs—a schema that consists of natural language, mathematical symbols, pictures, blueprints, videos of physical demonstrations, and so on. Again, anything that can at least in theory be digitized can be part of the schema. In principle, even things such as verbal instructions and tacit knowledge can in principle be coded into the schema; for example, an anthropologist could watch Larry work on his hand ax and could transcribe into the schema a detailed description of what he or she sees.

My definition of PTs is in many ways similar to the Traditional Economics notion of technology. Traditional Economic theory contains "production functions" that transform raw materials, capital, and labor into products and services. Technology is then defined as the method by which that transformation occurs. But while technology is typically an exogenous black box in Traditional theory, we will look into its structure as an evolutionary system and attempt to understand how the black box works.

We can next imagine one of our vastly larger-than-the-universe design spaces, this time the Library of All Possible Physical Technologies.[7] Like our other libraries, it is finite at any point in time, its size defined by the length of the longest and most complex readable schema, but it is unbounded and can grow (or shrink) over time. We can imagine this library with near-infinite shelves of blueprints, designs, instructions, and recipes for transforming matter, energy, and information in various ways.

And just like our other design spaces, the vast, vast majority of designs in the Library of All Possible Physical Technologies are junk. Even though the designs may be physically realizable, most are boring, nonsensical, or absurd. The library is full of bicycles with square wheels, water jugs with holes in the bottom, and hammers made of cheese—and these are among the most coherent designs. Economically viable product and service designs are an even more infinitesimally tiny subset of the total library. Nearly all the functionally coherent designs have no economic value at all. The job of technology evolution, therefore, is to find the workable PT needles in the immense haystack of useless junk. It is then up to economic evolution to find the even-smaller subset of PTs that have economic value.

Physical Technology Readers

As with the other design spaces we have discussed, to qualify as a schema, a Physical Technology must be able to be read by a schema reader. Thus, we need someone, or something, to take the information in a PT and turn it into a real-world pattern of matter, energy, and information. That is, we need someone to take the instructions for building a house and actually turn it into a house. Again, our standard is not that the schemata contain so much information that just anyone can do it, but rather that a qualified reader could read the plans and make the object or provide the service. Thus, we would expect that a team of qualified house builders could use the PTs for house building to render the design for a house, or that a team of Eli Lilly scientists and technicians could use a set of pharmaceutical PTs to make the drug raloxifene. As before, the instructions for the PT do not have to exist in one document, but, rather, can be scattered around in various documents, as well as the knowledge in people's heads. The key principle is that the instructions could in theory (if not in practice) be memorialized in some form and transmitted to other readers. Finally, just as in the Library of Mendel and the Library of Smith, schemata and their readers coevolve. For example, as house builder skills and methods change, so do house designs, and as house designs change, so do the types of builders who are needed to build them.

One might counter that some aspects of tacit knowledge just cannot be captured in a schema. But if knowledge cannot be captured in any way, then neither can it be transmitted. We will call such knowledge *art* and exclude it from the library. For evolution to function, knowledge must be transmittable (and therefore able to be codified in some form). If Larry has some tacit knowledge about how to make particularly beautifully formed hand axes, but he cannot encode or transmit the knowledge in any way, then that knowledge will, sadly, die with Larry and not be a part of future hand ax PT evolution.

Early on in human history, PTs were simply the rules of thumb for describing how to create a tool ("use this rock, flake three times each side . . .") and were initially transmitted by way of imitation, grunts, and body language. Nonverbal signals are a pretty low-bandwidth method for coding and transmitting schema, which, of course, limit the size and complexity of the PT design space. Moreover, grunts and the like are not a very reliable communications method. Errors inevitably crept into early PT transmissions, yet for evolution to work properly, there must be a minimum fidelity in the transmission of information.[8] Thus, language was an enormous breakthrough in the ability to encode and transmit larger and more complex PTs and to do so much more accurately. The archaeological record shows a dramatic burst in toolmaking innovation and variety during the late Paleolithic period. During that epoch, work emerged in a greater variety of materials, and new designs such as fishhooks and sewing needles appeared. Although there is much debate as to exactly when our language abilities formed, some researchers believe that the sudden radiation in tool design is strong evidence of the development of language.[9]

Physical Technology Feeds Its Own Growth

One of the most remarkable things about human Physical Technology is how each new invention creates both the possibility of, and the need for, more inventions. Stuart Kauffman has noted that the invention of the internal combustion engine led to the invention of the automobile, which led to the invention of inflatable rubber tires, windshield wipers, asphalt paving, roadside motels, fast food, toll booths, and drive-through wedding chapels in Las Vegas.[10] Each invention opens up new niches for future inventions, and components from one invention are often recycled into new forms. As discussed earlier in the book, some inventions, such as the automobile, set off major avalanches of change, and some set off only small avalanches (the size of which Kauffman believes follow a power law). Nevertheless, all inventions have ripple effects, no matter how small.[11] Why does technology have this exponential, bootstrapping quality? How does technology feed its own growth?

Physical Technologies, like other schemata, have a modular, building-block character to them. Any PT can be thought of as coding for both *components* and an *architecture*.[12] A house has components (e.g., rooms, plumbing systems, windows) as well as an overall design (e.g., mock Tudor). A Shiatsu massage, likewise, has individual components (e.g., how to stretch the hamstrings) as well as a design for combining them.

Even something as primitive as a hand ax can be thought of in this way. A hand ax is basically a stone that has had its sides chipped by another stone into a sharp edge. One can think of the components of a hand ax as the part of the stone that the user grips and the part of the stone that is fashioned into the cutting edge. The architecture is the overall design itself, in this case, a hand grip with a cutting edge. The various combinations of components and architecture define the number of possible variations of the design. For example, there might be two variations of hand grips—say, a squat, round shape that is gripped in the palm, and a more tubelike shape that the user wraps the hand around. And there might be two variations on blade design—say, one that is flaked on just one side, and another that is flaked on both sides. We might also have variants at the architectural level, for example, a large version or a small version, or a granite version or a flint version. With these dimensions defined, we can then list possible variants of hand axes, for example, {large / granite / round / double-flaked}, {large / flint / round / single-flaked}, {large / granite / tube / double-flaked}, and so on, through sixteen variants of hand axes. We also can describe variants of much more complex artifacts in this way. Think of an automobile {V6 / 1.8 liter / 200 horsepower / four-door / leather seats / etc.} or a personal computer {2 GHz Pentium 4 / 128 MB memory / 80 GB hard drive / 4X CD burner / etc.}.[13]

It is this combinatorial property of components and architectures that gives PT space its vastly larger-than-the-universe size. It also means that innovations tend to cause PT space to unfold exponentially. Let's say there are two ways to make a hand ax, flake it on one side (single-flaked) and flake it on both sides (double-flaked). Then one day, hominid Harry stumbles onto a better way of shaping ax blades. In his new method of "fine flaking," he uses progressively smaller rocks to break off finer pieces and make a sharper edge. So we now have three blade types: single-flaked, double-flaked, and fine-flaked. With this single innovation, the number of possible hand ax variants jumps from 16 to 24. Or, returning to the measure of product variety we used in chapter 1, we can say the number of potential SKUs discovered in PT space jumped by 8 SKUs, or 50 percent, with just one innovation. Likewise, each time Intel adds a new variant to its microprocessor lineup, the number of potential SKUs in the computer market takes a huge jump.

Innovations in architectures can also cause jumps in SKUs. Let's say the innovative Harry one day takes a large, tube-shaped hand ax, and instead of flaking a sharp blade, he fashions it into a slightly dull point.[14] Even though this may at first look like a minor component innovation, it turns out to be an entirely new architecture—a stone mortar that can be used for grinding up nuts, mashing grains, and other useful things. With no further innovation, right away Harry has added 4 new potential SKUs to the stone tool market: {large / granite mortar}, {small / granite mortar}, {large / flint mortar}, and {small / flint mortar}. The number of SKUs added by an innovation climbs exponentially with the complexity of the artifact. An architecture with just two components and two variants on each component has 4 possible SKUs, an architecture with three components and three variants per component has 27, and an architecture with four components and four variants per component has 256. Architectural innovations can also lead to new innovations in components. The development of the personal computer architecture, for example, spurred widespread innovation in component design. Thus, each innovation sends shockwaves both big and small through PT space, and the number of possible SKUs unfolds exponentially with each act of invention.

Yet only an infinitesimally small fraction of the *possible* SKUs in PT space will ever be thought of, let alone explored or realized into products or services. Although there may be thousands, or even tens of thousands, of personal computer variants currently available in the market, only a minuscule fraction of the possible total computer variants are ever made and sold. Apple offers a computer with a PowerPC processor in screaming translucent orange. Dell offers a computer with a Pentium processor in basic black. No one has yet found good reason to offer a computer with a Pentium processor in screaming translucent orange, and thus, such a variant remains a potential, but not yet realized SKU in PT space. Thus, a key impact of new inventions is not only do they add actual new SKUs to an economy, but they also open up the space of *potential* SKUs as well. Each invention creates further headroom for more inventions, and PT space spirals up from hand axes to Kubrick's image of a spaceship circling the earth.

Technology Evolution by Deductive-Tinkering

In chapter 9, we discussed how the fitness landscapes associated with evolutionary systems tend to be rough-correlated, that is, neither a completely random jumble, nor a perfectly ordered landscape with a single peak. Evolutionary landscapes are typically somewhere in between, like the Alps. An important question for Physical Technology space is whether its fitness landscape is rough-correlated as well, because this will determine whether evolution is the best way to search it.

A rough-correlated PT space makes intuitive sense. It means that closely related designs in the space will generally have similar levels of fitness. For example, we would expect that two engines of the same design, but with slightly different parameters for their spark plugs, would probably have similar, though not identical, performance. However, this general correlation is not perfect; most small variations in spark plug design might not matter very much, but some differences might matter a lot and cause the engine not to function. Thus, while the landscape is correlated with high peaks tending to be near other high peaks, the landscape is also rough and jagged, with plateaus and Swiss cheese holes.[15]

A further piece of evidence in favor of the rough-correlated PT space hypothesis is essentially an existence proof. As discussed, evolution is a highly effective algorithm for searching rough-correlated spaces, and the evolutionary process tends to create rough-correlated spaces.[16] Thus, if we can show that the process by which people engage in PT innovation follows an evolutionary search process, then it is likely that PT space is rough-correlated.

As one considers the possibility that PT innovation is an evolutionary process, a natural reaction is, "But evolution is a blind, random process, while technology innovation is directed by human rationality and intention. How do we square that circle?" The answer is that there is nothing fundamental in the nature of the evolutionary algorithm that says intentionality and rationality cannot play a role, nor does anything say the process must be completely random. At its core, evolution is an iterative process of experimentation, selection, and then amplification of things that work. The random part of the process in biological evolution is the creation of variety for selection to act on.[17] But even this is far from completely random. Mutations may be random, but recombination in sexual creatures is not. Competition for mates ensures that fit organisms have a higher probability of pairing off with other fit organisms.

The only requirement is that the algorithm be fed a sufficient variety of experiments for selection to act on. The experiments must cover a broad enough swath of the fitness landscape to give the algorithm a fighting chance of finding high peaks. From the algorithm's point of view, it doesn't really matter how the process achieves that diversity. In the case of humans searching PT space, the evolutionary algorithm gets its diversity of experiments through what I will call deductive-tinkering. My use of the term *deductive-tinkering* is an amalgam of ideas from the psychologist Donald Campbell and from Herbert Simon's notion of "purposeful adaptation."[18] Basically, humans use two cognitive processes in the act of invention. One is their deductive, logical thinking facilities. In its unsophisticated form, deduction is a hominid making the mental connection that a club can be used as a weapon to kill prey, as in the scene in *2001*. In its sophisticated form, deduction is an engineer from Intel using theories of quantum mechanics to figure out what the limits are in packing circuits onto a chip.

The second part of the model, the tinkering part, is where we simply try stuff. As much as modern engineering uses science, there is still a lot of "let's try it and see what happens."[19] There are numerous well-known stories of people stumbling onto useful inventions. For example, in the 1980s, the 3M chemist Spence Silver was trying to make stronger adhesives and accidentally made one that was weaker. His colleague Art Fry then used the weak adhesive to make a sticky bookmark, which eventually morphed into the now-ubiquitous Post-it Note.[20] The Post-it Note was not discovered by deductive logic alone; serendipitous tinkering played a major role as well. As Henry Petroski, an engineering professor at Duke University, has put it, "Form follows failure."[21] Now, underlying the gut feel of tinkering, there are undoubtedly the workings of unconscious inductive cognitive processes, associative thinking, and reasoning by analogy, so tinkering is not a truly random process, either. Nevertheless, tinkering does the job of increasing the spread of experiments beyond what we would come up with using deduction alone.

In addition to deductive logic and inductive tinkering, an element of random craziness also informs what humans try. For example, Larry Walters, a thirty-three-year-old California truck driver, went to Sears one day in 1982, bought a lawn chair, strapped forty-five helium-filled weather balloons to it, and, with a cooler of beer and an air pistol, soared sixteen thousand feet into the air, disrupting air traffic across all of Southern California.[22] He originally intended to land by shooting the balloons with his pistol, but in his nervousness at being sixteen thousand feet in the air, he dropped the pistol after only popping a couple of balloons. After several hours, he slowly drifted back to earth, where his contraption became entangled in power lines, blacking out most of Long Beach. Eventually, Walters managed to clamber down to safety. Walters was apparently not interested in deductively testing any theories of aeronautics; nor was he researching the commercial potential of flying lawn chairs—he simply wanted to fly. Even with all our scientific, deductive engineering and our careful inductive experimentation, there will always be a few people out there trying crazy things. Although the flying lawn chair has not emerged as a major new technology, the crazy stuff has the effect of keeping the spread of experiments in PT space quite wide, and every once in a while, something works.

To picture the effects of the deductive-tinkering model, imagine a spot on an alpinelike, rough-correlated fitness landscape. This spot represents the design for a particular PT, for example, a microchip design. Then, draw a range of experiments on the landscape around that point. Your drawing might look something like figure 11-1. We would see tentacle-like fingers of exploration emanating from the current design. The emanations are the highly directed branches of deductive exploration. These branches would go to areas of the landscape that theory, science, and past experience say are fruitful, and would avoid areas not expected to be fruitful. In our microchip example, these branches would represent the carefully thought out, incremental efforts by the chip's engineers to improve its design. Next, we would see oozing around the fingerlike branches a region of tinkering experimentation. This would represent the bolder, more speculative efforts of chip designers to explore more risky ideas. Finally, we would see a few random blobs in the landscape; these are people trying things for the heck of it. The distribution of experiments over the landscape would not be the same shape as if the experiments

FIGURE 11-1

Deductive-Tinkering on the Landscape

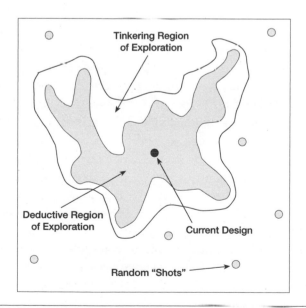

FIGURE 11-2

Deductive-Tinkering Versus Random Mutation and Crossover

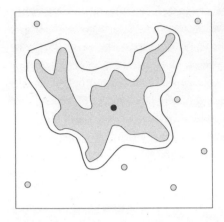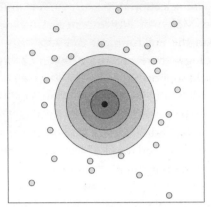

While the pattern created by deductive-tinkering (left) may be different from random mutation and crossover (right), both create a spread of experiments on the landscape and provide evolution with a source of differentiation.

were driven by random mutation and crossover (figure 11-2). But the key point is, the spread would be large enough for evolution to do its job.

Selection on the Physical Technology Landscape

Deductive-tinkering thus provides a mechanism for the variation of Physical Technologies. How, then, does selection work, and what determines fitness on the PT landscape?

As with variation, the process is different from biological evolution, but still consistent with the basic workings of the general algorithm. All PTs have a purpose, a functionality of some kind.[23] Designs for cell phones exist so that we can communicate, designs for coffee cups exist for holding coffee, and designs for plastic souvenir snow globes exist to remind us of that great trip to Montreal. Physical Technologies are selected according to their fitness for their purpose, whatever that purpose is. We thus look for PTs that meet their purposes better than alternative PTs do. By "better," I mean that they are more effective in meeting their purpose and are more economically efficient at it than the alternatives. Thus, the survival and widespread use of PTs for making snow globes is prima facie evidence that many people have found the globes to be both effective and efficient at fulfilling their purpose of providing entertainment and a bit of memorabilia. The globes' continued survival shows that on a relative basis, they stack up well in their competitive environment against souvenir coffee cups, tacky tea towels, and T-shirts that say "My friend went to Montreal and all I got was this lousy T-shirt."

For selection to occur in an evolutionary system, the system needs what Joel Mokyr of Northwestern University calls *superfecundity*—more designs than the environment can support—which thus creates competition.[24] In biology, there are more potential organism designs than any ecosystem could support. In technology, there are more possible PTs than people could possibly use, for example, more possible trinket designs than the tourists of the world could ever want. Evolution works in PT space because we have a superfecundity of PTs that compete with each other, and because people over time tend to select PTs that are the most effective and efficient in fulfilling their purposes.

Imitation Is the Sincerest Form of Flattery

Our last stop on our evolutionary checklist is replication. A key test for whether evolution is working is that successful designs should grow in frequency in the overall population of designs. In biology, the process is fairly straightforward. Genes that contribute to fitness have a higher probability of being passed on to the next generation than do genes that do not contribute to fitness. Thus, fit genes increase in frequency. But how does it work for technology? How do Physical Technologies replicate and thus grow in the population of PTs?

Quite simply, PTs that provide benefits to people get copied. For example, the first PT for making molded bricks was discovered in Mesopotamia around 5000 BC.[25] This highly useful invention was widely copied, and through deductive-tinkering, all sorts of variants on PTs for brick making evolved. The information for making bricks was stored in people's heads, was embedded in the artifacts themselves, and recorded in written descriptions. People watched and copied, masters taught apprentices, people looked at bricks themselves for clues, descriptions were eventually written down, and the art of brick making rapidly radiated to the four corners of the world.

Physical Technologies are thus replicated as humans spread them from one individual's head to another, as artifacts embodying the PTs are copied, and as the PTs are written down on stone tablets, printed in books, and put on Web pages. We can think of PTs as having a "market share" that fluctuates over time as successful PTs spread and unsuccessful ones die out. For example, PTs related to bricks had their heyday in London in the Victorian era, but then in the twentieth century, lost share to PTs using glass and steel. We can thus say that brick PTs enjoyed a replication advantage for a period, but this then diminished as other competing PTs grew in popularity.

With the outlines of a model for Physical Technology evolution in place, we can now look briefly at some of its implications. First, we will see how the rough-correlated geometry of the landscape helps explain the phenomenon of technology S-curves. Second, we will examine how the modularity and interrelationships between PTs account for the impact of disruptive technologies. And finally, we will look at how science has changed the process of PT evolution itself.

Explaining Technology S-Curves

In the 1980s, my colleague at McKinsey & Company, Richard Foster, developed a theory of the natural life cycle of technologies and described it in his book *Innovation: The Attacker's Advantage*.[26] Foster's theory was based on observations and case histories ranging from sailing ships to microprocessors. He found a strikingly consistent pattern in the cases and data he studied. In the early days of a new technology, performance is poor and progress slow. However, after a period of investment and tinkering with various designs, the performance of the technology suddenly takes off on an exponential improvement curve. During this period, each dollar invested in R&D yields substantial gains in performance from the technology. But as the technology matures, the curve of performance improvement begins to taper off. Diminishing returns on investment begin to set in. Foster called this pattern the S-curve, because a graph of the level of effort invested in improving a technology versus its performance gives an S shape (figure 11-3).

The second part of Foster's theory was that once returns on investment in one technology begin to tail off, entrepreneurs begin to have an incentive to look for new technologies. Early progress tends to be slow but eventually reaches the takeoff point, and the new technology replaces the old one as the market "jumps S-curves." Foster's message to companies was that the period of discontinuity between S-curves is a vulnerable point for incumbents. Established players tend to focus on milking as much value as possible out of old technologies. Typically, they expect the gains in performance of the past to continue. The players downplay the threat from new technologies even as their own performance flattens out. This leaves the incumbents susceptible to attack from smaller innovators, who are focused on the new technology.

If the fitness landscape of Physical Technology space is indeed rough-correlated, then we would expect to see exactly the types of S-curves observed by Foster. Stuart Kauffman notes that in the early days of the bicycle,

FIGURE 11-3

Technology S-Curves

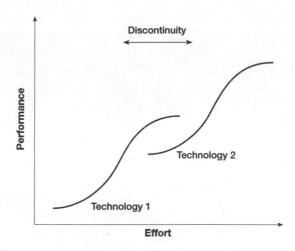

there was a plethora of experimental designs—big front wheels, small back wheels, various steering mechanisms, and so on.[27] But once the now-familiar architecture for two equal-sized wheels was worked out, improvements in the basic design came rapidly and the performance of bicycles soared. Then, after this period of progress, the top of the S curve was reached and further improvements were limited to refinements in various components, such as better gears and lighter frame materials, within a largely fixed overall architecture. Over time, new architectures such as the racing bike and the mountain bike were discovered, and journeys up new S-curves began.

To see such a story in terms of the fitness landscape, let's say that a certain spot represents the very first bicycle design and has a certain level of fitness associated with it (figure 11-4). All around this spot are potential design variations that are waiting to be discovered. Areas near the original spot represent small changes in bicycle design; areas farther away represent more radical innovations. With the goal of improving the fitness of the bicycle, you start some experiments and begin tinkering with your current design to see if some variations will improve or reduce its performance. In fitness-landscape terms, this is equivalent to exploring around your immediate area and seeing where the higher peaks and lower valleys are located.

Since you are starting with the very first bicycle design ever discovered, there are limitless variations that have never been tried before. Many of these variations could possibly lead to higher fitness, but more could lead to lower

FIGURE 11-4

Rough-Correlated Technology Landscapes Lead to S-Curves

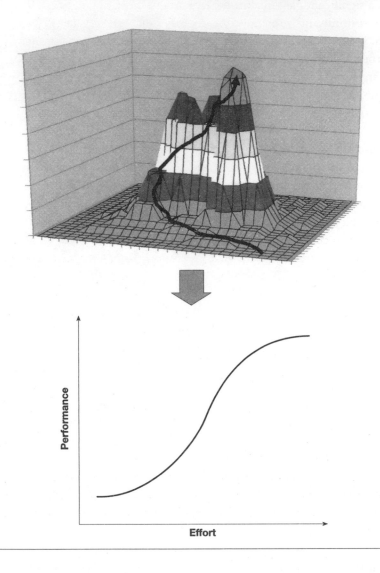

fitness, because bad ways to build a bicycle always outnumber good ones. Once you have identified the direction of the good designs—the high peaks on the landscape—you start heading that way. At first, though, your progress is slow, as you tinker with various experiments and try different paths. The high peaks are off in the distance, and you are just in the foothills. But after some initial wandering, you hit on a good design (e.g., two equal wheels, rear-wheel powered), which is equivalent to finding a good route up into the highlands. For a period, your ascent in fitness is very rapid; each step you take yields a significant gain in altitude. Eventually, though, you begin to close in on the summit and your upward progress slows. As you climb higher and higher, you notice something important; with each step, the number of possible routes upward decreases by a constant fraction. At the beginning, you faced any number of potential directions and untried designs. But once you set on your path and neared the summit, the number of potential paths upward began to shrink to increasingly incremental improvements.

If the fitness landscape of PT space were perfectly random, we would not see S-curves. The payoff to investment in a given technology would also be random, as any step on the landscape would yield a random change in fitness. If, at the other extreme, the fitness landscape of PT space were smooth and perfectly correlated (Mount Fuji–like), then there would be only one supreme bicycle design. We wouldn't have bicycle gearheads arguing over whether a Specialized S-Works Model 04 is better than a Cannondale R500. Nor would we have the discontinuity of jumping from one S-curve to another. In a perfectly correlated space, once the summit of design was attained, there would be nowhere else to go. Rather, S-curves are the natural result of the geometry of rough-correlated fitness landscapes.

Disruptive Technologies

In his book *The Innovator's Dilemma*, Clayton Christensen, a professor at Harvard Business School, asked why the jumps from one S-curve to another are so often major stumbling points for large, successful companies. In a careful study of the evolution of the computer hard-disk industry, Christensen found that what appear to be small changes in technology can often be highly disruptive.

Christensen claimed that whether a technology is disruptive depends less on how radical a technological advance it is, and more on its specific effect on the S-curve. If a technology pushes performance up an existing S-curve, even very rapidly, then the technology tends to preserve the power of existing players. However, when a technology requires a new S-curve, particularly when it starts at a worse price-performance point than the current technology, the newer technology tends to be disruptive and to change the industry structure. This is because any executive in a successful incumbent company would have a difficult time justifying investing resources in a technology that offers, at least initially, worse price performance. The first 3.5-inch disks were slow and expensive and held little data; an executive at a leading 5-inch disk company would reasonably ask, "Why would our customers want that?" By the time a new technology begins to climb the new S-curve, the incumbents of the old technology are stuck fighting a rear-guard battle to catch up, a battle they usually lose.

This "innovator's dilemma," as Christensen called it, makes perfect sense in the context of a rough-correlated landscape for Physical Technology space. As hard-disk designs shrank from 14 inches to 1.8 inches over time, the challenge was more than just making the same product smaller. Instead, it required significant changes to numerous components, new manufacturing techniques, and replacing many mechanical parts with electronic ones. While the changes might on the surface appear incremental, in fitness-landscape terms, these were big jumps. Although we have been visualizing fitness landscapes in three dimensions for convenience, the modularity of designs means they are really hugely multidimensional constructions. If one changes five components in a design, then one is moving across five dimensions of the landscape. "Distance" in the fitness landscape is a function of *both* the number of dimensions changing and amount of change in each dimension. Thus, the occurrence of many changes across many dimensions, as in the shifts in hard-disk size, qualifies as a major move on the landscape.

Almost by definition, architectural innovations require changing many things at once, whether the transition is from sailing ships to steamships, or racing bikes to mountain bikes. In a detailed study of the semiconductor equipment industry, Rebecca Henderson of MIT and Kim Clark of Harvard Business School showed that architectural innovations tend to be more disruptive of industry structure than innovations in individual components.[28] By viewing innovation as a search across a fitness landscape, we can see the common thread running through the work of Foster, Christensen, and Henderson and Clark: it is very difficult for successful, incumbent companies to make long jumps in the PT landscape. When you are on top of a local peak, there are far more ways to go down in fitness than up, and leaping to a new architecture appears highly risky. From the perspective of an entrepreneur or a new entrant starting in the low valley of a new architecture, there are lots of ways up and many new, untried peaks to explore. Most attempts up from the entrepreneurial valley will wind up in dead-end canyons or on disappointing short peaks. But with enough explorers working away, someone will eventually find an attractive route up.[29]

The Scientific Revolution: Reprogramming Evolution

A critical feature of Physical Technology evolution is that the fingers of deductive exploration have a higher probability of hitting high-fitness peaks versus experimental tinkering or a purely random search. Though far from perfect, human deduction is extremely helpful for seeing the potential consequences of actions, and for performing mental simulations rather than having to build everything. For 99.9 percent of human history, the reach of our deductive capabilities was relatively limited, and the deductive-tinkering model was far more tinkering than deduction. Humans had many PTs that worked, but did not know why they worked or how they worked. Despite these limitations, humans and their ancestors produced a slowly growing stream of inventions over a period of 2.5 million years.

Then, as we discussed in chapter 1, around 1750, something quite extraordinary happened; PT space and the consequent SKU count in the economy exploded. The trigger was the scientific revolution. The origins of the scientific revolution began around 1500 with the resurrection of classical knowledge during the Italian Renaissance, which reignited interest in natural phenomena. This renewed interest was pursued in the sixteenth century by figures such as Leonardo da Vinci and Nicolaus Copernicus. In many ways, however, da Vinci and Copernicus were still more tinkerers than scientists. It wasn't until the seventeenth century, following Francis Bacon's articulation of the scientific method and Galileo's establishment of the role of experiment, that the groundwork was laid for the tremendous advances of Isaac Newton, Robert Boyle, and others later in the century. Science then set off on an exponential curve of discovery that we are still riding today.[30]

The impact of science has essentially been to dramatically increase the hit rate of deductive insights. Deduction thus suddenly began to play a much bigger role in the deductive-tinkering mix. Deductive scientific theories did not completely replace tinkering; any engineer will tell you that what works in theory does not always work in practice. But the balance was tipped toward a very potent combination of the two, thereby dramatically increasing the speed with which evolution could find high peaks in the PT landscape.

Technology evolution is not a mere metaphor. It is the result of humankind's deductive-tinkering search through the near-infinite possibilities of Physical Technology space. The nature of the process of differentiation, selection, and replication in this substrate is different from that of biology, but it is an evolutionary process nonetheless. This means that PT evolution follows the same general laws that apply to other evolutionary systems. It also means that PT evolution exhibits behaviors common to other evolutionary systems such as the tendency of innovations to spur further innovations, and the punctuated-equilibrium nature of technology change. But PT evolution has a characteristic that is unique to human systems—we can reprogram our own evolutionary search algorithm. The invention of science has enabled humankind to unfold PT space at an explosive rate, and the consequent innovations of the industrial and information revolutions have transformed society and the planet. Having traveled from "The Dawn of Man" to a world of orbiting spaceships, we now turn back to our hominid friends, for Physical Technology is only half of the story.

CHAPTER TWELVE

Social Technology

FROM HUNTER-GATHERERS TO MULTINATIONALS

IN 2002, WILLIAM EASTERLY of the Institute for International Economics and Ross Levine of the University of Minnesota conducted a detailed study of seventy-two rich and poor countries and asked, "What makes one country richer than another?"[1] One might assume that the major determinants of national wealth include factors such as the existence of natural resources, the competence of government policies, and the relative sophistication of a country's Physical Technologies. Easterly and Levine found that while these factors all mattered to a degree, the most significant factor was the state of a nation's Social Technology. The rule of law, the existence of property rights, a well-organized banking system, economic transparency, a lack of corruption, and other social and institutional factors played a far greater role in determining national economic success than did any other category of factors. Even countries with few resources and incompetent governments did reasonably well if they had strong, well-developed Social Technologies. On the flip side, no countries with poor Social Technologies performed well, no matter how well endowed they were with resources or how disciplined their macroeconomic policies were.

Not only do Social Technologies affect the performance of a nation-state, but they also explain differences in performance at the more granular levels of industries and companies. During the late 1990s, economists began to notice a rapid rise in the productivity of the U.S. economy. At first, researchers looked to PTs for an explanation. There had been massive investments in computing power over the previous two decades, and a leading hypothesis was that the economy was at long last seeing the payoff from that investment.

However, my colleagues at McKinsey & Company's Global Institute were skeptical and delved underneath the headline productivity figures.[2] They found that the real driver of increased productivity was changes in how companies were organizing and managing themselves—in other words, innovations in Social Technologies.

One of the industries the McKinsey team examined in depth was retail, and in particular the impact of Wal-Mart on overall sector productivity. Wal-Mart's innovations in large-store formats and highly efficient logistical systems in the 1980s and early 1990s enabled the company to be 40 percent more productive than its competitors. This challenge in turn forced its competitors to imitate Wal-Mart's organizational innovations and raise their own productivity 28 percent in the late 1990s. Meanwhile, Wal-Mart continued to increase its own productivity a further 22 percent. This particular innovation race in Social Technologies in the retail sector alone accounted for *nearly a quarter* of the growth in overall U.S. productivity during the period. Similar Social Technology innovation races in five other sectors made up virtually all the rest. Computers certainly played a vital role in this story; without them, Wal-Mart's sophisticated logistics processes would not be possible. But computer technology played an enabling rather than a primary role; it was the innovations in organization and processes that yielded the dramatic productivity gains.

Let's Get Organized

In the previous chapter, I defined Physical Technologies as methods and designs for transforming collections of matter, energy, and information from one state into another in pursuit of a goal or goals. Social Technologies can be defined similarly:[3]

> Social Technologies *(STs) are methods and designs for organizing people in pursuit of a goal or goals.*

A group of people might come together and organize themselves to start a company, to form a religion, or to create a Friday night bowling league. Such acts of organizing are always in pursuit of a goal, whether it is profits, spiritual enlightenment, or a bit of fun. Just as PTs are methods for creating order in the physical realm to meet human needs, STs are methods for creating order in the social realm also to meet human needs.

The term *Social Technologies* is a close cousin of a term used by economists: *institutions.* Nobel Prize winner Douglass North defines institutions as "the rules of the game in a society."[4] Institutions are one ingredient in organizing, but I intend for my definition of STs to be somewhat broader and include other ingredients such as structures, roles, processes, and cultural norms. Social Technologies include all the elements necessary for organizing. The STs of a soccer team include not just the rules of the game, but also the job description of the goalkeeper, the cultural norms of the team, and whether the team fields three strikers at the front or two strikers and a sweeper at the rear. While the STs of a soccer team would include a complete description of the team's organizational methods, it would *not* include the strategy used by the team. Thus, statements such as "attack on the left" or "focus on short passes" would not be included. In an economic context, such strategies are a part of a Business Plan. This is a distinction we will return to later in the book.

How Social Technologies Evolve

Given this definition of STs, it should come as no surprise that we can construct a theoretical design space for them, a Library of All Possible Social Technologies. We will follow the same path we traveled for imagining the Physical Technology design space. In the ST library are schemata that code for specific designs and instructions for creating social structures. We can imagine writing out instructions for organizing a Yanomamö hunting party, describing the organizational structure of GE, or laying out European banking regulations. These instruction sets might include natural-language text, charts, and tables that include descriptions of the organizational structure, roles, decision processes, formal rules, incentive systems, codes of behavior, and so on. As before, we can imagine these STs encoded in multivolume sets of 500-page books— a vastly-larger-than-the-universe Library of All Possible Social Technologies.

As with PTs and Business Plans, in the real world, some STs exist in writing, but many exist only in people's heads. Social Technologies don't actually have to be written down, but in principle could be written down to a sufficient degree that a qualified reader could act on them to realize the design. So a Yanomamö hunter could understand the schema for a hunting band, a GE executive could understand the GE organization description, and an appropriately experienced EU bureaucrat could understand the banking regulatory structure.

Like the other design spaces we have discussed, the library of STs has three important attributes. First, like its PT cousin, the ST design space is self-feeding and exponentially unfolding.[5] Each ST breakthrough creates more headroom for the next set of breakthroughs—the invention of money enabled the invention of accounting, which enabled the invention of the joint stock company, which enabled the invention of stock markets, and so on.

Second, STs have a modular, building-block quality to them. For example, the organizational design of a large multinational corporation is a collection of modules that includes designs for organizing its business units, designs for its accounting and control systems, designs for its committee structure, and designs for its cultural norms of behavior.[6]

Third, the fitness landscape associated with ST design space is highly likely to be rough-correlated. Small differences in ST designs tend to yield small differences in relative fitness, but occasionally, small changes will make a ST either unworkable or much better. Thus, the ST fitness landscape, like our other fitness landscapes, has an alpine, rough-correlated shape, with flat spots, Swiss cheese holes, and the occasional portal to higher ground. A prediction from this assumption is that just as we observed S-curves and disruptive technologies in PT space, we would expect to see the equivalent in ST space. History seems to bear this out.[7] For example, the jump from hunter-gatherer ST to settled agriculture can be regarded as a major shift in the S-curve of human economic organization.[8] Likewise, Henry Ford's 1914 development of a radical new way of organizing manufacturing—the production line—was a highly disruptive ST that changed the structure of the early automotive industry, as well as many other industries.[9]

Deductive-Tinkering in Social Technology Space

If the Social Technology fitness landscape is indeed rough-correlated, then a further implication is that a highly effective way to search it is our grand-champion search algorithm—evolution. Just as people use deductive-tinkering to search Physical Technology space, they use deductive-tinkering to search for fit STs in ST space. For example, when Henry Ford and his team developed the production line, they didn't just sit down and deductively theorize about it on paper.[10] Nor did they merely try random experiments. Instead, they used a bit of both. Ford was motivated by the desire to manufacture a car that "the masses" could afford. To do this, he needed to reduce the number of skilled craftsmen in his manufacturing process, thus enabling more of the work to be done by less skilled and less expensive workers. Ford was familiar with advances by the U.S. Ordnance Department's Springfield (Massachusetts) Armory in using standardized interchangeable parts in its manufacturing process, and while he and his team probably did not read much theoretical economics, they were generally familiar with views on the benefits of labor specialization. Armed with a set of deductive hypotheses, Ford began experimenting with different configurations of his plant between 1908 and 1912. After four years of tinkering, in 1913 he struck on the key insight that the car itself should move along the production line rather than the workers, and by 1914, he had implemented a fully working, moving assembly line.

In STs, the ratio of deduction to tinkering is more weighted toward the latter than is the case with PTs. Despite advances in economics and organization theory, there is still far more art than science in activities such as redesigning a company's organization or creating a central banking system, as compared with building a jet aircraft or designing a new heart drug. The pattern of exploration on the fitness landscape of ST space has thus historically featured relatively few directed fingers of deduction and more clouds of trial-and-error exploration. One of the promises of Complexity Economics is that, over time, it will push the art-science boundary in ST a step further toward science. Despite the lesser role of deduction in ST space, the process of searching for fit STs using deductive-tinkering is nonetheless an evolutionary process. People conduct experiments with various STs, and then over time, successful designs tend to persist, while less successful ones fade away. Successful designs tend to be amplified as they are copied, attract more resources, and spread. For example, Ford's innovation of the moving assembly line spread rapidly through the manufacturing sector, displacing other STs, and remains standard practice today.[11]

There are tight linkages between PTs and STs. As humans move across the fitness landscape of PTs, they cause rumblings, earthquakes, and other upheavals in the landscape of STs, and vice versa. An advance in PT such as the ox-drawn plow could only have happened after the ST innovation of village-based agriculture (try carrying a plow as a nomad). Likewise, as mentioned earlier, many management innovations in the modern era have depended heavily on advances in computing and communications technology. In fact, the agricultural, industrial, and information revolutions can each be viewed as coevolutionary merry-go-rounds of advances in PTs leading to new forms of STs, which in turn were crucial for further advances in PTs, and so on.

Competing to Cooperate

We can next ask, what drives humanity's deductive-tinkering search through Social Technology space? What spurs us to constantly seek out new and better ways of organizing ourselves? The answer lies in the magic of non-zero-sum games.

In chapter 10, I noted the distinction between zero-sum games, in which one person's gain is another person's loss, and non-zero-sum games, in which both people can be made better off by cooperating. Cooperation in non-zero-sum games has a $1 + 1 = 3$ logic, whereby if you scratch my back, I'll scratch yours, and together we can do something neither can do as well on our own and we both benefit. Non-zero-sum cooperation is one of those Good Tricks of survival that has been widely employed by biological evolution. Dogs hunt in packs, termites collectively build mounds, fish swim in schools, and, like most primates, members of *Homo sapiens* live in groups.

But while the benefits of cooperation in non-zero-sum games are substantial, as the Prisoner's Dilemma showed us, there is often a tension between cooperating for the greater good and pursuing one's narrow self-interest.[12] In his thought-provoking book, *Non Zero*, the journalist and science writer Robert Wright argues that much of human history can be viewed as the outcome of this central tension between cooperation and self-interest.[13] Wright claims that the process of bootstrapping social complexity, from simple hunter-gatherer tribes to organized villages to nation-states and global corporations, has been the result of humans innovating new ways to cooperate across larger and larger scales and devising ways to play increasingly complex and profitable non-zero-sum games. He notes that in a world where resources are finite at any given moment, there are competitive pressures to cooperate. Over time, societies that are better able to organize themselves will socially, economically, and militarily dominate societies that are less successful at creating cooperative structures. Thus, it is the competition to cooperate that drives social innovation.

Recasting Wright's thesis in the language we have developed, we can view the deductive-tinkering search through the ST fitness landscape as a quest for STs that enable people to play and capture the benefits of non-zero-sum games. Social Technology fitness will therefore depend on three factors. First, the ST must provide the potential for non-zero-sum payoffs. Second, it must provide methods for allocating the payoffs in such a way that people have an incentive to play the game. And third, the ST must have mechanisms for managing the problem of defection. Let's take a closer look at each factor.

Non-Zero Magic

There are four basic sources of $1 + 1 = 3$ magic in non-zero-sum games. All four have been well known to Traditional Economic theory for a long time. First is the division of labor. As discussed in chapter 2, this benefit was pointed out by Adam Smith over two centuries ago. If two people have even slightly different skill sets, mutual gain can be created by each person's focusing on what he or she does best and then trading. If Larry is a good hunter and Harry a good ax maker, then Larry is better off stalking game than futilely pounding rocks, and vice versa.

Second is the heterogeneity of people. Their different needs and tastes create opportunities to trade for mutual benefit (something we saw in Sugarscape). Charles Darwin observed the benefits of this type of trade while interacting with Fuegian Indians during his voyage on HMS *Beagle*: "both parties laughing, wondering, gaping at each other; we pitying them, for giving us good fish and crabs for rags, [etc.]; they grasping at the chance of finding people so foolish to exchange such splendid ornaments for a good supper."[14]

Third are the benefits of increasing returns to scale, a concept discussed in chapter 3. A lone hunter, for example, might invest 500 kilocalories (kcal) of energy in a few hours of hunting, and have a 20 percent chance of killing an animal worth 2,500 kcal of food. Thus, his expected return would equal 500 kcal, and he would just break even. Now imagine he joins two others to form a hunting party. The three still invest 500 kcal each, but their odds of getting a kill now jump to 90 percent. Thus, the expected value becomes 750 kcal each (90 percent of 2,500 kcal, divided by three). Simply by joining the group, our hominid hunter has made a 250-kcal profit on his investment and greatly reduced his risk.

Fourth, and finally, cooperation helps smooth out uncertainties over time. If one hunting band has a successful day and another does not, the successful band can share its bounty with the unsuccessful group under the proviso that the others do the same when the situations are reversed (and perhaps the payback will include some interest). Cooperation is thus a Good Trick for mitigating risks. If you are on your own and have a run of bad luck, you starve. But if you are in a cooperative group, your colleagues can tide you over until you can pay them back.

Dividing the Spoils

These four sources of non-zero-sum gains can be mixed and matched in various contexts to create a near-infinite number of ways that people can cooperate for their mutual benefit. But for people to have an incentive to cooperate, they must receive some share of the spoils. How the gains of cooperation are divided up is therefore a crucial question. If the rewards are distributed in the wrong way, then cooperation collapses and the non-zero-sum gains evaporate.

Allocating the payoffs from cooperation is where John Nash (profiled in the popular book and film *A Beautiful Mind*) first made his mark with a brilliant paper in 1950 titled "The Bargaining Problem."[15] In the paper, Nash asked the simple question, how will two bargainers come to agreement? How much meat will Harry give Larry for the hand ax? As simple as it sounds, the problem stumped economists for generations. Nash's elegant solution was to say that how two or more bargainers split up the gains from exchange depends on how much each values the benefits of the deal, and what the parties' alternatives are. Each looks for his or her best deal assuming everyone else is looking for the best deal, too, and the trade is made at the point at which *no one has any incentive to change position, given the actions of the other.*

This point became known as the *Nash equilibrium*. Thus, as Harry and Larry haggle over the ax, they eventually find a point at which both are happy to trade and neither can improve his position without blowing the deal—they make the trade. Both walk away better off than they would have been had they not traded at all, thus capturing the non-zero-sum gains of cooperation.

But the existence of a Nash equilibrium does not guarantee a happy, cooperative result. In the single-round Prisoner's Dilemma, the Nash equilibrium is the solution in which both prisoners rat on each other and go to jail. This is because, if you are one of the prisoners and you don't know whether your colleague will talk or stay silent, you are better off talking. As your colleague in crime faces the same incentives, you can assume that he will talk, too. Nash's theorem tells us that for non-zero-sum games to result in cooperation, either the payoffs need to be structured such that everyone's best response is to cooperate, or the players need some mechanism for coordinating their responses. For example, let's say the prisoners have a mafia boss who promises to kill anyone who testifies and to reward anyone who keeps quiet after being released from jail. That would change the payoff structure and move the Nash equilibrium to a point at which both clam up and go free. Likewise, if the prisoners were allowed to communicate and knew what the other had been offered, they could coordinate their responses and avoid the defection trap. This last solution, however, would still have the possibility that one prisoner could nevertheless sell out the other for gain; after all, there is no honor among thieves. This leads to our third critical factor in ST fitness; for STs to be fit, they must have mechanisms for dealing with those who don't play nice.

Cheaters (Mostly) Never Win and Winners (Mostly) Never Cheat

The incentive to cheat means that cooperation is inherently difficult to achieve and potentially unstable even once attained. One hunter might run just a bit slower than his friends and expend only 400 kcal, and yet, so long as his colleagues don't notice his free riding, he will still get his 750-kcal meal. Likewise, the meat I give you for that nice hand ax might be rather old and tough, or I might give you only five ounces instead of the agreed-upon six. The selfish logic of biological evolution says that if cheaters cheat and get away with it, they improve their chances of passing their cheating genes onto their offspring. Thus, cheating confers an evolutionary advantage.

But if biological selection gives cheating genes an advantage over sucker genes, how, then, does cooperation get a foothold in a population? The answer is that the gains from cooperation are so powerful that cooperating genes have an advantage over cheating genes—but only if the genes aren't naive, don't let themselves be suckers, and ensure that cheaters get punished.[16] To survive, cooperating genes need some sophisticated defense mechanisms. Recall our earlier discussion of Kristian Lindgren's model. In the Prisoner's Dilemma, if the players play for just one round, both players have an incentive to rat on each other. When the game is repeated, however, and no one knows when it will end, the dynamics become much more complex. The types of robust, successful strategies that evolve usually have a logic along the lines of this: "I will begin on the assumption of mutual cooperation. If you cheat on me, however, not only will I refuse to cooperate, but I will punish you, even to my own near-term detriment. After some time, though, I might forgive you and try cooperating again, just in case your cheating was an error or a miscommunication, or on the chance you have reformed your ways. If, however, you cheat again, the probability of my forgiving you again will become lower and my punishment even more terrible."[17]

Just as evolution produced this kind of logic in the world of Lindgren's computer model, so too did evolution produce this kind of logic in the minds and instincts of our ancestors. Earlier in the book, we discussed a series of experiments called the ultimatum game in which researchers gave two subjects a pool of money and asked one person to decide on how to split it, and if the other agreed the split was fair, each could keep his or her share. If the partner rejected the split, however, neither got any money. The results of these reciprocity experiments were striking. Economic logic says that people should accept any offer of a split, no matter how small, because some money is always better than no money. In test after test, however, subjects rejected offers that were perceived as unfair, even to their own detriment. The results were consistent across cultures around the world, including hunter-gatherer cultures. Other games and experiments confirm the consistent and deep-rooted nature of human cooperative-reciprocity behavior.[18] Evolution has steered us in a direction whereby we are naturally inclined to be cooperative to capture the riches of non-zero-sum gains. Nevertheless, it has also equipped us with a sensitivity to cheating, expectations of fairness, and a willingness to mete out punishment to those we believe have crossed the line. In effect, evolution has programmed into our mental software sophisticated, intuitive "Nash equilibrium finders" and "fairness detectors" that enable groups of humans to form coalitions that are at least reasonably stable and resistant to attack by free riders and cheaters.[19]

Our reciprocity software, however, is not hardwired—it can adapt to local circumstances. When we are in an environment in which most of our experience is of other people's cooperation and reciprocation and in which social norms give us signals that people can be trusted (e.g., people tell admiring stories about self-sacrificing, trustworthy types), then our mental cooperation software will tend to be biased toward cooperating. It also will be more surprised and more forgiving when it encounters an example of defection or cheating. In essence, our minds statistically sample the population around us, and if people are usually cooperative, then when we encounter a cheater, we will tend to assume that the person's behavior is probably the result of an error or misunderstanding. In contrast, in a low-cooperation, high-cheating environment with social norms that don't support cooperation (e.g., the stories are all about thieves, and people tell you to "watch your back"), our cognitive cooperation software biases us toward being suspicious. We react harshly to the first signs of cheating, forgive only slowly if at all, and are likely to resist cooperating until given a sign of cooperation from the other party first.

The local tuning of reciprocity norms can create very complex dynamics at the level of populations. High-cooperation societies can see collapses in cooperation if cheating reaches a critical mass; low-cooperation societies can get stuck in uncooperative, economically impoverished dead ends; and when people from different cooperative traditions mix, it can lead to misunderstanding and turmoil.[20] The same issues can arise in organizations too. As we will discuss in chapter 16, high-cooperation, high-trust cultures in companies tend to lead to higher economic performance, and mergers between companies can run into significant problems when populations that have evolved different trust parameters are suddenly thrown together.

Thus, Social Technologies that are better at tapping into sources of non-zero-sum gains, finding cooperative Nash equilibriums for allocating those gains, and managing the defection problem will be higher on the fitness landscape than those that do not. As people have deductively tinkered their way across the landscape in search of fit STs, humankind has evolved increasingly complex and sophisticated social structures for addressing these three issues.

From Family Units to Business Units

The journey of Social Technology evolution began with our genetic predisposition to cooperate most closely with near kin.[21] Family members, after all, share some of our genes, and helping them helps increase the odds that those genes are passed on to the next generation. Our ancestors' earliest cooperative social structure was thus the family, with hominid family habits somewhere between profligate chimpanzees and monogamous apes. In most hunter-gatherer tribes, polygynous men took multiple wives if they could, and the higher the status of the male, the more mates.[22] Early humans tended to be polygynous, but unlike chimps, the males did generally stick around and invest in their mates and offspring, creating relatively stable family units.

Some societies never advanced beyond this most basic of social structures. Robert Wright notes, for example, that the Nunamiut Eskimos and Shoshone Indians were until quite recently organized around family units, with little social structure beyond that.[23]

The first step up the social structure ladder was cooperative hunting bands. The basic caloric logic of hunting bands—you get more to eat—is so compelling that most present-day hunter-gatherer societies and, by implication, most early societies discovered this form of cooperation. However, cooperative hunting bands in most early societies were relatively small scale and were made up of mostly kin or near kin.

The big bang in social cooperation came with the advent of settled agriculture. Physical Technologies for domesticating crops were independently discovered in various parts of the world beginning around eleven thousand years ago.[24] The increased calories and reduced risks of settled agriculture enabled settlements to become more permanent and the size of human groupings to rise significantly, which meant that cooperation began to extend beyond clans of family members. This in turn opened up a slew of new non-zero-sum games.[25] Cooperative groups could tap economies of scale such as the ability to build shelters and other structures that could not be built with only a few family members, could glean benefits from the division of labor in creating artifacts, and could pursue trade between distant villages.

However, all these innovations in cooperation created a new issue: Nash's problem of how to divide the resultant wealth. The sexual hierarchy of our primate background provided a natural answer to this, what Robert Wright and others call the "Big Man Society."[26] In our closest primate relatives, as in many other species, males compete with each other for sexual access to females. Big, strong, clever, and aggressive males push away weaker males for access to females, causing their big, strong, clever, and aggressive genes to be passed on to subsequent generations. In polygynous societies such as those of early humans, the more dominant the male, the more mates, and the more mates, the more offspring. This created a hierarchy of high-status and low-status males. As groups of early humans coalesced into societies of nonrelatives, this sexual hierarchy quite naturally transferred into a socioeconomic status hierarchy for dividing up the spoils of cooperation. The two hierarchies are, of course, two sides of the same coin: the characteristics of sexual dominance (e.g., size, intelligence, and aggressiveness) in our ancestral environment also tended to translate into economic success, and being economically well-off tended to translate into sexual status, as wealthy men could provide more resources for mates and offspring.[27] Thus, from ancient Greek myths to modern tabloid newspapers, humankind's three favorite topics of conversation—sex, money, and status—have been linked from our earliest days.

As discussed, hierarchy is not very much in vogue. No one likes dictators. Corporations are urged to flatten themselves into teams, and business leaders are supposed to resist the temptation to strut around their organizations as the alpha male or alpha female. Yet, the theory of networks shows that hierarchy plays a critical role in any information-processing system, whether it is a computer chip, the Internet, the human brain, or the economy. To tap into the benefits of a division of labor and economies of scale, someone needs to divide up tasks, coordinate their execution, bring things back together, and allocate the spoils. In early societies, that someone was usually a sexually dominant male. Wright describes the role of such a "Big Man" in an early American northwest coastal tribe:

> The chief planner was the political leader, the "Big Man." He held the allegiance of a clan, maybe a village. He orchestrated the building of salmon traps or fish cellars, and he made sure that some villagers specialized in, say making canoes that other villagers could then use. To pay for all of this he would take one-fifth, or even half, of a hunter's kill. Some of this revenue would be returned to the people in the form of chief-sponsored feasts . . .
>
> Needless to say, the Big Man skimmed a little off the top. He lived in a nicer-than-average house and owned a nicer-than-average wardrobe.[28]

One can see that it is not a terribly far distance to modern CEOs and politicians.

Once humans had the invention of hierarchy, it was then a simple step to the nested structure of hierarchy within hierarchy. We can just imagine the progression: at some point, a successful Big Man with a growing village to run does not have enough time to keep his eye on salmon trap production, so he appoints his younger brother or best friend to run that aspect of village life—and voilà, the business unit is born. The Big Man boss has reporting to him minibosses, who in turn have minibosses reporting to them. Hierarchy facilitates the division of labor and the processing of information. It is pervasive in all human social structures, ranging from hunter-gatherer tribes to neighborhood bowling leagues to big corporations.[29]

Peace, Love, and Understanding

While social and economic hierarchies have important information-processing benefits, such structures are inherently unstable. There is constant competition for the top spots, and inevitable succession battles when the Big Man loses his effectiveness or dies. Organizational turmoil is very costly, while stability has many benefits. Stable organizations have the ability to accumulate knowledge and skills over time, play non-zero games with longer-term (and potentially more lucrative) payoffs, and provide more certainty for the participants, thus attracting their cooperation at lower cost. In primate troops, the method of hierarchy management is fairly straightforward. A large, clever, aggressive male dominates the group, until another larger, cleverer, more aggressive male topples him in a violent coup. Unfortunately, this method of hierarchy management is still used today by dictatorships, organized-crime syndicates, and other unsavory social organizations.

With the advent of agriculture and larger, more permanent settlements, a series of innovations were developed for managing power transfers in hierarchies without (or at least with less) costly violence. These innovations included primogeniture (e.g., a prince becoming a king) and the selection of leaders by "elders" (e.g., an Afghani *loya jirga* or a papal election by cardinals). Relatively more recent innovations include democratic elections with universal suffrage, and shareholder governance of corporations. Interestingly, despite the layers of civility in the modern versions of these processes, the threat of physical force always lurks below the surface. If a U.S. president were ever to refuse to leave the White House after losing a valid election, some rather large men in dark sunglasses would presumably cart him or her away. Nonetheless, Social Technologies for managing changes in hierarchical structure have been crucial in enabling organizations to maintain stability and endure over time.

Not only does competition within hierarchies need to be managed, but competition *between* members of different hierarchies also presents both threats and opportunities. Human groups need STs that enable cooperation between complete strangers. The first problem that strangers must overcome when they meet is that they don't know whether to trust each other. The parameters for their norms of cooperation and reciprocity behaviors might be very different, and one party might take advantage of the other in a transaction. Thus, people need STs for figuring out whom they can and cannot trust beyond their immediate kin. The first such ST extending beyond individual villages was undoubtedly tribal identity. By identifying "your people" versus "outsiders," you could efficiently find people with whom you were more likely to share social norms. And since your interactions in a tribe were likely to be repeated over time, you were less likely to get ripped off or to have destructive miscommunications.

Historically, trading networks have tended to develop first and most strongly within tribal, ethnic, and religious groups. Consider the Mayan trading network that covered a large swath of Mexico, Guatemala, and Belize from 250 to 900 AD; the extensive Muslim trading networks that stretched from North Africa through the Middle East and into Central Asia over the past thousand years; and the Ivy League–dominated Wall Street firms. The ugly side of this tagging of "your people" versus "outsiders" is discrimination, which is inherently self-limiting. In the absence of other information, tagging may be a strategy that reduces risk, but it also excludes a larger world of potentially beneficial relationships.

In a sense, exclusionary tagging is like having a closed computing environment in which only computers of the same brand can talk to each other (e.g., IBMs to IBMs, Dells to Dells)—there are benefits to standard protocols for communications and behavior, but at the cost of scalability. Thus, a major breakthrough in ST was the development of an open protocol to enable strangers to cooperate: the rule of law. Laws enable complete strangers, with different backgrounds, histories, ethnicities, and social norms, to conduct business with each other with greatly reduced risk. For example, a major investment such as buying a home can be intimidating even with all the protection of property law, building codes, and insurance. Imagine what it would be like if such transactions were completely unregulated. There is a powerful correlation between the wealth of a society and the existence of written laws with mechanisms for enforcement and adjudication.[30] Establishing the rule of law is considered a critical hurdle by development economists when they are trying to stimulate growth in poor countries, and countries without strong legal systems inevitably fall back on tagging as a less efficient and socially divisive substitute. Laws, of course, don't completely replace trust, and societies can become dysfunctional if social trust breaks down and people over rely on legal institutions (witness the increasing litigiousness of U.S. society). Nevertheless, complex, large-scale cooperation is impossible without a well-functioning legal and regulatory system to provide protocols for cooperation.

Communications is also critical in engendering cooperative behavior. Thus, the development of language increased dramatically the potential for social and economic cooperation, unlocking a host of new non-zero-sum gains. There is much debate on when language developed—the admittedly wide range of estimates is from 30,000 years ago to around 1 million years ago.[31] Regardless, language probably developed well after toolmaking, for which there is evidence from 2.5 million years ago. Consequently, there was a phase of human economic activity that was prelinguistic and thus inherently limited in its level of complexity. Just as language transformed humankind's ability to create Physical Technologies, so too did it transform the creation of STs. One can imagine the advantage that language genes must have carried with them; as vocabulary rises, the space of beneficial, cooperative social games opens up exponentially. Imagine trying to negotiate a complex deal with someone if you could use only grunts, gestures, and facial expressions. Now imagine trying it with fifty words of bad, tourist-quality French. Now imagine it with the fluent language skills of a native speaker.

Once language was developed, a series of PT innovations further enhanced its value in cooperative activities. Writing, which appeared around 5,000 years ago (and thus by the standards of human history is a relatively recent invention), enabled people to disseminate knowledge more widely and to preserve it more accurately over time. It is doubtful whether the highly complex societies of ancient Egypt, Greece, or Rome would have been possible without writing. The emergence of European society from its tribal Dark Ages was certainly facilitated by the printing press, and the social innovations of the industrial revolution would not have been possible without reliable mail service. Nor could the complexities of modern global corporations be managed without telephones, faxes, and e-mail.

Building Computers Out of People

We have noted that a number of key Social Technologies innovations have an information-processing angle to them and earlier that "networks of information-processing things" have the ability to compute. Once the evolution of STs reached the stage at which large numbers of people could form cooperative networks and had the means for communicating and storing significant amounts of data, human organizations took on a different character—they became capable of emergent computation.[32]

Organizations of people have the ability to process information and solve complex problems that individuals cannot process or solve on their own. British Petroleum (BP), for example, can be thought of as a computer built for solving the problem of how to extract oil and gas from locations around the world, refine it, and then distribute it to millions of energy users. At BP, there is no one who can tell you, in full detail, just how that immensely complex problem is solved. Think of the vast flows of data flowing into BP on a daily basis and of all the decisions that need to be made, decisions ranging from board-level judgments to the shift schedule for a rig in the North Sea. As much as we like to think of a CEO as being in command, it is impossible for a CEO even as capable as John Browne to be aware of more than a tiny fraction of the thousands and perhaps even millions of decisions being made at any given moment in a large organization. Yet, the hugely complex problem of finding, extracting, refining, and distributing oil is solved in a highly distributed fashion, day in and day out.

Just like an anthill, or the brain, human organizations exhibit a form of networked emergent intelligence. The University of California, San Diego, anthropologist and cognitive scientist Edwin Hutchins has studied the problem-solving capabilities of individuals versus organized groups in a variety of settings. He concluded that organizations are capable of having collective, emergent capabilities that do not exist individually within the group.[33] In essence, not only is BP smarter than any one of its people, it is also smarter than the sum of its people.

One can debate the role of large global corporations such as BP in society. But even the most hardened corporate critic would have to admit that an organization such as BP, with its 103,000 employees in over a hundred countries around the world, is a marvel of human cooperation. The vast majority of its people have never met and never will meet, but are bound together in a web of social structures, norms, protocols, legal structures, and incentives that enable them to work together for a common purpose. If one extends that web of cooperation beyond BP's immediate employees to include its 1.3 million shareholders and thousands of supplier and other partner companies, then the scale of a social structure such as BP becomes even more remarkable.

For an organization of BP's size and complexity to exist, it must sit atop a vast mountain of ST innovations that society has evolved over millennia. These innovations include such STs as money, which was first used around 2,600 years ago in Mesopotamia and provides in essence a universal utility converter—it enables one person's economic needs and wants to be translated into the same units as someone else's needs and wants.[34] Likewise, BP would have a difficult time functioning without a central nervous system of financial information provided by the ST of double-entry accounting, originally developed by Italian merchants in the thirteenth century.[35] Nor could BP even exist in its current form without the invention of the limited-liability joint stock corporation, invented by the British Parliament in a series of Acts between 1825 and 1862.[36] While BP depends on a legacy of STs to function, it is also a participant in the economic evolutionary system as its managers deductively-tinker their way to new methods of organizing and managing, and as successful STs are adopted and spread both within BP and outside it.

From the biological heritage of our primate origins, we inherited an inclination to cooperate for mutual gain and a compulsion to compete in dominance hierarchies, and eventually our developing human brains gave us language. From these humble beginnings sprang an evolutionary process of deductive-tinkering over tens of thousands of years as humans experimented with various ways of organizing their social and economic activities. The inherent non-zero-sum riches found in cooperation rewarded those STs that worked, and over time, humankind found increasingly effective Good Tricks for organizational success. As our species evolved its way through the rough-correlated landscape of ST design space, people were able to build on the tricks that worked, with each successful innovation yielding the possibility of even more future possibilities. As such innovations improved the ability of organizations to process information and solve problems, richer and richer areas of the ST fitness landscape were opened up. Simultaneously, ST space coevolved with Physical Technology space as discoveries in each sphere fed new possibilities in the other.

We have gone from hand axes to spacecraft, and from hunting bands to multinational corporations. We still have not gone the full distance in our journey from the Yanomamö to New Yorkers, but we are closing in, and in the next chapter, we will put the final pieces of economic evolution together.

CHAPTER THIRTEEN

Economic Evolution

FROM BIG MEN TO MARKETS

WE HAVE OUTLINED a generic model of evolution and have been mapping that model onto the substrate of economic systems. In chapter 10, I introduced the idea that economic evolution can be viewed as a search for fit designs in a design space of All Possible Business Plans, or the Library of Smith. In chapters 11 and 12, I then described how the evolution of Physical and Social Technologies provides critical building blocks for economic evolution. In this chapter, we will see how it all comes together as the process of economic evolution unfolds in the world of businesses and markets.

If we run down our checklist from the generic model of evolution, we can see that we have most of the elements of a complete model. We have defined a design space for economic evolution (the Library of Smith), a schema that codes for those designs (Business Plans), a set of building blocks that underlie the designs (PTs and STs), a schema reader that turns Business Plans into reality (management teams), and an environment where evolutionary competition occurs (the marketplace). There are, however, two important blanks remaining to be filled in.

First, we need to define the *interactors* in economic evolution. In the biological implementation of evolution, individual organisms play the role of interactor; they interact with each other and their environment, and do the evolutionary work of living and dying. What is it that does the "living and dying" in the economic substrate?

Second, we need to identify the units of selection in economic evolution. In the biological implementation, selection acts on genes.[1] How does selection work in an economic context?

These two questions have a long history of discussion and debate in evolutionary economics.[2] I will present a perspective that is consistent with the computational view of evolution that we have been following and that fits into the overall framework of Complexity Economics. With our model complete, we will then use it to look more deeply into the workings of markets, to gain a new perspective on the Cambrian explosion of economic novelty that began around 1750, and, in the next chapter, delve into the origin of wealth itself.

Businesses Do the "Living and Dying"

In the generic model, schemata code for the construction of interactors. As mentioned, in a biological context, the schemata of DNA code for organisms that play the role of interactors. The way I have defined things, it follows naturally that if Business Plans are the schemata in economic systems, and Business Plans code for the construction of businesses, then the interactors in economies must be businesses—it is businesses that do the "living and the dying."

This then begs the question of just what a business is. We also need to draw a distinction between businesses, which are an economic concept, and firms, which are legal entities and therefore a Social Technology.

Building on our definitions of Physical and Social Technologies, we can define a business as follows:

> A business is a person, or an organized group of people, who transforms matter, energy, and information from one state into another with the goal of making a profit.

Thus, a business can be Harry the hominid transforming rocks into hand axes and exchanging them for meat, with the goal of getting more calories from the meat than expended in hand-ax production. The definition also works for IBM transforming bits of metal, plastic, silicon, electricity, and the energy of its workers into computers, which it intends to sell for a profit. The definition works for service businesses as well. For example, a shoe-shine stand might use shoe wax and a bit of elbow grease to transform unshined shoes into shined shoes with the goal of a profit. Importantly, the definition also excludes activities such as a school bake sale. Although a bake sale involves the transformation of eggs, sugar, flour, and the energies of parents and children into cookies, it does so with charitable rather than profit-making intentions (we will return to the definition of profits and their role as a goal in business in chapters 16 and 17).

Given this definition, the distinction between a business and a firm is most easily seen in a multibusiness company such as GE. General Electric is a single corporate entity, but has distinct businesses in plastics, lighting, media, financial services, and so on. Most large corporations are in fact collections of businesses. Coke, for example, divides itself up by both geography (e.g., Coke North America, Coke Asia) and by its drink products. Many smaller firms, however, are just single businesses. For example, the firm "Eighteenth Street News-Mags" might just own the single business of a corner shop.

We can then define a firm as follows:

A firm is one or more businesses controlled in common by a person or group of people.

In modern terms, firms take on different legal forms: sole proprietorships, partnerships, and corporations. But even without such formal STs, we can say that Harry was in effect the sole proprietor of his hand-ax-making business, because he controlled it. Likewise, a Yanomamö hunting party can be viewed as a type of partnership that controls its hunting business (note that I have used the word *control* rather than *own,* as ownership implies the ST of property rights). And finally, we can claim that GE is a firm because all of its diverse businesses are ultimately controlled by the same group of shareholders.

With the preceding definitions in mind, I would argue that businesses—and not firms—are the interactors in the evolutionary system. As the name implies, interactors are the entities in evolutionary systems that interact with each other and their environment and experience different rates of success against the selection pressures of their environment. For a one-business firm, the distinction does not matter much; the business and the firm are essentially one and the same—if the corner shop business of Eighteenth Street News-Mags succeeds or fails, then the firm Eighteenth Street News-Mags succeeds or fails. But in the case of GE, the interactions with customers, suppliers, and competitors happen primarily at the level of individual business units, not at the firm level. It is not GE the firm that succeeds or fails in the plastics business, it is GE Plastics. And if GE Plastics failed as a business, it would be a financial blow to GE, but GE as a firm would probably survive as it would continue to pursue its many other businesses.

The next level of distinction is between businesses and individual products and services. For example, one could argue whether GE Plastics is in fact a business or is an entity itself made up of multiple businesses such as Lexan and Noryl. Again, the key attribute of a business is that it provides the focal point for interactions. Thus, in distinguishing between a business and product and service lines, one should look for coherence across a set of dimensions such as a common set of customers, competitors, geography, technologies, or suppliers. The corner shop is a single business rather than a milk business and a newspaper business because the same customers tend to buy both milk and newspapers, the shop's primary competitors are other corner shops, and the focal point of interactions is at the shop level. Meanwhile, a pharmaceutical firm might own a heart-drug business and a cancer-drug business in which each business has a distinctive set of customers, competitors, and technologies.

There is inevitably some ambiguity and subjectivity in drawing these boundaries, and the issue of what constitutes a business unit versus a product or service line is the subject of regular debate in many companies. In the end, we will take a pragmatic and empirical approach and assume that management teams are best placed to make these distinctions. We will thus say that the interactors in economic evolution are the business units as defined by the companies themselves (thus, we'll leave it to GE to decide whether Lexan is a business or a product). This approach has the further benefit of capturing the dynamism of these boundaries. As the environment shifts and as technologies, customers, and competitors change, management teams periodically reassess and change business unit boundaries.

Units of Selection

Businesses are thus the interactors that struggle in survival-of-the-fittest competition in economic evolution. But it would be a mistake to assume that this means that businesses are the unit of evolutionary selection, just as it would be a mistake to assume that selection acts on organisms in biological systems.[3] To fully see how evolution does its work, we need to drop down yet another level.

You will recall our earlier discussion of the evolutionary logic that "good replicators replicate." In the generic model of evolution, the units of selection are sections of schemata that code for "traits" that distinguish one interactor from another in the competition to survive and replicate. In the case of biology, those bits of schemata are genes. For example, if a certain set of genes creates better camouflage for an organism than another set of genes creates, and camouflage provides its wearers with a differential advantage in survival and reproduction, then that set of genes will grow in frequency in the population over time.

What are the units of selection in economic evolution? Given that units of selection are sections of schemata, they must be bits of Business Plans. But which bits? How would we recognize them? And at what level of granularity? Is a unit of selection, for example, a marketing strategy, or might it be the Physical Technology for a particular product?

We can only answer these questions by looking backward in time and asking, what made a difference in the competitive success of a business? If a difference in store format helped Borders bookstores take a few points of market share from Barnes & Noble over a period, then store format was at that time a unit of selection. If a difference in the inventory management system had no impact, then during that period, it was not a unit of selection (although it could become one at some future point).

It sounds a bit circular to say that the units of selection are whatever the environment is selecting for (and against). But we have no choice; fitness functions are highly complex, multidimensional, and change over time. One cannot say a priori what the system is selecting for; one can only observe selection retrospectively, and thus only take an empirical, backward-looking approach to defining units of selection.

This backward-looking and empirical approach is true in biology as well. The definition of a gene is equally fuzzy. The popular conception is that the gene for a trait such as long legs is whatever DNA sequence is responsible for long legs. The reality, however, is that there is no specific, neat DNA sequence solely coding for the trait long legs. DNA is less like a simple blueprint and more like a dense and complex switching network. The trait long legs is made up of a host of interacting submodules, all of which are potentially heritable (e.g., hormones regulating bone growth, processes for muscle construction), yet those modules are also made of submodules, and so on, until one gets to the level of individual proteins themselves. And those same modules may be involved in processes underlying any number of other traits. Biologists thus take a practical and empirical approach to gene identification. For example, some diseases are caused by a missing protein; scientists will search for the sequence of DNA responsible for that protein and announce they have found the gene for the disease, even though the particular strand of DNA may be involved in a number of other mechanisms, too. Thus, a "gene" is merely a convenient label for bits of schemata scattered along the DNA and involved in coding for a heritable trait that could provide some basis for differential survival and reproduction.

We will take a similarly pragmatic and empirical approach in identifying the units of selection in economic evolution and define a new term, a module, as follows:

> A module *is a component of a Business Plan that has provided in the past, or could provide in the future, a basis for differential selection between businesses in a competitive environment.*

One way to think of modules is to ask, "If I were a manager of a business, what kinds of things might I try varying to improve the performance of that business?" For example, one might launch a new sales campaign, redesign the customer service process, introduce new cost control disciplines, or enhance products. Any of the activities that provided a basis for differentiating the performance of the business would be a module (or more precisely, the bits of Business Plan that coded for those activities would be the module).

There is strong evidence that people are able to retrospectively identify modules. An entire industry of consultants, business school professors, and gurus work to identify and spread business "best practices," which in effect are modules ("worst practices" are modules too, just not very fit ones).[4] These researchers study companies in search of practices that in the past have led to business success, and describe those practices in written documents and verbal presentations (i.e., encode them into schemata) thus transmitting them to management teams (i.e., qualified schema readers). The management teams then attempt to implement the practices in their organizations to provide a differential source of competitive advantage (i.e., act as a unit of selection).

Like our other definitions, this one has an inevitable element of subjectivity and judgment. There are often many and complex causes of differences in performance between businesses (just as the contributions to fitness in organisms are extremely complex). As we will discuss in chapter 15, a best practice module that was a unit of selection in the past may not be a source of advantage in the future. Nonetheless, evolutionary selection is not acting on Business Plans as a whole, but on elements within Business Plans.

Finally, the question of units of selection remains the subject of debate and research in both economics and biology. Various proposals have been put forward over the years for units of selection in economic systems (Richard Nelson and Sidney Winter's "routines," for example) and more generally in social systems (Richard Dawkins's concept of "memes," or Robert Boyd and Peter Richerson's "cultural variants").[5] Each of these terms has its own conceptual strengths and weaknesses, and the notion of modules draws on these other ideas. My purpose in introducing a new term is simply to ensure consistency with the generic computational model of evolution that we have been building, and to clarify the distinction between schemata, interactors, and units of selection in an economic context.

Strategy Glue

The term *module* has a further connotation. As previously discussed, evolutionary schemata have a building-block, combinatorial character to them (this is what makes their design spaces so enormous), and the term *module* is meant to imply that Business Plans are amalgamations of modules and that one can create variants of Business Plans by mixing and matching different modules. If one opens up a real business plan from a real company (as opposed to the theoretical Business Plans we have been discussing) and looks at the table of contents, one will typically see headings such as these:[6]

- The market environment

- Strategy

- Products and services

- Operations

- Marketing and sales

- Organization

Each of these component pieces of a Business Plan has subcomponents and sub-subcomponents. For example, within the Business Plan of a chemicals business, there might be a product module that describes how the business will provide specialty carbon-fiber materials for the aviation industry. That module will be built on a cluster of Physical Technologies for making carbon-fiber materials. Likewise, in the marketing and sales section, there might be a module on selling those products using a direct sales force. That module in turn will be built on a number of Social Technologies for organizing, managing, and motivating salespeople.

Business Plans are thus built up from atomistic PTs and STs, which are combined into modules, which are then further combined into Business Plans. The glue that binds it all together is strategy. We will discuss strategy more extensively in chapter 15, but for the moment, we can think of a strategy as a hypothesis about what combinations of modules will be profitable in a given environment. For example, an entrepreneur might hypothesize that combining PTs borrowed from Apple on creating easy-to-use electronic devices, with STs borrowed from Dell on Internet sales and logistics, along with a proprietary design he or she has created for a new gadget, might be a winning combination. Such a hypothesis would be a strategy. The entrepreneur could then write up a Business Plan describing the strategy and set off to the venture capital firms of Silicon Valley for funding. Business Plans are where PTs and STs meet, under the umbrella of strategies, to be made real as businesses in the economic world.

Differentiation: From Entrepreneurs to Bureaucrats

The players in the evolutionary play have now been cast, and it is time to set the plot in motion and see how the process of evolution unfolds in the economic substrate. In previous chapters, we saw how deductive-tinkering provides a mechanism for differentiation in Physical Technology and Social Technology space. The same principle applies to the differentiation of Business Plans. Managers do the best they can to rationally deduce what they hope will be a successful Plan. But then, as James Collins and Jerry Porras describe in their study of long-surviving companies, *Built to Last,* it comes down to "trying a lot of stuff and keeping what works."[7] At any point in time, there is a staggering diversity of Business Plan experiments going on, ranging from Vodafone's launch of 3G mobile Internet services in the United Kingdom, to BP's exploration of its options for business in Russia, to the switch to a new brand of beans by a corner shop in Bolivia to see if its customers would like them. Thus, deductive-tinkering in Business Plan space provides enormous differentiation, or superfecundity, for selection to act on. Developing successful Business Plans, like developing new STs, is more art than science. Thus, while it is not a completely blind process like biological evolution, Business Plan differentiation still involves a lot more tinkering than deduction.

At one end of the spectrum are entrepreneurs who innovate entirely new Business Plans. The entrepreneurial process is a form of deductive-tinkering, as entrepreneurs take modules of various Business Plans, shuffle them in new ways, or import new PTs or STs into the business world. The founders of The Home Depot, for example, took the suburban-superstore retail format and combined it with do-it-yourself building supplies to come up with a novel and successful Business Plan.

The great English economist Alfred Marshall compared entrepreneurs to medieval knights and hailed them as the heroes of capitalism.[8] But, from the point of view of evolution, they are not the only source of economic innovation and therefore not the only heroes. Middle managers can be heroes too. Imagine a middle manager in building 12, cubicle 23Q, of Mega Corp., Inc., who has just proposed a new procedure for managing product warranty claims. This middle manager uses the same deductive-tinkering process used by the bold entrepreneur (albeit perhaps with less vision and flair) as he attempts to rationally plan his actions, and then adjust and try things as he gets feedback from the environment (which includes both customers and his boss). From an evolutionary perspective this middle manager is just as important a source of Business Plan diversity as the entrepreneur—perhaps even more so.

The alpinelike shape of the fitness landscape means that evolution needs a spectrum of jumps to be effective in its search. Most innovations should be minor, short jumps because the vast majority of radical long-jump innovations will be failures. The middle manager in cube 23Q has a higher probability of succeeding with his incremental innovation than the bold plan of the entrepreneur. But some medium and long jumps are required as well to keep evolution from getting stuck on local peaks. Evolution thus needs both the plodding bureaucrat and the wild-eyed entrepreneur.

Selection: Big Men Versus Markets

Once differentiation in Business Plans is achieved through the deductive-tinkering of entrepreneurs, managers, and bureaucrats, how are Plans selected? Over its history, humankind has evolved two methods of economic selection: Big Men and markets.[9] We will discuss each in turn.

In the early days of the economy, the selection process was fairly straightforward—survival. If your Business Plan for combining Physical Technologies (e.g., bows and arrows) and Social Technologies (e.g., hunting party) under a strategy (e.g., hunt impalas near the river) was successful, then your caloric revenues were greater than your caloric expenses. This caloric profit enabled you to do things like invest in children. Calorically profitable Business Plans then had a higher chance of being replicated by attracting more participants, and propagated over time by being adopted by the next generation. Other Business Plans (e.g., use slingshots and hunt ostriches on the plains) that were less successful in their caloric profits would tend to lose resources to more successful plans and die out as either their adherents shifted to different plans or the adherents themselves died out.

As society and the economy grew more complicated, however, the feedback loop of selection became less direct, with intermediate, socially driven selection cropping up. The first collision between selection and society undoubtedly came when the first Big Man said, "Let's give this nice, fertile plot of land to my third wife's cousin (who is a lousy farmer) instead of to Mr. X (who is an excellent farmer)." We can safely assume that political meddling in economic affairs is as old as both politics and economics themselves. Such decisions favoring poor Business Plans (the cousin's) over good Business Plans (Mr. X's) do not last long in an environment where everyone was on the edge of survival—if the Big Man did this often enough, then either the Big Man's tribe would perish under his leadership or he'd be overthrown in a revolt. But once a society had crossed the survival threshold (particularly after the advent of settled agriculture), such social short-circuiting of the selection process became not just possible, but ever more likely as the group grew richer.

If a tribe is generally surviving and the Big Man's graft, corruption, or incompetence isn't life threatening, then relatively few people may even be aware of the additional wealth their tribe is giving up. As Robert Wright points out, competition puts some checks and balances on this; eventually, another Big Man might come along promising to do better and topple the old one, or the poorly performing tribe might be violently taken over by a better-organized one.[10] But there is nothing to guarantee that the new Big Man or tribe will turn out any better than the old one. Thus, the main impact of political interference in the process of Business Plan selection is to slow down evolution's clock-speed. In extreme cases, chiefs, kings, dictators, and other Big Men can actually stop economic evolution in its tracks, and as long as people are merely close to starving, as opposed to actually starving, such evolutionary dead ends can last for very long periods.

The Big Man system of Business Plan selection has a further problem: Big Men distort the fitness function itself. One of the features of evolutionary algorithms is that they are brilliant at adapting to whatever fitness criteria they are given. As we saw earlier, when the computer researcher Karl Sims selected his artificial creatures for their fitness in swimming, he got an amazing array of clever swimmers. When he switched the fitness criteria to moving across land, fins and tails were dropped in favor of legs and snake bodies. When engineers employ artificial evolution to do things such as design semiconductors, software, or new drugs, they have to be extremely careful in how they specify the fitness function, because the wrong fitness function inevitably leads to the wrong design. In a Big Man system, the fitness function maximized is the wealth and power of the Big Man (and his cronies), rather than the overall economic wealth of the society. Thus, the creative, entrepreneurial, and deductive-tinkering energies of the population are directed toward pleasing the Big Man. The immense mansions and palaces dotting the world, from grand French chateaus to the Hermitage in Russia, that delight tourists with their extravagant displays of riches are testaments to the effectiveness of economic evolution in maximizing the fitness function of Big Man wealth.

The only alternative selection system to Big Men that humans have thus far devised is markets. Markets are both an ancient and a recent invention. On the one hand, free markets have existed ever since Harry and Larry first traded an ax for meat. While such informal, bilateral trade has existed throughout history, the first evidence of organized markets is much more recent, dating back to the development of settled agriculture in the Fertile Crescent and the rise of cities such as Ur and Babylon, circa 7000 to 5000 BC.[11]

One of the great accomplishments of Traditional Economics was to show in effect that the fitness function that markets attempt to satisfy is the overall welfare of the people participating in them. In a Big Man economy, a business lives or dies by political favor. In a market-based economy, a business lives or dies by whether its customers like and are willing to pay for its products and services. In a Big Man economy, resources are directed toward the ventures that best line the pockets of the Big Men. In a market economy, resources are directed to ventures that make the best economic use of them.

All economies throughout history have in truth been some mixture of Big Men and markets. People in our hunter-gatherer past were often free to trade with each other as long as it didn't displease the Big Man, and assuming he got his cut. The traders in the bazaars of Babylon and the Agora of Athens were "licensed" to be there by political connections, taxes, bribes, and other fees to the hierarchy. Even in the Soviet Union, one of the most tightly controlled Big Man hierarchies in history, about a fifth of its economic activity was in the free-trading black market.

For the vast bulk of human history, though, Big Men have dominated Business Plan selection, and markets have played either a secondary or an underground role. For example, the economist William Baumol estimates that the aristocratic hierarchies of feudal Europe controlled over 80 percent of economic output.[12] It was not until about three hundred years ago that the balance of power between Big Men and markets began to flip. We will return to this history shortly, but we will first look at just how selection works in market-based systems.

How Selection Works in Market Systems

If selection is relatively straightforward in Big Man economies, it is a bit more complex in market-based economies. From an evolutionary perspective, the defining feature of a market economy is that markets provide the ultimate power in Business Plan selection. This does not mean that there are no Big Man hierarchies in market economies—on the contrary, as anyone from Karl Marx to a modern-day antiglobalization protester would be quick to point out, capitalist societies are full of robber barons, corporate chieftains, and other fat cats. The organization charts of large, modern corporations look little different from those of any other Big Man hierarchy (especially because much of the corporate world is still dominated by Big Men and not that many Big Women). Yet, the way one achieves fat-cat status in a capitalist society is by having one's Business Plans preferred by the market (and therefore society) versus the alternatives.

Market-based economies operate a dual layer system of Business Plan selection. The vast majority of economic decisions are still made by hierarchies, in this case, the hierarchies of corporations. As the business historian Alfred Chandler observed in the 1970s, the "visible hand" of corporate hierarchies makes far more economic decisions than Adam Smith's "invisible hand" of the market.[13] But, sitting on top of these massive hierarchies is a thin, but crucial layer, in which the hierarchies meet the market. Market economies are systems of evolutionarily competing hierarchies.

We have already discussed how deductive-tinkering creates differentiation among Business Plans. Let's look more closely at how differentiation works in a market context and how interaction with the environment then leads to Business Plan selection.

Let's imagine a senior executive who is in charge of a business unit in a large firm. She is trying to think of modifications to her Business Plan, modifications that will increase her unit's profits. The first thing she does is generate various options for the business: "I could try expanding product line A, introducing new service B, cutting costs here, reorganizing there," and so on. Each option involves varying some set of modules of the Business Plan. In generating these options, she applies all her cognitive abilities: some of the ideas come from deductive thinking about the business, some come from analogies and pattern recognition from other experiences (e.g., "this worked in my prior company"), some ideas may come from imitation (e.g., "my competitor launched this product, and it was a success"), and some ideas may be transmitted to her from others (e.g., "David in marketing mentioned this, which might be a good idea").

Once our business unit head has a set of options, she will then perform some mental simulations to think through which options would be best. When she has winnowed down the options in her head, she might then go to the next stage of further option generation and testing. She might ask colleagues for additional ideas, or request that they do their own mental simulations on her ideas and get back to her. She and her colleagues will then create a further refined list of options, on which they then might perform simulations that are more formal. For example, they might create spreadsheet models, try pilot schemes, analyze costs, or commission market research. The options will be assessed yet again by the team. Perhaps the options will also be discussed and debated with higher-level executives in the parent firm. Eventually, the business unit leader will select one or more options, make her decisions, and change the existing Business Plan into the new one. This will result in actions in the physical world: budgets and people will be allocated, products will change, marketing campaigns will be altered, and so on. Once the actions take shape in the physical world, then the market will render its judgement; sales will either go up or go down, profits will increase or decrease, and the management team will thus receive feedback on the success or failure of its Business Plan.

The process is not always this formal or this explicit, but the basic idea is that there is an iterative loop of option generation, testing, and selection. The loop begins in the mental models of the individual agents, eventually winds its way through groups of agents, and then leads to actions in the real world. Thus, option selection works at multiple levels: in the mental models of individual agents, within the organizational hierarchy, and ultimately in the marketplace itself.

Replication: Amplifying Success

The final step of the evolutionary algorithm is replication. In biological evolution, replication occurs either through cell division or sexual reproduction. Genes that contribute to an organism's ability to survive and reproduce tend to get replicated. So the effect of replication is that, over time, fit genes increase in *frequency* in a population, and unfit genes diminish in frequency or disappear. In biological systems, frequency is measured by asking what percentage of the population contains a particular gene. By measuring frequency, one is asking in effect how many interactors (e.g., humans) have a particular unit of selection (e.g., the genes for blue eyes) in the total population of interactors (e.g., 20 percent).

If we applied the same measure of replication success to economic systems, we would ask what percentage of the population of businesses contained a particular module. However, we run into a problem with this measure. The size of the interactors in most species varies by only a small amount. For example, grown humans range roughly between three feet and eight feet tall, which is less than one order of magnitude. Yet, the interactors in economics, namely, businesses, can vary in size from a one-person shoe-shine stand to the upstream petroleum business of Exxon Mobil, a difference of around 10^9 orders of magnitude. Somehow, we need to account for the fact that a Business Plan module that is replicated in five shoe-shine stands does not have quite the same economic impact as one replicated in five major oil companies.

One way around this problem is to note that in biology, the notion of frequency is really an abstraction of a more fundamental measure. Instead of asking what percentage of organisms contains a gene, we could equivalently ask what percentage of a species' total biomass contains the gene. This measure is even truer to the philosophy of the gene-centered view, as it asks what percentage of a finite pool of chemical and energy resources (measured in biomass) is controlled or influenced by the particular gene. Since the average biomass per organism tends not to vary too much for most species, we can view frequency or percentage of population as an-easier-to-measure proxy. Thus, when we ask what percentage of human biomass has its fitness influenced by genes for blue eyes, the answer would still be roughly 20 percent. This percentage-of-resources view is also more consistent with our substrate-neutral approach to evolution, as it can be applied to systems ranging from computers (e.g., percentage of computing resources), to Lego blocks (e.g., percentage of block mass).

Thus, we will take the percentage-of-resources approach and measure replication success by the percentage of resources whose fitness is influenced by a particular Business Plan module. These resources might include money, people, plant and equipment, or even intangible assets such as brand awareness, technical knowledge, and customer relationships—any resources that are in finite supply and over which businesses compete (the percentage-of-resources approach is also consistent with what economists refer to as the "resource-based view of the firm," a topic we will return to in chapter 16).[14] And since we are now talking about a continuous rather than discrete measure, we will say that a successful Business Plan module is *amplified,* rather than replicated. Thus, a Business Plan module is amplified in Business Plan space if its influence over resources grows over time.[15]

We can now revisit our discussion of selection and look at how successful Business Plan modules might be amplified and rewarded with influence over more resources. First, we will go back inside the head of our imaginary business unit leader. As she considers various options for her Business Plan, she makes a decision and selects a particular configuration of modules that she believes will be successful. She then rewards that configuration by implementing the Plan and directing people, money, and other resources toward its execution. Thus, the particular modules she selected have been amplified with more control over resources. The ten other options that she considered and threw out were not rewarded, and at least in her business, those modules have died out for now. Let's say that the early results of her Business Plan look very promising, as sales have grown and profits are up. The senior corporate-level team is impressed and would like to try some of the same modules (e.g., a new approach to sales) in other businesses in the firm. More money and people are directed at implementing those modules, which are therefore further amplified.

A few months later, one of her competitors notices the changes and copies the modules, thus further amplifying them because the modules now influence the resources in the second company as well. Partly as a result of the success of the module, both companies grow, attracting more capital from banks and the stock market. The module's influence is thus amplified yet again. Finally, our business unit leader decides to buy a smaller company that has not adopted the module. One of her rationales for the acquisition is the opportunity to implement the module and bring the target company up to best practice. After the deal, the module is implemented in the acquired company, which amplifies the module's scope of influence yet again. Recalling the biological maxim "good replicators replicate," one can take a "module's-eye" view in the economic world and see that "good amplifiers amplify."

Thus, we can see a variety of mechanisms at work for transmitting and amplifying Business Plan modules. They include the mental simulation and decision making of a single person, the problem solving and decision making of a group, imitation within and outside an organization, the direction of resources toward successful modules by the market, and the takeover of one business by another.

Economic Evolution in a Nutshell

We now have all the elements of an evolutionary model for searching the Library of Smith for fit Business Plans. We have seen how Business Plans are instructions for creating businesses that can be implemented by qualified Business Plan readers. These instructions bind Physical Technologies and Social Technologies together into modules under a strategy. Business Plans are differentiated through the deductive-tinkering of agents as they search for potentially profitable plans. While the distribution of experiments created by this process differs from the purely random differentiation of biological evolution, it nonetheless feeds the evolutionary algorithm with a superfecundity of Business Plans for selection to act on.

The process of selection is nested and occurs at several levels, ranging from the mental simulations of individuals to the problem-solving activities of groups. Further selection occurs as Business Plans percolate up and down the hierarchies of organizations, but then at some point the plans are implemented and the market renders its judgment.

Finally, successful modules are rewarded by gaining influence over more resources. Success for a module comes at two levels. The first level is within an organization, when a Business Plan is implemented and is given resources for its execution, for example, when people and money are invested in executing a plan. The second level is when modules are expressed in the marketplace and rewarded with growth and more capital by customers and financial markets. This is a winnowing process; the superfecundity of Business Plans means that far more plan options are considered within an organization than can be implemented, and far more plans are tried in the market than can succeed. As selection does its work, fit modules eventually gain influence over a larger and larger percentage of the total resource base of the economy. This is a highly dynamic process; what is fit today may or may not be fit tomorrow. Thus, the evolutionary process never stops, as modules come and go and as businesses rise and fall, adapting to the needs of the marketplace.

Beyond the basic machinery of the evolutionary algorithm, we would not expect any particular similarities between economic evolution and biological evolution.[16] For example, the notion that units of selection follow "descent with modification" through discrete generations in biological evolution, but hop around from Business Plan to Business Plan in economic evolution, does not make the process any less evolutionary, just different. Likewise, the ability of humans to use their brains and have foresight implies that the mechanisms for differentiation and selection are very different in economic systems versus biological systems, but again are evolutionary nonetheless.

Moreover, nothing in my proposed framework presupposes the existence of modern STs such as organized markets, money, private property, corporations, or even writing. The same processes apply for Harry the hominid contemplating how to get more meat for his hand axes as they do for a senior executive at a modern multinational considering strategies for China.

In Praise of Markets—for Different Reasons

If there is one thing Traditional economists agree on, it is that markets are good—markets may not always be perfect and they do have some well-identified failings, but when they work, they are hard to beat. This conclusion, built on the foundation of general equilibrium, stood at the center of the twentieth-century ideological debates of the Cold War and continues to provide the intellectual basis for global capitalism today. An evolutionary view of the economy leads one to agree with the broad view that markets are good, but for some very different reasons.

Traditional Economics emphasizes that markets are the best method for allocating resources in a way that optimizes the welfare of society under equilibrium conditions.[17] The problem, as we have seen, is that in the real world, equilibrium conditions are never met. But if the equilibrium assumptions of Traditional Economics are wrong, how can we be sure markets are a good thing?

Following the framework I have just outlined, we can reinterpret markets as an evolutionary search mechanism. Markets provide incentives for the deductive-tinkering process of differentiation. They then critically provide a fitness function and selection process that represents the broad needs of the population (and not just the needs of a few Big Men). Finally, they provide a means of shifting resources toward fit modules and away from unfit ones, thus amplifying the fit modules' influence.

In short, the reason that markets work so well comes down to what evolutionary theorists refer to as Orgel's Second Rule (named after biochemist Leslie Orgel), which says, "Evolution is cleverer than you are." Even a highly rational, intelligent, benevolent Big Man would not be able to beat an evolutionary algorithm in finding peaks in the economic fitness landscape. Markets win over command and control, not because of their *efficiency* at resource allocation in equilibrium, but because of their *effectiveness* at innovation in disequilibrium.

Complexity economists don't ignore the allocative role of markets.[18] They tend to think markets are pretty good at that, too, and generally better than the Big Man alternative. But while Traditional economists like to talk about the "perfect efficiency" of markets in equilibrium, Complexity economists often view market efficiency as a more relative notion. The Complexity view is that an ideal state of perfect efficiency may not actually exist, and even if it did, the disequilibrium nature of markets would probably prevent it from ever being reached. Markets can never be perfectly efficient, just as the engine of a car can never be made 100 percent thermodynamically efficient. The reason that markets are good at allocation has more to do with their computational efficiency as a distributed processing system (i.e., they get the right signals to the right people), than with their ability to reach a mythical global equilibrium.[19]

The empirical record of markets points to their success as an evolutionary mechanism. As the economist William Baumol has said, free markets have historically been "innovation machines."[20] Take a look at your own material surroundings—how many of the SKUs in your environment were invented, or otherwise designed (as opposed to merely manufactured), in Big Man economies? With few exceptions, the vast bulk of Physical Technology and Social Technology innovations of the modern world have come from a handful of market-oriented economies. And the few Big Man economy innovations, such as Soviet advances in aircraft design, have typically been motivated by military, not economic, needs.

None of this is to say that market-oriented societies are perfect. The societies of the rich capitalist world have critical problems with inequality, environmental destruction, and health crises such as AIDS. And there is strong evidence that the rampant materialism of these societies does not necessarily make people happier.[21] Impoverished Big Man societies have these same problems as well, but usually to a worse degree with fewer resources to address them and a lower likelihood that new, innovative approaches will solve them. Finally, the evolutionary view of markets does not diminish the difficulties that many countries have had in making the transition from Big Man to market economies—transitions that inevitably involve wrenching social change. In chapter 18, we will see that the Complexity view also provides a different perspective on the limitations and weaknesses of markets. But the bottom line is that people vote with their feet, and the record of worldwide immigration flows, particularly in the modern era, has consistently been from Big Man economies to market-oriented economies.

The Complexity view of markets thus leads to an appreciation of the strengths of markets in enabling innovation and growth. Perhaps one of the most eloquent critiques of Big Man economic systems was given by Václav Havel, a former dissident who spent time in the jails of communist Czechoslovakia and later became president of the democratic Czech Republic: "The essence of life is infinitely and mysteriously multiform, and therefore it cannot be contained or planned for, in its fullness and variability, by any central intelligence."[22]

Meta-Innovations: Revisiting 1750

At the beginning of the book, I noted that one of the most startling events in human history was the explosion in wealth and economic complexity that began around 1750 and continues to the present day. With our evolutionary framework, we can begin to see not just what happened but also how and why it happened. During this period, a set of innovations in Social Technologies significantly boosted the clock-speed of economic evolution itself.

In chapter 11, we discussed the first meta-innovation, the scientific revolution. Prior to 1500, human knowledge was primarily built by trial and error. The advent of science accelerated the pace of human search through Physical Technology space and vastly increased the effectiveness of both rational deduction and experimental tinkering.[23]

The second meta-innovation was the rise of organized markets. The development of market-based economies did not occur in a big bang, but rather was the result of two centuries of ST evolution. Two key events that initiated this change were the creation of parliamentary democracy in England, and the American Revolution.

During 1509–1547, Henry VIII of England was as Big a Man as they come, and an absolute ruler of his kingdom. But by 1690, after a century of upheaval and reform, England was a constitutional monarchy. Parliament took control of the government's purse strings and established the Bank of England to manage the nation's currency.[24] In addition, during this period, important steps were taken to secure the rule of law and to protect individual property rights. The Petition of Right in 1628 and the Habeas Corpus Act of 1679 were particularly important. All these foundational changes in Social Technology enabled the economy to transform over the next century from a feudal, hierarchical, Big Man society, to a market economy, with a growing merchant class, competitive private businesses, and capital markets. Although other European powers retained more top-down control of their economies, institutional reforms also took place in a number of other countries, particularly in Northern Europe, enabling market forces to slowly plant roots across the continent.

The American Revolution starting in 1776 (the same year that Adam Smith published his great work) was the second major boost to the development of market economies. The historian Paul Johnson notes that the economic approach of the British to their colonies was very different from the approach of the other major European powers.[25] France, Spain, and Portugal each transplanted highly centralized and hierarchical systems of political, military, and religious command to their New World holdings, which in turn led to top-down control of their fledgling economies. The British, on the other hand, were too cheap to go to the trouble of investing in the large military resources needed to institute that kind of control. There were more pressing concerns elsewhere in the empire, such as Britain's always-complex relationships with the Continent. Thus, the British American colonies evolved as scattered settlements of highly independent farmers and merchants. From its earliest days, British North America was an "anything goes" kind of place of free trade, free ideas, and free religion. Whenever the British or local colonial authorities attempted to clamp down, the inhabitants would simply head for wilder lands farther away from any source of control.

Thus, by the time the revolution came in 1776, the new nation had already experienced a century of relative economic freedom and had developed an egalitarian, populist culture that was naturally suspicious of Big Man control. The colonies also had a large and wealthy middle class. Johnson notes that the typical east coast American farmer in 1750 had between sixty to one hundred acres of land, ten head of cattle, sixteen sheep, six pigs, two horses, and a team of oxen. Average families had six to seven children, of whom four or five typically survived to adulthood, and only 3 to 5 percent of middle-aged males were poor.[26] By the time of the revolution, America's free-market experiment had been an astounding success; in 1700, America's GDP was 5 percent of Britain's and, by 1775, was 40 percent, which, as Johnson notes, "was one of the highest growth-rates the world has ever witnessed."[27]

By the end of the eighteenth century, the ST foundations had been laid for market economies in North America, Britain, and to varying degrees, other parts of Northern Europe. They were still not quite the market systems that we would recognize today. For example, banking systems were quite primitive and the limited liability joint stock corporation had not been invented yet. But the Big Men were pushed out of Business Plan selection, and entrepreneurship flourished.

These were also the geographies where science had put down its deepest roots. It is thus not surprising that these same regions were then the focal point for the industrial revolution. Through the nineteenth and twentieth centuries science yielded a dramatic acceleration in the discovery of new PTs, and markets enabled the rapid evolution of Business Plans for turning those PTs into products and services. A virtuous cycle of PT, ST, and Business Plan innovation ensued, leading to the greatest period of economic growth the world has ever known.

CHAPTER FOURTEEN

A New Definition of Wealth

FIT ORDER

IT WAS 1948, and Nicholas Georgescu-Roegen and his wife were terrified. They had managed to smuggle themselves, hidden in barrels, aboard a freighter bound from their native Romania to Istanbul.[1] They knew that if they were caught, they would be killed.

Georgescu-Roegen was an economist and had been working for the postwar Romanian government. He had been trained at the Sorbonne in Paris and studied under Joseph Schumpeter at Harvard before returning to Romania in the 1930s. The years after the war had been chaotic and fraught with power struggles over Romania's future. But in the peace agreement of 1947, the Western powers bowed to the reality of the Red Army's occupation of Bucharest, and by the end of the year, the Soviets had installed a totalitarian regime. Members of the previous government were purged and put through show trials, and some were executed. For Georgescu-Roegen, it was time to get out.

He and his wife eventually made it to America, where he was offered a position on the faculty at Vanderbilt University in Nashville. For the next twenty years, Georgescu-Roegen made seminal contributions to Traditional Economic theory. His mathematical virtuosity made him a rising star, and Paul Samuelson, the Neoclassicist in chief, bestowed on him the ultimate accolade: "an economist's economist." But in 1966, at the age of sixty, the star turned rebel when he engaged in a blistering attack on Traditional theory.[2] He then looked to evolutionary theory and physics for answers to the shortcomings of Traditional Economics and, in 1971, published his magnum opus, *The Entropy Law and the Economic Process*.[3]

In this chapter, we will see that Georgescu-Roegen's ideas were well ahead of their time. The basic insight in *The Entropy Law and the Economic Process* is that economic activity is fundamentally about order creation, and that evolution is the mechanism by which that order is created. We will examine Georgescu-Roegen's groundbreaking ideas, bring them up to date with current science, and integrate them with the evolutionary model outlined over the previous chapters. In doing so, we will arrive at our destination: a new perspective on the origin of wealth.

Cranks and Half-Baked Speculators

In his book, Georgescu-Roegen argued that while the biological form of the human species continues to evolve slowly, or "endosomatically," through our genes, we are at the same time rapidly evolving "exosomatically" through our culture. Georgescu-Roegen was not the first person to make this observation. Darwin saw this as an implication of his theory, and in the 1950s, the Catholic theologian Pierre Teilhard de Chardin developed a philosophy based on the idea of endosomatic and exosomatic evolution.[4] Nor was Georgescu-Roegen the only economist at the time looking to cultural evolution for answers. Friedrich Hayek wrote about cultural evolution in his 1960 book, *The Constitution of Liberty*, and Kenneth Boulding published his theory of cultural and economic evolution in the 1970s.[5] But Georgescu-Roegen was unique in his ability to ground his theory in science, in particular the connection between evolution and thermodynamics.

In chapter 3, we discussed the Second Law of Thermodynamics, the principle that the universe is inevitably moving from a state of low entropy to a state of high entropy. Left to its own devices, the world drifts from order to disorder. But if one puts energy into an open system, one can temporarily fight rising entropy and create order in a local part of the universe. The Second Law, however, must get its due, and any open system with decreasing entropy must ultimately export its entropy back into the universe in the form of heat and waste so that the total entropy of the universe continues to rise. It also means that an open system must maintain a flow of energy into it to keep fighting entropy; if the energy is cut off, order can no longer be maintained and the system decays and dissipates.

The Second Law has fundamentally shaped evolution in the biological world.[6] From a thermodynamic perspective, an organism is a collection of highly ordered molecules. All organisms have some form of barrier, such as a membrane, skin, or shell, that keeps their ordered insides distinct from the disordered outside. Maintaining that distinction between inside and outside requires energy. We can say that the molecules inside the boundary are ordered because the probability of getting the particular pattern of chemicals inside an organism from random molecular motion alone is infinitesimally low. For example, it is extremely unlikely that randomly moving molecules would spontaneously assemble themselves into a fully functioning bacterium. New York University biochemist Robert Shapiro likens this to the odds of a tornado in a junkyard creating a Boeing 747.[7] Thus, every organism needs a source of energy to maintain and grow its complex internal order, and all life gives off heat and waste materials as entropy is paid back to the universe. When that process stops, the organism's molecules are returned to the disorder of the environment—death is a surrender to the Second Law.

The Second Law thus provides a basic constraint on all life: over time, energy inputs must be greater than energy expenditures. All organisms must make a thermodynamic "profit" to survive and reproduce. The design for an organism can be thought of as a strategy for making thermodynamic profits long enough to reproduce, before the Second Law eventually catches up. An African elephant is a strategy for making thermodynamic profits and reproducing in the environment of the African bush, and a Coronatae jellyfish is a strategy for making thermodynamic profits and reproducing in the environment of the deep ocean. The Coronatae jellyfish is a particularly successful strategy, as it has been consistently profitable for about 200 million years. Competition for the energy and materials needed for order creation is, of course, intense; plants compete for ground, water, and sunlight, and many species have the strategy of stealing energy and materials from other species by eating them. Biological evolution has been a 3-billion-year quest for thermodynamically profitable strategies in a competitive and ever-changing world.

In *The Entropy Law and the Economic Process*, Georgescu-Roegen observed that, just as in biological systems, "the economic process materially consists of a transformation of high entropy into low entropy."[8] Georgescu-Roegen chided Traditional Economics for ignoring the role of entropy in economics and claimed that Neoclassical theory in effect violated the laws of physics by not recognizing thermodynamic constraints in its models.[9] He said it was akin to "ignor[ing] the difference between the actual world and the Garden of Eden," and called the Neoclassical production function a "conjuring trick."[10]

Georgescu-Roegen's critique was never answered by the economic establishment, and his book slipped into semiobscurity.[11] One of his conclusions was a stark warning that the inevitable by-product of economic entropy reduction is pollution. His ideas were picked up by the environmental movement, and thus, most economists today categorize him as an environmental economist and forget that he set out a major challenge to the entire edifice of Traditional theory.[12]

Perhaps one reason that Georgescu-Roegen was ignored was that the entropy concept has had a dismal history in economics. Many researchers over the decades have looked for metaphorical equivalents of entropy and energy in economics, such as an equivalence between money and entropy, or likening budget constraints to the conservation of energy.[13] As Paul Samuelson (who as I noted praised Georgescu-Roegen's contributions to Traditional theory) said in his 1970 Nobel Prize lecture: "How many dreary papers have I had to referee in which the author is looking for something that corresponds to entropy or to one or another form of energy?"[14] And in a 1972 paper, he went further: "And I may add that the sign of a crank or half-baked speculator in the social sciences is his search for something in the social system that corresponds to the physicist's notion of 'entropy.'"[15]

Samuelson was right. As we have discussed, such metaphorical comparisons tend to produce nonsense (though, of course, the irony is that this was exactly what Walras, Jevons, and the other founders of Traditional theory did). But Georgescu-Roegen was no crank, and he wasn't looking for something *like* entropy in economics. Instead, he was arguing, as I did in chapter 3, that economic systems exist in the real physical world and, therefore, they must obey the same law of entropy as everything else in the universe does.[16] As the British astrophysicist Sir Arthur Eddington once famously remarked, "If your theory is found to be against the second law of Thermodynamics I can give you no hope; there is nothing for it but to collapse in deepest humiliation."[17]

A Proposal: Three Conditions for Value Creation

Georgescu-Roegen made three important observations that fundamentally connect the idea of the economy as an evolving, complex system with our question of the origin of wealth.

First, he noted that processes that create economic value are inherently irreversible. Time in economic systems has a one-way arrow—or as he put it, you cannot burn the same lump of coal to power a locomotive twice.[18]

Second, as he wrote, "Casual observation suffices now to prove that *our whole economic life feeds on low entropy*, to wit, cloth, lumber, china, copper, etc. . . . all of which are highly ordered structures."[19] As noted before, economic processes are all about using energy to turn relatively low-ordered raw materials and information into more highly ordered products and services.

And third, while creating products and services is an inherently order-creating activity, not all order has economic value. As Georgescu-Roegen coyly noted, "No man can use the low entropy of poisonous mushrooms and not all men struggle for that contained in seaweed or beetles."[20]

I will go a step beyond Georgescu-Roegen's claims now and propose that taken together, these three observations tell us exactly what conditions have to be met for economic value to be created, which leads us to a new definition of wealth itself. To add more precision to Georgescu-Roegen's observations, I will restate them in more formal terms and refer to them collectively as the *G-R Conditions*.

A pattern of matter, energy, and or information has economic value if the following three conditions are jointly met:

1. IRREVERSIBILITY. All value-creating economic transformations and transactions are thermodynamically irreversible.

2. ENTROPY. All value-creating economic transformations and transactions reduce entropy locally within the economic system, while increasing entropy globally.

3. FITNESS. All value-creating economic transformations and transactions produce artifacts and or actions that are fit for human purposes.

We will discuss each condition in turn.

Irreversibility: Breaking Eggs to Make an Omelet

Earlier, we defined a *business* as "a person, or an organized group of people, who transforms matter, energy, and information from one state into another with the goal of making a profit." Likewise, I also defined Physical and Social Technologies in terms of transformations. The notion of transforming things from one state to another is a thermodynamic concept.[21] The nineteenth-century French engineer Sadi Carnot divided all transformations into two types: reversible and irreversible. The earth orbiting the sun is an example of a *reversible* transformation (we can call it a transformation, because its position is transformed from one point to another over time). There is no particular reason why the earth orbits in the direction it does; nothing in Newton's equations says it couldn't just as easily orbit the other way. If we saw a movie of the earth orbiting in one direction and then the other, we would not be able to tell which was the forward and which was the backward version, as the transformation of the earth's position would be perfectly symmetrical in time.[22] In contrast, if we saw a movie of a milk bottle falling off a table and smashing on the ground, and then saw the film run backward, we would easily know which version was which. A smashing milk bottle is an *irreversible* process.

At the macroscopic level of our lives and of economic phenomena, one thing we can count on is that time runs in only one direction.[23] It is the Second Law of Thermodynamics that gives time its arrow. Our brains intuitively know that entropy increases, and the only way to decrease entropy is through energy and work. Thus, if we watched a film of a milk bottle being smashed or a drop of ink dispersing in water, we would see the order of those systems decreasing and know that time was running forward. If we saw the smashed milk bottle spontaneously jump up and fix itself, or the inky water reassemble into a neat drop, we would know that time was running backward—such order creation does not just happen on its own. But if we saw a person carefully gluing the milk bottle back together again and refilling it, we would believe that time was running forward again because we would see someone putting energy into the system to create order. As the physicist Richard Feynman used to note, a good test was, if the film of a transformation ran backward and the audience laughed, then the process was irreversible.[24]

Irreversibility is thus intimately tied to entropy and order creation. This link occurs through the laws of probability. A useful way to think about order is to ask what the probability is of a particular state of things occurring just through the random motion of molecules. If you pour milk into a cup of coffee and just let it sit for a while without stirring it, eventually the milk will dissipate into the coffee as the random motion of the various molecules that make up coffee and milk jostle each other and the drink reaches an even temperature. You would be quite surprised if you looked at your coffee cup after a few minutes and saw all the black coffee sitting neatly on one side of the cup and all the white milk sitting on the other side. In theory, the random jostling of the coffee and milk molecules *could* lead to such an outcome purely by chance, but it is a "not in the lifetime of the universe" kind of probability. Now imagine that we put a barrier in the middle of your coffee milk mixture, and that the barrier has a molecular-sized trapdoor operated by a little nano-technology robot. The nanobot is programmed to sort the coffee and milk molecules, pushing them to either side of the barrier. Whenever a randomly moving milk molecule bumps on one side of the door, the machine opens it and lets the milk through. Whenever the machine senses a coffee molecule bumping the other side of the door, it opens the door in that direction and lets the coffee through. Over time, the machine sorts the coffee and milk to different sides of the cup. The little nanobot is in effect increasing order (decreasing entropy) in the coffee cup by *creating a lower-probability state than existed before*. However, this order comes at an inescapable price. We would have to feed the nanobot energy to do its work, and in return the nanobot would give off heat. Thus, entropy would decrease locally within the coffee cup, but still increase in the wider universe around it. In physics, such an imaginary molecular sorting device is known as Maxwell's Demon, after James Clerk Maxwell, who proposed this thought experiment in 1867 (in the original, the sorting device was an "observant and neat-fingered" demon).[25] After about 140 years of debate, theorizing, and experiments, scientists have concluded that Maxwell's Demon cannot reverse the flow of entropy without some source of energy—there is no order for free.

In essence, Georgescu-Roegen was saying that if the universe cannot escape the Second Law, then neither can economics.[26] The transformations or other processes that create economic value are thermodynamically irreversible. This does not mean that it is impossible to reverse a value-creating process. Rather, it means that it takes energy to make things and it takes energy to un-make things. In economic systems, time has an arrow. Think, for example, of the process of making paper. Trees are cut down in the forest and loaded onto trucks, the wood is turned into pulp and mixed with chemicals to make a slurry, and the slurry is pressed into rolls, dried, and cut into sheets. It would be very hard to make a tree again out of a pile of paper. To use Feynman's test, if we were to watch a film of pulp turning into logs, the logs jumping off trucks and so on, we would instantly know it was running backward. Likewise, films of automobiles disassembling themselves, planes flying backward, or bank tellers un-typing things in their computers would all give the audience a chuckle.

It is possible, however, to imagine one form of value-creating economic transformation that would be perfectly reversible. In 1982, the IBM physicist Charles Bennett demonstrated the theoretical possibility of a reversible computer—that is, a machine that can perform computations both forward and backward without any thermodynamic loss. Such a computer, if it existed, could do economically useful work and yet be reversible, and thus seemingly violate the first G-R Condition. But in subsequent work, Bennett's IBM colleague Rolf Landauer showed that such a reversible computer would require infinite memory storage. As soon as the computer began to erase information in its memory to make way for new information, it would be carrying out an irreversible process. Thus, as long as we have some finite bound on the economy (i.e., the economy is a subsystem of the universe and not the universe itself), then Georgescu-Roegen's theory is safe and the proposed condition of economic irreversibility is not violated.[27]

The first G-R Condition thus claims that all products and services with economic value are produced by thermodynamically irreversible transformations. To put it simply, you can't make an omelet without breaking some eggs.

You might have noticed that in the phrasing of the irreversibility condition, I have added the word *transactions* to the word *transformations*. This is because economic value is created not only in the production of goods and services, but also in their exchange. As discussed earlier in the book, Traditional Economics has long recognized this point, which arises out of people's differing preferences; trading creates value by better matching the configuration of goods and services in the world to people's preferences. Just as value-creating production is irreversible, so too is value-creating trade.[28] In intuitive terms, if two people agree to a trade because it is mutually beneficial (value creating), then they will not want to undo the trade and reverse it immediately afterward. Doing so would make them each lose the value of the trade (unless, of course, new information—such as information that the traded good is faulty—had been revealed and caused one of the people to change his or her mind).

From a physical, thermodynamic perspective, however, it is a bit trickier to characterize trading. For example, if we watched two people trade a Hank Aaron baseball card for a Babe Ruth baseball card, we could not tell whether the trade was forward or backward—was it Ruth for Aaron or Aaron for Ruth? This is because there is some hidden information we need to know—each trader's preferences and existing stock of baseball cards. Now, let's say we asked a market researcher to survey both traders before the trade and query them on who their favorite baseball players are and what cards they hold. We would then see a better match between their preferences and their collection of cards after the trade than before, and thus we would know which way the trade was running.[29] We would also know that the two traders would not want to immediately undo their deal. Thus, the transaction is irreversible in a thermodynamic sense.

Irreversibility is a necessary but *not* a sufficient condition for value creation. It is not hard to imagine irreversible processes that are value destroying; hurricanes, explosions, and incompetent management teams all destroy value in ways that take energy to reverse. The first G-R Condition gives time an arrow in economic systems, but we need the second condition to give entropy an arrow and further narrow down the transformations and transactions that are value creating.

Decreasing Entropy: Are Pink Cars and Bombs Value Creating?

The second G-R Condition, "All value-creating economic transformations and transactions reduce entropy locally within the economic system, while increasing entropy globally" enables us to distinguish throwing a rock through a window versus repairing it. Any process that creates value must be both irreversible and entropy lowering.

Most economic transformations lower entropy in an obvious way, as Georgescu-Roegen's examples of cloth, lumber, china, and copper illustrated. But aren't there economic transformations that involve raising entropy? For example, might not the demolishing of a building create value? Or what about making bombs for the military?

I would argue that demolishing a building is an intermediate step in a larger economic transformation, and not a complete transformation in and of itself, just like turning trees into wood pulp is an intermediate step in making paper. People don't demolish a building just for the sake of demolishing a building.[30] Buildings are demolished as a step in building another building, or in reclaiming the land for some other purpose (e.g., building a highway or even returning the land to nature).[31] The same argument holds true for rubbish disposal, environmental cleanup, and recycling, all of which can be viewed as part of the larger transformation process of creating a product or service in the first place (this is one reason environmentalists like Georgescu-Roegen's ideas: production and cleanup are viewed in an integrated fashion). The role of destruction as an intermediate step in value creation holds in biological systems as well. Before your body can create new order in its cells and systems, your digestive system must break down the nicely ordered packages of chemicals and energy that are in your food. Again, the adage that you can't make an omelet without breaking some eggs holds true.

Explosives, however, are a somewhat different matter. The act of transforming a bunch of chemicals into dynamite or a plastic explosive is an entropy-decreasing activity. The explosives maker uses energy and knowledge to take disordered molecules and order them in neat, high-potential energy packages that can be used to do useful work such as mining or demolition. From a thermodynamic perspective, the random motion of molecules is highly unlikely to spontaneously order themselves into a stick of dynamite. However, when the military uses explosives to blow up enemy targets, it may be doing something important to defend national security, but no one would argue that the use of a bomb is an economically value-creating transformation. Manufacturing a bomb lowers entropy and creates value (evidence for which is the fact that someone is willing to pay for it), but then *using* the bomb raises the entropy of enemy assets by blowing them up; the act destroys rather than creates economic value. Warfare inevitably raises entropy as it turns the hard-won order of economies into rubble, and the biological order of human bodies into injury and death.

Thus far, I have been fairly casual in my use of the word *order,* assuming that, like Justice Stewart Potter's famous definition of pornography, "we know it when we see it." *Order,* however, can be an ambiguous and slippery concept. For example, I could sneak out in the middle of the night and paint every car in Ann Arbor, Michigan, bright pink.[32] It is difficult to say that this would be value creating—after all, the residents of Ann Arbor are likely to be pretty angry with me and unlikely to pay me for my efforts. I could argue, however, that I have decreased entropy. After all, I expended energy to create a lower-probability configuration of the world. That is, a city of all pink cars is less likely than one with a random mix of car colors. But you could also argue that the activity was actually entropy increasing. By painting every car pink, I destroyed information—after my paint job, it would be a lot harder for people to identify their particular car. Thus, I may have expended energy to do it, but it is no better than throwing a rock through a window or any other act of vandalism. So, is painting cars pink order creating or information destroying?

It depends on your point of view. This is a key point in understanding the concept of order. *What constitutes order versus disorder must be measured relative to something.* To a traffic planner in a helicopter trying to count the number of cars in Ann Arbor, painting all the cars pink might be order creating, because it would help her spot cars more easily and accurately—she might even be willing to pay me something to do it. But from the perspective of a car owner, it is order destroying because of the information lost (the information lost is the previous car color, the fact that the owner might like pink less than the previous color is a separate issue; we will cover preferences in the next section).

This relative nature of order is a well-known issue in thermodynamics. The Polish physicist Wojciech Zurek gives as an example that he calls "the shuffling trick."[33] A magician shows you a deck of cards; the deck is perfectly ordered by value and suit (the two of hearts is followed by the three of hearts, and so on, and likewise for each of the other three suits). The magician then shuffles the deck very thoroughly, completely randomizing it. He then shows you the random deck. Next, he hands you another deck of cards, also perfectly ordered by value and suit, and bets you twenty dollars that you cannot do what he just did. Thinking, "how hard can it be to shuffle a card deck?" you accept the bet and give the neatly ordered deck a really good shuffling until it looks nice and random. You hand it back to the magician with a smile and await your twenty dollars. But then he says, "You lost the bet. In my shuffled deck, the order was queen of spades, ten of clubs, four of diamonds, and so on. Your deck looks nothing like mine—you owe me twenty bucks!" The point of the parable is that any one configuration of the deck of cards is just as likely or unlikely as any other—you have the same odds of shuffling the deck into perfect value and suit order as you do into any other particular order. We merely have picked one particular configuration out of all of the equally possible configurations and called it "ordered" because of the arbitrary meanings of the set of symbols printed on the cards.

Consequently, low entropy might indeed be *necessary* for something to have economic value, but defining what kinds of order are valuable and what kinds are not seems rather subjective—order is in the eye of the beholder. Our first two G-R Conditions thus leave us with necessity but not sufficiency for value creation.

Fitness (Part 1): An Evolutionary View of Preferences

Irreversibility and order are fundamentally connected to economic value creation, but we need some way of understanding why humans prefer certain kinds of order to others, why we prefer having cars of individual colors and a crunchy apple over a crunchy beetle. One approach would be to take the route of Traditional Economics and simply assume that humans have preferences, that those preferences are ordered in a logical way, and that people act in such a way as to maximize their satisfaction of those preferences. Under this approach, we don't need to know what those preferences are—they are revealed as people trade and consume—and we don't need to know how they are formed or how they might change over time. Following this view, wealth would simply be "whatever patterns of order that people prefer." But this is somewhat unsatisfactory, as much of the action is shifted into a mysterious, exogenous black box called *preferences*. So, let's see if we can open the box a bit, look inside, and connect it into the larger evolutionary framework we have been building.[34] Why do we want what we want? Why might you want a nice dinner, a new set of clothes, a trip to a tropical island, a red sports car, or a diamond necklace? And why might you prefer the diamond necklace to the nice dinner?

Preferences are a psychological phenomenon. Freud postulated that our material needs are driven by the animal drives of our id and kept in check by our superego—thus, our economic preferences are the result of battles between "I really want that expensive car now!" and "But I need to save for my children's education!" B. F. Skinner, on the other hand, thought that preferences were essentially learned. So, a Skinnerian might say that we want the fancy car because we have learned from society that fancy cars are desirable, and the maker of the car has taught us to want it by exposing us to alluring marketing messages. A further theory that is somewhere between Freud's animal drives and Skinner's learned behavior was developed in the 1960s by the psychologist Abraham Maslow. He claimed that humans have a "hierarchy of needs" that start with basic physical needs for food, water, sex, shelter, sleep, and so forth, and then go to higher level needs such as self-esteem and social esteem. Thus, a middle-class person who has already fulfilled his or her basic needs for food and shelter might splash out on a fancy car or clothes as a way of fulfilling his or her need for social esteem. The highest level of the Maslow hierarchy is *self-actualization*. When you reach megamillionaire status and have everything, you can then put your materialism aside and do good works, go off to Tibet to find yourself, or sit in your hot tub contemplating the meaning of life. This is why the really rich Hollywood stars are the ones eating vegan food and going to Buddhist monasteries—it is only the B-list celebs driving the Ferraris.

Although Maslow organizes our needs into a useful (but arguably ad hoc) framework, his theory does not answer the deeper question of where those needs come from, and *why* as consumers we prefer some things over others. An answer to these deeper questions may come from more recent work in evolutionary psychology.[35] Evolutionary psychology claims that our genes built our brains with one purpose: to get our genes into the next generation. People often confuse evolutionary psychology with a view that all behavior is genetically determined. No evolutionary psychologist would claim that someone's preference for Burger King over McDonald's is in his or her genes. Rather, what evolutionary psychologists claim is that many of our behaviors are the way they are because they helped our ancestors survive and reproduce in the African savanna around 100,000 to 500,000 years ago, or what evolutionary psychologists refer to as the *ancestral environment*. While all humans have common behaviors (e.g., desires for food, sex, and social status), humans are also very adaptable, and as Robert Wright has put it, those behaviors become *tuned* to the local environment.[36] To an evolutionary psychologist, "nature versus nurture" is not a very interesting question, because both factors are clearly involved in determining behavior. Rather, the interesting questions are, why did the "nature" part evolve, and how does the environment affect and tune the "nurture" part, and how do the two sides of human behavior interact with each other?

In anthropological observations of hunter-gatherer tribes, one can see how preference behaviors are directly related to things that help people survive in their environment, compete for status, reproduce, and nurture their children. It is more difficult to see this connection through all the abstractions of modern life, but an evolutionary psychologist would say that lurking beneath our modern economic preferences is the evolutionary shadow of our hunter-gatherer lifestyle in the African savanna. According to the U.S. Bureau of Labor Statistics, 90 percent of U.S. consumer spending belongs to seven major categories.[37] If one looks at these categories from the perspective of evolutionary psychology, a pattern begins to emerge:

- HOUSING (32 percent of expenditures). We tend to value housing that protects us physically from the elements, provides a good environment for our family, and shows our social status through the house's size, the way it is decorated, and where it is located. The evolutionary benefits of a shelter that protects us and is good for raising children are clear. Housing as a measure of social status and wealth goes back as far as archeological evidence of human settlements.[38] The MIT cognitive scientist Steven Pinker even claims that some of our modern preferences for what makes an attractive physical environment have a basis in what were evolutionary successful environments during our early history.[39]

- TRANSPORT (20 percent). Transportation enables us to earn a living as well as visit and bond with relatives and friends. Males also sometimes use transport to signal social status and (attempt to) attract females.

- FOOD (14 percent). The evolutionary necessity of food is obvious. However our particular tastes that value certain foods, especially rich, sweet, and fatty foods, evolved because these foods were scarce and nutritiously valuable in the ancestral environment.[40] Numerous businesses, from McDonald's to fancy French restaurants, make a living meeting tastes that, as Robert Wright has noted, evolved long before saturated fats were available on every street corner and most people had sedentary jobs.[41]

- LIFE INSURANCE AND PENSIONS (9 percent). Life insurance is a way of helping maximize the chances that your genetic progeny and mate survive if you meet an untimely end. Pensions help ensure that after you have reproduced and your offspring are full grown, you can still survive despite your diminished evolutionary value.

- HEALTH CARE (5 percent). The evolutionary benefits of good health care are clear, and as evolutionary theory would predict, we tend to be most concerned about the health of ourselves and our close genetic kin.

- CLOTHING (5 percent). Beyond the basic survival benefits of clothing in protecting us from the elements, we tend to use clothing to show status, to signal membership in a particular group, and to attract mates. A Cartier watch might show that you are a person of high status, your choice in footwear can identify you as a member of the hip-hop tribe or tax-accountant tribe, and that sexy strapless dress or snazzy suit is sure to attract a potential mate. This is not just true of luxury goods. Even more practical brands play on these same needs, but with a different message. For example, a male dressed in Lands' End might be signaling, "I am part of the sensible chinos and blue-shirt middle class; I am a reliable mate and don't feel a need to show off."

- ENTERTAINMENT, MEDIA, AND COMMUNICATIONS (5 percent). Even our notions of fun have residual connections to evolutionary benefits, such as bonding with friends and building coalitions over a dinner, or seeking to attract a mate in a bar. Sports, with their battles for dominance and chest beating, feed off drives that go back to our prehominid days. Likewise, stories, news, gossip, and information in general had enormous survival benefits in the ancestral environment. One study of mobile-phone usage noted that users participated in "social grooming," using the phones to build and maintain their social networks in much the same way other primates use physical grooming to build and maintain theirs.[42] Another study found male mobile-phone users were more likely to flash fancy phones and conspicuously talk on them when in front of females than when alone or in front of males, thus using the phones to signal wealth, status, and social connection— all factors that increased the chances of successful reproduction in the ancestral environment.[43]

Fitness (Part 2): Pushing Our Own Pleasure Buttons

Big Macs, Porsches, Jimmy Choo shoes, and mobile phones did not exist in the African savanna of our early hunter-gatherer days. Nevertheless, many of the drives that evolved to increase the odds of survival and reproduction in that environment still make themselves felt in our needs, desires, and emotions today, and help explain why we want the things we want in our modern consumer society.

While there may be an evolutionary logic for why we spend so much on food, shelter, clothing, health care, and perhaps even cell phones, there are some things we buy for which it is much harder to see an evolutionary connection. For example, why would we want to spend money to buy a painting or listen to music? A cynic might say these are also related to signals of status and attempts to attract mates. As Pinker notes, "What better proof that you have money to spare than to spend it on doodads . . . that don't fill the belly or keep the rain out."[44] Throughout history, it is the rich who have been most involved in supporting the arts. Many people would claim, however, that the pleasure of an aesthetic experience has value in and of itself, and it is not only the rich who enjoy such experiences. How does desiring art connect to evolutionary advantage in the ancestral environment? The answer is, it doesn't. According to evolutionary psychologists, art is what is known in evolutionary theory as an *exaptation*—a side effect of something we evolved for other reasons. We may have evolved ideas about what constitutes a beautiful scene, an attractive face, or a pleasant sound, for other reasons. For example, people around the world are attracted to scenes with water, high ground, shady trees, and so on, which might have as much to do with survival in the ancestral environment as aesthetics. Likewise, faces regarded as beautiful tend to be symmetrical, which is a sign of youth and reproductive health.

Pinker refers to art as "mental cheesecake."[45] Cheesecake did not exist in the ancestral environment, yet many people crave it. They crave it because we evolved cravings for fats and sugars, both of which were rare treats in earlier times, and quite good for putting on fat stores for lean times and helping children grow. And, just as we later learned how to make cheesecake to feed our earlier-evolved physical cravings, we learned how to make art to feed our earlier-evolved mental cravings for attractive images and sounds. None of this is to deny the intense and genuine emotions felt when experiencing art, nor the uniqueness of the genius involved in creating it; evolutionary psychology merely provides some insight into why it might exist in the first place.

The human psyche thus evolved a variety of pleasure and pain buttons in the ancestral environment because those buttons helped people survive and reproduce. But large-brained, nimble-handed humans have figured out how to push their own mental pleasure buttons (and avoid the pain buttons) in a variety of ingenious ways, ranging from McDonald's to haute cuisine, and from pornography to high art. Traditional Economics has tended to historically focus on differences in preferences. But the more interesting question is, in a world of 6.4 billion people, why is there so much similarity in preferences? Why, much to the chagrin of nutritionists and antiglobalization protesters, do people around the world like fizzy, sweet drinks such as Coca-Cola? Why do teens from Russia to Brazil crave the latest Nike sneakers? And why was the television show *Bay Watch* a big hit in both the suburbs of the United States and small villages in rural China? To evolutionary psychologists, the answers are obvious—sugary drinks, objects that convey status, and sexually desirable people push mental pleasure buttons that evolved long ago. While the application of evolutionary psychology to studying economic preferences and consumer behavior is still new and somewhat speculative, it can give us insight into the question of why some forms of order are more appealing to humans than others.

Moving back to our framework of economic evolution, we can then see that our evolving preferences provide a fitness constraint on Business Plan evolution, and that Business Plans and preferences coevolve. This is what evolutionary theorists refer to as *niche construction;* as organisms evolve, they have impacts on their environment, which in turn influences their evolution.[46] For example, plants process carbon dioxide and emit oxygen, while aerobic organisms (e.g., worms, fish, mammals) process oxygen and emit carbon dioxide. The two groups of organisms have coevolved over time, changing the composition of the atmosphere from 1 percent oxygen in the Proterozoic era to 21 percent today, which in turn provides a fitness constraint on future evolution.

In the economic realm, there is coevolution between our needs and tastes and the Business Plans that evolve to meet them. For example, our hearing evolved as a survival mechanism in our primate past and was well adapted to picking out useful patterns of sound in the environment of the African savanna (e.g., the presence of game or predators), and evolved further as humans gained language capabilities. Music developed sometime around 30,000 years ago as an exaptation, or "auditory cheesecake," to appeal to our evolved hearing and mental capabilities.[47] The desire for an MP3 player thus is not directly related to our survival and reproduction. Nor could we have had a desire for an MP3 player before it was invented. However, for the reasons just described, humans evolved a taste for music, and ever since, Business Plans have been developed to compete to satisfy that urge—from making and trading bone flutes and skin drums, to selling guitars, harmonicas, and, later, transistor radios and MP3 players. Thus, while our desire to hear music is quite old and has an evolutionary logic behind it, the solutions for meeting that desire have evolved significantly over time. Our preferences drive Business Plan evolution, and Business Plan evolution influences the evolution of our preferences.

The Universal Utility Function

Taken together, the three G-R Conditions say that economic activity is fundamentally about order creation. Faced with the disorder and randomness of the world, humans spend most of their waking hours ordering their environment in various ways to make it a more hospitable and enjoyable place. We order our world by transforming energy, matter, and information into the goods and services we want, and we have discovered the evolutionary Good Trick that by cooperating, specializing, and trading, we can create even more order than we otherwise could on our own. But what is the purpose of all our scurrying, buzzing, furtive order creation? Why do we do it?

At this point, Georgescu-Roegen took a slightly mystical turn and claimed that all our order-creating activity is aimed at increasing human happiness. He reached for an explanation that goes back to Bentham's notion of utility— that there is a mysterious ether, what Georgescu-Roegen called a *psychic flux*, that constantly flows through people and is a measure of their instantaneous happiness at a point in time.[48] In evolutionary terms, Georgescu-Roegen was saying that the fitness function of all our entropy-lowering activities is individual human happiness.

Here I will depart from Georgescu-Roegen, because I see a less mystical and more scientifically grounded alternative. In biological evolutionary theory, there is just a single, universal utility function—the replication of genes. From the gene's-eye view, our genes built our bodies as a strategy for replicating themselves. A part of that strategy was to give our bodies large brains that enabled humans to live in complex, cooperative social environments and build tools. Those brains were built to serve the purpose of replicating the genes that built them. As a result, the brain developed goals, preferences, and drives that were consistent with surviving, mating, and bringing up young in the ancestral environment. We have used our large brains to order our environment to meet the needs of our goals, preferences, and drives.

As Richard Dawkins has made clear, serving the historical replication interests of our genes is *not* the same thing as serving our current interests in happiness.[49] Our genes give us cravings for fats and sugars that were in short supply in the ancestral environment, yet in the modern world, these nutrients do us more harm than good. Likewise, our genes give us the emotional potential for irrational fits of rage. This was likely a good strategy in prelanguage hunter-gatherer days, when punishment was the other half of the cooperation equation, and the potential for communications was limited. But in modern society, with laws, norms, and other mechanisms for enforcing good behavior, such irrational outbursts can do more harm than good. Evolution doesn't give a whit about our happiness, and it doesn't necessarily give us goals, preferences, and drives that lead us to happier states. All evolution gives us is strategies that happened to have served our survival and replication interests in the past. By logic that is all it can give us.

Although the spiritual implications of this are beyond the scope of this book, it does explain one mystery of modern life: why doesn't money buy happiness? This isn't just a cliché; it is an empirical fact. A number of psychologists, including Nobel Prize winner Daniel Kahneman of Princeton, have carefully studied the causes of human happiness across cultures and over time.[50] They have found a strong direct genetic link that explains about 50 percent of happiness. Given that scientists know that there is a powerful biochemical basis for happiness in the brain (which is why antidepressant drugs work for many people), it is not surprising that genetics has some influence on the relative happiness of our individual brain chemistry. But that leaves the other 50 percent. In their review, Kahneman and his colleagues found that factors such as marriage, social relationships, employment, social status, and physical environment all had significant effects. Again, from an evolutionary perspective, it is not surprising that having a mate, social bonds, high status, and a comfortable environment all trigger "happy" chemicals in the brain—those were all critical factors for successful genetic replication in the ancestral environment.

The absolute level of one's wealth does have an impact on happiness, but not in a linear progression. People who are very poor and struggling for survival tend to be less happy. Once people reach the level at which their basic needs are met, however, the correlation between wealth and happiness plateaus significantly. Past that threshold, people tend to view wealth on a relative and not an absolute basis. Increases in wealth, especially unexpected ones, make us happy, but then we are quick to return to our baseline happiness. An unexpected pay raise might make you celebrate for a couple of months, but then you get used to the extra money and after a while begin to think you are underpaid again. Studies of lottery winners show a similar pattern in which they initially experience great joy, expect their life's problems to be solved, and then later regress to their baseline happiness or even below it. Again, this attitude toward wealth makes evolutionary sense. One can imagine how, in a competitive world, striving, wealth-accumulating, restless, never-satisfied genes would beat out satiated, fat-and-happy genes. Greed may not be good for our own happiness or the happiness of others, but a certain amount of it (kept in check by our social norms and structures) has historically been good for getting our genes replicated.

Wealth Is "Fit Order"

All wealth is created by thermodynamically irreversible, entropy-lowering processes. The act of creating wealth is an act of creating order, but not all order is wealth creating. Individual minds, organizations, and markets churn through Business Plans seeking different forms of economic order, and where the markets propose, consumers dispose. They select forms of order that meet their needs, fulfilling drives and preferences that may seem modern, but have deep historical roots in the universal utility function of our genes. Wealth is thus a form of anti-entropy. It is a form of order, but not just any order—it is *fit order*. Patterns of economic order, in the form of products and services, compete with each other to be needed, desired, and even craved by consumers. We can retrospectively say that patterns of economic order that are successful in the competition to meet our preferences are *fit*, and the Business Plan modules that contribute to the creation of fit economic order are then amplified over time. And just as species and their environments coevolve, the competitive ecosystem of Business Plans and the preferences of consumers coevolve, making fitness a contingent concept, whereby what is fit today may or may not be fit tomorrow.

We can relate the idea of wealth as "fit order" back to Traditional notions of economic value. In the Classical period, economists thought that the wellspring of value in the economy lay on the supply side, that value was derived from factors of production. For example, Cantillon believed that value was a function of how much scarce land was used in making a product, Marx saw labor as the ultimate source of value, and Ricardo added that capital was essential as well. With Jevons and the Marginalists, the theory of value swung over to the demand side, as they argued that value was determined by people's relative utilities for goods. In the Neoclassical synthesis, the two sides were fused: scarce factors of production met individual preferences through the mechanism of markets, and value was simply whatever two people were willing to trade for. If a widget maker was willing to sell a widget for one dollar and a consumer was willing to buy a widget for one dollar, then the value of a widget was one dollar.

The evolutionary view of value also has a supply and a demand side. On the supply side, things with low entropy have value. By definition, things with low entropy are scarce and require energy, materials, and information for their creation. On the demand side, our preferences determine the relative attractiveness of products and services competing for our attention. As in Traditional Economics, the two sides meet through the mechanism of markets, which find Business Plans that match scarce order with individual preferences. Money is a Social Technology that enables us to keep score in these interactions. The value of a widget is still one dollar in Complexity Economics, but we can gain a deeper understanding as to why.

Economic wealth and biological wealth are thermodynamically the same sort of phenomena, and not just metaphorically. Both are systems of locally low entropy, patterns of order that evolved over time under the constraint of fitness functions. Both are forms of fit order. And the fitness function of the economy—our tastes and preferences—is fundamentally linked to the fitness function of the biological world—the replication of genes. *The economy is ultimately a genetic replication strategy.* It is yet another evolutionary Good Trick, along with leopard camouflage, bat radar, and fruit-fly eyes. The economy is a massively complex Good Trick built on the complex Good Tricks of big brains, nimble toolmaking hands, cooperative instincts, language, and culture.[51]

If wealth is indeed fit order, then we can use another more familiar word to describe it. In physics, order is the same thing as information, and thus we can also think of wealth as fit information; in other words, *knowledge*. Information on its own can be worthless. Knowledge on the other hand is information that is useful, that we can do something with, that is fit for some purpose. So we have come full circle; the founder of Traditional growth theory, Robert Solow, was right. The origin of wealth is knowledge. Yet rather than treating knowledge as an assumption, an exogenous input, a mysterious process outside the bounds of economics, the Complexity-based view I have outlined puts the creation of knowledge at the endogenous heart of the economy.[52]

Evolution is a knowledge-creation machine—a learning algorithm.[53] Think of all the knowledge embedded in the ingenious designs of the biological world. A grasshopper is an engineering marvel, a storehouse of knowledge of physics, chemistry, and biomechanics—knowledge that is beyond the bounds of current human ability to replicate. A grasshopper is also a snapshot of knowledge about the environment it evolved in, the foods that were good to eat, the predators that needed to be defended against, and the strategies that worked well for attracting mates and ensuring the survival of progeny. There are terabytes of knowledge embedded in a single grasshopper. Now think of the mind-bogglingly immense amount of knowledge embedded in the entirety of the biosphere. All the order and complexity, all the knowledge, was created and assembled by the simplest of recipes: differentiate, select, replicate, and repeat.

Now, look around the room you are in and think of all the knowledge embedded in the objects around you. The carpentry involved in making your chair; the cotton-growing, fabric-making, and fashion-designing knowledge embedded in your clothes; the knowledge of electricity and materials embedded in your light; and all the knowledge embedded in your books. The sheer volume of knowledge in the econosphere is as staggering as that in the biosphere. The econosphere, too, was created by differentiate, select, amplify, and repeat.

We have found the answer to our quest. Wealth is knowledge and its origin is evolution.

Did We Pass the Test?

At the beginning of the book, I described a test that any theory claiming to explain the creation of wealth must pass. The theory must be able to start in a "state of nature" with a group of people and a set of natural resources, and create a history that shows decreasing entropy and growing complexity, organization, diversity, and wealth over time. The theory must take us from stone-tool-making hominids to chardonnay-quaffing New Yorkers and do so in the discontinuous, explosive, punctuated-equilibrium pattern of the historical record. In addition, the theory must do all this without reaching outside itself for key dynamics, and with a minimum of ad hoc assumptions. And finally, the theory must be consistent with, and not contradict, other well-accepted theories in the sciences.

This is a tall order and such a theory does not yet fully exist. But I believe it is achievable. Over the past five chapters, I have synthesized the work of many people into a sketch of what such a theory might look like. We can in essence "start" the model in our hominid past, circa 2.5 million years ago, with the initial point in Physical Technology space of the invention of the first stone hand-ax tool, and the initial point in Social Technology space of small bands of close kin. The only exogenous factors are physical inputs of energy and matter and outputs of heat and waste. The only exogenous dynamics are biological, such as the growth of human deductive-tinkering brains, the development of speech, and the evolution of basic preferences. Once set up, the search through PT, ST, and Business Plan spaces would be off and running, each coevolving and feeding off the other, and each expanding exponentially with successive discoveries. Out of these three design spaces, we would see emerge a pattern of gradual initial development with punctuated periods of rapid and slow change, but with an accelerating trend toward lower entropy, greater complexity and diversity, and growing wealth. Notably, such a trend toward greater order and wealth is not the inevitable result of evolution; the right conditions must be present. Nor is there any guarantee that if we "played the tape" of evolution again (to use a phrase from Stephen Jay Gould), we would end up with the same economy we have today. Evolution is an accumulation of millions of tiny accidents and contingent twists and turns; even small changes in that history can lead to very different outcomes.[54] But such a theory would help us understand the conditions needed for economic complexity to arise and grow, and the broad parameters that have enabled the development of the economy we have today.

Georgescu-Roegen's insights, articulated in the three G-R Conditions, provide a potentially important grounding point for any such theory. In fact, one could argue that the first two conditions, irreversibility and decreasing entropy, constitute empirical laws of economics. As this is a fairly strong statement, I should briefly clarify what I mean by a law. In general, when something is observed to be a universal regularity in nature with no known exceptions, it is said to be a *law*.[55] A law in and of itself does not necessarily explain *why* the regularity exists; it merely notes that it *does*. A theory, on the other hand, provides explanations for why regularities exist and how they work. Science is at its strongest when we have both empirical laws and deep, theoretical explanations for those laws. The laws of thermodynamics themselves, for example, are empirical regularities, but science also has a deep, quantum-level understanding of why those regularities exist. In contrast, as we saw in chapter 3, what usually goes for laws in economics are, on closer examination, rough approximations. The first two G-R Conditions can be viewed as laws because they are empirically testable and, I would argue, hold true without exception (try to think of something that you have paid for that is not the result of an irreversible process with decreasing entropy). The third G-R Condition is a bit trickier, because as we have noted, fitness is only observable post facto, and our only real way of observing economic fitness is by seeing if people have been willing to pay or trade for something. The third G-R Condition is thus more of a logical construct than an empirical law.

There is still some distance and many years of research to go before we have a rigorous, mathematical, empirically tested evolutionary model of the economy that addresses all these issues. But the broad body of work in Complexity Economics I have described in parts 2 and 3 shows that many pieces of the puzzle are already in place and that such a theory is not only possible, but highly likely in the years to come. Undoubtedly, some conjectures discussed in these chapters will turn out to be wrong or in need of revision, but the broad arc leading us away from an equilibrium view of the economy toward an evolutionary, Complexity-based perspective is clear. The implications of this paradigm shift are many and far-reaching and will be our subject in part 4.

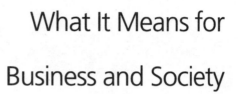

PART IV

What It Means for

Business and Society

Nature, to be commanded,
must be obeyed.

—Francis Bacon

CHAPTER FIFTEEN

Strategy

RACING THE RED QUEEN

THE MESSAGE of Traditional Economics is that if humans can just behave rationally enough, and if we possess enough information, then the economy will be revealed as a universe of clockwork predictability. Even the uncertainty of Traditional Economics is of the well-behaved kind.[1] The dream of a clockwork universe ended for science in the twentieth century, and is ending for economics in the twenty-first. The economy is too complex, too nonlinear, too dynamic, and too sensitive to the twists and turns of chance to be amenable to prediction over anything but the very shortest of terms.[2] Even if we were as rational as possible and had all the information we could want, the computational complexity of the economy is such that the future would happen before we would have time to predict it.[3]

This is a sobering message. Particularly as we routinely expect people to make economic decisions that require just such long-term predictions. This is not merely an issue for economists attempting to forecast the wiggles of GDP or inflation. CEOs are expected to determine whether one business strategy will deliver better results in the future than another. Investors are expected to determine whether one investment approach will yield a higher return in the future than another. And political leaders are expected to determine whether one policy will better serve the needs of society in the future than another.

If the message of Complexity Economics is correct, where does this leave us? Today, we muddle through. CEOs, investors, and policy makers use their powers of rationality as best they can. They make their predictions and decisions and are sometimes right and sometimes wrong; they experiment, adjust course, and deductively-tinker their way along. Is the message of Complexity Economics that we will never do better than that?

While Complexity Economics strips away our illusions of control over our economic fate, it also hands us a lever—a lever that we have always possessed but never fully appreciated. *We may not be able to predict or direct economic evolution, but we can design our institutions and societies to be better or worse evolvers.*

We have already seen evidence of the power of this lever. Over the eighteenth and nineteenth centuries, humankind evolved the Social Technologies of science and markets, leading to an acceleration of economic evolution and the greatest explosion in wealth creation ever seen. The message of Complexity Economics is that evolution may indeed be cleverer than we are, but rather than outsmart it, we can understand it and harness its power to serve human purposes. How we do this will be our theme in part 4, beginning with business strategy.

Are You Committed?

There are almost as many definitions of business strategy as there are business school professors and management gurus.[4] One of the first definitions, and still one of the best, is from the business historian Alfred Chandler's 1962 classic, *Strategy and Structure*:

> Strategy can be defined as the determination of the basic long-term goals and objectives of an enterprise, and the adoption of courses of action and the allocation of resources necessary for carrying out these goals.[5]

Chandler's definition is a good place to start, because it captures two points that have been critical to how managers have defined strategy ever since. First, strategy is inherently forward looking. To develop a strategy, one must make a determination about where one wants to be in the future. Second, strategy is about creating a plan for getting to the desired future state and committing to a course of action defined by that plan.

These two elements are at the heart of strategy development in most companies.[6] The planning process typically begins with a situation analysis that reviews the current state of the company and industry. The management team then assesses critical trends affecting customers, competitors, technologies, and so on, leading to a prediction of future scenarios and an assessment of attractive positions in those scenarios. An attractive position is one where the company has a *sustainable competitive advantage* enabling it to earn greater profits than its industry peers.

Traditional Economics predicts that in the equilibrium of perfect competition, no company will make profits above the minimum return required by providers of capital. In his seminal work in the 1980s, Harvard Business

School professor Michael Porter proposed that the only way for companies to earn profits above the bare minimum is to create sources of competitive advantage that (legally) reduce competition and increase the market power of the company.[7] Sources of competitive advantage help a company either achieve lower costs or differentiate its products and include factors such as proprietary technologies, strong brands, and privileged relationships with key partners.[8] For example, Wal-Mart's combination of proprietary methods for managing logistics and inventory, its well-known brand, and its power over suppliers enable it to earn higher profits than earned by its retail competitors.

Once a position of sustainable competitive advantage has been identified for the predicted future state, a plan needs to be developed for getting there. Another Harvard Business School professor, Pankaj Ghemawat, has observed that all strategic plans involve what he calls *commitment*.[9] Truly strategic choices are *difficult or costly to reverse once made*. Such hard-to-reverse commitments might include entering a new market, making an acquisition, and investing in a particular brand position. The level of commitment distinguishes strategic from tactical decisions. For example, a price cut might be a tactical decision if it is easy to reverse (e.g., one can easily raise prices again after holding a sale). Or a price cut might be a strategic decision if, as in the case of Wal-Mart, it is a long-term, widely publicized commitment to have "Everyday low prices." Such a commitment would be difficult to back away from later. When the Spanish conquistador Cortés landed on the southeastern Mexican coast in 1519, he ordered his men to burn their ships, thus forcing them to march inland—that is commitment.

Building a position of sustainable competitive advantage requires commitment, because by definition a position that does not require commitment is easy to imitate. For example, it is easy for one retailer to follow another in holding a temporary sale, but it is a bigger deal to commit to "Everyday low prices." It is the irreversibility of commitment decisions that makes strategy risky. If strategic decisions were easy or cost less to reverse, strategy would be risk-free. Ghemawat's point thus relates directly to the first G-R Condition discussed in the previous chapter: without irreversibility, there is no wealth creation, and it is irreversibility that makes wealth creation risky.

The standard approach to strategy thus hinges on two fundamental assumptions: first, that one can make confident predictions about what strategies will be successful in the future, and second, that one can make strategic commitments that will result in sustainable competitive advantage. Companies invest billions of dollars on the back of these assumptions every day. Unfortunately, both assumptions are wrong.

A $270 Billion Frozen Accident

There are people who make a hobby of "alternative history," imagining how history would be different if small, chance events had gone another way. One of my favorite examples is a story I first heard from the physicist Murray Gell-Mann.[10] In the late 1800s, "Buffalo Bill" Cody created a show called Buffalo Bill's Wild West Show, which toured the United States, putting on exhibitions of gun fighting, horsemanship, and other cowboy skills. One of the show's most popular acts was a woman named Phoebe Moses, nicknamed Annie Oakley. Annie was reputed to have been able to shoot the head off of a running quail by age twelve, and in Buffalo Bill's show, she put on a demonstration of marksmanship that included shooting flames off candles, and corks out of bottles. For her grand finale, Annie would announce that she would shoot the end off a lit cigarette held in a man's mouth, and ask for a brave volunteer from the audience. Since no one was ever courageous enough to come forward, Annie hid her husband, Frank, in the audience. He would "volunteer," and they would complete the trick together. In 1890, when the Wild West Show was touring Europe, a young crown prince (and later, kaiser), Wilhelm, was in the audience. When the grand finale came, much to Annie's surprise, the macho crown prince stood up and volunteered. The future German kaiser strode into the ring, placed the cigarette in his mouth, and stood ready. Annie, who had been up late the night before in the local beer garden, was unnerved by this unexpected development. She lined the cigarette up in her sights, squeezed . . . and hit it right on target.

Many people have speculated that if at that moment, there had been a slight tremor in Annie's hand, then World War I might never have happened. If World War I had not happened, 8.5 million soldiers and 13 million civilian lives would have been saved. Furthermore, if Annie's hand had trembled and World War I had not happened, Hitler would not have risen from the ashes of a defeated Germany, and Lenin would not have overthrown a demoralized Russian government. The entire course of twentieth-century history might have been changed by the merest quiver of a hand at a critical moment. Yet, at the time, there was no way anyone could have known the momentous nature of the event.

The Annie Oakley story is an example of what Gell-Mann calls a *frozen accident*—a tiny chance event that determines which branch history takes.[11] The nonlinear, dynamic nature of complex adaptive systems means that although such events might be small, the divergence in the paths of history can be quite large.

Business history is also built on an accumulation of frozen accidents. One of the most famous in modern times occurred during the summer of 1980, when IBM was preparing to launch its first personal computer and enter the fast-growing market pioneered by Apple. IBM approached a small company with forty employees in Bellevue, Washington. The company, called Microsoft, was run by a Harvard dropout named Bill Gates and his friend Paul Allen. IBM wanted to talk to the small company about creating a version of the programming language BASIC for the new PC. At their meeting, IBM asked Gates for his advice on what operating system (OS) the new machine should run. Gates suggested that IBM talk to Gary Kildall of Digital Research, whose CP/M operating system had become the standard in the hobbyist world of microcomputers. But Kildall was suspicious of the blue suits from IBM, and when IBM tried to meet him, he went hot-air ballooning, leaving his wife and lawyer to talk to the bewildered executives, along with instructions not to sign even a confidentiality agreement. The frustrated IBM executives returned to Gates and asked if he would be interested in the OS project. Despite never having written an OS, Gates said yes. He then turned around and licensed a product appropriately named Quick and Dirty Operating System, or Q-DOS, from a small company called Seattle Computer Products for $50,000, modified it, and then relicensed it to IBM as PC-DOS. As IBM and Microsoft were going through the final language for the agreement, Gates asked for a small change. He wanted to retain the rights to sell his DOS on non-IBM machines in a version called MS-DOS. Gates was giving the company a good price, and IBM was more interested in PC hardware than software sales, so it agreed. The contract was signed on August 12, 1981. The rest, as they say, is history. Today, Microsoft is a company worth $270 billion while IBM is worth $140 billion.

This vignette is full of frozen accidents: what if Kildall hadn't gone hot-air ballooning? What if Seattle Computer Products hadn't agreed to license Q-DOS? What if Gates hadn't gotten the final language changed in the contract? Any one of those small changes would have dramatically altered the course of business history. Yet, just like Annie Oakley and her audience, no one could have foreseen the historic consequences of those events at the time.

"The Future Ain't What It Used to Be"

One might reply that uncertainty is neither a new issue in economics nor a new one in strategic planning.[12] Much of Traditional Economics is devoted to understanding uncertainty, and strategic planners apply a variety of tools, including scenario analysis, to managing uncertainty.[13] We have to remember, however, that Traditional Economics makes a big assumption about what kind of uncertainty we face. When economists model uncertainty, they typically model it as randomness.[14] This is because randomness is well behaved and one can use statistical laws to make predictions about random systems. However, the type of uncertainty we saw in the Annie Oakley and Microsoft stories is the not-quite-regular, not-quite-random kind we saw in chapter 8. Random events play a role—the quiver of a finger here, a chance meeting there—but it is the dynamic, nonlinear structure of the system itself that magnifies small events into history-changing outcomes. This kind of uncertainty is better characterized by punctuated equilibrium and power laws than normal randomness.

The combination of punctuated equilibrium and power laws in complex adaptive systems is almost fiendishly designed to lull people into a sense of self-confidence, and then pull a nasty surprise. You will recall from chapter 6 that our minds are superb pattern-recognizers. We tend to make predictions by looking for patterns in the past and then extrapolating those patterns out into the future. More often than not, this works quite well (if it didn't, evolution would not have built our brains that way). Most of the time, the world is fairly stable. Quite often, conventional strategy analysis can tell us very useful things, and we are able to make accurate-enough short-term predictions. But the frequent occurrence of "stable" periods between punctuation points only gives us a false sense of predictability—there is nothing more dangerous than a "stable" industry.[15] Likewise, the existence of power laws means that big changes are far more likely to occur than the expectations our mental models give us on the basis of past experience.[16]

The following scenario has been played out repeatedly in industry after industry.[17] A young startup becomes successful and grows into a large company. The pattern-recognizing minds of the executives at the top of the company look at their success and say, "Aha, we've got this industry figured out." The leadership of the company then extrapolates the current pattern into the future and comes up with a strategic plan. The strategy works, and the company continues to be successful. The longer the industry remains relatively stable, the more convinced the management team becomes that it really understands what is going on and is able to predict where the business is going. The more convinced of this management becomes, the more precisely and specifically it tunes its assets, skills, and people to succeeding in the environment it has been experiencing. Then one day, Annie's hand trembles— a new technology is developed, a competitor has an idea, or consumer tastes begin to shift—and no one in the senior management team even knows about it. History has branched, and the world starts to change. At first, the pattern-recognizing minds of the company's leaders can't believe the changes are really occurring. They believe that the problems they are experiencing are just a temporary anomaly and demand more evidence—after all, they've had their industry figured out for a long time. But while the executive team waits for more evidence, the world keeps changing and the avalanche accelerates. The company is now in the middle of a punctuation point, and the management suddenly finds itself in a new game and stuck with the wrong mental models, the wrong assets, and the wrong skills. If the company is fortunate and the change is not too big or too fast, it might struggle through and survive. But if the change is large and quick, then the company dies or is taken over by someone more attuned to the new environment.

We thus have a problem. On the one hand, strategic planning requires us to make predictions about the future to make strategic commitments. On the other hand, we have a near-infinite number of possible future states, and which branch we take may depend on a series of impossible-to-predict frozen accidents. At the same time, the punctuated nature of change tricks our pattern-recognizing minds into thinking that the world is more stable than it really is. But to add to the doom and gloom, as we will now see, dealing with uncertainty is only half of the battle.

The Myth of Sustainable Competitive Advantage

In the seventeenth and eighteenth centuries, the British East India Company had the mother-of-all strategic positions. The company made today's Microsoft look like a timid mom-and-pop shop by comparison. It completely monopolized trade in four countries, had worldwide interests ranging from coffee and woolens to opium, had its own private army and navy, was empowered by the crown to declare war when its business interests were threatened, and effectively ruled over a fifth of the world's population. The British East India Company surely would have been at the top of any "most admired (and feared) companies" list in its day. Yet, despite all its economies of scale and scope, its barriers to competition, its privileged relationships, and its many core competencies (such as brutally oppressing the natives), during the nineteenth century its massive wall of competitive advantage crumbled in the face of technological innovation and the entry of new competitors, and in 1873, the company went out of business.[18] Although the British East India Company had a good, long run, in the end, the world changed and it didn't.

All competitive advantage is temporary.[19] Some advantages last longer than others, but all sources of advantage have a finite shelf life. While this may sound like a truism, the observation is often forgotten in the never-ending quest for "excellent" companies that build sustainable competitive advantages and allegedly outperform their industry peers year after year. My bookshelf is filled with books that tell the inspiring stories of such great companies, what they did to succeed, and how if your company does the same things they did, it can be a great company, too. These books include classics such as *In Search of Excellence*, by Tom Peters and Bob Waterman; *Built to Last*, by Jim Collins and Jerry Porras; and books written by admired managers such as Jack Welch and Larry Bossidy.

Intriguingly, though, just on the other side of my shelf are the "Why Great Companies Fail" books. This section includes bestsellers such as Clay Christensen's *Innovator's Dilemma* and Gary Hamel's *Leading the Revolution*. These books tell the terrifying stories of how big, once-successful companies blew it; of how industry-changing innovations, cumbersome bureaucracy, and hubris caused once mighty institutions to go down in flames. The basic message of these books is that to avoid their grim fate, your company needs to constantly innovate and to combine the might of a corporate giant with the nimbleness of a startup. This message is usually illustrated by examples of young, up-and-coming companies that are giving hell to doomed incumbents.

The fascinating thing about these books is that the same companies show up on both sides of the shelf. In the early 1980s, IBM was an "excellent" company and then moved over to the "blew it" books in the 1990s. Apple has traversed the full length of the bookshelf, starting off as a young up-and-comer, moving into "excellent" territory, then shifting to "blew it," and now has moved back to the "excellent" side with its recent successes under Steve Jobs. A shockingly large number of the original *In Search of Excellence* companies such as Amdahl, Digital Equipment Corporation, Westinghouse, Atari, Polaroid, and Kmart have fallen off the bookshelf completely into bankruptcy, breakup, or acquisition. Many others, such as Xerox and Lockheed Martin, are still around, but their performance declined precipitously soon after they were praised as role models. Two of the most lavishly praised companies in the 1990s, Enron and WORLDCOM, blew themselves up in spectacular and tragic fashion in 2002.

But while many companies fail, surely there must be *some* "excellent" companies that have built sustainable competitive advantages and maintained high levels of performance over long periods. Dick Foster and Sarah Kaplan, my former colleagues at McKinsey, examine this question in their book *Creative Destruction* by looking at the oldest league table in business, the *Forbes* 100.[20] In 1917, Bertie Forbes, the founder of *Forbes* magazine, published his first *Forbes* 100 list of the largest U.S. companies. In 1987, to celebrate the list's seventieth anniversary, the magazine republished the original list and asked, "where are they now?" The majority of the one hundred companies on the original list, sixty-one, had in one way or another ceased to exist, either merging into other companies or going bankrupt.[21] Of the survivors, twenty-one were still around but had dropped out of the top one hundred, and only eighteen, including such venerable names as Procter & Gamble, Exxon, and Citibank, were still in the elite group. These eighteen companies, as Foster and Kaplan note, were grand-champion survivors, weathering the storms of the Great Depression, World War II, the inflationary 1970s, the merger-and-acquisition turmoil of the 1980s, and the technology revolution of the 1990s. So, they must be great performers, the truly "excellent" companies, right? Wrong. With the exception of GE and Kodak, every one of them underperformed the average growth in stock market value during that seventy-year period, and since 1987, Kodak's performance has dropped off as well, leaving GE the sole original *Forbes* 100 company to survive *and* outperform the market over the past eight decades.[22] As another reference point, Foster and Kaplan also looked at the five hundred companies that started in the Standard & Poor's (S&P) 500 when it was formed in 1957, and found that only seventy-four survived until 1997. Moreover, as a group, the seventy-four survivors underperformed the overall S&P 500 index by 20 percent.

Taken together and viewed over a longer time frame, the story the "excellent company" books tell is *not* one of sustainable competitive advantage and enduring high performance. Rather, it is a story of the ephemeral nature of competitive advantage, and the incredible dynamism of markets as companies rise and fall.

Strategy Is a Red Queen Race

In two major studies published in 2002 and 2005, Robert Wiggins of the University of Memphis and Tim Ruefli of the University of Texas added some statistical rigor to the question of competitive advantage.[23] They examined a sample of 6,772 companies across forty industries from 1974 to 1997 and stratified the companies into superior, inferior, and modal (i.e., middle of the pack) performers relative to their industries.[24] The researchers addressed two errors common in many "excellence"-style studies. First, Wiggins and Ruefli ensured that the superior performance of the top firms was statistically significant. In a big enough roomful of people flipping coins, someone will inevitably get a streak of heads; Wiggins and Ruefli wanted to ensure that the patterns they were seeing were not just due to luck. Second, by using a series of rolling five-year windows, they also ensured that the performance was persistent, not dependent on just a few really good years and not overly sensitive to the particular time frame examined.

Their findings confirmed that true competitive advantage is both rare and relatively short-lived.[25] They found that only 5 percent of the companies in their sample ever achieved a period of superior performance lasting ten years or more. Only thirty-two companies, or less than 0.5 percent, made it twenty years, and only three companies (American Home Products, Eli Lilly, and

3M), or 0.04 percent, sustained high performance to the fifty-year mark. Wiggins and Ruefli also found that the intensity of competition increased during the twenty-three-year sample period. The average duration of periods of competitive advantage declined, companies churned in and out of the superior performance stratum faster and faster, and the chances of losing a superior position roughly doubled over the time frame of the study.[26]

Wiggins and Ruefli also showed that there is no such thing as a safe, stable industry. They split their sample into high-tech and low-tech groups, and while the velocity of change was somewhat faster for the high-tech group, they found that the same broad patterns occurred across all industries. As they described their findings, Wiggins and Ruefli noted that Schumpeter's ghost was alive and well; the "gales of creative destruction" were blowing harder than ever.

While Wiggins and Ruefli's data presents a major challenge to notions of strategy based on Traditional Economics, the patterns they identified would come as no surprise to an evolutionary biologist. Competitive advantage is rare and short-lived in the biological world as well. Indeed, it is exactly what one would expect in an evolutionary system. In biological systems, species are locked in a never-ending coevolutionary arms race with each other. As we noted earlier, a predator species might evolve faster running speed, its prey might then evolve better camouflage, while the predator might then evolve a sharper sense of smell, and so on, indefinitely, with no rest for the evolutionary weary. Biologists refer to such coevolutionary spirals as *Red Queen races,* named after the Red Queen in Lewis Carroll's *Through the Looking Glass.* It was she who said, "In this place it takes all the running you can do, to keep in the same place."[27]

There is no such thing as winning a Red Queen race; the best you can ever do is run faster than the competition. Recall Kristian Lindgren's evolutionary Prisoner's Dilemma model discussed in chapter 10, there was no final answer to the question "what is the best strategy?" Successful Prisoner's Dilemma strategies inevitably evoked reactions and innovations from other strategies, causing the ecosystem of strategies to change, and thus causing what constitutes a winning strategy to change over time. In evolutionary systems, *sustainable* competitive advantage does not exist; there is only a never-ending race to create new sources of temporary advantage.

This then changes our definition of an excellent company from one that has continuous high performance for very long periods (an achievement that is almost non-nonexistent) to one that can string together a series of temporary advantages over time—in other words, a strong runner in the Red Queen race.[28] Inevitably, it is impossible to perfectly time the decline of one source of advantage with the rise of another, and thus we would expect to see such companies exhibit a pattern in which they rise into the top ranks of performance, get knocked down, but like a tough boxer, get back up to fight and win again. Wiggins and Ruefli found evidence of exactly these sorts of companies. They screened their database for companies that were in the superior stratum during one five-year window and then dipped into the middle or poor performing stratum at some point, and then returned to superior performance for at least another five years. Examples included some well-known names such as Johnson & Johnson and Merck, but also less well-known companies such as Family Dollar Stores and Illinois Tool Works.[29] The number of companies achieving this pattern of repeat excellence was small, only 1 percent of the sample, but growing slightly over time, perhaps evidence that as competitive intensity increases, more companies are learning how to be repeat innovators.

Companies Don't Innovate; Markets Do

The virtual nonexistence of excellence that lasts multiple decades (again, less than 0.5 percent), and the extreme rarity of repeated excellence (again, 1 percent), brings us to a brutal truth about most companies. Markets are highly dynamic, but the vast majority of companies are not.

In fact, according to the sociologist Michael Hannan and management researcher John Freeman, companies are essentially inert. In the 1970s, Hannan and Freeman began a series of landmark studies on the "organizational ecology" of markets.[30] The evidence from these studies shows that while there is a tremendous amount of innovation and change in the economy at the level of markets, there is much less change at the level of individual companies. Their conclusion was that change in the economy is driven more by the entry and exit of firms than by the adaptation of individual companies. For example, the semiconductor industry did not make the shift from transistors in the 1950s to very large-scale integration (VLSI) chips in the 1980s because the leading companies of the day such as Hughes, Transitron, and Philco adapted.[31] Rather, the change came because the companies were replaced by other companies such as Intel, Hitachi, and Philips. Out of the original top ten semiconductor companies, only Texas Instruments and Motorola managed to survive the shift. And again, while such shifts may be more dramatic in technology industries, research by a number of organizational ecologists has shown that the dynamism of company populations over time is widespread across all industries.[32]

It is this dynamic pattern of entry and exit that explains Foster and Kaplan's somewhat paradoxical finding that as a group, the long-term survivors in the S&P 500 underperformed the average. It is the constant entry of newcomers that keeps the average up.

Again, these empirical findings should come as no surprise to us. In part 3, we discussed how businesses play the role of interactors in the evolutionary system of market economies. From the market's point of view, each business is an experiment in Business Plan space; some succeed and are amplified, while others fail and disappear. The firms that own these businesses then rise and fall with their fate. These findings show that the process of differentiating, selecting, and amplifying Business Plans works better at the level of the market than inside the walls of most companies. As Foster and Kaplan put it, "markets create more surprise and innovation than do corporations."[33]

Companies are Big Man (today we should say, Big Person) hierarchies with all their human foibles and distortions, while markets are almost pure evolutionary machines. Companies have an inherent disadvantage in that they can never have the same diversity of Business Plans as contained in the market as a whole. Nor can they ever perfectly mirror the selection pressures of actual markets or have the nearly infinite resources of the capital markets to invest in amplifying and scaling up Business Plans that succeed. From the unsentimental perspective of the evolutionary algorithm, businesses are just experimental grist for the evolutionary mill.

So far, I have painted a fairly depressing picture. Strategy is about making long-term commitments that will result in competitive advantage. But we can't predict the future very well due to the contingencies of frozen accidents. Furthermore, competitive advantage is rare, temporary, and appears to be lasting ever-shorter amounts of time. Finally, evidence shows that the vast majority of companies are poor runners in the Red Queen race and unable to keep up with the pace of adaptation in their markets.

The question then is, can we do better? Can we design companies that are more adaptable than those we have today? And specifically, can we avoid the problem of prediction and develop a more robust and adaptable approach to strategy?[34]

Strategy as a Portfolio of Experiments

The key to doing better is to "bring evolution inside" and get the wheels of differentiation, selection, and amplification spinning *within* a company's four walls. Rather than thinking of strategy as a single plan built on predictions of the future, we should think of strategy as a *portfolio of experiments,* a population of competing Business Plans that evolves over time.[35] We will look at the elements of such an approach shortly, but first, an example will help illustrate what a portfolio of strategic experiments looks like.

Let's return to the Microsoft story and imagine it is now the year 1987, six years after Gates signed the contract with IBM. The still nascent PC industry has just gone through a period of explosive growth.[36] No one has ridden that growth harder than Microsoft. But MS-DOS is now coming to the end of its natural life cycle. Customers are beginning to look for a replacement operating system that will take better advantage of the graphics and greater power of the new generation of machines. A change in the S-curve is coming, and the industry is far from certain how things will work out. Despite its success, Microsoft was still a $346 million minnow in 1987 compared to the multibillion-dollar giants hungrily eyeing its lucrative position. IBM was developing its own powerful multitasking OS/2 system; AT&T was leading a consortium of other companies, including Sun Microsystems and Xerox, to create a user-friendly version of the widely admired Unix operating system; and Hewlett-Packard and Digital Equipment Corporation were pushing their own version of Unix. Apple was also still a threat, consistently out-innovating the rest of the industry, and its highly graphical Macintosh was selling well.

We can imagine the options that Microsoft faced at this point. Option one: Gates could make an enormous "bet the company" gamble by investing in building a new operating system called Windows and attempt to migrate his base of DOS users to the new standard, ideally before a competitor would reach critical mass with its own system. Option two: he could exit the operating-system part of the market, cede that to his larger, better-funded competitors, and instead focus on applications for which Microsoft's small size and nimbleness might be more of an advantage. Or, option three: he could sell the company or otherwise team up with one of his major competitors. While Microsoft would lose its independence with option three, such a move would probably tip the balance of power in favor of whichever company he chose to partner with.

All these options would involve big commitments to hard-to-reverse courses of action and involve major risks. The conventional wisdom is that Gates chose option one, and the big bet paid off, enabling Microsoft to continue its dominance of desktop operating systems and spend the next decade fighting antitrust regulators. But that is not actually what happened. What Gates and his team did was much more interesting—they simultaneously pursued six strategic experiments.

First, Microsoft continued to invest in MS-DOS. Although everyone was predicting the operating system's demise, it still had an enormous customer base. Many customers were very cautious about switching, and each version of DOS was incrementally more powerful than the last. There was still some chance that DOS would continue to morph and evolve and provide what customers wanted for some time.

Second, Microsoft saw IBM as a real threat. Big Blue was still a powerhouse on the hardware side in 1987 and wanted to regain control of the operating-system market. But IBM also knew it would be risky to go it alone. As Michael Corleone said in *The Godfather, Part II,* "Keep your friends close, but your enemies closer." Gates and IBM agreed to turn IBM's OS/2 operating-system project into a joint venture.

Third, Microsoft saw Unix as a lesser threat than IBM, but a threat nonetheless. Microsoft held discussions with various companies, including AT&T, about participating in joint efforts on Unix. The discussions kept Microsoft's options open and the company plugged into what was going on, but also fueled speculation about Microsoft's Unix strategy. This had the benefit of creating additional uncertainty for the Unix advocates and slowing their progress.

Fourth, in addition to playing the Unix alliance game, Microsoft bought a major stake in the largest seller of Unix systems on PCs, a company called the Santa Cruz Operation. Thus, if Unix did take off, Microsoft would at least have a product of its own in the market.

Fifth, Gates did not pull back on investing in applications, but continued to build that business at the same time, despite the strain on resources. In particular, Microsoft built its position in software for the Apple Macintosh, passing Apple itself, as the leading supplier. This provided a hedge in case Apple capitalized on the discontinuity in the market to push its own operating system ahead.

Sixth and finally, Gates made major investments in Windows. Windows was intended to be the best of all worlds. It was built on DOS and backward-compatible with DOS applications, it was multitasking like OS/2 and Unix, and it was easy to use like the Macintosh. But most importantly, it would keep control of the PC operating-system market firmly in Microsoft's hands. Success with Windows was clearly the company's most preferred outcome.

What Gates created was *not* a focused big bet, but a portfolio of strategic options. One way of interpreting what Gates did was that he set a high-level aspiration—to be the leading PC software company—and then he created a portfolio of strategic experiments that had the possibility of evolving toward that aspiration.

It is important to remember that in 1987, Windows was far from a certain winner. Version 1.0 was launched in 1985 but sold very poorly, and Version 2.0, launched in 1987, was plagued with technical problems and delays. It wasn't until Version 3.0 appeared in 1990 that Microsoft's future lock on the operating-system market was assured. Annie's hand could have twitched in another direction; if IBM had been a bit faster with OS/2, if the Unix companies had gotten their act together, or if Microsoft had suffered further glitches with Windows, history could potentially have taken a very different branch.

Rather than try to predict the future, Gates created a population of competing Business Plans *within* Microsoft that mirrored the evolutionary competition going on outside in the marketplace. Microsoft thus was able to evolve its way into the future. Eventually, each of the other initiatives was killed off or scaled down, and Windows was amplified to become the focus of the company's operating-system efforts. At the time, Gates was heavily criticized for this portfolio approach. Journalists cried that Microsoft had no strategy and was confused and adrift; they wondered when Gates was going to make up his mind. Likewise, it was difficult for those working inside the company to find themselves competing directly with their colleagues down the hall. There is no evidence that Bill Gates looked to evolutionary theory or was thinking about fitness landscapes when designing this strategy. Yet, regardless of how the approach was specifically developed, the effect was to create an adaptive strategy that was robust against the twists and turns of potential history. Microsoft has continued this approach and today has a portfolio of competing experiments in areas ranging from the Web to corporate computing, home entertainment, and mobile devices.

There are some general lessons that can be learned from a portfolio-of-experiments approach to strategy. First, management needs to create a *context* for strategy. Constructing a portfolio of experiments requires a collective understanding of the current situation and shared aspirations among the management team. Second, management needs a process for *differentiating* Business Plans that results in a portfolio of diverse Plans. Third, the organization needs to create a *selection* environment that mirrors the environment in the market. Fourth and finally, processes need to be established that enable the *amplification* of successful Business Plans and the elimination of unsuccessful Plans. We will discuss each of these key points in turn.

Context: Creating Prepared Minds

I once worked with a very gruff, pragmatic senior executive who claimed not to believe in strategic planning, saying that it was a bunch of "pointy-headed nonsense." He was also very successful. He had taken a hodgepodge of industrial businesses in tough markets and managed to squeeze very good growth and margins out of them over a number of years. One day, I saw the advance materials for a strategic planning off-site and noticed that the analyses prepared by this executive and his team were by far the best in the binder.

The next day, I asked him, given that he had claimed not to believe in strategic planning, why he and his team had put so much effort into the analysis. His reply was, "I don't believe in planning. I do this so that we have prepared minds." Once I recovered from hearing this no-nonsense executive quoting Louis Pasteur ("chance favors the prepared mind"), the almost Zen-like wisdom of his remark sunk in. As he explained it, he and his team did not use the tools of conventional strategy analysis to make crystal-ball predictions about the future. Rather, they used the tools to provide context for making real-time decisions and to help them deal with all the uncertainties they knew would come their way. As we continued our discussion, he explained that the strategic planning exercise was a critical way to get his senior team to communicate. It gave them a common frame of reference for their businesses, a shared understanding of the facts, and a language for talking to each other.[37]

A former senior executive at GE Capital told me about a similar philosophy he had in planning for acquisitions. He saw the point of strategic planning not as predicting the future, but as a learning exercise to prepare people for a future that was inherently uncertain. For example, he noted that he never knew when an important acquisition opportunity might arise. Even though he did not have a plan that said "we will buy companies X,Y, and Z," if company X did come up for sale, his team could get an offer on the table more quickly and with fewer contingencies than anyone else could, thus increasing the probability of success. The members of his team could do this because they had already gone through the discussion about the market, knew a lot about company X, understood how it would impact their economics, and so on. They already had a shared view on what the acquisition would mean for them. In other words, they had prepared minds.

The message is *not* to tear up your strategy books, but to think of the tools of conventional strategy analysis as *having a different purpose*. The purpose is not to get to the "answer" of a single focused five-year plan based on predictions of the future, but rather to create "prepared minds." This requires thinking about whose minds it is important to prepare and how one can best go about doing that.

For most companies, this shift in perspective implies a major redesign of the strategic planning process. Most processes are focused on creating plans and making decisions rather than learning. A planning process focused on learning has three major attributes.[38]

First, the process should be focused on structuring in-depth discussion and debate among principal decision makers. Typical planning processes result in underlings presenting slides to senior decision makers in precooked dog-and-pony shows—very little learning goes on in such meetings. Instead, the focus should be on creating a forum in which senior decision makers meet to roll up their sleeves and wrestle intensely with the issues (and some-times each other).[39] Such forums need to be small (if too many lieutenants are in the room, the senior people won't speak openly) and have adequate time—a full day per business unit per year for the CEO and top team is a good rule of thumb, versus the hour or two typical in most company off-sites.

Second, the process must be fueled by facts and analysis. If only opinions are brought to the table, chances are that everyone will leave the room with the same mental models he or she walked in with. This means intense prepa-ration in the months leading up to the strategy conversation, and while staff and consultants can help, the senior principals need to be fully engaged in the preparation as well. A shared understanding of a common fact base is the single most valuable outcome of the process.

Third, there must be other forums clearly designated for decision making. If the strategy process becomes overburdened with near-term decisions on budgets, setting targets, and allocating capital, then learning goes out the window. The decision-making forums should be linked to, but separate from, the strategic learning process. Again, the focus of the strategy forum should be setting context to inform the design and management of the portfolio of experiments.

Differentiation: How Bushy Is Your Strategic Tree?

Typical strategic planning processes focus on chopping down the branches of the strategy decision tree, eliminating options, and making choices and com-mitments. In contrast, an evolutionary approach to strategy emphasizes cre-ating choices, keeping options open, and making the tree of possibilities as bushy as possible at any point in time. Options have value.[40] An evolving portfolio of strategic experiments gives the management team more choices, which means better odds that some of the choices will be right, or, as my McKinsey colleague Lowell Bryan calls it, "loading the dice."[41] The objective is to be able to make lots of small bets, and only make big bets as a part of amplifying successful experiments when uncertainties are much lower. Being forced to make all-or-nothing bets under uncertainty means that a company is boxed in—the opposite of a bushy strategic tree. While the media may laud the courage and vision of CEOs who take big, swinging bets, they are just as happy to pillory the CEOs whose big bets don't pay off.

Evolution needs a superfecundity of Business Plans to do its work. Of course, no one company can match the diversity of Business Plans in the market as a whole, but most companies operate at the other extreme and only have a single plan at work for each of their businesses. When it comes to Business Plan diversity, companies are often their own worst enemies. This is because there is an inherent tension between the need to explore and innovate and the need to exploit and execute.[42] Successful, efficient operations require focus and discipline. They require clear leadership and direction. In contrast, an evolutionary strategy requires tolerance of people going in different directions at once and experimenting with risky ideas. Likewise, the feedback loops on execution are tight and measurable; one can see the results each quarter. In comparison, the feedback loops on strategy evolution are hard to measure and may take multiple years. Finally, people hate redundancy— managers are always looking to make things more efficient by squeezing out slack capacity—yet by definition, diversity requires redundancy, overlap, and excess capacity. Thus, the drive for operational efficiency, while a necessary and worthy goal, often has the unintended side effect of lowering the diversity of strategic experiments and the company's stock of internally competing Business Plans.

In addition to creating a portfolio with a sufficient number of experiments, the competing Business Plans also need to be spread across the fitness landscape in such a way as to maximize the effectiveness of the evolutionary search process. As we saw earlier, one of the reasons evolution is so effective at exploring rough-correlated landscapes is that it mixes the length of its jumps. In biology, a combination of mutations and sexual recombination ensures a mix of short and long jumps. When thinking of "jump distance" in the Business Plan landscape, we should consider three dimensions: risk, relatedness, and time horizon. Risk refers to all the uncertainties that can affect the outcome of a strategic experiment, and the degree of irreversibility of the commitment. Relatedness refers to how close or how far the experiment is from the experience, skills, and assets the business already has.[43] Time horizon refers to the expected time to payoff from the experiments.

For example, in the Microsoft case, the company's Unix initiatives were relatively high risk, long term, and less related to the company's existing offering than were the other experiments. In contrast, Windows itself was probably medium on these dimensions, and arguably OS/2 was the lowest risk experiment, as it was technically less ambitious than Windows, and co-opted their most dangerous competitor. Thus, Microsoft had a fairly good spread of bets across the landscape. The exact number of strategic experiments in the portfolio and their distribution across these dimensions is ultimately a matter of judgment and specific to a business's circumstances, but the number should clearly be more than one, which is what most businesses typically have.

A common retort to the idea of a portfolio of strategies is that not every company can afford to pursue six strategies at once the way Microsoft did. But remember, at the time, Microsoft was the smallest and most resource constrained of its competitor group. It was not the case that Microsoft pursued six operating-system Business Plans and IBM pursued twelve—IBM basically pursued one. Moreover, not all options get the same level of commitment. For Microsoft, a Windows victory was the preferred outcome, and that initiative received the most investment. Organizations do have finite resources, but that is not usually what holds them back from pursuing a portfolio of options; rather, it is the mind-sets of the executives, and the processes and culture of the organization.

Finally, it is important to note that a diversity of Business Plans is not the same thing as a diversity of businesses. In the 1960s, it was fashionable to argue that companies should create diversified portfolios of businesses to reduce their risk—for example, one business might do well in economic upturns, while another might perform well in downturns. This resulted in the creation of poor-performing conglomerates of unrelated businesses, many of which were later broken up by corporate raiders. Wiggins and Ruefli's data and other studies show that there are significant performance benefits for firms remaining focused on a limited number of businesses.[44] What I am advocating is very different—*within* a business, there should be a portfolio of strategies. For example, Microsoft's portfolio of experiments was entirely within the operating-system business.

Selection Pressure: Setting Aspirations

Business Plan selection is another area that many companies struggle with. Companies intend to apply selection pressures that mirror the selection pressures at work in the market, but once the signal from the market enters the walls of the company, it is distorted "like a fun-house mirror," as one senior executive put it. Inside companies, there are a host of selection pressures that simply do not exist in the marketplace, such as "This has been the CEO's favorite idea, and he will lose face if he backs away from it," or "This is my division's turf." Such distortions stemming from internal politics, bureaucracy, and other factors are not usually the result of ill intent; they are just the result of being in an organization of real-world human beings. As we discussed earlier in the book, psychologists have found numerous biases and systematic misperceptions to which people are subject, as well as a deeply ingrained instinct to compete for status in social hierarchies. These human foibles inevitably affect how organizations interpret signals from the marketplace.

There are two ways to fight back against the fun-house mirror effect. The first is fairly obvious, and that is to improve the quantity, quality, and speed of information flowing from the marketplace into the organization. Such information includes detailed sales and customer data, market research, customer satisfaction surveys, competitor intelligence, and so on. When feedback from the market is missing or sketchy, opinions and politics tend to fill the information vacuum and distort Business Plan selection.

The second is a bit trickier. CEOs and senior executive teams play a critical role in creating the *selection environment* within their organizations through a variety of mechanisms. These range from the formal, such as compensation systems and promotion processes, to the more informal, such as the themes the CEO talks about in meetings. Collectively, these mechanisms create a set of signals that tell people what kinds of behaviors and decisions will be rewarded. When a group of middle managers is sitting in a room, debating the merits of a Business Plan, these signals inevitably play a role in shaping their thinking on which types of plans get support and which do not. It is important that this internal selection environment be carefully and thoughtfully engineered. CEOs and senior team members can only ever be aware of a small fraction of the decisions going on in their organizations. Many key selection decisions inevitably happen under the senior radar; a well-thought-out selection environment helps ensure that those decisions reflect both market realities and company priorities.

One important lever for shaping the internal selection environment is company aspirations. Most companies have missions, visions, values, and other such aspirational statements. For many companies, such statements exist on colorful posters on the walls at corporate headquarters to impress visitors—but the words have little impact on what people actually do. A few senior executive teams, however, are able to use company aspirations to beam market signals into their organizations and shape decision making.

There is a wide literature on what makes for a good aspiration and how to develop and communicate one.[45] For our purposes, however, four characteristics are essential if the aspirations are to play an effective role in Business Plan selection.

First, the aspirations must be carried around in the brains of lots of people in the organization. As James Collins and Jerry Porras put it in *Built to Last,* an effective aspiration "engages people—it reaches out and grabs them in the gut. It is tangible, energizing, highly focused. People 'get it' right away; it takes little or no explanation."[46] In contrast, most company aspiration statements don't grab anyone, and they just sound like PR pabulum. In their research, Collins and Porras looked at scores of aspirations and cite as one of the all-time greats Jack Welch's aspiration for GE in the 1980s: "Become No. 1 or No. 2 in every market we serve and revolutionize this company to have the speed and agility of a small enterprise."[47] Collins and Porras contrast this with the "Total Quality, Market Leadership, Technology Driven . . . " blah, blah, blah of (the formerly excellent) Westinghouse. Welch's vision is clear, challenging, emotive, and memorable. But words alone do not ensure that an aspiration is carried around in people's heads. Welch ensured that the idea of No. 1 or No. 2 was wired into compensation plans, performance evaluations, and business unit reviews, and he talked about it obsessively.[48] In short, he built a selection environment around the aspiration, thus shaping the thinking of thousands of people and the hundreds of thousands of decisions that determined which Business Plans would live and which would die. In the 1980s, a Plan for a new GE product that would boost a No. 3 business past its competitors into the No. 2 slot would get a lot of attention and resources. Likewise, a Plan to invest in a business that was No. 5, even if it was very profitable, would not get support unless the results promised to be material enough to pull the business into the top slots. Welch ensured that the selection pressures created by the aspiration had real consequences—how many of Welch's top executives do you think were running No. 3 or No. 4 businesses?

Second, the aspiration must capture an important insight about the selection pressures that the outside world is subjecting the organization to. When Jack Welch announced his famous No. 1 or No. 2 aspiration in 1981, GE was on the verge of being broken up. At the time, the company was selling for a "conglomerate discount"; that is, the individual value of its wide range of businesses, ranging from plastics to appliances to aircraft parts, added up to more than the value of GE in total. Also at the time, several flamboyant corporate raiders were trolling for companies that could be taken over and broken up for parts. Welch was under tremendous pressure from GE shareholders to raise the value of GE and eliminate the conglomerate discount. "No. 1 or No. 2" was Welch's method for taking that external selection pressure, interpreting it, and beaming it back into the organization in a way that was easy for everyone to understand, had emotional appeal, and was actionable. Just saying "We have to get rid of the conglomerate discount" would not have done it. Yet, the competitive managers favored by GE's talent selection process could emotionally relate to the "No. 1 or No. 2" challenge.

Third, one must strike an important balance in formulating an aspiration. It needs to be specific enough to provide a selection pressure, but not so specific as to require the ability to predict the future. The aspiration to be "a company that cares about its people," for example, is too bland and generic; no one really knows what to do with statements like that. But the aspiration to be "the leading whalebone corset manufacturer in northern England" makes, perhaps, unwarranted assumptions about the future opportunities for whalebone corsets in northern England. Welch's "No. 1 or No. 2" aspiration strikes the proper balance, as does Henry Ford's "to build a car for the multitudes." Ford's vision was explicit enough to provide selection pressures, for example, "does a particular change in the Business Plan lower car costs and make it more affordable to the average person?" Or, "does a new feature make the car more reliable for people with little mechanical training?" Yet, Ford's vision was general enough to allow for lots of deductive-tinkering on how the goal would be achieved. One cannot escape prediction entirely. Ford's goal presupposes that there would be a market for such a car, but in 1907, when only rich people could afford a car, it was a pretty safe bet that a "car for the multitudes," if it could be built, would be a big hit. Again, the idea is to make the aspiration reflect an important insight about the selection pressures at work in the external marketplace.

Fourth, and finally, a good aspiration provides a powerful motivating force to keep the company in constant motion, trying new things, and supporting the ethic of experimentation. In evolutionary systems, stasis on the fitness landscape is a recipe for extinction—if you ever stop experimenting and moving, you're done for. To be adaptive, a company must be restless, never satisfied with its progress, constantly searching and experimenting. As Intel's former chairman Andy Grove put it, "Only the paranoid survive." In the case of GE, after Welch laid down his aspiration, claiming, "Being No. 1 or No. 2 wasn't merely an objective. It was a requirement," you can bet that anyone running a No. 3 or No. 4 business was in motion, trying new things.

No aspiration lasts forever, though. As the selection pressures in the external environment change, so too must the aspirations providing internal selection pressures. Over time, aspirations are either achieved, as in Ford's case, or their relevance changes. While GE never got to the point that literally every GE business was "No. 1 or No. 2," by the end of the 1980s, Welch and his team had either fixed or sold off most of the poorer-performing businesses, the conglomerate discount was gone, and most of the businesses were running well. Thus, Welch moved on to other aspirations, such as globalization and building GE's presence in service businesses.

Amplification: Swarming Like Bees

Even when a company defies the odds and manages to develop and select promising business ideas, it often has a difficult time scaling them up. The stories of big companies failing to nurture successful new ideas under their noses are the stuff of legend. By definition, companies have a limited supply of talent and capital compared with the vast pools of both assets in the wider marketplace. In the internal competition for talent and capital, large-legacy businesses inevitably have the upper hand. Younger, more experimental businesses are often starved for capital, are run by the "B-team," and get inadequate senior management time. Or they get absorbed into a larger, more established business that kills them. The processes for allocating talent and capital in most companies also tend to work on relatively slow clock-speeds compared with the larger market—stock traders can shift capital between companies in milliseconds, versus the months or years it can take inside companies. And finally, many companies distort their resource allocation decisions by measuring large, old, established businesses in the same way they measure young, small ones. Big companies are fundamentally geared toward exploiting their legacy businesses and strategies; this is what they focus their talent and resources on and what they measure. In contrast, markets are geared toward finding and fueling what is new and growing.

An evolutionary approach to strategy emphasizes keeping the strategy tree bushy and the options open for as long as possible. But irreversibility—the first G-R Condition of wealth creation—cannot be avoided forever, and at some point, difficult-to-reverse commitments must be made. Companies are hierarchies, and senior management must ultimately make commitments and allocate finite resources. How do we make such decisions in an evolutionary context?

CapitalOne, a growing and innovative credit-card company, explicitly uses strategy-by-experiment to search for new fitness peaks in the financial services landscape. When asked how CapitalOne determines which experiments to scale up and which to kill off, one senior executive answered by describing a phenomenon seen in the behavior of honeybees. Bees spread out from their hive in a search pattern looking for good sources of nectar. When a bee is successful in finding nectar, it returns to the nest and does a little waggle dance in front of the other bees. The more nectar there is, the more excited the dance; the more excited the dance, the more bees swarm out to exploit the flower field. When the field starts to run dry, the bees return to the nest and await the next dancer.[49] The CapitalOne executive said, "We look at how much the bees are dancing. If they're dancing a lot we swarm all over the opportunity."[50]

To continue with the bee analogy, there are three important factors in successful amplification: knowing where the "nectar" is in the portfolio of experiments, having some spare "bees" around to swarm onto attractive opportunities, and having an ability to shift from one "field" to the next as the situation changes.

First, one must know which initiatives are promising and which are not. There must be explicit market feedback mechanisms built into the portfolio of experiments. Every Business Plan must have clear, thoughtful measures of success and a plan for collecting data in as close to real time as possible. One mistake many companies make is applying the same performance metrics to all their businesses and strategic experiments. The logic is usually driven by a desire to please the financial markets, for example, "the market measures us on earnings and return on capital at the corporate level, so we will measure all our businesses that way as well." But these measures tend to be more appropriate for later-stage, mature businesses and may not give an appropriate picture of newer, more experimental ventures. In such businesses, milestone measures such as hiring a key executive, winning early customers, and meeting budget targets may be more appropriate. Second, financial measures are often lagging indicators of the market's feedback. Other, more operational measures, such as customer satisfaction, assembly time, sales per square foot, employee turnover, and rework time, when added to financial data, may provide a more complete, real-time picture of a strategy experiment's health than would standard accounting-based financial measures alone. For an evolutionary approach to work, one needs real-time feedback on where the nectar is, and thus each strategy experiment must have a custom-built *balanced scorecard* and the measurement systems for carrying it out.[51] I elaborate on the concept later in the book, but briefly, a balanced scorecard is a set of performance metrics that is designed to provide visibility into value creation in a specific business. Balanced scorecards take a multidimensional view of performance and thus typically contain both financial and non-financial metrics.

Second, for evolution to work, the system must have slack capacity to experiment with (i.e., bees to do the swarming). If a company's total resources are fully committed to executing its legacy Business Plans, it will be incapable of evolving any new ones. One mistake that many companies make is to use the budgeting process to harvest all the slack capacity out of their businesses and put it under centralized corporate control. Typically, the corporate center then controls a pot of money for new initiatives. The problem with this approach is that, inevitably, the bandwidth of the senior executives is limited for approving resource decisions, and they are too far removed from the front lines to be the best judges of the success or failure of small-scale experiments. Thus, the initiatives tend to be too few and too large. It is important to push the slack resources down into the business units and give the units responsibility and accountability for creating and funding their portfolios of experiments. The senior team, however, still needs to make some high-level allocation decisions. In a rough-correlated landscape, high peaks tend to be near other high peaks, so it makes sense to overallocate resources to businesses whose initiatives are showing signs of success on the balance-scorecard metrics and to underallocate to those that are struggling. Again, this may mean a shift in the pattern of resource allocation, as resources move from being allocated on the basis of current business size, to an allocation based on the emerging results of new growth initiatives.

This leads to the third and final point: the allocation of resources among experiments needs to be fairly flexible and changeable in real time. Real-time feedback, balanced scorecards, and decentralized decision making aren't much use unless they lead to real-time adjustments in the portfolio. Yet few companies are able to adjust resources up or down as feedback comes in during the year—budgets are locked in annually, and contingency processes tend to be very short term and involve limited funds. Because centralized corporate processes are inherently too slow to address this issue, the only way to make resource allocation more real time is, again, to push more discretionary control over resources deeper into the organization. The business heads need to know what their slack is and then be able to measure the performance of those resources rather than just plowing their slack into "business as usual." If they don't have good uses for the slack, the leaders should have incentives to give it back. Likewise, they should have incentives to take resources from unproductive and unpromising experiments and reallocate them.

An Adaptive Mind-Set

Corporate leaders are expected to be bold generals who forecast the future, devise grand strategies, lead their troops into glorious battle—and then are fired at the first lost skirmish. It takes a courageous executive to push back against this mind-set, admit the inherent uncertainty of the future, and emphasize learning and adapting over predicting and planning.

Indeed, one's mind-set is perhaps the most important factor in creating an adaptive approach to strategy. One way to picture an adaptive mind-set is to think more like a venture capitalist than a manager.[52] Venture capital firms are, in essence, portfolios of strategy experiments. Their portfolios contain a variety of investments with a spread of risk, relatedness, and time horizon. Venture capital portfolios will often have more than one investment in the same industry segment, in essence trying a variety of Business Plans and betting that at least one will find a high-fitness peak. The position of venture capitalists is somewhere between the market's broad coverage of the fitness landscape and the narrow coverage of most single companies. Venture capitalists are also very quick to scale up successful enterprises and very ruthless in cutting their losses. Although they tend to focus hard on the short-term performance of their investments, venture capitalists also use a broad, long-term investment thesis and return targets to provide selection pressures. Few venture capitalists would have the hubris to make point predictions of the industries they invest in, nor do they spend much time in conventional strategic planning. Rather, venture capitalists use their portfolios to learn their way into the future and thus generate high returns out of some of the riskiest and fastest-changing markets in the business world.

The conventional wisdom is that an innovative mind-set is one that tolerates risk, ambiguity, and a lack of control.[53] The approach that I have outlined does not require such a mind-set—rather, it requires a redefinition of these concepts. Instead of taking big, risky bets to innovate, take many small ones and only bet big on stuff that works. Pursuing multiple Business Plans at the same time does not necessarily mean ambiguity if there is clarity in the selection pressures for good plans and bad plans. And while senior executives cannot necessarily control the outcomes of their strategic experiments, they can control the process of creating, selecting, and amplifying experiments to increase their odds of success.

In many ways, an adaptive mind-set is the opposite of what is conventionally considered a visionary approach. An adaptive mind-set is highly pragmatic. It values tangible facts about today more than guesses about tomorrow, doesn't expect that everything will work out as planned, and prefers lots of small failures to big ones. Above all, an adaptive mind-set is willing to say, "We learned something new; we need to change course."

Looking back on a period in the late 1980s, when BP made a number of critical strategic changes, Lord Browne, BP's CEO, described the process as "a series of steps, each building on the last, but without a predetermined plan. We did what was necessary, and as we made progress or ran into problems it became obvious what needed doing next." Rodney Chase, deputy group chief executive, added: "It wasn't a straight line. We made mistakes and not everything worked. But we realised we were learning by doing. Every stumble taught us something."[54]

CHAPTER SIXTEEN

Organization

A SOCIETY OF MINDS

WESTINGHOUSE and General Electric were the twin titans of early twentieth-century American industry.[1] Both were founded by charismatic inventors, Westinghouse by George Westinghouse Jr., and GE by Thomas Edison. Both GE and Westinghouse were early pioneers in the technologies of railroads and electricity generation. Both companies suffered during the Great Depression, served at the heart of the American war effort during the 1940s, and rode the postwar boom in products ranging from refrigerators to radios. In the 1950s and 1960s, the two great rivals were both household names.

But the postwar boom faded in the 1970s, and the two companies came under increasing pressure. Westinghouse's growth began to stall, its margins declined, and the company developed into a sprawling and bureaucratic behemoth. As the company struggled, it diversified into increasingly unrelated businesses such as real estate. During the 1980s, Westinghouse began shedding businesses and closing factories. By the end of the decade, the company had sold most of its transportation and industrial businesses. In the mid-1990s, in a last-ditch attempt to turn its fortunes around, Westinghouse tried to refashion itself into a media company by acquiring the CBS television network. But it was to no avail. By the new millennium, George Westinghouse's once great company was no more. CBS was acquired by Viacom, the remaining businesses were sold off piecemeal, and the Westinghouse brand name went to a division of British Nuclear Fuels.

GE also had its share of stumbles in the difficult climate of the 1970s and 1980s. It too battled maturing markets, slowing growth, and rising bureaucracy. Yet the company somehow managed to win those battles and achieve world-beating levels of performance in the 1990s. During those decades, GE underwent a dramatic transformation, evolving from a largely industrial and durable-goods conglomerate into a postindustrial financial services, media, and technology company. By the end of the century, GE was the most valuable company in the world.

Social Architecture and Adaptability

How could two companies in essentially the same industries, with such similar histories, and with almost identical strategic positions end up with such vastly different fates? Why was GE able to adapt and Westinghouse not? Some like to point to the charismatic leadership of GE CEO Jack Welch during this period as the key difference. But those who have studied GE closely, including Welch himself, contend that there was a lot more to the story than that.[2]

GE is a company that has reinvented itself several times in its long history, and Welch's revitalization of the company in the 1980s was only the most recent occurrence. GE's history is full of stumbles, including almost running out of cash in 1893, seeing Westinghouse's alternating-current electricity technology become the U.S. standard rather than its own direct-current technology, serious economic difficulties during the Great Depression, a major ethics scandal in the 1950s, and a period of malaise in the 1970s. But, consistent with the pattern of excellence we defined in the previous chapter, the company has repeatedly bounced back to enjoy runs of superb performance and has shown a remarkable ability to morph itself as the economy has changed.

From its earliest days, GE has been more than a company. Beginning with CEO Charles Coffin's leadership in the early 1900s, GE became an institution, with a legendarily strong culture and values. As James Collins and Jerry Porras point out in *Built to Last*, Westinghouse never managed to build that kind of institutional foundation.[3] Welch was both a product of GE's culture and, as CEO, its most forceful champion. Welch referred to the combination of GE's people, structure, and culture as the company's "social architecture" and believed it was the secret behind the company's unique ability to both perform and adapt.[4] He was also confident that a social architecture was something so difficult for any competitor to create, it was a secret he didn't mind talking about openly.[5]

The thesis of this chapter is that Welch was right, and that the design of a firm's social architecture plays a major role in determining how adaptable that organization will be. We will define a *social architecture* as having three components:

- The *behaviors* of the individual people in the organization.

- The *structures and processes* that align people and resources in pursuit of an organization's goals.

- The *culture* that emerges from the interactions of people in the organization with each other and their environment.

But before we can understand what makes for an effective social architecture, we need first to examine just what organizations are and why they often appear so resistant to change. We will thus begin by discussing what organizations are and why they exist, and place them in our evolutionary framework. We will then look at various barriers to adaptability that organizations face, discovering that several deep-rooted factors stack the deck against organizational change. Finally, we will see how the design of a firm's social architecture can counteract many of these barriers, particularly when the social architecture relies less on the "hardware" of structure and more on the "software" of culture to drive desired behaviors. By building an effective social architecture, a company can further bring evolution inside and become a faster runner in the Red Queen race.

Organizations Are Complex Adaptive Systems

If one asks a group of academics to define an organization, one will get a broad range of answers depending on whether the respondents are economists, sociologists, psychologists, anthropologists, or legal scholars. Each of these fields has studied organizations from its unique perspective, and each perspective has useful insights.[6] But one perspective cuts across these fields and offers a unifying view: organizations are complex adaptive systems.[7]

Organizations are made up of individual agents who dynamically interact with each other; agents' rules of behavior and networks of interactions change in response to changes in the environment; and agents' interactions produce emergent macro-level patterns of behavior. When one says something like "Ford had a good quarter," or "Sony is an innovative company," one is speaking of the emergent result of the actions and interactions of tens of thousands of people. Firms are complex adaptive systems nested within the larger complex adaptive system of the economy.

The classification of organizations as complex adaptive systems will prove to be useful, but we need to narrow things down further. Other groupings of humans, for example, people caught in a traffic jam, might also be considered a complex adaptive system, but we wouldn't call them an organization. To help make this distinction, we will use a definition from Howard Aldrich, a sociologist at the University of North Carolina:

> Organizations *are goal directed, boundary-maintaining, and socially constructed systems of human activity.*[8]

In other words, organizations are designed and built for a purpose. An organization's goals provide a force that motivates action—there is a current state and a desired state, and actions are taken to close the gap between the two. In human organizations, the goals might be to make money (a business), help children (a charity), or win a championship (a sports team). The existence of collective goals and coordinated activity helps distinguish what we normally think of as organizations from other human groupings, such as traffic jams or a circle of friends.[9]

As Aldrich's definition also notes, organizations are *boundary maintaining*. This is a point the German social philosopher Max Weber commented on in the early twentieth century: organizations distinguish between members and nonmembers. Companies carefully screen potential employees, citizens elect politicians into government bodies, and religions have ceremonies to welcome new members. In more general terms, we can say that organizations are open thermodynamic systems. There is a boundary distinguishing the inside world from the outside world, and the goals of the organization drive activities that lower entropy inside the organizational system relative to the outside environment.

Finally, as Aldrich puts it, "organizations have activity systems for accomplishing work, which can include processing raw materials, information, or people."[10] In the parlance we developed in part 3, organizations carry out thermodynamically irreversible transformations on matter, energy, and information, converting high-entropy inputs into lower-entropy outputs. The transformations are carried out in pursuit of the organization's goals. Thus, we can view organizations as vehicles for creating "fit order," or wealth.

Why Firms Exist

In part 3, I proposed that businesses are the interactors in economic evolution. Firms, in turn, are collections of one or more business units under the control of a common group of people. Thus, in basic terms, firms are organizations that develop and execute Business Plans with the collective goal of making a profit.

But why do firms exist?[11] Previously, I noted that cooperation has a $1 + 1 = 3$, non-zero-sum magic to it. By dividing tasks and cooperating, we can do things together that no person can do on his or her own and reap the rewards. But this answers the question "why do we organize?" not "why do we form organizations?" Why aren't we all just freelancers who come together to cooperate on specific tasks and then disband when we are done? Why do we create more permanent structures such as partnerships and corporations?

These were the provocative questions asked in 1937 by a young industrial lawyer named Ronald Coase in a seminal article, "The Nature of the Firm."[12] Coase's answer was simple but insightful—people form organizations to minimize "transaction costs." If a house builder and a carpenter are only going to work together once on a specific job, it might make sense for them simply to write a contract for that job and get on with it. If, however, they are going to work together repeatedly on multiple jobs, and perhaps in multiple roles, then it would be very expensive to write new contracts for each new job and role. In that case, it might be cheaper for them to form some sort of enduring relationship in an organization, perhaps as partners, or one might hire the other as an employee. In short, Coase said, if it is cheaper to freelance, people will freelance, but if it is cheaper to pull people together into an organization, they will.

We can update Coase's idea for our evolutionary framework and say that not only might organizations be cheaper mechanisms for cooperation in some circumstances, but they might also enable people to reach parts of Business Plan design space unobtainable just by contracting. In short, organizations are better vehicles for exploiting Business Plan space and thus better vehicles for wealth creation. There are four reasons for this.

First is a problem that economists refer to as *incomplete contracts*.[13] No matter how clever the lawyers are, no contract can ever cover all possible contingencies; life is simply too complex. The more complex the cooperation required, the more likely the contract will be incomplete. The problem of incomplete contracts restricts freelancing to relatively simple parts of Business Plan space.

Second is a factor economists call the *holdup problem*.[14] As discussed, wealth creation requires hard-to-reverse commitments. Often, those commitments take the form of investments in *specific assets*. As the name implies, such assets are designed to do something specific for a production process, but are not much use for other purposes. For example, a pizza oven is terrific at baking pizzas, but not very useful for cooking other things. The problem of incomplete contracts means that in a group of freelancers, there is always a risk that the contracts will unravel and someone will be stuck with expensive and hard-to-sell specific assets. The other freelancers can then "hold up" the owner of the assets and threaten to quit unless they get a better deal. By creating shared ownership of assets and aligning the interests of participants, organizations reduce the risk of investing in specific assets and making hard-to-reverse commitments.

Third, organizations provide a structure for cooperation to endure over long periods, even as the specific agents involved change. Some projects take many years to complete—for example, discovering, testing, and producing a new drug can take a decade or more. Yet individual human beings do inconvenient things like quit, get fired, move to another company, get sick, or even die. If GlaxoSmithKline had to disband and restart every time someone left the company, it would not get much done. By creating cooperative structures that outlive the participation of individual agents, organizations again enable us to reach for much more complex Business Plans than we could obtain in a purely freelance economy.

Fourth and finally, organizations provide a vehicle for collective learning. We are accustomed to thinking of learning as an individual activity. However, in a series of experiments during the 1950s, the French scientist Pierre Grassé demonstrated that organizations could learn, too.[15] As human organizations are a bit complicated, Grassé, a zoologist, conducted his experiments on a simpler form of organization—termite colonies. When termites build their nests, they construct pillars of soil that provide structural support and help with ventilation. Remarkably, the pillars are very regularly spaced from each other and of even height. Given that termites don't have much individual intelligence and limited communications abilities, Grassé wondered how they could collectively learn to do this. Careful observation convinced Grassé that the termites were learning through their *joint work product*. As a termite began to construct a pillar, this clicked on simple IF-THEN rules in other termites to pitch in and help. The existence of a pillar also clicked on other rules to prevent the termites' building in certain areas, which gave the pillars even spacing. In essence, the termites "read" the information embedded in the pillars (their joint work product) and responded accordingly. For example, if a pillar was low, a termite would add more earth; if it was high, the termite would move on to another pillar; and the termites would avoid building other pillars within a certain radius of existing pillars. Grassé termed this form of learning *stimergy*.[16]

Humans do the same thing. We cooperatively create artifacts that contain embedded information, and we change our behavior in response to the information embedded in those artifacts. Think, for example, of a group of architects working on a design for a building. One person might modify a blueprint and pass it on to a colleague for further modification. The colleague then gives it to an engineer, who might pass it on to someone else, and so on, and the design is modified in an iterative group-learning process. The blueprint (the joint work product) contains embedded information and is the vehicle for collective learning. Organizations are full of documents, diagrams, computers, and other physical artifacts that enable stimergistic learning, despite a changing cast of agents. Following our framework from part 3, organizations thus play the critical role of providing a storehouse, or a collective memory, for schemata.

Note that there is a difference between *learning* and *adapting*. Learning is the acquisition of knowledge in pursuit of a goal, while adapting is changing in response to selection pressures from one's environment. Although adapting requires the acquisition of knowledge, and learning can occur in response to environmental pressures, we will find it useful to maintain a distinction between the two terms. As we will see, while organizations are generally good at learning, they tend to have more trouble at adapting.

Building on Coase's original insight, we can see that there are enormous advantages to an economy made up of organizations, compared with one made up of contractual freelancers. The overarching effect is that organizations give us the ability to reach vast swaths of Business Plan design space that we would otherwise not be able to reach. As our methods for organizing—our Social Technologies—have evolved, this has enabled us to build organizations that are more and more sophisticated, which in turn have enabled us to discover and execute increasingly complex and wealth-creating Business Plans.[17]

Executing and Adapting

Any economic organization faces two basic challenges: first, it must execute its current set of Business Plans to survive the challenges of today, and second, it must adapt those Plans to survive the challenges of tomorrow.

Executing and adapting are the ultimate imperatives for any design in an evolutionary system.[18] In a world governed by the Second Law of Thermodynamics, successful exploitation of one's niche in the current environment is a necessary condition for survival—calories in must be greater than calories out, and money in must be greater than money out. But, as we also know, the shelf life of strategies in evolutionary systems can be quite short, so one must continuously explore new strategies, or risk finding oneself stuck in a poor position when the environment inevitably changes. But because the processes of executing and adapting each require resources, there is a natural tension in the system. How much should be invested in executing for today versus adapting for tomorrow? In business organizations, there is a constant competition for money, people, and senior management time between the need to perform in the short run and the equally critical need to invest and innovate for the long run.

Tom Peters and Bob Waterman were among the first popular management writers to draw attention to the managerial implications of this challenge in their 1982 *In Search of Excellence*.[19] They argued that organizations must simultaneously be "tight" in executing and "loose" in adapting. This dialectic has been a central theme in management writing ever since: Collins and Porras noted the importance of both "control" and "creativity" in *Built to Last*,

Dick Foster and Sarah Kaplan describe the need to balance "operating" and "innovating" in *Creative Destruction*, and Michael Tushman and Charles O'Reilly paint their vision of "ambidextrous" organizations that can do both, in *Winning Through Innovation*.[20] One of the best-known and most-cited papers in the academic world on this topic was written in 1991 by Stanford's James March, who used the memorable terms "exploration" and "exploitation."[21] While each writer's language and nuances are different, it is no coincidence that this yin-yang theme of opposing challenges keeps cropping up. But as we saw in the previous chapter, the evidence suggests that companies are generally better at the executing half of the dialectic than the adapting half.

Some might argue that this is just the natural order of things, that economic evolution is best handled at the market level and organizations should merely be execution machines. Let markets explore and firms exploit. But there is an argument to be made that greater intracompany adaptation would be better for society. Adaptation reduces the frictional losses associated with company failures and unemployment. When a company fails to adapt, the intransigence can have tragic consequences for individual lives and local communities. In addition, the lack of organizational adaptability is not strictly a concern of businesses. Many other types of organizations, ranging from nonprofits, to governments and military bodies, suffer from the same issue.[22]

Now that we have a perspective on what organizations are and why they exist, we can begin to examine why their performance on the executing side versus the adapting side of the equation is so heavily weighted toward execution. Using the perspective that organizations are complex adaptive systems, we will examine them from three levels:

THE LEVEL OF INDIVIDUAL AGENTS. What is it about our mental models that makes it hard for individuals to adapt?

THE STRUCTURE OF ORGANIZATIONS. How do hierarchies, complexity catastrophes, and the configuration of resources create barriers to adaptation?

EMERGENCE. How do corporate cultures play a critical role in emergent organizational behavior?

These three levels correspond to the three elements in our earlier definition of a social architecture: behavior, structure, and culture. In essence, the purpose of a social architecture is to address each of these levels, break down the barriers to adaptability, and enable the organization to achieve a balance between near-term performance and long-term evolution.

Individuals: Through Rose-Colored Glasses

How well an organization adapts is partly a function of the adaptability of the minds of the individuals in it. This is a question not only of the minds at the top, but also of the minds up and down the hierarchy—it doesn't help much if the CEO "gets" the need for change but no one else does, or if the young managers see it but the codgers on the executive committee don't. But "getting it" is challenging. Recent work in cognitive science shows that people tend to learn within the context of a mental model. And while humans are good at adding new information to their existing mental models, they have a more difficult time changing those models at a more fundamental level. In short, we tend to get stuck in our ways.

We will look at four reasons for poor individual adaptability: First, people have a bias toward overoptimism, which can reduce the felt need for change. Second, people also have a natural bias toward loss aversion, making them less likely to take certain kinds of risks. Third, the way we categorize the world and structure our mental models can get in the way of change. And fourth, the punctuated-equilibrium nature of change tends to favor leadership styles that are more rigid than ones that are more flexible.[23]

To begin changing their mental models, people must first perceive a need to change. They must see a gap between their goals and the current state and trajectory of the world. Moreover, fundamental change often requires that people believe something bad will happen unless things change. Accounts of events inside the U.S. government during the months before September 11 tell of mental models stuck in earlier paradigms: Central Intelligence Agency analysts still in Cold War mode, Federal Bureau of Investigation agents more accustomed to fighting crime bosses than terrorists, and politicians seeing the world through a prism of nation-states.[24] Despite much evidence on the threat that Al-Qaeda presented, it was not until tragedy struck that people were shocked into beginning to make the necessary adaptations. People have a general bias toward spinning their reality in positive ways and ignoring uncomfortable facts. It takes a real jolt to make them see that everything is not OK.

Dan Lovallo, a researcher at the Australian Graduate School of Management, and Nobel Prize winner Daniel Kahneman of Princeton refer to such optimism in the face of countervailing facts as *delusional optimism*.[25] As evidence of its prevalence, they point to persistent overoptimism in management forecasts and plans. For example, a Rand Corporation study of forty-four construction projects for chemical-processing plants found that, on average, the plants cost twice their initial projections and produced only three-quarters of their expected capacity. In the real world, forecasts are often missed, projects run late, technologies don't work as expected, and mergers are less successful than hoped for. The bias toward overoptimism is part of a deep-rooted human desire to believe in ourselves and our abilities. Lovallo and Kahneman cite another study, in which a million students were given a survey and 70 percent rated themselves above average in leadership ability, while only 2 percent rated themselves below average.

Another contributing factor is that executives are often selected for their optimism. Optimists are more enjoyable to work with, while pessimists can be perceived as disloyal. As Lovallo and Kahneman note: "The bearers of bad news tend to become pariahs, shunned and ignored by other employees. When pessimistic opinions are suppressed, while optimistic ones are rewarded, an organization's ability to think critically is undermined. The optimistic biases of individual employees become mutually reinforcing, and unrealistic views of the future are validated by the group."[26]

This means that one is likely to find a greater proportion of optimists as one gets nearer the top of the organizational ladder. This then creates a barrier to adaptability because the optimists feel a less acute need to change than do realists.

Lovallo and Kahneman's recommended solution is to ensure that outside views and data are regularly brought into the organization. For example, if you are going to build a chemical plant, look at the record of the other forty-four cases. One can also battle overoptimism by fostering a culture of realism. Jack Welch was infamous for popping the unduly optimistic bubbles of his people, and one of his dicta was that managers must "face reality [and] see things as they are . . . not the way they wished it would be."[27]

Individuals: Adaptability and Loss Aversion

Daniel Kahneman has also demonstrated that people have a further trait that hinders adaptability—a bias toward loss aversion. For example, if you are offered the bet of winning $1,500 or losing $1,000 on the flip of a coin, Traditional Economic rationality says you should always take the bet, but numerous experiments show that most people won't. People tend to view winning $1,500 as "nice to have," while losing $1,000 is a "disaster." This greater concern over losing manifests itself in nonmonetary situations as well, such as when someone is more concerned about looking like a fool during an important presentation than he or she is worried about making a case.

This general bias toward loss aversion naturally makes companies more cautious in exploring and more focused on exploiting. Exploring is by definition a more uncertain activity, and more fraught with downside risk. But there is a more subtle effect as well. In judging risk, people tend to look at relative scale rather than absolute scale. A CEO might view a $100 million decision as a big bet and be loss averse, but view a $1 million decision as small potatoes and be much less loss averse. A midlevel manager, however, might view the $1 million decision with the same trepidation as that felt by the CEO over the $100 million bet. This means that both decisions might be treated with the same level of risk aversion. Yet logically, the organization should be far more risk averse toward the $100 million bet. But the punishment for the middle manager (e.g., getting fired) for blowing a $1 million bet is personally just as negative as the pain for the CEO on losing his or her $100 million bet—in fact, the CEO, strapped into a golden parachute, might actually have a softer fall. As Kahneman points out, this gamblers' relativism means that organizations are often too risk averse for small bets made at lower levels of the hierarchy, and insufficiently risk averse for large bets made at the top levels.

But risk aversion against small bets flies in the face of the need to experiment. In the previous chapter, we saw that evolution works best when it has a diverse selection of small bets to work with across different levels of risk. When companies deny themselves a portfolio of small risks, they get strategically boxed in and end up placing all their chips on big-bet investments and on mergers and acquisitions. Making mid- and lower-level managers *less* accountable for their small-scale bets would foster more experimentation and, with it, greater adaptability.

Individuals: The Price of Experience

In chapter 6, we discussed how the cognitive scientist John Holland and his colleagues portray human mental models as organized into "default hierarchies."[28] Concepts are grouped together in hierarchical structures (e.g., small, blue, buzzing things are categorized as "flies"), and our decision-action rules use specific information when we have it, but fall back on default rules when things are uncertain.

The structure of a default hierarchy has a great benefit in that it allows people to take action even when they don't have complete information. And it allows people to fine-tune their actions and learn as they get more specific information and experience. On the down side, this structure can make experience a double-edged sword.[29] When we are young and inexperienced, our default hierarchies are fairly shallow, so our views of the world are more general than specific. This way of thinking has both advantages and disadvantages. The advantage is that our mental models are easily changeable. New experiences are readily absorbed, and reorganizing the hierarchy is not very difficult, because there isn't that much to reorganize. The disadvantage is that there is a lower probability of having the right response to a given situation. Thus, the stereotype of young people being more adaptable in their thinking, but also more likely to do something inappropriate, is not entirely unwarranted.

As we gain experience with age, our default hierarchies fill up and the situation reverses. We have a larger collection of specific experiences and more feedback on what has worked and what has not. Our mental models grow into highly complex structures of categories, interlinked rules, and weightings. We become less likely to perceive anything as totally new, and instead try to relate new knowledge to previous experiences and group those experiences into existing categories. Once in a while, we encounter something outside our realm of experience, and we then have to create a new, high-level category or rearrange existing categories. As our mental models become more complex, such major rearrangements become more difficult. Reorganizing an older, more experienced mental model is like reorganizing General Motors, whereas reorganizing a younger, less experienced model is more akin to reorganizing a small startup. Our mental models thus tend to settle over time, and it takes progressively bigger and bigger shocks to shake them up.

In essence, we balance exploring and exploiting over our lifetimes. The early emphasis is on exploring while we form our mental models and get feedback from the environment, but eventually we settle into a groove, and the emphasis shifts to exploiting the model we have developed. This is not an "ageist" argument, and certainly there are examples of fuddy-duddy twenty-year-olds and adaptable seventy-year-olds. But in broad terms, the structures of our mental models do change over time, and there are strengths and weaknesses at each stage of development.

The implications for organizations, however, are important. Stable mental models work well in stable environments, which is to say, most of the time. However, as we noted previously, the punctuated nature of change in complex adaptive systems is almost perniciously designed to lull our pattern-recognizing, rule-building minds into a sense of stability and then hit us with big changes. Firms tend to be organized as hierarchies, with the people who are most experienced sitting at the top. This arrangement presents a trade-off: the mental models at the top are likely to be some of the best for the purposes of execution in a stable environment, but less capable of exploring, and less likely to adapt to environmental shifts. The result can be significant inertia in an organization when environmental change does occur. This mental model inertia helps explain why many turnaround situations involve wholesale changes in top management. It is often easier and faster to simply change the people than to change their mental models.

If resistance to change in experienced mental models is a deep feature of human cognition, then how can we guard against it? A good starting point is simple acknowledgment of it at the top. Those running organizations must recognize that, while their wisdom may be highly valuable, their sensitivity to change and flexibility may be low. Likewise, their seniority may intimidate junior people, who are usually more aware of changes in the environment and have different perspectives. Perhaps the most important counter to this effect is to deliberately create a diversity of ages and experiences in the top management team and board. If everyone on the executive committee and on the board has gray hair, it is a bad sign; likewise, if no one does (e.g., many of the 1990s dot-coms), it is also a bad sign. But age isn't the only dimension that should be diverse; the range of experiences should be as well—different industries, functional backgrounds, international experiences, entrepreneurial experiences, corporate experiences, nonbusiness experiences, and so on. A diverse set of mental models at the top raises the probability that at least one of them will pick up on important changes in the environment and have fresh ideas about how to respond to them. To make a diversity of mental models effective, however, the senior leadership team must also embrace a nonhierarchical culture that is open to challenge and debate. An authoritarian CEO can easily suppress what would otherwise be a vibrant and diverse management team.

Individuals: "Rigids" Versus "Flexibles"

During the 1980 British Conservative Party annual conference, in one of the most famous speeches of her career, Prime Minister Margaret Thatcher vigorously defended her government's record. After a "winter of discontent" filled with strikes and violent protests, Thatcher defiantly refused to back away from her course of economic reform, declaring, "To those waiting with bated breath for that favourite media catchphrase, the 'U' turn, I have only one thing to say: You turn if you want to. The lady's not for turning."[30] Thatcher was a legendarily firm leader. The Iron Lady had a clear vision and ideology for how Britain should be governed, rarely deviated from that course, and was deaf to the cries of her critics. Some people loved her for her strong-willed leadership; others loathed her for her insensitivity and uncompromising rigidity.

In contrast, U.S. President Bill Clinton was often referred to in the press as "the Great Waffler." He was frequently criticized for having no fixed ideology, his willingness to compromise, his desire to keep his options open, and his sensitivity to poll results. Yet, these same qualities of flexibility and sensitivity to his environment enabled Clinton to get reelected governor of Arkansas after a difficult first term, as well as bounce back from the disastrous mid-term election of 1994 to win a second presidential term in 1996. Those qualities also enabled him to push through a number of controversial programs, ranging from welfare reform to the North American Free Trade Agreement, despite a sharply divided Congress. Some people loved Clinton for his listening skills, his adaptability, and his ability to forge consensus. Others couldn't stand him for his prevarications and his wheeling and dealing.

Two archetypical leaders, the Iron Lady versus the Comeback Kid, the rigid commander versus the flexible consensus builder, each with pluses and minuses, and each with great successes and failures. These are also archetypes we have probably encountered in our own experiences (although undoubtedly in more diluted form). Given the existence of rigid versus flexible leadership styles, it then follows to ask whether these contrasting styles might have anything to do with rigid versus flexible organizations.

This is a question that Johns Hopkins University economist Joseph Harrington Jr. asked in his research. He began by building a relatively simple model that portrays an organization as a hierarchy. Agents enter at the bottom of the hierarchy and are promoted or fired on the basis of their performance, and those who make it to the top eventually leave at a mandatory retirement age.[31] In Harrington's model, there are two types of agents, rigid Margaret Thatcher types and flexible Bill Clinton types. The agents in the hierarchy must make a decision each period and play either strategy A or B. There is an external environment for which either A or B is a better choice, and each agent's performance is partly determined by how its decisions fit with that environment.

Rigid agents essentially are born with their decisions already made. They always play the same strategy, consistently A or consistently B, no matter what is going on in the external environment. In contrast, the Flexible agents look at what the environment demands, and play either A or B as the situation warrants.

One would think that the Flexible agents would always win, because their decisions always fit with the demands of the environment. But there was one other factor at work. Harrington assumed that experience makes a difference. Thus, if one agent had played strategy A five times in its life and another had only played A three times, the more experienced agent would do better. Overall agent performance was thus a function of both matching the strategy to the environment, *and* experience. Harrington then portrayed the decision on whether to promote a particular agent in the hierarchy as a competition, with higher-performing agents rising to the top and lower-performing agents leaving. So, who won? Who made it to the top—Rigids or Flexibles?

The answer was, it depended on what the environment looked like. If the environment was perfectly random, flipping back and forth between favoring A and B without any bias, then Flexible agents won and tended to dominate the upper echelons of the organization. In such an environment, Rigid agents had a fifty-fifty chance of being wrong each round and rarely lived long enough to gain much experience.

If, however, the environment was more stable and there was a bias toward one strategy, say, the environment favored B, then the Rigid agents dominated. The reason for this is that the Rigid agents playing the B strategy in this example had a better than fifty-fifty chance of being right, and thus better than even odds of being promoted each round. Plus, whenever a Rigid playing the favored strategy (again, we'll assume B) met a Flexible playing that same strategy, the Rigid would win because of its deeper experience— the Rigid had always played B, whereas the Flexible had only sometimes played B. Even when the environment called for A, sometimes the Rigid would survive because it had a one-in-three chance of meeting another Rigid B each round, in which case the winner would be whichever Rigid B had more experience, or in the case of a tie, a coin flip. Thus, the upper echelons of the organization tended to comprise like-minded Rigids playing the favored strategy. The bottom line was, in a stable environment, experience counts—not all the Rigids made it to the top, but more often than not, they did.

This clearly is a highly simplistic model, but it does capture the essence of a dynamic seen in real-world organizations. If the environment is biased toward one type of strategy, people who diligently follow that particular strategy will be more likely to rise to the top, beating out the more-adaptable types. But when the environment changes, the organization is stuck with people who can't change with it.

Harrington added a further dose of realism to his model. Instead of having an environment that randomly changes between A and B (again with some bias toward one or the other), he switched to an environment that looks more like the punctuated-equilibrium pattern of change we have discussed. In a punctuated-equilibrium pattern the As and Bs would come in clusters, thus the environment might be stable for quite some time (e.g., all As), then go through a period of volatility (e.g., start flipping between As and Bs), and then settle into a new pattern (e.g., all Bs) for some time. He found that the punctuated-equilibrium pattern further reinforced the dominance of the Rigids at the top. The intuitive explanation is that during the long, stable periods, the Rigids who played the appropriate strategy have a significant advantage due to their deep experience, and they rise to the top. Things hum along nicely until the punctuation point comes. Then, the old Rigids are suddenly no longer playing the right strategy and are wiped out. In the transition, some Flexibles run things for a while, but when the environment eventually settles down, a new generation of Rigids rises to the top and the cycle repeats. Despite the simplicity of Harrington's model, this pattern is eerily similar to the patterns of management change many large companies experience.

Harrington notes that the less frequent, more abrupt, and more severe the transitions, the more dominant the Rigids are and the more disastrous the situation is when the environment actually shifts. In environments that are more continuously volatile, the Flexibles tend to do better. Harrington measured the economic efficiency of his model organizations during these transitions and found that the amount of economic loss was directly related to the number of Flexibles the organization managed to hold on to during the stable period. Organizations that drove out the Flexibles and were dominated by Rigids tended to do very well during the stable period (e.g., met all their earnings targets), but then really blew up when the punctuation point hit. In contrast, organizations that managed to hang on to a reserve of Flexibles and maintained a better mix between the two types did somewhat worse during the stable era (they were less efficient), but managed the adaptive transitions much more smoothly.

Structure: How Much Hierarchy?

We will now step up a level, from individual agents to looking at the impact organizational structure has on the issue of adaptability. Jack Welch has referred to structure as the "hardware" side of organization—the design of reporting relationships, managerial processes, and the configuration of the firm's resources.[32] Earlier in the book, we discussed the beneficial role that hierarchy plays in organizations. It enables the network structure to be organized in such a way that decisions can be made without everyone having to talk to everyone else, and thus prevent the gridlock of complexity catastrophes. Organizations with insufficient hierarchy have difficulty changing and adapting because the density of communications is too high, and the need for consensus slows down decision making. But the section in chapter 7 was titled "Two Cheers for Hierarchy!" not three cheers. In this section, we will see that hierarchy, while necessary, can also get in the way of adaptability.

Scott Page, a political scientist and associate director of the Center for the Study of Complex Systems at the University of Michigan, has examined the question, why do organizations evolve different amounts of hierarchy?[33] Why are some organizations broad and flat, while others are narrow and deep? He hypothesized that organizational structure was related to the nature of the problems that organizations solve. Organizations solve a bewildering array of problems, ranging from how to produce a product or provide a service, to how to hire people and how to manage the company's finances. These problems also have varying degrees of difficulty. For example, coordinating two people in their efforts to clean a house might be seen as a relatively simple problem, whereas coordinating a few thousand people to construct an Airbus A380 is a much more difficult problem.

Page proposed that there are two dimensions to the difficulty of an economic coordination problem. One dimension is how hard it is to decompose the problem into chunks that can be solved in parallel. For example, the house cleaners might divide their work such that one person cleans the kitchen while another is cleaning the bathroom. The difficulty of the parallel tasks is then measured by the time it takes to do the biggest task (e.g., the kitchen might take longer). The second dimension is the number of steps that need to be done sequentially. For example, in assembling an A380, one might have to carefully sequence the assembly of the fuel tanks and the control surfaces to build a wing, which then has to be sequenced into the overall assembly of the aircraft. The more sequential steps involved, the harder it is (and the longer it takes) to find the exact right sequence to reach the desired goal. A problem in which each chunk of work takes a long time, and lots of chunks have to be carefully sequenced, can be considered a difficult problem.

Page posited that organizations evolve to match the nature and difficulty of the problems they are trying to solve. In rough terms, if the problem can easily be chunked into parallel tasks and doesn't require much sequencing, then the organization will reflect this simplicity and tend to be broad and flat. If the problem cannot be easily divided up and has numerous sequential steps, then the organizational hierarchy will tend to be narrow and deep. For example, in a law firm, small teams of lawyers can work on client cases in parallel, with relatively little coordination across the teams. We would thus expect a law firm to have a relatively flat organizational structure, and in fact most large law firms have only four or five layers between the junior associates and the senior partners. In contrast, designing and building a jet aircraft requires a complex mixture of carefully sequenced and parallel steps and thus requires many coordinators and traffic cops to make sure it all comes together. We would thus expect an organization like Airbus to have many layers between the frontline workers riveting parts together, and the senior executives at the top.

Not only does this relationship between hierarchy and level of difficulty help explain why organizations in different industries might have different structural forms, but it also shows us that executing and adapting within an organization might require different structures. In very general terms, execution tasks involve coordinating numerous complex sequential and parallel processes, and thus require deep hierarchies. In contrast, exploration activities usually require broad, flat organizations. A portfolio of strategic experiments usually comprises a set of small teams, with some basic coordination at the overall portfolio level, but for the most part, the teams work in parallel and fairly autonomously. The differing nature of execution problems versus exploration problems creates a natural tension. Execution organizations, with their big, deep hierarchies, are designed to solve large, complex problems and excel at control, efficiency, and accountability. They are not designed for undertaking many small tasks in parallel, with an emphasis on speed, flexibility, and autonomy and a high tolerance for redundancy and small failures.

Consequently, companies rarely see exploration activities arising organically out of their mainstream execution hierarchies—it is a mismatch between the organizational structure and the nature of the problem. It is also why at many companies, when senior management sees a need for exploration, they pull small teams out of the hierarchy, put them in separate buildings, and create various forms of Skunk Works to pursue innovation initiatives. Such initiatives can be successful. Apple Computer's Macintosh, for example, was famously developed by a small, autonomous team with a pirate flag flying from the mast of its separate building.

Skunk Works that are separate from the execution hierarchy may often be the only way to address this mismatch. But there are two pitfalls that such approaches often run into. First, if all such exploration initiatives are run and funded by the corporate center, then the organization will inevitably explore only a limited section of the fitness landscape—the section that happens to be on the radar screen of senior management. Second, there are often problems reintegrating such initiates back into the mainstream organization. Reintegration is, of course, essential if a successful initiative is eventually to be amplified. Both issues are made easier when, in addition to the corporate portfolio, the business units also have the resources and autonomy to run portfolios of experiments themselves. This enables a broader exploration of the landscape and provides a more natural path for reintegrating successful initiatives back into the organization.

Structure: The Coevolution of Resources and Business Plans

Long before the tension between exploration and exploitation became popular in management circles, in 1959 an economist at the London School of Economics named Edith Penrose published a slim, but highly influential volume titled *The Theory of the Growth of the Firm*.[34] Penrose viewed company growth as a process of search and exploration, where management teams seek out new opportunities in their environment, and then use the *resources* of their firm to exploit those opportunities. Penrose primarily discussed the physical (e.g., plant and equipment) and human (e.g., management talent, employee skills) resources of firms, but modern theorists have extended her definition to include less tangible but equally important resources such as knowledge, brands, reputations, and relationships. In short, resources are what management teams draw on to exploit opportunities.[35]

Penrose's theory has two implications. First, a firm's resources are determined by the particular opportunities a management team wants to exploit. If a management team sees good opportunities in nanotechnology, it will hire researchers with nanotechnology experience, it will buy machines for fabricating nanotechnology devices, and it will attempt to build a brand and reputation for expertise in nanotechnology. But the flip side is that the resources a company has at a particular point in time define and limit its ability to explore. If, for example, a management team is running a fish-processing plant and the CEO wakes up one morning enamored by nanotechnology, that may be all well and good. There may in fact be opportunities in nanotechnology, but the company's resources (workers good at filleting fish, canning machines, and a brand such as "Taste O'Sea") will define the company's opportunity set as things related to fish processing, not nanotechnology.

We can recast Penrose's ideas in the terminology we developed in part 3.[36] Management teams use deductive-tinkering to search for profitable Business Plans, but their search is limited to plans that they believe they can execute, which in turn is determined by the state of the organization's resources at the time. But as plans are executed, management changes the configuration of resources and thus changes the space of possible future Business Plans. There is thus a continuous, coevolutionary loop between Business Plans and firm resources.

This coevolution between plans and resources creates path dependence in the structure of organizations and provides another important barrier to adaptation. One cannot simply leap from being a fish-processing company to being a nanotechnology star, even if the environment rewards nanotechnology companies more than it rewards fish-processing companies. More precisely, such a change *should not* occur; investment bankers might be only too happy to sell the fish-processing company a nanotechnology business if it had the cash, but the fish-processing management team would not have the requisite skills or experience to successfully run the nanotechnology business. Westinghouse tried such a "sow's ear into a silk purse" move when it attempted to rapidly transform itself from an industrial company into a media company, with predictable results.

Major changes in industry and strategic focus can successfully occur, but in a step-by-step evolutionary fashion, rather than through single leaps. In their classic 1990 article, "The Core Competence of the Corporation," C. K.

Prahalad and Gary Hamel described how Canon built on its resources in its photography and lithography businesses (in particular, optics and precision mechanics) to go into the photocopier business.[37] This move in turn created opportunities in laser printers and faxes. These opportunities required the company to build capabilities in microelectronics, which in turn enabled Canon to become a leader in digital photography, providing both cameras and printers. Over time, resources and opportunities chase each other.

The path-dependent nature of resources and the coevolutionary loop between Business Plans and resources thus add another factor that inhibits adaptability. A firm might simply be stuck with the wrong set of resources for the direction it needs to go, and reconfiguring those resources may take more time and money than are available.

Penrose's theory further reinforces the need for portfolios of strategic experiments. Not only do such portfolios create a greater diversity of Business Plans within organizations, but the initiatives in such portfolios also create a greater diversity of resources. Setting up an initiative usually involves hiring new people, developing new skills, buying assets, and so on. Returning to the Microsoft example, to explore the potential of both Windows and Unix, Gates had to hire people who had skills in each area, including Unix programmers, and he also bought the rights to an existing Unix-based operating system for PCs. Thus, if the market had swung toward Unix, not only would he have had the feedback from his Business Plan experiment, but he would also have had a core set of Unix resources to build on. Without this experiment, he could have been caught without any deep Unix expertise or assets.

Culture: Rules of Behavior

We will now discuss the third and final level of our social architecture framework: the level of organizational culture. I have placed culture at the top of the framework because it is an emergent characteristic of organizations. As noted before, when we make statements such as "Emerson Electric has a performance-oriented culture" we are making statements about the emergent result of thousands of individual decisions and behaviors.[38]

Culture is often a fuzzy term for which a wide variety of definitions have been put forward over the years.[39] For our purposes, I will use a definition that fits with our evolutionary framework, but is similar in spirit to a widely used definition from the anthropologists Robert Boyd and Peter Richerson:

> Culture *is an emergent characteristic of a group of agents and is determined by the agents' rules of behavior (or norms) for acting in their social environment and for interacting with each other. Cultural rules are socially transmitted and learned.*[40]

Cultural norms are in short the rules of thumb for behaving in a social environment. Norms are "should" or "ought" statements about what is considered the right, appropriate, or the expected thing to do, by the society or organization in a given situation.[41]

We can think of culture in an organizational context as a set of concentric rings, moving from the most widely shared norms, to ones that are more specific and individual. In the outermost ring are the norms that virtually all humans share. Evidence from anthropologists and cognitive scientists shows that a relatively small set of norms comes as standard equipment in human minds and is likely the product of our biological evolution.[42] For example, murder is a universal prohibition, and likewise, as we saw earlier, all societies have norms about reciprocal behavior. The specific tunings of these basic norms, however, are accomplished through a process of imitation and teaching and are thus culturally transmitted. For example, what constitutes murder might differ by society (e.g., definitions of "honor" killings, self-defense, and war), and as we saw in chapter 6, what constitutes fairness might differ by society.[43]

Moving inward, to the next ring, we see a vast universe of culturally specific norms. These norms have evolved in particular societies and are transmitted from person to person over time, from parent to child, from teacher to student, from boss to worker, from friend to friend, and so on. Culturally specific norms are spread through a variety of channels, such as stories, music, religion, writing, and the media. These norms often cover a very wide set of behaviors, ranging from sexual norms, to how guests are treated, to how to signal respect for another person. Such rules of behavior produce endless sources of friction when people from different cultures collide, as well as endless sources of humor when tourists try to navigate their way in a strange country. Within the broad swath of societal norms, there are often subgroups, and sub-subgroups, as determined by geography, religion, or other factors. In this way, one can speak of German culture, as well as Bavarian culture, as well as Catholic Bavarian culture.

We can then locate organizational culture at the next ring heading inward. Organizational cultures always exist in the broader context of societal cultures and, more generally, human culture. But organizations, including companies, develop their own unique cultures over time. We can think of these as the rules of behavior for interacting within a specific organization. For example, an organization might have a culture in which junior people feel free to speak up and express their views, or it might be an authoritarian culture in which junior staff defer to their seniors. Alternatively, a company might have a culture in which commitments are flexible and not taken very seriously, or one in which commitments are considered binding and there are serious consequences for missing them. The key is that these are organization-specific and not just general societal traits. For example, both Sony and Matsushita share cultural traits that one would identify as Japanese. Beyond these shared Japanese traits, however, one would find quite different rules of behavior that are particular to each company. It is this subset that we can think of as the organizational culture.

Many companies and management books use the term *values* when discussing corporate culture, and we should distinguish between values and norms. *Values* are statements of belief about what is important, such as "we value an egalitarian approach to teamwork." *Norms,* on the other hand, are statements with "should" or "ought" in them, such as "you should behave in a nonhierarchical way when working in teams." Values and norms tend to go in pairs of beliefs and behaviors (e.g., egalitarian beliefs and nonhierarchical behaviors). Many companies use the terms interchangeably, but I will use the terms *norms,* or *cultural rules,* to emphasize that what matters is the translation into individual behavior.

Finally, located in the innermost circle are individual norms. Every person has an individual set of rules of behavior that he or she follows. People at Matsushita might all share human norms, Japanese norms, and various Matsushita organizational norms, but they are still individuals and will differ in their behaviors. The way we can distinguish between idiosyncratic norms and organizational, societal, or human norms is to ask how widely shared the norms are. For example, one person in her youth might learn that individual initiative is rewarded, while another might come to believe that the best policy is to keep her head down and go with the flow. If initiative taking is a common feature in a society, then we would say it is a broad societal norm; if it is randomly scattered in the society but common in a particular organization, then initiative taking would be an organizational norm. Finally, if this rule of behavior was randomly scattered in the organization, but certain individuals had it, then it would be an individual norm.

Culture: The Ten Commandments

In one sense, it is obvious how culture affects organizational performance. If all (or even most) of the employees in a company behave in a particular way, that behavior will affect overall company performance. The more interesting question is which behaviors are desirable, and which ones are not.

Naturally, the norms that contribute to company success are likely to be highly specific to a company, its industry, its particular Business Plans, the competitive circumstances, and so on. But just as Tolstoy famously said, "All happy families resemble one another, but each unhappy family is unhappy in its own way," a handful of traits seem to crop up with regularity in studies of the cultures of high-performing and adaptive companies.[44]

I have collected some of these traits into a list of ten norms. This is not meant to be a definitive list, and one could certainly debate what should or should not be on the list. Rather, the list is meant merely to be illustrative of the types of norms that various researchers have identified. I have grouped the norms into three categories. The first relates to individual performance: "how should I behave when I am on my own and no one is watching?" The second describes cooperative behavior: "how should I behave when interacting with others?" And the third describes behaviors that facilitate exploration and innovation.

Performing norms

1. PERFORMANCE ORIENTATION. Always do your best, go the extra mile, take initiative, and continuously improve yourself.

2. HONESTY. Be honest with others, be honest with yourself, be transparent and face reality.

3. MERITOCRACY. Reward people on the basis of merit.

Cooperating norms

4. MUTUAL TRUST. Trust your colleagues' motivation, and trust in their skills to get the job done.

5. RECIPROCITY. Live the golden rule; do unto others as you would have them do unto you.

6. SHARED PURPOSE. Put the organization's interests ahead of your own, and behave as if everyone is in it together.

Innovating norms

7. NONHIERARCHICAL. Junior people are expected to challenge senior people, and what matters is the quality of an idea, not the title of the person saying it.

8. OPENNESS. Be curious, open to outside thinking, and willing to experiment; seek the best, wherever it is.

9. FACT-BASED. Find out the facts; it is facts, not opinions, that ultimately count.

10. CHALLENGE. Feel a sense of competitive urgency; it is a race without a finish line.

Simply read from a list, these norms have a somewhat motherhood-and-apple-pie quality to them. They are very easy to declare and easy to agree with. The hard part is weaving them into the social fabric of a large organization and getting hundreds, thousands, or even hundreds of thousands of people of all sorts of backgrounds and personalities to follow them.

Nonetheless, some firms do succeed in "walking the talk" for at least a subset of these norms. Johnson & Johnson is well known for its "Credo," which was written by Robert W. Johnson Jr. in 1943 and has been a guide to behavior in the company ever since. The Credo advocates a shared higher purpose of "serving the sick and those who treat them" (norm 6), principles of meritocracy (norm 3), and ethical behavior (norm 2). Johnson & Johnson founder Robert W. Johnson Sr. once famously proclaimed, "Failure is our most important product," signaling a willingness to experiment and take risks (norm 8).[45]

The Firm that I am affiliated with, McKinsey & Company, is also well known for its strong culture. A number of norms have been drilled into the heads of new associates since Marvin Bower, the Firm's guiding influence for fifty-nine years, developed them in the 1940s and 1950s.[46] The wording has evolved over time, but the core concepts have endured. McKinsey is "one Firm" across the world, a concept that fosters norms of mutual trust and reciprocity (norms 4 and 5). It is also a "caring meritocracy" (norm 3), and a "nonhierarchical Firm" (norm 7). Its norm of "positive lasting impact on clients" gives McKinsey's associates and partners a shared purpose (norm 6). Finally, its "up or out" policy that people are either promoted or leave creates an intense performance culture (norms 1 and 10).

General Electric, too, has a famously competitive, performance-oriented culture driven by concepts such as "A" players, "fix it, close it, or sell it," and the four Es of leadership (energy, edge, energizer, and execution).[47] One of Jack Welch's most famous bits of jargon, the "boundaryless organization," speaks directly to norm 8. Another Welchism, "facing reality," addresses norm 2, while the notion of "A" ideas being recognized, regardless of rank, reflects norm 7.

In all probability, there is no company that truly lives all ten norms. Even the highly praised GE sometimes falls short (at least anecdotally) on some of the cooperative norms. And individual organizations inevitably have particular interpretations and emphasize different aspects of these norms. The key point is not that the particular norms I have sketched should be carved in stone tablets, but simply that it is possible to identify cultural rules that, if widely used in a population, would be likely to have a positive effect on macro performance.

Culture: Inherent Tensions

Each of these norms plays a critical role in the executing-versus-adapting story and in reducing the dependency of the organization on structure and process.

Individual performance norms clearly have an important impact on execution. But they also play a role in adaptation. If individual performance norms are deeply embedded in an organization and succeed in driving individual behavior, then the hierarchy and processes don't have to be quite so tight and restrictive to achieve good performance. If the hierarchy and centralized control processes don't have to be so tight, this in turn enables the organization to have more slack resources for experimentation and to drive responsibility closer to the frontline. When individual performance norms are poor, the hierarchy tends to crack down and tighten processes, perhaps succeeding in boosting execution, but damaging the organization's ability to adapt.

Cooperative norms also have important effects on both adaptation and execution. In low-trust, low-cooperation environments, interactions between agents must be spelled out in great detail, with numerous rules and little flexibility. One sees this in organizations in which labor and management have poor relations and unions have stepped in with detailed contracts that specify which person can pick up which screwdriver. Norms that foster trust and cooperation allow people to use their brains to determine what is best, given the circumstances, creating both better performance and the possibility of experimentation and improvement.

Finally, norms for individual performance, trust, and cooperative behavior are all necessary but not sufficient conditions for adaptation. There must be an additional set of norms that push individuals to explore and take risks. Furthermore, there must be norms that help protect such individuals in the organization (e.g., norms 7 and 9) and give them the space to innovate.

Taken together, norms from each of these three categories can help an organization minimize the rigidity of the "hardware" side of things and substitute the "software" of culture for hierarchy and process. If widely adopted and practiced, such norms would undoubtedly have a positive emergent effect on most organizations.

The reality for most organizations, however, is that they truly live few, if any, of these norms. Despite what may be written on posters in the company lobby or on plastic cubes on people's desks, at many companies, values and culture are not top management priorities. In such companies, the culture evolves organically through the interactions of employees, with little shaping by senior management. Such organizational cultures tend to be a mixture of strengths and weaknesses. For example, some organizations may be strong on individual performance norms, but weak on cooperative norms, or vice versa. There are inherent tensions between the norms in the top-ten list, for example, the tensions between an intense, performance-oriented meritocracy and the need for teamwork. Unless these tensions are actively managed through senior leadership and reinforced by the structural side of the organization, some subset of the norms inevitably comes to dominate. It is thus virtually impossible for a set of norms that is balanced across individual performance, cooperation, and innovation to arise organically without strong leadership.

Creating an Adaptive Social Architecture

We have touched on a number of factors that might explain why organizations generally don't adapt as quickly or successfully as markets do:

Individuals

- Human mental models tend to be biased toward optimism, dulling our ability to recognize the need for change.

- A natural bias toward loss aversion causes people to systematically underinvest in experimentation.

- As our mental models gain experience in a stable environment, they become more effective in that environment, but at the price of reduced flexibility.

- In a stable environment, organizational hierarchies tend to favor the promotion of people with experience and skills executing the current business model (Rigids) over people whose skill sets are more oriented toward exploring and adapting (Flexibles).

Structure

- The challenges of executing complex production and service processes drive organizations to develop deep, densely connected hierarchies. Yet these structures are not well suited to the tasks of exploration, which require flatter, more autonomous organizational structures.

- The coevolutionary relationship between Business Plans and resources constrains the space of Business Plans that a firm can explore, and path dependence in resources limits the ability and speed with which an organization can shift to a new Business Plan.

Culture

- Strong cultural norms are critical to adaptability because they enable organizations to reduce centralized hierarchical control without sacrificing execution performance.

- There are, however, inherent tensions in cultural norms that encourage individual performance, cooperation, and innovation; these tensions must be actively managed by the organization's senior leadership.

Executing and adapting appear to be irreconcilable opposites, and the empirical data we discussed in the previous chapter suggests that most companies are destined to favor the former over the latter. But by understanding the sources of this schism, we can also begin to see the outlines of a potential solution. By shifting the central lever of management from the hardware of organizational structure to the software of culture, we can begin to address each of these issues.

At a crude level, there are fundamentally only two ways of running a large organization. One is to use the structure of management hierarchy. We can define roles, goals, tasks, and procedures; then measure individual and group performance against those goals; and reward and punish accordingly. Such a structure serves to reduce the degrees of freedom of individual agents and constrain them to desired behaviors. The benefits of this approach are control, reliability, and predictability. Using the structure lever increases the odds that people will do what they are supposed to do, and not do what they are not supposed to do. Although I've described the use of hierarchy in rather unflattering terms, it can be very satisfying for people to have a well-defined role, interesting tasks to carry out, and clear measures of success—particularly if it pays well. Without such hierarchical structures, we'd still be in caves rubbing sticks together to make fire.

The second method still requires the skeleton of hierarchy, but uses less command-and-control muscle on the bones. Rather than using structure and process to guide individual behavior, an organization can rely more heavily on culture. The primary advantage of a culturally driven organization is that cultural rules tend to be more flexible than structures. Cultural rules provide general guidance, but leave the "how" up to the individual. In short, they require individuals to use their brains.

Cultural rules can be used to address each of the issues we have identified. Overoptimism and risk aversion can be counterbalanced with cultural norms that encourage people to face reality, make fact-based decisions, and take thoughtful risks. Likewise, the entrenchment of senior mental models can be addressed by a nonhierarchical culture that creates not just an expectation that junior people will speak their minds, but an obligation (McKinsey calls this "the obligation to dissent"). The rigid-versus-flexible issue can be mitigated by a culture that embraces a diversity of management styles and that values both execution and innovation skill sets. Finally, the structural issues that tend to favor execution hierarchies over portfolios of experiments can also be offset by changes in culture. In particular, boosting individual performance and cooperation norms can enable a looser hierarchical structure without a consequent loss in near-term performance. This in turn enables resources and responsibility for experimentation to be pushed deeper into the organization.

Moving to a more culturally led management approach does not mean abandoning the hardware of structure and process. On the contrary, as we have noted, a social architecture needs both. Rather, it means that the hardware and software sides of the organization must be consistent and mutually reinforcing. One can work backward and ask, if the objective is to better balance executing and adapting, then what kind of culture would support that objective, and what kind of structure and processes would support that culture? For example, if one of the desired norms is individual accountability, but there are no rewards for those who achieve targets, and no penalties for those who miss, then the norm will merely be empty words. Likewise, norms around innovating and risk taking need to be supported by a constellation of budgeting, human resources, and performance processes.

Perhaps the most critical hardware levers in a social architecture are a company's human resources and training processes. Rather than fight human nature, strong-culture companies recognize that it is far easier to hire the right people who culturally fit than it is to create them. Thus, these companies have a very strong perspective on what kind of candidates have the "right DNA" for the organization, and actively screen for those qualities. But even though the new hires might have the right raw material, strong-culture companies don't assume that new hires will adopt the culture simply through osmosis. Instead, such companies have carefully engineered induction processes that introduce new recruits to the norms and then reinforce the norms in training and other programs throughout the person's career. Evaluation and promotion further reinforce the culture by explicitly rewarding those who live the norms and by withholding rewards from, or punishing, those who do not. People receive a consistent message on the culture from these processes, literally from their first interview to retirement.

Finally, senior management behavior and communications play an enormous role in building and perpetuating a culturally led social architecture. It is a cliché, but nonetheless true, that if senior management does not walk the talk and model the desired norms, then no one else will. As mentioned before, carefully balanced systems of cultural norms do not arise organically, and thus all strong-culture companies have sometime in their history had a CEO who played the role of chief cultural architect and enforcement officer.

These individuals carefully designed the set of desired norms for their companies, personally and passionately ensured consistency against those norms by their senior team, drove the norms deep into their organizations, and then created mechanisms to ensure that the norms would be perpetuated. Over time, once a culture is well established, cultural design and enforcement can (and should) become the collective responsibility of the senior team, but during the crucial period when the culture is being built, there is no substitute for personal CEO leadership.

Communications is also naturally important, and cognitive science tells us that most corporate change programs are 180 degrees backward.[48] Humans are fairly stubborn creatures and don't just immediately change their mental models and behaviors in responses to speeches from their bosses, or because of PowerPoint presentations or plastic cubes with inspirational messages. Instead of trying to appeal to our fact-based, deductive sides, corporate change programs need to address the story-loving, pattern-recognizing, more emotional, inductive side of human cognition. People need to be jolted from their existing mental models and see an urgent and personal gap between the way things are and the way things need to be. A change program needs to have a fact-based argument underlying it, but the emphasis in communications should be on stories, analogies, and patterns to help people see the issues. Most change programs are also very passive, with lots of communications cascading down from on high. But learning is interactive, and thus a change program needs to get people to personally grapple with the issues.

Many executives find the idea of sound bites mildly distasteful and associate them with politicians. But the reality of human cognition is that we remember short, catchy, rhythmic phrases that use alliteration, metaphor, humorous twists, or other tricks. Jack Welch was the master of the carefully engineered sound bite and used them with great effect to drive norms of behavior into the GE organization.[49] Finally, intense repetition is essential. There is a reason why religious leaders see their flocks weekly, and why politicians give the same stump speech until they are blue in the face—our minds tend to weight messages by frequency as much as quality.

This way of managing is not easy and is therefore rare. As Robert Wiggins and Tim Ruefli pointed out, companies with a pattern of adaptability and repeat success comprise only 1 percent of the corporate population. GE, Hewlett-Packard, IBM, Johnson & Johnson, British Petroleum, DuPont, Procter & Gamble, and Goldman Sachs are a few of the often-cited examples of companies that have managed to build adaptive social architectures.[50] None of these companies is perfect, but each has had repeated runs of high performance, has bounced back from periods of adversity, and has endured over long periods of time despite vast changes in their environments.

A Society of Minds

One of the questions Edith Penrose asked in her *Theory of the Growth of the Firm* was, what, if any, are the fundamental constraints on firm size and growth?[51] She identified two. The first is the ability to manage complexity. At some point, an organization can simply become, as Penrose put it, "too big . . . to be efficiently handled."[52] The outer envelope of this constraint, however, has continued to advance, as our Physical and Social Technologies have evolved. Clearly, it is easier to run a large, global organization with computers, telephones, airplanes, and modern management techniques than it is with letters, carrier pigeons, steamships, and nineteenth-century STs. Indeed, there is evidence that this constraint has loosened over time, as the average number of employees in a *Fortune* 500 company has nearly tripled, from around 16,000 in 1955 when the list was first published, to nearly 48,000 in 2003.[53]

The second constraint Penrose identified was knowledge. A firm can only grow as fast as its knowledge.[54] And, since knowledge is the product of evolutionary processes, we can say that a firm can only grow as fast as its evolutionary processes allow it to grow. Although the size of organizations in the economy has grown, the shape of the distribution of both firm size and growth rates has remained remarkably stable. According to work by Robert Axtell at the Brookings Institution and Gene Stanley at Boston University, both are distributed according to our old friend, the power law.[55] The existence of these power laws suggests that there are indeed constraints at work on the system. One can hypothesize that perhaps it is Penrose's second constraint that is holding us back. Our PTs and STs have enabled organizations to develop coordinating, controlling, and executing abilities that are far ahead of their innovating and knowledge-creating abilities.

If true, this means that we are operating at a level vastly below our human potential. The great cognitive scientist and artificial intelligence researcher Marvin Minsky observed that what we call "intelligence" is not a singular thing; rather, it is an emergent phenomenon that arises from the collective interactions of many individual parts. The magic of intelligence is that when those parts are organized in a particular way, they can do things that no individual part could do on its own. Minsky called this description of intelligence "the society of mind."[56]

We can think of human organizations as passing through three stages of development. The first stage was the evolution of STs that enabled strangers to reliably cooperate with each other. The second stage was the creation of large-scale organizations that could exploit the PTs of the industrial revolution. But perhaps now we are at the beginning of a third stage. We are only just now learning how to create "societies of minds" in our largest organizations.

Most organizations tap only a small fraction of the brainpower of their people. The hierarchical command-and-control organizations that arose out of the industrial age enabled humans to achieve cooperation on scales once unimaginable and execute Business Plan designs of immense complexity. Nevertheless, the inherent rigidities of these structures ultimately limit them to being evolutionary fodder in the churnings of markets. But through the lever of culture, companies can create true societies within their organizations and free the minds of their people. As in any society, along with freedom comes responsibility, and the culture must support performance and execution, as well as exploration and adaptation. Creating such a culture is truly "social engineering" with all the consequent risks and unpredictability associated with the phrase. But for companies that succeed, the reward is the creation of institutions that can be engines of wealth creation for generations to come.

CHAPTER SEVENTEEN

Finance

ECOSYSTEMS OF EXPECTATIONS

DURING THE SUMMER of 1998, John Meriwether, the CEO of the multi-billion dollar hedge fund Long-Term Capital, received an urgent phone call while on vacation. The month of August had been a nonstop roller coaster for the world's financial markets, with Asian economies toppling one after the other and wild gyrations in the U.S. markets. By the end of the month, the roller coaster had run off the rails. Long-Term Capital had lost $4.4 billion in the space of a few days.[1] Meriwether was ignominiously summoned back to Greenwich, Connecticut, to begin arranging an emergency bailout.

Crashing Nobel Prizes

The summer of 1998 may be remembered as the moment when one era of finance theory ended and a new one began. The great stock market crash of 1987 had shaken the foundations of the ivory tower, but the events of 1998 started it crumbling. The incredible volatility of the markets, the cascading of crashes from one market to another, and the sudden changes in perceptions of risk were all phenomena for which Traditional Economics offered little or no explanation. It was also the height of irony; the key architects of Long-Term Capital's investment strategy were also two of the fathers of modern finance theory, Robert Merton and Myron Scholes, both Nobel Prize winners. As Merton noted the day after Long-Term Capital's crash, "according to our models this just could not happen"—yet there it was, on the front page of the *Wall Street Journal*.[2]

More recent events have only served to raise further questions about the Traditional Economics view of finance theory. In the neat, rational, equilibrium world of Traditional finance, stock market bubbles do not exist. Yet, during the great bull market of 1997 to 2000, over \$12.7 trillion of value was added to U.S. financial markets, and then in the great fin de siècle bust, \$10.8 trillion evaporated just as quickly. The gap between the real world and the textbooks could no longer be ignored.

Finance is one of the few areas of economics in which theories and equations come straight out of academia and are almost immediately applied in the real world. The tools of Traditional finance are heavily used by investors, banks, corporate managers, and government policy makers. The decisions that ride on the back of these ideas range from billions of dollars in trading, to whether two companies will merge, to how central banks set interest rates. Thus, any claim that Traditional finance theory is wrong is an important claim indeed.

Finance theory is also unique in that it is the most empirically tested area of economics. Financial economists have an embarrassment of riches, with minute-by-minute data on the trading of tens of thousands of assets. They are also fortunate because financial markets tend to be old and keep good records, allowing economists to look at data not only at the minute-by-minute level, but also over decades. Unfortunately, as of late, all this data has not been kind to Traditional theory.

Forgotten Frenchmen and Dusty Libraries

In 1900, Louis Bachelier, a young French graduate student in mathematics at the Sorbonne, completed a dissertation titled "The Theory of Speculation."[3] In it, he made the remarkable claim that stock prices moved according to a *random walk*. As I described earlier in the book, a random walk is when something moves a random distance, in a random direction, at each increment in time. The radical implication of Bachelier's claim was that there was no more useful information in the path of a stock price over time than there was in the wanderings of a drunk down the streets of Paris. Unfortunately, the great dons of Bachelier's thesis committee were not convinced, and his work lay largely unnoticed for the next sixty years.[4]

Then, in 1954, a statistician named Jimmie Savage was rooting through the stacks of the University of Chicago library and happened upon a small, dusty book by one L. Bachelier, written in 1914. Intrigued, Savage sent a note about it to the legendary economist Paul Samuelson. Samuelson acquired a copy of Bachelier's thesis from the Sorbonne, and through Samuelson's influence, the random-walk hypothesis became a cornerstone of Traditional finance theory.

During the three decades following Samuelson's resurrection of Bachelier, an extraordinary group of economists that included Samuelson, Paul Cootner, Harry Markowitz, James Tobin, Franco Modigliani, Merton Miller, Fisher

Black, Myron Scholes, Eugene Fama, William Sharpe, and Robert Merton developed most of the major ideas of Traditional finance. In 1973, a Princeton University professor named Burton Malkiel published *A Random Walk Down Wall Street,* a book that neatly summarized the research of this era and popularized it for both Wall Street professionals and individual investors.[5] The book became a bestseller and a fixture of MBA courses, and an entire generation of traders and investors was raised on the ideas begun by the forgotten Frenchman.

Textbook Stock Picking

According to Traditional finance theory, the way we should value a stock (or any other financial instrument) is to look at the future cash flows we will get from the stock over time.[6] Let's imagine a company called Predictable Enterprises, which pays a dividend on its stock. Now, let's further imagine that we have a crystal ball and can perfectly forecast that Predictable Enterprises will pay a dividend of $10 per share per year for the next five years. Our crystal ball also tells us that in year six, the company will be taken over by Nobel Ventures for $100 in cash per share. By holding a share of this stock, one would receive a payout of $10 for five years, which equals $50, plus $100 in year six, for a total of $150 (we'll ignore taxes). So, the future value of one share of Predictable is $150. As we all know, however, a dollar today is worth more than a dollar tomorrow. You wouldn't buy the stock for $150 today simply to get back $150 in six years; you would want a return on your money. How much of a return you think is fair will depend on how risky the investment is and what your alternatives are. Imagine now that instead of having a crystal ball, you merely *expect* Predictable Enterprises to perform as just outlined. You aren't merely guessing; you have read all the company's reports, analyzed its position in the market, and used all the publicly available information to make your determination. But while you expect Predictable to perform in a certain way, you also know that it could do worse, or it could do better. You also know that instead of putting your money into Predictable with its associated risks, you could put your money into an interest-bearing bank account with a government guarantee and virtually no risk at all. So let's assume that you consider Predictable sufficiently risky that you need to earn a 10 percent return before you would think it worthwhile. If that was the case, then you would only be willing to pay $94 today for the stream of dividend payments that gives you back $150 over time. Such an investment would give you your 10 percent return.[7] The idea that investors value a dollar today more than a dollar tomorrow is called *discounting,* and the amount of discounting depends on the level of risk an investor believes he or she is taking on.

In the world of Traditional finance theory, all investors are rational and behave in this way. They search out all available information on a particular stock, form a set of expectations of future cash flows from holding the investment, assess the risks to come up with a discount rate, and then calculate what the stock is worth today. Thus, at a given moment, *the price of a stock reflects all the information available on the stock, and everyone's expectations based on that information*. Let's say you expected Predictable to grow and its dividend to rise from $10 to $11, $12, $13, and $14 for each of the years. Then today, you'd be willing to pay $101 to get your 10 percent return rather than $94. So, a stock that investors expect to grow in the future will have those expectations already built into the price today. Likewise, an expectation that future dividends will decline would cause your valuation to drop. Similarly, a change in your perception of the investment's risk would cause your discount rate to change, thus also changing the value you place on the stock.

Once you have digested all the available information and calculated the price you are willing to pay, in theory, the only reason you should change that price is if a *new piece of information* comes along that changes your future expectations. Thus, if you get the news that Predictable met another dividend payment of $10 and this was your expectation to begin with, you would continue to place a value of $94 on the stock. However, if instead you got unexpected news that Predictable was increasing its dividend, then your valuation would jump up by an appropriate amount.

So far, we have described how Traditional finance theory says individual investors make their decisions, but we need next to consider what happens when we have a number of investors trading with each other. Not everyone interprets information in the same way. One person might be optimistic about Predictable's prospects and value the stock at $101, and someone else, who is pessimistic, might value it at $87. The optimist would be willing to buy shares at any price up to $101, and the pessimist would be willing to sell shares at any price down to $87. There is thus a potential for these two individuals to trade. Now, imagine there are many people in the market, and they have a spectrum of expectations and a spectrum of holdings of the stock. We can then hold an auction that enables all of them to trade with each other and in essence sort themselves out, with the pessimists selling to the optimists. At some point, all the investors will hold as much stock as they want at just the price they want, and they won't have any incentives to trade anymore. At this point, where everyone is satisfied and no one wants to trade anymore, the market is in equilibrium and the price set at this point by the auctioneer is the *market price*. In effect, the market price represents a consensus view of all the expectations and information in the market.

Here in the story, the market should just sit in equilibrium at the market price, with no trading until a new piece of information hits the market. We can imagine everyone is drumming fingers, yawning, and hanging around the trading floor, and then there is a news flash that Predictable Enterprises has just received an unexpected big order for its products. This announcement sets off a flurry of activity as everyone tries to learn as much as possible about the news. The investors update their expectations of Predictable's future cash flow and risk, and come up with a new valuation, which in turn sets off a new round of trading. The trading occurs until everyone is happy again; the market reaches its equilibrium and goes back into quiet mode until the next news flash.

It is the efficiency of the market in digesting information that causes prices to move in a random walk. If everyone is absorbing all the available information and doing the calculations correctly, then the only thing that will cause Predictable's price to move is a new piece of news. Since Traditional Economics assumes that the arrival of news is random, and no one knows whether it will be good news or bad news, prices then move randomly as they are buffeted by the winds of news. However, because economies in the industrialized world have tended to grow on average a few percent a year, economists model the randomness of news as having a slight bias toward good news. Without knowing anything else about Predictable Enterprises, we would expect it to have slightly more good news than bad news as the company benefits from overall economic growth. This is referred to as a *random walk with drift*. Thus, while stock markets follow a random walk, stocks have still on average gone up over time.

Vegas, Churchill Downs, and Wall Street

An important implication of the random-walk hypothesis is that there is no useful information in past stock price movements. Whether a stock went up or down yesterday has no bearing on whether it will go up or down tomorrow—again, the only thing driving prices is news, which is random. If there were any patterns in past prices, rational investors would spot them, those patterns would be useful information, and investors would use them when setting their valuation. Their trading would then arbitrage the pattern out of the market, making it random again.

Furthermore, the combination of rational investors and arbitrage means that it is impossible to beat the market and generate higher returns than the market as a whole. This is known as the *efficient-markets hypothesis*. One of the theory's early architects, Eugene Fama of the University of Chicago, defines a market as efficient if prices "fully reflect" all the available and relevant information.[8] The idea is that if everyone is using the same formula to calculate prices (perfect rationality) and has access to the same information, then prices will reflect this. Since you can't be smarter than perfect rationality, the only way to come up with a price that better reflects the "true" value of the stock is to have information that other people do not have. But the release and use of information is regulated specifically to prevent "insiders" such as company officers, or their friends and families, from unfairly trading on information that other investors do not have. And when new information is released to the market, whether it is a company's earnings report or a government economic statistic, the availability of 24/7 news coverage and the Internet virtually guarantees that everyone gets the information at the same time. The implication of an efficient market is that there is no way to get an advantage and systematically beat the market. As Paul Samuelson once said, "It is not easy to get rich in Las Vegas, at Churchill Downs, or at the local Merrill Lynch office."[9]

At this point, you might say, hang on, what about Warren Buffet? Aren't there smart investors and dumb investors? A Traditional finance theorist would reply, yes, there are, but it is the smart investors who set the market price. Let's imagine we had a market with two types of investors: Warren Buffet investors, who scour all the latest information and use their brilliant minds to analyze it all perfectly, and Joe Six Pack investors, who buy stocks based on tips from taxi drivers and bartenders. When we put them together and start trading, the Warren Buffett investors will buy and sell from the Joe Six Packs, taking advantage of the Six Packs' ignorance until eventually the market price equals the Warren Buffet price and all the parties stop trading. The Joe Six Packs will lose their money and the Warren Buffets will clean up. Thus, over time, the amount of capital under control of the Warren Buffets will grow, and the capital of the Joe Six Packs will shrink, leaving most of the money in the hands of "smart" investors.[10] In real-world markets, the majority of capital is under the control of pension funds, mutual funds, and other professional investors, and it is these investors' trading that generally sets prices.

The Joe Six Packs might not stand a chance against the pros, but what about those charts in mutual-fund advertisements showing a particular fund beating the market averages and its competitors over time? According to the Traditional finance economists, there are two possible explanations. One is that the fund is taking on more risk than the market average. In an efficient market, one *can* generate higher returns than the market average, but there is no free lunch. The price one pays is higher risk, and so, on a risk-adjusted basis, one is still not beating the market. The second explanation is luck. Just as with "excellent" companies, if we take a snapshot of a group of mutual funds over a certain period, inevitably there will be some "excellent" mutual funds, just as someone in a room of coin flippers will inevitably get a good run of heads. As Malkiel noted in his 1973 book, a number of studies show that on average and over time, mutual funds and professional investors don't beat broad market indices such as the S&P 500 on a statistically significant, risk-adjusted basis; in fact, most of them trail the indices.[11]

Traditional finance theory has developed its ideas into a rigorous and coherent theory that can take us all the way from the behavior of individual investors up to the movements of global markets. It is in many ways one of the most elegant and highly developed branches of Traditional Economics.

Over the last two decades, however, reality has not been kind to the theory. As noted at the beginning of the chapter, events such as the crash of 1987 and the technology bubble of the 1990s have presented significant challenges to Traditional finance. But perhaps even more importantly, a new generation of empirical work using highly advanced statistical tools has called into question the theory's core tenets. From the vantage point of this work, one can say that at best, the theory is a rough approximation that works under certain circumstances; at worst, one can say it is plain and simply wrong. To cut to the heart of the matter, we need to establish three salient facts:

- First, a substantial body of empirical and experimental evidence shows that real-world investors look nothing like their theoretical, perfectly rational counterparts.[12] Investors do not discount in the way Traditional theory assumes; they have various biases regarding risk, are subject to framing errors in processing information, and use heuristics to make decisions. As we discussed more generally in chapter 6, this does not mean that investors are irrational or make decisions purely on emotion. Rather, they are "boundedly" and inductively rational, instead of perfectly and deductively rational. Suffice it to say that three decades of work leaves little doubt that perfect rationality is a poor approximation of economic reality.

- Second, Bachelier was wrong. Markets do not follow a random walk. We will review evidence that market data has considerable structure, which has all the signature characteristics of a complex adaptive system.

- Third, financial markets are not efficient in the Traditional Economics sense of the word, but as we will see, they are highly *effective* in an evolutionary sense.

Cotton Prices, Fat Tails, and Fractals

To begin to understand what is wrong with Traditional theory and what kind of a phenomenon financial markets actually are, we need to go back to the 1960s and IBM's massive research center in Yorktown Heights, New York. One of its bright, up-and-coming stars was a Polish-born, French-educated mathematician named Benoit Mandelbrot (I briefly mentioned Mandelbrot's work in chapter 8.[13] From his earliest days, Mandelbrot was something of a rebel. While French mathematics was obsessed with the Bourbakist program of pure logic, Mandelbrot was interested in the unfashionable topic of geometry and often preferred to draw pictures of data rather than write equations.

Mandelbrot was giving a lecture at Harvard in 1960, when he spied on a blackboard a picture that intrigued him. The picture was a graph of cotton price data that had been collected by Hendrik Houthakker, an economics professor. Houthakker had been plotting the daily changes or variances of the prices and trying to fit the data into a Gaussian, bell-shaped curve, as the random-walk hypothesis said it should. But he could not get the data to fit. Mandelbrot, however, thought he recognized the pattern the data was creating, and he took Houthakker's data back to Yorktown Heights in a box of computer punch cards. In 1963, Mandelbrot published the results of his analysis in a paper titled "The Variation of Certain Speculative Prices." In four strokes, he demolished the random-walk hypothesis: (1) the distribution of the data had much fatter tails than a bell-shaped curve had; in other words, there were more extreme price swings than a random walk would predict; (2) those extreme events were in fact quite extreme; a large proportion of the total variance was explained by just a few violent price movements; (3) there appeared to be some clustering of price movements in time, in other words, a pattern of punctuated equilibrium; and (4) the statistics describing the data were not stationary as the random walk predicted, but changed over time.[14]

Not only did Mandelbrot shoot down the random-walk hypothesis, but he also proposed an alternative. He suggested that the tails of the cotton price distribution followed a power law.[15] Mandelbrot's proposal neatly explained the fat tails and extreme volatility of the data—all features that the economist's random-walk hypothesis could not explain. In later work, Mandelbrot would describe financial market prices as having "fractal geometry"—not only was there structure to be found in financial data, but the structures appeared over multiple timescales from minutes to months, just like the patterns of fractal images that Mandelbrot made famous.[16]

When the 1963 paper was published, it evoked a hostile reaction. Paul Cootner, a leading advocate of the random-walk hypothesis, said, "Surely before consigning centuries of work to the ash pile, we should like to have some assurance that all of our work is truly useless."[17] A debate over the paper ensued, including a thoughtful critique by the University of Chicago's Eugene Fama.[18] But in a further paper published in 1967, Mandelbrot answered his critics and confirmed his results with additional data from wheat prices, railroad stocks, interest rates, and exchange rates.[19] Eventually, the debate died down and the economists moved on to other topics. Mandelbrot was an outsider, an IBM mathematician, not an economist. The random-walk hypothesis had the power of Traditional theory behind it, and at that time, there was no alternative theory behind Mandelbrot's result. The idea of complex adaptive systems and the tools to understand them would have to wait another two decades. Mandelbrot's papers were filed in the economists' drawer of "inconvenient anomalies" and, like Bachelier's earlier work, lay largely forgotten until a new generation would rediscover them.

"A Non-Random Walk Down Wall Street"

In 1986, a junior professor from MIT named Andy Lo and his collaborator, Craig MacKinlay of the Wharton School, presented a paper to a conference of august finance academics in which the pair claimed to have proved that the stock market does not follow a random walk. In their 1999 book, *A Non-Random Walk Down Wall Street,* they describe the stunned reaction they received.[20] As they proceeded with their talk, one participant, a senior and distinguished economist, confidently asserted that their results were impossible, and argued that they must have made a computer programming error.

But over the years that followed, their results were replicated, their programming was found to be sound, and their conclusion stood. Unlike Mandelbrot, Lo and MacKinlay were finance insiders, and the techniques they used in their study were in the mainstream of Traditional finance work. Prior to Lo and MacKinlay's paper, there had been decades of statistical tests of the random-walk hypothesis, but the tests had focused on the question of whether future stock prices could be predicted from past stock prices.[21] The answer to the tests was no, but as Lo and MacKinlay pointed out, while this answer is consistent with the random-walk hypothesis, it does not prove it. They asked a slightly different question: do any patterns or regularities that exist in the data depart from a purely random pattern in a statistically significant way?[22] Whether one could use any such patterns to make money was a different matter. Lo and MacKinlay found two patterns that provided powerful evidence against the random walk (both of which were consistent with Mandelbrot's findings). First, they found that there was a correlation between prices and time, and second, they discovered that the variance of market prices did not behave as the random-walk hypothesis said it should.[23]

Lo and MacKinlay spent much of the next decade answering various critiques of their result and buttressing it with further evidence. In addition, a host of other researchers, armed with increasingly powerful computers and statistical tools, began to uncover all sorts of interesting patterns in data from financial markets around the world.[24] The nails began to go into the random-walk coffin quite quickly. By the year 2000, in the seventh edition of his book, even Burton Malkiel, the author of *A Random Walk Down Wall Street,* had to admit that markets did not, in fact, follow a random walk.

Attack of the Econophysicists

At around the same time that Lo and MacKinlay were attacking the foundations of Traditional finance from inside the profession, another group of researchers began to storm the gates from the outside. On November 9, 1989, the Berlin Wall fell and the world celebrated. Suddenly everyone was talking about major cutbacks in defense spending and a "peace dividend." While this was great news for the world, to the thousands of physicists and mathematicians working in the U.S. national weapons labs such as Los Alamos and Sandia, a peace dividend meant unemployment. Likewise, on the other side of the world in the soon-to-be former USSR, the world-class scientists of the Soviet defense industry were about to lose their jobs as well. Concurrently, a booming Wall Street had an almost insatiable demand for highly trained mathematicians. Soon, demand found supply, and a flood of true-life rocket scientists from around the world ended up working at places like Goldman Sachs, Morgan Stanley, and various secretive hedge funds, where the scientists now competed with each other to price derivatives rather than to blow up the world.

At first, the physicists—most of them fairly young—simply digested the finance textbooks given to them and went about crunching their computer models looking for ways to make money. Eventually, though, many of them began to notice the disparities between the real world of data they were seeing and the textbook descriptions. At the same time, the breakthroughs in chaos theory, nonlinear dynamics, and complexity theory were going full throttle in the physics community. Inevitably, the physicists turned to these ideas for answers, and finance and complexity theory eventually met. Soon, the pages of traditional physical science journals such as *Physical Review Letters* and *Nature* began to fill up with articles on finance written by "econophysicists."[25] Through the 1990s, scientists such as Eugene Stanley, Jean-Phillippe Bouchard, Neil Johnson, Rosario Mantegna, and Didier Sornette resurrected and built on Mandelbrot's claims and began to confront Traditional finance with a vision of volatile, fat-tailed stock markets—a vision very different from the textbooks.[26]

One of the physicists who crossed over from the world of weapons labs into the world of Wall Street was Doyne Farmer. Farmer was one of the participants in the original Santa Fe Institute economics workshop, and we reviewed some of his work on power laws and stock markets in chapter 8. In 1991, Farmer quit his job as head of the Complex Systems Group at the Los Alamos National Laboratory to cofound, along with his longtime friend and fellow physicist, Norman Packard, a firm called the Prediction Company. The mission of their new firm was to apply the latest physics ideas to financial markets. A well-known figure in the physics community, Farmer had a reputation not only for his pioneering work in complex systems, but also for an attempt in his youth to use his physics knowledge to beat Las Vegas in roulette. He and several co-conspirators, including Packard, coded a nonlinear model of roulette into tiny computers that they installed in their shoes, and then set off to the casinos to make their fortune. They didn't quite make the millions that they had hoped for, but they were successful enough to inspire a Nevada state law forbidding computer-assisted gambling. The Prediction Company was their attempt at a "shoe computer" for the biggest casino of all— Wall Street. After eight years of working in real-world markets and trading for Prediction Company clients such as UBS, Farmer decided to return to academia and the Santa Fe Institute to apply what he had learned to the world of theory.[27]

Markets as Evolving Ecosystems

A fundamental claim of Traditional finance is that any patterns or signals in the market will be arbitraged away by ever vigilant and greedy investors. As noted earlier, Traditional finance assumes that all investors have access to the same information, and if there are any patterns in stock prices, investors will see them and take them into account in pricing decisions, thus driving the market back to its random walk. Farmer found, however, that the Traditional Economics notion of arbitrage suffers from the $20 bill problem of chapter 3. The equilibrium framing of Traditional finance causes economists to forget about time and forget that markets are dynamic systems. Farmer and his colleagues at the Prediction Company found that they could detect statistically significant signals in market data (figure 17-1).[28] These "signals" consisted of complex patterns and relationships between various factors that predicted future share prices (e.g., interest rates, trading volumes—as the signals were proprietary, they did not disclose exactly what they consisted of). Traditional theory says that any such signals, once discovered, should be arbitraged away immediately. But Farmer and his team found that the signals would persist over time, often for days, months, or even sometimes for as long as a decade (figure 17-1a). Often they would see the signals weaken over time, as traders

FIGURE 17-1

Signals Come and Go: Strength of Two Proprietary Predictive Signals, 1975–1998

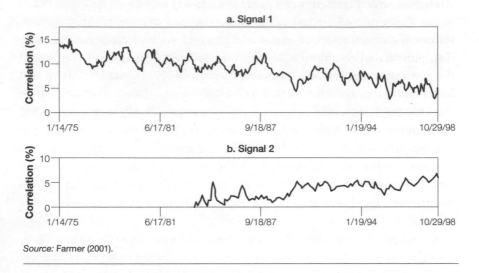

Source: Farmer (2001).

(including themselves) discovered and exploited them. But they also found that the complex, nonlinear dynamics of the markets meant that new signals were constantly being created even as old signals faded due to arbitrage (figure 17-1b).

In fact, the strong picture that Farmer got from his trading experience and research was that markets form a kind of evolving ecosystem. The markets are populated by heterogeneous traders and investors with a variety of mental models and strategies. As those agents interact with each other over time, they constantly learn and adapt their strategies—in fact, one could say they deductively-tinker their way through the Library of All Possible Investment Strategies. The complex interactions of these agents, their changing strategies, and new information from their environment causes patterns and trading opportunities to constantly appear and disappear over time.

The Santa Fe Institute's Brian Arthur poetically once called markets "ecosystems of expectations" to describe this interplay between agents and their strategies.[29] In chapter 6, we discussed the Santa Fe Artificial Stock Market Model built by Arthur, John Holland, and colleagues.[30] Their alternative to the perfectly rational idealization of Traditional finance was that investors are "inductively rational."[31] In the Santa Fe model, agents engaged in an evolutionary search for profitable strategies. Which strategies were successful at a particular time depended on the strategies the other agents in the market were using. Thus, a dynamic was created whereby particular combinations of strategies would create patterns or structures in the market, which in turn would change the behavior of other agents as they sought to exploit those strategies, which created further patterns causing other agents to react, and so on. The results of the Santa Fe model did a good job of replicating the key statistical characteristics of real-world markets, such as clustered volatility (i.e., punctuated equilibrium). Moreover, the model qualitatively replicated the coming-and-going of patterns that Farmer had observed.[32] The model had a limitation, however, in that its realism also made it complicated. The fact that the agents could choose from a near-infinite selection of possible strategies meant that the model was almost as difficult to understand as the real market itself. From his work in physics, Farmer also knew that complex macro behavior can sometimes be the result of quite simple micro behaviors. As Farmer put it, his goal was "not to formulate the most realistic possible market model, but rather to formulate the simplest model that is also reasonable."[33]

Leveraging his experience trading in real markets, Farmer began work on a new, simpler model.[34] Instead of allowing each agent to have its own "customized kitchen sink" of possible behaviors, he assumed that there were only three basic types of investors in the market.[35] First were the *value investors*, who buy or sell a stock on the basis of so-called fundamentals by looking at information signals such as a company's earnings, its growth, its competitive position, and so on. In effect, value investors are doing what Traditional theory says they should do.

The second type of agent was the *technical traders*. Instead of looking at the fundamentals, these investors looked at past prices and trading volumes to determine strategies. For example, they might see the price of a stock start to rise, and buy it to catch the rising tide. Traditional theory says that these investors should never make a profit, because if the market follows a random walk, there is no useful information in past prices. As Farmer noted, however, the real world is full of people trading with technical or hybrid technical-value strategies, so it was important to see what effect this group of investors might have on the market.

Farmer then added a third type of agent, a *liquidity trader*. This is someone who, for example, might be buying a house and sells a bunch of stock to get cash for the down payment. Traders like these aren't selling because they think the stock is over- or undervalued; they just need liquidity.

Farmer then put a final agent in his artificial market. The agent was not a trader, but nevertheless played a critical role: the *market maker*. Most Traditional finance models presuppose that the institutional details of how real world stock markets work do not matter much, and that prices are set by a

Walrasian auction.[36] As discussed earlier in the book, Léon Walras introduced the standard Traditional assumption that a godlike auctioneer matches buyers and sellers to set prices. Walras's inspiration for his auctioneer was the Paris Bourse from the late nineteenth century. But most modern financial markets moved on from Walrasian auctions long ago, and now employ *continuous double auctions* (continuous because the auction runs the entire time the market is open, and double because traders can both buy and sell). As we saw earlier, Farmer and his colleagues have shown that the institutional details of markets do play a significant role in market dynamics, particularly in generating power-law distributions of volatility. Although the market maker in this particular model was still a simplification compared to real world markets, it nonetheless was more realistic than the typical Traditional model as it used a continuous double auction rather than a Walrasian auction. This was important because it would ensure that the time dynamics of trading, and price impact of large orders, would be taken into account, versus the Walrasian assumption that everything happens at once.

Price Does Not Equal Value

Initially, Farmer created a market with just one fundamental agent and the market maker. Then he made it simpler still by assuming that the fundamental agent knew exactly what the true, perfectly rational value of the stock was at all times. In a bow to Traditional finance, Farmer also assumed that the true value followed a random walk. The fundamental agent was then given a simple trading rule: if the stock's price is less than fundamental value, buy; if it is higher, sell. The expectation was that this simple setup, with a perfectly rational agent and perfect information, would replicate the equilibrium conditions of Traditional finance, and as such, the market price would track the true value and follow a random walk.

It didn't (figure 17-2). Price and value did roughly track each other, but not perfectly. The cause was the same sort of time delay we examined in our discussion of dynamic systems in chapter 5. Recall the example of a shower in which there is a delay between turning the knob and the response in water temperature—at first you oscillate around the desired temperature, but then you eventually figure it out and the oscillations get smaller and smaller until you hit the target temperature. Now imagine that instead of there being a constant desired temperature, the desired temperature fluctuated randomly. In this case, the oscillations would never quite die down. Moreover, when the desired temperature took a big jump up, or a big dive down, you would be lagging even further behind and chasing it. Eventually, you would catch up, but you would overshoot it slightly. Thus, the actual temperature of your

FIGURE 17-2

Price Versus Value with a Rational Agent

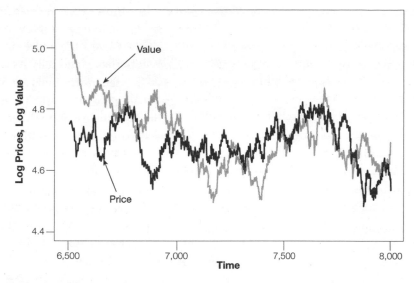

Source: Farmer and Joshi (2000).

shower would roughly track the random movements of the desired temperature over time, but not match it exactly. Your experience in the shower would look just like the graph in figure 17-2. In Farmer's model market, the small time delays between the actions of the trader and the response of the market maker created a dynamic relationship between the two, resulting in the less-than-perfect connection between price and value. The equilibrium view of Traditional finance simply assumes that everything happens all at once, and thus it hides these dynamics.

A Traditional Economist might reply, "Fine, but the deviations of price from value are unbiased, so we can just treat them as random noise, and the time delays involved in market making in the real world are very short, measured in seconds or minutes, so at timescales of days and weeks, this really shouldn't matter." But there is a counterargument. First, the deviations themselves aren't actually random. While the true value may be a random number, the price is determined by the dynamics of the trader's interacting with the market maker—it isn't noise; it is what physicists call *temporal structure*. That is, the prices formed by the interaction between the trader and the market maker have trends and momentum in them. Second, Farmer knew that while this temporal structure might start off having effects at the level of seconds and minutes, the structure might act like a grain of sand in an oyster and, through the dynamics of the system, lead to much-larger-scale patterns over time.

To show this, Farmer dropped a second type of agent into the model: a technical trader. Again, to keep things simple, he just assumed that the technical trader was a trend follower: when the price of the stock was going up, the trader bought; when it was going down, the trader sold. The effect of adding the technical trader into the mix was to amplify the dynamics. Returning to our shower example, imagine that you are again in the shower, trying to match the actual temperature to a randomly fluctuating desired temperature (in effect, you are the fundamental trader). But down in the basement, there is someone else turning the knobs of the water supply (the technical trader). Now, when you turn on the hot water to raise the temperature, there is a slight delay, but eventually the temperature starts to rise. Meanwhile, the technical trader in the basement sees the rising temperature and turns the control knob, putting even more hot water in the system, amplifying your action and causing the temperature to race up. You start to put on the cold to compensate, but you are now fighting against the technical trader's actions. Eventually, you put in enough cold and the temperature peaks and starts to drop—but then the technical shower-taker in the basement goes into reverse and starts sending cold water into the system. Your job of matching actual to desired temperature just got a whole lot harder. The minor fluctuations in the first scenario have now become major fluctuations, with long periods during which you are too hot or too cold, or even occasionally scalding or freezing.

This was in effect what happened in Farmer's model. The addition of a trend-following technical trader picked up on the temporal structure in prices and amplified it, and the dynamics of the fundamental and technical trader together created major, long-lasting departures from true value.[37] Farmer found that other real-world factors further amplified the separation of price and value. In particular, successful investors tend to reinvest their earnings, thus growing their capital and increasing the impact of their strategies on the market. So if a trend-following technical trader was successful for a period, its capital would grow driving price even further from value.

At this point, though, a Traditional economist might cry, "But what about arbitrage? Won't arbitragers drive price back to fundamental value?" According to Traditional finance, price and value *can* be different, but the difference is merely random, short-term noise as price bounces around the true value, and thus, on average, price equals value. As the departures from fundamental value are random and short term, no one can make any money from them, and thus the only sensible strategy is to be a fundamental investor. This assumption highlights a paradox built into the efficient-markets hypothesis. Milton Friedman first pointed out the paradox—markets need technical traders to arbitrage departures from fundamental value and keep markets efficient, but technical traders can't make any money in an efficient market and so will leave. It also brings up a related question that has bothered economists for decades. If markets are so efficient, and technical trading is not profitable, then why are there so many technical traders?

Farmer found an answer to the paradox. He took his model and set the fundamental value of the stock to a constant level. He then created a group of agents, *seasonal traders,* who simply bought and sold the stock in an alternating pattern. Their actions created a simple, regular, oscillating pattern in the price of the stock. Farmer next created a group of technical traders. He gave each technical trader a randomly generated strategy based on whether the price was going up or down during past periods (e.g., IF <price went down followed by up> THEN <buy> or IF <price went down followed by down again> THEN <sell>). Each agent was given a bit of money to start with, and successful trading agents would keep their profits and reinvest them. In effect, it was a simple evolutionary system. The agents would try various technical strategies, and the strategies that worked would be replicated and those that didn't would go bust. If Traditional finance was right, this should be a turkey shoot. Once the technical traders with the right strategy locked on to the oscillating pattern, their trading would counteract the oscillations and arbitrage the seasonal trading pattern out of the market, making it efficient again. But when Farmer ran his model, he found that something far more interesting happened.

At first, things went according to Traditional theory. Initially, the technical traders didn't have much money and so they didn't affect the price very much. But they quickly picked up on the oscillating pattern, started to arbitrage it, and, as they did, started to make a lot of money. With success, they started making bigger trades, which in turn began to affect the price. After some time, Farmer began to see the oscillations dampen as the traders arbitraged the inefficient pattern out of the market and brought it closer to the fundamental value of 21.5 (figure 17-3). After five thousand periods had passed, the oscillations were virtually gone, and the market looked as if it were rapidly approaching perfect efficiency. But then, volatility suddenly exploded, and prices began to move chaotically. What had happened was this: as the technical traders became richer, their trades became larger, and the large trades started introducing their own movements into the price. These movements created opportunities for other technical traders to try to arbitrage the patterns created by their fellow technical traders—when the technical traders had finished lunching on the seasonal traders, they began feeding off each other!

Farmer continued to run his model for many tens of thousands of iterations, and the crazy pattern just kept going and going. Notice that even

FIGURE 17-3

Fundamental Traders Fail to Arbitrage Technical Pattern

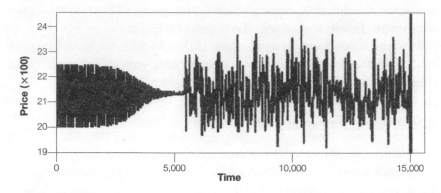

Source: Farmer (2001).

though the wild pattern after period five thousand in figure 17-3 looks random, it is not. The model is perfectly deterministic—there is no randomness in it at all—the emergent pattern is completely generated by the dynamics of the interacting agents. A Traditional economist might counter that the trading action between the technical traders is a zero-sum game, that money is just going from one technical pocket to another, and that on average, no one really makes any money from it. If they were perfectly rational, they would not play the game. They would exit at period five thousand, leaving the market in a pristine, efficient equilibrium. But as we have discussed, evidence shows that in real markets, people are not perfectly rational. Instead, people are biased toward optimism, believe they can do better than the next person, and learn as they go along. As investors experiment and try different strategies in the market, they leave in their wake patterns that other investors pick up on and exploit. As these other investors exploit those patterns, the result is new patterns, which still others pick up on, and so it goes. Some investors make money for a while, but then their fortunes turn. New investors enter and bring in more capital as they see opportunities, and some investors exit when their strategies fail. Farmer's model produced just the kind of behavior he witnessed in his real-world trading experience. As the complex dynamics of the market unfolded, patterns came and went over time, and the market moved in periods of quiet and storm.

Not only was Farmer's model consistent with his personal experience, it was also consistent with a large body of empirical evidence. First, Farmer's results replicated the key qualitative statistical characteristics of real-world data, including the fat tails that Mandelbrot discovered. Second, despite the claims of Traditional theory, a number of studies show that some forms of technical trading can be profitable.[38] Finally, several studies have shown that fundamental value only explains a small proportion of overall stock price movements. Figure 17-4b shows the results of one such study, and the similarity to the results from Farmer's model (figure 17-4a) is immediately apparent.[39] Note that this is not just a short-term effect; wide differences between value and price can last for multiyear periods, even over decades.

A New Definition of Market Efficiency

Are financial markets efficient? Examined through the lens of Complexity Economics, financial markets are an evolving ecosystem of competing trading strategies. Thus, asking whether markets are efficient makes about as much sense as asking whether the ecosystem of the Amazon rain forest is efficient. Efficient compared to what?

We can, however, ask a series of more meaningful and specific questions. Do the markets react very quickly to new information? Yes, absolutely. Numerous studies show that when news hits, markets react almost instantaneously.[40] The competitiveness of the market evolutionary system ensures this sensitivity—just as when a tender young leaf from the Amazonian tree canopy hits the rain forest floor, the vibrations set a host of insects charging down on it almost immediately. In fact, the markets have been getting faster at processing information over time with developments such as CNN, Bloomberg, the Internet, and immense amounts of computer power. Interestingly, Traditional theory predicts that with better information, prices should become less volatile relative to value, when in reality, the opposite has been happening. As the power of information and technology has increased, it appears to have made markets more volatile, not less so.[41] The evolutionary explanation is that as information technology improves, it opens up the design space of possible investment strategies and increases arbitrage and technical trading opportunities rather than decreasing them, and thus we have seen a dramatic rise in the number of so-called hedge funds.[42]

Are markets efficient at processing information? The answer again is yes. Markets are brilliant devices for sorting through vast amounts of information from large numbers of people and coming up with an aggregate view of what that information means.[43] There have been experiments using markets to forecast everything from election results to sports scores to Academy Awards results, and the markets often make predictions that are more accurate than either individual experts or simple polling.[44] This informational efficiency is a cornerstone of the efficient-markets hypothesis. However, the

FIGURE 17-4

Evolutionary Model Is Qualitatively Similar to Actual Data

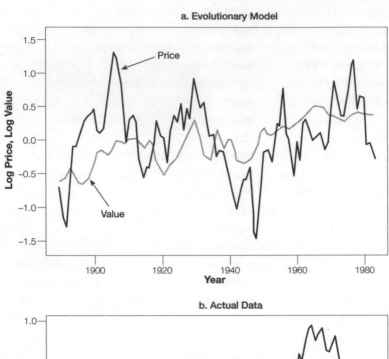

a. Evolutionary Model

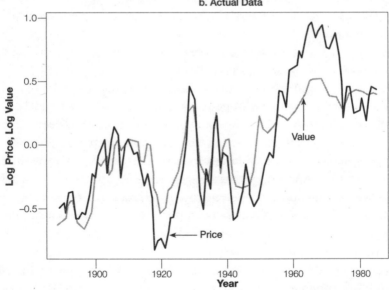

b. Actual Data

Source: Farmer (2002).

theory assumes that markets only use their great forecasting power on information related to a stock's fundamentals, while in the real world, traders also make bets on what they think other traders are doing and thinking. This more dynamic outlook puts the market in an infinite loop of forming expectations on the expectations of people's forming expectations of people who are forming expectations, and so on. This infinite regress was pointed out by John Maynard Keynes—"we devote our intelligence to anticipating what average opinion expects average opinion to be"—and was elaborated mathematically by Brian Arthur in his Bar Problem, discussed earlier in the book.[45] These expectations of expectations feed the evolutionary dynamics of the market, which means that while the markets are very powerful information processors, they are not efficient in the Traditional Economics sense of the word.

Are investors perfectly rational? No. But are investors self-interested? Yes, financial markets are not charities, and are driven by fear and greed as much as ever. Are investors smart? In general, yes, most money is managed by professionals who range from street-smart traders to PhD rocket scientists. Money managers have all the strengths of human beings, such as superb pattern recognition and creative learning capabilities, as well as all the weaknesses, including irrationalities and biases. Are markets competitive? The answer is, "highly." Seeing the stressed faces on any trading floor makes that clear. And with the deregulation of global capital flows, markets have only become more so.

Do smart, competitive investors arbitrage profitable opportunities and drive markets to efficiency? The answer is sometimes, but not always. Farmer has pointed out that Traditional theory makes two crucial assumptions about market efficiency.[46] First, in order for arbitrage to work, traders must be able to recognize strategies that make abnormal profits. Second, the amounts of money they put into trading abnormally profitable strategies must be enough to arbitrage the gains away and bring the market back to efficiency. Farmer notes that both of these assumptions are problematic in the real world. The measure of an abnormally profitable strategy is the *information ratio* (also known as the Sharpe ratio or return-to-risk ratio), which is the expected annual return divided by the expected standard deviation of that return. A strategy with high returns and low risk will thus have a high information ratio, while a low return, high-risk strategy will have a low information ratio. Most traders consider an information ratio of 1 as the sign of an attractive strategy. But as Farmer notes, learning the information ratio of a strategy takes time. If one assumes that returns are normally distributed (a bell curve) then the laws of statistics mean that it would take four years of data to be 95 percent confident that a trader's strategy had an information ratio of 1 (one can't rely on historical data alone because of the problem of data mining—one must actually test the strategy going forward). If the returns have fat tails (as data shows they do) then it takes even longer. Thus the rule of thumb, common among traders, that it takes five years of performance to know whether a strategy is any good or not is probably about right. This timescale is further lengthened by the "millionth monkey" problem. If enough traders are trading, then the odds are high that one of them will have a good five year run just by pure luck, further lengthening the time to confidently identify abnormally profitable strategies.

The second assumption has similar difficulties. Traditional theory assumes that infinite amounts of capital are instantaneously available for abnormally profitable strategies. But in the real world, successful traders need to accumulate capital over time. For example, if a trader started with $1 million and earned a 25 percent return (which would be very good) he or she would take thirty years to increase his or her funds under management to $1 billion. If in addition the trader doubled his or her capital every year from outside sources, it would still take ten years. It is possible for successful traders to raise large funds from outside investors much more quickly, but Farmer's point is that the timescale to establish a track record and then to raise the funds is measured in years. But markets do not stand still during periods of years, and profitable trading strategies can thus come and go on timescales faster than the market can arbitrage them to efficiency.

Are there magic formulas for getting rich? The answer is no. Samuelson was right when he said that it is hard to get rich in Las Vegas, Churchill Downs, or the local Merrill Lynch office. But he was wrong as to the reasons why. It is not because financial markets follow random walks; rather, it is because you would have a hard time getting rich in any competitive evolutionary environment, whether you are a trader on Wall Street or a tree frog in the Brazilian rain forest. There is an important difference, though, between Wall Street and Vegas. In Vegas, no matter how hard you try and how smart you are, you will never improve your odds (unless you bring a shoe computer). But Wall Street is not a game of pure chance—it is a highly dynamic, constantly evolving, complex system. Inevitably, at any point in time, some people will understand the system better than others and will get rich, at least for a while. Traditional Economics should ask itself, if financial markets are so efficient, then why does Wall Street seem to have a lot more Porsches and Ferraris than Main Street has? But competitive advantage is just as temporary in financial markets as it is in product and services markets. Inevitably, someone else will come along with a better idea, a cleverer strategy, or a more powerful technology and will take his or her moment in the sun.

The efficient-markets hypothesis is a myth born of nineteenth-century theories of equilibrium and Bachelier's random walk. Although Traditional market efficiency may not be a very meaningful concept, financial markets are highly *effective* evolutionary systems. Markets are the best Social Technology devised yet for integrating the views of large numbers of people to put prices on complex assets, and to allocate capital. Furthermore, the competitive intensity of markets ensures that they are fast at processing information, and that there is pressure on their participants to continuously innovate. Andrew Lo of MIT calls this evolutionary effectiveness of markets the "Adaptive Markets Hypothesis."[47] If there is a magic formula on New York's Wall Street, London's City, or the other markets of the world, it is differentiate, select, amplify, and repeat.

The Complexity Economics view of finance is still forming and many questions remain unanswered. But it is clear that the Traditional theories are inadequate and new approaches are needed. For Wall Street, the City, and other financial markets, the implications of Complexity finance are only just beginning to be felt. A number of firms, both major banks and hedge funds, are employing the statistical and modeling techniques of Complexity Economics in devising their investment strategies—and many of these firms either employ or are advised by various econophysicists and behavioral economists. Naturally, these firms are very secretive about what they are doing and the results they are achieving. But inevitably, complexity science will change the world of investing and will yield new innovations in the Red Queen race of investment strategy.

The impact on individual investors is likely to be longer term. Complexity finance does not change any of the broad guidance generally given to individual investors, such as the importance of diversifying one's portfolio or investing for the long term. But most innovations in finance eventually trickle down from institutional to retail investors, and at some point, funds employing these techniques are likely to become available to individual investors as well.

Implications for Managers

There is, however, another constituency for whom Complexity finance raises several important issues—business executives. Complexity finance affects the world of business in three areas. First, widely used methods for calculating a company's cost of capital may be wrong. Second, Complexity finance raises questions about the appropriateness of granting stock options in executive compensation. Third, and perhaps most importantly, it challenges us to think in new ways about the fundamental purpose of corporations and the nature of shareholder capitalism. We will discuss each in turn.

The Cost of Capital

A company's cost of capital sounds like a rather dry and technical subject. But it plays a crucial role in how senior executives make some of their most important decisions, including what investments to make, which strategies to follow, and whether to undertake a merger or an acquisition.[48]

All companies get their capital from someone, whether it is lent by banks or invested by shareholders. The providers of that capital need to be paid a return, and the cost of capital is simply the weighted average of the returns expected by the various providers of capital. For example, if half a firm's capital were from a bank loan at 6 percent interest and the other half from investors who were expecting a 12 percent return, then the firm's cost of capital would be 9 percent. This number, then, provides the company with a benchmark—any investments that management undertakes must provide at least a 9 percent return in order to pay for the cost of the capital employed. Since shareholders bear the risk of whether management succeeds in this task (debt-holders are protected from downside but do not share in the upside), any returns management generates above the cost of the capital benchmark create value for shareholders, and any returns below it destroy shareholder value.

Calculating exactly what that benchmark number is then takes on crucial importance in judging whether a management team is doing a good job. Unfortunately, the most widely used method for calculating this number is derived straight from the theories of Traditional finance. The standard method is known as the *capital asset pricing model*, or *CAPM*, and comes with all the usual assumptions about perfectly rational investors, efficient markets, and equilibrium.[49] But it also makes a crucial assumption about the way investors manage risk. Developed by University of Chicago economist Harry Markowitz in the 1950s, CAPM assumes that *all* investors hold portfolios of stocks that optimize the trade-off between risk and return. If everyone in the market owns such portfolios, they can then be combined to create the *market portfolio*. The risk of an individual stock is then measured relative to the theoretical market portfolio. This risk factor, known as a stock's *beta*, is then used to calculate the cost of equity, or the return that shareholders need to receive to make the risk worthwhile.

The problem is that no one, let alone everyone in the market, actually holds Markowitz's perfect portfolios.[50] Actually implementing Markowitz's idea is virtually impossible. For example, the theory assumes perfect information on company risk, an unlimited ability to sell stocks short, and the same time horizon for all investors. In addition, because risk and return profiles change, the market portfolio must be continuously updated. But in the real world adding, removing, and reweighting the stocks in a portfolio involves significant transaction costs, thus meaning that people do not reallocate their portfolio as often as the theory says they should. In fact, not even economists themselves can create the theoretical market portfolio, and when they test the theory, they simply use a weighted average of all the stocks in the market as a proxy.[51] The reality is that investment managers tend to be evaluated against much-easier-to-calculate indices such as the S&P 500 or FTSE 100, rather than Markowitz's theoretical market portfolio. Furthermore, evidence shows that managers "chase returns" rather than optimize risk-return trade-offs in the way CAPM assumes.[52]

Not surprisingly, the unrealistic assumptions in CAPM mean that the theory's predictions do poorly in empirical tests. Most importantly, the variable beta has been shown to have virtually no informational value as a measure of risk.[53] Consequently, the calculations for a company's cost of equity based on the CAPM formula are not very meaningful. To add insult to injury, using the CAPM in the real world requires a further set of assumptions and judgments. For example, calculations of the risk premium of equity over debt vary widely, depending on the particular index and periods used, and one has to make assumptions about what risk-free rate to use as well.[54] The bottom line is that from both theoretical and practical grounds, the CAPM has very questionable value as a method for calculating the cost of capital. Other alternatives, such as "multifactor models" (sometimes called the arbitrage pricing model), have been proposed, but these have been shown to share many of the same problems that CAPM has.[55]

Warren Buffett, "the Sage of Omaha," has summarized his views on the cost of capital: "Charlie [Munger] and I have not the faintest idea what our cost of capital is and we think the whole concept is fairly crazy. Frankly, I have never seen a cost of capital that makes sense to me."[56] Unfortunately, while Traditional methods for calculating the cost of capital are flawed, better alternatives have yet to be developed.[57] An important priority for the Complexity finance research program is to develop a methodology to replace CAPM, and a new way of measuring risk. At present, chief financial officers and other executives are stuck using the Traditional methods, but they should use these numbers with an enormous grain of salt, and thoroughly test the sensitivity of any decisions to the results of these calculations.

Do Stock Options Make Sense?

One of the results of the academic finance revolution of the 1970s was to make stock market performance the primary metric by which boards and management teams measure the success or failure of a corporation. This in turn created a movement to link executive compensation with stock market performance through the use of stock options.

The motivation and original idea behind this movement made great sense. Public corporations suffer from a built-in *principal-agent problem,* which pits the principals (shareholders) in a company against the agents (the CEO and his or her management team). On the one hand, shareholders want the company they own to be managed for the maximum value of their shares. On the other hand, the CEO and management team, if left to their own devices, might manage the company to maximize other things, like their salaries, the fancy artwork in the lobby, and the size of the corporate jet. In the 1960s and 1970s, numerous companies became virtual prisoners of their management teams, with CEOs who ran their companies into the ground while maximizing their salaries and egos. The Traditional finance professors did everyone a great service by reminding us that it is the shareholders who own a company and that CEOs and management teams work for those shareholders and not for themselves.

A logical way to align the interests of owners and management is to measure the management team on stock price performance and then give them financial incentives to do things that raise the share price. The view was that the best way to do this was to give managers stock options that would tie their future compensation to future stock performance. This idea caught on like wildfire in the 1980s, particularly as a wave of hostile takeovers put boards under pressure to improve their companies' share price performance. Thus, stock options jumped from 23 percent of the value of the median U.S. CEO's pay package in 1983, to 45 percent in 1998.[58]

It's a good idea in theory, but from the perspectives of both Complexity finance and actual practice, it is a bit more problematic. The fiduciary duty of management teams to serve shareholder interests is inscribed in law in most countries, and most Complexity economists would not disagree with the importance of the principal-agent issue. They would, however, point out a major problem. CEOs and management teams don't actually control stock prices. They control things such as strategy, costs, investments, and people, which in turn influence things such as revenue, profits, return on capital, and growth. The levers that CEOs and management teams have under their control affect a company's ability to create economic value, but only indirectly affect stock price.

Traditional economists argued that the practice of tying executive performance to stock price was fine because in an efficient market, the fundamentals that management influences also drive stock price, particularly in the long term. But as we have seen, in the real world, price does not always track value, and the deviations can be significant and last for years. There is, of course, *some* correlation between price and fundamental value, and the market is not completely insensitive to the actions of a management team, but the correlation is loose at best. In effect, we are judging CEOs on how well they drive a car with a very loose steering wheel.

As we have seen, the interplay between investment strategies, trader psychology, market institutional structures, and other factors beyond a management team's control can sometimes far outweigh fundamental factors in driving share price. For example, the enormous bubble in share prices during the 1990s made many CEOs incredibly rich for doing little more than riding the wave. Likewise, the bursting of the bubble had the opposite effect, taking down CEO compensation among both the stars and the dogs. Research by McKinsey & Company shows that from 1991 to 2000, about 70 percent of the returns of individual companies was due to market factors and that only about 30 percent was due to company-specific factors.[59] In theory, one could remove the effects of movements in broad market indices, but the relevance of the remaining component of price movement would still be questionable. Did the stock price go up because the market liked the CEO's new strategy, or because computers at several large hedge funds were locked in a multidimensional mathematical battle? There is no real way to know.

Wiring CEO compensation tightly into stock market performance has also inevitably changed CEO behavior. Some of it undoubtedly has been for the better, making CEOs feel more accountable for their company's performance. But it has also caused many CEOs to obsess over the twitches and ticks of the market and adopt a very short-term perspective toward managing what they think the market wants (usually the next quarter's earnings) rather than focusing on long-term value creation and building a strong, adaptive organization. We have also seen the dark downside of stock market obsession with the Enron, WORLDCOM, and Tyco scandals, in which management fear and greed led to earnings manipulation and outright fraud.

I am not claiming that CEOs and management teams have *no* influence on stock market performance—of course they do. But they are only one of many players in determining share price, and the fundamental signals they generate may often be drowned out by the cacophony of dynamics generated by a complex, evolving market. Nor am I arguing that CEOs should have no link to the performance of their stocks; we certainly don't want to go back to the bad old days of unaccountable CEOs holding shareholders hostage. But rather than holding CEOs accountable for an uncontrollable share price, we should hold them accountable for what they actually control: fundamental economic performance and long-term value creation. Since the early 1990s, Harvard Business School professor Robert Kaplan and his coauthor,

David Norton, have been advocating an approach to measuring corporate performance—an approach they call the *balanced scorecard*.[60] They note that no single metric, including share price, provides a complete picture of a company's performance. Instead, Kaplan and Norton recommend that each company analyze the factors that drive value creation in its business model, and custom-build a scorecard of measures around those factors. Such a scorecard should include a mixture of accounting, financial market, and other metrics (e.g., talent and customer metrics) that cover a firm's growth, profitability, and return on capital, as well as provide both backward-looking and forward-looking perspectives. The overall emphasis should be on the management team's success in creating economic value over the long term.[61]

Undoubtedly, new measures of company performance will be developed as research on financial markets continues. But in the meantime, such a scorecard can provide a more relevant basis for the performance contract between management and shareholders (and their representatives on the board) than just the gyrations of share price.

What Is the Goal of a Corporation?

If stock price movements are a questionable basis for measuring corporate performance, then this raises a larger question: what should the goal of a corporation be? Traditional economists agree that the purpose of corporations, or more generally, firms, is to serve the economic interests of society. As we saw early on, general equilibrium theory says that resources will be optimally allocated for society if managers seek to maximize the profits of their individual firms and if consumers seek to maximize their happiness from consumption. As John Maynard Keynes once put it, "Capitalism is the astounding belief that the most wickedest of men will do the most wickedest of things for the greatest good of everyone." So the best way managers can serve society is to maximize the profits of their enterprises.[62]

The goal of profit maximization, however, creates a problem. How do we know if management is truly maximizing its profits? Is a 10 percent profit good enough? How about 15 percent? What do we compare it to? In the view of Traditional Economics, the best judge of whether management is doing a good job is the capital markets. Self-interested investors will look to put their capital where it will earn the highest return for the risk involved. Since debt capital gets paid a fixed amount of interest, while equity returns swing with company profitability, shareholders are the best judges of whether management is doing a good job. Thus, profit maximization gets operationalized as *maximize shareholder value*.

In addition, many countries spell out legal obligations, or *fiduciary duties,* that boards and management teams have to serve the economic interests of shareholders. The United States and Great Britain go the farthest in elevating shareholders to a position of primacy. The legal systems of other countries, in particular many continental European countries and Japan, also provide management with fiduciary duties to shareholders, but shareholders are viewed as one of many *stakeholders* whose interests must be met. Among the stakeholders are employees (usually represented by labor unions), consumers, the communities in which the companies operate, and the government. For example, in Holland, large companies are required to have labor representatives on their boards, and the company's objective is defined as the continuity of the business rather than maximizing shareholder value. Advocates of shareholder capitalism argue that such stakeholder systems muddy the waters by trying to satisfy competing interest groups, leave management less accountable, and in fact serve overall society *less* well than shareholder-based systems. As evidence, shareholder advocates point to the high-productivity, high-growth, and high-employment economy that shareholder capitalism has created in the United States.[63]

This is not merely an academic issue. Questions over whose interests corporations should serve lie at the heart of heated debates over corporate governance reforms, corporate social-responsibility initiatives, antiglobalization protests, and the future of the European Union's economic model.[64]

Endure and Grow

Complexity Economics does not necessarily contradict the Traditional line of argument. Markets are still the most effective mechanism for pricing and allocating resources. Shareholders are still the legal owners of companies. And management must still be held accountable for its performance. But Complexity theory does offer a more nuanced view, raises some important questions, and suggests an alternative, objective function.

If we return to the first principles of our evolutionary framework, perhaps we can get some insights into the question of corporate objectives. As we discussed in chapter 9, evolutionary systems have a stark and pristine logic to them—good replicators get replicated. The objective function of any schema must be the survival and replication (or amplification) of its interactor. Any other objective function is a recipe for extinction. Translated into an economic context, this means that the objective of any Business Plan should be the survival and amplification of its business. It is therefore management's job to devise and execute Business Plans with this objective function. Put into more conventional terms, this means that it is management's job to devise and execute Plans that enable the businesses of their firm to endure and grow over time.

At first glance, an objective function of "enduring and growing" might sound closer to the Dutch objective of continuity than to the U.S. objective of maximizing shareholder value. But further reflection reveals that continuity and the maximization of shareholder value may not be so incompatible after all.

All evolutionary systems operate under a set of constraints imposed by the laws of thermodynamics. Survival and replication require flows of entropy-fighting energy, matter, and information. In biological systems, this means that all organisms face a thermodynamic profit constraint whereby calories ingested must, over time, be equal to or greater than calories burned. Good replicators are calorically profitable replicators, and they manage to be profitable in a competitive environment where resources are finite. Likewise, in economic systems, entropy reduction requires flows of energy, matter, and information (which in modern economies are measured in currencies), and all businesses face a profit constraint under which the inflows must be equal to or greater than the outflows.

In evolutionary systems, profitability is not an objective in and of itself; *rather, it is a fundamental constraint* that must be met if a business is to achieve the objective of survival and replication (or enduring and growing). The management thinker Charles Handy illustrates this distinction by noting that eating is a constraint on living (and a very vital one), but no one would claim that the purpose of life is to eat.[65]

But if we unpack the notion of profitability in an economic context, we find yet another set of constraints. To successfully execute a Business Plan, a management team must create an ecosystem of cooperation in and around the organization. First, capital must be attracted to the enterprise and the providers of that capital must see a potential return that is better than their alternative investment opportunities. Second, employees must be attracted and given incentives to work productively. Third, suppliers must see a profitable relationship with the business. And fourth, the business must provide goods and services that people want. But that is not the end of it. Management must also ensure that the business meets its legal obligations, pays its taxes, and does not do anything that causes the general populace to want to shut it down. Profitability is in fact a multidimensional problem in pleasing lots of people. In evolutionary terms, this is the economic fitness function: fit companies do a better job in meeting this multidimensional constraint than unfit ones do. Thus, from an evolutionary perspective, shareholder-ism versus stakeholder-ism is a false dichotomy. The fitness function is what it is—it doesn't matter whether one calls it shareholder-ism or stakeholder-ism—it is simply what a management team has to do for its business to endure and grow.

Shareholder-ism versus stakeholder-ism is also a false dichotomy in practical terms. Most advocates of shareholder capitalism acknowledge that a company that is unfair to its employees, breaks laws, and treats its customers poorly will be unlikely to provide good long-run returns to its shareholders. And most advocates of a stakeholder system admit that companies must generate a competitive return on capital to keep their investors on board. The key to this practical equivalence between shareholder and stakeholder systems is competitive markets; labor, capital, customers, and suppliers must all be able to go somewhere else.

But there is a further reason why Traditional Economics distinguishes shareholders from other stakeholders; only shareholders get the *residual claims* of the organization. In other words, they get what is left over after all the other claimants have been paid their due and are therefore at risk of the other stakeholders' raiding the company and leaving nothing for them. Consequently, shareholders are taking on more risk and need more protection. But everyone takes on risk in a cooperative venture—employees risk their careers, consumers risk whether a product will live up to expectations, and so on. If markets are free and competitive, then those risks should be reflected in prices (this is something Traditional economists should agree with). Equity capital is risky, but that is why it demands a higher return than debt capital.

Finally, some might argue that even if shareholder primacy is not a function of economics, it is enshrined in the law of a number of countries, particularly the United States. But this is not quite true, either. Such laws do spell out obligations to shareholders, but they also spell out obligations to all the other stakeholders as well. If any stakeholder is primary in the eyes of U.S. law, it is the U.S. government itself, which ensures that taxes take precedent over any other company obligation. The legal perspective is then no different from the evolutionary economic perspective; management must meet its obligations to *all* stakeholders.

Thus, from both an evolutionary and a practical perspective, paying a competitive return to one's shareholders is a constraint, not an objective, and while it may be a vitally important constraint, it is nonetheless only one of many constraints in the economic fitness function. This then brings us back to the objective itself. What does the objective "to endure and grow" mean?

To answer this question, we need to return to the subject of corporate excellence. Which is the more "excellent" company, Wang Laboratories, whose stock rose like a comet in the 1960s and 1970s, had world-beating performance for several years, but then flamed out and disappeared in the 1980s, or DuPont, whose stock has tended to underperform the broad market indices for much of its history, but has been around since 1802 and had $27 billion in revenue in 2005 and employed sixty thousand people?[66] Or what about Ye Olde Fighting Cocks Pub, which has been satisfying the refreshment needs of the citizens of Saint Albans, England, continuously since 795 AD, but has never grown beyond its modest size of a village pub?

Most people would intuitively say DuPont. While Wang grew spectacularly for a period, it did not endure, and while Ye Olde Fighting Cocks Pub has had impressive endurance, it has not grown. DuPont has managed to do both. Despite the fact that its stock has trailed the market average, as the Wangs of the world have entered and exited, DuPont grew from a start-up gunpowder maker to a major global chemicals, materials, and life sciences company and has endured for over two centuries. A Traditional economist would agree, since the total economic value created by DuPont over time has been much greater than that created by the other two (as measured by net present value). In fact, to endure and grow, DuPont has had to do everything a Traditional economist would claim it is supposed to do. It has had to be profitable, because unprofitable companies do not endure, and it has had to give its capital providers a competitive return (even if it has not been the highest return), as growth requires capital.[67]

One might then ask, "If Traditional Economics and Complexity Economics lead roughly to the same place, albeit by different routes, then what is the difference?" Perhaps the distinction between constraints and objectives is just academic word mincing.

The critical difference lies in how management teams apply these concepts. The objective of maximizing shareholder value has been operationalized by many management teams as an obsession with the swings in short-term stock price and quarterly earnings results. A survey of over four hundred chief financial officers conducted for the National Bureau of Economic Research found that the majority of companies viewed quarterly earnings as the key metric they should manage in the belief that by managing earnings, the companies would maximize their stock price.[68] Quarterly earnings announcements may indeed move prices, but as we have seen, such news may be far from the only thing moving prices. This fixation on quarterly earnings in turn often distorts management decision making. In the same survey, a majority of the CFOs said that they would forgo value-creating long-term investments if it meant missing analyst earnings estimates, and more than three-quarters said they would sacrifice economic value for a smooth earnings record.

A management team that was focused on enduring and growing would be likely to take a more balanced view.[69] The team members would focus on the levers that they could actually control, which would be the levers of economic value creation, rather than share price. Management would also more explicitly recognize the multidimensional nature of long-term survival and growth, and while shareholders would remain a vitally important constituency, a team pursuing endurance and growth would reallocate management time and attention toward actions that ensure healthy relationships with the full set of stakeholders. The focus on endurance of the institution as a goal would naturally encourage a long-term perspective on investment, and greater attention to building the foundations of longevity through factors such as a strong organizational culture. Meanwhile, an equally intense focus on growth would keep the pressure on performance high, provide a perpetual source of challenge, and spur innovation. Certainly, a company can grow but destroy economic value by investing in growth that is unprofitable or that earns an inadequate return on its capital. But again, the two objectives naturally balance each other—reckless investments in unprofitable growth endanger the goal of longevity, while too much conservatism in the name of institutional endurance runs counter to the goal of growth.

Not only would the objectives of endurance and growth help management clarify its raison d'être and better balance its decision making, but the objectives would also help management in communicating its goals to important constituencies, in particular, employees and external interest groups. Few employees jump out of bed in the morning fired up to maximize shareholder value. Most employees don't have stock options, and they view shareholders as big, rich, anonymous institutions. But employees can attach to the concepts of building a great, lasting institution that creates opportunities for people through growth.

Likewise, external constituencies, including politicians and activists, have a difficult time relating to maximizing shareholder value as the purpose of corporations. They see corporations as existing to serve the larger interests of society and, rightly or wrongly, don't buy the logic that serving shareholders is also serving society. This mind-set has created enormous communications problems in recent debates over corporate social responsibility and public relations headaches for many management teams.[70] Such constituencies would no doubt have an easier time seeing the connection between societal and corporate interests if the expressed goals of management were to build enduring institutions that provide products and services that people want, generate employment, pay taxes, operate within the law, maintain good relationships with external constituencies, and are innovating and growing to provide more of these societal benefits in the future.

Finally and not surprisingly, several studies have found that maximizing shareholder value is often not the lodestar of companies that, like DuPont, have both endured for a long time and grown to a large size. For example,

Arie de Gues, in *The Living Company*, a book based on a famous Royal Dutch/Shell study of twenty-seven large, long-lived companies, describes how the companies profiled saw their purpose as to "survive and thrive."[71] In a similar vein, James Collins and Jerry Porras, in *Built to Last*, studied eighteen long-lived companies and summarize their attitude as "more than profits." The authors add that for these companies, "profit is like oxygen, food, water, and blood for the body; they are not the *point* of life, but without them, there is no life."[72]

It is no coincidence that the objectives of enduring and growing echo the imperatives of executing and adapting discussed in the previous chapter. Both stem from the same evolutionary logic. The fact that companies are typically better at executing than adapting undoubtedly has a link to the short-term focus on earnings. Embracing the dual objectives of endurance and growth forces management to fully confront the inherent tensions in executing and adapting and creates pressure to strike a more equal balance between the two. In a competitive evolutionary environment, "endure and grow" is the *what*, and "adapt and execute" is the *how*. Enduring and growing are the timeless demands placed on designs in an evolutionary system.

CHAPTER EIGHTEEN

Politics and Policy

THE END OF LEFT VERSUS RIGHT

THE WORLD of economic ideas has always been linked to the world of politics, and historically, paradigm shifts in economic theory have led to reconfigurations of the political landscape. Adam Smith's ideas helped inspire a dramatic expansion in free trade in the nineteenth century. Karl Marx's theories provided the impetus for cataclysmic changes in the twentieth century. The Neoclassical paradigm laid the intellectual foundations of Western capitalist orthodoxy, while Keynesianism tempered that orthodoxy with a role for the state. In the period after World War II, state activism in Western economies grew to new heights, until challenged in the 1980s by Ronald Reagan and Margaret Thatcher, who in turn were inspired by the theories of economists such as Milton Friedman and Friedrich Hayek.

How will the ideas of Complexity Economics affect politics and policy? The time frame between the intellectual development of economic ideas and their larger impact on society has typically been measured in decades, if not longer. Marx published his *Communist Manifesto* in 1848, yet the Russian Revolution did not take place until 1917. Keynes published his most significant works in the 1930s, yet the greatest impact of his ideas was arguably not until the postwar period. Even two centuries after the publication of *The Wealth of Nations*, many political figures still seem to have a difficult time understanding the ideas of Adam Smith. While it may be some years before we feel the full impact of Complexity Economics on the public sphere, it is nonetheless intriguing to think about what some of those implications might be.

The first question most people ask about Complexity Economics in relation to politics is, whose side is it on? Does Complexity Economics lean towards the Right or the Left? Some might suspect that Complexity Economics favors the Right because of my claims that it takes a positive view of markets. Others might suspect that Complexity Economics tilts toward the Left, because I have also argued that markets are not as efficient as Traditional orthodoxy claims. In this chapter, I will propose that Complexity Economics is really neither Left nor Right. In fact, the Complexity approach to economics has the potential to make the historical framing of politics obsolete.

We will begin with a brief review of the history of the Left-Right framework. I will argue that there are two deeply rooted disagreements at the heart of this historical divide: one is a fundamental difference in how the two sides see human nature, and the other is a difference in views on the role of states versus markets. Complexity Economics offers a new perspective on both of these age-old debates that fits neatly into neither camp. We will then discuss examples of how Complexity Economics can be applied to issues in three areas: poverty in the developing world, the erosion of what researchers call "social capital" in the United States and other developed countries, and economic inequality. We will then close with some thoughts on future directions for Complexity Economics research.

A Framework Past Its Time

The idea of viewing politics on a spectrum from Left to Right has been impressive in its durability, lasting well over two hundred years. The terms originated in the layout of the French National Assembly, created during the Revolution of 1789. The Third Estate revolutionaries sat on the left side of the chamber, while the conservative First Estate royalists sat on the right. From its earliest days, the term *Left* had connotations of fighting for social progress, defending the less privileged, and remaking society for the better— but the term also had the whiff of utopianism. Likewise, the term *Right* had connotations of emphasizing individual freedom and responsibility, protecting social stability, and a belief in natural, incremental progress—but also had a subtext of defending the privileged and powerful. The economic dimensions of the Left-Right dichotomy were crystallized during the next century by the theories of Marx and Engels, and the epic battle between socialism and capitalism.[1] By the early twentieth century, the Left had become associated with policies advocating strong government intervention in the economy, ranging from outright ownership of economic assets in communist economies, to partial ownership and a regulatory role in social democracies, while the Right had become the haven of free-market advocates. Although the specific meanings of the terms continued to evolve, the broad dimensions of the divide remained constant through the mid- to late twentieth century: states versus markets, social liberalism versus social conservatism, and the needs of the many versus the rights of the individual.

After the Berlin Wall fell in 1989 and communism collapsed, Johns Hopkins University professor Francis Fukuyama boldly predicted that the great debate had finally been resolved and that the "End of History" had arrived.[2] During this period, a number of intellectuals and politicians attempted to reframe the terms of Left versus Right. In 1996 the Democratic Leadership Council in the United States published its New Progressive Declaration, and in 1998, Anthony Giddens (now Lord Giddens), the head of the London School of Economics and an adviser to Tony Blair, published a book titled The Third Way.[3] Both the "New Democrats" in the United States and "New Labour" in the United Kingdom, as they came to be called, argued for a position that sought to combine the wealth-generating success of capitalism with the humanitarian objectives of socialism—in essence directing capitalist means to socialist ends. This framing helped propel the economic ideologies of both the Clinton administration and the Blair government, and showed up in policies such as Clinton's reform of the U.S. welfare system, and Blair's attempts to inject market forces into the struggling British National Health Service. The idea of capitalism with a friendly face even had appeal to the Right side of the spectrum. George W. Bush's first election campaign was largely centered around the idea of "compassionate conservatism."

But history had not ended. The mobs on the streets of Seattle protesting the 1999 World Trade Organization meeting showed that the Left-Right divide was certainly alive. Likewise, many of Blair's reforms ran into rancorous opposition from the Left wing of his own party and stalled out, while Bush's compassionate conservatism turned out to mean sweeping tax cuts for the wealthy. The divide between Left and Right may have narrowed after the collapse of the Berlin Wall, but it did not go away.

To the extent that a third way was developed during the 1990s, it was based more on practical politics than on new economic theories. Both sides had learned the hard way that extreme, or purist, implementations of their models simply do not work. State-run utopias turn into bureaucratic nightmares, and free-market paradises lead to dysfunctional societies. Thus a century that included both Soviet gulags and the Great Depression ultimately forged a broad, pragmatic consensus that markets and states each have roles to play in society. Nonetheless, this centrist consensus left an intellectual vacuum. By the end of the twentieth century there was a feeling that the two poles symbolized by Marx and Smith were both wrong, but there was no new coherent framework to replace them. Despite the aspirations of its progenitors, the third way had evolved into a set of political tactics for winning elections from the center ground, rather than a truly new economic paradigm.[4]

It is this intellectual vacuum that Complexity Economics has the potential to fill. The Complexity approach to economics offers not just a muddled middle— it is neither Neoclassicism with a few market failures, nor socialism with a few market mechanisms—but a wholly new perspective. The fundamental question isn't Left versus Right; it is how best to evolve.

Human Nature and Strong Reciprocity

If one digs deeply into the Left-Right divide, down to its philosophical and historical core, one finds two conflicting views of human nature. On the Left is the view that human beings are inherently altruistic; that greed and selfishness stem not from human nature, but from the construction of the social order; and that humans can be made better through a more just society. The lineage of this view descends from Jean-Jacques Rousseau and Karl Marx.

On the Right is the view that human beings are inherently self-regarding and that the pursuit of self-interest is an inalienable right. The most effective system of government is one that accommodates rather than attempts to change this aspect of human nature. As the eighteenth-century Scottish philosopher David Hume put it, "in contriving any system of government . . . every man ought to be supposed to be a knave and to have no other end, in all his actions, than his private interests."[5] The Right claims, however, that if people pursue their self-interest through the mechanism of markets, then the general interests of society will be served as well. The lineage of this view descends from Hume, John Locke, and Thomas Hobbes.

One might be surprised *not* to see Adam Smith's name on this list. But as the economists Herbert Gintis, Samuel Bowles, and Ernst Fehr, and the anthropologist Robert Boyd point out, Smith actually took a more nuanced view. In his *Wealth of Nations,* Smith indeed showed how self-interest, mediated by markets, can lead to social benefit. But in his other great work, *The Theory of Moral Sentiments,* Smith also said, "How selfish soever man may be supposed, there are evidently some principles in his nature, which interest him in the fortunes of others."[6] In other words, Smith took a more rounded view of human behavior, one that acknowledged the coexistence of both the self-interested and altruistic sides of human nature.

Gintis and his colleagues claim that modern research shows that both the historical Left and Right views of human nature are too simplistic. For centuries, the question of the self-regarding versus the altruistic nature of humankind was a philosophical question and ultimately a matter of opinion. Since the 1980s, however, it has become a scientific question. A substantial body of evidence from controlled experiments, empirical studies, anthropological field work, and the application of game theory has now yielded an answer: Smith was basically right.

Human beings are neither inherently altruistic nor selfish; instead they are what researchers call *conditional cooperators* and *altruistic punishers*. Gintis and his colleagues refer to this type of behavior as *strong reciprocity* and define it as "a predisposition to cooperate with others, and to punish (even at personal cost if necessary) those who violate the norms of cooperation, even when it is implausible to expect these costs will be recovered at a later date."[7] This is the behavior we saw in our earlier discussion of the ultimatum game and the evolving Prisoner's Dilemma. In essence, people try to follow the Golden Rule, but with a slight twist: do unto others as you would have them do unto you (i.e., conditional cooperation)—but if others don't do unto you, then nail them, even at personal cost to yourself (i.e., altruistic punishment). People have a highly developed sense of whom they can trust and whom they cannot, to whom they owe favors and who owes favors to them, and whether they are being taken advantage of. As the old adage says, "Fool me once, shame on you: fool me twice, shame on me."

The universality of strong reciprocity behavior is staggering; it has been found in groups of people ranging from modern industrial societies, to remote hunter-gatherer tribes. There is a debate as to how much of this behavior is genetic versus cultural, but there are three pieces of evidence that point strongly to a genetic basis. First is the fact that strong reciprocity shows up in widely varying cultures—no society has been found that does not exhibit some form of it, thus indicating that its origins are not purely cultural.[8] Second is the fact that similar behaviors have been observed in a number of primate species.[9] And third, a biochemical basis for the behavior has been discovered in oxytocin, a brain hormone that plays a critical role in generating feelings of trust and eliciting cooperation in humans.[10] Although strong reciprocity appears to be universal, there is, however, a great diversity of ways in which different societies exhibit and enforce the behavior, thus making it likely that its development has been a case of coevolution between genes and culture.

The evolutionary logic for strong reciprocity is simple: in a world of non-zero-sum games, conditional cooperators perform better than agents following either purely selfish or purely altruistic strategies. Even though no single strategy dominated Kristian Lindgren's evolving Prisoner's Dilemma model, it is no coincidence that the strategies that rose to the top tended to be variations on the conditional cooperator theme. Likewise, when researchers surveyed results of the ultimatum game played by people around the world, they found that the society that came the closest to behaving according to the self-interested rationality assumed by Traditional Economics was the Machiguenga people of the

Peruvian rain forest. The Machiguenga's cultural norms for strong reciprocity are not as well developed as those of other societies, and as a result, Machiguenga culture is characterized by selfishness, mutual suspicion, and low cooperation. Their society has not advanced beyond family units of organization, and not surprisingly they were among the poorest people of the groups tested.[11]

A Traditional economist might argue that strong reciprocity is just another form of self-interest. After all, people cooperate to serve their own ends. Cooperation does indeed pay off in a non-zero-sum world, but there are two crucial distinctions between strong reciprocity and Traditional self-interest. First, Traditional *Homo economicus* does not care about the *process* of economic interaction, only whether the outcome maximizes the agent's self-interest. Experiments show, however, that real people care not only about outcomes, but about whether the process itself was fair. Second, as the ultimatum game shows, people will punish unfair behavior, even at a cost to themselves, and even if they have no hope of recovering that cost in the future. In other words, when people feel as if they've really been cheated, they can do some pretty crazy stuff. That is certainly a departure from self-interested rationality.

The economic and political ramifications of strong reciprocity may not be immediately obvious, but once we change the core assumptions of human behavior, a lot changes. As an example, consider the issue of public support for the welfare state.[12] In the 1930s through the 1960s, U.S. government programs to help the less fortunate generally enjoyed widespread popular support. That support dropped dramatically in the 1970s through the 1990s. The reasons for this drop have been the subject of much debate. Those on the Left argue that the lack of support stems from racism, as those receiving benefits are overwhelmingly minorities, and the rise of the selfish "me" generation during this period—in other words, a lack of altruism. The favored explanation of the Right is that people finally woke up to the ineffectuality of most welfare programs, thought it was a waste of their taxes, and wanted their money back—in other words, self-interest.

Using a combination of surveys, experiments, and focus groups, Christina Fong, Bowles, and Gintis found significant evidence that the swing in attitude was really due to neither of these explanations, but to strong reciprocity in action. When the social programs were instituted, those receiving benefits were viewed primarily as people who wanted jobs but who, because of bad luck and the vagaries of the economy, could not get them. Social norms supported the idea that such people deserve help. In more recent times, however, the popular perception has shifted to the idea that people on benefits are lazy, not interested in work, and abusing the generosity of society. Those behaviors violate reciprocity norms, and are seen as warranting the withdrawal of support and even punishment.

The authors suggest that social policies should be designed specifically to "mobilize rather than offend reciprocal values." For example, policies that are consistent with strong reciprocity include providing skills training for those who want to work, giving incentives for the poor to accumulate savings, supporting entrepreneurial activities in deprived areas, and improving educational opportunities for the disadvantaged. Likewise, strong reciprocity norms encourage people to categorize the disadvantaged into the deserving and undeserving. Programs that reflect this distinction tend to enjoy broad support. For example, state programs that provide unemployment insurance tend to be popular because workers pay into them while employed, and then if they have bad luck and are laid off, draw on the benefits. Likewise, Social Security has enjoyed over seventy years of popular bipartisan support largely because it is consistent with reciprocity norms—people cannot help getting old, and those who pay into the system benefit from it. On the other hand, programs that run counter to these norms and benefit "undeserving" people tend to be controversial; for example, welfare programs that give benefits with no reciprocal requirements such as work or training, or rehabilitation programs for drug users whose problems are viewed as a consequence of their own actions. But again, if reciprocal action is required (e.g., welfare recipients must work, or drug users must stay clean) then the programs tend to be popularly supported.

Strong reciprocity helps explain the attempts by the new Left in the United States and the United Kingdom to bring personal responsibility back into the progressive agenda. Clinton's reform of welfare to include work requirements, and Blair's campaign to be "tough on crime, and tough on the causes of crime" are prime examples. The Right has also begun to tap into these norms; for example, the faith-based initiatives supported by the Bush administration combine social goals with religiously inspired values of responsibility and reciprocity.

Human beings are neither the pure-hearted, altruistic creatures of Rousseau, nor the heartless, selfish creatures of Hume. Smith, the economist and moral philosopher, was ultimately right—humans are both. The Complexity Economics view on strong reciprocity means that the Left can finally turn away from Rousseau's notion that all social ills are society's fault, and admit a role for personal responsibility. And, likewise, the Right can turn away from Hume's notion that society must be constructed assuming the worst of human behavior, and admit a role for our more generous instincts.

Complexity Economics has shown, however, that individual agent behavior is only one piece of the puzzle. It is the combination of individual behavior and institutional structures that creates the emergent behavior of the system. This leads us to the next great debate between Left and Right—the role of markets versus states.

Left-Wing Utopias and Free Market Fantasies

As we saw in part 3, over its history, humankind has only developed two mechanisms for facilitating large-scale economic cooperation between strangers—hierarchies and markets.[13] There is an enormous variety of implementations contained within these two categories, but they all boil down to one or the other. Even forms of organization that are more egalitarian, such as communes and cooperatives, contain some form of hierarchical power structure.[14] The key distinction between a capitalist and a socialist economy from a Complexity Economics perspective is whether *the ultimate arbiter of economic fitness is a market or a hierarchy.*

In both capitalist and socialist systems, a process of Business Plan differentiation, selection, and amplification occurs within hierarchies. In capitalist economies, the process occurs in private-sector firms—this is Alfred Chandler's "visible hand" at work—while in socialist economies, it occurs in organizations controlled directly or indirectly by the state. In capitalist economies, however, the evolutionary process eventually filters up into the "thin layer" of the market—that is, the layer where Adam Smith's "invisible hand" provides the final word on Business Plan selection and amplification. In socialist economies, the thin layer of the market does not exist (or is dominated by the state), and the key evolutionary decisions on Business Plan selection and amplification are made within the hierarchies of government organizations.

The Critique of the Left

The Complexity Economics critique of a pure socialist economy is fairly straightforward and should not be a surprise at this point: the economy is simply too complex for the central planning required by socialism to work effectively. The argument has three key elements, two of which were developed by the great Austrian economist Friedrich Hayek in the 1930s and 1940s.[15]

The first is what Hayek called the "knowledge coordination problem."[16] The knowledge required to solve the problem of what to produce in an economy lies scattered all over society. It includes information on preferences embedded in people's heads, as well as information on costs, technologies, and so on. Collecting this information without market mechanisms is both a practical and a theoretical impossibility. By the time we surveyed the entire population on their preferences for the 10^{10} SKUs of goods and services in the economy (ignoring the fact that no one could complete such a survey in his or her lifetime), the information would be out of date as soon as it was collected. The same problem holds true with cost data.

This leads to the second problem, what Hayek called the "fatal conceit" of socialism.[17] If perfect rationality is a critical flaw in Neoclassical theory, it is just as big a problem for socialist theory. In fact, in a controversial article in 1933, the British economist H. D. Dickenson argued that there really was no difference between socialism and capitalism, because Walras's equations for market equilibrium could simply be solved by a socialist planner and get the same optimal result as a market.[18] Hayek countered that even if we were somehow able to collect all the data needed to do this, we would not be able to process it. Consistent with our earlier discussions, Hayek argued that human deductive rationality is simply not up to the job of understanding, predicting, and planning in a system as nonlinear and dynamic as the economy. In essence, Hayek was saying that perfect rationality is just as unrealistic in socialist theory as it is in Neoclassical theory.

The third critique builds from Hayek's two points and is a factor we discussed earlier. If we reject perfect rationality and instead rely on deductive-tinkering, then we need something to judge the success of our tinkering against; we need feedback on what are good Business Plans versus bad Business Plans. Without market mechanisms to provide that feedback, we are stuck with Hayek's knowledge coordination problem. In the absence of actual knowledge of what society wants, and with no mechanism for enforcing a selection of those things, the Big Man hierarchy of the state will simply produce whatever it decides to produce. As we discussed earlier, the natural tendency of Big Man power hierarchies is to do things that serve the interests of the Big Men. Thus, the fitness function in pure planned economies inevitably reflects the interests of the power hierarchies, and not those of society more broadly.

Thus, from a Complexity Economics perspective, markets play a critical role in collecting and processing information, as well as keeping power hierarchies in check by providing a fitness function for Business Plan selection. The vision of a neatly planned utopia does not square well with the messy reality of a complex adaptive system.

The Critique of the Right

The Complexity critique of the other side of the ideological divide is not so much a critique of capitalism itself, but rather a critique of the Neoclassically inspired Right-wing fantasy of how capitalism works. The argument has two key points.

First, while Complexity Economics views markets as both useful and necessary, it also knocks them off their optimally efficient pedestal. As we saw earlier, even financial markets, which are as close to textbook markets as one gets, operate far from their theoretical efficiency. This means that the tendency of some on the Right to automatically assume that markets are the answer to all problems in society is misguided. To be fair, most Traditional economists recognize the fallibility of the markets to some degree, and the literature is full of analyses of market failures. But the Complexity view would take us beyond Traditional market failures and would have us be skeptical of market solutions that depend on Traditional theory's usual array of unrealistic assumptions.

A small, but classic example was the deregulation of telephone directory enquiries in the United Kingdom. For fifty years, the United Kingdom had a single national number that one could call to find out a phone number. This monopoly was run by the formerly state-owned British Telecom (BT), and both the price and quality of the service were monitored and regulated by the government. The service was simple, worked well, and netted relatively few consumer complaints. In 2001, however, the government decided to deregulate the service and open it up to competition. The theory was that market competition would lead to lower prices and more innovative services. As predicted, a host of new companies entered; by 2004 there were 120 companies in the market. Theory and reality, however, quickly parted. Under the old system, there was only one number—"192"—and everyone remembered it. In the new system, with 120 competing numbers, few people could remember more than a handful of the new numbers. The new numbers were assigned by lottery, and the companies with the luck to get memorable numbers such as "118 118" quickly became new natural monopolies and captured the bulk of the traffic. In addition, for most people, directory calls are a very small expenditure and not worth the time and effort to seek out the lowest-priced provider. The result was that the new memorable numbers had higher prices and more service complaints than the old BT number. Furthermore, the new numbers were not truly national, as the regulations allowed telephone companies to restrict which numbers could be accessed from their networks—thus one might have to remember different numbers when calling from home, work, or a mobile. The realities of human cognition and the institutional design of the system were at odds with the simple world of Traditional theory, and thus the benefits of market competition did not materialize.[19]

Similar examples include the deregulation of the California electricity market, which led to serious electricity shortages in 2001, and the privatization of the British rail network, which has resulted in massively delayed train journeys ever since. None of this is to say that markets are bad and monopolies are good—again, Complexity Economics broadly supports the notion that markets are the best mechanism for economic evolution. Rather the point is that the Right has a tendency to view markets as the solution to all ills, based on the overly simplistic theories of Traditional economics. In each of these cases, the messy details of real human rationality and institutions did not match the theory, and the market solutions failed to deliver the social goods.

The second criticism is that the antigovernment stance of many on the Right looks very naive in the context of Complexity Economics. Neoclassical theory creates an ideal of economies existing in a pristine state of nature, free from the meddling of governments. It is in this idealized state that Pareto optimality is achieved and the maximum wealth for society is created. As soon as one starts interfering by layering on things such as taxes and regulations, one moves away from this ideal, and the amount of wealth created for society is reduced. Thus, the objective should be to restrain taxation and government expenditures to an absolute minimum. Likewise, the Right argues, while some basic regulation might be necessary for ensuring the functioning of markets, regulations generally have a distorting effect, interfere with natural price signals, and, like taxes, push the economy away from its ideal state. In an address to the White House Conference on Small Business in 1986, Ronald Reagan famously said, "Government's view of the economy could be summed up in a few short phrases: If it moves, tax it. If it keeps moving, regulate it. And if it stops moving, subsidize it."

But the antigovernment free marketers forget that economies don't exist in isolation. The economic evolutionary system is constructed out of a vast array of Social Technologies, many of which rely on government.[20] Market-based evolution requires a careful balance between cooperation and competition, and governments play a vital role in enabling their societies to strike this balance. Social Technologies such as contract law, consumer protection regulations, worker safety rules, and securities law all serve to engender cooperation and trust, while antitrust regulations serve to maintain healthy levels of competition.

Those on the Right in the United States often blame Franklin D. Roosevelt, a Democrat, for beginning the growth of government "interference" in the economy with the New Deal. But the key architect in positioning the government as a balancer of cooperation and competition was in fact a Republican and a different Roosevelt—Teddy.[21] His reforms during 1901 to 1909 in areas ranging from busting up the Rockefeller and Morgan trusts, to enacting the first food safety regulations, provided a critical institutional foundation for economic growth in the twentieth century.

One merely has to travel to developing countries with weak government institutions to see what life is like without these interventions. An economy can end up in a low-cooperation, low-competition dead end when government fails to play this role. Certainly, not all government regulations are good—there can, of course, be foolish, wasteful regulations. Nevertheless, the "government is the problem, not the solution" rhetoric of the Right undermines the essential role government institutions play in supporting the evolutionary effectiveness of the economic system.

Government as Fitness Function Shaper

Just as Complexity Economics provides a new perspective on the economic role of corporations, it also provides a new perspective on the economic role of governments. The Neoclassically inspired position of the Right has been that Pareto optimality is the most morally sound outcome for a free society, and as markets are the best institutional mechanism (in fact the only mechanism) for achieving Pareto optimality, the morally correct role of government is to ensure market efficiency. Any government actions that interfere with the market should be measured in cost-benefit terms against the losses in efficiency. Thus, for example, the Right often uses market efficiency arguments to oppose environmental regulations.

In contrast, a Complexity perspective would distinguish between two types of government action. Policies that get the government involved in differentiating, selecting, and amplifying Business Plans would be seen as interfering in economic evolution and have all of the problems discussed in the critique of socialist economies. Examples would include Japanese industrial policy that subsidizes and protects favored industries, French intervention in European banking mergers to favor its own national banks, or the U.S. government's energy policy favoring corn-based ethanol due to the political importance of Iowa. In contrast, policies that *shape the fitness environment*, while leaving Business Plan selection and amplification to market mechanisms, are a different matter. As we have seen, notions of efficiency in evolutionary systems are ephemeral. A Complexity perspective would say that government regulations form part of the fitness environment that companies compete in. As long as markets provide the mechanism for selecting and amplifying Business Plans, then the economic evolutionary process will innovate and adapt in response to those regulations.

For example, if voters tell their elected representatives that protecting the environment is a priority for society, then it is well within the government's purview to shape the economic fitness function to favor environmentally friendly Business Plans over environmentally unfriendly plans. Examples would include a carbon tax, emissions trading, or mandatory industry recycling requirements. In these cases the government is not selecting plans (e.g., whether fuel cells, ethanol, wind power, or some other Physical Technology is the best way to reduce emissions), but rather shaping the fitness environment in which plans will succeed or fail (e.g., in a world with a carbon tax a low-emissions plan will do better than a high-emissions plan).

This view of government as a fitness function shaper sits uneasily with both the Right and the Left. The Right is squeamish about the efficiency costs. But, as we have seen, the efficiency cost argument is inherently static— for example, if a carbon tax spurred innovations that dramatically lowered the cost of solar power, would that make the economy more or less efficient? The Left on the other hand tends to trust the rationality of bureaucrats more than the creative power of markets, and to prefer a more directive approach (e.g., preferring mandatory reduction targets for all power plants rather than emissions trading). One might argue, however, that if both the Right and the Left object, then it probably means we are on the right track.

The idea of government as a fitness function shaper, however, should be approached with caution for all of the reasons Hayek pointed out. We should be realistic about our ability to predict the effects of government shaping of the fitness function and the likelihood of unintended consequences. This does not mean that government cannot productively play such a role, but rather it means that there needs to be a willingness to experiment, collect feedback, and change course, none of which is ever politically easy. It also changes the terms of the debate from stale, ideological battles over market efficiency versus social goals, to practical discussions of how the evolutionary processes of the market can be better shaped to serve society's needs.

Complexity Economics thus changes our perspective not just on the ideological positions of Left and Right, but also on the two great institutions that they battle over: states and markets. The economic role of the state is to create an institutional framework that supports the evolutionary workings of markets, strikes an effective balance between cooperation and competition, and shapes the economic fitness function to best serve the needs of society. Consistent with norms of strong reciprocity, the state also has an obligation to ensure that all its citizens have an equal opportunity to participate in the economic system, and to provide a basic level of support for those who do not succeed in that system. The economic role of markets is to provide incentives for the discovery and differentiation of Business Plans, apply the fitness function shaped by consumers, technology, and the state in selection, and channel resources to selected plans for amplification. The question is not states versus markets—it is how to combine states *and* markets to create an effective evolutionary system.

We will now move on to looking at three areas of research where a Complexity-based perspective is shedding light on long-standing social problems. If Complexity Economics is still in its youth, then its application to public policy is in its infancy. In fact, not all of the researchers whose work I will discuss would explicitly consider themselves Complexity economists. I have included their work, however, because it fits well within the general themes of Complexity Economics and provides an illustration of where the Complexity perspective might lead us.

The common thread running through these examples is that micro-level behavior matters. As we have discussed, in complex adaptive systems the rules of individual agent behavior often have profound and sometimes unexpected effects on the macro performance of a system. We saw how the simple agent rules in Sugarscape led to a highly unequal distribution of wealth, how the agent strategies in the evolutionary Prisoner's Dilemma led to Schumpeterian gales of creative destruction, and how the behaviors of real people in the Beer Game led to waves of boom and bust. Traditional Economics has historically taken a narrow view of micro-level behavior—if everyone is assumed to be perfectly rational, then it makes no sense to explore how heterogeneous patterns of individual behavior affect macro-level outcomes. But as we will see, factors such as cultural norms, individual choices on where to live or what to watch on TV, and the behavior of parents may lie at the root of significant macroeconomic issues.

"Culture Matters"

According to the World Bank, the poorest country in the world in 2002 was the Democratic Republic of Congo, with an estimated income of $100 per head.[22] This is barely above the $92 per head estimated by J. Bradford DeLong for hunter-gatherer tribes of circa fifteen thousand years ago (see chapter 1). At the same time, the richest country in the world was Luxembourg, with an average income per head of $39,470, or to put it more viscerally, one Luxembourgian makes as much money each year as 394 Congolese. The divide between rich and poor in the world goes well beyond Congo and Luxembourg. At present, 21 percent of the world's population survives on less than $1 a day, including almost half of sub-Saharan Africa and a third of India and Southeast Asia.[23] As the economic historian David Landes has put it, "This world is roughly divided into three kinds of nations: those that spend lots of money to keep their weight down; those whose people eat to live; and those whose people don't know where their next meal is coming from."[24]

The candidates for the causes of this divide have historically fallen into Left and Right camps.[25] On the Left, favorite explanations include colonialism, racism, capitalist exploitation, and insufficient aid from rich countries. Meanwhile, the arguments on the Right have gravitated toward bad government, corruption, a lack of free markets, dependency on foreign aid, and even, subtly (and sometimes not so subtly), racial inferiority. In addition, a few less politically charged explanations have been put forward that include geography, climate, and particularly in Africa's case, the tragedy of near-constant warfare.[26]

In 1999, Harvard international studies professor Lawrence Harrison and his Harvard colleague Samuel Huntington (who famously predicted a clash of civilizations after the end of the Cold War) convened a symposium entitled "Cultural Values and Human Progress." The symposium tied together work that researchers around the world had been conducting for decades on the role of culture in economic development. The conference included well-known Western economists, historians, and social thinkers such as David Landes, Michael Porter, Jeffrey Sachs, Francis Fukuyama, and Nathan Glazer. But the conference didn't just include Western scholars abstractly discussing faraway cultures; it also included a number of researchers and social commentators from the countries under discussion, as well as practitioners from aid agencies. One of the outputs of the conference was a book, *Culture Matters,* whose title sums up the group's conclusion.[27]

In chapter 16, we defined culture as the emergent product of the micro rules of behavior followed by individuals, and discussed its role in the economic performance of organizations. Perhaps not surprisingly, the participants at the Harvard conference contended that culture plays a large role in the economic performance of nations too. In the case of nations, the rules or norms of behavior aren't merely acted out by thousands, but are acted out by millions.

Observations on the connection between culture and macroeconomic performance go back at least to the turn of the last century and the writings of the German sociologist Max Weber. But in the 1950s and 1960s, cultural explanations for economic outcomes fell out of favor for two reasons. The first was political correctness. As Landes put it, "culture . . . frightens scholars. It has a sulfuric odor of race and inheritance, an air of immutability."[28] The second reason was the dominance of Neoclassical economics. Culture has little place in a world of perfect rationality, and to the extent that it does, cultural rules must be self-interested, optimizing strategies, because otherwise, people would not use them.[29]

Fortunately, fears over political correctness have faded as scholars have shown that it is possible to have discussions about culture that are both scientifically fruitful, and respectful of the diversity of humankind. One must avoid the relativist trap and not shy away from statements about why the norms of one culture might be more supportive of economic development than those of another, but at the same time, one can recognize that there is no one cultural formula for economic success. In a world in which cultures as varied as Japan's and Norway's are among the most economically successful, such claims of one perfect formula are easily dismissed. Likewise, the rise of behavioral economics has reduced the influence of Neoclassical assumptions and brought the cultural horse inside the economic stable.

The multibillion-dollar question then is, which norms support economic development, and which norms don't? Much research remains to be done in this area, but various researchers, such as the Argentinean scholar Mariano Grondona, have proposed typologies of cultural rules.[30] The rules in these typologies fall roughly into the same three broad categories as did the organizational rules I presented in chapter 16. This should not be surprising, as both organizational and societal norms need to support the processes of economic evolution if they are to support wealth creation.

In the first category are norms related to individual behavior. These include norms that support a strong work ethic, individual accountability, and a belief that you are the protagonist of your own life and not at the whim of gods or Big Men. Fatalism greatly reduces personal incentives. It is also important to believe that there is a payoff to hard work and a moral life in this world, and not just in the next. Finally, economically successful cultures appear to strike a balance between optimism that improvement is possible, and realism about one's current situation.

In the second category are norms related to cooperative behavior. Foremost is a belief that life is a non-zero-sum game and that there are payoffs to cooperation. Societies that believe in a fixed pie of wealth have a difficult time engendering cooperation and tend to be low in mutual trust. Consistent with our discussion of strong reciprocity, it is important that the culture have norms that value generosity and fairness, but also sanction those who free ride and cheat.

The third category contains norms related to innovation.[31] Deductive-tinkering is much more effective if the deductive part is strong, and thus cultures that look to rational scientific explanations of the world rather than religious or magical explanations tend to be more innovative. Likewise, a culture needs to be tolerant of heresy and experimentation, as strict orthodoxy stifles innovation. Finally, it is important that the culture be supportive of competition and celebrate achievement, since overly egalitarian cultures reduce the incentives for risk taking.

One final norm is important to all three categories: how people view time. Cultures that live for today (or, conversely, are mired in the past) have problems across the board, ranging from low work ethic, to an inability to engage in complex cooperation and low levels of investment in innovation. Why work hard, and invest in cooperation and innovation if tomorrow doesn't matter? In contrast, cultures that have an ethic of investing for tomorrow tend to value work, have high intergenerational savings rates, demonstrate a willingness to sacrifice short-term pleasures for long-term gain, and enjoy high levels of cooperation.

Just like organizations, societies with hardworking, cooperative, innovative cultures would clearly facilitate the discovery, execution, and continued evolution of complex Business Plans. Likewise, serious deficiencies in any of these areas could potentially slow down or stop the wheels of economic evolution.

Again, there is no single way to implement these general types of norms. Japanese methods for encouraging stable cooperation may be quite different from Norwegian approaches, and no culture is equally strong across all areas. Moreover, rendering judgments on these norms does not necessarily imply moral judgments. Some of the norms have both economic and moral implications. For example, sanctions against cheating have economic as well as moral benefits. But many norms do not. For example, a live-for-today society might be just as moral as an invest-for-tomorrow society—just not as rich. Finally, while our focus is on economic success, it is not the only measure of societal health. For example, a society might have strong norms of tolerance and forgiveness that allow cheating to proliferate, thus weakening its ability to create large-scale, stable cooperation and reducing its economic achievements. But the very same norms might make it a warm, friendly, and even peaceful society.

Keeping these caveats in mind, one can begin to analyze the cultures of individual societies and assess the economic efficacy of their norms. One of the participants in the Harvard conference, Daniel Etounga-Mangeulle, an African business executive, noted that despite the diversity of African cultures, there is a "foundation of shared values, attitudes, and institutions that binds together the nations south of the Sahara."[32] He argued that too many of these common norms are on the wrong side of the cultural typology, and he highlighted two factors in African culture that he believes have particularly negative economic impacts: excessive concentrations of authority in individual Big Men (who often claim magical powers), and a view of time that focuses on the past and present, but not the future: "Without a dynamic perception of the future, there is no planning, no foresight, no scenario building, no policy to effect the course of events."

The impact of these norms is not just additive and linear over the population. As agents follow cultural norms they interact, and create complex dynamics. For example, let's examine the interplay between those who believe the world is a zero-sum game and those who see it as a non-zero-sum game. If your beliefs are biased toward seeing the world as a zero-sum game, then your objective will be to get your slice of the pie. You will view someone else's gain as your loss, and your proclivity to cooperate will be low. Rather than searching for new, more complex, and wealth-creating cooperative activities, people will invest their energies in finding ways to capture a greater share of existing wealth. It is not hard to imagine that thievery, dishonesty, and corruption will be higher in such a zero-sum society. The moral attitudes around such activities will also be different; for example, theft might be viewed as "I'm just taking my fair share" from someone who has more than his or her rightful share.

Now, imagine a population in which some agents think the economic pie is fixed, while others have a non-zero-sum view. Over time, as the non-zero-sum agents find ways to cooperate and create new wealth, they will be attacked by zero-sum agents trying to get their share. This conflict will lower the returns to cooperation, and eventually, the non-zero-sum agents will learn that cooperation doesn't pay and become zero-sum agents themselves. Non-zero-sum attitudes don't need to be an inherited, hardwired trait. One could have two populations in which people are born with the same natural distribution of attitudes and predispositions. But in the low-cooperation society, non-zero-sum attitudes are essentially beaten out of the agents over time and they eventually learn to become zero-sum agents. When researchers model these dynamics, they often find there is a tipping point: once a society is past a threshold ratio of noncooperators versus cooperators in a population, it becomes very hard to maintain large-scale cooperation, resulting in a "poverty trap."[33] Such tipping points mean that the vagaries of history can send one society down the low cooperation path into a poverty trap, while another society with the same predispositions to cooperate might bootstrap its way to riches. The dynamic interplay between cooperators and defectors can thus influence the evolution of norms and the level of trust in a society. Culture is not an immutable force; rather, it coevolves as people in a society interact with each other—culture is a product of history, and history is a product of culture.[34]

Numerous studies have shown that levels of trust vary widely across cultures.[35] In 1996, a major survey was conducted across a number of countries asking people (in their native language), "Generally speaking, would you say that most people can be trusted, or that you cannot be too careful in dealing with people?"[36] The diversity of responses was striking, ranging from the most trusting countries, where 65 percent of Norwegians and 60 percent of Swedes agreed they could trust people, down to a mere 5 percent of Peruvians and 3 percent of Brazilians.

There is an important correlation between trust and economic success (figure 18-1). High trust leads to economic cooperation, which leads to prosperity, which further enhances trust in a virtuous circle. But the circle can be vicious as well, with low trust leading to low cooperation, leading to poverty, and further eroding trust. The causal relationship is not perfect, however, because trust is not the only factor that determines levels of cooperation. For example, both Chinese and Indians rate themselves higher on trust than do Americans. One explanation is that while trust in the United States is low, Americans have been able to succeed economically despite this because of their strong Social Technologies, in particular, a tradition of respect for the rule of law. Another more gloomy explanation is that Americans are living off the

FIGURE 18-1

The Relationship Between Trust and Economic Performance

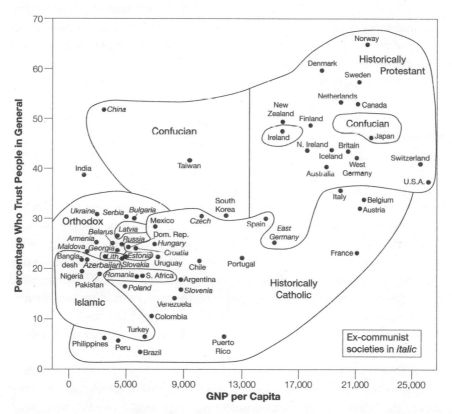

Source: Harrison and Huntington (2000). GNP per capita from World Bank estimates of purchasing power parity, in 1995 U.S. dollars.

social capital of their past, and unless it is rebuilt, trust will continue to erode. The idea that this erosion of trust will eventually catch up with the United States economically is a topic we will examine in the next section.

Francis Fukuyama has investigated why certain cultures have evolved high levels of social trust while others seem trapped in low-trust regimes. One of his conclusions is somewhat paradoxical: that societies with strong "family values" may have a difficult time evolving broader forms of social trust.[37] He argues that family-centric cultures, while having deep bonds of trust within families, tend to have narrower radii of trust outside families. In these cultures, economic networks are usually based on kin relationships, which naturally limit the scale to which the networks can grow. As examples, he cites the large proportion of small-scale, family-owned businesses in China, Korea, and Italy, and only a small number of global enterprises relative to the size of their economies. Meanwhile, societies with weaker family traditions, such as Japan, Germany, and Holland, evolved STs to help secure trust outside the bounds of family. These STs ranged from the early establishment of the rule of law, to voluntary and social organizations. Thus, while the bonds of trust within families may be weaker in relation to other cultures, the radius of trust is wider. It is remarkable, for example, that a country as small as Holland has evolved some of the largest corporations in the world, including Royal Dutch/Shell, Philips, and ABN Amro.

Karla Hoff of the World Bank and Arijit Sen of the Indian Statistical Institute also believe that overly strong family ties can have a negative impact on development.[38] In northern European Protestant traditions, families tend to be defined as the immediate nuclear family of parents and children, with weaker ties to grandparents, aunts, uncles, and cousins. In many African and South Asian traditions, the radius of family is larger and stronger, extending to grandparents, aunts, uncles, great aunts, great uncles, cousins, second cousins, and so on. These extended-family societies also have very strong norms on the sharing of economic wealth among family members. Richer family members are expected to help poorer family members. While the warm and fuzzy image of a large, extended family sharing with each other sounds very appealing and may have psychological and other benefits, in economic terms, it creates a basic problem. If you get a job, work hard, and accumulate a bit of savings, you will be rewarded by having your no-good, lazy second cousin come live with you, eat your food, and generally sponge off your hard-earned wages. This is what economists call a *moral hazard*. Extended definitions of family create incentives for free riding and lower the returns to work and savings. Hoff and Sen argue that not only does the extended family create problems at the individual level, but it can also further retard development as it extends into nepotism in business and government institutions.

The implications of culture for development policy are just beginning to be explored, but it is becoming clear that culture must be a part of the development equation. The World Bank economist William Easterly points out that between 1950 and 1995, the developed world provided more than $1 trillion in economic assistance to the developing world, yet the poverty rates in the vast majority of recipient countries barely budged, and many African countries have even slid backward since their independence in the 1960s.[39] While aid to alleviate severe and immediate symptoms of poverty remains critical, it is essential that people do more to understand and address the root causes. Although culture is certainly not the only root cause, programs that continue to ignore the cultural basis of poverty are undoubtedly doomed to failure.

Social Capital and the "Great Disruption"

In 2000, Robert Putnam, a professor of public policy at Harvard University, published *Bowling Alone,* a book that brought the term *social capital* into the public consciousness, and stimulated interest in the topic among both economists and policy makers.[40] Putnam defines social capital as the "connections among individuals—social networks and the norms of reciprocity and trustworthiness that arise from them."[41] In the terminology of Complexity Economics, if cultural norms provide the micro rules of agent behavior, then social capital is the emergent result of agents creating cooperative networks.

Not all cooperative activity, however, creates social capital. For example, the anonymous cooperation of trading in markets does not create social capital. A critical attribute of networks with social capital is that *the people in them have repeated personal interactions*—creating social capital is a contact sport. Typical examples of networks with social capital include local neighborhood associations, charities, religious organizations, sports teams, social clubs, civic groups, hobbyist organizations, and, of course, bowling leagues. Companies and other places of work are also significant sources of social capital, as many people spend the majority of their waking hours at work and build significant personal networks with their colleagues.

Putnam notes that while social capital is a friendly-sounding term, it is not always a good thing. Organized crime mobs and terrorist organizations can also have high degrees of trust between individuals, very effective networks, and strong (often brutally enforced) norms of behavior.[42] Lest someone be an FBI or a CIA informer, these violent groups' bonds of trust tend to be limited to close kin, members of their own religious or ethnic group, and other known associates, which, fortunately, puts a natural limit on their growth.

Since the 1970s, Putnam has been investigating the link between social capital and economic performance. As a part of this research, he has looked deeply into the significant differences in economic success between wealthy northern Italy and the poor south. In the introduction to his book *Making Democracy Work*, Putnam describes his visit to the government offices of the Puglia region in the south:

> In the dingy anteroom loll several indolent functionaries, though they are likely to be present only an hour or two each day and be unresponsive even then. The persistent visitor might discover that in the offices beyond stand only ghostly rows of empty desks. One mayor, frustrated at his inability to get action from the region's bureaucrats exploded to us, "They don't answer the mail, they don't [even] answer the telephone!"[43]

Putnam then contrasts this atmosphere with the government office of the Emilia-Romagna region in the north:

> Visiting the glass-walled regional headquarters is like entering a modern, high-tech firm. A brisk, courteous receptionist directs visitors to the appropriate office, where as likely as not, the relevant official will call up a computerized database on regional problems and policies . . . A legislative pioneer in many fields, the Emilian government has progressed from words to deeds, its effectiveness measured by dozens of daycare centers and industrial parks, repertory theatres and vocational training sites scattered throughout the region.[44]

From Puglia to Emilia-Romagna, it is a mere four hundred miles, or a six-hour drive. Both are populated by Italians, both have shared Italy's history; how can they be so utterly different in the effectiveness of their local governments?

Putnam locates the source of the dramatic difference between Italy's regions in a now familiar topic: low trust leading to an inability to achieve large-scale cooperation. Putnam argues that the differences in trust levels stem from the differing histories of the two regions, tracing back to medieval times. This history has resulted in two very different social capital inheritances. The south historically was monarchist, hierarchical, closed, and dominated by the church. Such hierarchical structures viewed civic organizations and business networks as threats to their power and discouraged them. Meanwhile the north was more egalitarian, communal, and open to trade, and later was influenced by the ideas of the Enlightenment. In such an environment, social networks grew and flourished.[45] As Putnam notes, history is path dependent, and the communal republics of the north gradually built their stock of social capital over centuries, while the monarchist republics of the south never managed to get the virtuous cycle of social capital development going. Over the long run, this dichotomy has translated into very different economic outcomes, with the north of Italy containing some of the richest and fastest-growing regions in the European Union, and the south containing some of the poorest.

In *Bowling Alone,* Putnam turned his sights on the United States to examine the question "What is the state of social capital in America?" The answer was "not good." He opens his book by describing the disappearance of half-century-old bridge clubs in Pennsylvania, the collapse of a century-old chapter of the National Association for the Advancement of Colored People (NAACP) in Virginia, and of Veterans of Foreign War posts, charity leagues, sewing circles, and marching bands across the land.[46] The anecdotal evidence is also supported by statistics. Trust in the U.S. government has fallen by half, from its peak of 40 percent in 1966 to 20 percent in 2003 (excepting a post-9/11 spike). Likewise, trust in business is down from 55 percent to 16 percent, and trust in religious institutions has fallen almost in half to 23 percent.[47] Perhaps even more alarming, trust between individuals has also steadily declined. The percentage of Americans agreeing with the statement "most people can be trusted" dropped from over 50 percent in 1968 to just above 30 percent in 2003. The significance of this decline in trust goes beyond the observation that it is more pleasant to live in a trusting society. As we saw earlier, there is evidence of an important connection between societal trust and macroeconomic performance.

Putnam's work is complemented by Francis Fukuyama, who further observes that several indicators of declining social capital began to move simultaneously in the 1960s, including a sevenfold increase in the violent crime rate from 1963 to 1993 (with some drop-off in more recent years) and equally enormous jumps in divorce rates and births to single mothers during the same period.[48] Fukuyama calls the period from 1960 to 2000 the "Great Disruption" and notes that the decline in social capital has not been unique to the United States, but has also happened (though to lesser degrees) in much of the rest of the developed world.

Both Fukuyama and Putnam agree that the causes are complex and not attributable to a single factor. Both also note that many of the causal factors have been a double-edged sword; on their own, the factors had positive benefits to people, but the emergent effect on society has been negative.

For example, both Fukuyama and Putnam cite the dramatic changes to family structure that occurred during this period, in particular, rising divorce rates and the entry of women into the workplace. Easier access to divorce has undoubtedly freed millions from unhappy marriages, but it has also had undeniable effects on children, their socialization, and their own bonds of trust.

Likewise, the opening of the workplace to women has had a momentous impact on enabling women to fulfill their individual potential. However, as Putnam notes, women have historically played a larger role in creating the social fabric of society than men have played. Women have usually been more involved in civic organizations, grassroots politics, and religious organizations. They have also historically tended to manage family social networks of friends and neighbors. Putnam cites a study showing that among women of equal age, socioeconomic, and marital status, being in the workforce cuts volunteering by 50 percent, informal visiting with friends 25 percent, club and church attendance by 15 percent, and entertaining by 10 percent.[49] Putnam does not criticize women for choosing to work outside the home; at an individual level, it may be both economically necessary and personally fulfilling. Rather, he merely notes that this micro-level change, replicated across millions of women during a relatively short time, has had an important macro-level effect.

Another important factor is the change in the physical layout of society, in particular, suburban sprawl. This has affected trust and the building of networks in multiple ways. First, there is simply more space between neighbors and fewer random chances to encounter each other and talk. Second, rather than walking in neighborhoods, people drive, which again means fewer chances to meet the neighbors and more time spent alone in the car. Also, the greater geographical separation of work and home and longer commutes has resulted in a drop-off in workplace socializing ("I'd love to meet after work, but I've got an hour commute to get home to my family"). The 1950s Ozzie-and-Harriet image of coworkers living down the road from each other and dropping by for an after-work martini is much less common today.

Another factor of immense consequence has been the isolating effect of mass media. Entertainment has dramatically shifted from a group activity of dance halls, concerts, pubs, bridge clubs, bowling leagues, and so on, to an individual activity. Radios, televisions, stereos, video games, home theaters, and the Internet have meant that an increasing portion of nonwork time is spent home alone or just with family. Just as important as the medium itself has been the message. The economics of the media industry drive participants to aim content at mass audiences, and thus programming tends to reflect the lowest common denominators of human emotion (some would argue that this is changing with the more tailored content of the Internet, but given the popularity of porn and gambling on the Web, this is questionable). For more than four decades, society has been fed a diet of murder and mayhem, not just in fiction programming, but in the news media as well. Humans have always loved stories of sex and violence, but the ability to call them up at the touch of a remote control or computer mouse, and vividly presented in television, movies, and computer games, is a new phenomenon in the context of human history. In chapter 6, we discussed the bias in human decision making known as "representativeness," referring to our limited skills in statistical reasoning and our tendency to misjudge probabilities based on unrepresentative samples. If one is exposed to a steady stream of murder stories, one will sub-consciously infer that murder is a pretty common thing and overestimate one's own chances of being murdered. This kind of fear engendered by the media further reduces trust and isolates people.

Just as with the case of women entering the workforce, people have cho-sen to live in suburbs, drive their cars, and watch television for perfectly valid reasons. Yet again, the macro-emergent effects of these individual choices have been an unexpected and worrying decline in social capital. The effects of this decline on long-term U.S. economic performance are as yet unknown, but they are not likely to be positive.

Given the structural and largely irreversible nature of the causes of the Great Disruption (e.g., few would advocate women returning to the home, and people won't give up their cars), the question of what can be done is dif-ficult. Putnam advocates an "agenda for social capitalists" that includes the following components:[50]

- Greater individual commitment to social involvement (and watching less TV)

- Programs in schools to help build norms of trust and social capital in the next generation

- Reforms to make workplaces more family friendly

- Better public transport and the rewriting of zoning laws

- Efforts to encourage voting and political involvement

Putnam admits that the challenge of such a multidimensional effort to rebuild American social capital is overwhelming, and our political institu-tions may not be up to the job of leading such a change.

Fukuyama is ultimately more optimistic. He argues that this is neither the first, nor surely the last Great Disruption that humankind has faced.[51] Taking an evolutionary view, he notes that human social systems are remarkably adaptive. He observes that past periods of social disruption saw multidecade declines in social capital, followed by a process of "re-norming" and then rebuilding of social capital. For example, Fukuyama cites the immense disrup-tion caused by the shift from an agricultural-based economy to an industrial-based one in the early nineteenth century, and the rises in petty crime, violence, alcoholism, out-of-wedlock birth, and other signs of social stress that accompanied it. He notes that a new social order and set of norms emerged in response to these changes during the Victorian period—a period generally regarded as quite high in social capital.

The issues around social capital and trust go beyond economics and touch virtually all facets of society.[52] The issues speak to a complex adaptive system in flux. Social capital does not get picked up on the radar screen of Traditional Economics, because the Traditional framework is concerned with the self-interested choices of rational individuals, and as long as everyone is choosing optimally for himself or herself, then everyone is choosing optimally for society. Complexity Economics takes a different perspective and allows that the complex interactions of a society mean that well-intentioned individual choices may sometimes yield surprising and not-always-desirable emergent outcomes. In this case, individual choices on factors as varied and seemingly disconnected as where to live, whether to work outside the home, or how to spend one's leisure time can lead to a dramatic decline in social cohesion.

While I agree with Fukuyama's evolutionary perspective and believe that we will find ways to adapt, evolutionary theory offers no guarantee of a one-way ticket toward greater social order and wealth. Evolutionary systems can experience collapse, dead ends, and poverty traps.[53] Thus, I agree with Putnam that a more proactive approach must be taken—an approach that spans individual behavior, schools, governments, civic institutions, and the media.

The issues around social capital are not easy to pigeonhole in the traditional Left-Right framework. On the one hand, the overarching point that cooperation lies at the core of economic prosperity is more resonant with the Left and cuts against the grain of the rugged individualism of the Right. Furthermore, those on the Left would argue that the decline in social capital presents a problem that has evolved within market economies across the Western world, and that markets alone will not solve. But on the other side of the political divide, those concerned by the decline in social capital tend to favor a return to old-fashioned values—trust in your neighbor, volunteerism, civic duty, religious involvement, and strong families—these have long been staples of the conservative Right. The argument does not lead us to a mushy position in the center with a bit of community and a bit of old-fashioned values, but rather pulls us hard in both directions simultaneously—a lot of community, a lot of old-fashioned values, and a critical role for government leadership.

Inequality, Social Mobility, and the Culture of Poverty

We have seen the relationships between poverty, culture, and social capital. We will add a further related issue to the list: inequality. As mentioned earlier, 21 percent of the world's population lives on less than $1 a day, which translates into well over a billion people. Furthermore, despite progress made by countries such as China and India, many economists would argue that worldwide inequality is growing.[54]

There is no doubt that economic inequality is as old as economies themselves. A. Y. Abul-Magd, a mathematician, has studied archeological data to understand the distribution of wealth in ancient Egyptian society.[55] Using the square footage of houses in a settlement populated circa 1370 to 1340 BC as a proxy for wealth, he estimated that the distribution of wealth was described by a Pareto distribution with parameters similar to those of modern societies.

Is Inequality Moral?

While inequality is persistent and pervasive, one can nonetheless ask, is it moral? The political commentator Matt Miller argues in his *Two Percent Solution* that how one answers that question is a key distinguishing feature of the Left-Right divide.[56]

Those on the Right say that if people are free to make their own choices in life, and markets are competitive, then the outcomes produced by free people and competitive markets will be morally sound. As Miller puts it, markets reward morally virtuous behavior such as "work, responsibility, thrift, innovation, and risk-taking." One can feel sympathy toward the less fortunate and show compassion, but there is no superior method for allocating resources. If one accepts markets as the best way to organize the economy, then one must accept their outcomes.

Those on the Left argue that markets are a social construct, built on Social Technologies created by human beings to serve their own purposes. If a market economy is a socially constructed system, then we must be responsible for its outcomes. Furthermore, within that system, it is not virtue alone that determines outcomes. The lottery of birth plays a big role, in particular, inherited intelligence, wealth, looks, race, and geographic location. Given the influence of these factors, as Miller puts it, "it makes no sense to think that market outcomes could be presumptively moral."

Again, the two opposing poles can be explained by the principle of strong reciprocity. In crude terms, if whether one is rich or poor is the result of one's own actions (the Right's argument), then people deserve what they get. But if it is largely a matter of luck or factors outside an individual's control (the Left's argument), then they don't.

As with the question of selfishness versus altruism, these views were for a long time simply a matter of opinion. But thanks to the work of many researchers, there is now a significant body of evidence on this subject.

Samuel Bowles of the Santa Fe Institute, Herb Gintis of the University of Massachusetts, and Melissa Osborne Groves of Towson University recently surveyed this work and concluded that neither the Left nor the Right is quite correct.[57]

A Lack of Social Mobility

For the Right to be correct, there must be high social mobility. Through grit, determination, and hard work, the Horatio Algers of the world must be able to rise from rags to riches. These stories do indeed happen, particularly in the United States, but overall social mobility in the U.S. is lower than one might think. A study by Tom Hertz of American University, using data from 6,273 families observed over thirty-two years (from 1968 to 2000), showed that mobility was particularly low at the very poor and very rich ends of the spectrum (see table 18-1). If a set of parents were in the highest decile of income (i.e., top 10 percent), there was a 29.6 percent chance that their children would also grow up to be in the highest decile. Furthermore, looking down the top decile column of the table, one can see that there was a 59.1 percent chance of that same child remaining upper class (upper 3 deciles), and only a very small probability of the child dropping to the bottom of the income distribution. Conversely, a child born to bottom decile parents had a 31.5 percent

TABLE 18-1

Influence of Parental Income on Child's Income Level at Adulthood

Child's probability (%) of reaching a particular income level at adulthood given parental income

	PARENTS' INCOME LEVEL		
	Top decile	Fifth decile	Bottom decile
Child's income level at adulthood			
Top decile	29.6	7.3	1.3
Upper 3 deciles	59.1	23.0	9.3
Middle 4 deciles	34.3	48.0	28.3
Lower 3 deciles	6.6	29.1	62.4
Bottom decile	1.5	7.3	31.5

Source: Data from Tom Hertz, "Mobility of Black and White Families," in Bowles, Gintis, and Osborne Groves, eds. (2005). Income measure is age-adjusted log family income. Adulthood defined as age 26 or above.

chance of staying in the bottom decile, a two-thirds chance of remaining lower class, and only a slim 1.3 percent chance of making the Horatio Alger climb to the top. Finally, children born to middle-class parents (fifth decile) were most likely to remain middle class. This lack of economic mobility was even more marked for blacks. Only 17 percent of whites born into the lowest decile remained there, while the figure was 42 percent for blacks.

"Aha!" cry those on the Left. "This is proof that we live in an unfair society that puts up barriers to achievement for the poor and minorities." But not so fast. The causes of this lack of mobility are much more varied, and we need to unpeel the proverbial onion to see what is going on.[58]

First, we need to account for the effect of money simply given to children by their parents. This factor explained about 12 percent of the correlation between parental and child incomes. This then leaves unexplained the differences in what the offspring actually earned.

We can next look at the ever-controversial nature-versus-nurture issue. Perhaps high-earning parents pass on their high-earning genes to their children. Studies of fraternal and genetic twins show that 12 percent of the correlation between parent and child earnings can be explained by genes, versus 28 percent by environment. In a separate study, only 5 percent of the earnings correlation was explained by IQ, which indicates that within the 12 percent explained by genes, other genetic traits, such as personality traits, must be at work, not just native intelligence (at least as measured by IQ). Thus, while genes are an important factor, they are not an overwhelming one.

Other studies have looked at environmental factors such as education and race. Poor parents are more likely to send their children to poor schools, and racial discrimination might be a factor in both parent and child poverty. Perhaps surprisingly, schooling only accounted for 10 percent of parent-child income correlation, which suggests that other environmental factors must be at play as well. And race, when controlled for other demographic factors, was only 7 percent, so there must be more to the black-white gap than meets the eye.

We thus have a mystery. There is a high correlation between parental and child income, so in effect wealth is inherited. But the two obvious inheritances from parents, cash and genes, only account for a modest part of the correlation. Meanwhile, environmental factors such as poor schools and racial discrimination appear not to close the explanatory gap. As these various factors account for only about a third of the total correlation, there is clearly something big that we get from our parents that is missing. Many researchers believe that the missing pieces from the equation are culturally driven behavior and social capital, the subjects of the previous two sections.

The "Culture of Poverty"

In a paper titled "The Apple Does Not Fall Far From the Tree," a team of five researchers studied correlations in behaviors between parents and children.[59] The team divided the behaviors into "prosocial behaviors," such as completing school, attending church, and joining school clubs, and "delinquent behaviors," such as drug use, sex before age fifteen, fighting, damaging property, and suspension from school. The researchers also looked at a number of personality traits that have economic consequences, such as self-esteem, depression, and shyness. They found, as the title of their paper suggests, substantial correlations between parents and children on these behaviors and personality traits. School-finishing, churchgoing club joiners were likely to have goody-two-shoes children, while brawling drug-takers were likely to have delinquents. Interestingly, the researchers did not find much effect from socioeconomic status; rich delinquents were about as likely to have delinquent children as were poor delinquents. Surprisingly, parenting style, measured on five dimensions (involvement, monitoring, child autonomy, emotional warmth, and cognitive stimulation), was much less significant than one might expect. It was the *behaviors* that parents themselves exhibited, not their parenting skills per se, that seemed to matter—the parental adage "do as I say and not as I do" does not appear to work.

The researchers concluded that parental behavior has a strong influence on child behavior (not surprising to any parent), which in turn had a strong influence on future child earnings. Undoubtedly some parental behaviors have a genetic basis; for example, behaviors such as substance addiction, and disorders such as depression, have well-known genetic components. But as shown by the twin studies, overall, genetic factors play only a modest role in predicting future income. The other source of inherited behavior is the cultural norms and values that parents pass on to their children, leading to the conclusion that inherited culture must play a substantial role in individual economic outcomes.[60]

Again, this should not be surprising. If the micro rules of cultural behavior play a critical role in the economic performance of organizations and societies, one could also reasonably expect them to play a role in individual economic outcomes as well. The observation that culture is largely inherited from one's parents, peer network, and local community provides a clear mechanism for at least partially explaining the lack of social mobility. If people in upper income strata have norms that encourage individual performance, cooperation, and innovation, those norms will be passed on to their children, who will then use those norms to achieve economic success, and in turn pass them on to their children. Likewise, people in lower income strata can become trapped with cultural norms that perpetuate antisocial and antieconomic behaviors across generations. In the 1960s Senator Daniel Patrick Moynihan famously identified the "culture of poverty" as a leading cause of the persistence of an economic underclass in the United States.

We can also extend this logic to argue that antisocial cultural norms lead to networks with weak social capital.[61] Thus, individuals from dysfunctional cultures will also benefit less from their friends, neighbors, and associates.[62] There will be fewer opportunities for cooperative activity, fewer exchanges of knowledge, and fewer opportunities to share risk. Young people will also have fewer role models and mentors willing to invest in them. In such cultures, the little social capital that exists may be found in less constructive groupings, such as gangs and networks of drug dealers. In contrast, those from prosocial cultures will experience the opposite. They will benefit significantly from the help of high-social-capital networks in which role models invest in the young, people use their networks to find jobs for each other, and success is celebrated and difficulties supported.

Rawlsian Logic and Policy

Where does this leave us in the Left-Right divide? The Right is correct in that individual responsibility still matters and positive behaviors often lead to positive outcomes. Cultural norms may explain the heritability and persistence of certain behaviors, but they do not morally excuse antisocial activities. Likewise, while social mobility may be lower than popularly perceived, the United States is still a relatively mobile society, particularly for the middle classes.

But the Left is also correct. The birth-lottery of endowed wealth, native intelligence, and race taken together do play an important role in explaining economic outcomes (even if their individual contributions are modest). The birth-lottery argument becomes even more compelling if one adds culture to the lottery; after all, one cannot choose the culture that one is born into.

From a policy perspective, neither the Left's nor the Right's usual solutions look very promising. Income redistribution does not address any of the behavioral issues (whether they stem from genes or culture), and a pure laissez-faire approach to the market does not seem right when it dooms so many people to a lifetime of poverty.

Miller argues that we should abandon the Left-Right framing of this issue and instead take a stance borrowed from the philosopher John Rawls.[63] We should ask ourselves the question, "If we did not know anything about our draw in the birth-lottery, what kind of a system would we want?" Thus, we would design the system *before* knowing whether we would be born to a wealthy investment banking family on the Upper East Side, or to a single-mother crack addict in the Bronx.

The answer to this thought experiment, Miller contends, is that we would design a system that combines equality of upside opportunity with a downside social safety net. First, we would want as much a chance of climbing out of the Bronx as possible, but at the same time would not want to be penalized if we had the luck of being born to the banking family. Thus, the focus would be on helping poor people get rich, rather than economically punishing the rich. In particular, we would want to ensure that the school in the Bronx is just as good as the school available to the banker's kid. We would also want to ensure that no unfair barriers, such as racism, were placed in the way. At the same time, we would want some downside protection. Even if the poor child works hard in school, he or she still might need some drug rehab for mom and help with food, housing, and health care to keep out of desperate straits. By the same token, the banker's kid might sleep better at night knowing that if the family's fortunes collapsed due to bad luck, there was some bottom to their fall.

Miller translates his Rawlsian logic into four specific policy proposals. The first is to create universal health coverage by providing tax subsidies to enable people to buy health insurance from competing private health plans. The second is to raise the quality of public education, particularly for poorer children, by dramatically raising teacher salaries in exchange for union agreement to allow pay for performance. The third is a proposal to further reform education through a "grand bargain" between liberals and conservatives that would allow competition via a voucher system in exchange for de-linking education spending from property taxes (which ensure the richest kids get the best schools), and raising overall investment in education. Fourth, and finally, is a federal guarantee of a "minimum living wage" to put a floor under people's incomes. Miller proposes to pay for these new initiatives by redirecting 2 percent of GDP to these priorities.

Miller's Rawlsian moral logic also has the benefit of appealing to our strong-reciprocity sense of fairness. Hard work and moral rectitude would be rewarded in these proposals but sloth would not, and bad luck would be treated with generosity. This appeal to strong reciprocity gives Miller's proposals a good chance of being popularly supported—politicians take note.

Changing Cultures and Creating a "Common Layer"

While Miller's proposals would certainly help remove barriers to advancement and protect some of the most vulnerable in society, they would not, however, address the deeper cultural basis of poverty and inequality. The subject of culture and poverty is a challenging one, particularly when it touches sensitive issues of race. Senator Moynihan, a Democrat and viewed by most as a liberal, was roundly attacked by the Left as a racist for his discussions of the culture of poverty in the 1960s. But a discussion of the culture of poverty does not automatically imply either a criticism of a particular minority cultures, nor carry a message that minorities need to "act white." Just as there is nothing intrinsically Japanese or Norwegian about norms that support hard work, cooperation, and innovation, there is nothing inherently black, white, or brown about those cultural attributes either. Indeed, the growing class of African American CEOs, senior government officials, leading academics, and professionals is testament to the power of those norms and behaviors in action (and the fact that the children of such people tend also to be successful is further evidence).[64]

While there is no immutable link between race and culture, there is a link between culture and history. We saw this in Putnam's study of northern versus southern Italy, and even in the simplified world of cooperating versus noncooperating agents in simulations. One can say that while overt racism has declined (but not been fully eliminated) as a barrier to economic mobility in America, the legacy of 250 years of slavery followed by a further 100 years of racial isolation has left its mark on the culture of many African American communities. The practical questions then are, what antisocial and antieconomic norms has that history created in the culture, and how can they be changed? This view reconciles the two often competing camps among African American political and religious leaders, between those on the Left who "blame society," versus those on the Right who advocate "personal responsibility." One can simultaneously acknowledge the wrongs of the past, while looking ahead to changes in norms and individual behaviors as the keys to escaping the cultural poverty trap.

The positive message of this view is that cultures can and do change, even in the course of a few generations. Furthermore, cultures can change in ways that encourage economic progress without sacrificing other positive norms that give a culture its unique identity. For example, both Spain and Ireland have experienced substantial cultural change as well as record-breaking economic growth since the 1970s. Yet both countries have retained their respective Spanish-ness and Irish-ness. Eliminating the culture of poverty requires the changing of cultural norms, but it does not require a complete homogenization of the tapestry of American culture.

That being said, however, all societies function better when there are broadly shared common norms. Trust tends to be higher and cooperation easier to create in homogeneous societies. A long-standing challenge for the United

States, and a growing challenge for European countries with large immigrant communities, is how to engender trust and cooperation in a multi-ethnic, multicultural society. In an ideal world one would have a common layer of strong norms of what it means to be American (or British, or Brazilian, etc.) broadly shared by society. This common layer would include norms that support both democracy (e.g., the right to freedom of expression, the importance of participating in the political process) and economic achievement (e.g., the rewarding of hard work and innovation, the importance of education and self-improvement). It is this common layer of shared culture that cements together a democracy and provides a counter to the culture of poverty. Under this common layer, however, would be the rich variety of norms, traditions, and beliefs that make multicultural societies so dynamic.

Creating the common layer, however, is a challenge that spans the political system, the education system, and the media. But it is a challenge that will become increasingly important as economic growth continues to leave too many citizens behind, and as societal tensions growing from immigration and globalization continue to rise. In many respects, America has been the most successful experiment in creating such a common layer. Excepting the historical exclusion of Native Americans and African Americans, the United States has had an unrivalled record in incorporating immigrants into its society and generating economic growth and opportunity. The documents created by the founding fathers were not just documents of law, they were statements of values. Those values served the country well for two centuries, but sometime during the social upheavals of the "Great Disruption," the mechanisms for transmitting, renewing, and reinforcing those values in the nation's families, schools, places of worship, media, and political institutions fell into disrepair.

Reinvigorating and updating its culture for the modern world may be one of the most important tasks the United States faces in the new century. But it is not a challenge for the United States alone. Europe faces similar issues with integrating a population of 23 million Muslims, and determining whether the European Union is a cultural as well as an economic and political entity. Likewise, the rapid economic growth of China and India will undoubtedly bring wrenching cultural change. And finally, as discussed earlier, economic growth in the most impoverished countries of the world will not occur without cultural change to complement aid, investment, and structural reforms.

Once again, none of these issues fits neatly into the Left-Right divide. As Senator Moynihan summed it up: "The central conservative truth is that it is culture, not politics, that determines the success of a society. The central liberal truth is that politics can change a culture and save it from itself."[65]

Future Directions

In this chapter, I have attempted to give a sampling of some of the research applying ideas from Complexity Economics to important questions of public policy. There are, however, several other areas for which Complexity Economics may help increase our understanding.

For example, Complexity Economics may not help us better forecast inflation but as discussed earlier, it can potentially help us manage macroeconomic policy more effectively by giving us new insights into the dynamics of the business cycle. A long-standing mystery of business cycles is why wages are too sticky and don't fall enough to prevent recessions. In a perfectly rational society we would absorb economic downturns by all taking small cuts in wages rather than through large scale layoffs. Strong reciprocity behavior may explain this conundrum as employees see wage cuts as unfair, and poor dynamic intuition means that they don't realize that the downturn will result in increased unemployment instead.[66]

Environmental issues provide a further example. The physical environment is itself a complex adaptive system. The spike in global wealth that began around 1750 has also generated an equally large spike in carbon emissions into the atmosphere. On the long timescales of the environment, the effect of the rapid growth in global wealth has been a dramatic, human-induced pulse of change into the global ecosystem. We are blindly conducting an experiment on the environment—an experiment whose results we do not yet know. Given the propensity of complex systems to have tipping points and undergo sudden regime changes and collapses, we should be very concerned by this experiment. According to one large-scale review, we are already overshooting the regenerative capacity of the earth and using up 1.2 times the carrying capacity of our planet.[67] Complexity Economics can contribute to this issue by helping us better understand the coevolution of the economy and the environment, by reconnecting economics and thermodynamics (all production processes have an environmental cost that needs to be accounted for), and by providing insights into why humans have been so slow to respond to this global issue.[68]

Finally, there is ongoing Complexity Economics research in areas ranging from healthcare system reform, to campaign finance reform, electoral system reform, international trade, and the deregulation of industries.[69] The commonality between these areas is that they all involve understanding complex adaptive systems that are undergoing change.

Complexity Economics is still a very new player in the public policy arena. Many of the ideas I have discussed in this chapter are still at a speculative stage, but every day, new research is being conducted and the pace of progress and understanding is accelerating.

Margaret Thatcher once said, "There is no such thing as Society. There are individual men and women, and there are families."[70] From the perspective of Complexity Economics, she was simply wrong. The interactions of millions of people, making decisions, engaging in strong reciprocal behavior, acting out their cultural norms, cooperating, competing, and going about their daily lives, creates an emergent phenomenon that we call society—a phenomenon as real as the emergent pattern of a whirlpool. Within society are the constructs of states, markets, and communities, the three of which together create the economic world that we live in. We may not be able to control or predict the future direction of society, but we can endeavor to ensure that these three elements work together to create wealth, social capital, and opportunity.

I have argued that Complexity Economics both transcends and obviates traditional Left-Right categorizations. It is not a mushy middle ground between the two poles, but rather a new perspective, a new dimension from which to view the problems. My personal hope is that by placing economics on a more scientific foundation, Complexity Economics can help reduce some of the bitter partisanship that has characterized political debate in the United States, particularly since the mid-1990s. After all, the citizens for whom policy makers work are not interested in who scores more points or who wins between the Left and Right; they just want to see their lives improve.

Throughout this book, I have claimed that two institutions have provided the foundations of economic evolution: markets and science. To that score, we should add a third: democracy. Democracy is itself an evolutionary system of policy ideas. As E. M. Forster exclaimed, "Two cheers for democracy: one because it admits variety and two because it permits criticism."[71] Over the coming years, Complexity Economics will inject a new burst of variety into debates about politics and policy. It will be up to the evolutionary workings of the democratic process to select and amplify those ideas that will best serve society.

Epilogue

THERE IS A MAASAI LEGEND that in the mid-eighteenth century, one of their great leaders had a dream of a white flock of birds that devastated their lands. The leader also dreamt of a giant snake that stretched inland from the sea and took away the Maasai people. The Maasai interpret the white birds as foretelling their encounter with European settlers, and the snake as foretelling the building of the Mombasa railroad. For over a century, ever since these forces arrived on their doorstep, the Maasai have struggled to preserve their ancient nomadic way of life.

As I sat in the hut of the Maasai elder, I thought about how the course of economic evolution had taken us to very different places. On the one hand, his life has many hardships that mine does not. This struck home when one of the village men showed us a wound that had become infected. We were able to treat the wound with antibiotics, a simple cure available to any Westerner for a few dollars, but without which the man might have lost the limb or even died. Yet, despite these hardships, I observed the smiles on the faces of the villagers, the beauty of their environment, and their close sense of community. In contrast, when I returned to London, I could not help but notice the frowning, stressed faces of some of the wealthiest people on earth.

I wondered where economic evolution would take us in the future. I wondered what dreams this current Maasai elder might be having about paved roads, mobile phones, and television. How long will the Maasai be able to resist these changes? When they inevitably come, will the Maasai adapt, or will they lose what it means to be Maasai? Most importantly, will these changes make them happier?

These questions are not just relevant to the Maasai, but to all of us. Economic evolution and growth bring with them unquestionable benefits. It is easy for rich Westerners to forget what life was like a mere eight generations ago, and still is like for over a third of the world's population. The past two centuries of explosive growth have freed billions from a Hobbesian existence of toil, hunger, and disease.[1] The next century could free billions more. But such growth is not without costs, ranging from "great disruptions" in age-old patterns of life to environmental damage.

There is a natural tendency to equate evolution with progress, whether it is the biological climb from amoeba to human, or the economic climb from the stone age to modernity. But evolutionary theorists like to remind us that there is nothing in evolution that guarantees progress. *Progress* itself is too subjective a term. All we can objectively say is that under certain conditions, evolution will over time lead to greater complexity, and in an economic context, that means greater wealth. But as the theorists would also tell us, the trend toward greater complexity is not a sure thing either; biological history is full of collapses and extinctions, and so too is human social history.[2]

There is thus no guarantee that we will stay on the explosive growth curve we have been riding since 1750. One must remember that such growth is a very recent phenomenon; thus far it has lasted for only 0.01 percent of human economic history. Staying on the growth path will require that we nurture and continue to evolve the Social Technologies that have provided its foundation: markets, science, and democracy. Even in the rich West, where these STs are the most deeply embedded, they should not be taken for granted. The United States, for example, has recently struggled with business scandals leading to a populist backlash against markets, a decline in science education, and a loss of competitiveness in its democracy (in the 2004 election, 98 percent of the members of Congress who stood for reelection were reelected).[3] Economic evolution depends on the health of these STs and their constant renewal must be a priority.

Continuing the growth curve will also require that markets, science, and democracy lay deeper roots in the rest of the world. The two current growth dynamos, India and China, have each made strides on this, but more remains to be done. In India, democracy is strong and science is making progress, but the record on market reform is patchy. Meanwhile China has dramatically opened its markets and made major investments in science, but still lags in democracy. Sadly, large parts of the world, particularly sub-Saharan Africa, remain largely untouched by any of the three STs. In these parts of the world corruption, superstition, and Big Men still rule. Patiently building the institutions and culture required to support economic evolution is the only path for these countries out of poverty.

There are reasons to be optimistic, however, that the growth curve will continue for some time to come. Earlier, I paraphrased Marvin Minsky and discussed the extraordinary things that people organized into a "society of minds" are capable of. The economy is now evolving into a society of minds on a planetwide scale. The evolution of Physical Technology is continuing to drop the cost, and raise the speed of human interactions at an exponential rate.[4] Almost the entire storehouse of human knowledge is in the process of being digitized and made available to anyone, anywhere on the planet. The global society of minds is in essence evolving a global memory. Finally, if India and China continue their reforms, then over 2.3 billion people will enter the world economy in the next generation. If one is hopeful, a further 650 million people from sub-Saharan Africa will join them sometime during this century. Innovations in Physical Technology, combined with this historic addition of minds to the global society of minds, will vastly increase the degrees of possibility for the system. We can only imagine what such a system will be capable of.

The continuing evolution and spread of Physical and Social Technologies thus give us reasons to be optimistic. But some would argue that the real risk to humankind is not that we will fall off the growth curve, but rather that we will stay on it. Three issues stand out. First, like Dr. Frankenstein's monster, our global economic creation may already be in the process of turning on its creator, devouring the resources of the earth and polluting its lands, seas, and sky. As mentioned before, the environment is a complex adaptive system itself, and the potential for tipping points, radical change, and even collapse are very real. Second, since the eighteenth century, the pace of PT evolution has far outstripped ST evolution. We are already wrestling with the effects of nuclear and genetic technology, and in the next generation's lifetime, artificial intelligence and nanotechnology will likely be added to the list. If our Social Technologies do not catch up, the risks of global catastrophe will continue to grow. Third, and finally, is the clash of cultures.[5] In earlier times, cultures tended to collide only at their geographic frontiers. Today they collide on a daily basis on television, over the Internet, and in our great multicultural cities. Unfortunately, humanity's record of sensitively managing cultural clashes, from the landing of Cortés in Mexico to the current tensions between Islam and the West, is not encouraging.[6]

Despite these challenges, in my view, the balance is tipped toward optimism, in no small part because it is now within our reach to understand complex human systems. We may not be able to predict or control these systems, but we can shape them through our actions.

Undoubtedly many of the actions needed to address these issues will require vision and wisdom from political and business leaders. But we should remember that in evolutionary systems, power comes not from the top down, but from the bottom up. Evolution is a blind process, and the evolutionary algorithm will respond to whatever fitness function it is given. If, as individual consumers, workers, and voters, we ask the economy and our political institutions to maximize our short-term needs, to fill materialistic lives with ever more stuff, and to do so without regard for the health of our planet or the lives of future generations, then that is what we will get.

But there is an alternative. Through the ways in which we spend our money, whom we choose to work for, our votes, and our voices, we can create a fitness function that requires our businesses, governments, and scientific institutions to take a longer-term view and to address the needs of global society in a broader and more sustainable way. If we create such a fitness function, then those institutions and our economy will by necessity adapt and respond to that call. Edmund Burke once said that a society is a "partnership not only between those who are living, but between those who are living, those who are dead, and those who are [yet] to be born."[7] We are all a part of the global society of minds, and how that society evolves is up to each of us.

NOTES

Preface

1. See Kuhn (1962). The quote is from Nicholas Wade's retrospective on Kuhn's work in *Science*, July 8, 1977, pp. 143–145.

2. It is commonly believed that the phrase "dismal science" was used by Thomas Carlyle to describe Malthus's theories (e.g., Samuelson and Nordhaus, 1998, p. 323, or Heilbroner, 1953, p. 76). This is actually incorrect. As Levy (2003) points out, the phrase was first used by Carlyle to further his appallingly racist views. Carlyle made the remark in an 1849 pamphlet titled "An Occasional Discourse on the Negro Question" during a period when economists such as J. S. Mill were arguing against the morality of slavery as a denial of fundamental human rights. When Carlyle used the now famous turn of phrase, he was mocking the alliance of economists and abolitionists.

3. From John Maynard Keynes's 1936 *The General Theory of Employment, Interest and Money*, ch 24, part V.

4. For examples, see Brown and Eisenhardt (1998), Clippinger (1999), Kelly and Allison (1999), Lissack and Roos (1999), Petzinger (1999), Koch (2000), Lewin and Regine (2000), Pascale, Millemann, and Gioja (2000), and Stacey, Griffin, and Shaw (2000).

Chapter One

1. From Smith (1776), ch. 4, p. 25.

2. The question of what makes people happy is studied by a subfield in psychology called *hedonic psychology*. Researchers have found that while one's absolute level of wealth is not a strong determinant of happiness compared with other factors such as genetics, relationships, and career fulfillment, the rate of change of wealth over time is indeed an important factor. See Kahneman, Diener, and Schwarz (1999) for a survey.

3. Krugman (1992), preface.

4. Stuart Kauffman opens his wonderful book *At Home in the Universe* (1995) with a look out his window in Santa Fe and asks the question "where does all of the order come from?" I am indebted to Stuart for helping me appreciate the centrality of this question in economics. Kauffman (2000), 211–241, discusses his views on the question of order in economics.

5. My example is inspired by the question "how does New York manage to feed itself?" which was raised as an example of self-organization in economics in the 1987 economics meeting at the Santa Fe Institute, a meeting that we will discuss later in the book. See Anderson, Arrow, and Pines (1988).

6. The technical definition of the word *complex* and measures of complexity are topics that we will discuss later in the book. Meanwhile, my usage is the term's common meaning. For a general discussion of definitions and measures of complexity, see Gell-Mann (1994) and Flake (1998). For a technical discussion, see Haken (2000).

7. Seabright (2004), pp. 13–26.

8. For detailed accounts of humankind's long-term economic history, see Diamond (1997), Wright (2000), Landes (1998), Jay (2000), Cameron and Neal (2003), and Seabright (2004).

9. The dates in this section are all highly approximate, as estimates vary significantly and new evidence is constantly causing researchers to reconsider elements of the chronology. The sources for this section were Jones et al. (1992) and Diamond (1997).

10. Horan, Bulte, and Shogren (2005).

11. Seabright (2004). Other species do have "economies" featuring colonies of individuals living together, divisions of labor, and trade in nutrients. These species range from social insects, to the creature *Physalis physalis* (known as a Portuguese man-of-war), which is not a single organism but rather a colony of single-celled organisms. Many of these species are haplodiploids, and the female members of the colony are all sisters. True sociality among nonrelatives is not unknown; as Seabright notes, it has been seen in sticklebacks, vampire bats, and other species. However, the sociality tends to be around specific tasks, within very small groups, and for limited periods. Extensive cooperation among large numbers of nonrelatives persisting over long periods does appear to be unique to humans. Nonetheless, the study of other social species and superorganisms provides fascinating insights into the dynamics and evolution of cooperation—insights that may be applicable to human economies as well. See, for example, Bonabeau, Dorigo, and Theraulaz (1999).

12. Horan, Bulte, and Shogren (2005).

13. This description of the Yanomamö is drawn from Chagnon (1992).

14. The $90 figure is based on an estimate of very long-run world GDP, by J. Bradford DeLong of the University of California–Berkeley (see DeLong's Web site, www.j-bradford-delong.net, for a description of the data and methodology). Although I could not find GDP figures specific to the Yanomamö, the Yanomamö live a lifestyle roughly typical of 10,000 to 15,000 years ago. According to DeLong's figures, this would place the Yanomamö at around $93 in GDP per capita (in constant 1990 dollars), but we should not put too fine a point on it and I have thus rounded the figure to $90. I have used GDP per person as a proxy for income, as the Yanomamö have very little savings and no government, so what is produced is consumed. As another reference point, the World Bank estimate of gross national income per capita for the world's least developed countries in the world is $280. Some example indicators of the relative development levels of these countries are 11.9 telephone lines per 1,000 people, 2.8 computers per 1,000, and 14 percent of roads paved. Estimating Yanomamö income at approximately one-third of this level, which also gives us $93 per capita, while not precise, is probably not unreasonable. New York City average income data is from New York State government statistics. Median income, however, is probably more informative than average, and the U.S. Census Bureau reports median household income in New York State averaged $43,160 for 2001–2003. But we know even less about income distribution in Yanomamö society, so I have simply compared averages.

15. Chagnon (1992) does much to explode the myth that life before the advent of technology was a kind of innocent Eden. For example, one-quarter of all Yanomamö males die violently, and the Yanomamö people also suffer from very high infant mortality. The overall mortality data for the Yanomamö averages 6.5 percent (calculated from the data given in ibid., p. 268, for the years 1987 to 1991). I have used the data for the most remote villages with the least modern contact, because this better approximates the ancestral hunter-gatherer lifestyle. The comparable figure for New Yorkers is 0.84 percent (from the 2002 U.S. Census). This rough comparison actually understates the difference, as Yanomamö demographics are significantly younger than the New Yorker demographics.

16. I am paraphrasing DeLong's statement from his study of long-run GDP. DeLong's actual words were these: "I know I at least would be extremely unhappy if I were handed my current income, told that I could spend it on goods at current prices, but that I was prohibited from buying anything not made before 1800." See www.j-bradford-delong.net.

17. Schwartz (2004) points out that such a wide array of choice does not, as economists have long assumed, necessarily mean an increase in welfare. I have used some of Schwartz's examples from pp. 9–22.

18. I was unable to find an exact measure of SKUs in any research on the Yanomamö. However, an informal counting of the items mentioned in Chagnon (1992) and some assumptions yielded an estimate of around 300 SKUs. As a further reference, I informally counted items on my visit to a Maasai village, a significantly more advanced society with far more contact with the modern world, and came up with approximately 800 SKUs.

19. Although I have not found any reliable estimates of the number of unique products and services on offer in a modern economy, one data point is at least instructive in the likely order of magnitude: the universal product code (UPC) system. The UPC system is an inaccurate measure itself, because not all final products have UPC codes, the vast majority of services (which in turn account for most consumption

in developed countries) do not, and UPC codes are also used for intermediate goods. Nonetheless, the code does give us one measure of product diversity. The current UPC system has twelve digits, of which two are administrative, meaning the unique product part of the code is ten digits. The manager of the system, the Universal Code Council, is running out of codes and recently moved to a thirteen-digit system. A full UPC system with ten numerically identifying digits implies 10 billion products. The hierarchical structure of the system, however, means that not all codes are available for all products. For example, if Pepsi runs out of its unique codes, it cannot use a code with digits assigned to Coke. Let's assume that the code utilization is 50 percent and, for sake of argument, that the number of false codes and number of uncoded products roughly cancels out and that the ratio of product SKUs to service SKUs in the economy is proportional to the ratio of product to service consumption (services were 59 percent of U.S. 2002 total consumption). Under these assumptions, we would have about 12 billion SKUs, or in the range of 10^{10}. A further cross-check is that if world GDP is $36.5 trillion, then this would imply an average of $3,650 in GDP per SKU, which seems to be about the right order of magnitude. Petroski (1992), 23, cites a few other numbers that help us get a sense of the magnitude of SKU diversity. He notes that 5 million patents have been issued in the United States alone and the Chemical Society's database contains over 10 million human-made chemical substances. Likewise, Schwartz (2004), pp. 9–22, gives a sampling of the staggering array of items found just in his local environment in Philadelphia. Whatever the true number of SKUs, it would clearly be very large. My calculation is intended merely to illustrate the complexity of the modern economy. A serious analysis of this topic would undoubtedly yield some very interesting results.

20. It is difficult to place the lifestyle of the Yanomamö exactly in our crude timeline. There is much controversy between researchers on the date of the first human colonization of the Americas, but it ranges from 10,000 to 35,000 years ago, with evidence of settlements in South America from about 15,000 years ago (Diamond, 1997, pp. 45–50). There is evidence of settled agriculture in various parts of the world starting around 10,000 years ago (p. 100). Given that the Yanomamö are descendents of people who migrated into the Americas, but that their economy is not one of settled agriculture, their lifestyle is probably typical of people living 10,000 to 15,000 years ago. Again, this observation is intended to be more illustrative than exact.

21. DeLong constructed this estimate out of seven data sets: a long-term estimate of population size by Kremer, three long-term series on GDP per capita, and three series on world GDP. The data and a description of how DeLong constructed the series are published under the title "Estimating World GDP, One Million B.C. to Present" on DeLong's Web site, www.j-bradford-delong.net. For the period from 2.5 million BC (roughly the appearance of the first tools) to the beginning of DeLong's series at 1 million BC (for which period he estimates GDP per capita at $92), I have simply assumed a linear extrapolation from zero. Naturally, any specific estimates over such a long period are highly speculative, but economic historians have significant evidence regarding the overall pattern that the data shows.

22. In looking at the curves for GDP per capita growth, one might initially (and not unreasonably) think that the sudden near-vertical bend in the curve is simply the result of exponential growth viewed over a very long period. However, plots of log GDP per capita reveal a nearly identical shape. Doyne Farmer of the Santa Fe Institute analyzed DeLong's data for his 2003 Ulam Lecture and concluded that the data exhibited double exponential growth (www.santafe.edu/~jdf). Given the degree to which the data series is an estimate, one cannot be conclusive regarding its functional form, but there is significant evidence that the rate of growth has been accelerating over time. See Bernstein (2004), pp. 17–23, for further discussion and data.

23. Ormerod (1994), p. 10, cites a 1982 study by Angus Maddison showing a related statistic, that Western economies grew as much in percentage terms between 1950 and 1970 as they did between 500 and 1500. Bernstein (2004) also discusses the Maddison data.

24. Landes (1969), p. 5.

25. I have borrowed the term *econosphere* from Stuart Kauffman; see Kauffman (2000), p. 211.

26. Darwin was, of course, the first to see evolution as an algorithm, although he did not articulate it in that specific way and did not have the later mathematical discoveries of Alan Turing, Kurt Gödel, or Alonzo Church to help him see the broader implications (Dennett, 1995, pp. 48–50). For popular expositions on the idea of evolution as an algorithm, see Dawkins (1976) and (1982) and Dennett (1995), in particular ch. 2, section 4, from which I have borrowed the term *substrate*. For a mathematical treatment, see Landweber and Winfree (2002).

27. See Paul Krugman's critique of the book *Bionomics*, by Michael Rothschild (Rothschild, 1990): "The Power of Biobabble," published on the *Slate* Web site, October 23, 1997.

28. See, for example, Holland (1975), Whitley (1993), Mitchell (1996), Landweber and Winfree (2002), and Crutchfield and Schuster (2003).

29. Hodgson (1993), p. 81, notes that it was actually the sociologist Herbert Spencer, not Darwin, who coined the term *survival of the fittest*. Hodgson goes on to defend Spencer's economic ideas, which he contends were insightful for their time. However, Spencer's ideas increasingly became hijacked at the turn of the century by Social Darwinists with political and racist agendas.

30. Dennett (1995), pp. 28–34 and 48–60. Richard Dawkins also eloquently made this point in 1986 in *The Blind Watchmaker*.

31. For a review of debates on Darwinism versus theories of "intelligent design" (creationism by another name), see Dembski and Ruse (2004).

32. Increasing complexity is not a *guaranteed* result of the evolutionary process. Rather, it is dependent on the implementation of the system and the tuning of its parameters. Kauffman (1993) argues that biological evolution has self-tuned its parameters to enable growth in complexity. However, while biological evolution has increased the average complexity of the biosphere and the complexity of the most complex organisms, that increase has been far from monotonic, as the various crashes of extinction and bursts of speciation in the fossil record show. Likewise, although the overall trend in economic evolution has been toward greater order and complexity, the historical record too shows it has been far from monotonic. See Wright (2000) and Cameron and Neal (2003).

33. Dennett (1995) and Kauffman (1995a), pp. 149–189, also make this point.

34. Paul Seabright, in his fascinating 2004 book *The Company of Strangers: A Natural History of Economic Life*, also uses the example of a shirt in his first chapter, although his purpose is to illustrate the intricate cooperation involved in the manufacture of even the most prosaic products in the global economy. My purpose is different and is to make a point about the evolution of designs. I only became aware of Seabright's book and his shirt example late in the process of editing and thus happened on shirts as my choice of illustration independently. Furthermore, during final editing Pietra Rivoli published her *The Travels of a T-Shirt in the Global Economy: An Economist Examines the Markets, Power, and Politics of World Trade* (John Wiley & Sons, 2005). Perhaps shirts will become the standard example of economic evolution and globalization, much as Adam Smith's pins have become the canonical example of the division of labor.

35. My use of the labels *Physical Technology* and *Social Technology* are from Nelson (2003) and will be defined more fully later in the book.

36. Social Technologies are similar but not identical to what economists refer to as institutions. I will more fully define Social Technologies in chapter 12 and make this distinction clearer.

37. Freeman and Soete (1997).

38. See Hodgson (1993) for an excellent history of evolutionary theory in economics.

39. Charles Darwin's *Autobiography*, p. 120, as quoted in Plotkin (1993), pp. 28–29.

40. Alfred Russell Wallace deserves credit for independently coming to many of the same insights that Darwin had. While Darwin was generous in recognizing Wallace's contributions (and afraid of being scooped), the historical record shows that Darwin did indeed get there first (Browne, 2002).

41. Thorstein Veblen, "Why Is Economics Not an Evolutionary Science?" *Quarterly Journal of Economics* 12 (1898), pp. 373–397, reprinted in Gherity (1965).

42. There has been controversy about Marshall's intent with this passage, but he repeated it in every edition of *Principles*, starting with the fifth. See Hodgson (1993), ch. 7, for a discussion of Marshall's thoughts on economics and evolution.

43. Hayek wrote repeatedly about linking evolution and what he called "spontaneous order." He was probably the first economist to look seriously at theories of self-organization developed by the chemist Ilya Prigogine. See Hodgson (1993), ch. 12, for a discussion. Also see Vriend (2002) on Hayek and complexity, and Colander (2000) for a historical survey of complexity thinking in economics.

44. Nelson and Winter (1982).

45. See Waldrop (1992), p. 82.

46. For a highly readable introduction to complex adaptive systems, see Waldrop (1992). There are also several other excellent popular books on the subject, including Gell-Mann (1994), Kauffman (1995a), Holland (1998), and Johnson (2001). Flake (1998) provides a nicely written and illustrated introductory text. For a comprehensive technical introduction, see Bar-Yam (1997). For a compendium of early papers and discussion, see Cowan, Pines, and Meltzer (1994).

47. For examples, see Anderson, Arrow, and Pines (1988), and Cowan, Pines, and Meltzer (1994).

48. I first heard Brian Arthur use the term "complexity economics" in a lecture in 1994. The first printed reference is in Arthur (1999) in *Science*: "Complexity economics is not a temporary adjunct to static economic theory, but theory at a more general, out-of-equilibrium level."

49. The notion of scientific programs was developed by the philosopher of science Imre Lakatos in the late 1960s. For an application to economic methodology, see Mark Blaug's essay in Hausman (1994), pp. 348–375. See Hands (2001) for further discussion.

Chapter Two

1. This account is adapted from various sources, including Waldrop (1992), news reports from the period, personal discussions with founding members of the Santa Fe Institute, and the Citigroup Web site.

2. Waldrop (1992), p. 91.

3. See, for example, Ormerod (1194), Keen (2001), and Fullbrook, ed. (2004).

4. Cassidy (1996). The article was widely discussed at the December 1996 annual meeting of the American Economics Association as well as at a subsequent meeting of over sixty leading economists at Stanford in January 1997.

5. See, for example, Colander, Holt, and Rosser (2004).

6. Quoted in Cassidy (1996).

7. Alan Greenspan, quoted in Andrews (2005).

8. At this point, I will not delve into a philosophical debate about whether economics is a science in the same way that, say, physics is. But I will contend that economics has aspirations to be scientific in the sense that the field's goals are to provide an understanding of human economic phenomena through explanations that are rigorous, logically consistent, and backed by empirical observation. For discussions of the status of economics as a science, see Hausman (1994) and Hands (2001). Evidence for economics' scientific aspirations can be found in virtually any economics textbook, or in the acceptance criteria for any refereed journal in the field.

9. For histories of economics, see Niehans (1990) and Backhouse (2002). For classic introductory textbooks, see Samuelson and Nordhaus (1998) and Stiglitz (1997). For a managerially oriented text, see Mansfield (1999).

10. Some readers will note that my characterization of the Traditional Economics consensus has a distinctly Anglo-American Neoclassical bias. This is because of the global dominance of those ideas, particularly in recent decades. Continental academics have typically given more prominence to historical and institutional views of economics than have their British and American counterparts. I will later discuss the relevance of those views to Complexity Economics.

11. Nelson and Winter (1982), pp. 6–11. I have added survey articles to my definition to admit more advanced material. I have also not followed Nelson and Winter's lead on their use of the label *orthodox economics* because I do not believe that Traditional Economics represents an orthodoxy anymore; as we will see, numerous economists and physical scientists disagree with many elements of the historical paradigm. For now, "Traditional" is a more accurate term. Nonetheless, Nelson and Winter's description of the strengths and weaknesses of their term orthodox economics holds for my definition of Traditional Economics as well.

12. Everyone has his or her favorite textbooks, but examples include, for microeconomics, Samuelson and Nordhaus (1998), Stiglitz (1997), and Mas-Colell, Whinston, and Green (1995). For macroeconomics examples, see Dornbusch and Fischer (1990), Mankiw (1994), Krugman and Obstfeld (1991), D. Romer (1996), Blanchard and Fischer (1989), and Heijdra and Van Der Ploeg (2002). For an example of the type of survey article I am referring to, see *Quarterly Journal of Economics* 115, nos. 1 and 4 (2000), in which, in celebration of the millennium, Harvard University's prestigious journal commissioned a series of six essays by leading economists on the question "What do we know about economics today that Marshall did not?" Examples of some recent survey monographs include Aghion et al. (2003) and Szenberg and Ramrattan (2004).

13. Baumol (2000), pp. 3–4, also notes that textbooks are a useful gauge of the state of the field because "the material selected for such a book can therefore be expected to focus on subjects deemed to shed light on the workings of the economy and the design of policy. They are intended to sum up the contributions of economics that really matter to others, and not just to those who labor at the frontiers of our discipline, sometimes perhaps, as Marshall put it, largely '. . . for the purpose of mathematical diversion' . . . It follows that the textbook criterion can indicate what economists believe others should glean from the work of our profession . . . that is, what [is] *useful.*"

14. There are, of course, exceptions. See, for example, Szenberg and Ramrattan (2004).

15. Not all Nobel laureates fall into what I have labeled the Traditional camp. For example, the work of Herbert Simon, Friedrich Hayek, Douglass North, and Daniel Kahneman have all provided critical foundations for the work of the Complexity economists.

16. In a review article, Colander (1999), pp. 6–7, provides a nice summary of what I am referring to as Traditional Economics: "Through the 1990s, economic researchers typically started with a set of principles: for example, utility-maximizing by consumers and profit-maximizing for firms, far-sighted individual rationality, and a belief in equilibrium, which meant that structurally, individual's decisions in the models fit reasonably well together. These principles were probably best embodied in Debreu's 1959 *Theory of Value*. During the second half of the 1900s, they first became comprehensively embedded in microeconomic models, and then, as Keynesian economics declined and New Classical macroeconomics became dominant in the 1980s, they spread to macroeconomics as well. By the late twentieth century, these principles formed the core of economist' vision of reality, in the sense that all economic models were built on these principles, or around variations of these principles like assumptions of bounded rationality or imperfect information."

17. See Backhouse (2002), pp. 13–17, for an overview of Xenophon's work.

18. Biographical details about Adam Smith are from Ross (1995), Niehans (1990), and Backhouse (2002). The origin of the term *classical economics* comes from Marx (Niehans, 1990, pp. 9–13). Marx himself is now commonly placed in this period, though he probably would have vociferously objected to being put in the same category as Adam Smith.

19. There are, of course, many important questions that economics has wrestled with. However, questions of the nature of economic value and its ultimate source, growth, and allocation have dominated the Classical, Marginalist, and Neoclassical periods (Niehans, 1990). More specific questions such as the role of money, the setting of prices, and the gains from exchange have typically been placed within the framework of these larger questions. A possible exception is phenomenological questions of the macroeconomy, such as the nature of unemployment. But the longtime quest of macroeconomics has been to integrate such questions into a more fundamental framework based on value, growth, and allocation.

20. Smith's intention to explicitly address both questions is clearly spelled out in the title of the first part of *The Wealth of Nations*: "Of the Causes of Improvement in the productive Powers of Labour [i.e., the origin of wealth], and of the Order according to which its Produce is naturally distributed among the different Ranks of the People [i.e., the allocation of Wealth]." Smith (1776), p. ix.

21. Smith also acknowledged the importance of technology and capital in boosting productivity, but saw those as ultimately driven by the division of labor; for example, the amount and type of machinery required would be determined by the organization of labor. See Backhouse (2002), p. 124.

22. Smith (1776), book 1, ch. 1, p. 4.

23. Niehans (1990), p. 60.

24. Smith (1776), book 1, ch. 2, p. 15.

25. Ibid., book 4, ch. 2, p. 482.

26. Ibid., p. 485.

27. For brevity, I have greatly simplified my description of Smith's view of supply and demand. Although Smith can be credited with the first clear articulation of the role of price in equilibrating supply and demand, his portrayal was not the modern form we are accustomed to. Smith postulated a "natural price" based on factor costs plus a "natural rate" of return on capital. If the market price were above the natural price, then consumers would reduce their demand, driving the price back to its "natural" level. Although the idea of a "natural" rate of return in the form of the zero-profit condition did survive in production theory, Smith had no theory of utility and budgets to provide constraining conditions on the demand side. Not until seventy-two years later, when John Stuart Mill published his *Principles of Political Economy*, would there be a complete theory of supply and demand, and then Marshall provided the famous X diagram in 1890. See Niehans (1990) and Backhouse (2002).

28. According to Niehans (1990), pp. 24–36, Cantillon was very specific and calculated this balancing point at 1.5 acres of land per head. At this point, according to Cantillon, wages would be at subsistence levels and the population neither starving nor growing.

29. For a description of Quesnay's *Tableau Économique*, see ibid., pp. 37–48. As an eighteenth-century physician, Quesnay believed that the health of the body depended on a balance of circulatory flows of humors (blood, bile, lymph, and phlegm), and there is a clear metaphorical connection between his medical views of bodily health and his views of economic health. For a discussion of the metaphor of the economy as circulatory system, see Mirowski (1989).

30. The term *lassez-faire*, however, is attributable to Pierre de Boisguilbert, a critic of the government of Louis XIV. See Backhouse (2002), p. 91.

31. Ibid., pp. 104–108, and Niehans (1990), pp. 73–76.

32. We will discuss theories of increasing returns in the next chapter, as well as in the context of positive feedback dynamics in part 2.

33. Turgot's work would later be extended and given analytical footing by Antoine Augustin Cournot and Johann Heinrich von Thünen. See Niehans (1990), pp. 164–187.

34. Ibid., pp. 123–126.

35. The notion of utility was first articulated by the Dutch mathematician Daniel Bernoulli in 1738. Bentham independently rediscovered it sixty years later and, unlike Bernoulli, did not give it a mathematical form. Bernoulli's discovery, however, failed to have a significant impact until much later, whereas Bentham's writings were highly influential on a subsequent generation of economists, including Mill and Ricardo and the later Neoclassicists. See ibid., pp. 118–137, and Backhouse (2002), pp. 132–165.

36. Backhouse (2002), p. 136.

37. While Bernoulli and Bentham had both postulated a diminishing marginal utility of income, neither had extended the concept to consumption or given it an analytic treatment. Thus, Niehans (1990), pp. 187–196, credits Gossen for the concept of diminishing marginal utility. For convenience, I have discussed Gossen's work in the section with Classical economists such as Smith, Turgot, and Bentham. However, on the basis of Gossen's analytic treatment of utility and as a contemporary of Cournot and von Thünen, Niehans properly classifies Gossen as an early Marginalist.

38. An autobiographical note by Walras on this incident is given in Ingrao and Israel (1990), p. 87.

39. Quoted in ibid., p. 88.

40. Mirowski (1989), Niehans (1990), and Backhouse (2002).

41. On the use of numerical examples in Classical economics, see Backhouse (2002), pp. 237–240. Prior to Walras and the Neoclassicists, early-nineteenth-century economists such as Antoine Cournot, Johann Heinrich von Thünen, and Hermann Heinrich Gossen used basic algebraic techniques and differential calculus. See ibid., pp. 166–168.

42. Stewart (1989).

43. Ingrao and Israel (1990).

44. Stewart (1989), p. 60.

45. Walras noted in various letters and articles the significant influence of Poinsot's book and other writings on rational mechanics in the development of his theories. See Ingrao and Israel (1990), p. 88, and Mirowski (1989), pp. 219–220.

46. Ingrao and Israel (1990), p. 88.

47. Walras never actually proved either the existence, the uniqueness, or the stability of his equilibrium; rather, he merely worked through the equations until he found one that satisfied the conditions. Such formal and general proofs would have to wait until the twentieth century, when von Neumann introduced fixed-point techniques to the field. See Mas-Colell, Whinston, and Green (1995), pp. 584–598, for existence and uniqueness proofs for Walrasian equilibria.

48. Mirowski (1989), pp. 243–248, provides an account of Walras's reactions to early criticisms about these assumptions.

49. Niehans (1990), pp. 197–207.

50. Quoted in ibid., pp. 197, 198.

51. Mirowski (1989), pp. 217, 256–257, notes the popularity of this text in spreading the key ideas of Lagrange, Maxwell, and Faraday within England. Jevons was known to have attended Faraday's lectures at the Royal Institution and followed the writings of Thomson, Maxwell, and Joule closely.

52. According to Mirowski (1989), p. 257, Jevons's initial metaphor of choice was a lever in equilibrium, a metaphor he used to derive his initial equations of exchange. Later, he broadened his conception to a more general notion of energetics and the mathematical use of field theory.

53. Quoted in ibid., p. 219.

54. Ibid., pp. 217–222. Niehans (1990), pp. 189, 201, notes that in the first edition of Jevons's *Principles*, it is not clear whether Jevons got his notion of diminishing marginal utility directly from Gossen, as Jevons merely notes that the principle is implied in the writings of a number of economists and refers only specifically to Richard Jennings. In the second edition, however, Jevons devotes six pages of the preface to Gossen and credits Gossen's originality.

55. Quoted in Mirowski (1989), p. 219.

56. Niehans (1990), pp. 259–266.

57. Niehans (1990), p. 265, notes that Pareto argued that in the absence of fixed costs, a central planner could only equal the market outcome, but with fixed costs, a central planner could achieve a superior outcome. As Niehans adds, this argument would be further developed by Hotelling's analysis of monopolistic competition in 1938.

58. From Voltaire's *Candide*, 1759, ch. 1.

59. Mirowski (1989), pp. 219–221.

60. Niehans (1990), pp. 420–444.

61. As Samuelson himself commented on the relationship between Hicks's book and his own, "Value and Capital was an expository tour de force of great originality, which built up a readership for the problems Foundations grappled with and for the expansion of mathematical economics that soon came." Quoted in Backhouse (2002), p. 259.

62. For an exposition of Samuelson's revealed preference theory, see Mas-Colell, Whinston, and Green (1995), pp. 5–16.

63. For an exposition of Arrow-Debreu general equilibrium, see ibid., pp. 691–693.

64. The debate over the efficiency of allocation in market economies versus centrally planned ones has a long history going back to Pareto and Enrico Barone. They each concluded that a central planner could do at least as well as a market since both the central planner and the market were simply solving a Walrasian system of equations. Oskar Lange argued that all that mattered from a social-welfare perspective is that the correct prices are used; he said it was irrelevant whether those prices were discovered by a market or by a central planner. Friedrich Hayek countered that in practical terms, it was impossible for any central planner to acquire all the information needed to calculate correct prices. The Soviet Union actually attempted to adopt Lange's technique and created massive mathematical models to calculate prices. History, however, would seem to have proven Hayek right. As we will discuss later, in developing his arguments on socialism, Hayek anticipated many of the key themes of Complexity Economics. See Niehans (1990) and Backhouse (2002) for histories of this debate, and Hayek (1988), Bernstein (2001), and Caldwell (2004) for discussions of Hayek's views.

65. Niehans (1990), pp. 445–451, and John Elliot's introduction in the 1983 edition of Schumpeter (1934).

66. Quoted by John Elliot in Schumpeter (1934), p. xix.

67. Ibid., p. xxiv.

68. Although it is fair to say that Neoclassical growth models, exemplified by the later work of Robert Solow and Paul Romer, dominated Traditional Economics at the end of the century, the Schumpeterian tradition of growth theory has also continued into the modern era. See Nelson (1996), Scherer (1999), and Helpman (2004) for discussions.

69. Niehans (1990), pp. 451–456, notes, however, the contributions of Roy Harrod during this period. Although Harrod was largely concerned with extending Keynes's theory of the business cycle and his mathematical skills were limited, he was an important transitional figure between Schumpeter and Solow.

70. In the spirit of full disclosure, Robert Solow has on occasion served as an adviser to McKinsey & Company, a firm I am associated with as well.

71. Solow (2000), pp. ix–xxvi.

72. The balanced-growth concept was introduced in an earlier *Econometrica* paper in 1953 coauthored with Paul Samuelson, but the full "Solow model," with exogenous population growth, was first described in Solow (1956).

73. For expositions of Solow's model, see Solow (2000), Barro and Sala-i-Martin (1995), and D. Romer (1996).

74. See P. M. Romer (1994), Aghion and Howitt (1998), and Barro and Sala-i-Martin (1995) for reviews.

75. P. M. Romer (1990).

76. Heijdra and Van Der Ploeg (2002).

77. For example, Michael Porter's widely used work on strategy has its roots in Neoclassical microeconomics. See Porter (1980) and (1985).

78. Niehans (1990), p. 491.

Chapter Three

1. This account is drawn from Waldrop (1992).

2. Anderson (1972).

3. In 1944, the physicist Erwin Schrödinger wrote "What Is Life?" a provocative essay that wrestles with these issues. For a modern discussion, see Haynie (2001).

4. In the spirit of full disclosure, the firm I am affiliated with, McKinsey & Company, has been a financial supporter of research at the Santa Fe Institute since 1994.

5. My description of this meeting is drawn from Waldrop (1992), pp. 136–197, Anderson, Arrow, and Pines (1988), and personal discussions with various of the meeting's participants.

6. Waldrop (1992), p. 142.

7. Quoted in Ingrao and Israel (1990), p. 158.

8. Ibid., p. 159.

9. Mirowski (1988), pp. 241–265, and Ingrao and Israel (1990), pp. 148–173, give accounts of the scientific critiques of the Marginalist program.

10. Friedman (1953).

11. Hands (2001), p. 53, notes the impact of the essay as "it is cited in almost every economics textbook." According to economic philosopher Daniel Hausman (1994), the essay is, half a century later, "the only essay in methodology that a large number of, perhaps majority of, economists have ever read."

12. H. Simon, "Problems of Methodology—Discussion," *American Economic Review: Papers and Proceedings* 53 (1963): 229–31, reprinted in Hausman (1994), pp. 214–216.

13. I am, of course, simplifying, but the logic is the same as Simon's example: "X-businessmen desire to maximize profits; Y-businessmen can and do make the calculations that identify the profit-maximizing course of action . . . [therefore] Z-prices and quantities are observed at those levels which maximize the profits of the firms in the market." Simon noted that Nagel had shown the fallacy of using the validity of Z to support X and Y, and further argued that one would need to observe X and Y to support the theory, even if Z were observed. Ibid.

14. D. M. Hausman, "Why Look Under the Hood?," in Hausman (1994), pp. 217–221.

15. For a summary of critiques of Friedman, see Hands (2001), pp. 53–60. I am greatly simplifying here. For a review and detailed references on the role of assumptions in science and economics, see ibid., and for an anthology of classic articles, see Hausman (1994). In the course of my discussion on economic methodology and philosophy of science, I will draw on various models, including Hempel's deductive-nomological (D-N) model, post-Kuhnian sociology of scientific knowledge (SSK), Lakatos's methodology of scientific research programs (MSRP), and Campbell's evolutionary epistemology.

16. The originator of the theory-as-map analogy is the philosopher of science Ronald Giere (Hands, 2001, p. 311). My explanation is drawn from Holland (1998), pp. 28–33. Also see Sterman (2002) for a discussion of models as approximations.

17. Axel Leijonhufvud, "Towards a Not-Too-Rational Macroeconomics," in Colander (1996), pp. 39–55.

18. See, for example, Kahneman, Slovic, and Tversky (1982).

19. Technology, of course, plays a role in establishing the bounds of "satisficing" behavior. For example, someday we might have the price of all nearby gas stations beamed to our cars via the wireless Internet and then be directed to the cheapest one via GPS, and the on-board computer might calculate the trade-off between gallons used in driving the extra distance and the cost saved. But even with more information available, people still engage in "satisficing," for example, you might switch the computer off because you can't be bothered to go the extra distance to save a few dollars and you think a nearer station might have cleaner bathrooms.

20. Behavioral game theory probably comes closest to incorporating behavioral, informational, and market-structure effects in an equilibrium setting. See Camerer (2003) for a survey. However, as Camerer notes (pp. 473–476), there is still some distance to go before all these effects are simultaneously incorporated in a realistic way.

21. Kirman and Gérard-Varet (1999) p. 10. There are exceptions. Kirman notes that the non-*tâtonnement* models of Hahn and Negishi explicitly deal with time. Steve Smale worked with dynamic models in the 1970s, and Richard Day in the 1980s and 1990s. I view concepts such as the Hicksian "week" as arbitrary index times that don't relate to real-world timescales (despite the name *week*), something that Hicks himself admitted (see Hicks, 1939, p. 122).

22. Imagine a process that randomly rains $20 bills on a geographic area. Also imagine that the population of that area is not evenly distributed, but clustered in an area we will call A. At some point, by random chance, there will be an accumulation of bills in a relatively unpopulated area (call it B). Once that accumulation is discovered, people will rush to area B to pick the bills up. But since this takes time, while they are gone, bills will pile up in area A. They will rush back to A. The macro pattern will be fluctuating stocks of bills in areas A and B.

23. For example, Richard Day (1994) and (1999) has done much to bring a dynamic perspective to the field (though his work is arguably in the gray zone between Traditional and Complexity Economics). Some might also argue that game theory and many macroeconomic models are dynamic, but again, in the majority of these models, the dynamics are paths to a preassumed equilibrium and there is no explicit recognition of either absolute or relative timescales. See Fudenberg and Tirole (1991) and Heijdra and Van Der Ploeg (2002) for examples.

24. See Anderson, Arrow, and Pines (1988), Arthur, Durlauf, and Lane (1997), Sterman (2000), and Durlauf and Young (2001) for discussions.

25. One can point to work such as "endogenous growth theory" (Aghion and Howitt, 1998) as a counterexample. However, as discussed previously, while such theories improve our understanding of the interaction between innovation and economic variables at an aggregate level, they merely place innovation in a black box within the bounds of the model and tell us little about what is inside the box. In part 3, I will make clearer what a fundamental and endogenous theory of innovation might look like.

26. See, for example, Crutchfield and Schuster (2003), pp. 65–78, 81–100.

27. Cutler, Poterba, and Summers (1989).

28. Mankiw (1994), p. 326.

29. Some researchers, such as Mordecai Kurz (1997), have attempted to model endogenous fluctuations within an equilibrium framework. Such work arguably falls in a gray zone between Traditional models and Complexity Economics approaches as I have defined the terms.

30. Arthur (1994a). Arthur's theories on increasing returns were popularized in the 1990s by the science writer Mitchell Waldrop (1992) and in a *New Yorker* column (January 12, 1998, pp. 32–37) by economics writer John Cassidy. In response, Princeton economist and *New York Times* columnist Paul Krugman wrote a scathing article in January 1998, "The Legend of Arthur," attacking Arthur's contributions on increasing returns. This in turn prompted responses in Arthur's defense from Waldrop and Cassidy. Nobel laureate Kenneth Arrow had the last word, strongly defending Arthur and arguing that Arthur had made important contributions to the modern understanding of increasing returns. Krugman's original column and the letters in reply are available at www.pkarchive.org.

31. Keynes (1923), p. 65.

32. Thomas Love Peacock (1835), "The March of Mind," ch. 2 in *Crotchet Castle*.

33. The argument that the purpose of science is explanation was put forward by the logical-empiricist school in the 1950s by figures such as Richard Braithwaite, Ernest Nagel, and Carl Hempel. For a classic articulation, see Hempel's deductive-nomological (D-N) model in Hempel (1965). For discussions in an economic context, see Hands (2001), pp. 82–88, and Hausman (1994), pp. 1–50.

34. For a classic lecture by Popper on this subject, see Klemke, Hollinger, and Kline (1980), pp. 19–34. For a modern discussion in an economic context, see Hands (2001), pp. 88–93.

35. I'm presenting a highly simplified view of science as an evolutionary process. See Hull (1988) and Plotkin (1993) for more complete discussions.

36. Kirman and Gérard-Varet (1999), p. 8.

37. See W. H. Greene (2000) for an introduction.

38. See, for example, Campbell, Lo, and MacKinlay (1997), Mandelbrot (1997), Lo and MacKinlay (1999), Mantegna and Stanley (2000), Shleifer (2000), Shiller (2000), Johnson, Jeffries, and Hui (2003), and Sornette (2003).

39. See, for example, Kagel and Roth (1995) and Camerer, Loewenstein, and Rabin (2004).

40. Paradoxically, while microeconomics typically ignores inventory effects, inventory dynamics have taken on growing importance in macroeconomic work. See, for example, Blanchard and Fischer (1989), pp. 301–308, 332–336. However, even these lagged models do not capture the full story. See Sterman (2000), pp. 661–842, for an account of the macro-level effects of inventory, backlog, and capacity; the account includes a truly dynamic model.

41. Lillo and Farmer (2004).

42. Samuelson and Nordhaus (1998), p. 681.

43. F. T. Cave (2004).

44. Montier (2002), pp. 29–31.

45. In fact, Kai Nagel, a computer scientist; Martin Shubik, an economist; and Maya Paczuski and Per Bak, both physicists, have built a model along these lines. See Nagel et al. (2000). Their model shows that the search for low prices and spatial dynamics combine to create price convergence, but with a lag and a distribution of prices with statistical similarities to real-world data.

46. As the highly regarded macroeconomist Olivier Blanchard (2000), p. 1402, notes, "macroeconomics today is solidly grounded in a general equilibrium structure. Modern models characterize the economy as being in temporary equilibrium."

47. Scarf and Hansen (1973) and Axtell (2002) and (2003).

48. Scarf and Hansen (1973).

49. Lo and MacKinlay (1999), pp. 26–40.

50. See Mandelbrot (1997), Lo and MacKinlay (1999), Mantegna and Stanley (2000), and Johnson, Jeffries, and Hui (2003) for reviews and discussions.

51. Sornette (2003) and Mandelbrot and Hudson (2004).

52. See, for example, LeBaron and Scheinkman (1989), LeBaron (1994), Farmer and Lo (1999), and Farmer (2001). See chapter 17 for a more complete discussion and further references.

53. Ijiri and Simon (1977). I am indebted to Doyne Farmer for making me aware of this quote.

54. B. Greene (1999).

55. For a discussion of the relationship between metaphor and scientific models, see Holland (1998). Also see Cartwright (1999) and Hands (2001).

56. Walras's inspiration was noted numerous times by Walras himself. See Mirowski (1989) and Ingrao and Israel (1990). For another example of metaphorical inspiration, see the table created by Irving Fisher showing the analogies between physics and economics concepts and reproduced in Mirowski (1989), p. 224.

57. Anderson, Arrow, and Pines (1988).

58. See von Baeyer (1998) for a nontechnical introduction to thermodynamics. See Kondepudi and Prigogine (1998) for a more technical account.

59. Specifically, Mirowski (1989) identifies income plus utility as the implicit conserved quantity on the consumption side (pp. 230–233) and output plus costs on the production side (pp. 314, 328) of canonical Neoclassical models. He notes the inherent contradictions and mixed units in these fixed quantities and attributes these inconsistencies to the lack of understanding of conservation principles by the protagonists. Smith and Foley (2002) provide a thorough mathematical exploration of the relationship between utility theory and thermodynamics and come to a somewhat different conclusion from Mirowski's, interpreting the conservation of commodities as the equivalent of the First Law.

60. As noted previously, it was not until the 1950s that Neoclassical economics and growth theory were united. However, as we will see in part 3, Neoclassical growth models still have a problem accounting for the creation of true novelty.

61. Lionel Robbins, "An Essay on the Nature and Significance of Economic Science," reprinted in Hausman (1994), pp. 83–110.

62. Samuelson and Nordhaus (1998), p. 4.

63. Murray Gell-Mann used this example in a talk he gave at McKinsey & Company in London on February 16, 2001. Richard Feynman also noted that if you took a film of some activity such as breaking windows and spilling milk and ran it in both directions, you could tell the backward direction, as it would be the one that made the audience laugh (von Bayer, 1998, p. 133). I'm not sure whether Feynman or Gell-Mann has the first claim to the "film test" of irreversibility and wouldn't dare speculate.

64. As the great British astrophysicist Sir Arthur Eddington once said, the Second Law "holds, I think, the supreme position among the laws of nature." Quoted in von Baeyer (1998), p. 56.

65. I was not able to locate a copy of the original 1867 first edition of Thomson and Tait's book that would have been used by Jevons. However, the British Library does have a copy of the 1890 fourth edition, and Thomson and Tait give a detailed account of what changed between the various editions. There was still no mention of entropy in the 1890 version.

66. In multiuniverse theories of physics, however, questions are sometimes raised about the possibility of interactions between universes through black holes or quantum effects.

67. Quoted in Waldrop (1992), p. 147.

68. The continued centrality of equilibrium analysis in modern Traditional Economics is illustrated by the following recent quotes: "A characteristic feature that distinguishes economics from other scientific fields is that, for us, the equations of equilibrium constitute the center of our discipline" (Mas-Colell, Whinston, and Green, 1995, p. 620). "Macroeconomics today is solidly grounded in a general equilibrium structure. Modern models characterize the economy as being in temporary equilibrium, given the implications of the past and the anticipations of the future" (Blanchard, 2000, p. 1402).

69. A major exception to this is Nicholas Georgescu-Roegen, who made this observation in the 1970s (Georgescu-Roegen, 1971). We will discuss his work further in later chapters.

70. As a closed system travels to a minimum-energy equilibrium, energy may be shuffled around and in the process create order. However, we can view the area where free energy is flowing and order is being created as an open subsystem within the larger closed system. For example, we can view the dissipation of the sun's energy as part of the grand reshuffling of energy in the closed system of the universe as it heads toward heat death, and the earth as an open subsystem within that larger closed system. We can likewise view the economy as an open subsystem within the open subsystem of human society, which is within the open subsystem of the earth's ecosystem, and so on.

71. The Classical economists all recognized the physical nature of the economy (e.g., Cantillon's or Quesnay's models), but this was lost in the abstractions of the Neoclassicists. In more recent times, the main progenitors of this view have been Nicholas Georgescu-Roegen (1971), whose work has inspired many in environmental economics (e.g., Daly, 1999), and Jay Forrester (1961), whose system dynamics methodology was famously applied to environmental issues in "The Limits to Growth" study in the 1970s (Meadows, Randers, and Meadows, 2004).

72. I was told this story while visiting the NASDAQ computer center in 1996. The center naturally has backup generators, but apparently the squirrel created a chain reaction of problems that caused a modest delay in getting the backup power on. But any stoppage in the market, even a small one, is taken very seriously. The market has since apparently been made squirrel-proof.

73. For example, Robert Solow has voiced this view: "It will occasionally turn out that some piece of economics is mathematically identical to some piece of utterly unrelated physics. (This has actually happened to me although I know absolutely nothing about physics.) I think this has no methodological significance but arises because everyone playing this sort of game tends to follow the line of least mathematical resistance." From T. Bender and C. Schorske, *American Academic Culture in Transformation* (Princeton, NJ: Princeton University Press, 1997), pp. 73–74, quoted in Mirowski (2002), p. 8n3.

74. While I will argue that the economy is best modeled as an open disequilibrium system, this does not mean that equilibrium techniques will not have their uses. Equilibrium analysis remains a very powerful tool and will undoubtedly continue to be useful to model special cases within the more general case of a complex adaptive economy. As we will see, just as game theory and certain equilibrium techniques have been very useful in understanding biological evolutionary systems (see Maynard Smith, 1982), they can be highly useful in Complexity Economics as well. The key distinction between Complexity and Traditional approaches is knowing that one is modeling an equilibrium as a special case or as an approximation of a more general disequilibrium setting, and thus knowing the limits of that special case or approximation.

75. For a discussion of the philosophy of mathematics and its properties as a language, see Devlin (2000), and Lakoff and Núñez (2000).

76. The most famous of these is the Bourbaki School, a French movement started in 1939 and active through the 1950s. The logical positivists also attempted to prove the pure objectivity of mathematics at about the same time, but that effort was subsequently abandoned. The peak of economics' flirtations with Bourbakism was Debreu's brilliant *Theory of Value* in 1959. See Ingrao and Israel (1990), pp. 280–288. The physical sciences largely abandoned Bourbakism in the 1950s and 1960s, but its influence in economics can continue to be seen in the purely axiomatic style of much work even in recent years. Alan Kirman, in Kirman and Gérard-Varet (1999), ch. 1, provides a critique of the "self-contained" yet "empirically empty" nature of much recent theoretical work in economics.

77. For a good nontechnical discussion of this issue, see Deutsch (1997), ch. 10.

78. This does not imply that only intuitive math objects are real. Physicists create all sorts of bizarre math objects that are not intuitive but have a real physical meaning. For example, superstring theory postulates eleven or maybe more dimensions in the universe. But again, the categorization and interpretation ultimately ties back to some interaction with the physical world, whether it is a sophisticated physics experiment or a child counting pebbles.

79. *Oxford Dictionary of Physics* (2000), pp. 158–159.

80. *Collins Dictionary of Economics* (2000), p. 164. Another example is from Stiglitz (1997), p. 88: "Physicists also speak of equilibrium in describing a weight hanging from a spring. Two forces are working on the weight. Gravity is pulling it down; the spring is pulling it up. When the weight is at rest, it is in equilibrium, with the two forces just offsetting each other . . . An economic equilibrium is established in just the same way."

81. This point about the contradiction between Neoclassical economics and the physical energy characteristics of the economy was first made by Nicholas Georgescu-Roegen in his 1971 masterwork, *The Entropy Law and the Economic Process*, a book we will discuss at length later. Daly (1999), pp. 75–88, provides a fascinating account of a debate between Georgescu-Roegen and Robert Solow on this issue.

82. This description is drawn from Anderson, Arrow, and Pines (1988), Waldrop (1992), and personal discussions with several of the participants.

83. See Arthur, Durlauf, and Lane (1997), Durlauf and Young (2001), Bowles, Gintis, and Osborne Groves (2005), Gintis et al. (2005), and the Santa Fe Institute Web site (www.santafe.edu) for examples.

84. For a discussion, see Krugman (1998).

Chapter Four

1. This description and quotations are excerpted from Seth Mydans, "In a Philippine Wasteland, a 'Living Metaphor,'" *International Herald Tribune* (reprinted from *The New York Times*), July 19, 2000, p. 1.

2. The question of economic origins did arise in the writings of some Classical economists, particularly Marx, but has never featured very strongly in Neoclassical economics. For example, it is not mentioned anywhere in Hicks's *Value and Capital* (1939). But it has, of course, played a role in the Austrian,

institutionalist, and historical schools. See, for example, Schumpeter (1934), Hayek (1948), North (1990) and (2005), Rosenberg and Birdzell (1986), and Mokyr (1990) and (2002).

3. Epstein and Axtell (1996). For a popular account of this work, also see Rauch (2002).

4. Brian Arthur of the Santa Fe Institute described a thought experiment very similar to Sugarscape in 1987; see Waldrop (1992), pp. 241–243.

5. Athough these rules are varied in the course of various experiments, this is a typical setup for many of the basic runs. See Epstein and Axtell (1996), ch. 2.

6. Epstein and Axtell (1996, pp. 71–82) also perform separate experiments on group formation by giving cultural "tags" to the agents.

7. Aghion et al. (2003), p. 368, provide a table of Gini coefficients, a measure of income inequality, with an average coefficient of 0.274 for nineteen developed countries. In the simplest version of Epstein and Axtell's model, their Gini coefficient begins at 0.23 and then evolves to a quite large 0.503 (Epstein and Axtell, 1996, p. 37). Runs of the "full" model with inheritance, trading, and so forth, give a result of 0.268, quite close to the coefficient seen in developed economies.

8. Epstein and Axtell (1996), pp. 54–68.

9. Ibid., pp. 94–137.

10. The agents' preferences for sugar versus spice were formulated in the Cobb-Douglas form, though the interpretation of this in the context of Sugarscape has some important differences from typical Neoclassical models (ibid., p. 97).

11. Thaler (1993) and Lo and MacKinlay (1999).

12. Axtell (2002).

13. Epstein and Axtell (1996), pp. 36–37, 154.

14. For a discussion of complexity and the history of economic thought, see Colander (2000). Also see Mirowski (2002).

15. For examples, see Anderson, Arrow, and Pines (1988), Arthur (1994a) and (1994c), Colander (1996), Arthur, Durlauf, and Lane (1997), Axelrod (1997a), Albin (1998), Lesourne and Orléan (1998), Prietula, Carley, and Gasser (1998), Young (1998), Gintis (2000), Durlauf and Young (2001), Rauch and Casella (2001), Camerer (2003), Johnson, Jefferies, and Hui (2003), Kollman, Miller, and Page (2003), and Bowles (2004).

Chapter Five

1. For popular overviews of dynamic systems, see Gleick (1987) and Stewart (1989). For introductory texts, see Devaney (1992), Flake (1998), and Kaplan and Glass (1995). For somewhat more advanced texts, see Strogatz (1994) and Bar-Yam (1997).

2. My example is inspired by Devaney's (1992), pp. 9–11, use of interest payments as an example of a dynamic system.

3. The stock and flow terminology is from *system dynamics*, a methodology for modeling dynamic systems. The classic reference is Forrester (1961). For a modern overview, see Sterman (2000), and for a popular introduction, see Senge (1990).

4. Sterman (2000), pp. 649–654.

5. Skidelsky (1994).

6. Technically, negative feedback can drive oscillations with increasing amplitude if there are sufficiently long delays between input and output, but the most common effect of negative feedback is dampening behavior.

7. Stewart (1989), pp. 60–72, and Mirowski (1989), p. 72.

8. For a history of the study of nonlinear systems, see Gleick (1987), Stewart (1989), and Devaney (1992).

9. Stewart (1989), pp. 81–84.

10. LeBaron (1994) notes evidence of nonlinearities in macroeconomic data.

11. For example, see Peters (1991) and Chorafas (1994).

12. See Brock, pp. 77–97, in Anderson, Arrow, and Pines (1988); Le Baron (1994); Brock, pp. 385–423, in Arthur, Durlauf, and Lane (1997); Mandelbrot (1997); Mantegna and Stanley (2000); Sornette (2003); and Johnson, Jeffries, and Hui (2003) for discussions.

13. Stewart (1989), pp. 60–62.

14. My section title is borrowed from the title of ch. 20 of Sterman (2000). In the spirit of full disclosure, Professor Sterman was one of my thesis advisers at MIT.

15. Ibid., pp. 791–798.

16. Although time is generally ignored in many Traditional models, some theoretical (noneconometric) models do feature explicit time delays. Sterman (2000), p. 798, notes that the traditional explanation for commodity cycles, the "cobweb model," does feature a first-order lag that enables it to oscillate in a stable limit cycle with a period equal to twice the normalized time period. However, as Sterman points out, it is a linear difference equation that is incapable of producing the more complex patterns found in real-world commodity cycles.

17. Ibid., pp. 798–841.

18. Ibid., pp. 824–828.

19. Paich and Sterman (1993).

20. Also see Sterman (1989a) and (1989b).

Chapter Six

1. This is a composite picture to illustrate typical rationality assumptions used in various Traditional Economic models, including completeness of preferences, transitivity, the weak axiom of revealed preference, the Walrasian budget set, expected utility under Knightian uncertainty, Diamond's consumption-versus-savings trade-offs, discounting behavior, and rational expectations.

2. See Pindyck and Rubinfeld (1989) for a good introductory discussion of consumer choice and rationality. See Mas-Colell et al. (1995) for a more advanced presentation. Also see D. Romer (1996) for a discussion of rationality in macroeconomics. For a discussion of economic decision theory and how it has been tested experimentally, see Plous (1993). Economists have explored other formulations of rationality, however, including various models that are more dynamic and include learning while still preserving equilibrium. See Kirman and Salmon (1995) for a review.

3. Simon (1992) and (1997).

4. See Selten (1990) for a review of the impact of bounded rationality. There are, of course, important exceptions, such as George Akerlof's revival of Keynesian economics using "boundedly" rational behavioral assumptions. See Akerlof and Yellen (1985).

5. Selten (1990). Interestingly, Herbert Simon and bounded rationality warrant only a brief mention in Samuelson and Nordhaus (1998), p. 178, and are not mentioned at all in Stiglitz (1997), Mas-Colell et al. (1995), Pindyck and Rubinfeld (1989), Dornbusch and Fischer (1990), or D. Romer (1996).

6. There has been progress in recent years, however, in formally modeling bounded rationality. See, for example, Rubinstein (1998) and Sterman (2000).

7. Camerer, Lowenstein, and Rabin (2004), p. 6, note that Kahneman and Tversky's 1979 paper in *Econometrica* introducing prospect theory is one of the most widely cited papers ever published in that journal. Kahneman, Slovic, and Tversky (1982) is a classic collection of their work.

8. For examples, histories, and surveys of behavioral economics, see Hogarth (1990), Thaler (1992), Plous (1993), Thaler (1993), Kagel and Roth (1995), Henrich et al. (2004), Montier (2002), and Camerer, Lowenstein, and Rabin (2004). For examples of integrating behavioral economics with theoretical work, see Camerer (2003) and Gintis et al. (2005). For discussions aimed at a management audience, see Russo and Schoemaker (1989), Bazerman (1998), and Dörner (1996).

9. For some recent discussions of behavioral economics in the popular press, see "Rethinking Thinking," *Economist*, December 18, 1999, pp. 63–65, Roger Lowenstein, "Exuberance Is Rational," *New York Times Sunday Magazine*, February 11, 2001, and Louis Uchitelle, "Some Economists Call Behavior a Key," *New York Times*, business section, February 11, 2001.

10. This example is excerpted from Bazerman (1998), p. 81. See Gintis et al. (2005) for a survey of work on reciprocity behavior.

11. See Kagel and Roth (1995), pp. 253–348, for a survey of ultimatum game results. See pp. 282–288 for cross-cultural results of the ultimatum game. Also see Henrich et al. (2001) for cross-cultural results with tribal cultures. See also Gintis et al. (2005).

12. Fehr and Gächter (2000).

13. "Primary Sources," *Atlantic Monthly*, April 2003, pp. 33–34.

14. Gintis et al. (2005), pp. 3–39.

15. A Traditional economist might then say, "Aha, there is a rational basis for reciprocity behavior. People assume there will be future interactions with each other and thus these strategies make sense in a repeated game." There are two replies to this: First, I never said the behavior was irrational; there is a logic to reciprocity and punishment. In fact, it is an evolutionary logic. But again going back to the Fehr and Gächter experiment, people tend to do this, *even when there is no possibility of future interactions*. Thus, it is

not perfectly rational in the narrow, Traditional Economics sense. The second reply is that people do engage in this behavior, whether or not there will be future interactions, because it is *heuristic* behavior rather than *calculated* behavior.

16. Quoted in "Rethinking Thinking," *The Economist*, December 18, 1999, p. 65.

17. For a managerially oriented summary of these biases, see Roxburgh (2003).

18. "The Price of Safety," *The Economist*, November 23, 2000.

19. This example is from James Surowiecki, "The Financial Page: Mind Over Money," *New Yorker*, April 23 and 30, 2001, p. 60.

20. See, for example, Fischer Black, in Thaler (1993), pp. 3–22.

21. Lewis (1985).

22. Deutsch (1997), pp. 131–140, provides a good popular description of a Turing Machine.

23. Those who view the brain as a material thing that computes—researchers like Steven Pinker (1997), Andy Clark (2001), and Daniel Dennett (1991)—tend to be in the pro-Turing-Machine camp. Others, such as Roger Penrose and David Gelernter, argue that in the brain, there are other factors at work (e.g., quantum effects) that are not yet understood, but take the brain out of the realm of Turing Machines.

24. For another example in addition to Arthur's bar problem discussed in this section, see Foster and Young's (2001) analysis of agent strategy in a penny-matching game.

25. Arthur (1994b).

26. More specifically, the fixed point in the bar problem is unstable and unreachable, given the information and coordination constraints placed on the agents. See ibid.

27. A wide literature has developed on a more generalized form of Arthur's bar problem known as the minority game. See, for example, Challet and Zhang (1997). The problem has also been applied in very interesting ways to finance theory; see Johnson, Jeffries, and Hui (2003), pp. 87–136.

28. For overviews and references, see Stillings et al. (1995) and Clark (1999) and (2001). For a popular introduction, see Pinker (1997).

29. Pinker (1997).

30. See Schank (1990). Also see McKee (2003) for a discussion of storytelling in a managerial context.

31. For a specific theory of analogy making, see Mitchell (1993).

32. Gilovich, Vallone, and Tversky (1985).

33. Clark (2001), p. 38.

34. Teaching a computer to order from a restaurant is not a trivial task. Roger Schank (1990) actually tried to do just that in the 1970s.

35. Brian Arthur pointed out this induction-versus-deduction contrast in 1992 in his Santa Fe Institute Working Paper 92–07-038.

36. See Holland et al. (1986) for a detailed account. Holland (1995) also presents some of the ideas in a form for a general audience.

37. This example is adapted from Holland (1995), pp. 43–62.

38. Holland et al. (1986), pp. 68–76.

39. Schank (1990), pp. 4–5, describes some experiments showing how people fall back on default responses when encountering unfamiliar questions.

40. See Mitchell (1993) for a detailed model and discussion of reasoning by analogy.

41. See Arthur (1995), and Arthur et al., "Asset Pricing Under Endogenous Expectations in an Artificial Stock Market," in Arthur, Durlauf, and Lane (1997), pp. 15–44.

42. The rule was similar to, but not exactly like, perfect rationality. The reason for this goes back to the problem of implementing perfect rationality on a Turing Machine; one can only create an approximation of perfect rationality on a computer.

Chapter Seven

1. Rauch and Casella (2001), pp. 3–5. Watts (2003) also gives an account of the history of the study of networks in a sociological and an economic context as well as references. Giddens (2001) in his introduction to sociology outlines how the field has historically viewed interaction networks.

2. See Watts (1999), ch. 2, for a summary and references.

3. For excellent general introductions to the topic of networks and references, see Watts (2003) and Barabási (2002). For a more technical introduction, see Watts (1999).

4. This example is from Kauffman (1995a), pp. 55–58. For a more technical discussion, see Kauffman (1993), pp. 307–310. Watts (2003), pp. 43–47, also discusses this example.

5. In Kauffman's original model (1993, pp. 307–310, and 1995, pp. 55–58), the ratio was 0.5. Subsequent work by Watts (2003), pp. 43–47, puts the ratio at 1.0.

6. See Gladwell (2000) for other examples of tipping points.

7. For a discussion in the context of consumer products and technology, see Farrell (1998).

8. Watts (2003).

9. Ibid., pp. 92–95, and Watts (1999), pp. 3–5. One can play the Bacon game on Tjaden's Web site, at www.oracleofbacon.org.

10. The number 510,829 is all actors or actresses with finite Bacon numbers. Of the sample, 10 percent had no connection or infinite Bacon numbers.

11. Watts (2003), pp. 121–129.

12. Ibid., pp. 39–40.

13. Watts (1999) and Newman (1999).

14. For the mathematics behind this calculation, see Newman (1999) pp. 3–4.

15. This slogan is a trademark of Sun Microsystems, Inc.

16. They are also a form of cellular automata, a concept that was invented by John von Neumann and that we will discuss in later chapters.

17. Kauffman (1995a), pp. 74–80.

18. Boolean networks are a particular type of cellular automaton. The physicist and mathematician Stephen Wolfram (2002), among others, has argued that the universe itself is a cellular automaton. In this case, it would follow that the economy is one, too. Again, all this is admittedly highly speculative; the key point is that computational views of economic phenomena are capable of generating interesting insights and are a rich area for research.

19. Using the IBM Blue Gene speed of 70.62 trillion floating-point calculations per second.

20. The inability to fully explore large networks could, however, change if quantum computers were eventually developed. See Johnson (2003) for a popular discussion.

21. This finding, though, is still controversial. While the Human Genome Project and the private company Celera Genomics claim 30,000, a figure now accepted by many scientists, Human Genome Sciences stands by earlier estimates at 100,000. See, for example, Cookson and Griffith (2001).

22. Kauffman (1993), pp. 191–203.

23. This example is drawn from news reports at the time, various profiles of Dell and IBM, and the companies' Web sites.

24. This view is consistent in many ways with Porter's (1996) idea of strategy as a process of making trade-offs among constraints in a business system.

25. Kauffman (1993), pp. 209–218.

26. Kauffman (1995a), pp. 252–271. We will look at Kauffman's idea of conflicting constraints in more detail in chapter 16. Also see Eisenhardt and Brown (1999) for a discussion of the managerial implications of conflicting constraints.

27. In chapter 16, we will look at the work of Scott Page, a computational economist at the University of Michigan, who has examined the role of hierarchy in the ability of a network to solve computationally difficult problems. See Page (1996).

28. Kauffman (1993), pp. 209–227.

29. Kauffman (1995a), pp. 84–92.

30. In addition to sensitivity to initial conditions and perturbations, chaos manifests itself in Boolean networks by longer median state cycles for a network of a given number of nodes. See Kauffman (1993), p. 197.

31. See, for example, Katzenbach and Smith (1993).

Chapter Eight

1. This account is adapted from Fischer (1996), pp. 35–37.

2. See Kennedy (1987) for examples.

3. Moore (1983) and Gordon (1986).

4. This idea of the economy as a propagation mechanism was first articulated by the Norwegian economist Ragnar Frisch, who used this approach to develop a model of business cycles in 1933. See Niehans (1990), pp. 372–378.

5. Heijdra and van der Ploeg (2002), pp. 477–539. Also Hartley, Salyer, and Hoover (1998).

6. A thought experiment will show why this is so. Imagine we take the input of the spoon tapping and code it as a bit string. We then run the bit string through a compression algorithm and compress it as much as possible. If the spoon tapping input is really random, we will not be able to compress it very much. We then code the output string and see that it is longer than the input string because one input tap may produce several oscillatory output wiggles. However, when we run the output through our compression algorithm, we will get back a string of equal or slightly longer length than our original (depending on the efficiency of our compression). We have thus neither fought entropy nor added real information to the input string; we have just added some "echoes" in the noise, which our compression algorithm has filtered back out. In contrast, if we took a random bit of string as input, say, 01001001011101001, and then did "work" (i.e., used energy to fight entropy) to rearrange the bits into an output of the same length reading 00000000011111111, this could be compressed further to the statement "print 0 nine times, print 1 eight times," which can then be coded in something fewer than seventeen bits. Thus, the work we did in rearranging bits added order to the string, enabling us to make the compressed version shorter than the input. Neither jelly-propagation mechanisms nor Real Business Cycle models can do the order-creating work to make their output strings compress to shorter length than their input strings. The classic technical discussion of order, entropy, and information compression is Shannon and Weaver (1949). See Gell-Mann (1994) for a popular discussion.

7. As Heijdra and van der Ploeg (2002), p. 528, note: "An important, somewhat disappointing, feature of the unit-elastic RBC model is its lack of internal propagation. For all cases considered, the impulse-response function for the output was virtually identical to the exogenous technology shock itself. The lack of propagation plagues not just the unit-elastic model but many other RBC models as well. For this reason, one of the currently active areas of research in the RBC literature concerns the development of models with stronger and more realistic internal propagation mechanisms." By "internal propagation," they mean the ability to add to the output signal a dynamic structure that was not present in the input signal.

8. For an account of Keynes's life during the Depression years, see Skidelsky (1994).

9. Krugman (1994) has a very good description of the evolution of Keynesian economics, and I have drawn on that description in my discussion here.

10. See Akerlof and Yellen (1985a) and (1985b). Also see Krugman (1994), pp. 206–220.

11. Heijdra and van der Ploeg (2002), pp. 359–403.

12. I am, of course, simplifying, and there are other alternatives. See, for example, the work of Stanford's Mordecai Kurz on endogenous fluctuations (Kurz, 1997). However, the Real Business Cycle and New Keynesian schools remain the currently dominant theories.

13. For example, the Akerlof-Yellen menu cost model (and subsequent versions) rely on a highly elastic labor supply, something not supported by the empirical literature (Heijdra and van der Ploeg, 2002, p. 402).

14. For some excellent popular discussions of emergence, see Holland (1998), Buchanan (2000), Johnson (2001), and Morowitz (2002).

15. See the short but seminal article by Anderson (1972).

16. Nijhout, Nadel, and Stein (1997).

17. The Russian economist Nicolai Kondratiev argued that the economy has a sixty-year "long-wave" cycle as well. See Sterman (1985) for a model and discussion.

18. Lotka (1956).

19. See Sterman (2000), pp. 684–708, for an overview and further references. See Senge (1990) for a popular discussion.

20. Sterman (1989a), (1989b), and (2000), pp. 684–698.

21. Sterman (1989b) has also found deterministic chaos arising in about 25 percent of the cases.

22. See Casti and Karlqvist (1991), ch. 9. Also see Sterman (2000), pp. 684–698.

23. The oscillations do not return to equilibrium in the time frame of the game. It is unlikely that they would return to equilibrium even over longer time frames without some coordinating mechanism (e.g., allow everyone to meet to coordinate orders). Even when players have played a second time (with a different order deck) after a lecture on the dynamic structure of the game, they still cannot achieve perfect rationality equilibrium.

24. Increased information in the Beer Game does not change the result regarding perfect rationality; again, the participants have all the information they need to calculate the rational equilibrium. Rather, the additional information recognizes the problems created by the anchor-and-adjust heuristic and improves the performance of that heuristic.

25. Sensier and van Dijk (2004).

26. See McCarthy and Zakrajšek (2002) for an analysis and further references.

27. One might note that I have just admitted an exogenous factor in the dampening of the business cycle. In my critique of Traditional theory, I have not denied that exogenous factors exist and have an impact, but rather critiqued the role they typically play in theory. In this case, my argument is that business cycles are an emergent property of endogenous dynamic structure (and thus are not caused exogenously), but exogenous factors such as technology change can affect the dynamic structure itself.

28. Gould and Eldridge (1993) and Gould (2002).

29. Gould (1989), p. 54.

30. See Gould (2002), pp. 774–775, for his account of the origin of the term. See pp. 824–839 for his description of what he meant by *equilibrium*.

31. See Bak (1996) for a discussion of avalanches and his sand-pile experiments. In financial markets, punctuated equilibrium presents itself as volatility that is correlated in time, known as the autoregressive conditional heteroscedasticity (ARCH) or generalized ARCH (GARCH) fact. See Mantegna and Stanley (2000) and Johnson, Jeffries, and Hui (2003).

32. See Girvan and Newman (2001) for a specific discussion on network structure in a social and biological context.

33. Jain and Krishna (2002a) and (2002b).

34. See, for example, Marx's *Critique of Political Economy* and Schumpeter's *Business Cycles: A Theoretical, Historical and Statistical Analysis of the Capitalist Process*.

35. See Lydia Adetunji, "Inventor Found Investors Not on His Wavelength," *Financial Times*, December 19, 2001, p. 5.

36. See Ziman (2000) for a review.

37. See, for example, Rosenberg (1982), pp. 55–80.

38. See Kauffman in Anderson, Arrow, and Pines (1988), pp. 125–146.

39. Baldwin and Clark (2000).

40. Cutler, Poterba, and Summers (1989).

41. This description is from Buchanan (2000), p. 35.

42. The distribution is called a power law because one variable is expressed as an exponential power of the other, for example, $f(x) = x^{-a}$, and thus $\log f(x) = -a \log x$, so a logarithmic graph of the function gives a straight line with slope of $-a$.

43. Bak (1996) and Buchanan (2000).

44. Niehans (1990), pp. 259–266.

45. Subsequent economists, starting in 1932 with Robert Gibrat's *Les Inégalités Économiques*, tried to reconcile Pareto's result with the Walrasian framework by claiming that Pareto's finding on income inequality was in reality lognormal. See Mandelbrot (1997), pp. 252–269, for a critique of the lognormal claim.

46. Mandelbrot (1997), pp. 371–411. Although Mandelbrot correctly identified the kurtosis and scale-free behavior of the tails, it has since been shown that the power law exponent of the tails is higher than Lévy-stable distribution he initially proposed. See Plerou et al. (2001).

47. From a presentation by H. Eugene Stanley at The Economy as an Evolving Complex Systems III Conference, Santa Fe Institute, November 16, 2001.

48. Plerou et al. (1999).

49. Axtell (2001).

50. Stanley et al. (1996) and Lee et al. (1998).

51. Farmer et al. (2004), Lillo and Farmer (2004), and Lillo, Szabolcs, and Farmer (2005).

52. See Szabolcs and Farmer (2005).

Chapter Nine

1. Dennett (1995).

2. Both Richard Dawkins (1986) and (1996) and Daniel Dennett (1995) have noted that the intuition that a design must have a designer is a powerful motivator for beliefs in creationism and that a lack of understanding of how evolution can create intelligent design on its own is an important reason that many people still believe in creationism or believe evolution is "just one theory." See Dembski and Ruse (2004) for an account of the debates on design.

3. Dawkins (1986).

4. See Sims (1994a) and (1994b) for a description of the experiments. In addition, photos of the evolved creatures can be viewed on Sims's Web site, at www.genarts.com/karl.

5. Dennett (1995).

6. In a sense, there was a "creator" in Sims's program as Sims established the conditions for evolution. In nature, we are close (but not quite there) to being able to tell the story from the Big Bang to the origin of life, to today. See Fry (1999), Solé and Goodwin (2000), Morowitz (2002), Schneider and Sagan (2005), and Lane (2005).

7. Dennett (1995), pp. 48–60.

8. LEGO is a registered trademark of The LEGO Group.

9. Kauffman (2000), pp. 223–225.

10. This example is inspired by Dennett's Library of Babel (1995, pp. 107–113). Dawkins (1996), pp. 180–203, uses a similar example with what he calls the Museum of All Shells.

11. Holland (1975) and (1995) and Mitchell (1996). Holland specifically uses the word *schema* to refer to the coding of building blocks. For ease of exposition, I will use the word more generally to refer to a coding of designs and later introduce the concept of building blocks.

12. Hull (1988).

13. Herbert Simon discussed the role of hierarchy and modularity in complex systems in a paper in 1962. See Simon (1996), pp. 183–216, for a reprinted and updated version.

14. Dawkins's terminology is different, but this is his point when he argues for the gene as the unit of selection. See Dawkins (1976) and (1982).

15. In principle, there is no reason why this *Gedankenexperiment* could not be carried out in real life, and one would expect interesting LEGO toys to evolve from it. The only barrier is that evolution does require many iterations and time, which may be beyond the limitations of patience of two seven-year-olds. This is why such experiments are typically implemented on computers, which do not tire so easily.

16. Dawkins (1976), pp. 15–20. This section also draws on Wilson (1992) and Fortey (1997).

17. See Fry (2000), Morowitz (2002), and Schneider and Sagan (2005) for discussions and further references.

18. Dawkins (1976).

19. Ibid.

20. These estimates are from Kauffman (1995a), p. 163.

21. Dennett (1995), pp. 111–113, notes that his example of the Library of Mendel was in turn inspired by Richard Dawkins's "biomorph land" from Dawkins (1986).

22. Design space size is defined by the length of the schema. Although there is no conceptual limit to the length of a schema, in any working evolutionary system, the length of a schema will be constrained by the workings of the schema reader. Infinitely long schemata are not possible, because they could not be read by any schema reader in finite time.

23. Dennett (1995), pp. 77–80.

24. This means that in reality, such a fitness landscape would have billions of dimensions. However, for ease of visualization and discussion, we will speak as if it has only three. See Kauffman (1993) and (1995) for a discussion of the dimensionality of fitness landscapes. We will also assume that codes with less than the maximum 10 billion base pairs are filled out with a "0" for the empty spaces, so moving one symbol at a time can also mean moving in the direction of longer or shorter genomes.

25. Fitness landscapes were first discussed by Sewall Wright in 1931. Their mathematical properties are extensively explored in Kauffman (1993). Excellent discussions for a general audience are found in Kauffman (1995a) and Dennett (1995).

26. Kauffman (1995a), pp. 161–189.

27. Crutchfield, pp. 101–133, in Crutchfield and Schuster (2003).

28. There are actually a variety of hill-climbing algorithms, and this particular one is called Random Mutation Hill Climbing. See Mitchell (1996), p. 129, for others.

29. Kauffman (1993) and (1995) discusses the effects of mixing long and short jumps in his *NK* model of a fitness landscape.

30. Kauffman (1995a), p. 180.

31. Crutchfield, pp. 101–133, in Crutchfield and Schuster (2003).

32. See Holland (1975) and (1995) and his discussions of the two-armed-bandit problem. March (1991) identified the tension of exploring versus exploiting in an organizational context. See Mitchell (1996), pp. 117–118, and Axelrod and Cohen (1999), pp. 43–50, for further discussions in an evolutionary context.

33. See Mitchell (1996), pp. 119–125, for the two-armed-bandit proof and a discussion.

34. Dennett (1995), pp. 77–78.

35. Dennett (1995), pp. 128–135.

36. There is a rich literature on the suitability of different search algorithms for varying landscape constructions; see Whitley (1993), Kauffman (1993), and Mitchell (1996). I am not claiming that evolution

is the best search algorithm for all types of problems, but merely that evolution has many useful characteristics for searching dynamic, rough-correlated landscapes. Nature provides an existence proof that evolution is not a bad way to address this type of search problem. It is possible that a superior algorithm could be found, though none has been yet.

37. None of these results are preordained. Evolution does not necessarily lead to increasing order or growth. But given the right parameters, it can. Thus, my caveat. Kaufman (1993) argues that biological evolution self-tunes to these parameters.

38. See Koza (1992) for examples.

39. See Hodgson (1993) for a historical account.

40. See, for example, Crutchfield and Schuster (2003), Koza (1992), and Mitchell (1996).

41. *Henry IV*, part 1, act II, scene iv, line 460.

Chapter Ten

1. Axelrod (1997a), p. xi.

2. For an introduction to game theory, see Fudenberg and Tirole (1991) and Gintis (2000). For a discussion for a business audience, see Brandenburger et al. (1997).

3. Bowles (2004), p. 24.

4. Since cooperation is strongly dominated in the single-round case, backward induction shows that both players defecting each round is also the subgame-perfect equilibrium for a finite repeated game. In the infinite-horizon game, the Always Defect strategy remains a subgame-perfect equilibrium, but if the discounting of future payoffs is sufficiently high, then a strategy that says "cooperate in the first round and continue to cooperate as long as the opponent does not defect, but if the opponent defects than defect for the rest of the game" is also subgame perfect. In the case of the finite but unknown horizon game, the results are indeterminate. See Fudenberg and Tirole (1991), pp. 110–111.

5. Axelrod (1984).

6. Axelrod (1997a), pp. 14–29.

7. Lindgren and Nordahl (1994); Lindgren, in Arthur et al. (1997), pp. 337–367; and Lindgren and Johansson, in Crutchfield and Schuster (2003), pp. 341–360.

8. The Game of Life is one of the best-known examples of a cellular automaton. See, for example, Wuensche and Lesser (1992) and Wolfram (1994) and (2002). It is fitting that game theory and cellular automata are combined in Lindgren's model, as both were central to the work of John von Neumann, who invented game theory along with Oskar von Morgenstern and cellular automata theory along with Stanislaw Ulam.

9. Ties are broken by a random number. Also, neighborhoods on the edge of the lattice wrap around to connect with the opposite edge, so the lattice is really a torus rather than a plane.

10. During these periods, the agents are playing evolutionary-stable strategies, the biological equivalent of Nash equilibriums. See Maynard Smith (1982).

11. Dennett (1995), pp. 107–111.

12. To see Dennett's trick, take his boxed-set tactic to an extreme. One could say that there is a Library of the Alphabet with only 100 books in it, each containing just a single character. Even though this library is quite small, it too contains every possible book; for example, *Moby Dick* is in a special 1,250,000-volume boxed set. Likewise, we could also have a Library Bigger Than Babel of all possible 5,000-page books.

13. As mentioned before, this is because for the schema reader to read the code and then render the design, the reader must read the code in finite time.

14. My notion of a Business Plan is consistent with, but somewhat broader than, the concept of an organizational blueprint articulated in Hannan and Freeman (1977). Hannan and Freeman define a *blueprint* as containing the organizational structure, processes, and goals of an organization. Under my definition of a Business Plan, these are contained within Social Technology, but in addition, a Business Plan contains the specific technology recipes used in its transformations (Physical Technologies) as well as a strategy. In addition, Hannan and Freeman propose that blueprints themselves are the unit of selection. As will be discussed later, my definitions of Business Plans are not the units of selection but rather the schemata for the interactor (businesses), and the units of selection are Business Plan modules.

15. This circular, coevolutionary relationship between management teams and their plans was first observed by the strategist and organizational theorist Edith Penrose in the 1950s. See Penrose (1959).

16. Nelson (2003).

17. Gould (2002).

Chapter Eleven

1. The original study of British tit birds opening milk bottles was by J. Fisher and R. A. Hind in 1949; the connection to the cultural transmission of learning was made by Dawkins (1982), p. 109.

2. At this point in human history, it was certainly grunts and body language. There is still much debate over when and how language evolved. The textbook answer is, somewhere between 30,000 and 100,000 years ago; see Jones et al. (1992), p. 137. However, some researchers such as MIT's Steven Pinker (1994), pp. 363–364, believe it may have been much earlier, corresponding with *Homo erectus*—as much as 1.5 million years ago. It is also possible that the evolution of language was fairly gradual and that there is thus no single point at which it appeared, but rather that it emerged over a long period. In any case, however, language is still much more recent than the toolmaking of *Homo habilis*. See Carruthers and Chamberlain (2000) and Cavalli-Sforza (2001) for further discussions.

3. Of course, like most cultural innovations, the "discovery" of trade was probably not a single act by a single set of individuals. Rather, such a useful Good Trick for survival (to use Dennett's phrase) was probably independently discovered by multiple groups of hominids at multiple times, and one of those groups was the eventual progenitor of *Homo sapiens*.

4. Horan, Bulte, and Shogren (2005).

5. There is a wide literature on technology innovation as an evolutionary process. See Ziman (2000) for an overview and further references. As Ziman points out (p. 3), "the basic analogy between biological and cultural evolution has often been remarked. From the middle of the nineteenth century onward, it was noted more or less independently by such eminent scholars as William Whewell, Karl Marx, Thomas Henry Huxley, Ernst Mach, William James and Georg Simmel. The basic idea has been extended by later authors such as Jean Piaget, Konrad Lorenz, Donald Campbell, Karl Popper and Jacques Monod." Also see Petroski (1992) and Baldwin and Clark (2000).

6. The term *Physical Technology* was introduced by Nelson (2003). While my definition is similar in spirit to Nelson's, the specific definition is my own. It is also built on the notion of techniques, developed by Joel Mokyr of Northwestern University. See Mokyr (1990), pp. 273–299; Mokyr, in ch. 5 of Ziman (2000), pp. 52–65; and Mokyr (2000).

7. Mokyr defines his design space as λ the set of *feasible techniques* and Ω the set of *useful knowledge*. My definition of PT space corresponds with λ. Mokyr's Ω then is what PT evolution searches for and is rendered into physical existence by schema readers.

8. Ridley (2001).

9. Cavalli-Sforza (2001), pp. 92–96, and Jones et al. (1992), pp. 107–143.

10. Stuart Kauffman, personal communications, October 1995. Kauffman describes this effect (what he calls economic webs) in Anderson, Arrow, and Pines (1988), pp. 125–146.

11. Kauffman (1993), pp. 395–402, and (2000), pp. 222–232.

12. The distinction between components and architecture has a long history in the literature on design; see Simon (1996) and Alexander (1997). This distinction recognizes that in problems of design, neither pure reductionism nor pure holism is sufficient, and rather, both views are required. See Braha and Maimon (1998), pp. 6–7. My use of the specific terms *architecture* and *component* follow Henderson and Clark (1990) and Baldwin and Clark (2000).

13. See Baldwin and Clark (2000) for a detailed discussion on the importance of modularity in design. See Braha and Maimon (1998), pp. 109–142, for a formal description of the mathematical representation of complex artifacts.

14. What we would view as very small innovations in stone tool design occurred over extremely long periods in early human history. Evidently, in the space of about 1.5 million years after the appearance of the first tools, our ancestors managed to invent only three variants: the hand ax, the chopper, and the cleaver. Things such as finely flaked blades, axes mounted on handles, and mortars and pestles did not appear until between 500,000 and 100,000 years ago. See Jones et al. (1992), pp. 350–360. I have ignored specific time frames in this discussion to make general points about the evolution of design.

15. Stuart Kauffman claims (somewhat controversially) that two factors lead to rough-correlated shapes in fitness landscapes: design modularity and fundamental constraints from physical laws. PTs have both these properties. We have already noted the modularity of PTs, and PTs are certainly constrained by physical laws. See Kauffman (1995a), pp. 191–206, and (1995b).

16. Ibid.

17. Ziman (2000), pp. 3–12, 41–51.

18. My term *deductive-tinkering* is derived from Donald Campbell's (1960) ideas on the role of blind variation and selective retention in the creative thought process, and Herbert Simon's (1996), pp. 51–83,

notion of purposeful adaptation. In addition, Boyd and Richerson (1985) build on Campbell in their idea of "biased transmission." Aldrich (1999), pp. 22–26, also distinguishes between intentional and blind variation. For a general discussion of evolution and the design process, see Braha and Maimon (1998), pp. 19–84. In addition, Kauffman (1995a), p. 202, observes that human technological evolution on fitness landscapes is a combination of both intentional thought and tinkering.

19. Even with the advance of science, iterative tinkering remains essential. Most complex design problems are deductively intractable. For a brief discussion of whether design problems can be solved in polynomial time (NP complete), see Braha and Maimon (1998), p. 25.

20. The story of the development of the Post-it Note's development can be found on the 3M Web site, www.3m.com. Post-it is a registered trademark of the 3M Corporation.

21. Petroski (1992), p. 22.

22. Many people think that this story is an urban legend or Internet myth, but it was reported by both the *New York Times* and the wire services on July 3, 1982, after the flight occurred, and on December 19, 1982, when Walters was fined for his misadventures by the Federal Aviation Administration. Tragically, Walters committed suicide in 1993. A play has subsequently been written about his life and dreams of flight.

23. This is again building on the ideas of Simon (1996).

24. Mokyr (1990); Mokyr, in Ziman (2000), pp. 52–65; and Mokyr (2000).

25. For a wonderful history of bricks and photographs showing the great variety of designs made with bricks (great proof of the building-block concept), see Campbell and Pryce (2003).

26. Foster (1986).

27. Kauffman (1995a), pp. 202–206. Kauffman uses the term *learning curve* to refer to the phenomenon of diminishing returns to investment in technology. However, in the terminology of the management literature, *learning curve* refers to declines in cost as a function of cumulative production, while the phenomenon Kauffman discusses is, following Foster (1986), referred to as an S-curve. Despite the confusion in terminology, Kauffman's points are correct when applied to S-curves.

28. Henderson and Clark (1990).

29. A natural follow-up question is, why don't incumbents do both? Why don't they exploit their existing fitness peaks while exploring for new ones? Henderson and Clark (1990) posit a set of internal organizational barriers for doing this, in particular with regard to architectural innovation. We will discuss this question in more depth later in the book.

30. See Jardine (1999), Dear (2001), and Gribbin (2002) for accounts of the scientific revolution.

Chapter Twelve

1. Easterly and Levine (2002). They use the standard term *institutions* to explain national economic-performance differentials. As described later in the book, I have incorporated institutions in my definition of Social Technologies.

2. Lewis et al. (2002) and Johnson (2002). See also "US Productivity Growth 1995–2000," available from the McKinsey Global Institute Web site. Also see Dorgan and Dowdy (2002) for a study on the impact of management techniques on macroeconomic productivity.

3. The term *Social Technology* was introduced by Nelson (2003). While my definition is similar in spirit to Nelson's, the specific definition is my own.

4. North (1990), p. 3. See Scott (2001) for a survey of alternative definitions of *institutions*.

5. In the late 1970s and early 1980s, both Herbert Simon and Richard Nelson and Sidney Winter articulated views that organizational design is the result of a process of evolutionary search. Simon's (1996), pp. 139–167, observations were in relation to economic institutions, while Nelson and Winter's (1982) observations were related to firms. For more recent examples of evolutionary views of institutions, see Loasby (1999), Hodgson (2002), and Bowles (2004).

6. Krames (2002).

7. Wright (2000) provides descriptions of many of the major shifts in STs.

8. For a detailed narrative of this transition, see Diamond (1997), pp. 83–193.

9. For a description, see Freeman and Soete (1997), pp. 141–148.

10. Ibid., pp. 137–138.

11. Chandler (1962).

12. Game theory has become central to economists' understanding of the evolution of social norms and institutions. See, for example, Axelrod (1984) and (1997a), Skyrms (1996), Young (1998), Gintis (2000), and Bowles (2004).

13. Wright (2000).

14. From Charles Darwin's *Autobiography*, quoted in Wright (1994), p. 194.

15. Yes, the book is better than the movie. See Sylvia Nasar's (1998) wonderful biography of Nash.

16. The evolution of cooperative behavior and particularly "altruistic" behavior remains controversial among evolutionary biologists and social scientists. See Sober and Wilson (1998) for a detailed account, as well as Seabright (2004). The stance I take generally follows the views of Dawkins (1976) and Maynard Smith (1982).

17. Lindgren and Nordahl (1994) and Arthur et al. (1997), pp. 337–367.

18. See Kagel and Roth (1995), pp. 253–348, for a survey of bargaining game results. See pp. 282–288 for cross-cultural results of the ultimatum game. Also see Henrich et al. (2004) for cross-cultural results with tribal cultures.

19. See Axelrod (1984) and (1997), Wright (1994), Ridley (1996), Pinker (1997), Buss (1999), Skyrms (1996), Sober and Wilson (1998), and Gintis et. al. (2005) for further discussions of the evolutionary basis of cooperative behavior.

20. Fukuyama (1995) and Harrison and Huntington (2000). Also see Maynard Smith (1982) and Axelrod (1997b).

21. Sober and Wilson (1998).

22. Early humans practiced *polygyny*, in which males tended to mate with multiple females, as opposed to *polygamy*, in which both males and females can mate with multiple partners. See Wright (1994), pp. 155–180.

23. Wright (2000), pp. 30–31.

24. Diamond (1997).

25. Seabright (2004).

26. Wright (2000), pp. 33–35.

27. See Wright (1994) for an in-depth discussion and references.

28. Wright (2000), p. 33.

29. As Wright (2000), pp. 39–41, points out, anthropologists have labeled some societies, such as the !Kung and Shoshone, as "relatively less hierarchical." He claims that this should be interpreted as "less complex hierarchies" rather than "egalitarian" and notes that these tribes may have in fact seen the complexities of their hierarchies decline as they were driven into less fertile lands by European settlers.

30. Easterly and Levine (2002).

31. See chapter 11, note 2 for a discussion of the evolution of language and references.

32. The information-computational view of organization arguably originates with Herbert Simon (e.g., Simon, 1992 and 1996). Cyert and March (1992) were also pioneers in this perspective. For modern examples, see Prietula et al. (1998), Kennedy and Eberhart (2001), and Monge and Contractor (2003).

33. Hutchins (1996).

34. Jay (2000), p. 38.

35. Ibid., pp. 121–122.

36. Micklethwait and Wooldridge (2003).

Chapter Thirteen

1. I am, of course, simplifying in stating that genes are the unit of selection in biology. This remains an area of active research. We will, however, generally follow the gene's-eye view of selection described in Dawkins (1976) and (1982).

2. See Nelson (1995), Hodgson (2002), and Knudsen (2002) for reviews.

3. Dawkins (1976) and (1982).

4. Best practice management research and business school cases provide evidence of the ability of people to retrospectively identify modules. For examples of best practice research see the Corporate Executive Board's Web site, www.executiveboard.com, and Harvard Business School's extensive case library at www.harvardbusinessonline.hbsp.harvard.edu (I have past affiliations with both the Corporate Executive Board and Harvard Business School).

5. See Nelson and Winter (1982), p. 14, for the original definition of routines, and Cohen and Sproull (1996) for discussions and further definitions. See Dawkins (1976), p. 192, for the original definition of memes, and Dawkins (1982), Dennett (1995), Lynch (1996), Brodie (1996), Blackmore (1999), Aunger (2000), and Shennan (2002) for discussions and debates on memetics. See Boyd and Richerson (1985), Dunbar, Knight, and Power (1999), Balkin (1998), Klein and Edgar (2002), Plotkin (2002), and Boyd and Richerson (2005) for other work and discussions of cultural evolution.

6. Amazon.com lists an amazing 97,041 books on how to write a Business Plan. A modest sampling indicates that they generally seem to follow this same basic formula. I can also personally attest to the commonality of this formula, as I once worked at a venture capital firm and read a few hundred business plans over the course of several years.

7. Collins and Porras (1994), pp. 140–168.

8. Niehans (1990), p. 447.

9. My points in this section echo earlier arguments made by Hayek (1948) and (1988).

10. Wright (2000).

11. Cameron and Neal (2003). For a history of markets, also see McMillan (2002) and Bevir and Trentmann (2004).

12. Baumol (2002).

13. Chandler (1977).

14. My use of the term *resources* in this context is consistent with its meaning in the management literature. See, for example, Wernerfelt (1984) and (1995) and Robert Grant, pp. 179–199, in Segal-Horn (1998) for a review and references.

15. Nelson and Winter (1982), pp. 119–121, and Nelson (1995), p. 69, make a similar point .

16. This point is emphasized by Nelson (1995).

17. While the emphasis on allocation is generally true, some Traditional economists have focused on the role of markets in innovation as well. In general, the approach has been to show how markets in equilibrium create the correct incentives for innovation and allocate resources to the innovators. See, for example, Aghion and Howitt (1998) and Baumol (2002).

18. See, for example, Gintis (2003).

19. Axtell (2002) and (2003).

20. From the title of Baumol (2002).

21. Kahneman, Diener, and Schwarz (1999) and Schwartz (2004).

22. From V. Havel, *Summer Meditations* (New York: Alfred A. Knopf, 1992), p. 62, quoted in McMillan (2002), p. 7.

23. Campbell (1960). For recent discussions of evolutionary epistemology, see Plotkin (1993) and Ziman (2000). See Hull (1988) for an evolutionary theory of science.

24. Cameron and Neal (2003), pp. 154–155.

25. Johnson (1997).

26. Ibid., pp. 94–95.

27. Ibid., p. 94.

Chapter Fourteen

1. Biographical details are from "The History of Economic Thought" Web site maintained by the New School University of New York, available at http://cepa.newschool.edu.

2. Georgescu-Roegen's attack was made in the introduction to his *Analytical Economics: Issues and Problems* (Cambridge, MA: Harvard University Press, 1966).

3. Georgescu-Roegen (1971).

4. See Teilhard de Chardin (1969) and a discussion of his work in Wright (2000).

5. Hayek (1960) and (1988), and Boulding (1978).

6. Schneider and Sagan (2005).

7. Cited in Kauffman (1995a), pp. 44–45.

8. Georgescu-Roegen (1971), p. 18.

9. Roegen (1971), Daly (1999), and Mirowski (1989).

10. Quoted in Daly (1999), pp. 78–79.

11. For over twenty years, Georgescu-Roegen repeatedly challenged Stiglitz and Solow (whom he saw as the two high priests of Traditional Economics) to a debate, to which they demurred. After Georgescu-Roegen's death, Solow finally agreed to answer a set of questions related to Georgescu-Roegen's critique. The frosty exchange, which readers can judge for themselves, was originally published in *Ecological Economics* 22, no. 3 (September 1997): 271–273, and is reprinted in Daly (1999), pp. 85–88.

12. While correct in broad principle, Georgescu-Roegen's sometimes apocalyptic tone on the environment reduced his credibility. For example, Georgescu-Roegen (1971), p. 21, predicted that by the year 2000, humankind would be living off artificial protein and that, at some point in the future, we would return to draft animals and plows as fossil fuel supplies ran out.

13. Georgescu-Roegen gives as an example the econometrician Harold T. Davis's work in the 1940s and the critique of his work by J. H. C. Lisman (ibid., p. 17). To show that physicists can be just as guilty of bad metaphor as economists can, Mirowski (1989), p. 367, provides the example of Robert Bordley in a 1983 paper.

14. Quoted in Mirowski (1989), p. 382.

15. Quoted in ibid., p. 383.

16. Some of Georgescu-Roegen's arguments look quaint or even wrong to modern eyes. His views on entropy critically lack the benefit of work on information theory carried out in the 1980s and 1990s, and his views on evolution were developed before computers enabled the mathematical exploration of evolutionary theory and the development of the algorithmic perspective. Nonetheless, the overall arc of his argument still holds up remarkably well.

17. A. S. Eddington, *The Nature of the Physical World* (New York: MacMillan, 1930), p. 74, quoted in Haynie (2001), p. xii.

18. Georgescu-Roegen (1971), pp. 6, 11, 196–198, 278.

19. Ibid., p. 277. Italics in original.

20. Ibid., p. 18.

21. See discussions of Gibbs's ensembles and the Onsager-Boltzmann equations in Keizer (1987).

22. The only way we could tell the direction of time would be if we had some reference point to a fixed set of stars. But this information would only be useful if we knew a priori what the "correct" orbit was. We can say the process is reversible because a space-alien physicist with no knowledge of our particular solar system could not distinguish the forward from the backward orbit, while any space alien familiar with the Second Law of Thermodynamics could tell the arrow of time from a movie of a smashing bottle of milk.

23. The directionality of time, and the relationship between time at the macroscopic and quantum levels, is a complex topic and the subject of continuing research. For non-technical discussions, see Prigogine (1996) and Deutsch (1997).

24. From von Baeyer (1998), p. 133.

25. For a history of Maxwell's Demon, see von Baeyer (1998).

26. The issue of reversibility is not explicitly addressed in Traditional Economics, but a look at Traditional theory through the lens of reversibility reveals some interesting contradictions. For example, trades are generally formulated as nonreversible, for example, a Walrasian auction. However, nothing inherent prevents someone from running Neoclassical production functions backward, for example, Cobb-Douglas. Thus, what gives Neoclassical theory an "arrow of time" (to the extent that it has one) is the arrangement of utilities and either initial endowments or exogenous shocks, which put the system out of equilibrium such that the utilities then pull the economy ahead in time through irreversible trades, such as in the canonical "Hicksian week." Interestingly, this microeconomic irreversibility due to utilities does not translate to macroeconomic irreversibility. Most macro models are either time reversible (e.g., Solow's growth model), or the arrow of time is given exogenously (e.g., the Diamond overlapping-generations model). This further demonstrates the lack of consistency and integration between the worlds of Traditional micro and macro theory.

27. I am grateful to Cosma Shalizi of the University of Michigan for pointing this issue out to me. For a description of Bennett and Landauer's work, see von Baeyer (1998), pp. 152–155.

28. Eric Smith of the Santa Fe Institute and Duncan Foley of the New School University have shown theoretically that one can create reversible economic transactions at the point at which consumers are indifferent to trade and maintain constant utility. Such transactions, however, do not satisfy the condition of creating value. See Smith and Foley (2002).

29. Work by the physicists Leo Szilard in the 1920s and further developed by Leon Brillouin in the 1950s showed that information acquisition inevitably results in a global increase in entropy, thus revealing the directionality of time. See von Baeyer (1998), pp. 146–152.

30. One could raise the question of people like vandals, who destroy things for pleasure. I would argue that while such people may be satisfying some psychological need, they are not creating economic value. In fact, taxpayers pay money to the police to stop such people. Thus, from the perspective of society, vandals are value destroying.

31. Even if we isolate this intermediate step of demolition and view it as a transformation in and of itself, we would see that while the entropy of the physical building is being increased, the entropy of the demolition firm is being decreased as it grows and hires people, organizes, buys equipment, creates knowledge about demolition, and so on—thus the local entropy in the economic system as a whole

decreases, and as the rubble of the building is returned to the environment, entropy in the universe increases.

32. I thank the participants of the University of Michigan–SFI Complexity Workshop in 2002 for suggesting this example.

33. I have adapted this example from von Baeyer's (1998), pp. 157–158, description.

34. Bowles (2004), pp. 93–126, provides a review of efforts to reconcile a theory of preferences with observed behavioral regularities from experimental economics. As far as I know, however, no work has been done to reconcile a theory of preferences with evolutionary psychology (Buss, 1999). In this section, I present some preliminary thoughts on the topic.

35. For overviews of evolutionary psychology, see Wright (1994), Pinker (1997) and (2002), Ridley (1997), and Buss (1999). Evolutionary psychology remains controversial; for a countervailing view, see the collection of essays in Rose and Rose (2001).

36. Wright (1994).

37. U.S. Department of Labor, Bureau of Labor Statistics, *Consumer Expenditures in 2000* (April 2002, available at www.bls.gov).

38. See, for example, Abul-Magd (2002).

39. Pinker (1997), pp. 374–378.

40. Ibid., pp. 378–385.

41. Wright (1994).

42. Research sponsored by the British telephone company BT Cellnet; see Fox (2002).

43. Study by the Norwegian telephone company Telenor; see www.telenor.no/fou/program/nomadiske/artikler.shtml.

44. Pinker (1997), p. 522.

45. Ibid., pp. 521–538.

46. Laland, Odling-Smee, and Feldman (2000) and Bowles and Gintis (2002).

47. The oldest known musical instruments are bird-bone flutes from 30,000 to 32,000 years ago. They were found in caves in southern Germany and France (Klein and Edgar, 2002, pp. 194–195). See Pinker (1997), pp. 528–538, on the evolution of music appreciation.

48. Georgescu-Roegen (1971), pp. 283–291.

49. Dawkins (1976) and (1998), Dennett (1995), and Wright (2000).

50. Kahneman et al. (1999) and Layard (2005).

51. See Wright (2000) for an eloquent discussion. Also see Horan, Bulte, and Shogren (2005) for evidence of economic activity as a source of advantage in human evolution.

52. Although knowledge historically lay at the exogenous boundaries of Neoclassical economics, researchers in management, organization studies, and sociology have made it central to their studies for some time. In particular, in the 1950s, Edith Penrose (1959) described how knowledge and organizational learning are crucial to wealth creation by firms. This led to a stream of research on the role of knowledge and learning in strategy and organization. For discussions, see Cohen and Sproull (1996), Mintzberg, Ahlstrand, and Lampel (1998), pp. 175–231, and Eisenhardt and Santos in Pettigrew, Thomas, and Whittington (2002), pp. 139–164.

53. See Plotkin (1993) for a discussion of theories of evolutionary epistemology.

54. Gould (2002).

55. In my definition of a scientific law, I am greatly simplifying a complex topic. See Hausman (1994), pp. 10–15, and Cartwright (1999), pp. 49–74, for discussions.

Chapter Fifteen

1. In the 1920s, Frank Knight made the distinction between "risk" with known probabilities and "uncertainty" with unknown probabilities. This presented a problem for the equilibrium framework, as uncertainty without a known probability distribution could not be modeled. The issue was resolved by Leonard Savage in his 1954 book, *The Foundations of Statistics* (New York: John Wiley & Sons), in which he proposed that agents be modeled as if they held well-defined probabilistic beliefs. Savage's subjective probability theory has since become the standard approach to modeling uncertainty in Traditional Economics. See Mas-Colell, Whinston, and Green (1995), pp. 167–215, for a modern treatment and references.

2. This does not deny that either short-term forecasting can improve or the odds that long-term forecasts will sometimes be right can improve. As data gathering, computer models, and scientific understanding of complex phenomena improve, so will forecasting of complex systems such as the weather and the economy (e.g., see "And Now, the War Forecast," *Economist Technology Quarterly*, September 17, 2005,

pp. 21–22). Rather, as discussed earlier in the book, the Complexity theory shows that there are fundamental limits to long-range forecasting in such systems.

3. Searches on fitness landscapes are generally regarded as NP Complete problems. See Flake (1998) for an introduction to NP Complete problems. See Weinberger (1996) for a discussion of NP Completeness and fitness landscapes. For a discussion on the difficulty of predicting evolution, see Grant and Grant (2002).

4. For surveys, see Mintzberg, Ahlstrand, and Lampel (1998) and Pettigrew, Thomas, and Whittington (2002).

5. Chandler (1962), p. 13.

6. Unfortunately, space does not allow a full review of the rich variety of views and approaches in the academic strategy literature. For an excellent overview geared toward a general audience, see Mintzberg, Ahlstrand, and Lampel (1998). For reviews that are more academically oriented, see Rumelt, Schendel, and Teece (1994) and Pettigrew, Thomas, and Whittington (2002). In this section, I am focusing on the strategy-as-positioning, or strategy-as-structure, school because of its wide application by businesses, consulting firms, and MBA courses. We will look at the resource-based view of the firm later in the book.

7. The concept of competitive advantage goes back to Joe Bain's 1959 *Industrial Organization* and Igor Ansoff's 1965 *Corporate Strategy*. Porter (1980) and (1985) then developed the concept into its canonical form. See Pettigrew, Thomas, and Whittington (2002), pp. 55–71, for a current review.

8. See Pettigrew, Thomas, and Whittington (2002), pp. 55–71, for a more complete taxonomy of sources of competitive advantage.

9. Ghemawat (1991).

10. Murray Gell-Mann told this story in a talk to McKinsey & Company's London office on February 16, 2001. As is typical, Murray did his research carefully and I have verified the basic facts of the story. However, there is some controversy over whether Crown Prince Wilhelm held the cigarette in his mouth or hand (see www.ormiston.com/annieoakley).

11. Gell-Mann (1994), pp. 133–134.

12. The quotation in the heading is from baseball great Yogi Berra (www.yogi-berra.com).

13. See Van der Hijden (1996) and Schwartz (1991) for discussions of scenario analysis. Also see Courtney (2001) for a discussion of strategy under uncertainty.

14. See Mas-Colell et al. (1995) for a presentation of the Traditional Economics approach to uncertainty.

15. Inductive systems in which firing rules are weighted by past success (e.g., those described by Holland et al., 1989), can lose their adaptability when in a stable environment for long periods, as rule structures become deep, specific, and heavily weighted.

16. Evidence for power laws in patterns of company growth, size, and performance are found in Lee et al. (1998), Axtell (2001), and Powell (2003). Camerer et al. (2004), pp. 9–12, provide a brief review and references on the heuristic processes by which people build probability judgments and the errors these processes produce.

17. Foster and Kaplan (2001), ch. 3, describe a similar scenario.

18. See Micklethwait and Wooldridge (2003) for a history. A small successor company trading tea and coffee under the East India Company name still exists today.

19. The relative sustainability of competitive advantage has been the subject of debate in the field of strategy since the 1980s. Wiggins and Ruefli (2005) provide a history of empirical results and a review of the debate. Wiggins and Ruefli (2002) provide evidence on the temporary nature of advantage.

20. Foster and Kaplan (2001).

21. Note that in a merger or an acquisition, the assets of the acquired company do not cease to exist, even if the ownership of them changes. However, I view this as "dropping off the list," because in the framework outlined in part 3, the assets are coming under the control of another Business Plan. The process of mergers and acquisitions is one mechanism by which successful Business Plans amplify their control over resources.

22. The measure of performance that Foster and Kaplan use is total returns to shareholders with dividends reinvested. Using a different measure (return on assets) and by combining the results of two studies, Wiggins and Ruefli (2002) identify three companies that both survived and had persistent superior performance from 1950 to 1997: American Home Products, Eli Lilly, and 3M, further confirming that the combination of long-term survival and high performance is exceedingly rare.

23. Wiggins and Ruefli (2002) and (2005).

24. Performance was measured by return on assets and Tobin's q. The results noted are for return on assets.

25. Competitive advantage itself is unobservable. Thus, what Wiggins and Ruefli were testing for was what competitive advantage is hypothesized to cause—long-term, sustained, superior performance relative to industry. There is a history of debate on the scientific validity and testability of competitive advantage due to its unobservable nature; see Powell (2002) for a discussion and prior references.

26. T. Ruefli, e-mail correspondence with author, September 25–26, 2005.

27. The term *Red Queen Principle* (which I have adapted as *Red Queen race*) was first applied to this phenomenon by the University of Chicago biologist Leigh van Valen, "A New Evolutionary Law," *Evolutionary Theory* 1 (1973): 1–30. See Kauffman (1995b) for a discussion on Red Queen races in biology and economics.

28. Since the mid-1980s, the field of strategy has roughly been divided into two major camps: the structure and the resources camps (Wernerfelt, 1984 and 1995; Henderson and Mitchell, 1997; Pettigrew, Thomas, and Whittington, 2002; and Hoopes, Madsen, and Walker, 2003). An evolutionary view would say that this is a dichotomy as false as "nature versus nurture." In fact, it is the same false dichotomy played out in a different substrate. What is referred to as *resources* in the strategy literature can be seen as an aspect of the Business Plan (schema) in a business (interactor), and *structure* can be seen as the environment the business operates in. In the evolutionary view, Business Plans evolve in response to selection pressures from the environment, and the environment is largely a function of the collection of Business Plans being executed by businesses (what evolutionary theorists refer to as niche construction). Thus, business performance cannot be seen as either a function of resources *or* a function of structure; rather, resources and structure dynamically coevolve and create each other over time. In the taxonomy of Mintzberg, Ahlstrand, and Lampel (1998), an evolutionary view rejects the design, planning, and positioning schools of strategy. It shares elements with, and provides a synthesis of, the entrepreneurial, cognitive, learning, power, cultural, environmental, and configuration schools. While it does not fully agree with any of these perspectives in isolation, the Complexity Economics perspective provides a theoretical foundation for many of the empirical observations and insights found across these various strands of literature.

29. T. Ruefli, e-mail correspondence with author, September 25–26, 2005. The measure for these companies was return on assets.

30. Hannan and Freeman (1977), (1984), and (1989), and Hannan and Carroll (1992).

31. Foster (1986), pp. 132–135, and Tushman and O'Reilly (1997), pp. 17–25.

32. See Hannan and Freeman (1989) and Baum and Singh (1994) for reviews and discussions.

33. Foster and Kaplan (2001), p. 20.

34. While the *practice* of strategy by most companies has not been very adaptive, evolution has been a topic of interest for management academics since the early 1980s. Building on the ideas of Boyd and Richerson (1985) on cultural evolution, Nelson and Winter (1982) in economics, and Campbell (1960) in epistemology, management scientists in the 1980s began to look at strategy from an evolutionary perspective. In particular, the Stanford University business school professor Robert Burgelman has led significant work in this area, see Burgelman (1983) and Barnett and Burgelman (1996). For a fascinating evolutionary account of Intel's strategy, see Burgelman (2002). Evolution has also often been referred to in popular books about management strategy. See, for example, Peters and Waterman (1982), p. 114, and Hamel (2000), pp. 264–269, 297–306.

35. The idea of thinking of strategies as real options has its origins in work by Avinash Dixit and Robert Pindyck (1994). In Beinhocker (1999), I look at creating a portfolio of options as an approach for an evolutionary search on a fitness landscape. My colleague at McKinsey, Lowell Bryan (2002), has explored the implications of this approach for management practice, referring to it as a "portfolio of initiatives."

36. This example is adapted from Beinhocker (1999).

37. This section is adapted from Beinhocker and Kaplan (2002).

38. My thinking on this topic has been heavily influenced by Dick Foster and Sarah Kaplan's work with Johnson & Johnson on a process that has become known as "Frameworks." See Foster and Kaplan (2001), ch. 11.

39. Mintzberg, Ahlstrand, and Lampel (1998), pp. 176–231.

40. See Dixit and Pindyck (1994), Copeland and Keenan (1998), and Leslie and Michaels (2000) for discussions of "real options" and strategy.

41. Bryan (2002).

42. This tension between exploring and exploiting has been noted by several authors, including Peters and Waterman (1982), March (1991), Collins and Porras (1994), Tushman and O'Reilly (1997), and Foster and Kaplan (2001).

43. Bryan (2002) refers to this as "familiarity."

44. Wiggins and Ruefli (2002), p. 95.

45. Three good starting points on aspirations are Collins and Porras (1994), Tushman and O'Reilly (1997), and Lencioni (2002).

46. Collins and Porras (1994), p. 94. While I criticized the assumption that there are excellent companies (as opposed to long-lived companies), I still believe that careful studies of company practices, such as *Built to Last*, can shed light on interesting ST innovations that companies have developed.

47. Quoted in Collins and Porras (1994), p. 95.

48. Welch (2001).

49. Bee foraging behavior has been studied in detail by entomologists and is a fascinating case of highly effective self-organized behavior. See Camazine et al. (2001), pp. 188–215.

50. Quoted from a presentation by J. Donehey and G. Overholser of CapitalOne, at the Embracing Complexity Conference, held by Ernst & Young, Boston, August 2–4, 1998. See Bonabeau and Meyer (2001) for a more detailed description of CapitalOne's approach.

51. Kaplan et al. (1996).

52. While I am advocating a venture capital mind-set, I am not advocating corporate venture investing. Most such efforts have been disappointing; see Campbell et al. (2003).

53. See, for example, Hamel (2000).

54. Berzins et al. (1998), p. 7.

Chapter Sixteen

1. This history is compiled from the Web sites of both companies (www.westinghousenuclear.com and www.ge.com) and from Collins and Porras (1994), Slater (1999), and Welch (2001).

2. Welch (2001) and Collins and Porras (1994).

3. Collins and Porras (1994).

4. Slater (1999) and Welch (2001).

5. Krames (2002) and Slater (1999).

6. For examples and reviews, see Arrow (1974), Simon (1997), Williamson and Winter (1991), Jensen (1998), Hatch (1997), Penrose (1959), Williamson (1990), Cyert and March (1963), Astely et al. (1983), Koza and Thoenig (1995), and Giddens (2001). For a postmodern perspective, see Hatch (1997).

7. For examples, see Nelson and Winter (1982), Aldrich (1999), Dosi, Nelson, and Winter (2000), Haken (2000), Lee et al. (1998), Lesourne and Orléan (1998), Morecroft and Sterman (1994), Prietula et al. (1998), Axelrod (1984) and (1997a), Axelrod and Cohen (1999), Durlauf and Young (2001), Young (1998), and Monge and Contractor (2003).

8. Aldrich (1999).

9. Cyert and March (1992) note that organizations themselves don't have goals; only individuals do. What we think of as organizational goals are the emergent result of the interaction of individual agent goals. Chester Barnard, in his 1938 classic *The Functions of the Executive* (Cambridge, MA: Harvard University Press). discussed the important role of management hierarchies in the alignment of individual goals into positive emergent goals. See Williamson (1995) for a current discussion of Barnard's theories.

10. Aldrich (1999), p. 4.

11. For a summary of the Traditional Economics perspective on why Firms exist, see Roberts (2004), pp. 74–117.

12. See Williamson and Winter (1993) for a modern review of Coase's work.

13. Ibid. and Williamson (1995).

14. Holmström and Roberts (1998).

15. Camazine et al. (2001), pp. 23–26.

16. In their classic 1988 paper "Organizational Learning" (reprinted in Cohen and Sproull, 1996, pp. 516–540), Levitt and March claim that "organizational learning is viewed as routine-based, history-dependent, and target-oriented." "Stimergistic" learning is consistent with this definition. Also see Hutchins (1996) on collective learning.

17. Wright (2000).

18. See Axelrod and Cohen (1999), pp. 43–50, for a discussion.

19. Peters and Waterman (1982). As we will discuss later, both Joseph Schumpeter and Edith Penrose get credit for identifying this dichotomy much earlier.

20. Collins and Porras (1994), Foster and Kaplan (2001), and Tushman and O'Reilly (1997).

21. March (1991).

22. A prime example is the difficulty health organizations and governments have had in adapting to the HIV/AIDS crisis; see "Help At Last," *The Economist*, November 29, 2003, p. 11.

23. These are not the only possible reasons for a lack of individual adaptability. See, for example, Cohen and Sproull (1996) and Camerer, Loewenstein, and Rabin (2004) for discussions. But these are each well-studied and potentially major contributors to mental model rigidity.

24. See, for example, Bob Woodward's *Bush at War* (New York: Simon & Schuster, 2002) and Richard Clarke's *Against All Enemies* (New York: Free Press, 2004).

25. Lovallo and Kahneman (2003).

26. Ibid., p. 5.

27. Welch (2001), p. 106.

28. Holland et al. (1986) and Holland (1995).

29. Given the dominance of hierarchies by older, more experienced people, surprisingly little research has been done on the impact of age and experience on mental model adaptability and decision making. Sternberg (1999), pp. 122–123, summarizes empirical evidence, and Holland et al. (1986), pp. 250–254, discuss the subject briefly in the context of default hierarchies. The views in this section are thus my own interpretation of Holland's model and somewhat speculative. There is an important opportunity for future research in this area.

30. Margaret Thatcher, "Special Report: Politics Past," speech given at Conservative Party conference, 1980; available at the Guardian Web site, politics.guardian.co.uk.

31. Harrington (1998).

32. Krames (2002), p. 105.

33. Page (1996).

34. Penrose (1959). However, credit for the first economist to identify this trade-off probably goes to Joseph Schumpeter in his 1934 *Theory of Economic Development*.

35. See Wernerfelt (1984) and (1995), Barney (1991), Henderson and Mitchell (1997), Segal-Horn (1998), Mintzberg, Ahlstrand, and Lampel (1998), and Dosi, Nelson, and Winter (2000) for discussions and references on the resource-based view of the Firm.

36. Penrose (1959) herself was very critical of many early attempts to apply evolutionary theory to economics. Her work was developed before modern theories of Universal Darwinism, and she quite rightly rejected the metaphorical use of biological ideas. Nonetheless, her own work is very compatible with evolutionary thinking and in her foreword to the third edition of her book, she favorably notes the evolutionary views of Nelson and Winter as well as Brian Loasby.

37. Prahalad and Hamel (1990). For other examples, see Baghai, Coley, and White (1999).

38. For an interesting simulation of culture emerging from agent interaction, see Prietula, Carley, and Gasser (1998), pp. 3–22.

39. In a 1952 study, Kroeber and Kluckhohn cited 164 definitions of *culture* in the anthropology and sociology literature. The number has undoubtedly risen since. See Boyd and Richerson (1985), p. 33.

40. This definition is narrower, but sympathetic with Boyd and Richerson's (1985), p. 2, definition: "By 'culture' we mean the transmission from one generation to the next, via teaching, and imitation of knowledge, values, and other factors that influence behavior." The key differences in my definition are the emergent character of culture and the focus on the cognitive rules that translate knowledge and values into behaviors rather than the knowledge and values per se. Finally, my interest is not all behaviors, but the subset of social behaviors. The key compatibilities are a view that culture is expressed through behavior, is socially learned, and is both vertically (e.g., through parents and superiors in a hierarchy) and horizontally (e.g., peers) transmitted. My definition is also compatible with memetic views of culture; see, for example, Balkin (1998), Aunger (2000), and Shennan (2002). My stance on memetics is agnostic, but my position depends on an evolutionary view of culture; see Dunbar et al. (1999) and Klein and Edgar (2002).

41. We can distinguish cultural norms from routines (Nelson and Winter, 1982) by asking whether the rules are firm-specific or Business-Plan-specific. For example, a chemical company might have various rules on how to produce its chemicals, how to market them, and so on. But these rules would potentially change with changes in its Business Plans and are thus routines. At the same time, the organization might also have safety norms that are specific to the company, but not to a particular Business Plan or even Business. Such norms would then be part of a company's safety culture rather than routines. Cultural norms and Business Plans (with their routines) coevolve; norms help enable certain Business Plans, and Business Plans require certain norms.

42. The idea that humans have a small set of universal norms wired into them by evolution is controversial, but is strongly supported by some. For an academic review, see Katz (2000). For popular discussions, see Wright (1994), Ridley (1996), and Pinker (2002).

43. Henrich et al. (2004).

44. Tolstoy quote from *Anna Karenina*, part I, ch. 1. The literature on corporate culture and its impact on performance and adaptability is extremely diverse, ranging from academic to popular. For a sampling

of perspectives, see Deal and Kennedy (1982), Peters and Waterman (1982), Kotter and Heskett (1992), Schein (1992), Howard and Haas (1993), Collins and Porras (1994), Cohen and Sproull (1996), de Gues (1997), Tushman and O'Reilly (1997), Aldrich (1999), Cohen and Prusak (2001), Collins (2001), Welch (2001), Bower (2003), and Roberts (2004).

45. Quoted in Collins and Porras (1994), p. 147.

46. See Edersheim (2004) for a biography of Bower. The current articulation of McKinsey's values can be viewed on its Web site www.mckinsey.com.

47. Krames (2002).

48. Gardner (2004).

49. Krames (2002).

50. See, for example, Collins and Porras (1994), Collins (2001), Slater (1999), Foster and Kaplan (2001), Tushman and O'Reilly (1997), and Roberts (2004).

51. Penrose (1959).

52. Ibid., p. 18.

53. Axtell (2001) also shows that the mean size of all companies captured in the U.S Census has gradually grown from 17.73 employees in 1988 to 19.00 in 1997.

54. See Penrose (1959), pp. xvi–xviii, 12–13, 18–19, 213–214, for her discussion of this issue.

55. Axtell (2001), Stanley et al. (1996), and Amaral et al. (1997) and (1998).

56. Minsky (1985).

Chapter Seventeen

1. See Lewis (1999) and Lowenstein (2000) for accounts of the failure of Long-Term Capital.

2. Lewis (1999).

3. This section is drawn from Peter Bernstein's (1992) excellent history of finance theory.

4. Ironically, five years after Bachelier submitted his thesis, Albert Einstein reinvented the theory in a different context. Building on work by Scottish botanist Robert Brown, Einstein developed a mathematical account of *Brownian motion*. The form of Brownian motion that is mathematically the same as Bachelier's random walk is continuous-time Brownian motion, which was formulated by Norbert Weiner in 1921 (Mandelbrot, 1997, p. 24).

5. Malkiel (1973).

6. For overviews of Traditional finance theory, see Brealey and Myers (1988), Cochrane (2005), and Ross (2005). Lengwiler (2004) describes the links between asset pricing and general equilibrium theory.

7. The figure of $94 is calculated by applying the present value (PV) formula to the stream of cash flows described in the text: $PV = \Sigma\, C_t / (1 + r_t)$, where C is the cash flow in year t, and r is the discount rate. For a description of how to use the PV formula, see Copeland et al. (1994).

8. Quoted in Campbell et al. (1997), p. 20.

9. Quoted in Bernstein (1992), p. 17.

10. For a discussion of "noise" traders and their impact on market equilibrium and further references, see Fischer Black, "Noise," in Thaler (1993), pp. 3–22.

11. Malkiel (1973), pp. 161–172.

12. Thaler (1993), Shleifer (2000), Montier (2002), and Camerer, Loewenstein, and Rabin (2004). For an opposing view, see Ross (2005).

13. The biographical profile of Mandelbrot is from Gleick (1987), pp. 83–90.

14. Mandelbrot's original 1963 article is reprinted in Mandelbrot (1997), pp. 371–411.

15. More specifically, Mandelbrot proposed that the data followed a Lévy-stable distribution, which is scale-free in the tail.

16. Mandelbrot and Hudson (2004).

17. Quoted in ibid., p. 166.

18. Fama's response is reprinted in Mandelbrot (1997), pp. 444–457.

19. Ibid., pp. 419–443.

20. Lo and MacKinlay (1999), p. 4.

21. The classic review of this work is Fama (1970). Lo and MacKinlay (1999), p. 13, give a complete list of references.

22. As Lo and MacKinlay (1999), p. 14, point out, they were not the first to ask this question or the first to get a result rejecting the random-walk hypothesis. Their results, however, were compelling enough to set off a program of debate and research, whereas for various reasons, other earlier researchers such as Mandelbrot were largely ignored.

23. Ibid., pp. 17–45. Houthakker pointed out the existence of clustered volatility in financial time series to Mandelbrot in the 1960s (Mandelbrot, 1997, and Mandelbrot and Hudson, 2004), and in a widely cited paper, Engle (1982) mathematically characterized the phenomenon.

24. See LeBaron (1989) and (1994), Campbell et al. (1997), and Lo and MacKinlay (1999) for surveys.

25. See Farmer (1999), Farmer and Lo (1999), Mantegna and Stanley (2000), Sornette (2003), and Johnson, Jeffries, and Hui (2003) for descriptions of the work of "econophysicists" and references.

26. For examples and further references, see Mantegna and Stanley (1996), Plerou et al. (1999), and Cont and Bouchaud (2000), and Sornette (2003).

27. For profiles of Farmer, see Gleick (1987) and Bass (1999). The firm I am affiliated with, McKinsey & Company, has provided financial support for Professor Farmer's research at the Santa Fe Institute.

28. Farmer (2001).

29. Brian Arthur first used the term "ocean of expectations" in Arthur (1995) and then an "ecology" of expectations in Arthur et al. (1997), p. 38. He then settled on "ecosystems of expectations" in later talks.

30. Arthur et al., "Asset Pricing Under Endogenous Expectations in an Artificial Stock Market," in Arthur, Durlauf, and Lane (1997), pp. 15–43.

31. Kahneman et al. (1982), Thaler (1993), Kagel et al. (1995), and Shleifer (2000).

32. LeBaron et al. (1999).

33. Farmer (1998), p. 5.

34. Farmer (1998) and (2002).

35. Farmer (2001), p. 64.

36. Although the Walrasian auction remained a widely used assumption in much microeconomic and finance work in the twentieth century, economists did not completely ignore other mechanisms. A subfield, *market microstructure*, studied the characteristics of different price-formation mechanisms. See O'Hara (1995) for a survey.

37. Real-world market makers have limits on their positions and are generally required to maintain flat inventories over some period. These requirements create risk-averse behavior, which in turn introduces trends into market dynamics through market maker trading. Farmer (1998), (2001), and (2002) discusses how market-maker risk aversion creates nonrandom temporal structure.

38. See, for example, Neftci (1991), Brock et al. (1992), and LeBaron (1998).

39. See Campbell et al. (1997), pp. 253–287, for a discussion and references.

40. See Bernard, "Stock Price Reactions to Earnings Announcements," in Thaler (1993), pp. 303–340, for a discussion and references.

41. See, for example, "A Survey of Risk," *Economist*, January 24, 2004, pp. 10–11.

42. For example, the volume of foreign-exchange trading has exploded with improved information technology and cannot be accounted for by increased trade flows, hedging, or other "fundamental" causes. Instead, improved technology has fueled significant growth in foreign-exchange speculation. As Farmer (1998), p. 4, notes, over $1 trillion in foreign exchange is traded daily, a volume 50 times greater than world daily GDP.

43. Surowiecki (2004).

44. For example, the Iowa Electronic Markets allows people to buy and sell shares on the basis of their predictions of the percentage of the vote they think candidates will receive in future elections. In the 2000 U.S. presidential election, the predictions from the market were more accurate than 75 percent of all six hundred polls taken. See Surowiecki (2003).

45. Keynes's famous "beauty contest" quote is from his 1936 *General Theory of Employment, Interest and Money*.

46. See Farmer (1998), pp. 44–45, and Farmer (2002), p. 935.

47. Lo (2004).

48. Copeland, Koller, and Murrin (2000).

49. See Brealey and Myers (1988) for textbook overviews of CAPM. See Cochrane (2005) for a mathematical treatment.

50. See Campbell, Lo, and MacKinlay (1997), pp. 188–217, and Montier (2002), pp. 81–86, for reviews of the empirical evidence on CAPM.

51. This problem was identified by Richard Roll in 1977. The usual proxy for the market portfolio is the value-weighted CRSP index.

52. Karceski (2002).

53. Debate on the relevance of beta goes back to Basu's (1977) discovery of the price-earning effect and Banz's (1981) discovery of the small company effect. See Campbell, Lo, and MacKinlay (1997), pp.

211–212, and Montier (2002), pp. 83–84, for reviews and references. Copeland, Koller, and Murrin (2000), pp. 224–226, observe, "If beta is not dead, then it's surely wounded."

54. The theory says the comparator should be the zero beta portfolio, but again a proxy, typically government debt, must be used, and one has to make choices in selecting the proxy, such as time frame, specific instrument, and issuing government.

55. See Campbell, Lo, and MacKinlay (1997), pp. 219–251, Lo and MacKinlay (1999), pp. 189–212, and Montier (2002), pp. 87–92, for reviews and references.

56. Andrew Hill, reported by *Financial Times*, May 14, 2003.

57. Alternative approaches do exist (e.g., McNulty et al., 2002, and Shefrin, 2005), but have yet to be integrated in a larger theoretical framework and empirically tested.

58. Copeland, Koller, and Murrin (2000), p. 7.

59. De Swaan and Harper (2003).

60. See Kaplan and Norton (1996) and (2000) for a description of the balanced-scorecard approach.

61. Dobbs and Koller (2005).

62. For a discussion, see Jensen (1998) and (2001), and Mas-Colell, Whinston, and Green (1995), pp. 152–154.

63. See, for example, Copeland, Koller, and Murrin (2000), pp. 3–15.

64. See, for example, Elkington (1999), Kelly (2003), Zadek (2004), and Bakan (2004).

65. Handy (2002).

66. DuPont's performance in 1917–1987 was a 7.2 percent compound annual average growth in market capitalization versus 7.5 percent for the U.S. market as a whole (Foster and Kaplan, 2001, p. 8). The total return on the stock from 1970 to 2004 was 510 percent versus 1,000 percent for the S&P 500. Likewise, during the window 1994–2004, the total return was 48 percent versus 149 percent for the S&P (DuPont company Web site, www.dupont.com).

67. Companies can, of course, grow from their own cash flow without outside investment, but such retained earnings that are not returned to shareholders but are reinvested in the business count as capital, too.

68. Graham, Harvey, and Rajgopal (2005).

69. Davis (2005a).

70. Davis (2005b)

71. See de Gues (1997), p. 11.

72. Collins and Porras (1994), pp. 48–79.

Chapter Eighteen

1. The association of the Left with a critique of private-property ownership, however, predates Marx and goes back to Rousseau's comments on the evils of private property and competition in his *Discours sur l'inégalité*, and in the preface to his play *Narcisse*. See Johnson (1988), p. 4.

2. Fukuyama (1992).

3. Giddens (1998) and (2000).

4. See Giddens (2000) for a discussion of critiques of the third way and his response.

5. From Hume's *Essays: Moral, Political and Literary* (1754), quoted in Gintis et al. (2005), p. 4.

6. Gintis et al. (2005), p. 3.

7. Ibid., p. 8.

8. Gintis et al. (2005) and Henrich et al. (2004).

9. See Silk in Gintis et al. (2005), pp. 43–75, regarding cooperation in primates.

10. See Damasio (2005) regarding oxytocin and trust.

11. Gintis et al. (2005), p. 29, and Heinrich et al. (2004), pp. 125–167.

12. Fong, Bowles, and Gintis, in Gintis et al. (2005), pp. 278–302.

13. Arrow (1974).

14. The idea that in our distant past, we humans lived in small-scale, communitarian groups has been shown by anthropologists to be a myth (Wright 2000). While the hierarchies of some cultures are more consultative and consensus oriented than others, they are hierarchies nonetheless. Even if such communitarian groups are possible on a small scale, the lessons of networks show that to avoid complexity catastrophes as they grow larger, groups need hierarchies and patching. As scale is a critical, non-zero-sum ingredient in economic growth, we are left with the alternatives of hierarchies or markets.

15. Hayek (1944), (1948), and (1988).

16. Hayek (1948), pp. 33–56, 77–91.

17. See Hayek (1980), p. 21.

18. The argument on socialist calculation was first raised by Barone in 1908, but Hayek's response was aimed at Dickenson's version of the argument. See Caldwell (2004), pp. 214–220.

19. The experience of U.K. directory enquiries deregulation was detailed in a documentary "Wrong Numbers," broadcast by BBC Two on May 20, 2004.

20. See Fligstein (2001).

21. Morris (2001).

22. World Bank, "2002 GNI Per Capita, Atlas Method." Data presented in U.S. dollars. Available on the World Bank Web site www.worldbank.org.

23. World Bank, "Global Poverty Monitoring Program, 2001." Data presented in U.S. dollars, 1993 PPP. Available on the World Bank Web site www.worldbank.org.

24. Landes (1998), p. xix.

25. North and Thomas (1973), Rosenberg and Birdzell (1986), and Landes (1998).

26. Diamond (1997).

27. Harrison and Huntington (2000).

28. Ibid., p. 2.

29. See Bednar and Page (2003) and Bowles (2001a) for examples of norm-producing models that may be individually suboptimal but survive through group selection.

30. Grondona, in Harrison and Huntington (2000), pp. 44–55.

31. A study by Thomas and Mueller (2000) shows common cultural norms among entrepreneurs from a variety of cultures.

32. Quoted in Harrison (2001).

33. See Hammond (2000) for an agent-based example.

34. The interplay between culture and experience may at least be partially mediated by neurochemical changes in the brain. For example, one's experience in society may change one's oxytocin set point and thus change one's trust behaviors. See Zak and Knack (2001), Zak (2003), and Glimcher (2002) and (2003).

35. Henrich et al. (2004).

36. Zak (2003). However, Gintis et al. (2005), p. 381, note that methodological questions have been raised about the usefulness of such surveys.

37. Fukuyama (1995), pp. 62–145.

38. Hoff and Sen (2001).

39. Easterly (2002).

40. Putnam (2000).

41. Ibid., p. 19.

42. Ibid., pp. 21–22.

43. Putnam (1993), p. 5.

44. Ibid., pp. 5–6.

45. See Padgett and Ansell's (1993) fascinating account of the complex social network of the Florentine Medicis.

46. Putnam (2000), pp. 15–17.

47. Purdy (2003). See also Fukuyama (1995).

48. Fukuyama (1999), pp. 31–44.

49. Putnam (2000), p. 195.

50. Ibid., pp. 402–414.

51. Fukuyama (1999), pp. 263–282.

52. Putnam (1993) and (2000), Fukuyama (1995) and (1999), Bowles, Choi, and Hopfensitz (2003), Skyrms (1996), Sober and Wilson (1998), and Bowles (2004).

53. Bowles (2004), p. 12.

54. See the World Bank's 2006 World Development Report for a discussion. Whether global inequality is actually growing (versus within country inequality), however, is the subject of debate. See the discussion of work by Stanley Fischer in "Global Inequality: More or Less Equal," *The Economist*, May 11, 2004.

55. Abul-Magd (2002).

56. Miller (2003), p. 50. Matt Miller is also a senior adviser to McKinsey & Company.

57. Arrow, Bowles, and Durlauf (2000), and Bowles, Gintis, and Osborne Groves (2005).

58. Ibid., pp. 1–22.

59. Duncan et al., in Bowles, Gintis, and Osborne Groves (2005), pp. 23–79. Also see Bowles, Gintis, and Osborne (2001).

60. Feldman, Otto, and Christiansen, in Arrow, Bowles, and Durlauf (2000), pp. 62–85.

61. Bowles (2001b).

62. Durlauf (2001) finds significant correlations between group membership and economic outcomes.

63. Miller (2003), pp. 69–91.

64. Hertz, in Bowles, Gintis, and Osborne Groves, eds. (2005), p. 188, shows that intergenerational income elasticity for blacks approaches that for whites above the ninth income decile.

65. Quoted in Harrison and Huntington (2000), p. xiv.

66. Bewley, in Gintis et al. (2005), pp. 303–338.

67. Wackernagel et al. (2002).

68. See, for example, Sterman and Sweeney (2002).

69. For examples, see Richards, ed. (2000), and Kollman, Miller, and Page, eds. (2003).

70. From an interview with *Woman's Own*, October 31, 1987, quoted in *The Oxford Dictionary of Quotations* (Oxford: Oxford University Press, 1999).

71. E. M. Forster, 1938, *Two Cheers for Democracy*.

Epilogue

1. See Fogel (2004) and Bernstein (2004).

2. See Diamond (2005).

3. Source: Analysis of data from the University of Michigan Library "Elections 2004" Web site (www.lib.umich.edu/govdocs/elec2004).

4. See Butler et al. (1997) and Johnson, Manyika, and Yee (2005).

5. See Huntington (1996).

6. See Kennedy (1987), Diamond (1997), and Wright (2000).

7. Edmund Burke, 1790. *Reflections on the Revolution in France.*

BIBLIOGRAPHY

Abul-Magd, A. Y. 2002. Wealth Distribution in Ancient Egyptian Society. *Physical Review E* 66: 057104.

Aghion, P., and Howitt, P. 1998. *Endogenous Growth Theory.* Cambridge, MA: MIT Press.

Aghion, P., Frydman, R., Stiglitz, J., and Woodford, M. 2003. *Knowledge, Information, and Expectations in Modern Macroeconomics: In Honor of Edmund S. Phelps.* Princeton, NJ: Princeton University Press.

Akerlof, G. A., and Yellen, J. L. 1985a. A Near-Rational Model of the Business Cycle, with Wage and Price Inertia. *Quarterly Journal of Economics, Supplement* 100: 823–838.

———. 1985b. Can Small Deviations from Rationality Make Significant Differences to Economic Equilibria? *American Economic Review* 75: 708–721.

Albin, P. S. 1998. *Barriers and Bounds to Rationality.* Princeton, NJ: Princeton University Press.

Alchian, A. A. 1950. Uncertainty, Evolution and Economic Theory. *Journal of Political Economy* 58: 211–221.

Aldrich, H. 1999. *Organizations Evolving.* London: Sage.

Alexander, C. 1997. *Notes on the Synthesis of Form.* Fourteenth edition. Cambridge, MA: Harvard University Press.

Amaral, L. A. N., Buldyrev, S. V., Havlin, S., Leschhorn, H., Maass, P., Salinger, M. A., Stanley, H. E., and Stanley, M. H. R. 1997. Scaling Behavior in Economics: I. Empirical Results for Company Growth. *Journal de Physique I,* 7: 621–633.

Amaral, L. A. N., Buldyrev, S. V., Havlin, S., Salinger, M. A., and Stanley, H. E. 1998. Power Law Scaling for System of Interacting Units With Complex Internal Structure. *Physical Review Letters* 80: 1385–1388.

Anderson, P. W. 1972. More Is Different. *Science* 177: 393–396.

Anderson, P. W., Arrow, K. J., and Pines, D., eds. 1988. *The Economy as an Evolving Complex System.* Redwood City, CA: Addison-Wesley.

Andrews, E. L. 2005. 'Maestro' Leaves Stellar Record and Murky Legacy. *International Herald Tribune,* August 26: 13 and 17.

Arrow, K. J. 1974. *The Limits of Organization.* New York: W.W. Norton.

Arrow, K., Bowles, S., and Durlauf, S., eds. 2000. *Meritocracy and Economic Inequality.* Princeton, NJ: Princeton University Press.

Arthur, W. B. 1992. On Learning and Adaptation in the Economy. Santa Fe Institute working paper 92–07–038.

———. 1994a. *Increasing Return and Path Dependence in the Economy.* Ann Arbor, MI: University of Michigan Press.

———. 1994b. Inductive Reasoning and Bounded Rationality (the El Farol Problem). *American Economic Review Papers and Proceedings* 84: 406–411.

———. 1994c. The End of Certainty in Economics. Talk delivered at the conference *Einstein Meets Magritte.* Free University of Brussels. Reprinted in *The Biology of Business,* J. H. Clippinger, ed., 1999. San Francisco: Jossey-Bass.

———. 1995. Complexity in Economic and Financial Markets. *Complexity* 1: 20–25.

———. 1999. Complexity and the Economy. *Science* 284: 107–109.

Arthur, W. B., Durlauf, S. N., and Lane, D. A., eds. 1997. *The Economy as an Evolving Complex System II*. Reading, MA: Addison-Wesley.

Astely, W. G., and Van de Ven, A. H. 1983. Central Perspectives and Debates in Organization Theory. *Administrative Science Quarterly* 28: 245–273.

Audretsch, D. B. 1995. *Innovation and Industry Evolution*. Cambridge, MA: MIT Press.

Aunger, R., ed. 2000. *Darwinizing Culture: The Status of Memetics as a Science*. Oxford: Oxford University Press.

Axelrod, R. 1984. *The Evolution of Cooperation*. 1990 edition. London: Penguin Books.

———. 1997a. *The Complexity of Cooperation*. Princeton, NJ: Princeton University Press.

———. 1997b. The Dissemination of Culture. *Journal of Conflict Resolution* 41, no. 2: 203–226.

Axelrod, R., and Cohen, M. D. 1999. *Harnessing Complexity*. New York: Free Press.

Axtell, R. L. 1999. The Emergence of Firms in a Population of Agents: Local Increasing Returns, Unstable Nash Equilibria, and Power Law Size Distributions. Brookings Institution, Center on Social and Economic Dynamics working paper, no. 3.

———. 2001. Zipf Distribution of U.S. Firm Sizes. *Science* 293: 1818–1820.

———. 2002. The Complexity of Exchange. Brookings Institution working paper.

———. 2003. Economics as Distributed Computation. Brookings Institution working paper.

Backhouse, R. E. 2002. *The Penguin History of Economics*. London: Penguin Books.

Baghai, M., Coley, S., and White, D. 1999. *The Alchemy of Growth: Kickstarting and Sustaining Growth in Your Company*. London: Orion Business Books.

Bak, P. 1996. *How Nature Works: The Science of Self-Organized Criticality*. New York: Springer-Verlag.

Bakan, J. 2004. *The Corporation: The Pathological Pursuit of Profit and Power*. London: Constable.

Baldwin, C. Y., and Clark, K. B. 2000. *Design Rules: The Power of Modularity*. Cambridge, MA: MIT Press.

Baldwin, W. L., and Scott, J. T. 1987. *Market Structure and Technological Change*. London: Harwood Academic Publishers.

Balkin, J. M. 1998. *Cultural Software*. New Haven, CT: Yale University Press.

Banz, R. 1981. The Relation Between Return and Market Value of Common Stocks. *Journal of Financial Economics* 9: 3–18.

Barabási, A-L. 2002. *Linked: The New Science of Networks*. Cambridge, MA: Perseus Publishing.

Barkow, J. H., Cosmides, L., and Tooby, J. 1992. *The Adapted Mind*. New York: Oxford University Press.

Barnett, W. P., and Burgelman, R. A., eds. 1996. Evolutionary Perspectives on Strategy. Special issue, *Strategic Management Journal*. 17 (Summer).

Barney, J. 1991. Firm Resources and Sustained Competitive Advantage. *Journal of Management* 17: 99–120.

Barro, R. J., and Sala-i-Martin, X. 1995. *Economic Growth*. 1999 edition. Cambridge, MA: MIT Press.

Bar-Yam, Y. 1997. *Dynamics of Complex Systems*. Reading, MA: Addison-Wesley.

Bass, T. A. 1999. *The Predictors*. New York: Henry Holt.

Basu, S. 1977. The Investment Performance of Common Stocks in Relation to Their Price Earnings Ratios: A Test of the Efficient Market Hypothesis. *Journal of Finance* 32: 663–682.

Baum, J. A. C., and Singh, J. V. 1994. *Evolutionary Dynamics of Organizations*. New York: Oxford University Press.

Baumol, W. J. 2000. What Marshall Didn't Know: On the Twentieth Century's Contributions to Economics. *The Quarterly Journal of Economics* CXV, no. 1 (February): 1–44.

———. 2002. *The Free-Market Innovation Machine: Analyzing the Growth Miracle of Capitalism*. Princeton, NJ: Princeton University Press.

Bazerman, M. 1998. *Judgment in Managerial Decision Making*. New York: John Wiley & Sons.

Bednar, J., and Page, S. 2003. Can Game(s) Theory Explain Culture? University of Michigan working paper, October 9.

Beinhocker, E. D. 1997. Strategy at the Edge of Chaos. *McKinsey Quarterly*, no. 1: 24–39.

———. 1999. Robust Adaptive Strategy. *Sloan Management Review* 40, no. 3 (Spring): 95–106.

Beinhocker, E. D., and Kaplan, S. 2002. Tired of Strategic Planning? In Risk and Resilience. Special edition, *McKinsey Quarterly*: 48–57.

Bernstein, P. L. 1992. *Capital Ideas*. New York: Free Press.

Bernstein, W. J. 2004. *The Birth of Plenty: How the Prosperity of the Modern World Was Created*. New York: McGraw-Hill.

Berzins, A., Podolny, J., and Roberts, J. 1998. British Petroleum (A): Growth and Performance. Graduate School of Business, Stanford University, Case 8–IB-16A, May 18.

Bevir, M., and Trentmann, F., eds. 2004. *Markets in Historical Context*. Cambridge, UK: Cambridge University Press.

Blackmore, S. 1999. *The Meme Machine*. New York: Oxford University Press.

Blanchard, O. J. 2000. What Do We Know About Macroeconomics That Fisher and Wicksell Did Not? *Quarterly Journal of Economics* CXV, no. 4 (November): 1375–1409.

Blanchard, O. J., and Fischer, S. 1989. *Lectures on Macroeconomics*. Cambridge, MA: MIT Press.

Bonabeau, E., Dorigo, M., and Theraulaz, G. 1999. *Swarm Intelligence, from Natural to Artificial Systems*. Oxford: Oxford University Press.

Bonabeau, E., and Meyer, C. 2001. Swarm Intelligence: A Whole New Way to Think About Business. *Harvard Business Review* (May–June): 106–114.

Bossidy, L., and Charan, R. 2002. *Execution: The Discipline of Getting Things Done*. New York: Crown Business Books.

Bouchaud, J. P., and Potters, M. 2000. *Theory of Financial Risks: From Statistical Physics to Risk Management*. Cambridge, UK: Cambridge University Press.

Boulding, K. E. 1978. *Ecodynamics: A New Theory of Societal Evolution*. Beverly Hills, CA: Sage Publications.

Bower, M. 2003. Company Philosophy: "The Way We Do Things Around Here." *McKinsey Quarterly*, no. 2. Reprinted from chapter 2 of M. Bower. 1966, *The Will to Manage* (New York: McGraw-Hill).

Bowles, S. 2001a. Individual Interactions, Group Conflicts, and the Evolution of Preferences. Chapter 6 in Durlauf and Young, eds. *Social Dynamics*. Washington, DC: Brookings Institution.

———. 2001b. The Evolution of Inequality. Santa Fe Institute Working Paper for the Poverty Traps Workshop, July 20–22.

———. 2004. *Microeconomics: Behavior, Institutions and Evolution*. New York: Russell Sage Foundation and Princeton, NJ: Princeton University Press.

Bowles, S., and Gintis, H. 2002. The Origins of Human Cooperation. Santa Fe Institute working paper 02–08–035, July 24.

Bowles, S., Gintis, H., and Osborne, M. 2001. The Determinants of Earnings: A Behavioral Approach. *Journal of Economic Literature* 39 (December): 1137–1176.

Bowles, S., Choi, J-K., Hopfensitz, A. 2003. The Co-Evolution of Individual Behaviors and Social Institutions. *Journal of Theoretical Biology* 223: 135–147.

Bowles, S., Gintis, H., and Osborne Groves, M., eds. 2005. *Unequal Chances: Family Background and Economic Success*. Princeton, NJ: Princeton University Press.

Boyd, R., and Richerson, P. J. 1985. *Culture and the Evolutionary Process*. Chicago: University of Chicago Press.

Boyd, R., and Richerson, P. J. 2005. *The Origin and Evolution of Cultures*. Oxford: Oxford University Press.

Braha, D., and Maimon, O. 1998. *A Mathematical Theory of Design: Foundations, Algorithms and Applications*. London: Kluwer Academic Publishers.

Brandenburger, A. M., and Nalebuff, B. J. 1997. *Co-Operation*. New York: Doubleday.

Brealey, R. A., and Myers, S. C. 1988. *Principles of Corporate Finance*. Third edition. New York: McGraw-Hill Publishing.

Brock, W., Lakonishok, J., and LeBaron, B. 1992. Simple Technical Trading Rules and the Stochastic Properties of Stock Returns. *Journal of Finance* 47, no. 5: 1731–1764.

Brodie, R. 1996. *Virus of the Mind*. Washington, DC: Integral Press.

Brown, A. 1999. *The Darwin Wars*. London: Simon & Schuster.

Brown, S. L., and Eisenhardt, K. M. 1998. *Competing on the Edge: Strategy as Structured Chaos*. Boston: Harvard Business School Press.

Browne, J. 1995. *Charles Darwin: Voyaging*. London: Pimlico.

———. 2002. *Charles Darwin: The Power of Place*. London: Pimlico.

Bryan, L. L. 2002. Just-in-Time Strategy for a Turbulent World. In Risk and Resilience. Special edition, *McKinsey Quarterly*: 17–27.

Bryan, L., Fraiser, J., Oppenheim, J., and Rall, W. 1999. *Race for the World: Strategies to Build a Great Global Firm*. Boston: Harvard Business School Press.

Buchanan, M. 2000. *Ubiquity: The Science of History . . . Or Why the World Is Simpler Than We Think*. London: Weidenfeld & Nicolson.

———. 2002. The Physics of the Trading Floor. *Nature* 415: 10–12.

Burgelman, R. A. 1983. A Model of the Interaction of Strategic Behavior, Corporate Context and the Concept of Strategy. *Academy of Management Review* 8: 61–70.

———. 2002. *Strategy Is Destiny: How Strategy-Making Shapes a Company's Future*. New York: Free Press.

Buss, D. M. 1999. *Evolutionary Psychology: The New Science of the Mind*. Boston: Allyn & Bacon.

Butler, P., Hall, T.W., Hanna, A.M., Mendonca, L., Auguste, B., Manyika, J., and Sahay, A. 1997. A Revolution in Interaction. *McKinsey Quarterly*, no. 1: 4–23.

Caldwell, B. 2004. *Hayek's Challenge: An Intellectual Biography of F. A. Hayek*. Chicago: University of Chicago Press.

Camazine, S., Deneubourg, J-L., Franks, N. R., Sneyd, J., Theraulaz, G., and Bonabeau, E., eds. 2001. *Self-Organization in Biological Systems*. Princeton, NJ: Princeton University Press.

Camerer, C. F. 2003. *Behavioral Game Theory: Experiments in Strategic Interaction*. Princeton, NJ: Princeton University Press.

Camerer, C. F., Lowenstein, G., and Rabin, M., eds. 2004. *Advances in Behavioral Economics*. Princeton, NJ: Princeton University Press.

Cameron, R., and Neal, L. 2003. *A Concise Economic History of the World: From Palaeolithic Times to the Present*. Fourth edition. Oxford: Oxford University Press.

Campbell, A., Birkinshaw, J., Morrison, A., and van Basten Batenburg, R. 2003. The Future of Corporate Venturing. *Sloan Management Review* 45, no. 1: 30–37.

Campbell, D. T. 1960. Blind Variation and Selective Retention in Creative Thought as in Other Knowledge Processes. *Psychological Review* 67: 380–400.

Campbell, J. W. P., and Pryce, W. 2003. *Brick: A World History*. London: Thames and Hudson.

Campbell, J. Y., Lo, A. W., and MacKinlay, A. C. 1997. *The Econometrics of Financial Markets*. Princeton, NJ: Princeton University Press.

Carruthers, P., and Chamberlain, A. 2000. *Evolution and the Human Mind: Modularity, Language, and Meta-Cognition*. Cambridge, UK: Cambridge University Press.

Cartwright, N. 1999. *The Dappled World: A Study of the Boundaries of Science*. Cambridge, UK: Cambridge University Press.

Cassidy, J. 1996. The Decline of Economics. *The New Yorker*, December 2: 50–60.

Casti, J. L. 1994. *Complexification*. New York: HarperCollins.

———. 1997. *Would-be Worlds*. New York: John Wiley & Sons.

Casti, J. L., and Karlqvist, A. 1991. *Beyond Belief*. Boca Raton, FL: CRC Press.

Cavalli-Sforza, L. L. 2001. *Genes, Peoples and Languages*. London: Penguin Books.

Cave, F. T. 2004. Economists and Politicians at a Loss as Eurozone's Price Disparities Increase. *Financial Times*, March 3.

Caves, R. 1982. *American Industry: Structure, Conduct, Performance*. Fifth edition. Englewood Cliffs, NJ: Prentice Hall.

Chagnon, N. A. 1992. *Yanomamo: The Last Days of Eden*. San Diego: Harcourt Brace & Company.

Challet, D., and Zhang, Y-C. 1997. Emergence of Cooperation and Organization in an Evolutionary Game. *Physica A* 246: 407–418.

Chandler, A. D. Jr. 1962. *Strategy and Structure: Chapters in the History of the American Industrial Enterprise*. 1990 edition. Cambridge, MA: MIT Press.

———. 1977. *The Visible Hand: The Managerial Revolution in American Business*. Cambridge, MA: Belknap Press of Harvard University Press.

———. 1990. *Scale and Scope: The Dynamics of Industrial Capitalism*. Cambridge, MA: Belknap Press of Harvard University Press.

Chorafas, D. N. 1994. *Chaos Theory in the Financial Markets*. Chicago: Probus Publishing Co.

Christensen, C. M. 1997. *The Innovator's Dilemma: When New Technologies Cause Great Firms to Fail*. Boston: Harvard Business School Press.

Churchill, G. A. 1991. *Marketing Research Methodological Foundations*. Fifth edition. Chicago: Dryden Press.

Clark, A. 1999. *Being There: Putting Brain, Body, and World Together Again*. Cambridge, MA: A Bradford Book, MIT Press.

———. 2001. *Mindware: An Introduction to the Philosophy of Cognitive Science*. New York: Oxford University Press.

Clippinger, J. H. III. 1999. *The Biology of Business: Decoding the Natural Laws of Enterprise*. San Francisco: Jossey-Bass.

Cochrane, J. H. 2005. *Asset Pricing*. Revised edition. Princeton, NJ: Princeton University Press.

Cohen, D., and Prusak, L. 2001. *In Good Company: How Social Capital Makes Organizations Work*. Boston: Harvard Business School Press.

Cohen, M. D., and Sproull, L. S., eds. 1996. *Organizational Learning*. Thousand Oaks, CA: Sage Publications.

Colander, D., ed. 1996. *Beyond Microfoundations: Post Walrasian Macroeconomics*, Cambridge: Cambridge University Press.

———. 1999. New Millenium Economics: How Did It Get This Way, and What Way is It? *Journal of Economic Perspectives* 14, no. 1 (Winter): 121–132.

————. 2000. *Complexity and the History of Economic Thought*. London: Routledge.

Colander, D., Holt, R. P. F., and Rosser, J. B. Jr. 2004. *The Changing Face of Economics: Conversations with Cutting Edge Economists*. Ann Arbor, MI: University of Michigan Press.

Collins, J. C. 2001. *Good to Great*. New York: HarperCollins.

Collins, J. C., and Porras, J. I. 1994. *Built to Last: Successful Habits of Visionary Companies*. New York: Harper-Business.

Cont, R., and Bouchaud, J. P. 2000. Herd Behavior and Aggregate Fluctuations in Financial Markets. *Macroeconomic Dynamics* 4: 1–27.

Cookson, C., and Griffith, V. 2001. UK: Inside Track—An Argument about Human Complexity. *Financial Times*, June 12.

Copeland, T. E., and Keenan, P. E. 1998. Making Real Options Real. *McKinsey Quarterly*, no. 3: 128–141.

Copeland, T., Koller, T., and Murrin, J. 2000. *Valuation: Measuring and Managing the Value of Companies*. Third edition. New York: John Wiley & Sons.

Courtney, H. 2001. *20/20 Foresight: Crafting Strategy in an Uncertain World*. Boston: Harvard Business School Press.

Cowan, G. A., Pines, D., and Meltzer, D. 1994. *Complexity. Metaphors, Models and Reality*. Cambridge, MA: Perseus Books.

Crutchfield, J. P., and Schuster, P. 2003. *Evolutionary Dynamics: Exploring the Interplay of Selection, Accident, Neutrality, and Function*. New York: Oxford University Press.

Cutler, D. M., Poterba, J. M., and Summers, L. H. 1989. What Moves Stock Prices? *Journal of Portfolio Management* (Spring): 4–12.

Cyert, R. M., and March, J. G. 1992. *A Behavioral Theory of the Firm*. Second edition. Oxford: Blackwell Publishers.

Daly, H. E. 1999. *Ecological Economics and the Ecology of Economics*. Northampton, MA: Edward Elgar.

Darmasio, A. 2005. Human Behavior: Brain Trust. *Nature* 435 (June): 571–572.

D'Aveni, R. A., and Gunther, R. 1994. *Hyper-Competition: Managing the Dynamics of Strategic Manoeuvring*. New York: Free Press.

Davis, I. 2005a. How to Escape the Short-term Trap. *Financial Times*, April 11.

————. 2005b. The Biggest Contract. *The Economist*, May 26.

Dawkins, R. 1976. *The Selfish Gene*. Oxford: Oxford University Press.

————. 1982. *The Extended Phenotype*. 1999 edition. Oxford: Oxford University Press.

————. 1986. *The Blind Watchmaker*. London: Longmans.

————. 1996. *Climbing Mount Improbable*. London: Penguin Books.

————. 1998. *Unweaving the Rainbow: Science, Delusions and the Appetite for Wonder*. Boston: Houghton Mifflin.

Day, R. H. 1994. *Complex Economic Dynamics*. Cambridge, MA: MIT Press.

————. 1999. *Complex Economic Dynamics (Volume II): An Introduction to Macroeconomic Dynamics*. Cambridge, MA: MIT Press.

Deal, T. E., and Kennedy, A. A. 1982. *Corporate Culture: The Rites and Rituals of Corporate Life*. 2000 edition. New York: Perseus Publishing.

Dear, P. 2001. *Revolutionizing the Sciences: European Knowledge and its Ambitions, 1500–1700*. Hampshire, UK: Palgrave.

De Geus, A. 1997. *The Living Company: Habits for Survival in a Turbulent Business Environment*. Boston: Harvard Business School Press.

Dembski, W., and Ruse, M. 2004. *Debating Design: From Darwin to DNA*. Cambridge, UK: Cambridge University Press.

Dennett, D. C. 1991. *Consciousness Explained*. Boston: Little, Brown.

————. 1995. *Darwin's Dangerous Idea*. New York: Touchstone.

De Soto, H. 2000. *The Mystery of Capital: Why Capitalism Triumphs in the West and Fails Everywhere Else*. New York: Basic Books.

De Swaan, J. C., and Harper, N. W. C. 2003. Getting What You Pay For with Stock Options. *McKinsey Quarterly*, no. 1: 152–155.

Deutsch, D. 1997. *The Fabric of Reality*. New York: Penguin Books.

Devaney, R. L. 1992. *A First Course in Chaotic Dynamical Systems*. Reading, MA: Addison-Wesley.

Devlin, K. 2000. *The Language of Mathematics: Making the Invisible Visible*. New York: W. H. Freeman.

Diamond, J. 1991. *The Rise and Fall of the Third Chimpanzee: How Our Animal Heritage Affects the Way We Live*. London: Vintage.

————. 1997. *Guns, Germs and Steel*. New York: W.W. Norton & Company.

————. 2005. *Collapse: How Societies Choose to Fail or Succeed*. New York: Viking Penguin.

Dixit, A. K., and Pindyck, R. S. 1994. *Investment Under Uncertainty.* Princeton, NJ: Princeton University Press.

Dobbs, R., and Koller, T. 2005. Measuring Long-Term Performance. In Value and Performance. Special edition, *McKinsey Quarterly*: 16–27.

Dorgan, S. J., and Dowdy, J. 2002. How Good Management Raises Productivity. *McKinsey Quarterly*, no. 4: 14–16.

Dornbusch, R., and Fischer, S. 1990. *Macroeconomics.* Fifth edition. New York: McGraw-Hill.

Dorner, D. 1996. *The Logic of Failure; Recognising and Avoiding Error in Complex Situations.* London: Merloyd Lawrence.

Dosi, G., Nelson, R. R., and Winter, S. G., eds. 2000. *The Nature and Dynamics of Organizational Capabilitites.* Oxford: Oxford University Press.

Dosi, G., Teece, D. J., and Chytry, J., eds. 1998. *Technology, Organization, and Competitiveness.* Oxford: Oxford University Press.

Dunbar, R., Knight, C., and Power, C., eds. 1999. *The Evolution of Culture.* Edinburgh: Edinburgh University Press.

Durlauf, S. N. 2001. The Membership Theory of Poverty: The Role of Group Affiliations in Determining Socioeconomic Outcomes. Working paper for the Santa Fe Institute workshop on "Poverty Traps," July 20–22.

Durlauf, S. N., and Young, H. P., eds. 2001. *Social Dynamics.* Washington, DC: Brookings Institution Press.

Easterly, W. 2002. *The Elusive Quest for Growth: Economists' Adventures and Misadventures in the Topics.* Cambridge, MA: MIT Press.

Easterly, W., and Levine, R. 2002. Tropics, Germs and Crops: How Endowments Influence Economic Development, NBER working paper 9106.

Edersheim, E. H. 2004. *McKinsey's Marvin Bower.* New York: John Wiley & Sons.

Eicher, T. S., and Turnovsky, S. J. 2003. *Inequality and Growth: Theory and Policy Implications.* Cambridge, MA: MIT Press.

Eisenhardt, K. M., and Brown, S. L. 1999. Patching: Re-stitching Business Portfolios in Dynamic Markets. *Harvard Business Review* (May–June): 72–80.

Elkington, J. 1999. *Cannibals with Forks: The Triple Bottom Line of 21st Century Business.* Oxford: Capstone.

Engle, R. 1982. Autoregressive Conditional Heteroscedasticity with Estimates of the Variance of United Kingdom Inflation. *Econometrica* 50: 987–1007.

Epstein, J. M. 1997. *Nonlinear Dynamics, Mathematical Biology and Social Science.* Reading, MA: Addison-Wesley.

Epstein, J. M., and Axtell, R. 1996. *Growing Artificial Societies.* Washington,DC: Brookings Institution Press. Cambridge, MA: MIT Press.

Ethiraj, S. K., and Levinthal, D. 2002. *Search for Architecture in Complex Worlds: An Evolutionary Perspective on Modularity and the Emergence of Dominant Design.* University of Michigan and University of Pennsylvania, Wharton School working paper (November).

Fama, E. 1970. Efficient Capital Markets: A Review of Theory and Empirical Work. *Journal of Finance* 25: 383–417.

Farmer, J. D. 1998. Market Force, Ecology, and Evolution. Santa Fe Institute working paper 98–12-117.

———. 2001. Toward Agent-Based Models for Investment. *Benchmarks and Attribution Analysis.* The Association for Investment Management and Research: 61–70.

———. 2002. Market Force, Ecology, and Evolution. *Industrial and Corporate Change* 11, no. 5: 895–953.

Farmer, J. D., Gillemot, L., Lillo, F., Szabolcs, M., and Sen, A. 2004. What Really Causes Large Price Changes? *Quantitative Finance* 4 (August): 383–397.

Farmer, J. D., and Lo, A. W. 1999. Frontiers of Finance: Evolution and Efficient Markets. *Proceedings of the National Academy of Science* 96: 9991–9992.

Farmer, J. D., Patelli, P., and Zovko, I. I. 2005. The Predictive Power of Zero Intelligence in Financial Markets. *Proceedings of the National Academy of Sciences* 102, no. 6: 2254–2259.

Farmer, J. D., Shubik, M., and Smith, E. 2005. Is Economics the Next Physical Science? *Physics Today* (September): 37–42.

Farrell, W. 1998. *How Hits Happen: Forecasting Predictability in a Chaotic Marketplace.* New York: Harper-Business.

Fehr, E., and Gächter, S. 2000. Cooperation and Punishment in Public Goods Experiments. *American Economic Review* 90, no. 4 (September): 980–994.

Feyerabend, P. 1975. *Against Method: Outline of an Anarchistic Theory of Knowledge.* London: New Left Books.

Fischer, D. H. 1996. *The Great Wave: Price Revolutions and the Rhythm of History.* New York: Oxford University Press.

Flake, G. W. 1998. *The Computational Beauty of Nature: Computer Explorations of Fractals, Chaos, Complex Systems and Adaption.* Cambridge, MA: MIT Press.

Fligstein, N. 2001. *The Architecture of Markets: An Economic Sociology of Twenty-First-Century Capitalist Societies.* Princeton, NJ: Princeton University Press.

Fogel, R. W. 2004. *The Escape From Hunger and Premature Death 1700–2100.* Cambridge, UK: Cambridge University Press.

Forrester, J. W. 1961. *Industrial Dynamics.* Cambridge, MA: MIT Press.

Forty, R. 1997. *Life: A Natural History of the First Four Billion Years of Life on Earth.* New York: Alfred A. Knopf.

Foster, D. P., and Young, H. P. 2001. On the Impossibility of Predicting the Behavior of Rational Agents. *The Proceedings of the National Academy of Sciences* 98, no. 22: 12848–12853.

Foster, R. 1986. *Innovation: The Attacker's Advantage.* New York: Summit Books.

Foster, R., and Kaplan, S. 2001. *Creative Destruction.* New York: Doubleday.

Fox, K. 2002. Evolution, Alienation and Gossip: The Role of Mobile Telecommunications in the 21st Century. Working paper of the Social Issues Research Centre, Oxford University.

Fox, R. F. 1988. *Energy and the Evolution of Life.* New York: W. H. Freeman.

Frank, S. A. 1998. *Foundations of Social Evolution.* Princeton, NJ: Princeton University Press.

Freeman, C., and Soete, L. 1997. *The Economics of Industrial Innovation.* Third edition. Cambridge, MA: MIT Press.

Friedman, M. 1953. *Essays in Positive Economics.* Chicago: University of Chicago Press.

———. 1962. *Capitalism and Freedom.* Fortieth anniversary edition, 2002. Chicago: University of Chicago Press.

Fry, I. 1999. *The Emergence of Life on Earth: A Historical and Scientific Overview.* London: Free Association Books.

Fudenberg, D., and Tirole, J. 1991. *Game Theory.* Cambridge, MA: MIT Press.

Fukuyama, F. 1992. *The End of History and the Last Man.* New York: Free Press.

———. 1995. *Trust.* New York: Free Press.

———. 1999. *The Great Disruption: Human Nature and the Reconstitution of Social Order.* New York: Free Press.

Fullbrook, E., ed. 2004. *A Guide to What's Wrong with Economics.* London: Anthem Press.

Gardner, H. 2004. *Changing Minds: The Art and Science of Changing Our Own and Other People's Minds.* Boston: Harvard Business School Press.

Gell-Mann, M. 1994. *The Quark and the Jaguar.* New York: W. H. Freeman.

Georgescu-Roegen, N. 1971. *The Entropy Law and the Economic Process.* Cambridge, MA: Harvard University Press.

Ghemawat, P. 1991. *Commitment: The Dynamic of Strategy.* New York: Free Press.

Ghemawat, P., Collins, D. J., Pisano, G. P., and Rivkin, J. W. 1999. *Strategy and the Business Landscape.* Reading, MA: Addison-Wesley.

Gherity, J. A. 1965. *Economic Thought: A Historical Anthology.* New York: Random House.

Giddens, A. 1998. *The Third Way: The Renewal of Social Democracy.* Cambridge, UK: Polity.

———. 2000. *The Third Way and Its Critics.* Cambridge, UK: Polity.

———. 2001. *Sociology.* 4th Edition. Cambridge, UK: Polity.

Gilovich, T., Vallone, R., and Tversky, A. 1985. The Hot Hand in Basketball: On the Misperception of Random Sequences. *Cognitive Psychology* 17: 295–314.

Gintis, H. 2000. *Game Theory Evolving: A Problem-Centered Introduction to Modeling Strategic Interaction.* Princeton, NJ: Princeton University Press.

———. 2003. Agent-Based Simulation of a General Equilibrium Economy with Complete and Incomplete Contracting. Working paper available from the author.

Gintis, H., Bowles, S., Boyd, R., and Fehr, E. 2005. *Moral Sentiments and Material Interests.* Cambridge, MA: MIT Press.

Girvan, M., and Newman, M. E. J. December 2001. *Community Structure in Social and Biological Networks,* Santa Fe Institute working paper 01-12-077.

Gladwell, M. 2000. *The Tipping Point: How Little Things Can Make a Big Difference.* Boston: Little, Brown.

Gleick, J. 1987. *Chaos: Making a New Science.* New York: Viking Penguin.

Glimcher, P. W. 2002. Decisions, Decisions, Decisions: Choosing a Biological Science of Choice. *Neuron* 36, no. 2: 323–332.

———. 2003. *Decisions, Uncertainty, and the Brain: The Science of Neuroeconomics.* Cambridge, MA: MIT Press.

Gordon, R. 1986. *The American Business Cycle: Continuity and Challenge.* National Bureau of Economic Research Studies in Business Cycles Series, vol 25. Chicago: University of Chicago Press.

Gould, S. J. 1989. *Wonderful Life: The Burgess Shale and the Nature of History.* New York: W.W. Norton.

———. 2002. *The Structure of Evolutionary Theory.* Cambridge, MA: Belknap Press of Harvard University Press.

Gould, S. J., and Eldridge, N. 1993. Punctuated Equilibrium Comes of Age. *Nature* 366: 223–227.

Gould, S. J., and Lewontin, R. 1979. The Spandrels of San Marco and the Panglossian Paradigm: A Critique of the Adaptionist Programme. *Proceedings of the Royal Society* B205: 581–598.

Graham, J. R., Harvey, C. R., and Rajgopal, S. 2005. The Economic Implications of Corporate Financial Reporting. NBER working paper no. 10550, January 11.

Grant, P. R., and Grant, B. R. 2002. Unpredictable Evolution in a 30-Year Study of Darwin's Finches. *Science* 296, 26 April: 707–711.

Greene, B. 1999. *The Elegant Universe: Superstrings, Hidden Dimensions, and the Quest for the Ultimate Theory.* London: Random House Publishing.

Greene, W. H. 2000. *Econometric Analysis.* Fourth edition. Englewood Cliffs, NJ: Prentice Hall.

Gribbin, J. 2002. *Science: A History 1543–2001.* London: Allen Lane / Penguin.

Haken, H. 2000. *Information and Self-Organization: A Macroscopic Approach to Complex Systems.* Second edition. Berlin: Springer-Verlag.

Hamel, G. 2000. *Leading the Revolution.* Boston: Harvard Business School Press.

Hamel, G., and Prahalad, C. K. 1994. *Competing for the Future.* Boston: Harvard Business School Press.

Hammond, R. 2000. Endogenous Transition Dynamics in Corruption: An Agent-Based Computer Model. The Brookings Institution, Center on Social and Economic Dynamics, working paper no. 19.

Hands, D. W. 2001. *Reflection Without Rules: Economic Methodology and Contemporary Science Theory.* New York: Cambridge University Press.

Handy, C. 2002. What's a Business For? *Harvard Business Review* (December): 49–55.

Hannan, M. T., and Carroll, G. R. 1992. *Dynamics of Organizational Populations: Density, Legitimation, and Competition.* New York: Oxford University Press.

Hannan, M. T., and Freeman, J. H. 1977. The Population Ecology of Organizations. *American Journal of Sociology* 1, no. 83: 929–964.

———. 1984. Structural Inertia and Organizational Change. *American Sociological Review* 49, no. 2 (April): 149–164.

———. 1989. *Organizational Ecology.* Cambridge, MA: Harvard University Press.

Harrington, J. E. Jr. 1998. The Social Selection of Flexible and Rigid Agents. *American Economic Review* 88, no. 1 (March): 63–82.

Harrison, L. E. 2001. To Modernize, Some Have to Change Their Culture. *International Herald Tribune,* Editorials / Opinion, March 1.

Harrison, L. E., and Huntington, S. P. 2000. *Culture Matters: How Values Shape Human Progress.* New York: Basic Books.

Hartley, J. E., Salyer, K. D., and Hoover, K. D., eds. 1998. *Real Business Cycles: A Reader.* London: Routledge.

Hatch, M. J. 1997. *Organization Theory: Modern Symbolic and Postmodern Perspectives.* Oxford: Oxford University Press.

Hausman, D. M. 1994. *The Philosophy of Economics.* Second edition. Cambridge: Cambridge University Press.

Hayek, F. A. 1944. *The Road to Serfdom.* 2001 edition. London: Routledge Classics.

———. 1948. *Individualism and Economic Order.* 1980 edition. Chicago: University of Chicago Press.

———. 1960. *The Constitution of Liberty.* 1976 edition. London: Routledge Classics.

———. 1988. *The Fatal Conceit: The Errors of Socialism.* 1991 edition. Chicago: University of Chicago Press.

Haynie, D. T. 2001. *Biological Thermodynamics.* Cambridge: Cambridge University Press.

Heijdra, B. J., and van der Ploeg, F. 2002. *Foundations of Modern Macroeconomics.* Oxford: Oxford University Press.

Heilbroner, R. L. 1953. *The Worldly Philosophers: The Lives, Times and Ideas of the Great Economic Thinkers.* 1972 edition. New York: Touchstone Books.

Helpman, E. 2004. *The Mystery of Economic Growth.* Cambridge, MA: Belknap Press of Harvard University Press.

Hempel, C. 1965. *Aspects of Scientific Explanation and Other Essays in the Philosophy of Science.* New York: Free Press.

Henderson, R., and Mitchell, W., eds. 1997. Organizational and Competitive Interactions. Special Issue. *Strategic Management Journal* 18 (July).

Henderson, R. M., and Clark, K. B. 1990. Architectural Innovation: The Reconfiguration of Existing Product Technologies and the Failure of Established Firms. *Administrative Science Quarterly*, no. 35: 9–30.

Henrich, J., Boyd, R., Bowles, S., Camerer, C., Fehr, E., and Gintis, H. 2004. *Foundations of Human Sociality: Economic Experiments and Ethnographic Evidence from Fifteen Small-Scale Societies*. Oxford: Oxford University Press.

Heymannn, D., and Leijonhufvud, A. 1995. *High Inflation*. Oxford: Oxford University Press.

Hicks, J. 1939. *Value and Capital*. Second edition. Oxford: Clarendon Press.

Hodgson, G. M. 1993. *Economics and Evolution*. Ann Arbor, MI: University of Michigan Press.

———. 2002. Darwinism in Economics: From Analogy to Ontology. *Journal of Evolutionary Economics* 12: 259–281.

Hodgson, G. M., ed. 2002. *A Modern Reader in Institutional and Evolutionary Economics*. Northampton, MA: Edward Elgar.

Hoff, K., and Sen, A. 2001. A Simple Theory of the Extended Family System and Market Barriers to the Poor. Santa Fe Institute Conference on Poverty Traps, working paper, July 20–22, 2001.

Hogarth, R. M. 1990. *Insights in Decision Making*. Chicago: University of Chicago Press.

Holland, J. H. 1975. *Adaption in Natural and Artificial Systems*. 1992 edition. Cambridge, MA: MIT Press.

———. 1995. *Hidden Order*. Reading, MA: Addison-Wesley.

———. 1998. *Emergence. From Chaos to Order*. Reading, MA: Addison-Wesley.

Holland, J. H., Holyoak, K. J., Nisbett, R. E., and Thagard, P. R. 1986. *Induction: Processes of Inference, Learning, and Discovery*. Cambridge, MA: MIT Press.

Holmstrom, B., and Roberts, J. 1998. The Boundaries of the Firm Revisited. *Journal of Economic Perspectives* 12: 73–94.

Hoopes, D. G., Madsen, T. L., and Walker, G., eds. 2003. Why Is There a Resource-Based View? Toward a Theory of Competitive Heterogeneity. *Strategic Management Journal*, Special issue 24 (October).

Horan, R. D., Bulte, E., and Shogren, J. 2005. How Trade Saved Humanity from Biological Exclusion: An Economic Theory of Neanderthal Extinction. *Journal of Economic Behavior and Organization*.

Howard, R., and Haas, R. D., eds. 1993. *The Learning Imperative: Managing People for Continuous Innovation*. Boston: Harvard Business School Press.

Huntington, S. P. 1996. *The Clash of Civilizations and the Remaking of the World Order*. New York: Simon & Schuster.

Hutchins, E. 1996. *Cognition in the Wild*. Cambridge, MA: MIT Press.

Hull, D. L. 1988. *Science as a Process: An Evolutionary Account of the Social and Conceptual Development of Science*. Chicago: University of Chicago Press.

Ijiri, Y., and Simon, H. A., eds. 1977. *Skew Distributions and the Sizes of Business Firms*. Amsterdam: North-Holland.

Ingrao, B., and Israel, G. 1990. *The Invisible Hand*. Cambridge, MA: MIT Press.

Jain, S., and Krishna, S. 2002a. Large Extinctions in an Evolutionary Model: The Role of Innovation and Keystone Species. *Proceedings of the National Academy of Science* 99, no. 4 (February 19): 2055–2060.

———. 2002b. Crashes, Recoveries, and Core Shifts in a Model of Evolving Networks. *Physical Review* E 65: 026103.

Jardine, L. 1999. *Ingenious Pursuits: Building the Scientific Revolution*. London: Abacus.

Jay, P. 2000. *Road to Riches or The Wealth of Man*. London: Weidenfeld & Nicolson.

Jensen, M. C. 1998. *Foundations of Organizational Strategy*. Cambridge, MA: Harvard University Press.

———. 2001. *A Theory of the Firm*. Cambridge, MA: Harvard University Press.

Johnson, B. C. 2002. Retail: The Wal-Mart Effect. *McKinsey Quarterly*, no 1: 40–43.

Johnson, B. C., Manyika, J. M., and Yee, L. A. 2005. The Next Revolution in Interactions. *McKinsey Quarterly*, no. 4: 20–33.

Johnson, G. 2001. All Science Is Computer Science. *New York Times*, March 25.

———. 2003. *A Shortcut Through Time: The Path to the Quantum Computer*. New York: Alfred Knopf.

Johnson, N. F., Jefferies, P., and Hui, P. M. 2003. *Financial Market Complexity: What Physics Can Tell Us About Market Behavior*. Oxford: Oxford University Press.

Johnson, P. 1988. *Intellectuals*. New York: Harper & Row.

———. 1997. *A History of the American People*. New York: HarperCollins.

Johnson, S. 2001. *Emergence: The Connected Lives of Ants, Brains, Cities, and Software*. London: Allen Lane.

Jones, S., Martin R., Pilbeam, D., and Bunney, S. 1992. *The Cambridge Encyclopedia of Human Evolution*. Cambridge: Cambridge University Press.

Kagel, J. H., and Roth, A. E. 1995. *The Handbook of Experimental Economics*. Princeton, NJ: Princeton University Press.

Kahneman, D., Slovic, P., and Tversky, A. 1982. *Judgement Under Uncertainty: Heuristics and Biases.* Cambridge: Cambridge University Press.

Kahneman, D., Diener, E., and Schwarz, N. eds. 1999. *Well-Being: The Foundations of Hedonic Psychology.* New York: Russell Sage Foundation.

Kaplan, D., and Glass, L. 1995. *Understanding Nonlinear Dynamics.* New York: Springer-Verlag.

Kaplan, R. S., Lowes, A., and Norton, D. P. 1996. *The Balanced Scorecard: Translating Strategy Into Action.* Cambridge, MA: Harvard Business School Press.

Kaplan, R. S., and Norton, D. P. 2000. *The Strategy-Focused Organization: How Balanced Scorecard Companies Thrive in the New Business Environment.* Boston: Harvard Business School Press.

Karceski, J. 2002. Returns-Chasing Behavior, Mutual Funds, and Beta's Death. *Journal of Financial and Quantitative Analysis* 37, no. 4 (December): 559–594.

Katz, L. D., ed. 2000. *Evolutionary Origins of Morality: Cross-Disciplinary Perspectives.* Bowling Green, OH: Imprint Academic.

Katzenbach, J. R., and Smith, D. K. 1993. *The Wisdom of Teams: Creating the High-Performance Organization.* Boston: Harvard Business School Press.

Kauffman, S. 1993. *The Origins of Order.* New York: Oxford University Press.

———. 1995a. *At Home in the Universe.* New York: Oxford University Press.

———. 1995b. Technology and Evolution: Escaping the Red Queen Effect. *McKinsey Quarterly*, no. 1: 119–129.

———. 2000. *Investigations.* New York: Oxford University Press.

Kay, J. 2003. *The Truth About Markets: Their Genuis, Their Limits, Their Follies.* London: Allen Lane.

Keen, S. 2001. *Debunking Economics: The Naked Emperor of the Social Sciences.* London: Zed Books.

Keizer, J. 1987. *Statistical Thermodynamics of Nonequilibrium Processes.* New York: Springer-Verlag.

Kelly, K. 1994. *Out of Control.* Reading, MA: Addison-Wesley.

Kelly, M. 2003. *The Divine Right of Capital: Dethroning the Corporate Aristocracy.* San Francisco: Berrett-Koehler.

Kelly, S., and Allison, M. A. 1999. *The Complexity Advantage.* New York: BusinessWeek Books/McGraw-Hill.

Kennedy, J., and Eberhart, R. C. 2001. *Swarm Intelligence.* San Francisco: Morgan Kauffmann.

Kennedy, P. 1987. *The Rise and Fall of the Great Powers: Economic Change and Military Conflict from 1500 to 2000.* New York: Random House.

Keynes, J. M. 1923. A Tract on Monetary Reform. *The Collected Writings of John Maynard Keynes*, vol. 4, 1977 edition. London: Palgrave MacMillan.

Kirman, A., and Gérard-Varet, L-A., eds. 1999. *Economics Beyond the Millennium.* New York: Oxford University Press.

Kirman, A., and Salmon, M. 1995. *Learning and Rationality in Economics.* Oxford: Blackwell.

Klein, B. H. 1977. *Dynamic Economics.* Cambridge, MA: Harvard University Press.

Klein, R. G., and Edgar, B. 2002. *The Dawn of Human Culture.* New York: John Wiley.

Klemke, E. D., Hollinger, R., and Kline, A. D. 1980. *Introductory Readings in the Philosophy of Science.* New York: Prometheus Books.

Knudsen, T. 2002. Economic Selection Theory. *Journal of Evolutionary Economics* 12: 443–470.

Koch, R. 2000. *The Natural Laws of Business.* New York: Doubleday.

Kohler, T. A., and Gumerman, G. J. 2000. *Dynamics in Human and Primate Societies.* New York: Oxford University Press.

Kollman, K., Miller, J. H., and Page, S. E. 2003. *Computational Models in Political Economy.* Cambridge, MA: MIT Press.

Kondepudi, D., and Prigogine, I. 1998. *Modern Thermodynamics: From Heat Engines to Dissipative Structures.* New York: John Wiley & Sons.

Kotter, J. P., and Heskett, J. L. 1992. *Corporate Culture and Performance.* New York: Free Press.

Koza, J. R. 1992. *Genetic Programming.* Cambridge, MA: MIT Press.

Koza, M. P., and Thoenig, J. C. 1995. Organizational Theory at the Crossroads: Some Reflections on European and United States Approaches to Organizational Research. *Organization Studies*, vol. 6: 1–8.

Krames, J. A. 2002. *The Jack Welch Lexicon of Leadership.* New York: McGraw-Hill.

Kremer, M. Population Growth and Technological Change: One Million B.C. to 1990. *Quarterly Journal of Economics* 108 (August): 681–716.

Krugman, P. 1992. *The Age of Diminished Expectations: U.S. Economics Policy in the 1990s.* Cambridge, MA: MIT Press.

———, 1994. *Peddling Prosperity: Economic Sense and Nonsense in the Age of Diminished Expectations.* New York: Norton.

———. 1996. *The Self-Organizing Economy.* Cambridge, MA: Blackwell Publishing.

———. 1997. The Power of Biobabble. *Slate,* October 23. http://www.slate.com/id/1925/.

———. 1998. Two Cheers for Formalism. *Economic Journal* 108: 1829–1836.

Krugman, P., and Obstfeld, M. 1991. *International Economics: Theory and Policy.* Second edition. New York: HarperCollins.

Kuhn, T. S. 1962. *The Structure of Scientific Revolutions.* Chicago: University of Chicago Press.

Kurz, M. 1997. *Endogenous Economic Fluctuations.* Berlin: Springer-Verlag.

Kurzweil, R. 1999. *The Age of Spiritual Machines: When Computers Exceed Human Intelligence.* New York: Viking Press.

Lakatos, I., and Musgrave, A. 1970. *Criticism and the Growth of Knowledge.* Cambridge, UK: Cambridge University Press.

Lakoff, G., and Núñez, R. E. 2000. *Where Mathematics Comes From: How the Embodied Mind Brings Mathematics into Being.* New York: Basics Books.

Laland, K. N., Odling-Smee, J., and Feldman, M. W. 2000. Niche Construction, Biological Evolution and Cultural Change. *Behavioral and Brain Sciences,* 23, no. 1: 131–146.

Landes, D. S. 1969. *Prometheus Unbound: Technological Change and Industrial Development in Western Europe from 1750 to the Present.* Cambridge: Cambridge University Press.

———. 1998. *The Wealth and Poverty of Nations.* New York: W.W. Norton.

Landweber, L. F., and Winfree, E., eds. 2002. *Evolution as Computation.* Berlin: Springer-Verlag.

Lane, N. 2005. *Power, Sex, Suicide: Mitochondria and the Meaning of Life.* Oxford: Oxford University Press.

Layard, R. 2005. *Happiness: Lessons from a New Science.* London: Allen Lane.

Leavitt, H. J. 2003. Why Hierarchies Thrive. *Harvard Business Review* (March): 96–102.

LeBaron, B. 1994. Chaos and Nonlinear Forecastability in Economics and Finance. *Philosophical Transactions of the Royal Society of London (A),* 348: 397–404.

———. 1998. An Evolutionary Bootstrap Method for Selecting Dynamic Trading Strategies. University of Wisconsin working paper.

———. 2000. Agent Based Computational Finance: Suggested Readings and Early Research. *Journal of Economic Dynamics and Control* 24: 679–702.

———. 2001a. Empirical Regularities from Interacting Long and Short Memory Investors in an Agent-Based Financial Market. *IEEE Transactions on Evolutionary Computation* 5: 442–455.

———. 2001b. Evolution and Time Horizons in an Agent-Based Stock Market. *Macroeconomic Dynamics* 5: 225–254.

LeBaron, B., Arthur, W. B., and Palmer, R. 1999. Time Series Properties of an Artificial Stock Market. *Journal of Economic Dynamics and Control* 23: 1487–1516.

LeBaron, B., Brock, W. A., and Lakonishok, J. 1992. Simple Technical Trading Rules and the Stochastic Properties of Stock Returns. *Journal of Finance* 47: 1731–1764.

LeBaron, B., and Scheinkman, J. A. 1989. Nonlinear Dynamics and Stock Returns. *Journal of Business* 62: 311–337.

Lee, Y., Amaral, L. A., Canning, D., Meyer, M., and Stanley, H. E. 1998. Universal Features in the Growth of Complex Organizations. *Physical Review Letters* 81, no. 15: 3275–3278.

Lencioni, P. M. 2002. Make Your Values Mean Something. *Harvard Business Review* (July–August): 113–117.

Lengwiler, Y. 2004. *Microfoundations of Financial Economics: An Introduction to General Equilibrium Asset Pricing.* Princeton, NJ: Princeton University Press.

Leslie, K. J., and Michaels, M. P. 2000. The Real Power of Real Options. *McKinsey Quarterly Strategy Anthology:* 97–108.

Lesourne, J., and Orléan, A. 1998. *Advances in Self-Organization and Evolutionary Economics.* London: Economica.

Levy, D. M. 2003. *How the Dismal Science Got its Name: Classical Economics and the Ur Text of Racial Politics.* Ann Arbor, MI: University of Michigan Press.

Lewin, R., and Regine, B. 2000. *The Soul at Work.* New York: Simon & Schuster.

Lewis, A. A. 1985. On Effectively Computable Realizations of Choice Functions. *Mathematical Social Sciences* 10: 43–80.

Lewis, M. 1999. How the Eggheads Cracked. *New York Times Magazine,* January 24: 24–77.

Lewis, W., Palmade, V., Regout, B., and Webb, A. P. 2002. What's Right with the U.S. Economy. *McKinsey Quarterly,* no. 1, 2002: 31–40.

Lillo, F., and Farmer, J. D. 2004. The Long Memory of the Efficient Market. *Studies in Nonlinear Dynamics & Econometrics* 8, no. 3, article 1.

Lillo, F., Szabolcs, M., and Farmer, J. D. 2005. Theory for Long Memory in Supply and Demand. *Physical Review E* 71: 066122.

Lindgren, K., and Nordahl, M. G. 1994. Evolutionary Dynamics of Spatial Games. *Physica D*, 75: 292–309.

Lissack, M., and Roos, J. 1999. *The Next Common Sense*. London: Nicholas Brealey Publishing.

Ljungqvist, L., and Sargent, T. J. 2000. *Recursive Macroeconomic Theory*. Cambridge, MA: MIT Press.

Lo, A. W. 2004. The Adaptive Markets Hypothesis: Market Efficiency from an Evolutionary Perspective. *Journal of Portfolio Management* 30: 15–29.

Lo, A. W., and MacKinlay, A. C. 1999. *A Non-Random Walk Down Wall Street*. Princeton, NJ: Princeton University Press.

Loasby, B. 1999. *Graz Schumpeter Lectures: Knowledge, Institutions and Evolution in Economics*. London: Routledge.

Lotka, A. 1956. *Elements of Mathematical Biology*. New York: Dover Publications.

Lovallo, D., and Kahneman, D. 2003. Delusions of Success: How Optimism Undermines Executives' Decisions. *Harvard Business Review* (July): 56–63.

Lowenstein, R. 2000. *When Genius Failed: The Rise and Fall of Long-Term Capital Management*. London: Fourth Estate.

Lucas, R. E. Jr. 2002. *Lectures on Economic Growth*. Cambridge, MA: Harvard University Press.

Lynch, A. 1996. *Thought Contagion*. New York: Basic Books.

Malkiel, B. G. 1973. *A Random Walk Down Wall Street*. Seventh edition. 2000. New York: W.W. Norton & Company.

Mandelbrot, B. B. 1997. *Fractals and Scaling in Finance*. New York: Springer.

Mandelbrot, B. B., and Hudson, R. L. 2004. *The (Mis)Behaviour of Markets: A Fractal View of Risk, Ruin and Reward*. London: Profile Books.

Mankiw, N. G. 1994. *Macroeconomics*. Second edition. New York: Worth Publishers.

Mansfield, E. 1999. *Managerial Economics: Theory, Applications and Cases*. New York: W.W. Norton & Company.

Mantegna, R. N., and Stanley, H. E. 2000. *An Introduction to Econophysics: Correlations and Complexity in Finance*. Cambridge: Cambridge University Press.

———. 1996. Turbulence and Financial Markets. *Nature* 383 (October 17): 587–588.

March, J. G. 1991. Exploration and Exploitation in Organizational Learning. *Organization Science* 2, no. 1 (February): 71–87.

March, J. G., Schulz, M., and Zhou, X. 2000. *The Dynamics of Rules: Change in Written Organizational Codes*. Stanford, CA: Stanford University Press.

Mas-Colell, A., Whinston, M. D., and Green, J. R. 1995. *Microeconomic Theory*. New York: Oxford University Press.

Maynard Smith, J. 1958. *The Theory of Evolution*. Cambridge: Cambridge University Press.

———. 1982. *Evolution and the Theory of Games*. Cambridge: Cambridge University Press.

Maynard Smith, J., and Szathmáry, E. 1999. *The Origins of Life*. Oxford: Oxford University Press.

McCarthy, J., and Zakrajšek, E. 2002. Inventory Dynamics and the Business Cycle: What Has Changed? U.S. Federal Reserve Board working paper, December 18.

McKee, R. 2003. Storytelling That Moves People. *Harvard Business Review* (June): 51–55.

McMillan, J. 2002. *Reinventing the Bazaar: A Natural History of Markets*. New York: Norton.

McNulty, J. J., Yeh, T. D., Schulze, W. S., and Lubatkin, M. H. 2002. What's Your Real Cost of Capital? *Harvard Business Review* (October): 114–121.

Meadows, D. H., Randers, J., and Meadows, D. L. 2004. *The Limits to Growth: The 30-Year Update*. White River Junction, VT: Chelsea Green Publishing.

Micklethwait, J., and Wooldridge, A. 2003. *The Company: A Short History of a Revolutionary Idea*. New York: Modern Library.

Miller, M. 2003. *The Two Percent Solution: Fixing America's Problems in Ways Liberals and Conservatives Can Love*. New York: Public Affairs.

Minsky, M. 1985. *The Society of Mind*. New York: Simon & Schuster.

Mintzberg, H., Ahlstrand, B., and Lampel, J. 1998. *Strategy Safari: A Guided Tour Through the Wilds of Strategic Management*. New York: Free Press.

Mintzberg, H., Quinn, J. B., and Ghoshal, S. 1998. *The Strategy Process*. Englewood Cliffs, NJ: Prentice Hall.

Mirowski, P. 1988. *Against Mechanism*. Totowa, NJ: Rowman & Littlefield.

———. 1989. *More Heat than Light: Economics as Social Physics, Physics as Nature's Economics*. Cambridge: Cambridge University Press.

———. 1994. *Natural Images in Economic Thought*. Cambridge, U.K.: Cambridge University Press.

———. 2002. *Machine Dreams: Economics Becomes a Cyborg Science*. Cambridge: Cambridge University Press.

Mitchell, M. 1993. *Analogy-Making as Perception*. Cambridge, MA: MIT Press.

———. 1996. *An Introduction to Genetic Algorithms*. Cambridge, MA: MIT Press.

Mokyr, J. 1990. *The Lever of Riches: Technological Creativity and Economic Progress.* Oxford: Oxford University Press.

———. 2000. Natural History and Economic History: Is Technological Change an Evolutionary Process? Northwestern University working paper (April).

———. 2002. *The Gifts of Athena: Historical Origins of the Knowledge Economy.* Princeton, NJ: Princeton University Press.

Monge, P. R., and Contractor, N. S. 2003. *Theories of Communications Networks.* Oxford: Oxford University Press.

Montgomery, C. A., and Porter, M. E. 1991. *Strategy: Seeking and Securing Competitive Advantage,* Boston: Harvard Business School Press.

Montier, J. 2002. *Behavioral Finance: Insights Into Irrational Minds and Markets.* Chichester, UK: John Wiley & Sons.

Moore, G. 1983. Business Cycles, Inflation and Forecasting. *National Bureau of Economic Research Studies in Business Cycles,* no. 24, Second edition. Cambridge, MA: Ballingham.

Morecroft, J. D. W., and Sternam, J. D. 1994. *Modelling for Learning Organizations.* Portland, OR: Productivity Press.

Morowitz, H. J. 2002. *The Emergence of Everything: How the World Became Complex.* Oxford: Oxford University Press.

Morris, E. 2001. *Theodore Rex.* New York: HarperCollins.

Nagel, K., Shubik, M., Paczuski, M., and Bak, P. 2000. Spatial Competition and Price Formation. Santa Fe Institute working paper 00–05–029, Elsevier Preprint.

National Bureau of Economic Research. 2000. *Macroeconomics Annual 1999.* NBER. Cambridge, MA: MIT Press.

Nasar, S. 1998. *A Beautiful Mind.* New York: Faber and Faber.

Neftci, S. N. 1991. Naive Trading Rules in Financial Markets and Wiener-Kolmogorov Prediction Theory: A Study of "Technical Analysis." *Journal of Business* 64, no. 4: 549–571.

Nelson, R. R. 1995. Recent Evolutionary Theorizing About Economic Change. *Journal of Economic Literature* XXXIII (March): 48–90.

———. 1996. *The Sources of Economic Growth.* Cambridge, MA: Harvard University Press.

———. 2003. Physical and Social Technologies and Their Evolution. Columbia University working paper, available from the author.

Nelson, R. R., and Winter, S. G. 1982. *An Evolutionary Theory of Economic Change.* Cambridge, MA: Belknap Press of Harvard University Press.

Newbold, P. 1995. *Statistics for Business and Economics.* Fourth Edition. Englewood Cliffs, NJ: Prentice Hall.

Newman, M. E. J. 1999. *Small Worlds: The Structure of Social Networks.* Santa Fe Institute working paper 99-12-080.

Newman, M. E. J., and Watts, D. J. 1999. *Scaling and Percolation in the Small-World Network Model.* Santa Fe Institute working paper 99–05–034.

Nicolis, G., and Prigogine, I. 1989. *Exploring Complexity: An Introduction.* New York: W. H. Freeman and Company.

Niehans, J. 1990. *A History of Economic Theory.* Baltimore, MD: John Hopkins University Press.

Nijhout, H. F., Nadel, L., and Stein, D. L. 1997 *Pattern Formation in the Physical and Biological Sciences.* Reading, MA: Addison-Wesley.

North, D. C. 1990. *Institutions, Institutional Change and Economic Performance.* Cambridge: Cambridge University Press.

———. 2005. *Understanding the Process of Economic Change.* Princeton, NJ: Princeton University Press.

North, D. C., and Thomas, R. P. 1973. *The Rise of the Western World: A New Economic History.* Cambridge: Cambridge University Press.

O'Hara, M. 1995. *Market Microstructure Theory.* Cambridge, MA: Blackwell Business.

Ormerod, P. 1994. *The Death of Economics.* 1997 North American edition. New York: John Wiley & Sons.

———. 1998. *Butterfly Economics.* New York: Pantheon Books.

Oswald, A. J. 1991. *Surveys in Economics.* vol. 2. Oxford: Blackwell.

Padgett, J. F., and Ansell, C. K. 1993. Robust Action and the Rise of the Medici, 1400–1434. *American Journal of Sociology* 98, no. 6 (May): 1259–1319.

Page, S. E. 1996. Two Measures of Difficulty. *Economic Theory* 8: 321–346.

Paich, M., and Sterman, J. 1993. Boom, Bust, and Failures to Learn in Experimental Markets. *Management Science* 39, no. 12: 1439–1458.

Pascale, R. T., Millemann, M., and Gioja, L. 2000. *Surfing the Edge of Chaos: The Laws of Nature and New Laws of Business.* New York: Crown Business.

Peak, D., and Frame, M. 1994. *Chaos Under Control.* Reading, MA: Addison-Wesley.

Penrose, E. 1959. *The Theory of the Growth of the Firm.* 1995 edition. Oxford: Oxford University Press.

Persky, J. 1992. Retrospectives: Pareto's Law. *Journal of Economic Perspectives* 2, 767–773.

Peters, E. E. 1991. *Chaos and Order in the Capital Markets: A New View of Cycles, Prices, and Market Volatility.* New York: John Wiley & Sons.

Peters, T. J., and Waterman, R. H. Jr. 1982. *In Search of Excellence: Lessons from America's Best-Run Companies.* New York: Warner Books.

Petroski, H. 1992. *The Evolution of Useful Things.* New York: Vintage Books.

Pettigrew, A., Thomas, H., and Whittington, R., eds. 2002. *Handbook of Strategy and Management.* London: Sage.

Petzinger, T. 1999. *The New Pioneers.* New York: Simon & Schuster.

Pindyck, R. S., and Rubinfeld, D. L. 1989. *Microeconomics.* New York: Macmillan.

Pinker, S. 1994. *The Language Instinct: How the Mind Creates Language.* New York: HarperCollins.

———. 1997. *How the Mind Works.* New York, London: W.W. Norton & Company.

———. 2002. *The Blank Slate: The Modern Denial of Human Nature.* London: Allen Lane-Penguin Press.

Plerou, V., Gopikrishnan, P., Amaral, L. A. N., Meyer, M., and Stanley, H. E. 1999. Scaling of the Distribution of Price Fluctuations of Individual Companies. *Physical Review* E 60: 6519–6529.

Plotkin, H. 1993. *Darwin Machines.* London: Penguin Books.

———. 2002. *The Imagined World Made Real: Toward a Natural Science of Culture.* London: Penguin Press.

Plous, S. 1993. *The Psychology of Judgment and Decision Making.* New York: McGraw-Hill.

Porter, M. E. 1980. *Competitive Strategy: Techniques for Analyzing Industries and Competitors.* New York: Free Press.

———. 1985. *Competitive Advantage: Creating and Sustaining Superior Performance.* New York: Free Press.

———. 1996. What Is Strategy? *Harvard Business Review* (November–December): 61–78.

Powell, T. C. 2002. The Philosophy of Strategy. *Strategic Management Journal* 23: 873–880.

———. 2003. Varieties of Competitive Parity. *Strategic Management Journal* 24: 61–86.

Prahalad, C. K., and Hamel, G. 1990. The Core Competence of the Corporation. *Harvard Business Review* (May–June): 79–91.

Prietula, M. J., Carley, K. M., and Gasser, L., eds. 1998. *Simulating Organizations.* Cambridge, MA: MIT Press.

Prigogine, I. 1996. *The End of Certainty: Time, Chaos, and the New Laws of Nature.* New York: Free Press.

Putnam, R. D. 1993. *Making Democracy Work: Civic Traditions in Modern Italy.* Princeton, NJ: Princeton University Press.

———. 2000. *Bowling Alone: The Collapse and Revival of American Community.* New York: Simon & Schuster.

Rauch, J. 2002. Seeing Around Corners. *Atlantic Monthly* 289, no. 4 (April).

Rauch, J. E., and Casella, A., eds. 2001. *Networks and Markets.* New York: Russell Sage Foundation.

Resnick, M. 1997. *Turtles, Termites and Traffic Jams.* Cambridge, MA: MIT Press.

Ridley, M. 1996. *The Origins of Virtue.* London: Penguin Books.

———. 2001. *The Cooperative Gene.* New York: Free Press.

Roberts, J. 2004. *The Modern Firm: Organizational Design for Performance and Growth.* Oxford: Oxford University Press.

Romer, D. 1996. *Advanced Macroeconomics.* New York: McGraw-Hill.

Romer, P. M. 1990. Endogenous Technological Change. *Journal of Political Economy* 98, no. 5: S71–S102.

———. 1994. The Origins of Endogenous Growth. *Journal of Economic Perspectives* 8, no. 1: 3–22.

Rose, H., and Rose, S., eds. 2001. *Alas Poor Darwin: Arguments Against Evolutionary Psychology.* London: Vintage.

Rosenberg, N. 1982. *Inside the Black Box: Technology and Economics.* Cambridge: Cambridge University Press.

———. 1994. *Exploring the Black Box: Technology, Economics, and History.* Cambridge: Cambridge University Press.

Rosenberg, N., and Birdzell, L. E. Jr. 1986. *How the West Grew Rich: The Economic Transformation of the Industrial World.* New York: Basic Books.

Ross, I. S. 1995. *The Life of Adam Smith.* Oxford: Clarendon Press.

Ross, S. A. 2005. *Neoclassical Finance.* Princeton, NJ: Princeton University Press.

Rothschild, M. 1990. *Bionomics: Economy as Ecosystem.* New York: Henry Holt and Co.

Roxburgh, C. F. 2003. Hidden Flaws in Strategy. *McKinsey Quarterly*, no. 2: 26–39.

Rubinstein, A. 1998. *Modeling Bounded Rationality.* Cambridge, MA: MIT Press.

Rumelt, R. P., Schendel, D. E., and Teece, D. J. 1994. *Fundamental Issues in Strategy. A Research Agenda*. Boston: Harvard Business School Press.

Russo, J. E., and Schoemaker, P. J. H. 1989. *Decision Traps*. New York: Fireside.

Samuelson, P. A., and Nordhaus, W. D. 1998. *Economics*. Sixteenth edition (International edition). Boston: Irwin McGraw-Hill.

Sargent, T. 1995. *Bounded Rationality in Macroeconomics*. New York: Oxford University Press.

Sato, Y., Akiyama, E., and Farmer, J. D. 2002. Chaos and Learning in a Simple Two Person Game. *Proceedings of the National Academy of Sciences* 99, no. 7: 4748–4751.

Scarf, H., and Hansen, T. 1973. *Computation of Economic Equilibrium*. New Haven, CT: Yale University Press.

Schank, R. C. 1990. *Tell Me a Story*. New York: Charles Scribner's Sons.

Schein, E. H. 1992. *Organizational Culture and Leadership*. Second edition. San Francisco: Jossey-Bass.

Scherer, F. M. 1999. *New Perspectives on Economic Growth and Technological Innovation*. Washington, DC: Brookings Institution Press.

Schneider, E. D., and Sagan, D. 2005. *Into the Cool: Energy Flow, Thermodynamics, and Life*. Chicago: University of Chicago Press.

Schumpeter, J. A. 1934. *The Theory of Economic Development*. 1983 edition. London: Transaction Publishers.

———. 1943. *Capitalism, Socialism and Democracy*. Fifth edition, 1976. London: Routledge.

Schwager, J. D. 1992. *The New Market Wizards: Conversations with America's Top Traders*. New York: HarperBusiness.

Schwartz, B. 2004. *The Paradox of Choice: Why More Is Less*. New York: HarperCollins.

Schwartz, P. 1991. *The Art of the Long View: Planning for the Future in an Uncertain World*. New York: Currency Doubleday.

Scott, W. R. 2001. *Institutions and Organizations*. Thousand Oaks, CA: Sage Publications.

Seabright, P. 2004. *The Company of Strangers: A Natural History of Economic Life*. Princeton, NJ: Princeton University Press.

Segal-Horn, S. 1998. *The Strategy Reader*. Milton Keynes, UK: Blackwell Business.

Selten, R. 1990. Bounded Rationality. *Journal of Institutional and Theoretical Economics* 46, no. 4 (December): 649–658.

Senge, P. M. 1990. *The Fifth Discipline*. New York: Currency Doubleday.

Sensier, M., and van Dijk, D. 2004. Testing for Volatility Changes in U.S. Macroeconomic Time Series. *Review of Economics and Statistics* 86, no. 3 (August): 833–839.

Shannon, C. E., and Weaver, W. 1949. *The Mathematical Theory of Communications*. 1963 Illini Books edition. Chicago: University of Illinois Press.

Shefrin, H. 2005. *A Behavioral Approach to Asset Pricing*. London: Elsevier Academic Press.

Shennan, S. 2002. *Genes, Memes and Human History: Darwinian Archaeology and Cultural Evolution*. London: Thames and Hudson.

Shiller, R. J. 2000. *Irrational Exuberance*. Princeton, NJ: Princeton University Press.

Shleifer, A. 2000. *Inefficient Markets: An Introduction to Behavioral Finance*. Oxford: Oxford University Press.

Simms, K. 1994a. *Evolving 3D Morphology and Behavior by Competition*. Cambridge, MA: MIT Press.

———. 1994b. Evolving Virtual Creatures. *Computer Graphics*, SIGGRAPH '94 Proceedings, July: 15–22.

Simon, H. A. 1978. Rational Decision-Making in Business Organizations. Nobel Memorial Lecture, December 8.

———. 1991. *Models of My Life*. New York: Basic Books.

———. 1992. *Economics, Bounded Rationality and the Cognitive Revolution*. Hampshire, UK: Edward Elgar Publishing.

———. 1996. *The Sciences of the Artificial*. Third edition. Cambridge, MA: MIT Press.

———. 1997. *Administrative Behavior*. Fourth edition. New York: Free Press.

Simpson Ross, I. 1995. *The Life of Adam Smith*. Oxford: Oxford University Press.

Skidelsky, R. 1994. *John Maynard Keynes: The Economist as Saviour 1920–1937*. London: Macmillan.

Skyrms, B. 1996. *Evolution of the Social Contract*. Cambridge: Cambridge University Press.

Slater, R. 1999. *Jack Welch and the GE Way: Management Insights and Leadership Secrets of the Legendary CEO*. New York: McGraw-Hill.

Smith, A. 1776. *The Wealth of Nations*. Reprint edition, 1994. New York: Modern Library.

Smith, D. E., and Foley, D. K. 2002. *Is Utility Theory So Different from Thermodynamics?* Santa Fe Institute working paper 02–04–016.

Sober, E., and Wilson, D. S. 1998. *Unto Others: The Evolution and Psychology of Unselfish Behavior*. Cambridge, MA: Harvard University Press.

Solé, R., and Goodwin, B. 2001. *Signs of Life: How Complexity Pervades Biology*. New York: Basic Books.

Solow, R. M. 1956. A Contribution to the Theory of Economic Growth. *Quarterly Journal of Economics* 70, no. 1: 65–94.

———. 2000. *Growth Theory: An Exposition.* Second edition. New York: Oxford University Press.

Sornette, D. 2003. *Why Stock Markets Crash: Critical Events in Financial Systems.* Princeton, NJ: Princeton University Press.

Soros, G. 1987. *The Alchemy of Finance: Reading the Mind of the Market.* New York: John Wiley & Sons.

Stacey, R. D., Griffin, D., and Shaw, P. 2000. *Complexity and Management.* London: Routledge.

Stanley, M. H. R., Amaral, L. A. N., Buldyrev, S. V., Havlin, S., Leschhorn, H., Maass, P., Salinger, M. A., and Stanley, H. E. 1996. Scaling Behavior in the Growth of Companies. *Nature* 379: 804–806.

Sterman, J. D. 1985. A Behavioral Model of the Economic Long Wave. *Journal of Economic Behavior and Organization* 6: 17–53.

———. 1989a. Modeling Managerial Behavior: Misperceptions of Feedback in a Dynamic Decision Making Experiment. *Management Science* 35, no. 3: 321–339.

———. 1989b. Deterministic Chaos in an Experimental Economic System. *Journal of Economic Behavior and Organization,* 12: 1–28.

———. 2000. *Business Dynamics.* New York: McGraw-Hill.

———. 2002. All Models Are Wrong: Reflections on Becoming a Systems Scientist. Jay Wright Forrester Prize Lecture. *System Dynamics Review* 18, no. 4: 501–531.

Sterman, J. D., and Sweeney, L. B. 2002. Cloudy Skies: Assessing Public Understanding of Global Warming. *System Dynamics Review* 18, no. 2: 207–240.

Sternberg, R. J., and Davidson, J. E. 1995. *The Nature of Insight.* Cambridge, MA: MIT Press.

Stewart, I. 1989. *Does God Play Dice? The Mathematics of Chaos.* Cambridge, MA: Basic Blackwell.

Stiglitz, J. 1997. *Economics.* Second edition. New York: W.W. Norton & Company.

Stiglitz, J. E. 2002. *Globalization and Its Discontents.* New York: W.W. Norton & Company.

Stillings, N. A., Weisler, S. E., Chase, C. H., Feinstein, M. H., Garfield, J. L., and Rissland, E. L. 1995. *Cognitive Science. An Introduction.* Second edition. Cambridge, MA: MIT Press.

Strogatz, S. 1994. *Nonlinear Dynamics and Chaos.* Cambridge, MA: Westview Press.

Suh, N. P. 1990. *The Principles of Design.* New York: Oxford University Press.

Surowiecki, J. 2003. The Financial Page: Decisions, Decisions. *New Yorker* (March 24): 33.

———. 2004. *The Wisdom of Crowds.* New York: Doubleday.

Sutton, R. S., and Barto, A. G. 1999. *Reinforcement Learning: An Introduction.* Cambridge, MA: MIT Press.

Szabolcs, M., and Farmer, J. D. 2005. An Empirical Model of Price Formation. Santa Fe Institute working paper 05-10-039.

Szenberg, M., and Ramrattan, L., eds. 2004. *New Frontiers in Economics.* Cambridge: Cambridge University Press.

Teilhard de Chardin, P. 1969. *The Future of Man.* New York: Harper Torchbooks.

Thaler, R. H. 1992. *The Winner's Curse: Paradoxes and Anomalies of Economic Life.* Princeton, NJ: Princeton University Press.

———. ed. 1993. *Advances in Behavioral Finance.* New York: Russell Sage Foundation.

Thomas, A. S., and Mueller, S. L. 2000. A Case for Comparative Entrepreneurship: Assessing the Relevance of Culture. *Journal of International Business Studies* 31, no. 2.

Tirole, J. 1988. *The Theory of Industrial Organization.* Cambridge, MA: MIT Press.

Tushman, M. L., and O'Reilly, C. A. 1997. *Winning Through Innovation: A Practical Guide to Leading Organizational Change and Renewal.* Boston: Harvard Business School Press.

Van der Hijden, K. 1996. *Scenarios: The Art of Strategic Conversation.* Boston: John Wiley & Sons.

Vega-Redondo, F. 1996. *Evolution, Games and Economic Behaviour.* New York: Oxford University Press.

von Baeyer, H. C. 1998. *Warmth Disperses and Time Passes: The History of Heat.* New York: Modern Library.

Von Neumann, J., and Morgenstern, O. 1944. *Theory of Games and Economic Behavior.* Sixtieth Anniversary Edition 2004. Princeton, NJ: Princeton University Press.

Vriend, N. J. 2002. Was Hayek an ACE? *Southern Economic Journal* 68, no. 4: 811–840.

Wackernagel, M., Schulz, N. B., Deumling, D., Linares, A. C., Jenkins, M., Kapos, V., Monfreda, C., Loh, J., Myers, N., Norgaard, R., and Randers, J. 2002. Tracking the Ecological Overshoot of the Human Economy. *Proceedings of the National Academy of Science* 99, no. 14 (July 9): 9266–9271.

Waldrop, M. M. 1992. *Complexity: The Emerging Science at the Edge of Order and Chaos.* New York: Touchstone.

Watts, D. J. 2003. *Six Degrees: The Science of a Connected Age.* New York: W.W. Norton.

———. 1999. *Small Worlds.* Princeton, NJ: Princeton University Press.

Weinberger, E. D. 1996. NP Completeness of Kauffman's N-K Model. Santa Fe Institute working paper 96-02-003.

Welch, J. 2001. *Jack: Straight from the Gut*. New York: Warner Business Books.

Wernerfelt, B. 1984. A Resource-based View of the Firm. *Strategic Management Journal* 5: 171–180.

———. 1995. The Resource-based View of the Firm: Ten Years After. *Strategic Management Journal* 16: 171–174.

Wheen, F. 1999. *Karl Marx*. London: Fourth Estate.

Whitley, L. D., ed. 1993. *Foundations of Genetic Algorithms 2*. San Mateo, CA: Morgan Kaufmann Publishers.

Wiggins, R. R., and Ruefli, T. W. 2002. Sustained Competitive Advantage: Temporal Dynamics and the Incidence and Persistence of Superior Economic Performance. *Organization Science* 13, no. 1: 81–105.

———. 2005. Schumpeter's Ghost: Is Hypercompetition Making the Best of Times Shorter? *Strategic Management Journal* 26: 887–911.

Williamson, O. E., ed. 1995. *Organization Theory: From Chester Barnard to Present*. Oxford: Oxford University Press.

Williamson, O. E., and Winter, S. G., eds. 1993. *The Nature of the Firm: Origins, Evolution, and Development*. New York: Oxford University Press.

Wilson, E. O. 1992. *The Diversity of Life*. New York: W.W. Norton & Company.

———. *Consilience: The Unity of Knowledge*. New York: Random House.

Wolfram, S. 1994. *Cellular Automata and Complexity*. Reading, MA: Addison- Wesley.

———. 2002. *A New Kind of Science*. Champaign, IL: Wolfram Media.

Wright, R. 1994. *The Moral Animal: Why We Are the Way We Are: The New Science of Evolutionary Psychology*. New York: Vintage Books.

———. 2000. *Non Zero: The Logic of Human Destiny*. New York: Pantheon Books.

Wuensche, A., and Lesser, M. J. 1992. *The Global Dynamics of Cellular Automata*. Reading, MA: Addison-Wesley.

———. 1998. Discrete Dynamical Networks and Their Attractor Basins. *Proceedings of Complex Systems 98*, University of New South Wales, Sydney, Australia. Also Santa Fe Institute working paper 98–11–101.

Young, H. P. 1998. *Individual Strategy and Social Structure: The Evolutionary Theory of Institutions*. Princeton, NJ: Princeton University Press.

Zadek, S. 2004. *The Civil Corporation: The New Economy of Corporate Citizenship*. London: Earthscan.

Zak, P. J. 2003. Trust. *The Journal of Financial Transformations*. CAPCO Institute: 17–24.

Zak, P. J., and Knack, S. 2001. Trust and Growth. *Economic Journal*, no. 111: 295–321.

Zarnowitz, V. 1992. Business Cycles: Theory, History, Indicators and Forecasting. *NBER Studies in Business Cycles*, vol. 27. Chicago: University of Chicago Press.

Ziman, J., ed. 2000. *Technological Innovation as an Evolutionary Process*. Cambridge, MA: Cambridge University Press.

Abul-Magd, A. Y., 441
accounting, mental, 122
Adams, Bob, 45
adaptability
  barriers to, 357–361
  hierarchy and, 364–366
  rigidity versus, 361–364
adaptation
  cooperation and, 373
  culture and, 368–374
  distinguished from learning, 355
  execution and, 355–356, 375
  individual role in, 357–364
  purposeful, 250
  social architecture for, 374–379
  structural role and, 364–368
Adaptive Markets Hypothesis, 403
adaptive walks, 208, 210–211, 215
adaptiveness, importance of, 347–348
aesthetics, evolutionary view of, 312–313
Africa
  cultural norms in, 431
  economic conditions in, 428, 452
African Americans, 448
  economic conditions of, 447
agents
  defined, 18
  inductive reasoning by, 129–130
  traditional view of, 141–142
agriculture
  as disruptive Social Technology, 271
  and hierarchy management, 273
Airbus A380, 365
aircraft industry, periodicity of, 110
Akerlof, George, 52, 166
Al-Qaeda, 357
Aldrich, Howard, 351, 352

algorithm
  defined, 12, 192
  evolution as, 189–190
  experimentation and, 249–250
  information-processing medium for, 201–202
  substrate-neutral, 192
altruism, 51, 121, 477
  failure of, 420
  selfishness versus, 441
altruistic punishment, 121, 419
Alvarez, Luis and Walter, 55
Amdahl, 330
American Home Products, 331
American Revolution, 296–297
amplification
  of Business Plans, 337, 345–347
  of fit designs, 196
analogies
  power of, 127
  rules and, 133–134
ancestral environment, 310
anchor and adjust, 171
AND, Boolean, 148
Anderson, Phil, 45, 48, 167
Anglo-American Cable Company, 174
Apple Computer, 248, 330
  Macintosh product of, 335, 336, 366
"The Apple Does Not Fall Far from the Tree," 444
arbitrage, 396, 397, 401
architecture
  effect of innovations in, 248
  of Physical Technologies, 247
Arkwright, Richard, 16, 40
Arrow, Kenneth, 38, 39, 43, 46, 464
art, as mental cheesecake, 312
Arthur, Brian, 19, 46, 47, 57, 74, 96, 123–125, 134, 135, 136, 137, 225, 392, 401, 458, 464

Arthur's Bar problem, 123–126, 401
artifacts, 241
Asimov, Isaac, 115
aspirations, 341–344
assembly-line technology, 264–265
assumptions
    overreliance on, 48–50
    role of, 50
    in Traditional Economics, 51–54
AstraZeneca, 182–184
At Home in the Universe (Kauffman), 455
AT&T, 336
Atari, 330
auctions, 93
    continuous double, 394
    See also Walrasian auctions
Australopethicus africanus, 6
automobile, economic importance of, 175,
    246–247
availability biases, 122
Axelrod, Robert, 96, 221, 224–225, 227
Axtell, Robert, 80, 81–83, 88–92, 94–95, 181, 378

Bachelier, Louis, 382, 387, 389, 485
Bacon, Francis, 259
bacteria, inductive problem solving by, 130
balanced growth, 41
balanced scorecard, 408
bank account, as dynamic system, 100, 102, 103
Bank of England, 296
Bargaining Problem, 267–268
Barnes & Noble, 8
Barone, Enrico, 462
Baumol, William, 295
Beagle, H.M.S., 266
Beautiful Mind, A, 267
Beer Distribution Game, 168–172, 185
behavior
    affecting economic status, 444
    norms of, 369
    scientific analysis of, 115
behavioral economics, 117–119
bell curve, 178, 388
Bennett, Charles, 305
Bentham, Jeremy, 27, 28, 34, 461
Berlin Wall, fall of, 390, 417
Bernardo, Father Joel, 79
Bernoulli, Daniel, 461
Bertrand, Joseph, 49
beta, of stock, 404
bias
    availability, 122
    and connection density, 157
    framing, 122
    of investors, 387
    in networks, 156–157
    and predictability, 157

biased transmission, 476
bicycles, technology evolution in, 254–255
bid-ask spread, 181
Big Man Society, 271–272
    criticism of, 295–296
    distortion of fitness function in, 288
    versus market economy, 287–289
bilateral trade, effects on equilibrium, 93
Black, Fisher, 383
Blair, Tony, 417, 421
Blanchard, Olivier, 166
Blind Watchmaker, The (Dawkins), 458
block creatures, 188–191
Blue Gene computer, 63
Boisguilbert, Pierre de, 460
Boole, George, 147
Boolean networks, 147, 226
    as cellular automata, 470
    scaling of, 148–150
Borges, Jorge Luis, 1, 233
Bossidy, Larry, 330
Bouchard, Jean-Phillippe, 390
Boulding, Kenneth, 300
boundaries, maintaining of, 352
bounded rationality, 118, 119, 387
Bourbakism, 466
Bower, Marvin, 372
Bowles, Samuel, 223, 418, 420, 440, 442
Bowling Alone (Putnam), 435
Boyd, Robert, 284, 368, 418
Boyle, Robert, 259
Brazil, trust levels in, 432
British East India Company, 329
British Nuclear Fuels, 349
British Petroleum (BP), 265, 286, 348, 377
British rail network, privatization of, 424
British Telecom (BT), 424
Brookings Institution, 80, 81–83
Browne, John, 275, 348
Brownian motion, 485
Bryan, Lowell, 339
Buffett, Warren, 138, 386, 405
building blocks, evolutionary, 197, 213, 214
building materials, evolution of, 253
Built to Last (Collins and Porras), 286, 330, 342,
    350, 355, 414
bureaucracy, 152, 154
Burger King, 310
Burke, Edmund, 454
Bush, George W., 417
business cycle
    damping of, 172
    oscillations of, 162–163
    real models of, 163–164
    wiggling-jelly model of, 163–164
Business Plans, 235–237, 474
    amplification of, 337, 344–347
    assessing success of, 292, 293, 337, 345–346

components of, 285
deductive-tinkering in, 286–287, 293
defined, 235–237
differentiation of, 286–287, 337
distortion of, 341–342
execution and adaptation of, 355–356, 409–411
goal of, 409–410
modules in, 283–285
replication of, 290–291
resources and, 367–368, 374
selection of, 287–291, 293
businesses
cultural norms of, 370–371
defined, 280
as design, 16
distinguished from firm, 280–282
as interactor, 281, 282
staticity of, 333–334
Butler, Frank, 326

Calopez, Paz, 79
Camerer, Colin, 119
Campbell, Donald, 250, 475
Camus, Albert, 234
Canon, adaptability of, 368
Cantillon, Richard, 27, 316
capital, cost of, 404–405
capital asset pricing model (CAPM), 404–405
capitalism, 36, 415, 422
Complexity view of, 423–426
equilibrium view of, 294
evolution of, 417
Keynesian view of, 408
shortcomings of, 289
versus socialism, 20, 38, 416
triumph of, 38
CapitalOne, 345
capuchin monkeys, tool use by, 241
Carlyle, Thomas, xi, 455
Carnot, Sadi, 303
Carroll, Lewis, 332
Cassidy, John, 22, 464
cattle industry, periodicity of, 110
CBS, 349
cellular automata, 96, 226, 470
Central Intelligence Agency, 357
challenge, as innovating norm, 371
Chandler, Alfred, 289, 324, 422
chaos, 104
in Boolean networks, 470
edge of, 157–158
graph of, 106
network disintegration into, 156
Chaos (Gleick), 99
Chase, Rodney, 348
cheating, versus cooperation, 268–270
chess, reasoning styles in, 128, 212

chimpanzees, tool use by, 241
China
economic progress in, 441, 452
family businesses in, 434
trust levels in, 433
Christensen, Clayton, 257–258, 330
Church, Alonzo, 457
Cisco Systems, 236–237
Citicorp, 331
1970s strategy of, 21
Santa Fe Institute collaboration, 46–48, 74
civilization, economics and, 8–10
Clark, Andy, 128
Clark, Kim, 175, 258
Classical economics, 24, 460
Clinton, Bill, 361–362, 417, 421
closed system
described, 68
distinguished from open system, 69
in economics, 71
clothing
consumer spending on, 311
design of, 14–15
clustered volatility, 393, 486. See also punctuated
equilibrium
coarse graining, 50
Coase, Ronald, 353, 355
cobweb diagrams, 102
Coca-Cola, 281, 313
Cody, Buffalo Bill, 326
coevolution, 201
Coffin, Charles, 350
cognitive science, 125
future of, 139
perspectives of, 126
collective memory, 354
Collins, James, 286, 330, 342, 350, 355, 414
commitment, strategic, 325
commodities markets, periodicity of, 109–113
communications
consumer spending on, 311
density of, 151–152
and development of cooperative behavior, 274
effective modes of, 377
evolution of media, 253
in social architecture, 376
technological innovation fueled by, 246
Communist Manifesto, The (Marx), 415
Company of Strangers, The (Seabright), 458
compassionate conservatism, 417
competition
in evolution, 214
as reality check, 287–288
in wealth creation, 26
competitive advantage, 324, 325
studies on, 331–333
temporary nature of, 329–331
unobservability of, 482

complements, in markets, 38
complex adaptive systems, 18
  evolution of, 458
  implications of viewing economy as, 19–20, 99
  management of, 378
  organizations as, 351–352
complexity catastrophe, 152, 156
Complexity Economics, xii, 19, 458
  adaptiveness of, 324
  advantages of, 185
  versus chaos, 107–108
  defined, 96–97
  emergent phenomena in, 168
  on finance, 388–409
  ground broken by, 96
  importance of, xiii, 20, 265
  and macroeconomic policy, 449
  message of, 323
  and politics, 415–416, 422–426, 450
  potential of, 418
  precursors of, 46–48, 74
  social implications of, 449–450
components, effects of innovations in, 247–248
computers. See also Physical Technologies (PTs)
  as networks, 147–148
  speed of, 63
condition-action rules, in induction, 130
conditional cooperation, 121, 419
Congo, Democratic Republic of, economy of, 428
Conservation of Energy, Principle of, 66
Constitution of Liberty (Hayek), 300
constraints, 201, 214
  caused by complexity, 158
  conflicts of, 158
  of networks, 152
consumer behavior
  categories of, 310–311
  preferences in, 37, 309–310
continuous innovation, evolution as, 216
Conway, John Horton, 226
cooperation
  and adaptation, 373
  agriculture and, 271
  cheating and, 268–270
  in Complexity Economics, 223
  in corporations, 276
  and economic system, 121, 267
  evolution of, 271
  in families, 270–271
  language and, 274
  and learning, 354
  norms for, 371, 373
  within organizations, 352–354, 410
coordination, problems in, 223
Cootner, Paul, 382, 388
Copernicus, Nicolaus, 259
copper industry, periodicity of, 110

"The Core Competency of the Corporation"
  (Prahalad and Hamel), 367–368
Coronatae jellyfish, 301
corporations. See firms; organizations
correspondence principle, 95
Cortés, Hernán, 325, 453
cotton prices, fluctuations of, 179–180
Cournot, Antoine, 461
Cowan, George, 45, 46
CP/M, 327
crash of August, 1998, 381
crash of October 19, 1987, 56, 381
creative destruction, 40, 332
Creative Destruction (Schumpeter), 330, 356
crossover, of schema components, 196
Crotchet Castle (Peacock), 57
Crutchfield, Jim, 204, 206, 210
Cuba, automotive industry in, 47
Cultural Values and Human Progress
  symposium, 429
cultural variants, 284
culture
  defined, 368–369, 484
  economic efficiency of, 431–435
  versus hierarchy, 375–376
  and history, 447
  management through, 375–376
  and national wealth, 428–435
  norms of, 369, 430–431
  organizational, 369–370
  political correctness and, 429
  of poverty, 444–445
  race and, 447
  reinvigoration of, 448
  ring metaphor for, 369
  rules of (see norms)
  tension inherent in, 372–374
  time view of, 431
  Traditional view of, 429
Culture Matters (Harrison and Huntington), 429
Cutler, David, 177, 178
Cyert, Richard, 118

Darwin, Charles, 13, 16, 17, 173, 216, 266, 300,
  457, 458
Darwin's Dangerous Idea (Dennett), 233
data, and economics, 59
Dawkins, Richard, 188, 199, 217, 284, 314, 458
Day, Richard, 53, 463
de Geus, Arie, 414
Debreu, Gérard, 39, 43, 460, 466
deduction, 127–129
  combined with induction, 250–252
deductive-tinkering model, 249–252, 475
  constraints on, 367
  and economic evolution, 285–287, 293

effects of, 259–260
  in PT space, 251–252, 253
  in ST space, 264–265
Deep Blue (chess computer), 128–129
default hierarchy, 133, 359
defection, 223
degrees of possibility, 152–154
Dell, Michael, 153
Dell Computer, 55, 248
  in PC market, 153
DeLong, J. Bradford, 9, 428, 456, 457
delusional optimism, 357–358
  combating of, 375
democratic institutions, 273, 296
Dennett, Daniel, 29, 30, 187, 190, 192, 193, 194,
    202, 209, 212, 233, 234, 236, 457, 458, 469,
    472–475
dense networks, 154, 155
Derrida, Bernard, 156
design, 187–188
  business as, 16
  clothing, 14–15
  evolutionary, 13–14
  intelligent, 14
design space, 193, 213
  finite nature of, 234–235
  requirements for, 235
  size of, 473
Dickenson, H. D., 423
differentiation
  of Business Plans, 286–287, 337
  in economic evolution, 285–287
  in evolution, 211
  importance of, 339–341
Digital Equipment Corporation, 330, 335
diminishing marginal utility, law of, 29
diminishing returns, 28, 57
dinosaurs, extinction of, 55
discounting, 383, 387
discrimination, 274
diseconomies of scale, 150, 152, 154
disequilibrium, 41, 60
  innovation in, 294
  open system, 70, 72
disk storage, evolution of, 257–258
division of labor, 266
divorce rates, in U.S., 437
DNA, 202. See also Library of Mendel
  information coding in, 203, 215
  lengthening of, 235
DuPont, 377, 411–412, 413, 487
dynamic equilibrium, 31
  in growth theory, 41
dynamic system
  defined, 100
  described, 100–101
  economy as, 100

examples of, 100
feedback in, 101, 102
nonlinearity in, 102–107
time delays in, 101–102

earnings, quarterly reports of, 412
earthquakes, distribution of, 178–179
earthworms, evolutionary view of, 13–14
Easterly, William, 261, 435
econometrics, 59
economic evolution, xi, xii, 13–14
  acceleration in 1750s, 280, 296, 449
  algorithm of, 293
  contrasts with other forms of evolution,
    293–294
  as design process, 14, 237–239
  differentiation in, 285–287
  history of, 16–17
  interactors in, 279, 281, 282
  irreversibility of, 302, 303–306
  order in, 302
  processes of, 15–16
  replication in, 291–293
  selection in, 287–291
  strategies in, 284–285
  technology in, 15–16
  units of selection in, 279, 282–284
economic forecasting, impossibility of, 109
economic history, 7–9
  evolutionary view of, 11–13
economics
  behavioral, 117–119
  Classical, 24
  as complex adaptive system, 19–20 (see also
    Complexity Economics)
  equilibrium view of, 17–18, 21–23, 27–29
  evolutionary view of, 16–18, 216–217, 318–319
    (see also economic evolution)
  experimental, 60
  historical attitudes toward, 57–58, 316
  importance of, xi–xii
  laws of, 13
  Keynesian, 164–165
  Malthusian view of, 16–17
  Marginalist, 29–36
  mathematics in, 30, 48–49
  Neoclassical, 24, 36–39, 40
  New Keynesian, 166–167
  orthodox, 459
  physics metaphors in, 29–33, 46–48, 65–71,
    466
  relation to politics, 415–416
  relation to science, 46–49, 459
  textbooks in, 459
  traditional view of (see Traditional
    Economics)

economies of scale, 149, 150, 267, 271, 272
economy
    as adaptive system, 19–20, 99
    complexity of, 5–6, 107–108
    computer modeling of idealized, 81–88
    cooperation as basis of, 121
    decreasing entropy of, 301–303
    as dynamic system, 100, 470
    as genetic replication strategy, 317
    misclassification of, 99
    as n-body problem, 108
    nonhuman manifestations of, 456
    as nonlinear system, 107–109
    origins of, 80, 242–243
    periodicities in, 109–110
    technology as essential for, 243
    trust as essential for, 433–434
econophysicists, 180, 390–391
econosphere, 11, 457
Eddington, Arthur, 302
edges, defined, 142
Edison, Thomas Alva, 40, 349
education, improvement of, 446
Edward II, king of England, 161
efficient-markets hypothesis, 23, 295, 385
    history of, 402
    shortcomings of, 387
Egypt, ancient, distribution of wealth in, 441
Einstein, Albert, xii, 75, 485
El Farol, 124
elder rule, 273
Eldredge, Niles, 173
electricity industry, 110, 424
Elements of a Pure Economics (Walras), 30, 48–49
Elements of Statics (Poinsot), 31
Eli Lilly, 331
Elster, Jon, 121
emergence, described, 167–168
emergent properties, defined, 86
Emilia-Romagna, government of, 436
endogenous evolution, 198
    mechanisms of, 198–202
endogenous growth theory, 42
endogenous variables, 40, 55
Engels, Friedrich, 416
England
    depression of 1315, 161
    inflation in, 1201–1993, 162
    parliamentary democracy in, 296
Enron, 330, 407
entertainment, consumer spending on, 311
entrepreneurs, 40, 286
entropy, 67–68
    decrease of, 214, 303, 306–308
    and economics, 301–302
    implications of, 300–301
    irreversibility and, 303–304

Second Law and, 67–68
    and value, 316–317
Entropy Law and the Economic Process, The (Georgescu-Roegen), 299–300, 301
environment, 81
    ancestral, 310
    for evolution, 214
environmentalism
    Complexity view of, 449
    and entropy reduction, 307
Epstein, Joshua, 80, 81–83, 88–92, 94–95
equilibrium, 17, 30–31
    as abstraction, 73
    closed, 66–67, 70
    dynamic, 31
    effect of shocks on, 55
    versus growth, 39–40
    and growth reconciled, 41–42
    illusoriness of, 60
    implications of, 52–56
    invisible hand and, 38
    as metaphor, 65–68
    multiple, 31
    Nash, 268
    punctuated, 173–175, 231, 328, 363–364, 393
    ramifications of ball-in-bowl model of, 54–56
    system, 17–18, 69
    temporary, 55–63, 64
    theoretical settling time of, 62–63
    types of, 31
equilibrium model, 465
    as abstraction, 73–74
    arguments in favor of, 72–73
    Arrow-Debreu system of, 38–39, 43
    as propagation mechanism, 163
equilibrium points, 30–31
    multiple, 31
    temporary, 55, 63, 64
equilibrium system, 17–18
errors, behavioral, 121, 122
Erdös, Paul, 142, 143
Essay on the Principle of Population (Malthus), 16
Etounga-Manguelle, Daniel, 431
Euler, Leonhard, 30
European Union
    cultural change in, 447–448
    executive of, 158
evolution
    adaptive nature of, 210–211, 214
    as algorithm, 12, 189–190, 192, 214, 317
    as biological concept, 12
    building blocks of, 197
    characteristics of, 213–216
    and complexity, 458
    constraints on, 410
    as continuous innovation, 216
    dead ends in, 440

as design process, 14
differentiated from progress, 452
differentiation in, 211
economic (*see* economic evolution)
as economic concept, 12–13, 16–17, 216–217, 318–319
endogenous, 198–202
endosomatic, 300
exosomatic, 300
exploration and exploitation in, 211
general laws of, 12
intention and rationality in, 249–250
as learning algorithm, 317
of market, 391–394
mass-extinction events and, 55
misconceptions about, 249
necessary conditions for, 213–214
of Physical Technology (*see* Physical Technology evolution)
recursivity of, 192
shaping of, 453–454
of Social Technology (*see* Social Technology evolution)
Evolution and the Theory of Games (Smith), 217
evolutionary stable strategies, 231
Evolutionary Theory of Economic Change (Nelson and Winter), 17, 217
exaptation, 238, 312
execution, and adaptation, 355–356, 375
exogenous shocks, 54, 55
exogenous variables, 40, 55
experience, and adaptability, 359–361
experimental economics, 60
exploration versus exploitation, 211–212, 213, 360, 482
explosives, entropic view of, 307
Exxon Mobil, 291, 330

fact-based, as innovating norm, 371
Fama, Eugene, 383, 385–386, 389
families
behaviors within, 444
cooperation in, 270–271
and economic development, 434
and trust, 434
Family Dollar Stores, 333
Faraday, Michael, 33, 461
Farmer, Doyne, 46, 181, 182, 184, 185, 391–398 *passim*, 401–402, 457
fatalism, 430
Federal Bureau of Investigation, 357
feedback, 130. *See also* negative feedback; positive feedback
feedback loop, 101
Fehr, Ernst, 119, 120, 418, 469
Feynman, Richard, 304

field theory, 34
finance
Complexity view of, 388–409
data and, 59–60
efficient-market hypothesis and, 385, 387, 402
random-walk hypothesis and, 383–385, 388, 389
relation between academia and business, 382
Traditional view of, 387
fine graining, 50
firms. *See also* corporations; organizations
capitalization of, 404–405, 410
distinguished from businesses, 280–282
goal of, 408–409
growth of, 366–367
legal forms of, 281
raison d'être of, 352–355, 409–411
societal role of, 413
First Law of Thermodynamics, 66–67
Fisher, David Hackett, 162
fit designs, 197, 214
fit order, 316
wealth as, 316–318
fitness
in economic evolution, 303
determining, 308–312
fitness functions, 195
government and, 426–427
role in evolution, 214, 288
and rough correlation, 203, 216
fitness landscape, 203–206
fixed-point attractors, 103, 104
flexibility, organizational importance of, 362–364, 376
flow, 100–101
Fong, Christina, 420
food, consumer spending on, 311
Forbes, Bertie, 330
Forced Moves, 212
Ford, Henry, 40, 264–265, 343–344
Forrester, Jay, 168
Forster, E. M., 450
Foster, Richard, 254, 258, 330, 331, 334, 356
Foundation (Asimov), 115
Foundations of Economic Analysis (Samuelson), 37
Foundations of Statistics (Savage), 480
fractal geometry, 388
framing bias, 122
France, eighteenth-century economy of, 27
free riding, 121
Freeman, John, 333
Friedman, Milton, 39, 49, 58, 165, 396, 415
Frisch, Ragnar, 470
frogs, learning by, 130–132, 133–134
frozen accident, 326
Fry, Art, 250
Fukuyama, Francis, 417, 429, 434, 437, 439, 440, 448

G-R conditions, 303, 319
  definition of, 303
  entropy reduction, 306–308
  fitness, 308–314
  irreversibility, 303–306
Gächter, Simon, 120, 469
Galilei, Galileo, 47, 50, 259
Game of Life, 225–226, 474
Game of Life/Prisoner's Dilemma, 227, 419
  change sensitivity in, 231–232
  evolution in, 230–231
  strategies in, 228–230, 232–233
game theory, 96, 222, 476
  applied to Complexity Economics, 223–233
  behavioral, 463
garbage dumps, economy of, 79–80
garbage in, garbage out (GIGO), 48
Gates, Bill, 127, 327, 335, 336, 337, 368
Gauss, Karl Friedrich, 178
Gaussian distribution, 178, 388
GDP, world, 9, 457
GE Capital, 338
Gell-Mann, Murray, 45, 67–68, 326, 465, 481
General Electric, 174, 281, 331, 377
  aspirations of, 342
  culture of, 372
  evolution of, 349–350
general equilibrium, 33, 38–39, 43
General Motors, 155
General Theory of Employment (Keynes), 101, 164
genes
  effects of, 314–315
  replication of, 228, 291
  as schema, 283
genomes, 149
Georgescu-Roegen, Nicholas, 299, 300, 301, 302, 305, 306, 307, 314, 319, 478, 479
Germany, family traditions in, 434
Ghemawat, Pankaj, 325
Gibrat, Robert, 472
Giddens, Anthony, 417
Gilovich, Thomas, 127
Gintis, Herbert, 119, 121, 418, 419, 420, 442
Glazer, Nathan, 429
Gleick, James, 99
goals, 130, 483
Gödel, Kurt, 457
Goldman Sachs, 377, 390
Good Tricks, 190, 191, 195, 200
Gossen, Hermann Heinrich, 29, 34, 461
Gould, Stephen Jay, 173, 319
government
  Complexity view of, 426
  evolution of, 271–274
  importance of, 425–246
  Left view of, 422
  and markets, 426–427

  Right view of, 425
  as shaper of fitness functions, 426–427
  trust and, 436–437
graining, fine versus coarse, 50
graph, defined, 142
Grassé, Pierre, 354
grasshopper, knowledge value of, 317
gravitation, 33–34
Great Depression, 164–165, 350
Great Disruption, 437, 448
  causes of, 438–439
Greece, Ancient, economy of, 9
greed, 27, 316
Greenspan, Alan, 22
Grondona, Mariano, 430
groups, effective size of, 158–159
Grove, Andy, 344
Groves, Melissa Osborne, 442
growth
  balanced, 41
  of the economy, 9–11
  endogenous, 42
  and equilibrium reconciled, 41–42
  versus equilibrium, 39
  in gales of creative destruction, 40
  of resources, 215
guaranteed minimum wage, 446
Gutenberg, Beno, 178

Habeas Corpus Act, 296
Hahn, Frank, 52
halogen lamp, emergence of, 174
Hamel, Gary, 330, 367
Hamilton, W. R., 30
Handy, Charles, 410
Hannan, Michael, 333
happiness, research on, 315, 455
Harrington, Joseph, Jr., 362, 363
Harrison, Lawrence, 429
Harrod, Roy, 462
Hatfield, England, train accident in, 122
Hausman, Daniel, 50
Havel, Václav, 295
Hayek, Friedrich, 17, 96, 216, 300, 415, 422–423, 427, 458, 459, 462
hedonic psychology, 455
Henderson, Rebecca, 258
Henry VIII, king of England, 296
Hertz, Tom, 442
heterogeneity
  defined, 83
  economic importance of, 266–267
Hewlett-Packard, 335, 377
Hicks, John, 37, 467
hierarchies
  and culture, 375–376

default, 133, 359
depth of, 364, 374
effect on adaptation, 364–366
evolution of, 94–95, 364
importance of, 272
instability of, 272–273
limitations of, 379
management of, 273
of networks, 154–156
origins of, 271
physical force and, 271, 273
rigidity of leaders in, 363–364, 374
role of age in, 484
Social Technologies (STs) for managing,
    273–274
and task complexity, 365–366
universality of, 422
hierarchy of needs, 309
Hildenbrand, Werner, 43
Hitachi, 333
Hitler, Adolf, 37, 326
Hobbes, Thomas, 418, 452
Hoff, Karla, 434
holdup problem, 353
Holland, John, 46, 70, 74, 96, 129, 130, 132, 134,
    135, 136, 137, 211, 225, 359, 392
Holyoak, Keith, 129
Home Depot, 286
Homo economicus, 116, 119, 139
Homo erectus, 7, 242
Homo habilis, 6–7, 242
Homo neanderthalis, 7
Homo sapiens, 7, 126. *See also* humans
honesty, as organizational norm, 371
Horan, Richard, 7
horizontal inequality, 87
housing, consumer spending on, 310
Houthakker, Hendrik, 388
Hughes, 333
Hull, David, 195
Human Genome Project, 149
humans
    experience of, 359–361
    information-processing capability of, 126
    loss aversion of, 358–359, 374
    overoptimism of, 357–358, 374
    unique characteristics of, 242
Hume, David, 418, 421
hunter-gatherer lifestyle, 7, 8
    cooperation in, 267, 271
Huntington, Samuel, 429
Hutcheson, Francis, 26
Hutchins, Edwin, 275

IBM, 330, 377, 388
    change sensitivity of, 157

and Microsoft, 326–327, 336, 341
    OS/2 product of, 335, 337, 340
    in PC market, 153
    stock prices of, 175–176
if-then rules, in induction, 130
Illinois Tool Works, 333
In Search of Excellence, 330, 355
incomplete contracts, 353
increasing returns, 42, 56–57
India
    economic conditions in, 428
    economic progress in, 441, 452
    trust levels in, 433
individuals. *See* humans
induction, 126
    combined with deductive logic, 250–252
    flexibility of, 129
    hierarchical nature of, 133
    human use of, 126–127
    mathematical models of, 129–130
    metaphor and other analogies in, 127
    universality of, 130
inductive rationality, 117, 125–126, 139
Industrial Revolution, 15, 16, 260, 297
inequality, 440
    cultural basis of, 447
    growth of, 441
    horizontal, 87
    ideological views on, 428–429
information
    access to, 52
    distinguished from knowledge, 317
information ratio, 401
information-processing organ, described, 126
innovation
    architectural versus component, 175, 247
    deductive-tinkering and, 249
    in disequilibrium, 294
    disruptive technologies and, 257–258
    evolution as, 216
    market role in, 295
    norms for, 371
    ripple effects from, 174–175, 247
    S-curves and, 254–257
    Schumpeter, theory of, 39–41
    unfolding space of, 247
Innovation: The Attacker's Advantage (Foster), 254
Innovator's Dilemma (Christensen), 257–258, 330
institutional investors, 386
institutions, 262, 476. *See also* Social Technologies
    (STs)
Intel, 333
intelligence, multifaceted nature of, 378
intelligent design, 14, 458, 472
interactors, 195, 213, 279
    businesses as, 281, 282
Internet, growth of, 143–144

inventory, 61, 111–112, 169–172
investors
    biases of, 387
    institutional, 386
    self-interest of, 401
    stock picking by, 383–385
    types of, 393–394, 397
invisible hand, 26, 38
Ireland, cultural change in, 447
irreversibility, 302
    described, 303
    of economic transformations, 303, 305–306, 345
    and entropy, 303–304
Italy
    family businesses in, 434
    government styles in, 436

Jaffé, William, 31
Jain, Sanjay, 173, 175, 231
Japan, 430, 434, 431, 447
Jevons, William Stanley, 33, 34–35, 47, 50, 68, 69, 70, 72, 117, 302, 316, 461
Jobs, Steve, 40, 330
Johnson, Neil, 390
Johnson, Paul, 296, 297
Johnson, Robert W., Jr. and Sr., 372
Johnson & Johnson, 333
    Credo of, 372
joint work product, learning through, 354
Joule, James Prescott, 66, 461
Joyce, James, 234
jumps
    random, 208, 209, 210–211
    spectrum of, 214
Jurassic Park, 194

Kagel, John, 119
Kahneman, Daniel, 52, 96, 119, 315, 357, 358, 359, 459
Kaplan, Robert, 407, 408
Kaplan, Sarah, 330, 331, 334, 356
Kasparov, Gary, 129
Kauffman, Stuart, 46, 143, 147, 150, 152, 154, 156, 157, 158, 192–193, 203, 209, 217, 226, 230, 246, 254, 455, 475
Kelvin, Lord, 33, 461
Kermit the Frog, 130–134
ketchup market, studies of, 62
Kevin Bacon game, 144–145
Keynes, John Maynard, xii, 57, 101, 164, 165, 401, 408
keystone species, 173–174
Kildall, Gary, 327
Kirman, Alan, 59

Kmart, 330
Knight, Frank, 480
knowledge
    accumulation in evolutionary systems, 215
    collective learning of, 354
    digitization of, 453
    distinguished from information, 317
    and growth, 378
    meta-innovation in gathering, 296
    wealth as, 317
knowledge coordination problem, 422
knowledge economy, 42
Kodak, 331
Korea, family businesses in, 434
Krishna, Sandeep, 173, 175, 231
Krugman, Paul, 5, 12, 464, 471
Kubrick, Stanley, 241
Kuhn, Thomas, xi

labor, division of, 266
Lagrange, J.-L. de, 30
laissez faire, 27, 460
Landauer, Rolf, 305
Landes, David, 11, 428, 429
Lange, Oskar, 462
Langton, Christopher, 96
language, evolution of, 274–275, 475
lattice graph, 142, 146
Laurent, Hermann, 49
law
    defined, 319
    rule of, 274, 296
law of diminishing marginal utility, 29
law of diminishing returns, 28
Leading the Revolution (Hamel), 330
learning
    collective, 354
    distinguished from adapting, 355
LeBaron, Blake, 134
Left (political)
    critique of, 422–423
    on economic fitness, 422
    on economic inequality, 428–429, 441, 445
    on economic predestination, 445
    on government, 422, 427
    on human nature, 418
    New, 421
    on private property, 487
    on social capital, 440
Left-Right political spectrum
    current alignments of, 416–417
    history of, 416–417
    outdated nature of, 417–418
    research on, 418–421
    world views and, 418–421
legal system, importance of, 274, 296

LEGO blocks, 192
    appeal of, 193
    design library of, 193–194
    as evolutionary metaphor, 194–198
Leibniz, G. W., 30
Leijonhufvud, Axel, 51, 52
Lenin, Vladimir, 326
Leonardo da Vinci, 259
Levine, Ross, 261
Lewis, Alain, 123
Lexan, 281
Library of Babel, 233
Library of LEGO, 193–198
Library of Mendel, 202
    assessment of fitness in members of,
        203–204
    god's-eye view over, 209–210
    searching through, 207–212
Library of Smith, 236–237, 279
life insurance, consumer spending on, 311
Lilly, Eli, 245
limit order book, 181
    effects attributed to, 182–184
    order of order placement in, 184
limited-liability joint stock corporation, origin of,
    276
Lindgren, Kristian, 225, 227–231, 269, 419
liquidity trading, 393
Living Company, The (de Geus), 414
Lo, Andy, 64, 389, 390
Locke, John, 418
Lockheed Martin, 330
Long-Term Capital, 381
long-term production capacity, 111
Los Alamos National Library, 45, 390
loss aversion, 357, 358–359, 374, 375
Lotka, Alfred, 168
Lovallo, Dan, 357, 358
Lowenstein, George, 119
Lucas, Robert, 39, 165–166
Lumbricus terrestris, 13–14
Luo people, 122
Luxembourg, economy of, 428

Maasai people, 451
Machiguenga people, 419–420
MacKinlay, Craig, 64, 389, 390
macroeconomics, 39, 460
    assumptions in, 81
    described, 163
    inventory effects in, 464
Maddison, Angus, 457
Making Democracy Work (Putnam, Leonardi, and
    Nanetti), 436
Malkiel, Burton, 383, 387, 390
Malthus, Thomas, 16, 17, 455

management
    balanced scorecard for, 407–408
    of complexity, 378
    through culture, 375–376
    fiduciary duties of, 409, 411, 412
    of hierarchies, 273
    long-term goals of, 412–413
    social architecture building through,
        376–377
    stock options for, 406, 407
Mandelbrot, Benoit, 175, 179–180, 388, 389, 390,
    399
Mankiw, Gregory, 22, 166
Mantegna, Rosario, 390
maps, like theories, 50
March, James, 118, 356
Marconi, Guglielmo, 174
Marginalist era of economics, 29–36, 66–68
market microstructure, 486
market orders, 181
market portfolio, 404–405
market price, for stock, 384
    correlated with time, 389
    fractal nature of, 388
    random-walk hypothesis and, 383–385, 389
    versus value, 394–399
market trading, 393–394
markets
    advantages of, 288–289
    allocative role of, 295, 462
    aspects of, 38
    commodities, 109–113
    competitive nature of, 399, 401
    Complexity view of, 295
    computer simulation of, 134–137
    and corporate returns, 407
    and economic evolution, 294–295, 296
    efficiency of, 23, 295, 399, 401–403, 462
    as evolutionary systems, 391–394, 403
    government role in, 427–428
    innovation spurred by, 333–334
    nonlinearity of, 392
    non-Walrasian, 52
    organizational ecology of, 333–334
    selection in, 289–291
    sufficient conditions for, 132
    time sensitivity of, 402
Markowitz, Harry, 382, 404, 405
Marshall, Alfred, 17, 27, 36–37, 53, 216, 286, 458,
    460
Marx, Karl, 20, 174, 289, 316, 415, 416, 417, 418,
    460, 487
Marxism, 13
Maslow, Abraham, 309–310
mass media, and social capital, 438–439
mass-extinction events, 55
    in punctuated equilibrium, 173

mathematics
  in economics, 30, 48–49
  as language, 71–72
Matsushita, 370
Maxwell, James Clerk, 33, 304, 461
Maxwell's Demon, 304
McDonald's, 310, 311, 313
McKinsey & Company
  culture of, 372
  Global Institute of, 262
  obligation to dissent in, 376
media, consumer spending on, 311
memes, 284
Mendel, Gregor, 202
mental accounting, 122
mental models, 130, 357, 359–361
Merck, 333
meritocracy, as organizational norm, 371
Merton, Robert, 381, 383
Mesopotamia, 276
metaphors
  evolution as, 12–13
  power of, 127
  role in science, 64–65
"The Methodology of Positive Economics"
    (Friedman), 49
Mexico, debt default of, 21
microchip, impact of, 175
microcomputers, 175
microeconomics, 39, 464
  assumptions in, 81
  described, 163
Microeconomics, 223
Microsoft
  and IBM, 326–327, 336
  strategy of, 335–336, 340–341
  Windows product of, 335, 336–337, 340
Milgram, Stanley, 144
Mill, John Stuart, 27, 460
Miller, Matt, 441, 445–446
Miller, Merton, 382
millionth monkey problem, 402
Minsky, Marvin, 378, 453
Mirowski, Philip, 67
mobile telephony, 175
Modigliani, Franco, 382
modularity, of technology, 175
module, of Business Plan, 283–285
Mokyr, Joel, 253, 475
money
  mental accounting of, 122
  origin of, 276
  as Social Technology, 317
Monier, James, 62
monkeys, tool use by, 241
Moore's law, 96, 149
moral hazards, 434

Morgan Stanley, 390
Moses, Phoebe, 326
Motorola, 333
Moynihan, Daniel Patrick, 445, 447, 448
MS-DOS, 32
Munger, Charlie, 405
music, evolution of, 313–314
Muslim trading networks, 273
mutations, 196, 229
  point, 228
  random, 249
  split, 228
mutual funds, long-term results of,
    386–387
mutual trust, as organizational norm, 371

n-body problems, 108
NASDAQ, 71
Nash, John, 267, 271
Nash equilibrium, 268
National Association for the Advancement of
    Colored People (NAACP), 437
national wealth
  cultural factors in, 428–435
  disparities in, 428
  factors affecting, 261
Native Americans, 448
Natural Theology (Paley), 188
"Nature of the Firm" (Coase), 353
naturefacts, 241
negative feedback, 56, 57, 101, 467
Negishi, Takashi, 52
Nelson, Richard, 15, 17, 24, 96, 217, 238, 284
Neoclassical economics, 24
  growth model of, 462
  history of, 36–39
  static nature of, 40
  synthesis of, 37, 38, 43
nepotism, 434
Netherlands, 434
network effect, 143
networks
  biological significance of, 141
  Boolean (*see* Boolean networks)
  computers as, 147–148
  dense, 154, 155
  diseconomies of scale in, 150, 152, 154
  economic significance of, 141
  economies of scale in, 149, 150
  hierarchical, 154–156
  lattice, 142
  Milgram experiment on, 144
  people as, 275–276
  physical scientific study of, 142
  random, 142
  scaling of, 148–150

and small-world effect, 145
    social, 146, 147
    technological significance of, 141
    tipping points of, 143–144
New Keynesian economics, 166–167
New Progressive Declaration, 417
New Yorker tribe, 8
Newman, Mark, 145, 146, 147, 173
Newton, Isaac, 30, 50, 74, 259
niche construction, 313
Nike, preference for, 313
Nisbett, Richard, 129
nodes, 142
    number of connections per, 150–151
nonhierarchicality, as innovating norm, 371
nonlinear systems, 102
    dynamic, 103
    path dependency of, 106
    sensitivity to initial conditions of, 106
    study of, 107
nonrandom walks, 64
Non-Random Walk Down Wall Street, A (Lo and
    MacKinlay), 389
non-Walrasian markets, 52
Non Zero, 266
non-zero-sum games, 222
    actors in, 266–267
    cooperation and, 265–267
    culture and, 430
    economic implications of, 432
    factors in, 267
Nordhaus, William, 67
normal distribution, 178, 388
norms, 369
    building a system of, 376–377
    company-specific, 370
    conflicts of, 420
    cooperating, 371, 373, 430
    distinguished from routines, 484
    distinguished from values, 370
    economic implications of, 431–435
    importance of, 375
    individual behavioral, 430
    innovating, 371, 430
    performing, 371, 373, 430
    tensions inherent in, 375
    time-related, 430–431
    typologies of, 430
North, Douglass, 96, 262, 459
Norton, David, 408
Norway, 430, 431, 447
    trust levels in, 432
Noryl, 281
novelty
    emergence of, 215
    potential for, 149
    response to, 133

nuclear arms race, Tit for Tat strategy and, 224
Nunamiut people, 271

Oakley, Annie, 326, 327
Ochondra, Maria Luz, 79
Oikonomikos, 24
Olduvai Gorge, 242
one price, "law" of, 61, 92
    as approximation, 61–62
open system
    described, 68–69
    economics as, 71–72
openness, as innovating norm, 371
operators, and schemata, 214
optimism, 374
    bias in favor of, 357–358
    among stock traders, 398
OR, Boolean, 148
order
    creation from randomness, 214
    described, 307–308
    relative nature of, 308
order fulfillment, and stock prices, 182
O'Reilly, Charles, 356
organizational cultures, 369–370
organizations. *See also* businesses; corporations;
    firms
    agents in, 356
    capabilities of, 276
    collective learning in, 354
    as complex adaptive systems, 351–352
    cooperation within, 276, 352–354
    culture versus hierarchy in, 375–376, 379
    defined, 351–352
    developmental stages of, 378–379
    emergent behaviors in, 356
    functions of, 364–365
    information-processing aspect of, 275
    initiation into, 376
    market responsiveness of, 410
    relations with suppliers, 410
    social architecture of, 350–351, 374–378
    structure of, 356
Orgel, Leslie, 294
Orgel's Second Rule, 294
Origin of Species, The (Darwin), 17, 173
Origins of Order (Kauffman), 217
orthodox economics, 459
Oscar II, king of Sweden, 31, 108
oscillatory systems, 168
    case study of, 168–172
overadaptation, 211
overoptimism, 357, 374
    combating of, 375
    among stock traders, 398
oxytocin, 419

Packard, Norman, 391
Page, Scott, 364, 365
Paich, Mark, 113
Palanpur, farming in, 223
Paley, William, 188
Palmer, Richard, 134
parallel search, 216
Pareto, Vilfredo, 35–36, 37, 86, 179, 180, 462
Pareto distribution, 86
Pareto optimality, 35, 38, 43, 93
Pareto superiority, 36
parliamentary democracy, 296
Pasteur, Louis, 338
path dependence, 106, 212–213
pattern recognition, 129. See also induction
payoff matrix, for non-zero-sum games, 222
PC-DOS, 327
Peacock, Thomas Love, 57
Penrose, Edith, 366–368, 378
pensions, consumer spending on, 311
perfect correlation, and fitness landscapes, 257
perfect rationality, 47, 116–117, 118, 323
    evidence against, 119–122, 170–171
    history of, 117–118
    impossibility of, 123, 423
    as misnomer, 125
perfect-rationality model, 116–117
    as bedrock of Traditional Economics, 118
    justification for, 139
performance orientation, as organizational
        norm, 371
periodic limit cycle, 104, 105
Peru, trust levels in, 432
pessimism, attitudes toward, 358
Peters, Tom, 330, 355
Petition of Right, 296
Petroski, Henry, 250
phase transition, defined, 143
Phelps, Edmund, 166
Philco, 333
Philips, 333, 434
Physalis physalis, 456
Physical Technologies (PTs), 15, 16, 238, 475
    aspects of, 244–245
    coevolution with schema readers, 246
    communication and, 246
    components and architecture of, 247
    defined, 244
    deductive-tinkering and, 250–252
    described, 243
    design space of (see Physical Technology space)
    evolution of (see Physical Technology
        evolution)
    examples of, 244
    importance of, 453
    coevolution with Social Technologies (STs), 265
    replication of, 253–254

schema for, 244–245
schema readers for, 245–246
self-reinforcing nature of, 246–252
superfecundity and, 253
Physical Technology (PT) evolution
    deductive-tinkering in, 250–252, 253, 260
    defined, 244
    disruptive, 257–258
    imitation in, 253–254
    rules of, 259
    S-curve and, 254–257
    in scientific revolution, 258–259
    schema readers, 245–246
    selection process in, 252–253
    superfecundity in, 253
Physical Technology (PT) space, 243–245
    deductive-tinkering in, 249–252
    exponential unfolding of, 246–248
    rough correlation of, 249
physics, and economics, 29–33, 46–48, 65–71, 99, 466
Physiocrats, 27
pin factory, and Adam Smith, 25
Pinker, Steven, 126, 310, 312
Planck number, 180
Plato, 126
Poincaré, Henri, 48, 49, 106, 107, 108
Poinsot, Louis, 31, 65, 461
point mutations, 228
Polaroid, 330
politics
    Complexity view of, 415–416, 450
    economics and, 415
    Left-Right framework of, 416–426
Popper, Karl, 58
populations, 214
Porras, Jerry, 286, 330, 342, 350, 355, 414
portals, in fitness landscape, 206
Porter, Michael, 325, 429
portfolio, market, 404–405
positive feedback, 56, 57, 101
Post-it Notes, 250
potential energy, 66
Poterba, James, 177
poverty
    combating, 445–446
    cultural basis of, 447
    culture of, 444–445
    determinants of, 443
    developing world, 428
    lack of social capital and, 443
    social immobility and, 442–443
power laws, 179–180, 328, 388, 472
Prahalad, C. K., 368
Prediction Company, 391
preferences
    in consumer behavior, 37
    evolutionary view of, 308–314

Prelec, Drazen, 119
price
  determinants of, 26, 29
  fluctuations in, 62, 399 (*see also* volatility)
  "law" of one, 61–62, 92
  related to stock value, 394–399
price priority rule, 182
Prigogine, Ilya, 70
primogeniture, 273
principal-agent problem, 406, 407
Principles of Economics (Marshall), 17, 34–35
Principles of Political Economy (Mill), 460
Prisoner's Dilemma, 221, 266
  combined with Game of Life, 227–231, 419
  cooperation and, 223
  multiple agent version of, 225
  payoff matrix for, 222
  repeated games, 224–225, 269
probability, laws of, 304
Procter & Gamble, 330, 377
production capacity, 61, 111
production line, as disruptive technology, 264–265
productivity, 25
  and growth, 41, 410
profit maximization, 408
profit motive, 26, 410
progress, differentiated from evolution, 452
Promised Land garbage dump, 79–80
propagation mechanism, described, 163
property taxes, and education, 446
Proust, Marcel, 235
psychic flux, 314
psychohistory, 115
public education, improvement of, 446
Puglia, bureaucracy in, 436
punctuated equilibrium, 173, 175, 231, 328
  clustered volatility, 393
  keystone species and, 173–174
  phases of, 174
  and rigidity, 363–364
purposeful adaptation, 250
Putnam, Robert, 435–439

Q-DOS, 327
quarterly earnings, as metric, 412
quasi-periodic limit cycle, 104, 105
Quesnay, François, 27, 460

Rabin, Mathew, 119
race, and culture, 447
radio, impact of, 174–175
raloxifene, 246
random friends, influence of, 146–147

random graph, defined, 142
random jumps, 208, 209
  in combination with adaptive walks, 210–211
random walk, 382–383
  with drift, 385
Random Walk Down Wall Street, A (Malkiel), 383, 390
random-walk theory, 63–64
  downfall of, 388, 389
  implications for investors, 385
  and stock prices, 383–385
randomness. *See also* chaos
  distinguished from uncertainty, 328
  in experimentation, 250, 251, 252
  in physics, 99
Rapoport, Anatol, 224
rationality
  bounded, 118, 119, 387
  inductive, 117, 125–126, 139
  perfect, 47, 116–117, 118, 123, 125
Rawls, John, 445–446
Reagan, Ronald, 415, 425
real business cycle models, 163–164
recession of 1982, 56
reciprocity. *See also* cooperation
  adaptation of, 269–270
  importance of, 121
  as organizational norm, 371
  strong, 419–421
  Traditional view of, 468–469
recursion, 214
Red Queen races, 332, 480
Reed, John, 21, 45
Remembrance of Things Past (Proust), 235
Renaissance, 259
Rényi, Alfréd, 142, 143
replication, 190, 200, 214
  of Business Plans, 291–293, 409–410
representativeness, cognitive error, 122
resources
  and Business Plans, 367–368, 374
  defined, 367
  growth of, 215–216
  strategic allocation of, 347
return-to-risk ratio, 401
reversible transformations, 303, 479
Ricardo, David, 316
Richerson, Peter, 284, 368
Richter, Charles, 178
Right (political)
  critique of, 423–426
  on economic inequality, 429, 441
  on government, 425, 427
  on individual responsibility, 445
  philosophical basis of, 418
  on social capital, 440

rigidity, 357, 374
    advantages and disadvantages of, 362–363, 379
    balancing with flexibility, 376
    and punctuated equilibrium, 363–364
risk
    aversion, 359, 375
    distinguished from uncertainty, 480
    mistakes in assessing, 122
Rivoli, Petra, 458
Robbins, Lionel, 67
Romer, Paul, 42, 462
Roosevelt, Franklin D., 425
Roosevelt, Theodore, 425
Roth, Alvin, 119
Rothschild, Michael, 457
rough correlation, 203, 216
    characteristics of, 206
    fitness landscape with, 206
    of Physical Technology space, 249
    of Social Technology space, 264
Rousseau, Jean-Jacques, 418, 421, 487
routines (units of selection), 284, 484
Royal Dutch/Shell, 434
Ruefli, Tim, 331, 332, 333, 377
Ruelle, David, 46
rule of law, 274, 296
rules
    organization of, in inductive system, 133–134
    of thumb, in induction, 130–133
Russell Sage Foundation, 45

Sachs, Jeffrey, 429
Samuelson, Paul, 36–37, 67, 299, 302, 382, 386,
    402, 462
Sandia National Laboratory, 390
Santa Cruz Operation, 336
Santa Fe Institute (SFI)
    economics workshop, 46–48, 74
    founding of, 45–46
Santa Fe Institute Artificial Stock Market, 134,
    392–393
    implications of, 137–138
    learning as factor in, 135
    rules in, 136–137
satisficing, 52, 118, 463
Savage, Leonard (Jimmie), 382, 480
Scarf, Herbert, 63
Schank, Roger, 126
Scheinkman, José, 46
Schelling, Thomas, 96
schema, 194, 213, 214
schema readers, 194, 213
Scholes, Myron, 381, 383
Schrödinger, Erwin, 462
Schumpeter, Joseph, 17, 39–40, 42, 174, 299, 332,
    428

science
    metaphor in, 65
    reductionist versus systemic, 45–46
scientific method, 47
scientific revolution, 258–259, 296
Seabright, Paul, 7, 458
seasonal traders, 397
Seattle Computer Products, 327
Second Law of Thermodynamics, 67–68, 71
    applied to economics, 300–301, 305
    and irreversibility, 303
selection
    in evolution, 196
    in markets, 289–291
    process of, 214
    of Physical Technologies (PTs), 252–253
    of Social Technologies (STs), 264–265
    units of, 279, 282–284
selection environment, 337, 342–343
self-actualization, 309
self-interest, 35
    benefits of, 26
    in Complexity Economics, 223
    of investors, 401
    Right-wing view of, 418
    and strong reciprocity, 420
Selfish Gene, The (Dawkins), 199, 217
selfishness, 121, 418, 441
Selten, Reinhard, 119
semiconductor equipment industry, evolution in,
    258
semiconductor industry, evolution of, 333
Sen, Arijit, 434
sex, economic effects of, 88–89
sexual recombination, nonrandom nature of, 249
Shakespeare, William, 65, 127, 217, 234
Shapiro, Robert, 301
shared purpose, as organizational norm, 371
shareholders, 409
    accountability to, 405–408, 410–411
    legal obligations to, 409, 411
    maximizing value for, 405–408, 412, 413
    residual claims of, 411
Sharpe, William, 383
Sharpe ratio, 401
shocks, exogenous, 54, 55
Shoshone people, 271
shuffling trick, 308
Silver, Spence, 250
Simon, Herbert, 49, 52, 96, 118, 119, 166, 250,
    459
Sims, Karl, 188, 195, 196, 225
    block-creature simulations of, 188–191, 233,
    288
Skinner, B. F., 309
Sloan, Alfred P., 155
Slovic, Paul, 119

Smale, Steve, 463
small-world effect, 145
Smith, Adam, 4, 20, 24–27, 35, 41, 121, 236, 266, 289, 296, 415, 417, 418, 421, 460
Smith, John Maynard, 217, 231
Smith, Vernon, 52, 119
social architecture
    adaptability of, 374–379
    building of, 375–376
    components of, 350–351
    and performance, 377–378
social capital, 435
    economic effects of, 435–436
    implications for government, 436–437
    importance of, 435
    suggestions for building, 439
    in United States, 437–439
Social Darwinism, 13, 458
social mobility, levels of, 442–443
social networks, 146, 147
Social Technologies (STs), 15–16, 238, 324, 476
    coevolution with Physical Technologies, 265
    components of, 261
    defined, 262
    described, 243
    and economic evolution, 296–297
    evolution of (see Social Technology evolution)
    importance of, 261–262
    as key to progress, 452
    modularity of, 263–264
    state of versus Physical Technologies, 453
Social Technology (ST) evolution, 263–264
    components of, 270–276
    of corporations, 275–276
    effects of, 276–277
    from family to business, 270–272
    of government, 271–274
    as non-zero-sum game, 266–270
    rough correlation in, 264
socialism, 415, 422
    versus capitalism, 20, 38, 416
    Complexity view of, 422–423
    "fatal conceit" of, 423
soft drinks, 313
Solow, Robert, 40–41, 43, 317, 462, 466
Sony, 370
Sornette, Didier, 390
Southeast Asia, economic conditions in, 428
Soviet Union
    planned economy of, 15
    price modeling in, 462
Spain, cultural change in, 447
specialization, effects of, 7, 25
specific assets, 353
Spence, Michael, 52
Spencer, Herbert, 13, 458
spinning frame, invention of, 16

split mutation, 228
Spock, embodying perfect-rationality model, 116–117
spontaneous order, 458
Springfield Armory, standardization in, 264
Stanley, Eugene, 180, 378, 390
Star Trek, 116
Sterman, John, 109, 111–114, 170
Stewart, Potter, 307
Stiglitz, Joseph, 22, 52
stimergy, 354
stock
    beta of, 404
    defined, 100
    relation to flow, 101
stock keeping units (SKUs), 9
stock markets
    crash of October 19, 1987, 178, 180
    crash of September 3, 1946, 178
    limit order book, effect of, 182–185
    movements, 1941–1987, 177–178
    reaction to news, 177–178
    trades, types of, 181
    volatility of, 180–185
stock options, 405–407
stock picking, 383–385, 393–394
storytelling, 126, 127
strategic planning, 337–339
strategy, 238, 482. See also Business Plans
    adaptiveness in, 347–348
    allocation of resources in, 347
    and Business Plans, 284–285
    commitment to, 325
    context for, 337–339
    conventional approach to, 325
    definitions of, 324
    differentiation in, 337, 339–341
    as portfolio of experiments, 334–337
    research on, 331–333
    selection environment in, 337, 342–343
    slack capacity and, 346
    structure and resource views of, 482
Strategy and Structure (Chandler), 324
Strauss, Johann, Jr., 241
Strauss, Richard, 241
string theory, 65
Strogatz, Steve, 144
strong reciprocity
    brain chemistry and, 410
    Complexity view of, 421
    described, 419
    evolutionary logic for, 419–420
    implications of, 421
    and self-interest, 420
    universality of, 419
structure. See hierarchies
student distribution, 184

substitutes, in markets, 38
substrates, 192
suburban sprawl, and social capital, 438
Sugarscape model, 80–83
    distribution of wealth in, 83–85
    evolution of economic system in, 95
    as example of Complexity Economics, 96
    growth of inequality in, 85–88
    hierarchy in, 94–95
    sex variable in, 88–89
    trade in, 89–93
Summers, Larry, 46, 177
Sun Microsystems, 147, 335
superfecundity, 253, 286
superstitious reasoning, 122
supply and demand, 27, 92
    damping of fluctuations in, 60–61, 111–114
    history of theory, 26–27, 32–33, 37, 460
    "law" of, 60–61
    as negative feedback system, 109, 111
Supreme Court, U.S., size of, 158
Sweden, trust levels in, 432
system dynamics, 467
systems
    closed, 68
    open, 68–69
    view of economics, 71–72
Szabolcs, Mike, 184

Tableau Economique (Quesnay), 27, 460
tagging, 273–274
    exclusionary, 274
Tait, Peter Guthrie, 33
tâtonnement, 33
Tayler, Paul, 134
technical trading, 393, 396, 397
technology. *See also* Physical Technologies (PTs);
    Social Technologies (STs)
  as basis for economy, 243
  commercialization of, 40
  development of, 175, 475
  evolution of, 243–244 (*see also* Physical
    Technology evolution; Social Technology
    evolution)
  modularity of, 175
  path of progress in, 40
  and satisficing, 463
  as variable, 55
  in virtuous economic cycle, 41–42
Teilhard de Chardin, Pierre, 300
telephone directory services, British,
    privatization of, 424
temporal structure, 395–396
temporary equilibria, 55, 63, 64
Texas Instruments, 333
Thagard, Paul, 129

Thaler, Richard, 119
Thatcher, Margaret, 361, 362, 415, 450
theory, functions of, 58, 115–116
Theory of the Growth of the Firm (Penrose), 366,
    378
Theory of Moral Sentiments (Smith), 25, 121, 418
Theory of Political Economy (Jevons), 34
Theory of Value, 460, 466
thermodynamics, laws of, 66–68
Third Way, The (Giddens), 417
Thompson, William Lord Kelvin, 33, 461
3M, 332
Through the Looking Glass (Carroll), 332
Thünen, Johann von, 461
time, 468
    cultural view of, 430–431
    directionality of, 479
time delays, 52–53
    in dynamic system, 101–102
    human responses to, 169–170
    in stock market, 394, 395
time priority rule, 182
tipping point, in network formation, 143
Tit for Tat strategy, 224
Tjaden, Brett, 144
Tobin, James, 382
Tolstoy, Leo, 370
tools, importance of, 241, 243
trade
    bilateral, 93
    evolution of, 273–274
    origin of, 7, 475
    Pareto view of, 35–36
    stock, types of, 181
    as uniquely human activity, 7
    volume of, 92
    in wealth creation, 25–26
Traditional Economics, 17–18, 27–29, 458, 460
    absence of time in, 52–53
    assumptions in, 51–52, 70
    challenge to, 21–23
    definition of, 24
    distinguished from Complexity Economics, 97
    equilibrium in, 38, 52–56, 324–325
    garbage in, garbage out problem of, 48
    Homo economicus in, 116–117
    influence of, 43
    on investor behavior, 383–385
    legacy of, 42–43
    and market efficiency, 401–402
    metaphor in, 64–74
    negative feedback in, 56
    perfect-rationality model in, 116–117, 323
    predictive inaccuracy of, 58–59
    random walk theory of, 63–64
    on strong reciprocity, 420
    on technology, 245

testing of, 58–60
and uncertainty, 327–328
transformation, defined, 303
Transitron, 333
transport, consumer spending on, 310
Travels of a T-Shirt in the Global Economy (Rivoli), 458
Treatise on Natural Philosophy (Kelvin), 33
trust. *See also* cooperation
   cultural views of, 432–434
   economic impact of, 433–434
   family values and, 434
   and government effectiveness, 436–437
   levels of, in U.S., 437
   as organizational norm, 371
   Social Technologies and, 434
Turgot, Jacques, 27–28
Turing, Alan, 123, 457
Turing machine, 123
Tushman, Michael, 356
Tversky, Amos, 52, 119, 127
Two Percent Solution, The (Miller), 441
2001: A Space Odyssey, 241–242, 250
Tyco, 407

ultimatum game, 119–120
uncertainty. *See also* chaos; randomness
   distinguished from randomness, 328
   distinguished from risk, 480
   effects of, 328–329
   Traditional view of, 327–328
United States
   assimilation of immigrants in, 448
   business scandals in, 452
   founding of, 296
   as free-market experiment, 297
   multiethnicity in, 448–449
   public welfare in, 420
   social capital in, 437
   trust levels in, 433, 437
units of selection, 279, 282–284
universal health care, 446
Universal Product Codes (UPC), 456–457
Unix, 335, 336, 337, 340
unstable equilibrium, 31
Utilitarianism, 28
utility, 28, 34, 37, 461

Vallone, Robert, 127
value
   evolutionary view of, 316–317
   related to price, 394–399
Value and Capital (Hicks), 37
value creation, irreversibility of, 302, 305–306
values, distinguished from norms, 370

"The Variation of Certain Speculative Prices" (Mandelbrot), 388
variations, of schemata, 214
Veblen, Thorsten, 17
venture capitalists, 347–348
Veterans of Foreign Wars, 437
Viacom, 349
virus, function of, 200
visible hand, 289, 422
Vodafone, 286
volatility
   clustered, 393, 486
   order book and, 182–184
   power laws and, 180–181
   trends in, 399
Voltaire, 36
Volterra, Vito, 49, 168
von Neumann, John, 96, 461
vouchers, educational, 446

Wade, Nicholas, 455
Wal-Mart
   competitive advantage of, 325
   productivity trends at, 262
   variety of products, 8
Waldrop, Mitchell, 22, 27, 464
Wall Street, 273
Wallace, Alfred Russell, 458
Walras, Léon, 29–33, 36, 43, 47–50, 64–66, 68–72, 75, 76, 99, 117, 118, 302, 394, 423, 461
Walrasian auctions, 93, 486
Walters, Larry, 250
Wang Laboratories, 411
war, entropy increase from, 307
water, properties of, 167
Waterman, Bob, 330, 355
Watts, Duncan, 144, 145, 146, 147, 173
wealth
   determinants of, 25–26, 261, 443
   entrepreneurship and, 40
   evolutionary view of, 14–15
   as fit order, 316–318
   and happiness, 315
   history of, 9, 10
   as knowledge, 317
   manifestations of, 3, 8
   origins of, 4
Wealth of Nations (Smith), 4, 25, 121, 415, 418, 460
weather forecasts, 58
Web, evolution of, 57
Weber, Max, 352, 429
Weisbuch, Gerard, 156
Welch, Jack, 127, 330, 342, 343, 344, 350, 372, 377
welfare state, 420

Westinghouse, 330
    mission statement of, 342–343
    rise and fall of, 349, 350
Westinghouse, George, 349
"What Is Life?" 462
Wiener, Norbert, 485
Wiggins, Robert, 331, 332, 333, 377
Wilhelm II, Kaiser of Germany, 326
Winning Through Innovation (Tushman and
        O'Reilly), 356
Winter, Sidney, 17, 24, 96, 217, 284
Wolfram, Stephen, 470
women
    entry into labor market, 437–438
    and social capital, 438
work, defined, 66
World Trade Organization, riots of 1999, 417
WORLDCOM, 330, 407
Wright, Robert, 266, 271, 287, 310, 311

Wright, Sewall, 203
Wriston, Walter, 21
writing, importance of, 275

Xenophon, 24
Xerox, 330, 335

Yanomamö tribe, 8
    GDP of, 456
    hardships in, 456
    lifestyle of, 8–9, 456–457
Ye Olde Fighting Cocks Pub, 412

zero-sum games, 222
    economic implications of, 431–432
Zurek, Wojciech, 308

ERIC D. BEINHOCKER is a Senior Advisor to McKinsey & Company, Inc., where he conducts research on economic, management, and public policy issues. He was previously a partner at McKinsey and a coleader of its global strategy practice.

His career has bridged both the business and academic worlds. He has been a software CEO, a venture capitalist, and an Executive Director of the Corporate Executive Board. He has also held research appointments at the Harvard Business School and the MIT Sloan School, and has been a visiting scholar at the Santa Fe Institute. He is a graduate of Dartmouth College and the MIT Sloan School where he was the Henry Ford II Scholar.

Fortune magazine has named Beinhocker a "Business Leader of the Next Century," and his writings on business and economics have appeared in a variety of publications, including the *Financial Times*. Originally from Boston, Massachusetts, he lives in London with his wife Tilly and their daughter Anna.